MOON HANDBOOKS®

MARYLAND & DELAWARE

view of Chesapeake City

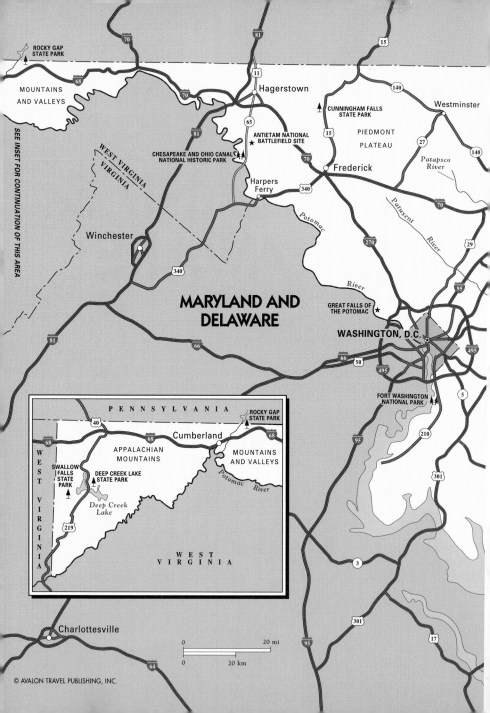

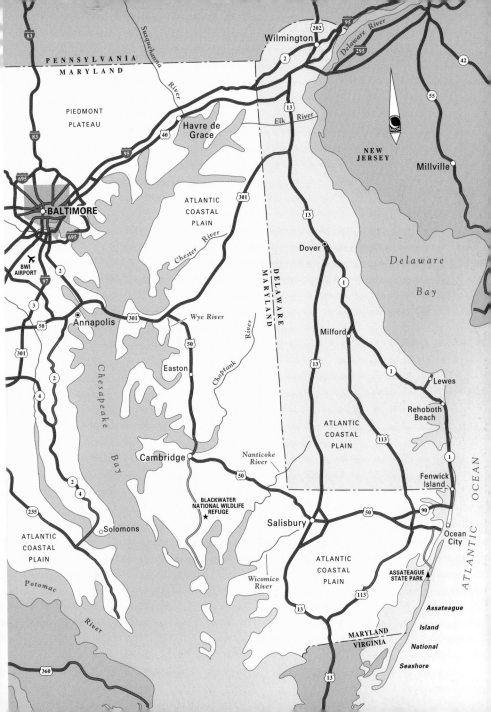

Baltimore Conservatory at
Druid Hill Park

MOON HANDBOOKS®

MARYLAND & DELAWARE

INCLUDING WASHINGTON, D.C.

SECOND EDITION

JOANNE MILLER

AVALON
TRAVEL

MAPS

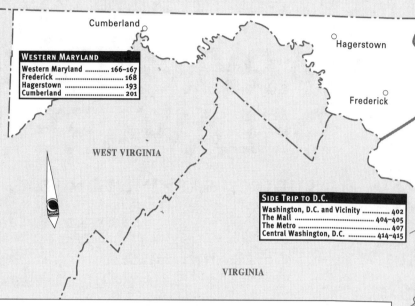

INTRODUCTION
Maryland 3
Delaware 313

PENNSYLVANIA

Cumberland

Hagerstown

WESTERN MARYLAND
Western Maryland 166–167
Frederick 168
Hagerstown 193
Cumberland 201

Frederick

WEST VIRGINIA

SIDE TRIP TO D.C.
Washington, D.C. and Vicinity 402
The Mall 404–405
The Metro 407
Central Washington, D.C. 414–415

VIRGINIA

MAP SYMBOLS

═══	Divided Highway	◯	State Highway	♠	State Park
━━━	Main Road	◉	State Capital	♠♠	National Park
────	Other Road	○	City/Town	☆	Regional Park
··········	Trail	★	Point of Interest	▲	Mountain
┝─┿─┥	Railroad	•	Accommodation	✈	Airport
⬡	Interstate	▼	Restaurant/Bar		
⬡	U.S. Highway	▪	Other Location		

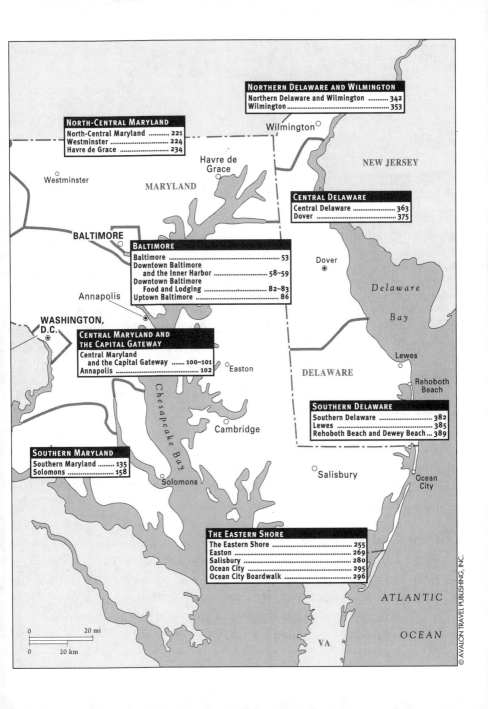

NORTHERN DELAWARE AND WILMINGTON
Northern Delaware and Wilmington 342
Wilmington 353

NORTH-CENTRAL MARYLAND
North-Central Maryland 221
Westminster 224
Havre de Grace 234

CENTRAL DELAWARE
Central Delaware 363
Dover 375

BALTIMORE
Baltimore 53
Downtown Baltimore
and the Inner Harbor 58–59
Downtown Baltimore
Food and Lodging 82–83
Uptown Baltimore 86

CENTRAL MARYLAND AND THE CAPITAL GATEWAY
Central Maryland
and the Capital Gateway 100–101
Annapolis 102

SOUTHERN DELAWARE
Southern Delaware 382
Lewes 385
Rehoboth Beach and Dewey Beach ... 389

SOUTHERN MARYLAND
Southern Maryland 135
Solomons 158

THE EASTERN SHORE
The Eastern Shore 255
Easton 269
Salisbury 280
Ocean City 295
Ocean City Boardwalk 296

Wilmington

NEW JERSEY

Westminster

Havre de Grace

MARYLAND

BALTIMORE

Dover

Delaware
Bay

Annapolis

WASHINGTON,
D.C.

Easton

Lewes

DELAWARE

Rehoboth
Beach

Chesapeake Bay

Cambridge

Salisbury

Ocean
City

Solomons

ATLANTIC

OCEAN

VA

0   20 mi

0   20 km

© AVALON TRAVEL PUBLISHING, INC.

Contents

MARYLAND 1

Introduction to Maryland 2

Founded as a place of refuge, the seventh state welcomes visitors today with a wealth of history and diverse natural beauty. See why Maryland is called "America in Miniature," with its rolling farmland, cool mountains, sandy peninsulas, and the mighty Chesapeake Bay at its heart.

The Land **4**; History **13**; The People **24**; Conduct and Customs **27**

On the Road in Maryland 29

What's your pleasure? Whether it's hiking the Appalachian Trail or sailing the bright waters of the bay, hunting for antiques or following the scenic National Road, get all the details to make the most of your trip here.

Outdoor Recreation **30**; Entertainment and Events **37**; Accommodations **40**; Food and Drink **43**; Transportation **44**; Information and Services **47**

Baltimore 52

Charm City earns its nickname with an offbeat spirit and small-town sweetness. Delve into the idiosyncratic worlds on display at the American Visionary Art Museum, embrace the macabre at Edgar Allan Poe's grave, or down a few beers in boisterous Fell's Point, where seafarers first cozied up to the bar more than two centuries ago.

Central Maryland and the Capital Gateway 97

This is the state's most populous area, where crowded suburbs give way to small towns and scenic parks, gardens, and wildlife refuges. If you're looking for architectural splendor, head to stately Annapolis. Home to the U.S. Naval Academy, the state capital enchants with its Georgian buildings, cobbled streets, and genteel yet lively atmosphere.

ANNE ARUNDEL COUNTY 98
  Annapolis and Environs; Greater Anne Arundel County
HOWARD COUNTY 111
  Ellicott City; Greater Howard County
MONTGOMERY COUNTY 116
PRINCE GEORGE'S COUNTY 123

Southern Maryland 134

Experience the past in the southern counties where Maryland was born. The fourth English settlement in North America, St. Mary's City transports visitors to colonial times through excavations and reconstructions. The 15-million-year-old fossils at Calvert Cliffs show a more ancient view. Back in the present, uncrowded villages and resorts host beach-goers, boaters, and anglers.

CHARLES COUNTY 138
  Cobb Island; Pomfret; Pope's Creek; Waldorf
ST. MARY'S COUNTY 146
CALVERT COUNTY 153
  Twin Beaches: Chesapeake Beach and North Beach; Solomons

Western Maryland 164

Historic Frederick acts as the gateway to both western Maryland and national memory. Pivotal Civil War battlefields Antietam and Monocacy, now peaceful, have become sites of pilgrimage. Outdoor enthusiasts should continue west into the Allegheny Mountains, where Deep Creek Lake offers hiking, skiing, and canoeing.

FREDERICK AND ENVIRONS 167
CROSSROADS OF THE CIVIL WAR 178
  Harpers Ferry National Historical Park; South Mountain; Antietam National
  Battlefield; Monocacy National Battlefield
HAGERSTOWN AND ENVIRONS 192
ORCHARD COUNTRY AND THE C&O CANAL 196
CUMBERLAND AND ENVIRONS 201
FAR WEST: GARRETT COUNTY 209
  Deep Creek Lake

North-Central Maryland 220

North-central Maryland is a mix of horse-breeding farms, rural country manors, and colonial ports, both sleepy and active. Here you'll also find some of the finest cycling routes in the country, where long, narrow roads weave along miles of marshland and glittering bay.

WESTMINSTER AND CARROLL COUNTY 223
BALTIMORE COUNTY 230
HARFORD COUNTY 232
  Havre de Grace

CECIL COUNTY 240
Village of North East; Village of Chesapeake City
KENT COUNTY 246
Chestertown; Village of Rock Hall; Greater Kent County

The Eastern Shore 254

East across the Chesapeake Bay Bridge you'll find thousands of miles of shoreline to explore, including "Miami of the North" Ocean City. Offshore, slow-paced Deal and Smith Islands offer a taste of the waterman's life, while wild horses roam freely on Assateague Island.

QUEEN ANNE'S COUNTY 257
Wye and Environs
TALBOT COUNTY 262
St. Michaels; Tilghman Island; Oxford; Easton
DORCHESTER COUNTY 272
Cambridge; East New Market; Secretary; Vienna; Bucktown; Hooper Island;
Taylors Island
SALISBURY AND WICOMICO COUNTY 278
Salisbury
SOMERSET COUNTY 284
Princess Anne; Deal Island; Smith Island; Crisfield
WORCESTER COUNTY 290
Snow Hill and Environs; Berlin
OCEAN CITY 294
Assateague Island

DELAWARE 311

Introduction to Delaware 312

A leader in industry, banking, and technology, this next-to-smallest state has an importance that far exceeds its area on the map. But thanks to its small size, Delaware's mix of urban sophistication, rural charm, and seaside delight can be sampled all in the same day.

The Land **314;** History **320;** The People **324**

On the Road in Delaware 327

Looking for the perfect greenway? Need advice on where (and what) to fish, or the easiest way to get around? You'll find all the inside information right here.

Outdoor Recreation **328;** Entertainment and Events **335;** Accommodations and Food **336;** Transportation **337;** Information and Services **338**

Northern Delaware and Wilmington 341

The name Du Pont is everywhere in the Brandywine Valley; the properties the family has bequeathed and their superb gardens provide a glimpse of how the other half once lived. Nearby, Wilmington is experiencing a renaissance, with a revitalized riverfront and a thriving restaurant scene.

BRANDYWINE VALLEY 343
WILMINGTON 352

Central Delaware 362

This is a golden country of back roads, wheat fields, and waving marsh grasses, where geese can be heard calling for miles. Wander the pebbled edges of the long coastline, tour the Amish country around Dover, or head to wonderfully preserved New Castle, where you can sit along the Delaware River and watch the ships—and the world—go by.

New Castle; Central Kent County: Odessa and Harrington; Dover and Environs

Southern Delaware 381

For lovers of sea and sand, the southern shore is Delaware. Each resort town is unique, from quiet Lewes to bustling Rehoboth to hard-partying Dewey Beach. Nearby, Cape Henlopen and Delaware Seashore State Parks offer summer at its finest.

Lewes; Rehoboth Beach and Dewey Beach; Bethany Beach and Fenwick Island; Sussex County Inland: Millsboro and Georgetown

Side Trip to D.C. 401

Tour grand monuments on the Mall, take in a show at the Kennedy Center, or soak up some knowledge at the Smithsonian. Or just explore city life in this most impressive of company towns. As befits the seat of the U.S. government, D.C. practically hums with energy.

The Mall; Tidal Basin; Capitol Hill; The White House; Old Downtown and the Federal Triangle; Adams-Morgan; Upper Northwest; Georgetown; East of the Capitol

Resources 435
SUGGESTED READING 436
INTERNET RESOURCES 439
INDEX 441

ABOUT THE AUTHOR
Joanne Miller

One of Joanne Miller's earliest memories is of being lulled by the hum of car wheels as she gazed out the window of a wine-colored Oldsmobile; the scenery changed from dense forests to cornfields to dry plains. Her father, a freelance photographer, was taking pictures in the U.S. National Parks System for *National Geographic.* By age 10 she had visited every state in the lower 48.

Comic books made interesting companions on the road; Scrooge McDuck introduced the South Pacific, Egypt's pyramids, and Jason and the Golden Fleece, all in an easy-to-follow four-color format. An appreciation of fine literature followed, in the form of Classics Illustrated *MacBeth,* which was a terrific ghost story. By the time Joanne was reading books with more words than pictures, she had written and illustrated one of her own: a primer on "How to Do Everything Right." Martha Stewart, eat your heart out.

After surviving her know-it-all teens, and adding Alaska, Hawaii, Japan, England, and Canada to her list of "been-theres," Joanne had her first in-depth encounter with Maryland and Delaware. After securing a B.A. in anthropology, she traveled through Mexico, and drove from Texas to Washington, D.C., seized by a desire to gawk at the Lincoln Memorial, and to cross the mighty, glittering Chesapeake. In the following years, she lived on the East Coast, returning to Delaware's beaches and following Civil War history and the briny scent of crab cakes south into Maryland's fine countryside.

She continues to live and write her own adventures in full color, whether it's canoeing among the fireflies on Deep Creek Lake, dodging feisty crabs on Smith Island's oyster-shell roads, or feeling the burn while climbing Baltimore's Washington Monument. Every place has its story, and Joanne makes the landscape come alive through words and pictures.

She is the author of *Moon Handbooks Pennsylvania* and *Moon Handbooks Chesapeake Bay* and is a frequent contributor to *Writer's Market* and *Novel & Short Story Writer's Market.* Among her published short stories, "Penance" was a finalist for the Raymond Carver Award. Currently, she is working on a novel of old San Francisco, *Land's End.*

Preface

When a writer takes on a book of this magnitude, it's like committing to a lover. Initial impressions are always superficial. Then, as time passes, one learns to read the Braille of another by running mental fingertips over conversations and listening hard to silences. Just so, one comes to know a place by pacing time on salt-blown promontories, canoeing marshy recesses, and walking—unknowing and unknown—through crowded urban streets. One thousand miles, ten thousand miles: I traveled to understand these places called Maryland and Delaware.

Below the surfaces of masonry, damp clay, and shifting sands lies the authentic nature of place and person. To truly know this nature takes years, and determined observation. One thousand hellos and goodbyes, nights caressed by warm softness, paths illuminated by fireflies; brilliance reflected on the water, golden seagrass waving impishly: one thousand memories, written in a book.

There is no place like Maryland. There is no place like Delaware. And the fact that there is a place like Washington, D.C., is a source of wonderment. I'm still in love, even though we live apart. Sometimes I dream about the Chesapeake; brackish water pumps through my heart, and I'm sailing on bright water, every flash of reflected sunlight a gold rush. Horseshoe crabs still scuttle over the stones of my imagination. I've been captured by the power of water, the power of wind. May you also know the glory of these beautiful places.

Maryland

Introduction to Maryland

To travel is to take a journey into yourself.

Dena Kaye

Sunlight on the bay is bewitching. This dancing light drew Native Americans to the shallow waters to gather food for their families. Hundreds of years later, Europeans, exhausted from the religious battles of the Reformation, saw heaven reflected on the gentle waves. The seat of this most wondrous of waters—*Terra Mariae,* Mary's land—was meant to welcome all who sought peace.

The mighty Chesapeake, and the land that caresses it, continue to enchant. Spun out from the hub of the bay, Maryland offers sandy peninsulas, fertile upland, and cool mountains. Bounty was and is everywhere, from shellfish and other seafood to thousands of acres of cultivated fields and farms teeming with livestock. Glittering cities rise above the coastal plain. How can one place be so many things?

Maryland and Virginia share water access to the Atlantic via Chesapeake Bay. East of the Chesapeake, a wide spit of land forms the Delmarva Peninsula (Delaware-Maryland-Virginia), a place of historic towns, low-lying farms, and fisheries. A chain of barrier islands runs along the lower part of the peninsula. Ocean City,

the *Maryland Dove,* docked at Historic St. Mary's City

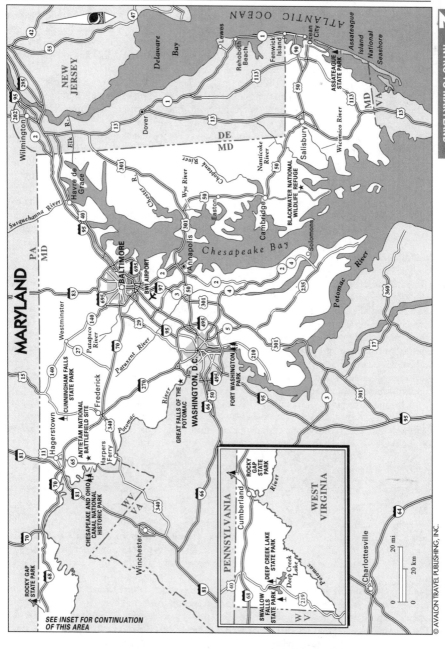

INTRO TO MARYLAND

Maryland, which lies at the southernmost end of one of these islands, is a renowned recreational surf-bathing and fishing resort. Assateague Island, just south of Ocean City across a narrow inlet, is a state and national preserve.

On the northern boundaries of the bay, farm and forest set the stage for wineries and horse farms. Here, the population becomes increasingly dense as it reaches Baltimore City on the northwest side of the bay. The old tobacco port of Baltimore grew into an industrial power during the 1800s, and today offers visitors a thousand pleasures. Baltimore features a world-class aquarium, art museums, and absolutely amazing food.

Hugging the west side of the Chesapeake, the great population centers of central Maryland stretch from Baltimore south to Washington, D.C. Annapolis, the wonderfully preserved state capital, lies at the western terminus of the bay bridge, linking west and east shores. The U.S. Naval Academy is one of many reasons to visit this charming town. Rockville, Bethesda, and Silver Spring form a few of the many suburban branches that spread from the city of Washington; the appearance of over-development is deceptive, however. Tracts of open land hug the Potomac River, while U.S. government facilities include a space exploration center, vast wildlife refuge, and agricultural center.

Surrounded by water—the Potomac River on the west and the Chesapeake on the east— southern Maryland is the birthplace of the state. St. Mary's City was the first colony, and today the winding waterways and farmlands are as bucolic as they were in Lord Baltimore's day. Solomons Island is a lovely base for exploring the ancient Calvert Cliffs and the rest of this quiet country.

The Piedmont Plateau spreads across the western part of the state, growing bumpy and sweet with pine as it enters the Appalachian Mountains. Far removed from salt spray, the west is a land of peaceful orchards and small farms scaling into gentle mountains, a place of warm fruit pies and black-water lakes: a different world, not three hours away from the bustle of Baltimore's inner harbor.

Today, light continues to dance on the bay, but the Chesapeake requires that the beauty and bounty it has conferred on so many generations be returned, in the form of conservation as well as appreciation. Maryland is a beautiful place; there is nowhere like it on earth. Nothing about it is austere. It was meant to answer a heart's desire, be it a silent and lonesome hike through pine woods or the mad whirl of a reel connecting with a big fish; canoes gliding on lakes of mirrored sky or salt spray peppering your face as your sailboat tacks into the wind. Perhaps your dreams are man-made: crab cakes, crispy on the outside, creamy within, and impossibly tender fried chicken; or ornate jewels made for heiresses and three-story-high glass walls with sharks circling behind. If you can imagine it, you will find it here, dancing in the sunlight, heaven captured and shared.

The Land

Maryland covers 10,460 square miles across three vastly different types of terrain. From east to west, bordering the Atlantic Ocean, the Tidewater consists of flat, sandy marshland surrounding the Chesapeake Bay. The land then rises into the rocky, fertile Piedmont Plateau, culminating in the ancient rounded mountaintops and piney forests of the Appalachians. At its narrowest point, between Garrett and Washington Counties in the west, it's less than two miles wide. The highest point in the state—also in the west—is 3,360-foot Backbone Mountain.

The Tidewater, or **Atlantic Coastal Plain,** is cut north-to-south by Chesapeake Bay, the largest estuary in the United States. The bay divides the region into the low-lying Eastern Shore—part of the Delmarva Peninsula—and the higher western shore. Soil in this area was partially submerged in the Atlantic Ocean several times during the Cenozoic era (roughly 65 million to 2 million years ago); as a consequence, the

© JOANNE MILLER

Amish farmers gather hay on Maryland's fertile farmland.

soil is sandy and full of clay and marl. The Miocene-period formations of the Cenozoic era are best exemplified by the Calvert Cliffs in Calvert County on the western shore. The cliffs are 13 miles long and rise to 100 feet; continuous bands of clay rich in marine fossils have been exposed over thousands of years. Prior to the Miocene, about 35 million years ago, the area was the site of an "event"—a comet, long since buried, hit earth in the region of the Chesapeake Bay. The impact was so great that sediments at ground zero were instantly heated to four thousand degrees Fahrenheit, melted, blasted out of the crater, rapidly chilled to glass, and thrown thousands of miles away. There's a little bit of the Chesapeake in Texas, buried in the sediments of the time period.

Westward over the plain is the **Piedmont Plateau,** a broad, rolling upland. Its streams flow gently and cut deep gorges until they reach the fall line. Here, the plateau ends dramatically, and its waters cascade to the plains below. The most spectacular of these is the **Great Falls of the Potomac,** 15 miles northwest of Washington, D.C. The numerous streams and creeks often have a reddish cast from the mineral-rich heavy clay soil.

Covering the extreme western part of the state, **the Appalachians** provide a spectacularly different topography. Mountains, such as Blue Ridge, Catoctin, Allegheny, Green Ridge, Great Savage, Meadow, Negro, and Sugar Loaf, divide the area into valleys. This region, which makes up one-fifth of Maryland's landmass, includes parts of Frederick County and the counties of Garrett, Allegany, and Washington. The most noteworthy valley, bordered on the east by South Mountain State Park, is the Hagerstown (or Antietam) Valley. It is an extension of the Cumberland Valley of Pennsylvania and is separated from the Shenandoah Valley of Virginia by the basin of the Potomac. The Antietam Valley is blessed with one of the most fertile soils of the eastern states, notable for its production of grain. The valley is also rich in limestone and a marble that, in color and evenness of texture, compares in quality with that of Tuscany.

Waterways

Maryland is laced with rivers and creeks; major drainage basins are the Potomac River, Chesapeake Bay, the Atlantic Ocean, and the Mississippi (in Garrett County). The waterways of the

CROSSING THE WATERS

In colonial Maryland, large commercial boats such as tobacco ships, wheat ships, and slave ships were common, and nearly everyone owned some sort of little bay craft. Canoes, punts, shallops, pinnaces, and sloops plied the waterways of the region, serving as fishing craft and general transportation.

The most precarious vessel was the log canoe, a fallen tree hollowed out by means of fire and axes, a method adopted from the Indians. Early watermen added two leg-of-mutton sails and a jib, making the boat considerably swifter and much more unstable. As time passed, single logs were bolted together to form a larger and much more bay-worthy log canoe, identified by the number of logs used in the base (six-log canoe, nine-log canoe). Other characteristic watercraft of the Chesapeake Bay are the bugeye, pungy, and the once-ubiquitous skipjack. All were used for oystering; bugeye and pungy are thought to be corrupt forms of the Scottish word for oysters, "buckie."

As more people streamed into the bay, a need for seaworthy vessels manned by skilled seamen grew. Packet sloops, decked vessels carrying 10–12 passengers, were the accepted mode of journeying between the bay's far-flung settlements.

Not all vessels plied the waters of the Chesapeake. With so many waterways to cross, ferries were common. Often, the ferry itself was little more than a flat-bottomed scow rowed or poled from shore to shore—on a narrow stream, the ferry might be pulled across hand-over-hand on a rope. One colonial-era ferry was nothing more than two lashed-together canoes; riders with horses had to stand the animal's front legs in one and hind legs in the other.

greater part of western Maryland course into the Potomac. These include the Monocacy (moh-NA-kah-see) River and the Conococheague (ka-no-ka-CHEEG), Antietam (an-TEE-tum), and Catoctin (ka-TOCK-tin) Creeks. The Potomac River, forming the boundary with Virginia on the south, is a principal water system for both states. From the time humans came to this area, it has afforded transportation and facilitated settlement up to the fall line. On the western shore, the Patuxent, Patapsco, Gunpowder, and Susquehanna (sus-kwa-HAN-na) Rivers all drain into Chesapeake Bay. The major Eastern Shore rivers—the Elk, Sassafras, Chester, Wye, Choptank, Nanticoke, Wicomico, and Manokin—have facilitated trade and nurtured towns and villages from colonial times to the present. Some of the waterways of western Maryland produce hydroelectric power; nearly all are used for commerce, fishing, and recreation.

Chesapeake Bay: This large and shallow (average depth outside the deep central channel: 21 feet) body of water dominates every facet of life in Maryland, particularly in the Tidewater region.

Chesapeake Bay is one of the world's largest estuaries and an international-class fishing area. Created within the last 15,000 years by the flooding of the lower valley of the Susquehanna, it is the final destination of hundreds of rivers, bays, and creeks. The bay is about 180 miles long and between five and 30 miles wide. The total shoreline of the bay and its tributaries in Maryland is about 4,000 miles. The total watershed is 74,000 square miles, a little greater than seven times the landmass.

More than 2.3 million people live within 20 miles of the bay and its tributaries. By the end of the 21st century, the population is forecast to grow to 12 million. The most populous city is Baltimore, but hundreds of cities, towns, and villages dot the shoreline. The way of life in many of them is determined in great measure by the bay, which has given meaning to the term "watermen"—those who make a living from the Chesapeake. From the earliest days of European settlement, the bay opened Maryland to the world, while settlements in other states often suffered economic and social isolation until railroads and canals arrived in the 19th century.

GEOGRAPHY

The most notable geographic feature of Maryland is the **Atlantic Coastal Plain,** formed by glacial advance and retreat, invasion and flooding by the Atlantic Ocean and Susquehanna River. From Baltimore south to Washington, D.C., the soil is made up of silts and clay. Southern Maryland is a combination of sand, silt, and clay; all of the southeastern shore and Atlantic shore is composed of homogenous silt, clay, shell beds, sand, and gravel. The Atlantic shore was once connected to Baltimore by land; a grass-covered, sandy valley composed of layers of sediment reached from the region of Queenstown across to Annapolis. As the waters rose at the end of the last ice age, the Susquehanna filled the valley and met the ocean, creating the Chesapeake Bay.

The **Piedmont Plateau** is a region of lowlands and gentle hills. The area is extremely fertile; the terrain, covering the hills like velvet in a jewel box, boasts some of the best farmland in the country. The northern section of the plateau has remained productive due, in large part, to the soil conservation methods practiced by Mennonite and Amish settlers who have dwelled there in large numbers since moving west from Philadelphia during the early days of the colonies.

South Mountain, on the southern state border near Gettysburg, marks the end of the Piedmont Plateau and the beginning of the Appalachians. Of all the mountain ranges of Appalachia, South Mountain is the oldest; structurally, it's a continuation of the Blue Ridge Mountains in Virginia.

The **Appalachian Mountains,** reaching up into the far northeast, tumble down through Pennsylvania into western Maryland. The Appalachians are a product of glacial carving, eons of ice scraping away neatly horizontal layers of rock, though the smooth, rounded, wooded hills near Deep Creek Lake are due more to steady erosion. In the northwest section of Maryland, south of Pittsburgh, the coal-mining valleys that contain the Youghiogheny (yock-a-GAY-nee) and Allegheny Rivers are deep, layered fissures marking the edge of the Appalachian Plateau.

CLIMATE

The climate of the state is as varied as its geography. In the eastern part, the buffering effects of the Chesapeake Bay and Atlantic Ocean create a moderate, insular climate. Mild winters (with an average of eight to 10 inches of short-lived snow) and summers of high humidity with generally warm days and nights are the norm. Temperatures are rarely excessive, though humidity certainly can be.

The climate of the western half of the state matches that of the interior of the continent, with cold air masses in winter from central Canada and the western United States bringing low temperatures and snow. In summer the winds of the Southwest and Gulf of Mexico bring hot humid air and rain through the lower elevations of the western counties, making the area as warm and sometimes as humid as the east. Rainfall averages two to four inches a month overall, with the greatest precipitation in July and August.

Best Times to Visit

Late summer in Maryland can seem almost tropical, so if your tolerance level for thick air is high, you'll enjoy all parts of the state. The west tends to be less humid than the areas that surround Chesapeake Bay, and many city dwellers escape to the higher elevation of Deep Creek Lake during the warmest months. Generally, off-season (late fall, winter, early spring) in any part of Maryland will yield a bounty of discounts and package deals. Though anglers and hunters are limited to their seasons, others will find that the best times to visit are determined by destination.

Ocean City and the Atlantic shore are favorite spots for visitors from the chilliest days of May (the water is *cold*) all the way through mid-October. September/October is an especially lovely time to be there—the summer crowds are gone, the water is warm, many hotels offer discounts, and the sun continues to light up the beach all day. Long, romantic (and very private) walks on the beach are yours during the winter, when some of the best restaurants and businesses stay open for the local trade.

If active outdoor sports are on your list, summer is an ideal time to go west. Hiking, biking, and water sports on the C&O Canal path and Deep Creek Lake are all the more enjoyable in fine weather; since many vacation at the shore, this leaves the western trails free of huddled masses. This is also the area to catch a bit of fall color. Maryland's premier ski resort welcomes visitors there in the winter—this is the area of concentration for all winter sports.

Autumn, winter, and spring are all good times to visit Baltimore, as the crowds are fewer and the attractions continue to entice. Fresh seafood is at its peak in the fall and winter, and the city's many fine restaurants make the most of it.

FLORA

Native plants require searching out, as most of the state has been cultivated since European settlement. Tobacco was the first crop, but because it demanded so much from the land, its cultivation decreased when market prices dropped after the American Revolution. Farmers began planting their fields with more renewable crops such as wheat, soy, and market vegetables. About one third of the land remains forested, though old-growth stands are rare.

Fortunately, cultivated fields encouraged the growth of wildflowers. Maryland's many varieties sparkle like jewels set in golden field grasses, and are often gathered for house bouquets. Native flora may be in short supply, but the many estate gardens and tree plantings—some maintained since colonial times—are truly spectacular. Many urban areas celebrate spring under the blooms of cherry and other decorative trees, including the 40-foot-tall Princess Paulownia, awash in royal purple flowers.

Native Trees

Trees characteristic of eastern hardwood forests—seven species of oaks, four species of hickories, five types of red and yellow maples, and beeches—are common, while the extreme west of the state extends into the northern and southern evergreen zones, with nine types of conifers, including white pine and spruce. Trees that grow easily and in large numbers without cultivation are the tulip poplar, yellow locust, yellow birch, pignut hickory, white oak (the state tree), and white ash. Crape myrtle and varieties of magnolia are found in the southern parts of the Atlantic Coastal Plain, where wild trees often remain shrub-size due to the sandy soil. Disease has depleted native species of elm and chestnut, though dogwood, hackberry, and sycamore continue to thrive. One of the country's most northern stands of bald cypress can be found in southern Maryland.

Shrubs and Flowers

In the spring and through the summer until fall, Maryland is festooned with wildflowers. Azalea, rhododendron, redbud, mountain laurel, and honeysuckle are common in shady areas. Sunny fields boast red wild bergamot, wild valerian, monument plant, wild rose, daisy, tiger lily, goldenrod, and black-eyed Susan, the state flower.

Under the forest canopy, spring brings the delicate wood violet to bloom alongside Indian pipe, spring beauty, Jack-in-the-pulpit, wild grapevine, Turks cap lily, trillium, Dutchman's breeches, and yellow lady slipper. Several types of ferns thrive along streams and rivers, among them bracken, New York fern, lady fern, and Christmas fern.

Along the shorelines, wildflowers hide among native grasses such as redhead grass, wild celery, eelgrass, and Widgeon grass; on the water, these natives have sometimes been supplanted by the ivory plumes of phragmites, an attractive but unwelcome foreign invader. One unusual wild find along the beaches is yucca, a flowering succulent normally associated with desert areas.

FAUNA
Mammals

Central Maryland is largely urban and suburban, which leaves little room for larger mammals common to the northern and southeastern regions of the United States. The raccoon, which has adapted to suburban intrusion, is an exception. However, the forests and fields of the Delmarva Peninsula and southern and western Maryland continue to support a variety of wildlife. White-tailed deer, once severely over-hunted and devastated by heavy deforestation, are slowly returning. Black bear and wildcat, though not considered endangered, are rarely seen in their western mountain habitats. Other animals common to North American forests, such as foxes, beavers, mink, raccoon, opossums, wood-chucks, striped skunks, gray and black squirrels, and wild rabbit have adapted and thrive in all areas with a bit of meadow. Muskrats, beaver, marsh rabbit, and otter inhabit the marshes. The endangered Delmarva fox squirrel, a victim of habitat encroachment, is on the way back.

Birds

Though habitat encroachment may challenge larger mammals, it's a windfall for species *aves.* Maryland is bird-watching heaven. Birders in Charles County in the central part of the state have spotted more than 321 varieties of birds of all types. The species list reads like poetry: Loons and grebes; gannets, pelicans, and cor-morants; herons and ibis; swans, geese, ducks; vultures, hawks, and falcons; turkeys, quail, rails; plovers and sandpipers; gulls and terns; doves and cuckoos; owls and nightjars; swifts, hum-mingbirds, kingfishers, and woodpeckers; fly-catchers; larks and swallows; jays and crows; chickadees, titmice, nuthatches, and creepers; wrens; kinglets, gnatcatchers, and thrushes; mim-ics, pipits, waxwings, and starlings; vireos and warblers; tanagers, sparrows, and finches. Nearly every county provides a bird-watching check-list; contact Charles County Tourism for theirs: P.O. Box B, La Plata, MD 20646, 301/645-0558 or 800/766-3386. A walk on any trail in the state will provide a glimpse of several winged beauties, including the rare indigo bunting and the Baltimore oriole (both spotted on Wye Is-land, Eastern Shore).

Perching Birds: Ravens, orioles, and blue-birds are found everywhere in the state. The brown-headed nuthatch is found in extreme southern areas, while mockingbirds, hawks, and crows are numerous throughout the coastal plain. Purple martins, largest of the American swal-lows, are valued for their voracious appetite for in-sects; refuges and farmers around the Chesapeake

Bay encourage the birds to nest by building mar-tin "hotels." The cardinal, Carolina wren, and tufted titmouse are often spotted in the Pied-mont Plateau. Thrushes, chestnut-sided war-blers, and many species of northern birds are commonly spotted in the mountainous areas. Nocturnal birds, the screech, great horned, and barred owls roam the skies in lightly wooded areas and suburbs year-round. Ground-nesting birds such as the bobwhite quail, Hungarian par-tridge, woodcock, wild turkey, and ring-necked pheasant are common in the woodlands.

Shore and Water Birds: These are perhaps the most symbolic of Maryland's birds. More than 40 varieties of ducks have been observed; year-round varieties include the canvasback, red-breasted merganser, black head mallard, black duck, and wood duck. Canada geese gather by the thousands on the edges of ponds and lakes during migratory season, as do tundra swans.

A shorebird, the killdeer, with its long legs and black double necklace, wades alongside the endangered piping plover (easily identifiable by the "peep peep" of its call), willits, avocets, seag-ulls, terns, and dozens of varieties of sandpipers on the shorelines. Ospreys, peregrine falcons, ea-gles, and other raptors nest and take to the skies along the Chesapeake. The great blue heron, a three-foot-tall wading bird, can be found nesting in trees in Chesapeake marshes.

Reptiles

Eight varieties of nonpoisonous snake inhabit Maryland: corn, yellow, rat, brown, king, striped water, water pilot, and scarlet. The two poiso-nous types are the timber rattlesnake in the mountain counties and the copperhead in the wetter areas.

The flesh of the now-common diamondback terrapin was so popular around the turn of the 20th century that the animal was nearly hunted into extinction. Snapping turtles, mud turtles, and eastern painted turtles are often seen near still water.

Amphibians

Frogs, newts, and salamanders inhabit the banks of streams, rivers, and catch basins. Common amphibians are the spotted salamander, purplish-black with yellow or orange spots; the marbled salamander, black with white or gray patches; the eastern tiger salamander, similar in marking to the marbled but with bright yellow, irregular spots; and the red-spotted newt, which spends part of its life strolling forest floors after rainstorms (they're also called efts in this stage, when they turn bright scarlet or orange).

Fish

The rivers and man-made lakes above and below the Great Falls of the Potomac contain such freshwater fish as largemouth and smallmouth bass, white perch, and varieties of sunfish and catfish. Northern pike have been introduced with some success into man-made Tridelphia and Pretty Boy Lakes. Trout, occasionally seeded in selected up-country waters, make their way into smaller streams.

Fish species in Chesapeake Bay overshadow those of all other localities. Perch, blue fish, striped bass (the state fish, also known as stripers or rockfish), and some 200 other varieties of finned fish are found there. Lower sections of the Chesapeake's tributaries are breeding grounds

BEAUTIFUL SWIMMER

Callinectes sapidus, the scientific name for Chesapeake Bay's blue crab, means "beautiful swimmer/tasty"—one of the most apt descriptions in the lexicon. The crustacean is equipped with paddle-like back legs that help propel it through the water on its endless quest for food. The blue's propensity to eat just about anything in its path has been a true saving grace. The Chesapeake Bay was one of the world's most productive ecosystems up until the 1960s. Disappearance of underwater grasses from great areas of the bottom of the shallow bay, combined with toxic wastes, added to the decline of the bay's fish and shellfish populations. The blue crab, however, is genetically primed to survive, rising and falling in the moving currents until feeding grounds are found.

The blue crab is hatched in deep water near the mouth of the bay, and produces a million eggs for every crab that reaches maturity. Like most marine creatures, the crab thrives in a narrow range of salinity, whereas the bay has a very wide range, from freshwater to Atlantic salt tides. The saltwater, being heavier, sinks to the bottom and flows in, while the fresh water flows out over it. The crab larvae are programmed by nature to rise and drop in the water and thus ride currents that take them to shallow, grassy feeding grounds.

A crab's life is one of continual expansion and release, from its first summer days as a plankton-sized zoea to its maturity, 12 to 18 months later, and beyond. As the crab increases in size, it needs to molt, or shed the old hard shell. The crab pumps water into its body to enlarge the new soft shell and within a few hours, the shell hardens (one of the primary reasons softshell, or molted, crabs are raised by aquaculture).

On maturity, the male crab attracts a female by strutting about, waving his claws and walking on tiptoes (the origin of stiletto-heeled shoes, no doubt). The lucky female backs underneath the male, who cradles her between his walking legs until she molts, at which time they mate. After the female's shell hardens again, the male releases her; he will remain in the bay until fall, while she journeys out to spawning areas near the mouth of the Chesapeake to lay her eggs in early winter.

The death of underwater grasses presents a problem: this is where the growing crabs hide to reach maturity. The lack of oxygen in the water, a product of algae growth, sometimes creates a phenomenon known as a "crab war," when crabs are driven up onto the land, fleeing the "dead" water. In spite of these hazards, the crab harvest increases and decreases without identifiable reasons; because of this phenomenon, crabs are not considered in jeopardy. However, scientists, watermen, and the millions of others who dwell on the bay are keeping a sharp lookout for signs of trouble with their beautiful swimmers.

for herring and shad in the early spring. (The prediction of when the shad will run has become a pseudo-religion among a certain set of anglers.) Formerly, because of pollution, only the spring breeders and catfish could be found on the Potomac River below the Falls; now the area is making a comeback.

Offshore from Ocean City, the Atlantic abounds in tuna, bluefish, dolphin, and occasionally marlin. Dolphin can be spotted from the shore, and occasionally come into the bay, sometimes with disastrous results. The National Fisheries Service warns against feeding or attempting to swim with the wild animals, as dozens of bites have been reported, and the animals are often injured by boat propellers.

Shellfish such as clams and blue crab—the symbol of the Chesapeake—are abundant but are always threatened by the effects of population growth around the Bay. Oysters have experienced a severe downturn in recent years.

ENVIRONMENTAL CONCERNS

Prior to the arrival of Europeans, most of Maryland was covered with old-growth forest and the Chesapeake teemed with oysters, crabs, and fish. Around 1676, an anonymous settler wrote: "The abundance of oysters is incredible. There are whole banks of them so that the ships must avoid them. A sloop, which was to land us at Kingscreek, struck an oyster bed, where we had to wait about two hours for the tide." A chart of the James River, published by the Dutch, shows seventeen "reefs." None exist today. Oysters, which filter and clean the water of the bay while feeding, were so abundant that they accomplished in a few days what now is done in a year.

Agricultural techniques, domestic livestock, and the runoff produced by both changed the face of the land. Marshes were drained for planting, which reduced the land's ability to filter storm water into the Chesapeake Bay watershed. By the late 1800s, hunting and habitat depletion severely reduced or wiped out once-abundant game animals, and pollution assaulted the bay from the lowest levels of the ecosystem to the top predators. Two thousand skipjacks and other boats dredged

---

PROTECTING THE BAY

In 1998, the Environmental Protection Agency announced an enhanced federal action plan that called for 50 new initiatives to help restore wetlands, replant 200 miles of streamside buffer forests, and curtail federal building in pristine fields in the area surrounding the nation's capital. Wetlands on federal land were to be restored at the rate of 100 acres net gain per year beginning in 2000. Dams and other obstacles on federal lands that prevented migratory fish from moving along waterways were to be identified and removed by the end of 2003.

Pollution prevention strategies are centered on cutting toxic discharges from federal facilities by 75 percent. Some of the chemicals of concern include lead, copper, cadmium, polychlorinated biphenyls (PCBs), and chlordane. Under the plan, special attention would be paid to cleaning the Anacostia River in the District of Columbia, the Elizabeth River in Virginia, and the Potomac and Upper Susquehanna Rivers in Maryland.

---

the bay and creek beds for oysters; a dozen railroad cars filled with shellfish left Baltimore daily to points west, as far as San Francisco.

The conservation movement and changes in the local economy—chiefly a reduced market for commercial game meat—began to reverse the damage at about the same time; wildlife and waterfowl have increased greatly in the past century. The waters of the bay, however, continue to be the subject of efforts to reduce pollution and sedimentation.

The Chesapeake Bay presents a graphic illustration of the chain of life. In the early 1980s, fishermen were the first to spot bright green mats spreading over the Potomac. The green was algae, tiny primitive plants, and they were a symptom of trouble. Algae populations had exploded thanks to an abundance of food: nutrient runoff (nitrogen and phosphorus) from farm fertilizers, waterside factories, sewage treatment plants, and automobiles. Minnows, small fish, and microscopic water animals were unable to consume all the algae, and the remainder sunk to the bottom of the bay. Bottom bacteria gorged on the bonanza, meanwhile robbing the water of oxygen, a condition known as anoxia. Other creatures that normally lived in these depleted zones were forced to leave—or suffocated. Fish and shellfish weren't the only victims. Algae shaded and choked submerged sea grasses (often called SAV, submerged aquatic vegetation), the "breeding farms" of the bay. In 1997, pollution was also blamed for an outbreak of pfiesteria, a flesh-eating microbe, which in turn was blamed for huge fish kills all over the bay, as well as skin problems reported by human swimmers. Though the pfiesteria threat has diminished, scientists are watchful; citizens are urged to call 888/584-3110 to report fish with lesions.

Numerous groups have banded together to monitor and improve the health of the bay, including The Chesapeake Bay Trust, the state of Maryland (which issues special "Treasure the Chesapeake" license plates and offers a tax-form donation choice), and scientists from Maryland, Virginia, Pennsylvania, Washington, D.C., and the Environmental Protection Agency. The turning point came in 1983, when sewage-treatment plants were put in place in cities around the bay and on major tributaries. The largest of these installations is the Blue Plains plant (aka the Craphouse Taj Mahal) on the Potomac River. Industrial wastes have proven to be a more difficult problem, as they do not flush out with the tides but settle to the bottom. The worst spot is in the James River, where the Allied Chemical Company dumped quantities of an ant-and-roach poison, Kepone. It's expected to stay in the water for many decades.

Richard Lacouture, a scientist with the Estuarine Research Center, Calvert County, says, "The bay isn't all that fragile. It has an amazing capacity to resist change. But that's not to say we haven't pushed it over the edge. We can never hope to see the bay that John Smith saw, or even the oystermen of the last century."

One success story has been the comeback of rockfish, or striped bass, the prime sport fish of the northern Atlantic Coast. Ninety percent of the coast's rockfish are hatched in the Chesapeake's tributaries. The population was almost wiped out by the early 1980s, and Maryland imposed a total ban on rockfish, naming it an endangered species. The ban was an economic disaster—7,500 jobs were lost on the East Coast—but the drastic effort was successful. In 1989, the rockfish count jumped up sharply and restrictions were eased, though the fish is still heavily monitored.

Oysters, once so plentiful, are being wiped out by pollution and two parasitic diseases, MSX and dermo. In efforts to study and combat the diseases, citizens have joined scientists through volunteer programs that count and check oyster sites. Two places to find out more about citizens' programs are the Estuarine Research Center, 10545 Mackall Rd., St. Leonard, MD 20685, 410/586-9700, and the National Aquarium of Baltimore, Conservation Dept., Pier 3, Baltimore, MD 21202, 410/659-4207. For information on the bay in general, contact the U.S. Fish and Wildlife Service, Chesapeake Bay Estuary Program, 180 Admiral Cochrane Dr., Ste. 535, Annapolis, MD 21401, 301/224-2732.

History

First People

Ancestors of Maryland's indigenous peoples, early hunter-gatherers, ranged across this part of North America between 9,000 and 12,000 years ago. Later tribal units were almost entirely of the Algonquian-speaking language family—the Piscataway and Yoacomocos (Wicomocos) on the western shore, and the Nanticokes, Wicomesse, Choptanks, Arseek, Cuscarawaoc, Pocomoke-Assateague, and Nause (reputed to be formidable sorcerers and poisoners) on the Eastern Shore.

Giovanni da Verrazano is thought to have visited the Atlantic coast near Chincoteague Bay in 1524. In 1526, Spanish explorers sailed into Chesapeake Bay and called it Santa Maria, a name that appears on a 1556 map. In 1608, Captain John Smith sailed into the Chesapeake and explored the eastern shoreline, finally choosing to settle in Virginia.

Lord Calvert Sees the Light

In 1580, George Calvert was born into a wealthy landowning family in Yorkshire, England. He served several terms in the House of Commons, and as Secretary of State and member of the Privy Council under King James I. He was knighted for exemplary service in 1619.

When Sir George was building his career, the Anglican Church was the official church of England; Henry VIII had broken with the Roman Catholic Church nearly a century before because of objections to his frequent spousal exchange program. Catholics were under perpetual suspicion of disloyalty to the crown, unable to hold public office or to hear Mass in public, and were fined for failing to attend Anglican services—an important source of income for the crown at the time.

At the age of 44, at the height of his political power, George Calvert announced that he had become a Roman Catholic, and subsequently resigned his public offices. Unable to lure him back into service, King James awarded him a barony in the Irish peerage; George Calvert became the first Lord Baltimore, which included a grant of land on the Avalon Peninsula, Newfoundland. Eager to explore his new real estate opportunity, Calvert journeyed there with his family and 40 others in 1628, and in his letters to King James wrote, "From the middlest of October to the middlest of May, there is a sad fare of wynter upon all this land." The next year, the colony moved en masse to Jamestown, Virginia. Meanwhile, in late 1631, a trapper named William Claiborne established a fur-trading post, the first permanent European settlement in Maryland, on Kent Island (off the Eastern Shore opposite Annapolis). This was to prove a thorn in the Calvert family's paw for years to come.

In Search of Fairer Climes

Lord Baltimore explored the Chesapeake, and returned to England to request a grant of land on the bay. His patron, James I, had died, but James's son, Charles I, granted him an enormous charter that included the Potomac River in its entirety, all of modern Maryland and Delaware, and a large strip of southern Pennsylvania, including much of Philadelphia (the northern boundary, the 40th parallel, runs roughly through the middle of today's Fairmount Park).

In addition, Lord Baltimore had near-royal rights over the territory, with the ability to make laws, create and summon militia, carry out judicial proceedings, and confer land grants and titles. Unlike the Virginia colony, Lord Baltimore's settlements were given the right to trade with countries other than England, all in return for one fifth of all gold and silver discovered in the new colony, plus an annual quitrent (similar to a lease payment) of two Indian arrows. He certainly knew how to make a deal.

George Calvert was determined to create something unknown in the old world: a land of religious tolerance for all people—including non-Christians—nearly 50 years before William Penn founded Pennsylvania on similar principles. Calvert's ambitions were a model of enlightened self-interest: the more people who came, the greater profits for him. The new land was to be named after King Charles's wife, Henrietta Maria—*Terra Mariae*, Mary's Land. However, George Calvert died before taking possession of the charter, and it was awarded to his 27-year-old heir, Cecil (Cecilius) Calvert, who promptly turned the day-to-day process of colonization over to his younger brothers Leonard and George.

The First Colonists

The Calverts' terms to new colonists were generous: Every adult journeying to Maryland would be granted 100 acres of land, and every child under 16 would receive 50 acres. If a new colonist brought servants provisioned with tools, clothes, and food, the colonist was also awarded 100 acres for each retainer. If he transported five men, he was to receive 1,000 acres (a manor) and could sit in judgment over local civil offenses, among other rights. For every grant of land, the grantee was to swear an oath of fealty to the proprietor, Cecil Calvert, and pay an annual sum of up to 20 pounds.

Men who indentured themselves were to receive 50 acres of land, an ox, a gun, two hoes, a new suit of woolen cloth, stockings, shoes, and hat upon conclusion of the term of service—usually four to seven years. Indentured women received a suit of clothes and three barrels of Indian corn (unequal wages are nothing new).

Though Lord Baltimore's intention was to offer a place of refuge to Catholics, the majority of the first group of more than 200 settlers to the new land were Protestant. This initial expedition left England in 1633 in two ships, the 360-ton *Ark* and the much smaller *Dove*. Cecil stayed home in England, and Leonard and George accompanied the first settlers and served as governor and deputy governor in Cecil's stead.

The passage was far from smooth. Anti-Catholic feeling still ran high, and a British naval vessel intercepted the ships, claiming the true nature of the expedition was to send reinforcements to Catholic Spain. Released a month later, the ships were separated by a fierce storm. The *Ark* headed for Barbados, where it was later joined by the *Dove*. The ships landed on St. Clement's Island, Maryland, March 25, 1634, and celebrated Catholic Mass.

St. Mary's

Leonard Calvert traveled up the Potomac in the *Dove*, accompanied by Captain Henry Fleet, a Virginia trader who spoke Algonquian. They negotiated with Piscataway and Yoacomoco; in exchange for 30 square miles of land, Calvert gave the Indians hatchets, axes, hoes, and cloth (Leonard had inherited the Calvert deal-making gene). The new settlement was named St. Mary's. The Yoacomocos welcomed the newcomers and traded freely with them; as with all successful European settlements in the New World, the natives' help and instruction proved to be the key to survival. Farming, the production of tobacco as a profit-making crop, the plantation system, and the abundance of the countryside brought relative prosperity and growth to the early colony. However, Henry Fleet raised doubts among the Yoacomoco, intimating that the newcomers were affiliated with Spain because of their Catholic propensities. Since the Spanish already held a reputation for evil among the tribes, relations cooled between the two groups.

It was believed that Fleet was influenced by William Claiborne, the trader who had settled on Kent Island in Chesapeake Bay before the Calverts had been granted their charter. Small groups of colonists were striking out from St. Mary's, looking for planting and trading opportunities—and some of them found their way to Kent Island. Claiborne argued that he, not the Calverts, owned Kent Island by reason of prior settlement. Though Leonard Calvert tried to appease Claiborne by extending trading rights to him, Claiborne's objection to the settlement of Maryland by the Calverts touched off Maryland's first naval engagement, setting Claiborne's ship against two Calvert vessels. Though Claiborne was defeated, he continued to harass the small colony. After several failed attempts to retake Kent Island, he returned to England, possibly taking Maryland's silver great seal of state ("Manly Deeds, Womanly Words") with him.

The Colonists Take Over

By 1652, encroaching European settlements forced shore tribes to abandon all but one of their villages and move north, into the territory of the

TOBACCO

Most planters came to the New World to grow one crop: tobacco. It had been the staple crop in Virginia since 1615, and its cultivation was responsible for considerable fortunes. The variety grown in Virginia was Sweet Scented, but another type of tobacco had been developed, called Oronoco after the Orinoco River, where it is thought to have originated. It was darker, larger-leaved, and stronger-smelling than Sweet Scented. Due to its ease of cultivation around the northern Tidewater, Oronoco became the most popular tobacco grown in Maryland. Its sharp-pointed leaves gave it the nickname "fox-eared," and planters who produced this crop were known as Oronocos. An anonymous journal of the day, using the creative style of spelling so common then, reads:

Between the months of March and April they sow the seed (which is much smaller than the Mustard seed) in small beds and patches digged up and made so by art, and about May the Plants commonly appear green in those beds. In June they are transplanted from their beds, and set in little hilocks in distant rowes, dug up for the same purpose; some twice or thrice they are weeded, and succoured [stripped of] . . . their illegitimate Leaves that would be peeping out from the body of the Stalk. They top the Plants as they find occasion in their predominating rankness: About the middle of September they cut the Tobacco down, and carry it into houses (made for that purpose), to bring it to its purity: And after it has attained, by a convenient attendance upon time, to its perfection, it is then tyed up in bundles, and packt into Hogs-heads, and then laid by for the Trade.

Susquehannocks. Also known as Conestogas, the Iroquois-speaking Susquehannocks lived at the head of the Chesapeake Bay and north along the Susquehanna River up into modern Pennsylvania. At first, the Susquehannocks and the Eastern Shore tribes allied, and raided the territory of the Piscataway, or Conoy, a confederation of Algonquian-speaking peoples (including the Yoacomocos) who occupied the Potomac Valley.

Throughout the mid-1600s, the Iroquois Confederation in southern New York state warred with the Susquehannocks, who abandoned their former strongholds on the river and moved south and west, into the lands of the Piscataway. During this time, a number of settlers in outlying areas were murdered, and Susquehannocks were accused of the crimes. Six chiefs parleyed with the colonists, claiming the murders had not been committed by the Susquehannocks, but by their Iroquois-allied enemies, the Seneca. The chiefs produced medals given to them by Governor Calvert. But the meeting ended badly: Five of

the six chiefs were slaughtered by the colonists, and one escaped. Outraged Susquehannock warriors moved south into Virginia, rampaging and pillaging colonial towns; other members of the tribe dispersed, wandering west and north, away from the spreading settlements.

Long-Distance Trouble

By 1649, King Charles was a prisoner of Protestant Reformation leaders (Roundheads) in England. In order to keep as inoffensive a profile as possible, Cecil Calvert, Lord Baltimore, removed the Catholic governor of Maryland and replaced him with a Protestant. Maryland was in a difficult situation: the tolerant Calverts had permitted Puritans (who as a group were largely responsible for removing power from the King in England) to settle in the area of Anne Arundel County. The Maryland Puritans refused to take an oath of allegiance to Lord Baltimore. The imprisoned King supported Lord Baltimore's claim to Maryland, and if Maryland failed to continue to recognize him as ruler, then Baltimore's claim could be invalidated.

In 1651, Oliver Cromwell, the nemesis of King Charles, defeated a pro-royal army in England and sent representatives (including, unfortunately for the Calverts, William Claiborne) to the New World to squelch rebellion in both Virginia and Maryland. By 1653, Cromwell had dissolved Parliament and named himself Lord Protector. In a bold and foolish move, Lord Baltimore declared that the province was to run under his laws once again, since England's Parliamentary legal system no longer existed.

Religious Intolerance

When William Claiborne heard of this, he convened a House of Burgesses in St. Mary's, and repealed the Act Concerning Religion of 1649, decreeing that anyone professing Roman Catholicism was to be prevented from practicing it. Maryland Catholics were kept out of public office, although they could acquire property; they were taxed twice and forbidden to worship publicly, and their priests were prevented from openly teaching or preaching.

In England, Cecil, Lord Baltimore, appealed directly to Cromwell, who eventually settled in his favor, once again giving the Calverts the right to proprietorship over *Terra Mariae*. To reassure the English Puritans in power that Protestants were not being persecuted in Maryland, Calvert himself rewrote the Act of Religious Toleration, keeping Claiborne's prohibitions against Catholics and further narrowing the once-broad declaration. Under the act only Christians were encouraged in the practice of their religion; Jews and other non-Christians who had formerly dwelt peacefully in the colony now came under scrutiny.

This Land Is Whose Land?

In 1638, the New Sweden Company built a fort and trading post near modern Wilmington, Delaware, but Maryland, deeply involved in its own religious turmoil, did nothing to remove the squatters. The Dutch, however, also had claims to Delaware, and sent Peter Stuyvesant to oust the Swedes and claim the land as part of Nieuw Netherland. Lord Baltimore's agents didn't

protest until 1659—however, the Dutch stubbornly refused to move until they were bested by the British in Europe.

In 1661, Charles Calvert, the son of Cecil, Lord Baltimore, took over the governorship of the colony, laying out the city of New Castle (in modern Delaware) as an outpost of Maryland. Upon Cecil's death, Charles became the third Lord Baltimore and the second Lord Proprietary of Maryland. Unfortunately, he failed to inherit his father's and grandfather's negotiating skills. By 1670, a joint Maryland-Virginia commission—surveyed by Edmund Scarbourge, a Virginian—"accidentally" shaved 23 square miles off Maryland's territory. It was only the beginning.

William's Weak Bottome

Oliver Cromwell died in 1658, and King Charles II was soon restored to the monarchy in Britain. In 1680, the rebel Quaker son of an aristocratic family, William Penn, agreed to exchange a debt owed his family by King Charles for land in the New World. Penn was determined to have deep-channel access to the Atlantic, even though his land grant was well above the point where the Delaware River met the sea. In fact, New Castle, the Maryland settlement in present-day Delaware, was considered to be the mouth of the Delaware River, and it was 20 miles south of Calvert's 40th-parallel border. Penn persuaded the Duke of York, King Charles's brother, to issue him a grant to New Castle plus a circle of territory 12 miles in radius, a swath of land from this circle down to Cape Henlopen, and a release of any claim York might have had to land above the 40th parallel. Penn was well aware that his claim to the territory wasn't based on fact; he commented on "the weak bottome of their Grant—the Duke of York never having had a grant from the king." Penn sailed to Maryland and met with Charles Calvert, Lord Baltimore, several times, trying to persuade him to deliver New Castle into his hands, using the York grant as leverage. Baltimore, unmoved, returned to England to plead his case, with Penn following shortly after. In 1685, King Charles died and was replaced by his brother, the Catholic King James II. Instead of supporting Baltimore, James granted Penn all

COLONIAL HOMES

Many examples of early Maryland architectural styles—catslides, telescopes, and plantation clusters—still exist around the state. Their enduring style was based on colonial practicality.

By 1657, the population of Maryland was approximately 10,000, largely farmers. The earliest home structures, built as one large room, were often divided in two by a plank wall. The larger room was used to conduct plantation business, and the smaller was for the family to withdraw to (the withdrawing, or drawing room). The house was often made of wood at front and back, brick at the ends, with double chimneys at either end—the space between them was bricked up and made into a "pent closet" for dry storage. A common way to expand the house was to add two or more "cell" rooms to the back, giving the rear half of the roof a longer distance to run than the front—called a "catslide house."

The fanciest homes were built on the same basic principles, perhaps one and a half or two stories instead of one. A house might have had a "stair case," a small one-room-sized enclosure, two stories high, to contain the stairs, which give the floor plan a squat T shape; and the gambrel roof would have been covered with cedar shingles instead of thatch. Sometimes the freestanding upper parts of the chimneys were set in a "diamond stack," catty-corner to the lower halves. Houses were not always enlarged; rather, a small house might have a larger one right beside it, and a larger one right beside that, so the row of houses looked like it could telescope into itself—a "telescope house."

A plantation consisted of a manor house and several outbuildings. On the western shore, plantation houses of the wealthy were made entirely of brick. On the Eastern Shore, homes were built of wood. It was a legal requirement in Maryland that every plantation have a name. Some like Littleham and Tilghman's Hope, reflected the owner's name, while others were fanciful: Penny Come Quick, Duck Pye, Coffin, Dear Bought, The Remains of My Lord's Gracious Grant Well Meaning.

A tidewater plantation house often consisted of a central block, two and a half stories high, containing a main hall, library, study, withdrawing room, lady's parlor, bedrooms, and an attic for storage. At either side of the main building, a narrow passage one story high (called a hypen) connected the main house with two buildings at either end. One of these one-and-a-half-story buildings was the kitchen, with rooms above for the cook and house servants. The other building was often used as a chapel for private services for Roman Catholics, and a schoolroom for the owner's children. The main house had two "front" doors—one that faced the road as an entryway, and the other, the "private" or "garden front" door that opened onto the gardens.

Plantations were entirely self-contained. Hidden from the main house by trees or hedges, a wind- or water-powered gristmill provided flour, and a group of log cabins were divided into sections for men's work (smokehouse, smithy, shoemaker, carpentry shop, cooperage, saw pit) and women's work (vegetable/herb garden, springhouse, icehouse, weaving-and-spinning house, storehouse, laundry, soap-making house, dovecote, chicken run, and orchards).

that was included under the grant of the Duke of York. Delaware was now a separate colony, though the Pennsylvania border remained indistinct. Further shady dealings involving faulty placement of Cape Henlopen on a map annexed another section of Maryland to Delaware.

End of the Colonial Era

Within the first three years of James's reign, his Protestant subjects overthrew him and replaced him with the Protestant rulers William and Mary. They removed all power from Lord Baltimore and made Maryland a vassal colony ruled from England for the next 25 years. Eventually, the Calvert family would regain the proprietorship over Maryland, only to lose it shortly thereafter during the Revolution. Under British rule, Quakers and other "dissenters" were taxed but allowed to practice their religions, but Catholics were forbidden to hear mass, make converts, keep school, or practice law. By the early 1700s, Maryland's capital was moved to Anne Arundel Town, renamed Annapolis, a combination of the word for city and the name of Britain's then-ruler, Queen Anne.

Maryland Goes West

As Annapolis thrived and became known as "The Athens of America," nearby arable land became less available; pioneers began to push inland up the Potomac and toward the mountains. Some were free and poor: failed Tidewater tobacco farmers, or former indentured servants who had worked out their time; but most were part of a new flood of immigrants. Germans from the Rhineland and the Palatine came to America at the urging of William Penn, and moved west and south from the port of Philadelphia. Scotch-Irish of Ulster Province also landed at Philadelphia, made their way to the Susquehanna, and turned south into Maryland. In 1729, a tobacco port on the Patapsco River was named after the colony's founder, Baltimore. Georgetown was established as a shipping port for tobacco. Hagerstown was settled in 1737, Frederick (named for the Prince of Wales) in 1745. In 1750, Cumberland, in the Allegheny Mountains, was a storehouse and trading post for the Ohio Company, a group of wealthy Virginia planters (including a young British Army officer named George Washington) and London merchants who wished to keep the Ohio Valley away from the French. French and English forces were expanding into Pennsylvania's rich Ohio Valley, forming alliances with Indian tribes and setting up encampments. As territorial hostilities heated up, young Washington published his journal—a chronicle of a soldier's life on the frontier—in the Annapolis *Maryland Gazette*. His words not only established him as a leader, but also gathered support in Annapolis for the French and Indian War.

The French Challenge

The British sent George Washington to northern Pennsylvania to demand an end to French interference in the Ohio Valley; he was politely rebuffed, then barely escaped assassination. Cumberland became a fort and an embarkation point for British troops. General Edward Braddock, fresh from England, marched from Cumberland with volunteers to rout the French from their encampment at Fort Duquesne (doo-KAIN) in what is now downtown Pittsburgh. Braddock was guilty of the same error that has felled American troops in other wars: he had no idea how to fight guerrilla style. When warned of an ambush by French-allied Hurons, he replied, "These savages may, indeed, be a formidable enemy to your raw American militia, but upon the King's regular and disciplined troops, sir, it is impossible they should make an impression." The general struggled alongside his troops in the thick of the fighting; he and two-thirds of his men died in the melee. The French controlled the west for the next three years, and their Indian allies began to raid and destroy outlying settlements.

Fort Cumberland was left with a skeleton garrison, and the few forces that remained withdrew to Fort Frederick at Big Pool. In 1757, British troops found Fort Duquesne abandoned and in ruins. The Battle of Quebec finally ended French domination in North America. After the treaty, old boundary disputes were again addressed (see the special topic "Mason and Dixon" in the Delaware Introduction chapter).

Pontiac's Rebellion

Not long after the French and Indian War, numerous Indian tribes in the northeast rose up under the Ottawa chief Pontiac, driving away the few European settlers who had returned to the western territory. One early pioneer and founder of Oldtown, Thomas Cresap, packed up his family and went east of Conoccocheague Creek (ca-NO-ca-cheek) near Williamsport, Maryland. With his older sons and some neighbors, Cresap began to raid Indian villages. His oldest son died during one of the skirmishes, as did a black volunteer, Nemesis, who is memorialized at Negro Mountain, Somerset County, Pennsylvania. The western frontier of Maryland remained free of European habitation until a treaty was signed with the Iroquois Confederation in 1768.

Throwing Off the Homeland

In 1765, twelve Frederick County justices repudiated the British Stamp Act, the colony's first official act of rebellion against the British. Marylanders had their own "tea party" in 1774 in Chestertown when the tea-carrying ship *Geddes* was burned in the city's harbor. On July 3, 1776, the state disavowed allegiance to the king; four months later, Maryland was the first of the former colonies to adopt a state constitution.

State representatives signed their own Declaration of Independence first, then sent Charles

FIRST CITIZEN CHARLES CARROLL

By the beginning of the 18th century, the Calvert family had regained the proprietorship of Maryland, and decisions regarding the citizenry were made by an Upper House (wealthy landed gentry), a Lower House (elected freemen), and a Governor. Around 1770, a proclamation by governor Sir Robert Eden increased taxes for the citizenry of Maryland in order to pay salaries of civil officers—many of whom were affluent members of the Upper House and cohorts of the Calverts. Marylanders had been grumbling about unfair taxes for several years, and this proclamation added fuel to the fire.

Daniel Dulany, a writer and supporter of the Calverts and Governor Eden, published a dialogue in 1773 between two fictional personages, "First Citizen" and "Second Citizen." The former spoke against the tax proclamation, while the latter answered with ease, upholding the governor's position.

A month later, a second letter appeared, in which the writer took "First Citizen's" side, claiming that he had been misquoted, correcting the errors and ably presenting the anti-proclamation argument. Dulany replied, starting a dialogue between the two, with Dulany consistently on the losing end. Dulany finally lashed out at his antagonist, calling him "an accurs'd Roman Catholic." The accursed in question was Charles Carroll III, son of one of the richest families in the New World.

Charles Carroll of Carrollton was educated by Jesuits at a secret academy in Cecil County, and at age 11 was sent to St. Omer in France, then to the College of Louis the Great in Paris, and finally to the Inner Temple in London, where he read law—knowing that, as a Catholic, he couldn't practice in Maryland. When Carroll drew his pen against the Upper House and governor, Marylanders feared taxation more than religious subversion—and Dulany's denunciation raised the populace's opinion of Catholics. Carroll replied, "I am as averse to having a religion crammed down people's throats as a proclamation. . . . I bear not the least dislike to the Church of England, though I am not within her pale, nor indeed to any other church; knaves and bigots, of all sects and denominations, I hate and despise."

The Lower House declared the governor's proclamation illegal, and Charles Carroll of Carrollton, known affectionately as First Citizen, began an unprecedented and meteoric rise in Maryland politics.

Carroll, Samuel Chase, Thomas Stone, and William Paca to Philadelphia to sign the Declaration composed by the Continental Congress. During the Revolutionary War, no fighting took place in the state, but Maryland troops distinguished themselves in battle throughout the colonies.

In the winter of 1776, Congress sent a delegation to Montreal to sound out French Canadians as allies to the American cause. Though not a delegate to the Continental Congress, Charles Carroll had attended its sessions as an unattached observer, and was asked to join the mission, along with his cousin, the priest John Carroll—Congress was hoping to impress the Catholic French Canadians with token Catholics. In a sterling example of "what goes around comes around," the French refused to help, citing the lack of freedom of American Catholics.

In August 1777, the British fleet was sighted in the approaches to Chesapeake Bay. There was a strong pro-British following in parts of the Eastern Shore, and Annapolis and Baltimore both girded for an invasion. Instead, the ships sailed up the Delaware River and landed troops below Philadelphia, the colonial capital. After George Washington was defeated at Brandywine Creek (Pennsylvania), Philadelphia was taken. The Revolutionary War dragged on until 1787, when both sides agreed to allow the colonies to form their own nation.

Washington nicknamed Maryland the Old Line State in honor of her valiant troops of the

TOCQUEVILLE ON DEMOCRACY

In 1789, during the French Revolution, Alexis de Tocqueville's grandfather and aunt were guillotined, and his parents were imprisoned. Tocqueville's reading on the subject of liberalism in England and America created a desire to investigate and explore democratic institutions. In 1830 the Bourbon dynasty fell, and Tocqueville, who had little stomach for the new government, was forced to take an oath of allegiance to the new monarch. He proposed a trip to America to report on prison reform there, and left in April 1831. After his return to France in 1832, Tocqueville completed his report on prison reform and then devoted himself to a more detailed study of democracy. He was enthusiastic regarding some American institutions, but wrote guardedly about others, including the power of public opinion and the effect on the arts in a democracy. Tocqueville found a wife's position in America happier and more respected than her European counterpart, and generally spoke favorably about the role of women in the democracy, though he lamented the feminine lack of musical and artistic sensibility. An aristocrat, he apparently had little understanding of the difficulty of tapping out a minuet after a morning of plowing the back forty.

In an 1831 conversation with Baltimore lawyer John Latrobe, Tocqueville commented on the blossoming of the once-repressed Maryland Catholics in the new democratic society:

[Catholics] are taking on an extraordinary increase, and [are] following a very clever policy. . . . In the last twenty years they have, with great skill, turned all their efforts toward education. They have established seminaries and schools (colleges). The best institutions of education in Maryland are Catholic; they even have schools in other states. These are full of Protestants. There is perhaps not a single young man of Maryland who, having received a good education, has not been brought up by Catholics. Although they take good care not to speak to the students about their beliefs, you can appreciate that they always exercise a certain influence. Furthermore, they have very adroitly turned most of their efforts to the education of women. They think that there where the mother is Catholic, the children must almost always be the same.

Continental Line. In April 1788, Maryland became the seventh state to ratify the new constitution. Two years later, the state conveyed 69.5 square miles to the new government for the District of Columbia: Washington, D.C.

Expansion

Baltimore, incorporated in 1797, grew rapidly as a port and shipbuilding and industrial center, overshadowing Annapolis in commerce and attaining a population of 26,500 (more than Boston) in 1800. Maryland's early years of statehood were spent in developing the state's resources. Unimpeded by the presence of British troops in the Revolution, Maryland got a healthy dose of war in 1812.

Britain and France had been at war since 1793, and Britain was infamous for impressing (seizing and forcing into labor) American sailors. In 1812, America declared war on Great Britain. England planned to cut the country in half at Chesapeake Bay; Maryland and federal forces were routed at the battle of Bladensburg, and British troops went on to burn Washington. Baltimore was spared capture, thanks to an intrepid stand at Fort McHenry against a 25-hour-long bombardment. While watching from a British treaty ship, Francis Scott Key penned a poem, "The Bombardment of Fort McHenry"; his publisher changed the title to a snappier "The Star-Spangled Banner." In 1815, the final battle of the war—Andrew Jackson's victory over British forces—took place in New Orleans, two weeks after a peace treaty had been signed.

Following the war, development of swift clipper ships and steam locomotives multiplied trade possibilities. New routes such as the National Road (U.S. 40), the Chesapeake and Delaware Canal (across the Delmarva Peninsula), the Chesapeake and Ohio Canal (along the Potomac River to the coalfields of Cumberland and western Maryland), and the Baltimore and Ohio (B&O) Railroad increased access from lands west of the Appalachians into Chesapeake ports. The B&O, begun in 1828, was the first U.S. passenger railroad. First Citizen Charles Carroll laid the cornerstone of the train depot in Baltimore, shortly before his death.

Slavery and the Dred Scott Decision

Mid-19th-century America experienced a heated battle over states' rights, particularly over the right of a state to declare slave ownership legal or illegal. In 1857, Dred Scott, a Missouri slave, claimed that he had become a free man when his master transported him temporarily into a free state. The case went all the way to the U.S. Supreme Court, and was heard before Chief Justice Roger Taney, a resident of Frederick, Maryland—and a slaveholder.

Five of the nine justices who served on the court supported slavery and slaveholding rights in the territories. The court ruled that all laws restricting the free movement of property—including, shamefully, human property—were unconstitutional; that no black person in the United States enjoyed "any rights which the White man was bound to respect." In principle, the Dred Scott decision meant that all the states and unincorporated territories were open to slavery; it undercut the makeshift solution of popular sovereignty (the right of each area to take its own position on slavery) in the territories. Rather than solving the sectional crisis, the court heightened tension. Several Southern slaveholding states seceded. Without an active declaration of war, Union troops fired on Fort Sumter, South Carolina, in 1861; the conflict had begun.

Civil War

In the mid-19th century, Maryland had almost equal numbers of slaves and free blacks. Marylanders were divided over the issue of slavery—southern Maryland and the Eastern Shore favored the South, while northern and western Maryland were pro-Union—and Maryland soldiers fought on both sides during the Civil War. When neighboring Virginia seceded, Maryland's presence within the Union became vital to the defense of Washington, D.C., and President Lincoln prevented secession by imposing military rule. Raids across the Potomac by Confederate cavalry were a constant threat. Fierce battles fought on Maryland soil included South Mountain and Antietam (both in 1862) and Monocacy (1864).

After the Civil War, manufacturing expanded

GLORY

After the bombing of Fort Sumter in 1861, the Civil War appeared to many a romantic interlude: a short-lived foray into glory. Few who volunteered for 90 days in the furious first days of blaring patriotism expected the war to outlast the term of their enlistment.

The first Confederate States of America flag sported seven stars in a circle representing the seceded states of South Carolina, Mississippi, Florida, Georgia, Louisiana, Texas, and Alabama. The circle of stars was later enlarged by Virginia, Arkansas, Tennessee, and North Carolina. A few border states below the Mason-Dixon line ostensibly stayed in the Union: Maryland, Delaware, Kentucky, Missouri, and West Virginia (which broke away from the larger state in 1863). Even after secession, thirty-four stars remained on the Union flag, representing all of the states.

The war lasted more than four years. Of the 1.2 million Southern boys who enlisted to the strains of "Dixie," 250,000 died. On the side of "Yankee Doodle" and the Union, 2.9 million signed up, and 348,000 never came home. In addition, 400,000 were wounded and a half million remained disabled after the war. Of the roughly 600,000 soldiers who met their end in the War Between the States, two-thirds died from disease, poor diet, and other non-battle-related injuries. Lack of clean water and spoiled food took their toll. Diarrhea was the biggest killer; many young men died of dysentery and typhoid fever. Others, who had never been exposed to common childhood diseases, died from measles and mumps before they saw battle. Ten black soldiers died for every white soldier. Sometimes the cure was worse than the illness: pneumonia was routinely treated with a mercury and chalk mixture that often caused insanity, ulcers, and tumors.

Clara Barton, who stated that her place was anywhere between the bullet and the battlefield, said, "If I were to speak of war, it would not be to show the glories . . . but the mischief and misery. . . . This is the side which history never shows."

rapidly and eventually emerged as the mainstay of the economy. Thousands of Greek, German, Italian, Russian, Polish, and other immigrants, together with newly freed blacks migrating from rural counties, flocked to take jobs in Baltimore's textile factories and other industries.

Modern Times

In 1904, Baltimore was devastated by fire but recovered to grow rapidly as World Wars I and II increased demand for the city's industrial products. The area was buffered from the worst effects of the Depression of the late 1920s thanks to its strong industrial base. As the fruits of American industry diminished in importance from the late 1950s to the present, Baltimore has turned increasingly to tourism. In the rest of the state, agriculture and aquaculture remain the mainstays of rural areas, while central Maryland enjoys a prosperity brought about by jobs in U.S. government–related research and services.

GOVERNMENT

Modern state government in Maryland is based on the Constitution of 1867. The Maryland legislature consists of a General Assembly, made up of a House and Senate. The governor serves a four-year term. Acting as a liaison between the executive and the legislature is the Board of Public Works—an agency composed of the governor, the controller of the treasury, and the treasurer. The executive branch is headed by the governor, who oversees 12 departments; the secretaries of the departments form the state cabinet.

The highest tribunal in the state is the Court of Appeals, a convention retained from the first Constitution of 1776. The court judges are appointed by the governor to serve a brief term, and then may be elected for a 10-year term. The governor designates the chief judge. A constitutional convention meeting in 1967 further modernized the government, as voters reacted negatively to changing the public election of many executive officials to appointment status.

Since the 19th century, commissioners serving both the legislative and executive functions have governed Maryland's counties. However, Montgomery, Prince George's, and Baltimore Counties have adopted charter governments with specialized departments and officers to perform functions once exercised by the boards of commissioners. In addition, more than 50 incorporated towns and cities hold charters. The largest have elected mayors, councils, and agencies of government service. The smallest town in Maryland is Port Tobacco, with 339 inhabitants. It dates to the colonial period, when it was an important tobacco inspection station.

Several times during Maryland's history, political machines dominated state politics, and each was swept away by reformers; unfortunately, government seems to attract those with questionable motives. Spiro T. Agnew, former governor of Maryland, was elected U.S. vice president in 1968 and 1972. In 1973, however, he resigned the office during an investigation of charges of graft while he was serving as a Maryland official. Governor Marvin Mandel, Agnew's successor, was indicted on similar charges in 1975, convicted in 1978 on charges of mail fraud and racketeering, and sentenced to jail. Forced by Maryland law to resign, Mandel resumed office for the 45 remaining hours of his term after the overturn on appeal (later reversed) of his conviction.

Today, the overriding issues concerning Maryland government are tax revenues and racial politics.

ECONOMY

Although Maryland's economic activity is varied, it centers principally on manufacturing, which employs more than a quarter of a million people. The center of manufacturing has been Baltimore since the end of the Revolution. Montgomery, Prince George's, and Washington Counties follow in importance. The leading manufactured products are metals, chiefly steel; food and related products; electrical machinery;

transportation equipment; and chemical and allied products.

Maryland ranks in the lowest 15 of the 50 states in total land under cultivation and value of agricultural products sold. At one time, less than .1 percent of the population derived income from dairy and poultry products; that's changed in recent years with the growth of the market for chicken. In western and southern Maryland and the Eastern Shore, a dense network of small farms produces greenhouse vegetables, corn, melons, and fruits for private use and local consumers, and there's a limited commercial soybean and tobacco market.

Fishing and forestry are important resources. Virginia and Maryland share the major fishing grounds, but more than half of the processing is in Maryland. Annapolis, Somerset, and Dorchester Counties on the Eastern Shore have more than half of the seafood processing plants. Almost 90 percent of seafood income comes from clams, crabs, and oysters. Two-thirds of forestry production is in sawn timber, and the remaining third consists of pulpwood, poles, and piling.

The existence of Washington, D.C., has greatly stimulated the economy of the surrounding areas of Maryland, including Prince George's and Montgomery Counties, which are considered part of the district's metropolitan area. Many federal institutions and agencies contribute markedly to the state's economic life, and the Washington-Baltimore "corridor" is responsible for more than half of the economic productivity of Maryland. The government—on the local, state, and federal level—employs more than 300,000 Marylanders.

The Port of Baltimore boasts the fourth largest foreign export trade in the United States and has been central to the Maryland economy since the mid-18th century. The Baltimore area has always offered excellent deep-water harbor facilities. The increased use of container shipping has led to modernization and has enhanced the port's ability to move bulk cargo. Ships can reach the port by way of both the southern end of Chesapeake Bay and the western end of the Chesapeake and Delaware Canal.

EDUCATION

In 17th-century plantation society, hired tutors or churchmen usually taught privileged children, and the gentry sent sons to study in England or on the continent. Only benevolent societies or generous teachers served poor youngsters.

The first signs of public interest in tax-supported education began in 1694 when the assembly taxed specific export items, ruling that the proceeds were to be used for schools. Twenty years later the law required the establishment of a school in every county, supported by taxation on imported blacks and Irish Catholic servants. The law met with indifferent success.

One of Maryland's leading colonial institutions was King William's school, founded in Annapolis in 1694. The school flourished because of the generosity of leading citizens and support from taxation. This academy—later known as St. John's College—lasted until the time of the Revolution, when, with Washington College, it formed the first state university.

Public education began in earnest in the years following the Revolution; a county received grants of money from the legislature if that county's citizens would provide the building and teachers. In 1826, the legislature voted to establish public schools throughout the state. Though schools in the cities flourished, education in the rest of the state lagged behind. Finally in 1864, the creation of a State Board of Education and the appointment of a superintendent of public education inaugurated the modern system. Racial segregation was gradually eliminated in schools following the U.S. Supreme Court decision of 1954.

Today Maryland boasts dozens of sites of higher learning. Johns Hopkins University in Baltimore and the University of Maryland College Park have gained worldwide recognition as centers of learning and research; the Peabody Institute in Baltimore enjoys an international reputation in the arts.

A major state library, Enoch Pratt in Baltimore, contains a large circulating library and special collections of rare books, manuscripts, and Marylandia. Among its precious collections are the papers and works of Edgar Allan Poe and H. L. Mencken. The nearby Peabody Library is distinctive for its rare books and musical publications.

The People

Historically, Marylanders have been seafarers and fishermen. Once completely dependent on a rural economy, the state now ranks 40th in farm acreage; southern Maryland south of Prince George's County and western Maryland beyond Frederick still exhibit a rural aspect, but these areas are not heavily populated. Much of the state is now urban, such as the densely populated "Washington gateway" that runs from Baltimore to Washington, D.C. More than half of the state's residents are concentrated in the metropolitan Baltimore area, and almost one-third of the people live in the suburban Washington, D.C., region.

Howard County, a southwestern suburb of Baltimore, is experiencing the greatest population growth, though the counties that surround Baltimore and the Washington gateway—Calvert, Charles, Carroll, and Frederick—are all expanding. Queen Anne's County, across the Bay Bridge, is also targeted for growth.

Generally, where Marylanders choose to live is affected by their age group. Families tend to live in the suburban areas that make up the Washington gateway; rural areas such as the Eastern Shore and southern and western Maryland have an older population; and the urban areas of Baltimore and Annapolis are largely made up of young adults. With marriage, young white couples depart to the suburbs, while black couples tend to remain in the cities.

Race relations continue to be a concern, particularly between blacks and whites. Relations were severely strained by the 1954 U.S. Supreme Court decision to end segregation, and widespread rioting occurred in the 1960s, mostly in Baltimore. Today, the city presents an interesting contrast to the picture many people have of a large

© JOANNE MILLER

Amish farm on the Eastern Shore

ropean nationalities to move to the Piedmont Plateau in the early 18th century. The Germans belonged to Pietistic faiths, such as Lutheranism, or were Mennonite, Amish, or Moravian.

LANGUAGE

English is the prevalent language in Maryland. However, you will find small pockets of traditional communities, such as Smith Island, whose members are reputed to speak a variation of Elizabethan English. Some claim it's more rural southern than historic speech, but it's all in the ear of the beholder.

RELIGION

The quest for religious freedom led to Maryland's founding and played a crucial role in the state's history. It was the desire of George Calvert to found a place where Roman Catholics could worship freely; Catholicism had been repressed in England since the early 16th century, following the founding of the Anglican Church, and came heavily under fire with the Protestant movement of the mid-16th century in Britain and on the Continent. The Roman Catholic Church, first and largest of the Christian churches, attached great significance to the infallibility and worldwide ministry of the pope and his representatives, priests—beliefs that directly challenged the sovereignty of kings and the Protestant belief that man had a direct line to God. Though they succeeded in planting the seeds of Catholicism and liberal religious freedom in America, the Calvert family was frustrated by the ongoing politics and power plays of the Protestant Reformation.

In the mid-17th century, the more extreme Protestants within the Church of England were called Puritans; they thought the English Reformation had not gone far enough and wanted to purify their national church by eliminating every shred of Catholic influence. A Puritan group settled south of Baltimore and worked—successfully—to unseat the Calverts and return control of the colony to England.

Though Puritans are no longer visible as

urban black population: Baltimore boasts some of the wealthiest black neighborhoods in America.

ETHNOGRAPHY

Maryland has always had a large black population. During the slavery era, Baltimore contained the highest free black population of all the northeastern slaveholding states and was second only to New Orleans in the number of "free people of color." Today, blacks constitute about 22 percent of the total population of the state. Nonwhite settlements are sharply localized. Baltimore contains the largest non-white population, while Garrett County has the smallest. Old slavery areas in southern Maryland and the Eastern Shore have seen a shift of blacks to cities. Chinese, Japanese, Filipinos, and displaced Indo-Chinese have also become a population segment in Maryland, and generally remain in urban areas.

Scotch-Irish, fleeing English persecution, and Palatine Germans, seeking relief from religious intolerance, were among the first non-English Eu-

BECOMING A SAINT

A simplistic view of the role of saints in the Catholic Church would be that they're valued for their closeness to God. Saints who have passed into the heavenly realm intercede for those who pray to them, repeating the penitent's prayer into God's ear with an amplified whisper.

All saints were once ordinary people. The Church has a regimented approach to canonization (the creation of a saint), and the process often takes decades. Though ancient saints were often martyrs, modern saints tend to be singled out more for their exemplary lives—often in the service of others—combined with four verifiable miracles. Mother Teresa, who worked with "the poorest of the poor," is currently a candidate for sainthood.

Another woman who dedicated her life to the less fortunate became America's first saint. Elizabeth Ann Seton grew up in comfortable circumstances in New York and married a wealthy businessman; she converted to Catholicism after the death of her husband. Her later years were spent serving as a pious and inspirational teacher of academic and religious subjects under the auspices of the church in Baltimore and on the American frontier in western Maryland; she founded St. Joseph's, the first parish academy, in Emmitsburg, to provide a place for her students to meet. Elizabeth Seton, who gave up everything she possessed to work with the children of settlers and Indians, also fostered a religious order—the Daughters (later Sisters) of Charity—devoted to helping the poor.

In 1935, more than a century after Mother Seton's death, a member of the order she founded was cured of cancer of the pancreas after prayers were offered asking for Mother Seton's intercession. In 1961, a four-year-old, Ann O'Neill of Baltimore, completely recovered from acute lymphatic leukemia after her family prayed for Mother Seton's help. In 1959, members of the Catholic Church in Rome examined every aspect of Seton's life, and declared her "venerable," the first step to canonization.

Shortly thereafter, Mother Seton's third miracle was given to Carl Klein, a construction worker with a rare and fatal brain disease who recovered completely after touching a reliquary with Mother Seton's remains and offering prayers. In 1963, after Mother Seton's miracles were investigated and declared authentic, Pope John XXIII beatified (declared "blessed") Elizabeth Seton, the second step in the canonization process. Her beatification ceremony was attended by Ann O'Neill, then 15 years old.

In 1974, Pope Paul VI waived the requirement for the fourth miracle and proclaimed Mother Elizabeth Ann Seton a saint. A magnificent basilica was built to honor her at Emmitsburg, near the former "frontier wilderness" she walked with her students.

such, another group of conservative Protestants remains highly visible in areas of the Eastern Shore and southern Maryland: Old Order Amish. The Amish have adopted a highly stylized, conservative style of dress (the predominant clothing color is black; married men are bearded; women's hair is always covered), along with a carefully maintained separation from "worldly" things like automobiles and computers. Amish farms are easily identified, especially during the fall harvest: Sheaves of wheat in the old-fashioned X shape are laid neatly in the field, picked up slowly and steadily by straw-hat-ted farmers pitch-forking the sheaves high up into the air on top of a horse-drawn wagon.

The Society of Friends, commonly called Quakers, was also part of the Protestant movement, though its members were nearly as reviled as Catholics, due to their firm belief that they owed allegiance to no one but God. Groups of believers moved south and west from Pennsylvania into Maryland during the colonial era. Quakers were instrumental in developing the Underground Railroad before the Civil War to transport slaves north from Virginia. One of the oldest—and still active—colonial-era meeting houses still exists outside Easton (see Talbot County in the Eastern Shore chapter).

Christianity, Buddhism, Judaism, and all other belief systems coexist peacefully in Maryland today. Though the Calverts never lived to see it, religious tolerance is the rule, much as they had planned; religion no longer plays the divisive role of the past.

Conduct and Customs

Carriages

Though it won't happen as often as in Pennsylvania, you'll occasionally come upon Amish families traveling by horse-drawn carriages. They don't drive on the interstates or highways, but they do use two-lane roads, so you're liable to encounter them anywhere in the state.

Carriages are impossible to miss; all carry red reflector triangles. In general, etiquette calls for automobile drivers to slow as they approach until a clear path for passing is available; then pass slowly—just fast enough to get around—and accelerate away, also slowly. You don't want to spook the horses; even though they're accustomed to cars, it's entirely possible to startle them.

Worship Meetings

If you have an interest in attending services in an unfamiliar religious tradition, use the following general guidelines. Methodist, Lutheran, and Catholic churches are open to visitors. In order to participate in the sharing of bread and wine at a Catholic church, however, you must be a baptized Catholic and recently confessed. Since the Catholic mass is highly ritualized, it's a good idea to sit in the back so you won't end up standing when everyone else kneels, etc. Quakers welcome everyone to their worship meetings and are quite tolerant in general. Mennonites are a measure *more* welcoming—missionary work plays a significant part in their beliefs. Old Order Amish meetings are closed to all but members (unless you know someone in the community).

Liquor Laws

Wine, liquor, and beer are served in bars, taverns, and most restaurants but are not available for take-out. All types of liquor are sold in grocery and liquor stores. Though the state has a dozen wineries, distribution is tightly controlled and the selection in stores may be limited—the best way to sample it is to visit the winery (they're almost all located in north-central Maryland).

Police

The interstates are regularly patrolled, and main highways also get a fair share of police passthroughs. Baltimore is a major American city whose police force and meter readers are on par with those of similar-sized municipalities. Suburbs along the entire Baltimore–Washington, D.C., corridor are regularly patrolled. One

© JOANNE MILLER

Mount Vernon Place United Methodist Church, Baltimore

thing to remember: even in the smallest town, a good portion of municipal income is derived from parking fines, and the days of $2 parking tickets are behind us. Though Maryland's rural areas seem far removed from the hustle and bustle, they are eminently civilized; houses are dotted throughout the landscape. Small towns may seem quite spread out, but the jurisdictions cover a lot of territory; law enforcement is often represented by part-time police or volunteers, who are occasionally overeager to nab out-of-staters, speeders, and other scofflaws. When nearing a town of any size, slow down and be careful.

On the Road in Maryland

Maryland truly has it all—the fine museums, natural history collections, and plethora of restaurants of Baltimore; hundreds of boating destinations and places to enjoy water sports on the Chesapeake, its tributaries, and Deep Creek Lake; and miles of trails, camping opportunities and outdoor recreation on the bay and in the mountains. The state also covers a lot of territory; though it's possible to drive from the eastern boundary at Delaware to the western edge at West Virginia, or around the Chesapeake Bay in a day, it makes much more sense to choose your delights. Fortunately, one of the best things about Maryland is that you can have breakfast in a Baltimore café and rustle up lunch at a rustic campsite.

The type of experience you choose and the amount of time you have will determine your destination. The Maryland chapters are divided into contiguous areas, based around Baltimore (the primary airport hub). Seeking big-city sightseeing mixed with a more rural experience? Then Baltimore and north-central Maryland are for you. A trip combining urban pleasures and American history might include Baltimore and central Maryland. If you prefer the outdoors far from

© JOANNE MILLER

Sideling Hill

the bright lights, consider western Maryland or the Eastern Shore. If a beach vacation is in order, try southern Maryland for its less-crowded beaches, or Ocean City on the Eastern Shore—it's where the action is. Are Civil War sites on your agenda? By all means, check out western Maryland and southern Maryland.

This chapter will give you a broad idea of what's available in the state, including specific destinations and festivals and events that take place throughout the year. There's so much to see and do, it's difficult to pack it all into one book—Maryland has a lot to offer, and by using this book as your guide, you'll discover a special place, restaurant, or scenic spot all your own.

Outdoor Recreation

Maryland's recreation areas make the great outdoors available to all, whether your inclination is backpacking the 185-mile Chesapeake and Ohio Canal trail, strolling through a historic home, clamming, or gliding in a silent canoe over ink-colored water. National parks offer a mix of activities, from active recreation to historic house tours, while state parks are more oriented toward outdoor activities. A chapter location is given for those parks detailed in this book.

PARKS

National Parks

The National Park Service maintains and administers five historical sites and museums. Fort McHenry National Monument and Historic Shrine (Baltimore chapter) is the birthplace of our national anthem and the scene of a historic naval assault during the War of 1812. Antietam National Battlefield and Monocacy National Battlefield (Western Maryland chapter) were the setting for significant Civil War battles; Antietam National Cemetery, near the battlefield, is the result of one of the bloodiest battles in our history.

Other National Park sites were created to retain the history of everyday life. Hampton National Historic Site, 535 Hampton Ln., Towson, MD 21286, 410/823-1309, north of Baltimore, is an elegant mansion set within 62 acres of parkland. Mansion tours start on the hour, 9 A.M.–4 P.M. A quick stroll will show off the wonderful formal gardens; a longer walk will reveal other buildings and hidden treasures. Thomas Stone National Historic Site (Southern

Maryland chapter) is the home of one of the colony's early movers and shakers.

The National Park Service is also responsible for a number of outdoor recreation sites. Greenbelt Park, 6565 Greenbelt Rd., Greenbelt, MD 20770, 301/344-3944, offers walking, hiking, and jogging on more than 12 miles of trails, biking on paved areas, picnicking, and overnight camping. The 174-site family campground is open year-round to tent camping, truck campers, and travel trailers, and offers modern restrooms with showers, drinking water, tables, and fire grills. Catoctin Mountain Park (Western Maryland chapter) is another popular venue in the forested mountains north of Frederick.

Assateague Island National Seashore (Eastern Shore chapter) and Chesapeake and Ohio Canal National Historical Park (Western Maryland chapter) are among two of the best-known national parks. Assateague, a barrier island on the Atlantic Ocean, is home to the famous wild pony herd. The C&O Canal offers a 184.5-mile towpath to hike or bike.

State Forests and Parks

Maryland has invested more than 280,000 acres in public land; there's a state forest or park within a 40-minute drive of any point in the state. Most of the state's 54 parks are open year-round, with most facilities (snack bars, swimming pools, and boat rentals) available from Memorial Day weekend to Labor Day. All state park day-use areas are open year-round, 8 A.M.–sunset, unless posted otherwise. All of Maryland's forests and parks are "trash free"—there are no trash receptacles in picnic or beach areas, and visitors are expected to pack out their own trash, a system that works surprisingly well. Because the terrain varies from park to park, the system offers a wide variety of outdoor activities, ranging from picnicking, swimming, boating, hiking, and camping to whitewater rafting and mountain biking. Boats must have current state registration. In icy weather, many of the parks offer winter sports: boating, fishing, skating, sledding, cross-country skiing, and snowmobile trails. In addition, many of the parks feature historical events and family-oriented activities throughout the year.

Maryland boasts a number of unusual state parks. Two island parks, Hart Miller Island, 410/592-2897, in the Chesapeake off Baltimore County, and St. Clement's Island, 301/872-5688, off St. Mary's County, offer pristine beaches only accessible by boat. Sideling Hill Exhibit Center, six miles west of Hancock (Western Maryland chapter); Soldier's Delight Natural Management Area, 5100 Deer Park Rd., Owings Mills, 410/922-3044, in Baltimore County; and Calvert Cliffs State Park (Southern Maryland chapter) offer unique natural geological features. Sideling Hill is on a mile-long, 340-foot-high section of exposed rock layers millions of years old; Soldier's Delight contains the only undisturbed serpentine barren in the state; and the Calvert Cliffs are made of 15-million-year-old fossils.

For general information on *all* Maryland state parks, call the State Forest and Park Service, 877/620-8367, or visit the website, www.dnr.state.md.us.

Wildlife Management Areas

Not all of Maryland's wild land is designated as state parkland. The State Forest and Park Service maintains 21 wildlife management areas for the purpose of conserving wildlife for sightseers and hunters. Though no facilities are offered, almost all of these areas are open to the public and accessible to hikers, horseback riders, snowmobilers, riders of all-terrain vehicles, and cross-country skiers. For information on management areas, call 877/620-8367, or visit www.dnr.state.md.us/publiclands.

ON LAND
Road Cycling

Maryland comes close to paradise as a destination for cyclists of all abilities. The state is laced with paved two-lane roads, and outside the Washington-Baltimore corridor, the roads are subject to little traffic. Western Maryland offers hilly terrain and breathtaking farmland, lake, and stream views; southern Maryland and the Eastern Shore are both flat as a crab cake and provide the cyclist with a wide variety of scenery, from fields of golden wheat to whispering marsh grasses. The water is never very far away. Southern Maryland and Kent County both publish bicycle-touring information, available from their respective tourism offices.

Hiking, Backpacking, and Trail Biking

The 2,167-mile Appalachian Trail—the longest continuous footpath in the world—runs through Maryland, stretching from the Maryland-Virginia border through South Mountain State Park (Western Maryland chapter) to Washington Monument State Park (the trail passes next to the monument). The trail continues north through Greenbrier State Park up to Blue Ridge Summit in Pennsylvania and beyond. The trail is open to hikers and backpackers, and the Maryland portion is saturated in Civil War history. The Appalachian Trail Conference (ATC) is an umbrella organization that coordinates and oversees some 30 groups that maintain sections of the trail from Maine to Georgia. They publish maps, a newsletter, and other information on the trail, and have a store in Harper's Ferry, Virginia (799 Washington St.); contact them at P.O. Box 807, Harper's Ferry, VA 25425, 304/535-6331, www.atconf.org. Another good website about the trail is www.fred.net/kathy/at.html.

The American Discovery Trail, or ADT (P.O. Box 20155, Washington, DC 20041-2155, 703/753-0149 or 800/663-2387, www.discoverytrail.org), is a new breed of national trail—part city, part small town, part forest, part mountains, part desert—all in one trail. Its 6,300 miles of connected multiuse trails stretch from Cape

SIGHTSEEING HIGHLIGHTS

Every section of Maryland has a wonderful variety of things to see and do. The urban areas feature sophisticated museums and developed historical sites; the outlying countryside is a recreational smorgasbord. Each chapter lists dozens of local highlights. This is a sampling:

Baltimore

No visit to Baltimore would be complete without a stop at **Fort McHenry,** the birthplace of our national anthem. The roundhouse at **B&O Railroad Museum** is a radiant monument to the iron horse, and the **Baltimore Museum of Industry** cleverly displays what built Baltimore. If a little workout is in order, a run up the steps of the **Washington Monument** will leave you gasping. Who'd have thought: the **Dr. Samuel D. Harris National Museum of Dentistry** is one of the most delightful collections in town. **Babe Ruth Birthplace and Orioles Museum** is unstinting in its appreciation of the great American game. Two world-class nature sites, the **National Aquarium in Baltimore** and the **Baltimore Zoo,** are must-sees. **Port Discovery,** ostensibly for kids, will delight every member of the family. Who could miss Baltimore's beauties, two outstanding art palaces with completely different foci: **Walters Art Museum** and the **American Visionary Art Museum,** and last, but certainly not least, beautiful old **Penn Station**?

Central Maryland and the Capital Gateway

The most populous area in Maryland has a number of attractions for sightseers. **Annapolis,** the state capital, has a tasty assortment of historic buildings, the U.S. Naval Academy (the J. P. Jones crypt and chapel are gorgeous), and many shops and restaurants. There are plenty of outdoor recreation and scenic spots, including **Patuxent Research Refuge/National Wildlife Visitor Center** and **Accokeek National Colonial Farm.** Two unusual sites are all about flight: **NASA/Goddard Space Flight Visitor Center** and **College Park Aviation Museum.** American history fans won't want to miss the **Surratt House Museum,** an integral part of the Abraham Lincoln assassination story.

Southern Maryland

The southern counties, among Maryland's more rural areas, are the cradle of the state. History and outdoor recreation are the big draws here. Maryland's colonial past (**St. Clement's Island–Potomac River Museum, Historic St. Mary's City**), the Civil War (**Dr. Samuel A. Mudd House Museum, Pt. Lookout State Park**)—and even ancient history (**Calvert Cliffs State Park**)—are yours to explore and enjoy. If your interests are more contemporary, you'll appreciate the **Calvert Marine Museum** with its restored lighthouse, and the unusual combination of art and nature at **Annmarie Garden** on St. John.

Western Maryland

The west, including the charming town of **Frederick,** is home to important Civil War sites and history—**Antietam Battlefield** and the **National Museum of Civil War Medicine,** among many others. A beautiful cathedral, the **National Shrine of St. Elizabeth Ann Seton** honors America's first Catholic saint. Two completely different museums, the **Washington County Museum of Fine Arts** and **Thrasher Carriage Museum,** both offer outstanding displays. The **C&O Canal National Historical Park** is one of the nation's exemplary recreation areas, though **Swallow Falls State Park** and **Deep Creek Lake** both offer a bounty of activities and captivating scenery.

North-Central Maryland

The northern territory closest to Pennsylvania's Piedmont is a region of produce farms, horse breeders, and watermen's communities—and some of the finest bicycle tour routes in the nation. Most of Maryland's vineyards are here, along with several outstanding state parks. The **Havre de Grace Decoy Museum** presents appealing exhibits on the art of carving. **Ladew Topiary Gardens,** a handsomely appointed private home converted to a museum and park, features some of the most amusing plants on the planet. Tanks, tanks a lot (and a bomb or two) can be found at the **U.S. Army Ordnance Museum.** North-central is home to a number of charming villages, among them **Chesapeake City, Chestertown,** and **Rock Hall.**

The Eastern Shore

A peaceful interlude and plenty of picturesque scenery can be found on the Eastern Shore. **Wye Island,** and the village of **Wye,** are often in the news as the site of peace accords. Former watermen's villages, like **St. Michaels** and **Easton,** have taken on a new gloss of sophistication. Attractions such as the **Chesapeake Bay Maritime Museum** and outstanding **Ward Museum of Wildfowl Art** are popular; but less showy venues such as the **Old Third Haven Meeting House, Jane's Island State Park,** and **Blackwater National Wildlife Refuge** are equally interesting. A boat trip to **Smith Island** may relax you into dreamland, but you'll wake up when you return to Crisfield for the fascinating **Tawes Historical Museum walking tour.** The biggest and best-known destination on the Eastern Shore is **Ocean City,** with its fabulous beach, boardwalk, **Life-Saving Station Museum,** and a variety of amusement parks, shopping, and restaurants.

ON THE ROAD/MARYLAND

Henlopen State Park, Delaware, to Pt. Reyes National Seashore, California. The ADT incorporates trails designed for hiking and bicycle and equestrian use. The Maryland portion passes through the Eastern Shore over the Bay Bridge through Annapolis to Washington, D.C.

Though it lacks the length of the Appalachian Trail and ADT, the C&O Canal towpath (Western Maryland chapter) is an exceptional hike or bike. It begins in Washington, D.C., and follows the Potomac River to Cumberland, more than 100 miles to the east. The sights are varied, and include a French and Indian War site near Big Pool, Fort Frederick, considered the best-preserved pre–Revolutionary War stone fort in America. The C&O Canal is one of nine National Recreation Trails in Maryland designated for hikers, bikers, and backpackers by the rails-to-trails movement, which converts unused railroad corridors and canal paths to multiuse trails. For the most part, the towpath isn't paved, but it's an easy and level road.

Gunpowder Falls State Park north of Baltimore (410/592-2897) offers numerous scenic areas and over 100 miles of hiking trails. The park maintains the North Central rails-to-trails route for hikers, bikers, and equestrians; it extends 21 miles from Ashland to the Maryland-Pennsylvania border.

Fishing

Fishing—freshwater, bay, and surf—is a consuming activity in Maryland. Freshwater species, often supplemented by state breeding programs, inhabit thousands of lakes, rivers, ponds, and streams. Nearly all of the state parks offer fishing opportunities: St. Mary's River State Park north of Great Mills in southern Maryland (310/872-5389) is known for its bass fishing, and Choptank River Fishing Pier in Cambridge on the Eastern Shore (410/820-1668) offers two public piers. Surf fishing is available at Sandy Point State Park at the base of the Bay Bridge below Annapolis (Central Maryland chapter), and Assateague State Park (410/641-2120) has miles of ocean frontage.

Fishing is strictly controlled by the Maryland Department of Natural Resources. Licenses are

Maryland's parks offer fine fishing.

required for anyone over the age of 16. Freshwater licenses cost roughly $10 for residents and $20 for nonresidents, and a trout stamp (allowing an angler to fish in catch-and-return trout management areas and to possess trout taken from nontidal waters) is an additional $5. A freshwater license allows an individual to fish in the fresh waters of Maryland from January 1 through December 31; a five-day nontidal license ($6) allows residents and non-residents to fish in the freshwaters of Maryland for five consecutive fishing days. Sportfishing (bay and surf) licenses run $9 for residents and $14 for nonresidents; a five-day Bay Sport license is available for $6. Head boats (fishing boats that charge by the head) include a boat license charge in their fees, so no additional license is required. For more information or to submit license applications, contact any DNR Service Center (in Annapolis, Cumberland, or Centreville) or the Maryland Department of Natural Resources, Licensing and Registration Service, 580 Taylor Ave., Tawes State Office Building/C-1, Annapolis, MD 21401, 410/260-8200. The DNR has an informative website, www.dnr.state.md.us/service/license.htm, and applications are available online.

No license is required for those who love to play in the mud; crabbing and clamming are available to anyone who wants to bait a trap or dig a hole anywhere along the marshes in the state. Assawoman Bay and Isle of Wight Bay, both east of Ocean City, are popular spots.

Hunting

The Maryland Department of Natural Resources also administers the state's hunting program through its Wildlife & Heritage Division (410/260-8540). Hunting is a time-honored tradition in Maryland, and related expenditures add millions of dollars to the state's coffers; about 95 percent of Maryland's state budget for wildlife programs comes from these sources. Revenues from hunting licenses and federal excise taxes on hunting equipment provide for the scientific investigation, protection, and management of wildlife. In a blazing example of enlightened self-interest, the hunting community is often the first to support and appreciate wildlife resources and the ecological principles upon which scientific wildlife management is based. Hunting promotes a personal desire to restore and improve wildlife habitat.

Among the game seasons available to hunters are migratory game bird, waterfowl, furbearers, forest game, upland game, deer (antlerless and antlered), and sika deer. All hunters are required to be licensed, and hunting licenses are valid from the date of issue to July 31, except the three-day nonresident license; the state offers a variety of licenses based on type of game and other factors. A Resident Basic License (about $25) allows you to hunt or trap all legal game in season except deer and waterfowl. A Harvest Information Program (HIP) permit is required to hunt all migratory game birds. Deer and waterfowl stamps may also be required for use with these licenses. Nonresidents of Maryland are required to present a valid I.D., and pay a fee of $86–130. This license allows nonresidents of Maryland to hunt all legal game except waterfowl and deer during bow and muzzleloader seasons. Bow and Muzzleloader Stamps as well as waterfowl stamps may be purchased for use with this license. A license is also required for nonresidents to trap in Maryland. For

more information, contact Permits Coordinator, DNR Wildlife & Heritage Division, 580 Taylor Ave., E-1, Annapolis, MD 21401, 410/260-8200, www.dnr.state.md.us/service/license.htm; applications are available online.

Stamps are similar to stamps in a passport; they allow a licensed hunter to approach a certain type of game or use a specified weapon. Among the stamps currently available for an extra charge are the Maryland Migratory Waterfowl Stamp, Federal Migratory Bird Hunting and Conservation Stamp, Deer Stamp, Bow Stamp, and Muzzleloader Stamp. Licenses and stamps are available by applying in person at any DNR Sport License Agent. Call any DNR Licensing and Registration Service Center (Annapolis Service Center, 580 Taylor Ave., P.O. Box 1869, Annapolis, MD 21404-1869, 410/260-3220; Western Service Center, 3 Pershing St., Rm. 103, Cumberland, MD 21502, 301/777-2134; East Central Service Center, 120 Broadway Ave., Rm. 207, Centreville, MD 21617, 410/758-5252) for the location of an agent near you or visit them online at www.dnr.state.md.us/service/netag2.html. Federal Migratory Bird Hunting and Conservation Stamps are available at post offices and National Wildlife Refuges, or by calling 800/STAMP24 (800/782-6724).

Golf

The state boasts hundreds of public golf courses, in every region, with a heavy concentration on the Eastern Shore. Individual chapters list courses, facilities, and contact information.

IN THE WATER
Boating and Sailing

The State of Maryland offers many opportunities for those who bring their own vessels. You can launch in fresh or saltwater and see hundreds of different plants and animals along Maryland's 4,360 miles of tidal shorelines. Some 17,000 miles of waterways, including 42 rivers, flow into the 1,726 square miles of the Chesapeake Bay. There are 623 square miles of inland water areas and 31 miles of Atlantic Ocean coastline.

All commercial or recreational **power boats**

must be registered in Maryland if equipped with any kind of primary or auxiliary mechanical propulsion and used principally in Maryland. Boats registered with the U.S. Coast Guard are exempt. Licensing fees include excise tax equal to 5 percent of the purchase price of the vessel, motor, and accessories (excluding the trailer) or the current fair market value; a $2 title fee; and a $24 registration fee (vessels 16 feet in length or less, propelled by a motor of 7.5 horsepower or less, are exempt from the fee). The registration is valid for the calendar year in which it's issued plus the subsequent year. Boat registration is handled by the Maryland Department of Natural Resources Service Centers (Annapolis Metropolitan Area, 580 Taylor Ave., Annapolis, MD 21401, 410/260-3220; Central Maryland, 2 Bond St., Bel Air, MD 21014, 410/836-4550; Dundalk Service Center, 7701 Wise Ave., Baltimore, MD 21222, 410/284-1654; Eastern Maryland, 201 Baptist St. #22, Salisbury, MD 21801, 410/543-6700; East Central Maryland, 120 Broadway Ave., Centreville, MD 21617, 410/819-4100; Southern Maryland, 6904 Hallowing Point Rd., Prince Frederick, MD 20678, 410/535-3382; Western Maryland, 3 Pershing St., Rm. 103, Cumberland, MD 21502, 301/777-2134). You can download forms from www.dnr.state.md.us/boating/registration.

Central Maryland is all about the Chesapeake, and the bay is all about **sailing** (though there are plenty of motor yachts on the water). Every town on the bay has a marina, and visitors who don't bring their own vessels can rent passenger space on a bewildering range of boat designs for an hour or several days. The Chesapeake is also the home of boat-and-breakfasts—a sail combined with an overnight. Some of the most popular stops for pleasure boating enthusiasts (and best places to sightsee) are Solomons Island (Southern Maryland chapter), Annapolis (Central Maryland and the Capital Gateway chapter), Rock Hall and Chestertown (Northern Maryland chapter), and St. Michaels (Eastern Shore chapter).

Kayaking and Canoeing

The Potomac River is only partially navigable for

sailing on Chesapeake Bay

small craft; certain areas, such as the river around Big Pool, are considered safe. A good place for information on the river is the Chesapeake & Ohio Canal National Historic Park. The state's other large rivers, among them the Susquehanna, Patapsco, Patuxent, and Pokomoke, are almost entirely navigable (the Pokomoke seems to be made for quiet paddling). Hundreds of smaller streams throughout the state provide adventure for canoeing enthusiasts, and Deep Creek Lake and Rocky Gap State Park (both in western Maryland) are indicative of the state's few but fine lakes. Many commercial riverside liveries rent canoes and kayaks. Exploring the marshy shoreline of the Chesapeake in a sea kayak is a particularly good way to see waterfowl and wildlife, particularly during seasonal migrations. While rounding a marsh on the Manokin River not far from Princess Anne in Somerset County, I came upon 150 Canada geese taking a break on the water.

Swimming, Surfing, and Personal Watercraft

Freshwater swimming is available at dozens of parks around the state, among them Swallow Falls State Park (waters rush through a canyon over boulders—very popular and scenic), Rocky Gap (lake with beaches), and Cunningham Falls State Park (lake and streams) in the west. Several state parks offer public Olympic-size swimming pools, as do larger municipalities. Point Lookout (Southern Maryland chapter) and Sandy Point State Park (Central Maryland chapter) offer bay beaches, as does Janes Island State Park (Eastern Shore chapter). Assateague Island State Park on the Eastern Shore features ocean beaches for swimming and surfing.

Ocean City has its own surfing culture (the city has erected a statue in memory of a young local surfer); though the waves will never rival Hawaii's, there are still plenty of good rides. Personal watercraft (also known as Jet-Skis) rentals are popular here, most often used on the calmer waters of Assawoman Bay, on the west side of the peninsula. Personal watercraft are also used frequently on Deep Creek Lake in western Maryland. Equipment rentals are available in both areas.

WINTER SPORTS

Because of Maryland's comparatively mild winters, most cold-weather activity takes place in the western part of the state.

Maryland's only downhill ski area, Wisp, is just north of Deep Creek Lake. Several additional downhill ski areas are just across the Pennsylvania border in the Laurel Highlands south of Pittsburgh (Seven Springs, Hidden Valley, and Laurel Ridge State Park), and north of Hagerstown (Blue Knob State Park).

Herrington Manor State Park, not far from Wisp, offers cross-country skiing and snowshoeing, with equipment rental. Nearby New Germany State Park also opens cross-country trails, and both parks have winter rental cabins. Ice fishing is also permitted (see the Western Maryland chapter).

Deep Creek Lake State Park offers six miles of snowmobile trails in winter, and many other parks offer limited snowmobile trails.

ON THE ROAD/MARYLAND

Entertainment and Events

SHOPPING

Every village in Maryland has at least one antiques dealer, and most have several; shoppers will never run out of places to look. Malls are equally ubiquitous, though the queen of all mall strips has to be the road between Rockville, Maryland, and Washington, D.C.—every U.S. retailer and a few Europeans appear to have at least one shop on this "miracle mile." A close contender is the town of Columbia, a planned community that was built with the pleasures of commerce in mind.

Like most older American cities, Baltimore's former downtown shopping area has dispersed to outlying areas, but boutique browsing is still a pastime in the inner harbor and surrounding upscale neighborhoods. Annapolis features lots of interesting small shops, some oriented unerringly to T-shirt and key-chain fans. Ocean City is built for amusement and offers a variety of shopping, from malls to tiny discount outlets.

ARTS AND ENTERTAINMENT

Enormous amounts of wealth have been concentrated in Baltimore. The city offers spectacular fine-art museums and galleries, as well as a multitude of cultural performances including an accomplished symphony, vocal performances, and dance. The city's aquarium and science and industrial museums deserve to be ranked among the best in the United States.

Ocean City's venues often feature big-name rock bands, singers, comedians, and other entertainers. Almost every county has at least one music showcase and a local theater troupe that performs musicals and plays.

Don't overlook smaller rural history, maritime, and art museums. The collections, such as those of the Washington County Museum of Fine Arts in Hagerstown and the Calvert Marine Museum on Solomons Island, are often exceptional.

FESTIVALS AND EVENTS

Maryland offers a host of celebrations, from tiny village festivals and sweeping agricultural fairs to paeans to the state's spokes-crustacean. Though January and February are quiet months for events, May through December are filled with festivals and activities large and small. An annotated list of festivals and special events by month is included in each chapter; a statewide sampling follows:

March/April

The **Bunny Bonanzoo** is one of Baltimore's oldest and best-loved Eastertide traditions, featuring a bunny hop and egg hunt among other activities at the wonderful Baltimore Zoo.

The prestigious **Ward World Championship Wildfowl Carving Competition,** which has been held in Salisbury since 1970, includes a weekend of activities.

The **Maryland Sheep & Wool Festival** will warm the cockles of your heart as well as offer opportunities to learn "Rug Braiding" and "Hands-on Beginning Shepherd Skills," among dozens of other classes, exhibits, and displays. It's held at the Howard County Fairgrounds in West Friendship.

The last week in April through the first week in May is time for the **Salisbury Dogwood Festival,** when the town is covered in bloom and hosts special events.

Gladiator meets *Private Ryan* in the annual **Marching Through Time** living history encampment in Glenn Dale (Prince George's County). More than 300 reenactors represent Roman citizens, World War II soldiers, and everything in between.

The **John Wilkes Booth Escape Route Tour** gives participants the chance to follow the trail of the president's assassin in considerably more comfort than Booth himself.

May

The **Preakness,** second jewel in horse racing's Triple Crown, takes over the city of Baltimore in May. There's a parade with marching bands, floats, and equestrian units, and dozens of related events and parties. The race is held at Pimlico Race Course.

Another "only in Baltimore" event, the **Living American Flag Program** features 4,000 grade-school kids who gather at Fort McHenry to re-create the first American flag with a huge mosaic of colored cards.

For more than 100 years, the **Baltimore Watercolor Society's Mid-Atlantic Regional Watercolor Exhibition** has drawn some of the best artists in the region. The event is held at the Strathmore Hall Arts Center, Bethesda/Rockville.

The three-day **Mid-Atlantic Maritime Arts Festival,** on the grounds of the Chesapeake Bay Maritime Museum, St. Michaels, features ship models, maritime paintings, crafts, music, seafood, and more.

In sympathy with Boston, Chestertown residents boarded the British brigantine *Geddes* in 1774 and dumped its tea shipment into the Chester River. The **Chestertown Tea Party Festival** commemorates the event with a colonial parade, music, food, boat rides, and historical reenactments.

Sharpsburg (Washington County) is home to the oldest **Memorial Day Parade** in America, a tradition started after the Civil War to honor returning veterans. The parade is followed by a ceremony in the National Cemetery.

June

The **Chesapeake Bay Bridge Walk** gives participants a chance to enjoy views from the bridge in a 4.3-mile-long stroll.

From June through September, Baltimore hosts **weekend festivals** celebrating its varied ethnic heritage. The festivals all feature food, music, and live entertainment, and include Greek, Jewish, and Latino cultures, among many others.

The **Annual Antique & Classic Boat Festival,** held at the Chesapeake Bay Maritime Museum, St. Michaels, features more than 100 classic boats and automobiles in a judged show. There are also seminars and special exhibits.

Columbia Festival of the Arts is 10 days of performing arts at Lake Kittamaqundi in Columbia, including two weekends of free performances in addition to ticketed performances, workshops, and master classes. Past years have featured Branford Marsalis, Rick Danko, and many others. While you're in town for music, don't miss **Jazzfest,** presented in partnership with the Festival of the Arts. Jazz greats Jimmy McGriff and Hank Crawford have performed at prior festivals, and events include concerts, workshops, and the "House of Jazz"—dinner and continuous live entertainment.

Summer Solstice is celebrated at Accokeek Foundation in southern Maryland with boat rides, demonstrations, lawn games, and walks along the river.

A gathering of tribes celebrate their heritage at the **American Indian Pow-Wow and Festival** in Waldorf with native regalia, crafts, food, drinks, songs, and dances.

Once known as the marriage capital of the world for its lack of barriers to getting hitched in a hurry, Elkton celebrates **National Marriage Day** with an outdoor wedding and opportunities to take and renew vows.

July

Fireworks? The **Navy Surface Warfare Center** has a shell or two—some consider its Fourth of July celebration to be the best in southern Maryland. It's held in the Village Green Park in Indian Head.

Traditional country and bluegrass music fills the air at the **Fiddler's and Banjo Contests,** Friendsville (Garrett County). Spontaneous clogging appreciated!

The **Lotus Blossom Festival** stars acres of lily and lotus blossoms; it's held in mid-July at Lilypons Water Gardens in Buckeystown.

August

The official state sport of Maryland is . . . jousting, of course! Calvert County hosts a **Jousting Tournament** in Port Republic along with a bazaar and country supper.

North Beach celebrates **Bayfest** with 150 craft

vendors, live music, antique cars, and kids' activities, all held on the town's beautiful beachfront.

More than 300 juried artists and craftspeople display their wares at the annual **Havre de Grace Art Show** at Tydings Memorial Park.

Ocean City's **White Marlin Open** offers cash prizes of $850,000 with more than 250 boats competing for record catches of white marlin, blue marlin, wahoo, tuna, and shark.

September

The **Annual Skipjack Races & Festival** is held early in September on Deal Island. Food, arts and crafts, and family activities are part of the fun.

The **Pemberton Colonial Fair,** held outside Salisbury, combines 18th-century games, performances (including period dancing, dressage, and other horse events), and booths on the grounds of an authentic colonial manor house.

A benefit for Howard Community College, the **Columbia Classic Grand Prix** is a day of steeplechase, equestrian events, and parades, with displays and food.

The **Grand Militia Muster** in Historic St. Mary's City is the largest gathering of 17th-century reenactment units in the United States.

Bivalves 'R' us: **St. Mary's County Oyster Festival** is home of the national oyster shucking championship and the national oyster cook-off.

October

On **Tilghman Island Day,** the village is filled with exhibits and seafood. Visitors can watch skipjack and workboat races, listen to music, and bid in an auction.

Olde Princess Anne Days have been going on since the late 1950s, and are as popular as ever. The historic house and garden tour and colonial fair takes place over two days.

The Historical Society of Talbot County in Easton holds **Heritage Weekend,** an antique show and sale that includes appraisals.

A popular 35-minute walk, **Ghosts of the Patapsco Female Institute,** weaves through the spooky ruins of the old girls' school. Come in costume with a flashlight. Boo!

Cakewalkin' in Western Maryland! Hagerstown hosts its own version of the **Alsatia**

Mummer's Parade, an event with 150 units, bands, and floats.

Schifferstadt Museum celebrates **Oktoberfest** with oompah bands, food, and crafts.

Every year in October, the Lexington Market presents its **Chocolate Festival,** with the seductive bean in all forms. Tasting, music, games, and demonstrations round out the four-day celebration.

November

Celebrate mollusk madness at **Oysterfest,** and learn to shuck, tong, and nipper from local watermen. Prepared oysters are for sale, and visitors can slurp to live music between boat rides. It's held on the grounds of the Chesapeake Bay Maritime Museum, St. Michaels.

The **Waterfowl Festival** takes over the town of Easton (literally—the streets are closed and decorated). This is one of the biggest events on the Eastern Shore, featuring art, sculpture, duck stamps, crafts, demonstrations, food, music, and more.

Baltimore celebrates turkey day with a **Thanksgiving Day Parade** on Pratt Street with floats, marching bands, and of course, good old Santa.

December

Historic St. Mary's City presents a number of holiday events, including a Christmas concert in the Old State House and an evening of feasting and madrigals.

Colonial Christmas at Smallwood State Park features colonial decorations, costumed docents, and cooking demonstrations.

Annapolis's historic district, which is justifiably famous, hosts **Annapolis by Candlelight** with more than a dozen private homes open for touring.

On a more electrified note, three areas in central Maryland sponsor light displays. **Lights on the Bay** at Sandy Point State Park features a two-mile drive with 50 animated and stationary holiday displays. Another illuminating event, the **Symphony of Lights** in Columbia is a spectacular drive-through display of holiday lights. And Seneca Creek State Park near Gaithersburg offers a 3.5-mile drive, **Winter Lights.**

Antietam National Battlefield, Sharpsburg, sets out 23,110 luminaries along a 4.5-mile route to honor Civil War soldiers killed and wounded during the three days of battle there. The **Memorial Illumination** has been an annual event for more than a decade.

The Baltimore **Lighted Boat Parade** features more than 50 decorated boats and other pleasure craft.

Accommodations

Maryland affords the traveler a huge variety of accommodations, from low-end and midrange chain motels and hotels to bed-and-breakfasts, luxury hotels, and full-package resorts. Budget travelers will do best at inexpensive chain motels and camps. There are two American Youth Hostel (AYH) branches (in Baltimore and Knoxville, near Harper's Ferry), and a few universities and colleges that make dormitory rooms available during the summer.

CAMPING

Eighteen Maryland state parks offer camping, available April–October with a few April–De-cember exceptions. Some campsites, like those at Assateague State Park, may be reserved. Campsites vary, including "improved" (room to park a car and motor home, camping trailer, or tent, with water, washhouses, and toilets nearby); "unimproved" (room for one car and a camping trailer or tent, toilets and water nearby); and "primitive" (pit toilets only). Fees for day use vary from free to $10, and all charge for overnight camping and cabin use. Seven parks rent "camper cabins," one-room cabins with beds and electricity, outside fireplaces, and washhouse; or "cabins," with at least one bedroom, electricity, kitchen, refrigerator, and shower.

Not every state recreation area is covered in

STATEWIDE HOTEL AND MOTEL CHAINS

The following chains have facilities throughout the state, usually in the larger towns. For specific locations or to book rooms, call the 800 number below for each chain directly. (Rooms may also be booked through a travel agent.)

HOTEL/MOTEL	TELEPHONE	WEBSITE
Best Western	800/528-1234	www.bestwestern.com
Comfort Inn	800/221-2222	www.comfortinn.com
Days Inn	800/325-2525	www.daysinn.com
Econolodge	800/553-2666	www.econolodge.com
Embassy Suites	800/362-2779	www.embassysuites.com
Hampton Inn	800/HAMPTON (800/426-7866)	www.hamptoninnweekends.com
Holiday Inn	800/HOLIDAY (800/465-4329)	www.holiday-inn.com
Howard Johnson	800/446-4656	www.hojo.com
Marriott	800/228-9290	www.marriott.com
Quality Inn	800/228-5151	www.qualityinn.com
Red Roof Inn	800/THE ROOF (800/843-7663)	www.redroof.com
Sheraton	800/325-3535	www.sheraton.com

this book, but an excellent general map with facility information on all parks and forests is available by contacting the State of Maryland Department of Natural Resources; State Forest and Park Service; 580 Taylor Ave., E-3, Annapolis, MD 21401. State park and forest campsites, cabins, and shelters can be reserved May 1–Sept. 30 by calling 888/432-2267, or online at www.reservations.dnr.state.md.us, Mon.–Fri. 8 A.M.–8 P.M. For October 1–April 30 arrivals, call the specific park for information regarding facility use and availability.

Maryland also has plenty of private campgrounds, often with extra conveniences such as swimming pools, playgrounds, and stores.

UNDER $50

Outside of the Baltimore-Washington corridor, it's not difficult to find basic low-cost accommodations averaging $50 a night—usually small, family-run motels and occasional guest houses (private homes that rent rooms for the night to travelers). Since most don't advertise, it will take some driving around (and some asking around, especially in the local café) to find a place.

American Youth Hostels (AYH) is a branch of Hostelling International (HI), an organization with affiliates all over the world. Despite the name, youth hostel accommodations are open to people of all ages, though you must be a member of either HI or AYH. To purchase a one-year membership (the cost is $28 for adults 18–54, free for those 17 and under, and $18 for those over 55), get in touch with the branch of HI nearest you or contact HI USA, 8401 Colesville Rd., Ste. 600, Silver Spring, MD 20910, 301/495-1240, www.hiayh.org. If you're not a member and are planning a one-night stay, you'll be charged a $3 "temporary membership fee" (which can be applied to a full membership) in addition to the room rate. Most AYH facilities offer dorm-style rooms, with men and women housed separately, and a few smaller family-size rooms. Visitors are responsible for their own bedding (most hostels rent sheets for a nominal fee), towels, and meals; bathrooms are shared and a communal kitchen is available. Hostels in Maryland average $12 a night. Though it's all right to show up at a hostel in the late afternoon to book a room, it's a better idea to book at least a week—preferably a month—ahead during the summer months. Hostelling International publishes guidebooks to its facilities all over the world and also runs a reservation service.

Another source of budget stays are colleges and universities in Maryland that rent out dorm rooms during summer break (and sometimes several months longer). The average room has two single beds and a private or shared bath, is near inexpensive food service sources, and ranges in cost from $15 to $40 per day. The best way to find out which educational facilities are renting is by calling the college or university directly—some institutions have developed summer programs and now save their facilities for student accommodation only. Maryland currently lists two facilities open to the public, one in Baltimore and one outside Washington, D.C., but more are added every year.

$50–75

Chain hotels and motels offer convenient accommodations priced in the $45–60 range, though some—especially in Baltimore and the larger towns—are more upscale.

$75–100

At more than $90 a night, hotels in Baltimore, Washington Gateway, and most of the resort areas and larger towns tend to be expensive. Always ask about discounts and packages; these are established to draw in travelers and families with low-season rates and "kids stay free" bargains.

Another option is the bed-and-breakfast, which offers a more homelike stay, often in a historic house. Though prices average $75 to well over $100, they frequently include a charming room, a private bath, and a hearty breakfast, served along with the interesting conversation of fellow travelers. Since most B&Bs are locally owned, the hosts are likely to be great sources of unadvertised information about the area. Lone travelers often prefer the homey feel and friendliness of a B&B to the anonymity of a hotel. Lists of local bed-and-breakfasts are frequently available from the information/tourist sources listed in the specific destination chapters of this book.

Another option, inns are often renovated historic wayfarers' lodgings and usually provide private baths but no breakfast. (Those that do provide breakfast are sometimes listed interchangeably with bed-and-breakfasts.) Inns frequently have more rooms to offer and aren't as intimate as a B&B.

OVER $100

Top-level accommodations generally offer packages with rates below $150 per night in the off-season, but prices can soar well beyond $300 per night depending on room and season. Baltimore's Inn at the Colonnade and Harbor Court typify big-city luxury accommodations; both have received numerous international awards and accolades for service and surroundings. A few B&Bs are also in the luxury category, thanks to their locations—St. Michaels and Oxford in particular. Most B&Bs, regardless of location, provide equally elegant surroundings for less money. Resorts that offer multiple entertainment options as well as lodging also fall into the luxury category, such as Turf Valley in Ellicott City.

Food and Drink

FOOD

In Maryland, you'll find two things on every menu, regardless of the size or style of the restaurant: seafood and chicken. The state produces raw materials in quantity; the Chesapeake provides the glub and thousands of commercial chicken farms provide the cluck. Ethnic eateries such as Thai, Chinese, Mexican, West Indian, Jewish, Italian, and others may be found in Baltimore and larger cities.

Seafood

Seafood restaurants are the McDonald's of Maryland. Crabs, clams, and oysters require a great deal of hand-processing, and as a result, are comparatively expensive; even in small towns the tariff can be high. Crab is served in some form from one end of the state to the other. Tomato-based Maryland crab soup and crab cakes are ubiquitous, and usually good everywhere. Soft-shell crabs are aqua-farmed, and are available year-round. The once-plentiful bay oyster is suffering an ebb, so most oysters served on the menu are from elsewhere. Rockfish (striped bass) is fresh and wonderful. Take advantage of the exceptional variety and freshness of the bay and ocean bounty.

Gourmet

Baltimore is a great food town. There are so many good restaurants that it's impossible to do them justice, though I've tried to vote with my stomach as much as possible. Bethesda is a mini-version of Baltimore, especially in the ethnic restaurant category.

Farm Markets

For fresh foods that you can prepare yourself, try shopping at Maryland's farm markets. From spring until late autumn, local farmers bring produce and meats into the villages and towns to sell directly to the consumer (Baltimore has its own farmers' market in the summer). Many farm markets are casual open-air affairs, often with a flea market attached. Western Maryland produces abundant crops of peaches and apples, and corn, melons, and other produce is available everywhere in roadside stands outside urban Maryland.

WINERIES AND BREWERIES

Maryland isn't known for wine, at least not for now. The number of wineries in the state grows every year (more than 10 at this writing), and if the problem of chronic grape shortages is solved over time with successful plantings, the state may rewrite the book on mid-Atlantic vintages. Grape growers harvest an average of 450 tons a year, but the wineries produce more than 300,000 bottles of wine, often with juice purchased from out of state. The majority of Maryland vintners are still on the learning curve, but that doesn't stop them from giving great parties. The annual **Maryland Wine Festival** is a two-day event at the Carroll County Farm Museum near Westminster, usually held the third weekend in September (call 800/654-4645 for more information). Vintners have formed the Association of Maryland Wineries (800/237-WINE or 800/237-9463, www .marylandwine.com), and one of its primary goals is to modify the state's restrictive laws that prohibit wineries from shipping wine directly to customers (you may buy it at the winery and carry it home, but they can't send you a bottle or a case). Currently, each winery must go through distributors to make their wines available to the public, and the distributorship is limited to a few wine and liquor stores—a good reason to visit each winery and sample the wares. In spite of that, Maryland wine sales in 2002 reached $5 million, an 11 percent increase over 2001. Maryland wineries also reported significant increases in the number of stores that began carrying Maryland wine, and the number of visitors to the wineries also increased in 2002 by as much as 200 percent at some wineries.

Microbreweries have sprouted up in towns and villages all over the state, and the brews are uniformly excellent. Baltimore, Frederick, and

Ocean City all have their own breweries with local distribution and pubs that mix hearty food with creative beers.

You must be 21 to buy or drink alcohol. Bars close at 2 A.M. All types of liquor are sold in grocery and liquor stores.

Transportation

GETTING THERE

By Air

Baltimore-Washington International (BWI, 410/859-7111 or 800/I-FLY-BWI or 800/435-9294), 10 miles south of Baltimore and 30 miles north of Washington, D.C., is the state's major airport, with international traffic from 31 foreign and domestic carriers. US Airways has a hub there and operates flights daily to and from all major U.S. cities and commuter flights to many Maryland destinations. Washington National Airport (703/661-2700) and Washington Dulles International Airport (703/419-8000) in Virginia also serve Maryland.

Smaller airports connect the traveler with every

AIRLINE PHONE NUMBERS

The following airlines fly into Baltimore:

AIRLINE	TELEPHONE	WEBSITE
Domestic carriers:		
American Airlines	800/433-7300	www.aa.com
America West Airlines	800/235-9292	www.americawest.com
Continental Airlines	800/525-0280	www.continental.com
Delta Airlines	800/221-1212	www.delta.com
Northwest Airlines	800/225-2525	www.nwa.com
Southwest Airlines	800/435-9792	www.iflyswa.com
United Airlines	800/241-6522	www.ual.com
US Airways	800/428-4322	www.usairways.com
International carriers:		
Air Jamaica	800/523-5585	www.airjamaica.com
Air Ontario/Air Canada	888/247-2262	www.aircanada.ca
British Airways	800/247-9297	www.british-airways.com
El Al Israel Airlines	800/223-6700	www.elal.co.il
Icelandair	800/223-5500	www.icelandair.is
Commuter and limited-route airlines:		
Frontier Airlines	800/432-1359	www.flyfrontier.com
Midway Airlines	800/446-4392	www.midwayair.com
Pro Air	800/939-9551	www.proair.com

THE NATIONAL ROAD

Prior to the coming of Europeans, Native American hunters and traders used an ancient trail, Nemacolin's Path, as the main and perhaps only crossing over the Allegheny Mountains from the marshes of Delaware. After colonists had settled the mid-Atlantic coasts, they looked toward the frontier—particularly the region of modern Pittsburgh. Nemacolin's Path became the main route of travel for early settlers, though it remained little more than a narrow walkway, suitable for lone travelers or those in single file. George Washington used the road on his journey north to negotiate with the French over the Ohio River valley. When General Braddock marched west from Fort Cumberland in 1755, hoping to wrest the area from French control, his ill-fated troop of British soldiers straggled along Nemacolin's Path.

In the early 19th century, President Thomas Jefferson and the National Congress appropriated funds to build a toll road from Cumberland, Maryland, to Wheeling, West Virginia, on Nemacolin's Path; they hoped, literally, to capitalize on the steady westward movement of the new nation's citizens. This National Pike, built through the investment of farmers and businessmen, connected with the Philadelphia Wagon Road near Hagerstown, Maryland, creating the first through path from Chesapeake Bay to the Ohio River, and on to the Mississippi River. Tollbooths were established every few miles along the widened, tamped-earth and log road. Stagecoaches, dray wagons, Conestoga wagons loaded with a family's possessions, horses and riders, and foot travelers all found the convenience of the road outweighed the costs. Not all agreed: resentment frequently arose against those hired to collect the toll, and tollgates and toll-houses were torn down. Under common law, farmers taking grain to mill could pass a turnpike toll for free; shrewd travelers sometimes carried grain bags full of bran to defraud toll takers. Rough side roads, "shun-pikes," were developed to avoid payment. One notice posted on a toll-gate read, "We ast you not to collect no more tole, you must Not collect one cent if you do we are Going to Destroy your House with fire and Denamite. . . . We don't want to do this but we want a Free Road and are agoing to have it."

The author of that anonymous threat finally did get his or her demand met, though nearly a century later. With the advent of the speedy and convenient railroad, the Old National Pike fell into disuse. However, when automobiles became the preferred mode of transportation, the road revived and prospered. Though modern (toll) turnpikes carry much of the heavy traffic nearby, the old National Road—much improved by asphalt and finally toll-free—still appeals to those with a taste for the scenic and historic.

ON THE ROAD/MARYLAND

region. Cambridge Airport, Easton Municipal Airport, Ocean City Municipal Airport, and Salisbury-Wicomico County Regional Airport serve the Eastern Shore. St. Mary's County Airport is in southern Maryland, and Greater Cumberland Regional Airport, Washington County Regional Airport (Hagerstown), and Frederick Municipal Airport serve western Maryland.

By Rail

Amtrak has eight rail stations in the Maryland area, including Washington's Union Station, Baltimore's Penn Station, and West Virginia's Harpers Ferry Station. Amtrak's Capitol Limited stops in Pittsburgh; Connellsville, Pennsylvania; Cumberland, Maryland; Martinsburg, West Virginia; Harpers Ferry, West Virginia; Rockville, Maryland; Washington, D.C.; Baltimore; Philadelphia; and New York City. Amtrak may be reached by calling 800/USA-RAIL (800/872-7725). The Amtrak line connects directly to the Maryland Area Rail Commuter (MARC) system, a Monday–Friday commuter service with 75 trains on three lines in the Baltimore-Washington corridor, eight Maryland counties, and northeastern West Virginia. Call 800/325-RAIL (800/325-7725) for routes and schedules.

By Bus

Greyhound offers dozens of connecting routes from all over the United States and within the state. Call 800/822-2662 for specific departure times and destinations; they'll give schedules and prices over the phone.

By Car

There is one official toll road in Maryland, I-95, a four-lane that runs from the northeastern border of Delaware through Baltimore to the Washington, D.C., Beltway ($2, northbound). It also goes through the Fort McHenry Tunnel ($1).

U.S. 40, one to four lanes built on the old colonial toll road, parallels I-95 from Delaware to Baltimore, then heads west alongside I-70 from Baltimore to Hancock (then I-70 turns north to Pennsylvania) and I-68 from Hancock to the western Maryland border and beyond. The latter two are high-speed roads that vary between two and four lanes; U.S. 40 rambles alongside like a distracted mule tethered to a wagon. Another major route is U.S. 50, which runs east-west from Annapolis over the Bay Bridge (eastbound $2.50); with two to four lanes, it turns south, then east to Ocean City. I-83 is the main high-speed route from Baltimore to Pennsylvania; I-270 performs that function from Washington, D.C., to Frederick. I-495/I-95 loops around Washington, D.C., and I-695 circles the city of Baltimore and crosses the Francis Scott Key Bridge ($1). I-895 is a short stretch south of Baltimore through the Baltimore Harbor Tunnel ($1). Information on the latest toll rates and access to maps is available online at www.mdot.state.md.us.

By Water

Maryland is a boater's paradise, and most of the state's counties are accessible by boat along the Potomac River, Chesapeake Bay, and the Atlantic Ocean. Every town on the water has a marina; for information on pleasure-boating facilities, call the Marine Trade Association, 410/269-0741. The Port of Baltimore has hosted a number of impressive luxury liners, including the *Queen Elizabeth II*. It's a port of call for 15 cruise ships with destinations in the Caribbean and Europe.

Maryland is a boater's paradise.

Call the Port of Baltimore for more information, 410/385-4454.

GETTING AROUND

Interstate and Intrastate Mass Transit

MARC commuter trains run Monday–Friday on three lines. The Brunswick Line runs between Martinsburg, West Virginia, and Washington, D.C.; the Camden Line connects Baltimore's Inner Harbor and Washington, D.C., and the Penn Line links Perryville, midtown Baltimore, and Washington, D.C. (800/325-RAIL or 800/325-7725).

Washington Metro Rapid Transit (202/637-7000) features five **subway** lines that travel from downtown Washington to Maryland and Virginia. Baltimore Metro (410/539-5000) operates between the city and the northwestern suburb of Owings Mills, with links to an aboveground light rail system between northern Anne Arundel County and Timonium in Baltimore County.

Intercity Mass Transit

The Maryland Transit Authority (MTA) runs

75 bus lines in the city of Baltimore and throughout the state. For schedules and routes, call 410/539-5000, or visit www.mtamaryland.com. The Washington Metropolitan Area Transit Authority operates Metrobus (Metro) in Washington, D.C., and the surrounding Maryland suburbs (202/637-7000).

By Car

Hundreds of little Maryland kids must be traumatized every year when asked to draw an outline of their state in school. What mnemonic device can one possibly use? Seagull with a broken wing? A lumpy rendition of the letters "TL"? Just as the outline fails to fit a mold, so does the state. Auto travel is the best way to appreciate Maryland's rural beauty and also to visit some of its less accessible attractions. One of the advantages of travel in Maryland is proximity: in each of the state's divisions as laid out in this book, visitors have the choice of spending less than three hours point-to-point on the road, or far longer, depending on chosen routes.

The highway speed limit in Maryland is 65 mph unless posted otherwise. Children under three must ride in approved safety seats, and drivers and front-seat passengers must wear seat belts.

Historically, the Chesapeake Bay and its tributaries allowed the development of cheap water transport, but at the same time complicated land transportation. Bridges of every description abound throughout the state. Major projects joined the state's many smaller ones; the completion in 1952 of the four-mile Chesapeake Bay Bridge facilitated travel from the Eastern Shore to the western. The completion of the Baltimore Harbor Bridge (1957), Fort McHenry Tunnel (1985), and the Francis Scott Key Bridge across the Patapsco River (1977) helped to move traffic around Baltimore. Along with bridges and tunnels, the state maintains an active ferry system, serviced by the Maryland State Highway Administration. A map of ferry services is available by calling 800/252-8776, or online at www.mdot.state.md.us.

ON THE ROAD/MARYLAND

Information and Services

VISAS AND OFFICIALDOM

Overseas visitors need a passport and a visa to enter the United States. This means (except for diplomats, students, or refugees) a nonimmigrant visitor's visa. You must obtain this in advance at a U.S. consulate or embassy abroad. Residents of western European and Commonwealth countries usually receive these readily; residents of other countries may have to provide the consulate with proof of "sufficient personal funds" before the visa is issued.

Upon your arrival in the United States, an immigration inspector will decide on the time validity of your visa—the maximum duration of a temporary visitor's visa (B-1 or B-2) is six months. If your U.S. visa has expired, you can still enter the country (for a stay of 29 days or shorter) with a transit visa, but you may be required to show proof of onward travel, such as an airplane ticket or ship travel voucher.

SPECIAL INTERESTS

Though urban areas pose the usual threats to visitors traveling alone, seniors, students, and gay and lesbian travelers will find few difficulties along the road in Maryland. The state's city dwellers are ethnically mixed, but the rural population tends to be of white, western European origin. In spite of this, locals are generally blasé about those who appear "different" (Washington, D.C., brings in plenty of international visitors). Newcomers are seldom met with suspicion, and a friendly, polite attitude will win over the most conservative Marylander. Helpful and friendly people can be found everywhere in the state.

Tourism-oriented Baltimore offers advantages and facilities for travelers with disabilities, including wheelchair access, and services for hearing- and vision-impaired visitors. Outside the city's boundaries, however, access and services are limited. The Maryland Relay Service (MRS)

LYME DISEASE LOOKOUT

During years with mild winters, insect populations that are normally depleted by cold explode in the spring and summer. One of the most unpleasant of these is the deer tick, a tiny (pinhead-sized) black bloodsucker that can cause health problems a million times bigger than himself.

When the deer tick has managed to burrow into a host (that's some unlucky mammal, possibly you) for more than 15 hours, during the blood extraction process he will expel bacteria into the host's bloodstream. The bacteria, which can be one or a combination of hundreds of strains, may result in Lyme disease. Most people don't even realize that a tick is attached to them, as there's no pain or itching, and the tick drops off by itself in about three days.

Lyme disease manifests in several ways. Most victims experience flu-like symptoms—headache, nausea, muscle and/or joint pain—about three days after the initial infection. It's easy to mistake this for a bout of food poisoning, as it usually lasts less than 12 hours, then disappears. During the next few days, only about a third of all victims experience a telltale "bulls-eye rash," a red center with a red circle around it that can occur anyplace on the body (and sometimes several places). About three weeks after the initial infection, victims begin to develop arthritis symptoms, usually on one side. The pain is constant, and sometimes moves from joint to joint. The pain may appear to be muscle or tendon strain that just doesn't go away. This is accompanied by severe fatigue, and as time passes, depression, mental confusion, forgetfulness, and other rashes. It doesn't get better by itself.

Lyme disease is supposedly completely treatable with antibiotics, and the sooner treatment begins after infection, the more effective and complete the recovery. However, the disease is often ignored and frequently misdiagnosed; to complicate matters, medicos differ on length and type of treatment. There are blood and urine tests, which vary greatly in effectiveness—at best, the most effective test can only identify a few different strains of the many possible strains of bacteria.

If you even suspect you've been infected, insist on immediate treatment. Keep the tick if you have it (it can be tested), but keep in mind that a percentage of people who are infected don't register on a blood test or have a bulls-eye rash. Experts recommend 21 to 90 days of doxycycline, 100 mg two to three times per day (30 days is the average, and most victims don't experience a relapse after this dose and duration). Chronic Lyme disease—usually misdiagnosed or untreated for months or years after an initial infection—requires more intensive and longer therapy. Some people report relief from the use of traditional Chinese medicine (herbs), acupuncture, and energy-movement touch therapies such as Jin Shin Jyutsu.

The best offense is a good defense. When hiking in wooded areas with long grasses (a favorite tick hangout), wear long pants—preferably light in color—tucked into your socks. Long-sleeved, cuffed shirts are also good, but always check exposed skin by sight and by running your hand over your skin (you may not see them, but you can feel them). Don't forget to check face and hair. Not all ticks are dangerous, just as not all mosquitoes carry malaria; but when it comes to Lyme disease, it's better to be safe than sorry. For additional information on Lyme disease, click on www.LymeAlliance.org.

is a free statewide phone service that links standard voice telephones with text-telephone (TTY) users. The website is www.mdrelay.org; access number is 771 in Maryland or 800/201-7165 for the voiceline.

HEALTH AND SAFETY

Falling ill in a strange place can happen to anyone, but fear shouldn't prevent visitors from enjoying the varied charms of Maryland. Travelers who take regular medication should take enough to cover their expected stay, though most prescriptions are readily available throughout the state.

Baltimore, Ocean City, Frederick, and towns in the Washington, D.C., gateway all have excellent hospitals, pharmacies, and emergency medical services; extensive police services; and fire stations. Firefighters are frequently trained in emergency medical procedures. Any of these services are only minutes away by phone (dial 911 in case of emergency, and the appropriate agency will respond, whether it's an ambulance for transport to a hospital or a police officer). Hospitals often require some form of assurance of payment upon admittance, usually medical insurance billable in the United States, cash, or credit cards.

Police and fire services are free to everyone. Street crime is more common in the urban areas—pickpocket theft, car break-ins, and muggings are the crimes most reported by visitors. Baltimore makes major efforts to educate and protect travelers. The usual rules apply: leave the 24-karat dog collar at home, and don't use large-denomination paper money as origami or stroll aimlessly in questionable neighborhoods—leave that to the police decoys. Crime against visitors in the smaller cities is virtually unknown, and the villages and rural areas are quite safe. Occasional vandalism on parked cars in state park parking lots has been reported, however, so make sure everything is in the trunk and out of sight.

As the town size decreases, so do the number of health and safety services. Cities with populations of more than 1,000 are minimally equipped with small police and firefighting forces, and a clinic that will handle emergency health problems. In villages and rural areas of less than 1,000, these services are provided by visiting medical personnel and volunteer police and firefighters. The dangers of snakebite, bear or wildcat maulings, tick bites, and other wildlife-encounter indignities are negligible outside the more isolated hiking trails. Use the emergency procedures outlined below to get help.

Highway Patrol cars are frequently seen on the interstates and highways of more than two lanes, but are seldom seen on the millions of miles of two-lane roads that net the state—a boon to those who trifle with speed limits, but a problem for those who are lost or have suffered an auto breakdown. Fortunately, there's usually some kind of dwelling within walking distance if an emergency occurs. People are remarkably helpful, but respect their privacy. Knock on the door, then step away so they can get a good look at you. Be prepared to ask your questions through the door, and request that they call the emergency service for you. Sometimes, you'll be invited in for coffee and cake.

Emergency Services

In any of the larger cities and towns, police and medical emergency services can be reached by dialing 911 (there is no charge for the call if you make it from a public phone). Since so much of the state is rural and the towns and villages may be far between, however, a 911 call may not get a response. In that case, call the operator (dial "0") for the number of the local clinic and park or police authorities. State parks are usually staffed full-time during the day and an office on the premises will dispatch necessary help.

MONEY
Currency

U.S. paper currency is all the same size, and most of the bills are the same color, too. If you're not acquainted with it, you would be well advised to familiarize yourself with the common denominations to avoid making expensive mistakes. Paper currency (bills) comes in denominations of $1, $2 (uncommon), $5, $10, $20, $50, and $100. Bills larger than $100 are not in common usage. There are presently two different editions of $5, $10, $20, $50, and $100 bills in circulation; though they both bear a portrait of the same person, older bills have "little heads"—smaller portraits—and new bills have "big heads with a ghost"—a shadow portrait on the right-hand side that shows when held up to the light. The 2004 version of the $20 bill will feature colored ink and other anti-counterfeiting measures.

Coins in circulation come in denominations of one cent (called a penny, it's 1/100 of $1), five cents (a nickel), 10 cents (a dime), 25 cents (a quarter), 50 cents (a half-dollar; it's rarely used), and $1 (called a Sacajawea dollar; gold in color, it's rarely used). Quarters released since 1999 feature various designs on the back that honor the 50 states. Maryland's quarter bears the dome of the Maryland Statehouse and the phrase "The Old Line State."

ATMs

Maryland generally participates in all the benefits and conveniences of modern life, including automated teller machines (ATMs) and instant credit-card approval. However, a vast majority of Maryland is rural, and you will find that many of the state's smaller settlements and villages don't have banks or ATMs and won't accept payment by personal check. For this reason, you should carry a reasonable amount of cash (enough for a room and food) when heading to the hinterlands. A rule of thumb: if a town has a stoplight, it probably has a bank branch, and possibly an ATM. Almost all ATMs are equipped to handle Cirrus and other bank cash-transfer requests.

COMMUNICATIONS AND MEDIA

Newspapers

Maryland has been a pioneer in journalism since the colonial period. Beginning in 1727 with the *Maryland Gazette* of Annapolis, newspapers and printing developed rapidly during the Revolution. Today, more than 50 towns publish newspapers, some full of local merchants' ads and the latest high-school basketball victories.

The newspaper with the greatest readership and influence in the state is the ***Baltimore Sun,*** established in 1837. Its daily and evening editions exceed 170,000 each and its Sunday readership is more than 300,000. Also widely read is the award-winning ***Washington Post.*** Both Washington, D.C., and Baltimore also boast wide selections of specialized, alternative, and free papers.

Magazines

Baltimore is a glossy "city" monthly magazine that focuses on local food, fads, and fashion. The articles are well written and fun, and the restaurant review section in the back of each issue is informative. Call 800/365-2808 for subscription information, or check them out on the Web at www.baltimoremag.com.

Tidewater Times was established in 1952 as a specialized monthly magazine aimed at visitors, prospective land buyers, and others for whom the Eastern Shore had special allure. The articles are quite good. For rate or subscription information, contact the Tidewater Times, P.O. Box 1141, Easton, MD 21601, 410/226-0422, www.tidewatertimes.com.

Mid-Atlantic is published 10 times a year, with three annual guides. It's a slick and well-illustrated contemporary magazine that covers the entire region. For subscription information, call 800/777-0999.

Radio and Television

Radio and television are dominated by the centers of mass media in the area, Baltimore and Washington, D.C.

TOURIST INFORMATION AND MAPS

Tourist Information

The **Maryland Office of Tourism,** 217 E. Redwood St., Baltimore, MD 21298, 800/462-9443, www.mdisfun.org, is stocked with brochures on every part of the state, and you can talk with a friendly and knowledgeable volunteer if you have questions. The "starter" book, *Destination Maryland,* outlines the state's attractions. Several websites offer information for visitors: www.maryland.com and delmarweb .com/maryland/travel.html are two good ones.

The Department of Natural Resources, 580 Taylor Ave., E-3, Annapolis, MD 21401, 410/ 974-3771 or 800/830-3974, www.dnr.state .md.us/index.html, publishes a free *Maryland State Forests and Parks Guide* that includes general information on all state park and forest facilities, plus individual phone numbers for more detailed maps and reservations.

Maps and Directions

Maryland marks its roads and streets well, with few exceptions—it's a lot harder to get lost here than in, say, Pennsylvania. Maryland Tourism sends a Maryland Transportation Services map along with its information packet, and other maps, such as *Scenic Routes,* are available. The map the state provides is not perfect: a few of the back roads that were marked "paved" weren't. An auto club map (AAA), though not quite as detailed, proved to be quite accurate. If you're planning on auto-touring in any of the rural counties, a local map is highly recommended—they can often be acquired through the county tourism office before your trip, or at a gas station while on the road.

Time and Tax

Maryland is in the Eastern Standard Time zone.

In the larger cities, merchants keep longer hours and days, but elsewhere, food, clothing, and general-goods stores are normally open Mon.–Sat. 10 A.M.–6 P.M. Many shops close on Sunday, and those that cater primarily to tourists often shorten their hours (or close entirely, as in Ocean City) during the winter months. Hotels, inns, and bed-and-breakfasts are generally open daily year-round. Some restaurants are open daily, but most close one day a week, often Sunday, Monday, or Tuesday. Many restaurants open early, around 6 A.M., and stop serving at 10 P.M.

State sales tax is 5 percent. Restaurants and hotels usually charge a premium tax over the state tax, totaling an average of 11 percent.

WHAT TO TAKE

Temperatures in the winter months occasionally drop below zero, depending on where you are. In western Maryland, expect the coldest weather, and dress accordingly. For the rest of the state, take plenty of clothing that can be layered. Summer is uniformly warm and humid, and shorts and T-shirts are common in both the rural areas and the cities. A common style of dress year-round is "sailing preppy"—short-sleeved knit shirts with collars, khaki or navy shorts or pants, and loafers or boat shoes. The look is Ralph Lauren/Talbot's/Lands' End.

If you're traveling by auto, the interstates and large highways have frequent rest stops; however, if you plan to tour the back roads, take both toilet paper and snacks. The villages in the rural areas are few and far between, and there's no guarantee that stores will be present, let alone open, even during the day. For back-road touring, a map bought at a local gas station is a must, and a compass isn't a bad idea, either.

Electrical Appliances

The electrical current in use in Maryland is the same as in the rest of the United States. It functions on 110 volts, 60 cycles of alternating current (AC). Appliances requiring the normal European voltage of 220 will not work.

WEIGHTS AND MEASURES

The United States does not use the metric system; instead, it measures distance in inches, feet, yards, and miles (see the conversion table at the back of this book). In the United States, dry weights are measured in ounces and pounds, and liquid weights in ounces, pints, quarts, and gallons. Temperature is measured using the Fahrenheit, not the Celsius, scale.

Baltimore

At first, I had a tough time getting a handle on Baltimore. My idea of what the city was kept slipping away, as hard to pin down as the weather. In June, Baltimore might as well have been on the equator: thunderstorms and bright sun battled it out every day. My impressions of the city came and went like the clouds. Baltimore (people here actually call it BAL-mer) began to take shape when I took to the streets on foot. People are casually friendly—all kinds engaged me in conversation. On Howard Street, a thin young man carried a rusted but quite good Eames chair down the street; he'd found it in the junkyard and wanted to sell it to the antique dealers there—he asked me how much I thought he could get. Two passersby chimed in with their opinions. An elderly man on Charles Street emerged from a bookstore and asked me the proper French translation of the phrase "a man without money." But the sweetness emanating from the people on the street is balanced by the rumble of rough

neighborhoods not far from the center of town and the increased cost of living in Baltimore thanks to a booming tourist business; still, there are plenty of good deals here.

My only real complaint about Baltimore is that not enough people called me "hon." Every native Baltimorean I talked to not only told me what a great place it was to grow up in, but that people from waitresses to taxi drivers would address me in terms of endearment. Baltimore has not only changed from the days of H. L. Mencken, but it has changed in the last few decades—more for the better, in spite of my lack of "hon's."

Baltimore, a tobacco port founded in 1729, was named for the baronial title of the Calvert family, proprietors of Maryland. The city's strategic location spurred its growth, and by the time of the American Revolution, it was a thriving seaport. The city served as the seat of the Continental Congress while Philadelphia was under

Baltimore Harbor

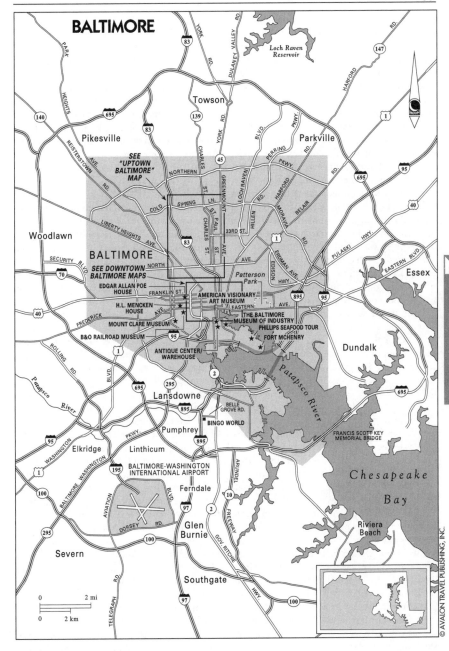

BALTIMORE

YORK RD.

83

DULANEY VALLEY RD.

Loch Raven
Reservoir

147

PARK HEIGHTS

140

695

Towson

139

83

1

MOON

Pikesville

Parkville

REISTERSTOWN RD.

SEE "UPTOWN
BALTIMORE"
MAP

CHARLES ST.

YORK RD.

45

NORTHERN

PERRING PKWY.

695

95

LIBERTY HEIGHTS AVE.

COLD SPRING LN.

ST. PAUL ST.

CHARLES ST.

GREENMOUNT AVE.

33RD ST.

LOCH RAVEN RD.

HILLEN RD.

HARFORD RD.

MORAVIA

BELAIR

40

Woodlawn

SECURITY BLVD.

70

BALTIMORE

*SEE DOWNTOWN
BALTIMORE MAPS*

83

NORTH AVE.

1

AVE.

ERDMAN AVE.

EDISON HWY.

PULASKI HWY.

EASTERN BLVD.

Essex

EDGAR ALLAN POE
HOUSE

FRANKLIN ST.

*Patterson
Park*

40

H.L. MENCKEN
HOUSE

FREDERICK

AVE.

★ AMERICAN VISIONARY
ART MUSEUM

EASTERN AVE.

895

95

MOUNT CLARE MUSEUM ★

★ THE BALTIMORE
MUSEUM OF INDUSTRY

ROLLING RD.

B&O RAILROAD MUSEUM

95

★ PHILLIPS SEAFOOD TOUR
★ FORT McHENRY

Dundalk

1

ANTIQUE CENTER/
WAREHOUSE

BLVD.

2

Patapsco River

695

*Patapsco
River*

695

Lansdowne

895

BELLE
GROVE RD.

FRANCIS SCOTT KEY
MEMORIAL BRIDGE

Pumphrey

■ BINGO WORLD

895

95

WASHINGTON

Elkridge

Linthicum

PKWY.

Chesapeake

100

1

195

BALTIMORE-WASHINGTON
INTERNATIONAL AIRPORT

AVIATION BLVD.

Ferndale

97

2

10

ARUNDEL

Bay

BALTIMORE-WASHINGTON

295

DORSEY RD.

Glen
Burnie

GOV. RITCHIE HWY.

FREEWAY

Riviera
Beach

Severn

100

Southgate

97

100

0   2 mi

0   2 km

TELEGRAPH RD.

BALTIMORE

British siege in 1776–77. The British took pleasure some years later in bombarding Fort McHenry during the War of 1812. However, Baltimore's booming commerce wasn't threatened until the opening of the Erie Canal in 1825. Always on the ball, business interests in the city prompted construction of the first U.S. railroad here, the Baltimore and Ohio, begun in 1827.

The site of numerous riots between Southern and Northern sympathizers during the Civil War, Baltimore remained within the Union but under martial law throughout the war. During the latter half of the 19th century the city was transformed from a mercantile to an industrial center. Baltimore built itself on the muscular biceps of the workingman (and -woman). In 1904 a fire destroyed most of the downtown business district, but recovery was rapid. Baltimore's continued growth in the 20th century has been due in large part to its port facilities, which have expanded from the original all-purpose piers to the present 45 miles of developed waterfront.

From its gracious Victorian days as a haunt of the upper crust to its current status as renaissance city, Baltimore has seen both good times and bad, but its robustness stems from the people who go home at night to a little place on a side street, and settle in with a beer by the blue-white light of the tube. The industrial strength that kept the city alive through economic hard times has fallen upon hard times itself. As in many vital centers of American production, jobs have gone elsewhere; what is left, however, are the products of determination—the fruits of Baltimore's will to survive and prosper. Against all odds, it has become a magnet for visitors, a wonderful place full of things to see and do.

Like that other phoenix of a city, Pittsburgh, Baltimore is a city of neighborhoods. Mount Vernon and Belvedere were society neighborhoods in center city; Fell's Point and Canton were port villages, as was Federal Hill. Highlandtown (pronounced HA-len-town) and Greektown were both villages east of the main part of town that have retained their individuality in spite of being swallowed up by the spread of the big city. All have a particular charm: history, shopping, great places to eat.

Plenty of money has remained in town. Johns Hopkins University, the Peabody Conservatory of Music, and Maryland Institute College of Art are a few of many world-famous institutions of higher learning in the city. There are well-endowed art collections, state-of-the-art science and natural history museums, a fantastic zoo, and good restaurants too numerous to count. Baltimore has become a playground for families—what could be more endearing than that? And the people are great.

NEIGHBORHOODS

Baltimore is made up of dozens of small neighborhoods, many of which are exclusively residential. **Mount Vernon,** site of the Washington Tower, and **Belvedere,** east of Mount Vernon, were easily the most socially prominent neighborhoods in Baltimore during the 19th century, and have remained architecturally interesting. **Bolton Hill,** southwest of the Maryland Institute of Art, is another still-fashionable area of 19th-century townhouses; F. Scott and Zelda Fitzgerald, radio star Gary Moore, and the Cone sisters all lived there. Farther north, **Hampden** was a New England–style mill town that has long since become part of the city.

Other neighborhoods that were once outlying villages have become tourist areas. One is **Fell's Point,** a shipbuilding and trading port east of the city. The streets are named after British places and people; row houses predate the Civil War, and were built for workers who labored at what was once Baltimore's deepest port. Today, Fell's Point offers visitors numerous shops, galleries, and restaurants; walking tours originate from the visitor center (808 S. Ann St., 410/675-6750). Further east, **Canton** also retains many of its original structures, and some consider it the most authentic of old Baltimore neighborhoods. Homes in these neighborhoods are often sheathed in "formstone," a white or colored fake stone wall-covering sold as part of a widespread scam during the mid-1950s (characters in the film *Tin Men* are based on formstone salesmen).

Continuing east on Eastern Avenue, drivers will pass under a rail bridge decorated with a

© JOANNE MILLER

Belvedere townhouses

blue and white "key" pattern that marks the beginning of **Greektown.** This ethnic enclave has retained the shops and restaurants of the immigrants who settled there. Another wonderful neighborhood that has preserved a distinct personality is **Little Italy,** from Pratt Street to President Street, on the inner harbor. The restaurants are justly famous in both areas.

Federal Hill, southwest of the inner harbor, is a once-outlying village that has been absorbed by the city. This 30-block area has become an upscale haven of beautiful older houses, restaurants, and shops. Homes in the tree-lined residential area of **Otterbein,** just to the west of Federal Hill, were once available to homesteaders for $1 a year.

Mount Vernon Place and Belvedere Walking Tour

In the last few hundred years, this still-elegant but slightly worn section of Baltimore provided the stage for international romance, literary history, and proper etiquette, with a little muckraking thrown in as well.

The tour starts at 11 W. Mulberry Street, built by John H. B. Latrobe around 1830. An engi-

neer who practiced law, Latrobe represented the B&O Railroad and other big businesses in Baltimore; however, his wealth came from the invention of the Latrobe Stove, an enclosed fireplace he invented in order to keep his wife from retreating to her native Natchez, Mississippi, during Baltimore winters. As part of his civic duty, Latrobe judged a literary contest and awarded first prize of $50 to the orphaned son of a local pioneer family, Edgar Allan Poe. The story, "A Ms. Found in a Bottle," was Poe's first published work. Within a few years, Poe became famous for his fiction; he invented both the detective and horror genres with stories such as *Murders in the Rue Morgue, The Pit and the Pendulum,* and *Masque of the Red Death.* However, proper Baltimoreans found him "unstable as water," and employment opportunities were nil—a difficult situation for a young man who had secretly married his 13-year-old first cousin and was struggling to support both her and her mother. Poe lived in other cities (including Philadelphia), but came home to Baltimore in his later years, lived in a house on Amity Street, and is buried in Westminster Cemetery along with his wife.

Around the corner, the building that once

occupied 417 N. Charles Street was the birth-place of novelist Upton Sinclair; it was demolished in 1969. The son of a Baltimore "Establishment" family, Sinclair shocked the world when he exposed the meatpacking industry in his 1906 work, *The Jungle*. Sensitive to political corruption and social injustice, he wrote about venereal disease (*Damaged Goods*, 1913), Christian hypocrisy (*The Profits of Religion*, 1918), and the shortcomings of American journalism (*The Brass Check*, 1919). Sinclair released some of his works himself when commercial publishers refused them, notably *Upton Sinclair Presents William Fox* (1933), which exposed financial chicanery in the film industry. In 1934 Sinclair ran as the Democratic candidate for governor of California on the EPIC (End Poverty in California) program. Narrowly defeated, he returned to writing, turning out 11 novels featuring protagonist Lanny Budd—confidant of international leaders, intimately involved in intrigues before and during both World Wars. The third novel in the series, *Dragon's Teeth* (1942), about Hitler's rise to power, won a Pulitzer Prize in 1943.

In Baltimore, one man threw away his crown for a wife, and another threw away his wife for a crown. Head north on Charles Street and make a left on Madison, then a right on Cathedral Street. Light from the Tiffany and Lafarge stained glass windows of Emmanuel Episcopal Church, 811 Cathedral St., bathed the baptism of Wallis Warfield in 1896. Warfield later captured the heart of a king (read on). Farther up the street at the corner of Cathedral and Read, the Medical Arts building sits on the site of Betsey Patterson Bonaparte's last home. Patterson married Jerome Bonaparte, the youngest brother of Napoleon, in 1803. Two years later, Napoleon had the marriage annulled so that Jerome could marry Catherine of Wurttemberg and become king of Westphalia. Jerome commanded an army in the invasion of Russia in 1812. After taking part in the Battle of Waterloo (1815), he fled France. He later returned and witnessed the establishment of the Second French Empire under his nephew Napoleon III. Betsey remained in Baltimore until her death.

Writer and journalist H. L. Mencken lived at 704 Cathedral Street with his wife, Sarah, from

H. L. MENCKEN ON BALTIMORE

A Baltimorean by birth and choice, Henry Louis Mencken was America's most prominent journalist, book reviewer, and political commentator of the early 20th century. His father owned the Mencken Cigar Company of Baltimore, and his son (known as H. L.) was seldom seen without a stogie in hand. A skeptic by nature, Mencken was sure in his opinions and wicked with his prose, and his writings often criticized the government and organized religion. Though he often worked out of New York City, he chose to live in Baltimore, for these reasons, outlined in *Happy Days* (New York: Alfred A. Knopf, 1940):

The city into which I was born in 1880 had a reputation all over for what the English, in their real-estate advertising, are fond of calling the amenities. So far as I have been able to discover by a labored search of contemporary travel-books, no literary tourist, however waspish he may have been about Washington, Niagara Falls, the prairies of the West, or even Boston and New York, ever gave Baltimore a bad notice. They all agree, often with lubricious gloats and gurgles, (a) that its indigenous victualry was unsurpassed in the Republic, (b) that its native . . . females of all ages up to thirty-five were of incomparable pulchritude, and as amiable as they were lovely, and (c) that its home-life was spacious, charming, full of creature comforts, and highly conducive to the facile and orderly propagation of the species.

1930 until her death after a long illness in 1935. Mencken is considered the most influential American editor, essayist, and social critic of the first half of the 20th century. He began his career as a reporter for the *Baltimore Morning Herald;* in 1905, he became a controversial columnist for the *Baltimore Evening Sun.* One of his essays, "Puritanism as a Literary Force" (1917), interpreted Puritanism as the root of most American problems; "The Sahara of the Bozart" (1920) slammed southern culture and literature, which ironically helped inspire the southern literary renaissance of the 1920s and 1930s. Mencken's influence waned in the 1930s; he adamantly opposed Roosevelt's New Deal programs, and his acerbic style was better suited to more prosperous times. Mencken's most celebrated work includes essays collected in the six-volume *Prejudices* (1919–27), and book-length musings on playwright George Bernard Shaw (1905), philosopher Friedrich Nietzsche (1908), and women (1917).

To the east, 14 E. Chase Street was the home of a young lady who was to become the arbiter of polite society in America during the mid-20th century, Emily Post. A government agent once visited Post in order to review her tax papers—her book *Etiquette* was a national best-seller—and commented, "No woman has a right to make so much money."

A few blocks north and east, 212 E. Biddle Street housed Johns Hopkins medical student Gertrude Stein, daughter of a wealthy Pittsburgh family. Ms. Stein eventually gave up on medicine and began writing. One of her works, "Three Lives," is set in Baltimore. Her experimental style prompted H. L. Mencken to remark, "She made English easier to write, and harder to read." After moving to Paris, Ms. Stein talked the Cone sisters from Baltimore into investing in impressionist art, much of which is now in the Baltimore Museum of Art.

Stein's neighbor across the way at 215 E. Biddle Street was none other than Wallis Warfield, all grown up. She wed her first husband in Christ Church on Chase and Paul Streets; they divorced a few years later. Edward VII had already been crowned King of England in 1936 when he met Wallis Warfield Simpson. Political opposition to his marrying a divorcée forced him to abdicate later that year—he retained the title of Duke of Windsor. He and Simpson wed in 1937 and lived in France until their deaths.

Sights

The **National Historic Seaport of Baltimore** is a concept, rather than a place, and includes several of the major attractions on the waterfront. A single ticket purchase of $16 for adults, less for children under 12, includes one admission to all the attractions listed below (Fort McHenry requires an additional entry fee for those 17 and older), and a full day's passage on a water taxi to each site and other harbor destinations. The ticket may be used at any time for a full year following purchase, but is only good for one day. This is a true bargain, considering that each of the sites included on the ticket charges admission: Top of the World, the Maritime Museum (Lightship *Chesapeake,* US Submarine *Torsk,* US Coast Guard Cutter *Taney,* and the Seven-Foot Knoll Lighthouse), Baltimore Museum of Industry, and the Steam Tug *Baltimore,* visiting ships, and the fireboat base at Fort McHenry. Access to the water taxi will also get you to Federal Hill and its sites and restaurants, Fell's Point and its attractions, and Canton's modern shopping center. Unfortunately, it's impossible to do all these things in one day, but it's possible to take in the first three, have coffee in Fell's Point, and zip over to Federal Hill for dinner (or vice versa) before dropping from exhaustion. You'll end up saving at least $5 per person.

HISTORIC SITES

Fort McHenry, E. Fort Ave., 410/962-4290, www.nps.gov/fomc, played an active role in our nation's history from 1776 through World War II. Built during the Revolutionary War, the earth-walled, star-shaped stronghold called Fort

DOWNTOWN BALTIMORE AND THE INNER HARBOR

BALTIMORE

ANTIQUE ROW ★

MADISON ST.

★ EUBIE BLAKE NATIONAL
JAZZ MUSEUM

★ MT. VERNON
PL. U.M.C.

★ CENTER
STAGE

MONUMENT ST   WALTERS
GALLERY

THE GEORGE
PEABODY LIBRARY

MARYLAND HISTORICAL
SOCIETY MUSEUM   WASHINGTON
MONUMENT

CENTRE   ST.

MOTHER SETON
HOUSE ★

FRANKLIN

CATHEDRAL OF
THE ASSUMPTION ST.

ENOCH PRATT
FREE LIBRARY

CITY GALLERY

MULBERRY   ST.

SARATOGA   ST.   BALTIMORE
FARMER'S MARKET ★

LEXINGTON
MARKET ★

ST. JUDE SHRINE
★
FAYETTE

WESTMINSTER CEMETERY
HALL AND BURYING GROUND
★
BALTIMORE

BALTIMORE CENTER FOR
THE PERFORMING ARTS ★

★ BALTIMORE ARENA

DR. SAMUEL D. HARRIS
NATIONAL MUSEUM OF
DENTISTRY ★

LOMBARD   ST.

BROMO SELTZER
TOWER
★

THE GALLERY AT
HARBORPLACE
★

PRATT

BABE RUTH BIRTHPLACE AND ★
ORIOLES MUSEUM

TOP OF THE WORLD
OBSERVATION LEVEL ★

WASHINGTON   ST.

CONWAY   ST.

*Inner
Harbor*

ORIOLE PARK AT
CAMDEN YARDS

LEE   ST.

MARYLAND SCIENCE
CENTER
★

395

KEY

Federal Hill

MARTIN LUTHER KING JR. BLVD.

GREENE   PACA   EUTAW   HOWARD   CHARLES   SAINT PAUL   CALVERT   LIGHT ST.   HARBORPLACE

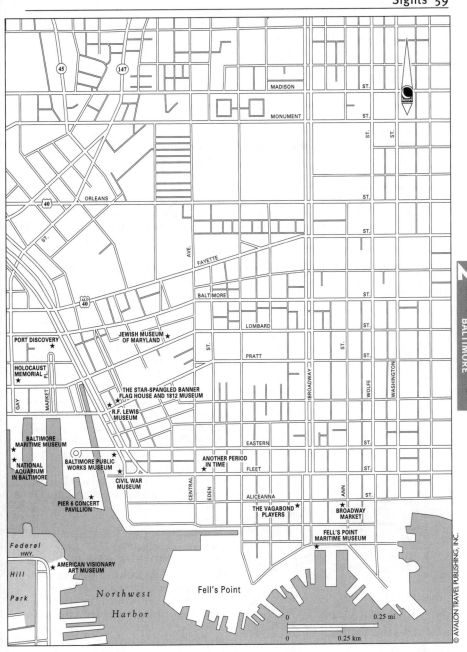

BALTIMORE

45

147

MADISON ST.

MONUMENT ST.

ST.

ST.

40

ORLEANS ST.

ST.

AVE.

FAYETTE

ALT 40

BALTIMORE ST.

LOMBARD ST.

PORT DISCOVERY ★
JEWISH MUSEUM OF MARYLAND ★
PRATT ST.

HOLOCAUST MEMORIAL ★

BROADWAY

WOLFE

WASHINGTON

THE STAR-SPANGLED BANNER FLAG HOUSE AND 1812 MUSEUM ★

GAY
MARKET PL.

R.F. LEWIS MUSEUM ★

BALTIMORE MARITIME MUSEUM ★
EASTERN ST.

NATIONAL AQUARIUM IN BALTIMORE ★

BALTIMORE PUBLIC WORKS MUSEUM ★
ANOTHER PERIOD IN TIME ★
FLEET ST.

CIVIL WAR MUSEUM

CENTRAL

EDEN

ALICEANNA

ANN ST.

PIER 6 CONCERT PAVILLION ★

THE VAGABOND PLAYERS ★

BROADWAY MARKET ★

FELL'S POINT MARITIME MUSEUM ★

© AVALON TRAVEL PUBLISHING, INC.

Federal HWY.

Hill

AMERICAN VISIONARY ART MUSEUM ★

Park

Northwest

Harbor

Fell's Point

0   0.25 mi

0   0.25 km

Whetstone was surrounded on three sides by water. Ships sailing into Baltimore would have to pass the fort first, and the site was far enough from Baltimore to protect the port without endangering the city.

The Revolutionary War ended without an attack on Baltimore. However, improvements to the fort continued. In 1798, French engineer Jean Foncin was selected to plan a new fort. James McHenry, secretary of war under President George Washington, was instrumental in supporting its construction. The fort was renamed in his honor.

The fort found lasting fame during the War of 1812. British naval vessels attacked in September 1814. For 25 hours the British bombarded Fort McHenry from ships anchored in the Patapsco River. The fort's defenders held firm, and Baltimore was saved. It was during this bombardment that Francis Scott Key was inspired to pen the poem that became our national anthem.

During the Civil War, the fort's guns were turned toward the city. Union troops were sta-tioned at Fort McHenry to keep Baltimore out of the hands of those who would have Maryland join the Southern rebellion. The fort also held political prisoners suspected of being Confederate sympathizers, often without trial. Following the Battle of Gettysburg in early July 1863, nearly 7,000 Confederate soldiers were detained in the fort.

Fort McHenry continued its military service to the country until July 20, 1912, when the last active garrison left the fort. From 1915 to 1917, Baltimore used the site as a popular city park and beach. In 1917, the U.S. Army once again occupied the site to establish a hospital for returning wounded veterans of World War I. It was the largest military hospital in the United States, with more than 100 temporary buildings. Some of the earliest developments in the fields of reconstructive surgery and neurosurgery were made there. When the war ended, the need for the hospital slowly diminished, and in 1925 the hospital buildings were torn down.

During that year, Fort McHenry was made a national park, and it was transferred to the care of the National Park Service in 1933. Fort McHenry was designated a National Monument and Historic Shrine in 1939. It is America's only Historic Shrine.

During World War II the fort served as a Coast Guard Training Center for fire control and port defense. From June–Labor Day, it's open daily 8 A.M.–7:45 P.M.; 8 A.M.–4:45 P.M. the rest of the year. A $5 admission is charged to enter the fort, although access to the surrounding park grounds is free. A boat shuttle departs every half-hour (weather permitting) Memorial Day–Labor Day 11 A.M.–5:30 P.M. from Light Street pier to the fort ($5).

The **Baltimore Civil War Museum,** President Street Station, 601 President St., 410/385-5188, www.mdhs.org/explore/baltcivilwar.html, is best reached on foot after parking in the nearby industrial neighborhood—the roads are a bit confusing. The museum displays artifacts and details detailing Baltimore's history in the conflict; the President Street Station was the site of mob riots during the early part of the war. This small museum's displays are interesting

Fort McHenry

© JOANNE MILLER

A COLLISION HAS TAKEN PLACE

Baltimore has the dubious distinction of being the site of the first blood spilled in the Civil War. Maryland was deeply torn in its loyalties; though it was officially a Southern slave state below the Mason-Dixon Line, its strategic position surrounding the capital made it imperative that Maryland's loyalties remain with the Union. The citizens of Baltimore did not necessarily agree with this idea.

On April 19, 1861, four days after President Lincoln called for a muster of troops to defend Washington, a Massachusetts regiment reached Baltimore's President Street station by rail at around 10 A.M. The troops were to remain in the cars, which were to be hitched to horses and pulled several blocks west to the Camden station rails, where they would continue on to the capital. An angry pro-Southern mob attacked the train with paving stones and managed to halt the last two cars. Roughly 100 uniformed Union soldiers were forced to leave the cars, and marched through the mob of 3,000, continually being pelted by rocks and eventually gunfire. Finally, their commander ordered them to load their rifles and protect themselves.

A short distance away, 10 companies of unarmed troops from Pennsylvania endured a two-hour assault trapped in rail cars, covering themselves as well as possible from the rain of stones and shattered window glass. The mob dragged trees and other debris across the tracks to prevent the troop trains from moving toward the capital. Eventually, the police—slow to oppose such large numbers of rioters and possibly moved by Southern sympathies—managed to clear the tracks and free the trains. Three soldiers, eight rioters, and one bystander died in the melee.

Shortly after the confrontation, the governor of Maryland, Thomas Hicks, and George Brown, mayor of Baltimore, wrote to the President: "Sir, A collision between the citizens and the Northern troops has taken place in Baltimore, and the excitement is fearful. Send no more troops here. We will endeavor to prevent all bloodshed."

President Lincoln, prizing Baltimore's strategic position, placed the city under martial law. A month later, Union troops built a fort and positioned cannons and gun emplacements on Federal Hill. Baltimore's citizens would not be permitted to collide with the Federal government again for the duration of the war.

BALTIMORE

and well put together; it's a worthy stop for Civil War buffs. One panel tells the story of Henry "Box" Brown, a slave shipped from Richmond, Virginia, through Baltimore to Philadelphia by abolitionist James A. Smith. Brown spent 26 hours in a crate; when it was opened, he sang, "I waited patiently for the Lord, and he heard my prayer." Smith tried to ship two more slaves, but was caught—he served eight years in prison. The museum is open daily 10 A.M.–5 P.M. Admission is $4 adults, $3 seniors and kids, and if you can round up a Civil War veteran, they get in for free.

The **B&O Railroad Museum,** 901 W. Pratt St., 410/752-2490, www.borail.org, is one of the finest rail collections and sites in America, and the home of the B&O rail roundhouse and Mount Clare Station. The first passenger trains in

the New World headed west to Ellicott's Mills from here in 1830; America's first steam engine, the **Tom Thumb,** originated from here; and in 1844, Mount Clare received Samuel F. B. Morse's famous telegraph message, "What hath God wrought?" from Washington, D.C. The museum features exhibits, replicas, and artifacts of railroading, including models and replicas from the "Fair of the Iron Horse" in 1927. It's hard to believe that almost 4 percent of the total population of America worked for the railroads in 1925. Even if railroad lore isn't one of your interests, stop by to take a look at the roundhouse. Built in 1884, 240 feet across and 123 feet high, this magnificent building holds machines that ran the rails, from the earliest "grasshopper" locomotives to the 320-ton monster steam engine **Allegheny,** and beyond to the diesel era. Early coach cars look like elegant little houses on wheels. The equipment is beautifully maintained, and the smell of wood, oil, and polish will transport you back to the days of coach travel. The outside yard features trains and more trains. The museum is open daily 10 A.M.–5 P.M.; parking is safe and plentiful. Admission is $6.50.

The broad-based collections of the **Maryland Historical Society Museum and Library,** 201 W. Monument St., 410/685-3750, www.mdhs .org, touch every part of Maryland's history. Interactive displays give the feel of a boat's pilot house, ship's chandlery, and a sailor's life in the 1880s; the Civil War is depicted in letters and photographs; and rooms are filled with displays of 20th-century fine and decorative arts. There are paintings by the Peales, a Claire McCardell Costume and Textile Gallery with changing exhibitions (see the special topic The American Look in the Western Maryland chapter), an original draft of the poem that became our national anthem, and a gallery of sporting art. Families will appreciate the "history haversacks" for kids that contain a pack of parent-child pastimes, scav-

enger hunts, crafts, and other hands-on activities to be used during self-guided treks through the exhibitions. The museum is open Wed.–Fri. 10 A.M.–5 P.M., Saturday 9 A.M.–5 P.M., Sunday 11 A.M.–5 P.M. Admission is $4.

HISTORIC HOMES

Mount Clare Museum, Carroll Park, 1500 Washington Blvd., 410/837-3262, was the home of Charles Carroll, the barrister—one of the non-Catholic Carrolls. Once set on a bucolic hill far from the center of Baltimore, the house now adorns a sometimes-seedy city park—but if you're interested in authentic furnishings and decor from the 1760s, this is a must-see. It's the only 18th-century museum house in Maryland to contain so many of the daily artifacts of life belonging to the builder of the house and used by the family. Many of the items were hunted down and reclaimed by the staff from repositories on the Eastern Shore, often from descendants of Mrs. Carroll (Margaret Tilghman). Portraits of the Carrolls painted by Charles Willson Peale in

THOSE CONFUSING CARROLLS

Though the name Charles Carroll of Carrollton is familiar to anyone interested in the Revolutionary War years, the number of historic homes with the name of Carroll attached may lead one to think that, like George Washington, Charles Carroll slept everywhere. In fact, each of the Carroll historic homes belonged to different relatives and different generations of the same family.

Charles Carroll (1660–1720), the Irish settler (C.C.I.S.) and family patriarch, was the first attorney general of Maryland. He left us without a home to visit in America. However, his son, Charles Carroll of Annapolis (C.C.O.A., 1702–1782), left us a lovely mansion in that town overlooking the harbor. His (C.C.O.A.'s) son was Charles Carroll of Carrollton (C.C.O.C., 1737–1832), the signer of the Declaration of Independence, who lived outside Buckeystown, a property that remains private. Mount Clare, Baltimore home of Charles Carroll, Barrister (C.C.B.), a cousin and contemporary of C.C.O.C.'s—though from the Protestant side of the family—is now part of a public park.

C.C.O.C.'s son, Charles Carroll of Homewood (C.C.O.H., 1775–1825), built the Homewood house on what is now the campus of Johns Hopkins University with money received as a wedding gift from his dear old dad. Funds dried up, however, as junior continued to "improve" the property. Undaunted, C.C.O.H. and his wife, Harriet Chew, had several children, among them Charles Carroll of Doughoregan (C.C.O.D., also known as The Colonel, 1801–1862). Though descendants of the Carrolls continue to reside in Maryland, they now prefer to keep their homes to themselves.

1770–71 hang in the house, and rotating exhibits—a recent one included ladies' fans from the period—add extra interest. Tours are given Tues.–Fri. at 11 A.M., noon, 1 P.M., 2 P.M., and 3 P.M., and on the weekends at 1 P.M., 2 P.M., and 3 P.M. Admission is $5.

Homewood House Museum, on the campus of Johns Hopkins University, 3400 N. Charles St., 410/516-5589, www.jhu.edu/~hwdhouse/homewood.html, is the country home of Charles Carroll, Jr., son of Charles Carroll of Carrollton. He built the Federal-style house in 1801; the home is decorated with fine 18th- and 19th-century furnishings. It's open Tues.–Sat. 11 A.M.–4 P.M., Sunday noon–4 P.M. All tours are guided and begin on the hour and half hour; the last tour begins at 3:30 p.m. Admission is $6 adults, $5 seniors, $3 students.

Evergreen, 4545 N. Charles St., 410/516-0341, is another property maintained by Johns Hopkins University—no Carrolls here, though. This 48-room Italianate house on 26 acres was the home of former ambassador John Work Garrett, who converted the gymnasium into a theater designed by famous Russian émigré Léon Bakst, a designer for Diaghilev and the Ballets Russe. The Garretts supported many of the arts of Baltimore in the 1920s–30s, and the house reflects their interests and taste: a rare-book library, Tiffany chandeliers, Japanese netsuke, and blue-and-white Chinese porcelain are all on display. The house is open for tours on the Mon.–Fri. 10 A.M.–4 P.M., Sat.–Sun. 1–4 P.M. Admission is $6.

The Star-Spangled Banner Flag House and Museum, 844 E. Pratt St., 410/837-1793, www.flaghouse.org, is the home of Ms. Mary Pickersgill, flag and banner maker. During the summer of 1813, the British threatened to attack Baltimore, and the defenses at Fort McHenry were subsequently strengthened. The commandant, Major George Armistead, ordered a flag "so large that the British will have no difficulty seeing it from a distance." Ms. Pickersgill, with the help of her mother, daughter, and two nieces, sewed the 30- by 34-foot flag—bigger than the house—by hand. They went to a neighborhood brewery to have room to spread out the blue

field on which they placed 15 stars. For her services, Mary was paid $405.90 (the receipt is in the house), and the sturdy flag went on to stream gallantly through bombs bursting in air. The house contains furniture from the period, and the visitors center features a video about the War of 1812 and the flag. In the garden, there's a stone map of the United States with each state cut from stone native to that state.

A highlight of the museum is the Great Flag Window that is the same size, color, and design as the original flag. The house and museum are open Tues.–Sat. 10 A.M.–4 P.M. Admission is $6. (The flag itself is displayed at the Smithsonian Institution in Washington, D.C., where it has undergone a massive conservation procedure. See the National Museum of American History in the Washington, D.C., chapter.)

ON THE WATER

The **Baltimore Maritime Museum,** is a collection of four very different types of seagoing vessels clustered near the Baltimore Aquarium on Pier 3, 410/396-3453. If you'd like to see what living and working on a ship might be like, you have several to choose from. Each vessel provides detailed operating and historical information.

The U.S. Coast Guard Cutter *Taney* is the last surviving ship from the December 7, 1941, attack on Pearl Harbor. She served as a command ship at Okinawa, a fleet escort in the Atlantic and Mediterranean, and a medical ship in Vietnam—and is the last ship afloat that participated in the search for Amelia Earhart.

The Lightship *Chesapeake*—so called because her mast-head light, foghorn, and bell helped guide mariners to safe harbor during storms—was built in 1930. She's built for strength; her gigantic anchors held her on station during the worst of storms.

The Seven-Foot Knoll Lighthouse, built in 1855, marked the entrance to the Baltimore Harbor for 135 years before being moved to its current site on dry land. Unfortunately, the interior serves as offices rather than being an authentic re-creation of a lighthouse keeper's home (see Calvert Marine Museum, Southern Maryland chapter).

It's a creepy thrill indeed to walk through what seems like an endless parade of tight little doors on the USS *Torsk*, a World War II submarine built in 1944. It holds the record for most dives, having submerged 11,884 times. Think about that when you're inspecting those tiny bunks. Not recommended for claustrophobics.

The tour requires walking and climbing in some tight spaces. The Maritime Museum is open Feb.–Nov. daily 10 A.M.–6 P.M., Dec.–Jan. Fri.–Sun. 9 A.M.–5 P.M. Admission is $7.

Fell's Point Maritime Museum, 1724 Thames St., 410/732-0278, displays artifacts and tells the story of those who earned their living on the water. Now a trendy residential neighborhood, Fell's Point was the site of Baltimore's first shipyard in the 1730s, and was home to a thriving maritime industry through the mid-19th century. The museum is open Thurs.–Mon. 10 A.M.–5 P.M. Admission is $4.

LITERARY SIGHTS

Though it's now privately owned, the **H. L. Mencken House,** 1524 Hollins St. on Washington Square, deserves a nod and a smile as tribute to one of the most popular writers of the 20th century. Please don't disturb the residents. Mr. Mencken would find that not at all amiable.

It's highly unlikely that you'll want to do much more than drive by the **Edgar Allan Poe House,** 203 N. Amity St., since the neighborhood has slipped well past marginal into the nether regions. However, a visit to Poe's grave at the old **Westminster Cemetery Hall and Burying Ground,** 500 W. Baltimore St., 410/706-2072, might be in order. Visitors leave flowers, notes, and the occasional empty pint bottle on the grave of the famous author and his wife; the church next to the burying ground is periodically open for a tour of the catacombs beneath. The cemetery is open daily 8 A.M.–dusk, and entry is free. Churchyard and catacomb tours are given Apr.–July, first and third Friday of each month, 6:30 P.M. Tours are by reservation only and a tour fee of $4 is charged.

The George Peabody Library, 17 E. Mount Vernon Pl., 410/659-8257, dates from the

THE TELL-TALE HEART

Edgar Allan Poe lived in Baltimore from 1829 to 1836 and died here in 1849 at age 40. At the time of his death, he was relatively unknown and quite poor; he was buried in the back of an old cemetery (the Western Burying Ground) on the edge of town with barely a stone marking his grave.

Legend has it that years later, Baltimore's schoolchildren initiated a "Pennies for Poe" campaign through which they hoped to raise enough money to move Poe's grave to a more prominent location in the cemetery (now named Westminster) and mark it with a more worthy headstone. They couldn't collect the money they needed, but the city chipped in and helped them out. Now it's a tradition for visitors to the grave to leave pennies on the tombstone.

Every year since 1949, a mysterious stranger clad in a three-quarter-length black coat and fedora has visited the grave on Poe's birthday. The stranger places his hands on Poe's tombstone and appears to pray. A moment later he is gone, leaving three roses and a bottle of cognac. The three roses are thought to represent the poet, his wife, and her mother. All are buried in the tiny cemetery.

The identity of the mysterious stranger has remained a riddle since the ritual began. The original visitor carried on the tradition until 1993, when he left a cryptic note saying, "The torch will be passed."

founding of the Peabody Institute in 1857. Reflecting the scholarly interests of the 19th century, the library consists of a general reference collection on virtually every subject but music; the 255,000 volumes date from the 16th to the early 20th centuries.

George Peabody embodied the classic rags-to-riches story. Born to a poor family in Massachusetts, he became wealthy as an investment banker in England, and, as an investment, started a dry goods firm in Baltimore in 1814. Peabody financed the westward expansion of American railroads and, when he retired, sold his interest in the investment bank to his partners, J. P. Morgan and his father; the company eventually became the House of Morgan. In the years that followed, Peabody created museums of natural history, archaeology, and ethnology at Yale and Harvard, the Peabody Museum in Salem, Massachusetts, and a number of philanthropic foundations. On his death in 1869, he bequeathed the Peabody Institute and Library to Baltimore.

Even if you aren't here for the books, come inside to see the extraordinary architectural details of the building—the stack room contains five tiers of ornamental cast-iron balconies that rise upward to a skylight that forms the ceiling. You will, as one local writer predicted, say "Wow." Though the books are noncirculating, the library is open to the public for day use Mon.–Fri. 9 A.M.–3 P.M.

Enoch Pratt, a merchant banker who made his fortune in Maryland, gifted the city with an entire free library system. The **Enoch Pratt Free Library** consists of 26 branches and the Central Library, 400 Cathedral St., 410/396-5500, www.pratt.lib.md.us, which is the state library resource center. The central library is another historic building illuminated by a spectacular skylight. The Pratt libraries maintain several special collections. Among them are 5,500 volumes of the work of H. L. Mencken, and 325 volumes and manuscripts of the works of Edgar Allan Poe. The children's reading room, with its fountain and fireplace, is a delightful place to visit for readings and other special events. Pratt books are circulating to those with a local address and library card. The Central Library is also a good place to pick up free newspapers, neighborhood flyers, and bus schedules.

BALTIMORE CITY LIFE

The **Baltimore Museum of Industry,** 1415 Key Highway, 410/727-4808, www.thebmi.org, is one of my favorite places in the city, and I'm not alone—it was chosen as Baltimore's "Best Hands-On Museum for Kids" by *Baltimore Magazine* for several years running. Inside the converted oyster cannery that serves as the museum's home, workers have constructed an abbreviated version of Baltimore's industries: an oyster cannery, print shop, bank, store, movie theater, garment fac-

I SCREAM, YOU SCREAM

In the middle of the 19th century, a Baltimore dairyman named Jacob Fussell made daily rounds delivering milk. The cream he was unable to sell was stored on ice, and when he turned that extra product into ice cream, his customers raved. Soon Fussell stopped selling milk and devoted his dairy to the production of the sweet treat. In 1851, he opened the first ice cream factory in America, and soon was churning out ice cream up and down the East Coast. One of his old delivery trucks is on display at the Baltimore Museum of Industry.

tory, and more. Each of these "businesses" is put into action by a worker/guide who talks about the industry and its heyday. Often, visitors can join in, cranking out a handbill on the 1880 job press, or making cans in the oyster company assembly line. In addition to the many live exhibits, there are plenty of colorful and informative displays on the companies and products that originated in Baltimore—many have become household names in America and beyond. "Born in Baltimore, raised everywhere" was the slogan of Gans Brothers umbrellas—the city was the umbrella capital of America until the last umbrella factory of Polan, Katz and Co. (the first to introduce colored umbrellas) closed in 1981.

Also of interest is a wall of Baltimore "firsts"— the first gas lights, the first street lighted by gas (not Light Street, as you might suppose, but Howard Street), straws and drinking cups produced by the Sweetheart Company, Black & Decker's cordless drill, Howard Head's aluminum skis, the first phone system, and of course, Bromo-Seltzer, created by Isaac Emerson in 1890 and named for a then-active Italian volcano, Mt. Bromo. The "miracle cream" Noxzema debuted here in 1914, mixed up in a coffee pot in the backroom of Dr. Lloyd Bunting's pharmacy.

BMI also offers revolving displays, a research library, and trips, by reservation, on the steam tug *Baltimore*. The museum is open Mon.–Sat. 10 A.M.–4 P.M. Admission is $10 adults, $5 seniors, students, and children.

The **Baltimore Public Works Museum,** 751 Eastern Ave., 410/396-5565, is undeniably unique. If you've ever wondered how tunnels, roads, bridges, clean water, wastewater, and recycling systems are created and maintained in a big city, this is your opportunity to learn. Baltimore is proud of its public works programs; the city pioneered the first gas streetlight (1816), the first earthen dam (at Druid Lake, 1875), and the formula for chlorinating water to prevent waterborne diseases. The museum is housed in a beautiful 1911 pumping station, and reveals the city's infrastructure through exhibits, video presentations, interactive computers (where visitors can build their own city), and Streetscape—an outdoor maze of drains, conduits, and pipes. Who'd have thought sewage could be so much fun? It's open Wed.–Sun. 10 A.M.–4 P.M. Admission is $2.50.

In 1859, Baltimore laid its first horse-powered rail transportation system; within a few years, electricity replaced horseflesh. The long-distance transportation provided by the colorful electrified trolleys made it possible for the busy seaport town to expand out from the harbor to create the many neighborhoods that characterize it today. In fact, the first successful commercial electric railway in the United States was the Baltimore-Hampden run, built in 1885. The **Baltimore Streetcar Museum,** 1901 Falls Rd., 410/547-0264, www.baltimoremd.com/streetcar, is the result of the efforts of local volunteers to preserve an important part of the city's past. The museum chronicles the early days with an audiovisual presentation, *Trolley—The Car That Built Our Cities,* pictorial displays of the town in the 1940s and 1950s, and of course, the railcars themselves. The yard and car house contain both unrestored and restored cars from every era of Baltimore's past. The museum also features an antique trolley for a rocking, clanging ride into history on a short rail trip. The "trolleymen" are all volunteers, dressed as authentic conductors—and they know everything about these early transportation systems you'll ever need to ask. It's open June–Oct. Saturday noon–5 P.M., year-round Sunday noon–5 P.M. The $5 admission price includes the museum exhibits, car house, and unlimited rides on the streetcar line.

Penn Station, 1500 N. Charles St., 410/291-4263, is an elegant building that's still as engaging as it was in the heyday of railroads. This glistening glass-and-stone palace is the place to catch the train; there's also a great little candy store inside, with the city's best candy apples (cinnamon and caramel). Temporary parking out front makes it easy to pop in for a pit stop, a snack, and to check arrivals and departures on the clicking-clacking flip boards.

ONLY IN BALTIMORE

Attention athletes: the challenge is to make it up the spiraling 228 steps of the **Washington Monument,** 609 Washington Pl., 410/396-7837, without clinging to the walls and gasping more than once. Baltimoreans are proud that this monument to the father of our country predates the D.C. model by decades. In fact, the architect, Robert Mills, honed his skills in

a sunny Sunday in downtown Baltimore

© JOANNE MILLER

BALTIMORE

Baltimore and went on to create the obelisk in the capital. The most embarrassing thing about the monument is that sound carries throughout the tower better than a two-block phone connection, so everyone knows when you're winded. The rewards at the top are bragging rights, great views, and several years' worth of graffiti (you can rest while you're reading). There's a little gallery with historic displays on the bottom floor. It's open Wed.–Sun. 10 A.M.–4 P.M., and admission is $1.

The **Dr. Samuel D. Harris National Museum of Dentistry,** 31 S. Greene St., 410/706-0600, www.dentalmuseum.org, will leave you smiling beyond all expectations. The faint scent of clove oil in the lobby may bring back an unpleasant memory or two of being strapped to the chair, but that will be dispelled the minute you enter this clever, informative, and entertaining museum. Video games—including tooth jukeboxes that play silent film clips and old commercials ("You'll wonder where the yellow

THE BABE

Katherine Ruth moved into the home of her father, Pius Schamberger, when her birth time grew near to escape the noise and congestion of the apartment above her husband's saloon a few blocks away. George Herman Ruth was born there, at 216 Emory St., in 1895. Ruth grew up a product of a rough neighborhood; by the time he was seven, his parents deemed him incorrigible, and he was sent to St. Mary's Industrial School, a Catholic institution for orphans and delinquent boys.

By the time he was 19, he had established a reputation as the best young athlete in Baltimore, particularly when it came to baseball. The owner of the minor league Baltimore Orioles, Jack Dunn, signed Ruth to his first professional contract, and at the same time, assumed Ruth's legal guardianship. Other team members called the rookie "Jack Dunn's baby," which the local press shortened to "Babe."

Threatened by financial ruin, Dunn sold Babe and several other players to the Boston Red Sox within the year. That same year, 1914, Ruth married his first wife, Helen, who was to die tragically in a fire in 1929. Ruth played for the Red Sox for more than five seasons, becoming one of the American League's greatest left-handed pitchers. In 1916, he established a World Series record by pitching 29 consecutive scoreless innings in series play. In spite of his pitching ability, the Sox switched Ruth to the outfield so he would have more chances at bat.

In short order, Ruth established himself as a great home-run hitter. Traditional power hitters of the time were belting 8–12 homers per season, and Ruth doubled, then tripled those numbers—to a high of 60 home runs per season after he joined the New York Yankees in 1920. Hank Aaron finally broke the Babe's 714-hit career home run record, but not until decades later. Yankee Stadium was built to accommodate the huge crowds that came to see the Babe, and sportswriters dubbed it "The House That Ruth Built." In the 1920s, Babe Ruth *was* baseball. The newspapers followed his giant appetites for food, drink, and social life, and he became an American icon, congratulated by presidents and adored by kids. This was an affection he returned, and the press worshipfully followed his visits to hospitals and interaction with his young fans. Ruth married his second wife, Claire, in 1929, and adopted her daughter by a previous marriage shortly after. In one newsreel, he told the press that Claire was going to be his new trainer, and watch out for him, but age and years of high living had taken their toll.

Babe Ruth retired from baseball in 1935, capitalizing on his fame to appear (badly) in a few Hollywood films. He attempted to become the manager of a big-league ballclub; a desire that was blocked, he felt, by Major League owners. Nonetheless, he made appearances at ballparks around the country for the rest of his life. He died of throat cancer in 1948, and is buried in the Gates of Heaven Cemetery in Hawthorn, New York.

BALTIMORE

went . . .")—make learning fun for all ages. Changing exhibits, which have included the amazing feats of "iron jaw" performers, a "Match the Smile to the Celebrity" game, and an array of fancy toothbrushes, might make you consider becoming a dentist. Kids may decide to take time out on tooth-shaped chairs while their elders inspect George Washington's authentic dentures. (Surprise! They're not made out of wood.) It's an appealing mix of gear, lore, and gadgets associated with dentistry and teeth. In case you're overwhelmed with oral angst, you can always petition St. Appolonia, patron saint of dentists and sufferers of dental pain. Make sure to stop by this clever museum, and don't forget to brush. Museum hours are Wed.–Sat. 10 A.M.–4 P.M., Sunday 1–4 P.M. Admission is $4.50.

If you're looking for scandalous details of a hero's life, you won't find them at the **Babe Ruth Birthplace and Orioles Museum,** 216 Emory St., 410/727-1539, www.baberuthmuseum.com. It's the bats, the balls, the legend; a sprightly film and artifacts chronicle the Babe's life and concentrate on his rough childhood, larger-than-life talents, and love for kids, and skim over his excesses. But you leave feeling great about the Babe, and even more enthusiastic about the game. My question is, does "The Homer That Saved Little Johnny," in which Babe Ruth promised a severely ill boy that he would "knock a homer" for him against St. Louis in the 1926 World Series, count as a miracle? The Babe hit three homers, and Little Johnny recovered. If there ever was a patron saint of baseball, it would have to be George Herman Ruth. There's also historical information about the Orioles and rotating exhibits; a recent display addressed the historic Cuba-Orioles game. The museum is open Apr.–Oct. daily 10 A.M.–5 P.M. (until 7 P.M. on all Orioles home game days), Nov.–Mar. daily 10 A.M.–4 P.M. Admission is $6.

The **Eubie Blake National Jazz Museum and Cultural Center,** 847 N. Howard St., 410/625-3113, www.eubieblake.org, Eubieblake@erols .com, is a repository of memorabilia of the legendary ragtime and musical theater composer, as well as displays on other jazz greats born in Baltimore: Billie Holiday, Chick Webb, Cab Calloway,

© JOANNE MILLER

Bromo Seltzer Tower

and others. The gallery features a new exhibition each month, and provides instruction in visual and performing arts to the community. Regular hours are not established, so contact them directly for times and admission fees.

What soccer is to the West Coast, lacrosse is to the East. The **Lacrosse Museum and National Hall of Fame,** 113 W. University Pkwy, 410/235-6882, www.lacrosse.org, celebrates the game, from its origins as a stickball game played by Native Americans prior to European settlement to today's modern teams. Home to USLacrosse national headquarters, an umbrella organization for lacrosse clubs across the nation, the museum's displays depict the fast-moving game's history, equipment, and stars—both men and women. Pro football veteran Jim Brown's picture graces the hall of fame: he played for Syracuse University in 1957. Lacrosse is played internationally, with world championship competitions every four years (the 2002 world championship was in Perth,

Australia), and America sports some of the best teams in the world. The U.S. men's team has won every world championship except one, in 1978, when Canada took the title, and the University of Maryland women's team has won five national championships. The museum is open June–Jan. Mon.–Fri 10 A.M.–3 P.M., Feb.–May Tues.–Sat. 10 A.M.–3 P.M. Admission is $3.

The name Phillips is invariably associated with seafood in this part of the world; the Phillips family built a restaurant empire in Maryland from the humble beginnings of a single fishing boat on Hoopers Island. Now visitors can take the **Phillips Seafood Tour,** 1215 E. Fort Ave., 443/263-1200, www.phillipsfoods.com, a walk through the Phillips' processing plant. There, millions of crab cakes will dance before your eyes—but the best part is the samples. Call for tour times and availabilities.

Top of the World Observation Level and Museum, World Trade Center, 401 E. Pratt St., 410/837-VIEW (837-8439), offers panoramic views of the city and well-designed displays of Baltimore history and cultural life. Architect I. M. Pei designed the World Trade Center as a showplace; the elevator takes you directly to the 27th floor. It's open daily Memorial Day–Labor Day 10 A.M.–9 P.M., rest of the year Wed.–Sun. 10 A.M.–6 P.M. Admission is $4.

It's hard to miss the **Bromo Seltzer Tower,** 21 S. Eutaw St., as its clock with four faces can be seen from much of the city. At one time, a giant whirling blue Bromo Seltzer bottle capped the crenellated tower, but neighbors complained that the eerie blue light kept them awake at night. At least they always knew what time it was.

ETHNIC MUSEUMS AND SITES

What do you do when an interesting museum is in a marginal location? **Great Blacks in Wax,** 1601-03 E. North Ave., 410/563-3404, www .greatblacksinwax.org, is on the main drag of one of Baltimore's tougher neighborhoods—the good news is that it's the focal point of a revitalization movement. The museum is set up in an old theater; though the displays don't even flirt with high-tech, the idea—of pride in the ac-

complishment and achievement of blacks from ancient times to the present—is absolutely on target. A replica of a slave ship, similar to those that brought the ancestors of most American blacks to this continent, provides considerable food for thought in terms of understanding the courage, strength, and adaptability it takes to survive in a hostile world. The museum is open Jan. 15–Oct. 14 Tues.– Sat. 9 A.M.–6 P.M., Sunday noon–6 P.M.; Oct. 15–Jan. 14 Tues.–Sat. 9 A.M.–5 P.M., Sunday noon–5 P.M.; also open Monday during February and July–Aug. and Martin Luther King's Day 10 A.M.–4 P.M. Admission is $6.

The East Coast's largest museum chronicling the history of African Americans, the **Reginald F. Lewis Museum of African American History and Culture,** Pratt and President Streets, 410/333-1130, www.africanamericanculture.org, houses artifacts and exhibits that cover 350 years of Maryland history. Inside, there's a genealogy center, theater, recording studio for oral history, gift shop, and café in addition to the galleries. Contact the museum for hours and admission fees.

Jewish Museum of Maryland

The **Jewish Museum of Maryland,** 15 Lloyd St., 410/732-6400, www.jhsm.org, concentrates on preserving Maryland's Jewish history and culture through its collection of photographs, papers, and objects. This is no dry historical treatise, though—the rotating exhibits are interesting and well designed. One recent exhibit focused on Jewish life in Maryland's small towns. The story of Jewish participation in the building of Baltimore is a fascinating one. Jewish families began to settle in Baltimore in the Fell's Point area early in the 19th century. By the 1840s, more than 1,000 lived on the eastern edge of the city. The Civil War brought a new prosperity, and wealthy Jewish businessmen built elegant homes and the stately Oheb Shalom temple on Eutaw Place. Lloyd Street Synagogue, the third-oldest standing synagogue in the country and the first in Maryland (1845), is next door to the museum, as is the B'nai Israel Synagogue, built in 1876.

Call to arrange a guided tour. There is an excellent gift shop on the premises; the museum is open Tues.–Thurs. and Sunday noon–4 P.M. Admission is $3.

The **Holocaust Memorial,** at the intersection of Water, Gay, and Lombard Streets, 410/837-4636, is a sculptural reminder of World War II devastation and the hopes of new generations for a more tolerant future.

CHURCHES

Basilica of the Assumption, Cathedral and Mulberry Streets, 410/727-3565, www.baltimore-basilica.org, was historically the Mother Church of Roman Catholicism in the United States, the chief church encompassing the vast Diocese of Baltimore that extended from Maine to Georgia and west to the Mississippi. The building was initiated by the first U.S. archbishop, John Carroll (brother of Charles Carroll of Carrollton), who is buried in a crypt on the site. Benjamin Henry Latrobe, architect of the U.S. Capitol, donated the design. The cornerstone for the church was laid in 1806; however, the War of 1812 delayed completion until the early 1920s. The importance of the stately basilica was underscored by visits from Pope John Paul II in

1995 and Mother Teresa in 1996. The building's central dome features a radiant portrait of Mary rising into heaven; the entire church is redolent of a century of frankincense. The basilica is often open to visitors during the day (call ahead to make sure); regularly scheduled tours begin each Sunday at noon, and private tours are available by appointment.

The Greek Orthodox **Cathedral of the Annunciation,** 24 W. Preston St. at Maryland Avenue, is a magnificent domed building enclosing gilded icons, ornate woodwork, and mosaics. Over the entrance, the Greek inscription reads "House of God, Gate of Heaven." Unlike many orthodox churches, this one has benches so attendees can sit rather than stand during the service. Though the church is locked when not in use, stop by the office during the week and ask to be admitted.

St. Jude Shrine, Paca and Saratoga Streets, 410/685-6026, www.stjudeshrine.org, is dedicated to the Catholic patron saint of hopeless cases and lost causes, St. Jude Thaddeus. Though the body of St. Jude rests in St. Peter's in Rome, this small church was dedicated in 1917 and has been going strong ever since. The shrine is open most days, and masses are held daily.

Lovely Lane United Methodist Church, 2200 St. Paul St., 410/889-4458, was designed by the New York architect Stanford White (who was shot to death by his lover's husband, causing a sensational trial in the early years of the 20th century—but that's another story). This massive, sturdy granite building is the mother church of American Methodism, and a museum on the premises exhibits historical materials related to the founding of the sect. Guided tours are offered July 1–Labor Day Mon.–Fri. 9 A.M.–3 P.M. and Sunday at 11 A.M. Hours vary the rest of the year. Donations are appreciated.

Mother Seton House, 600 N. Paca St., 410/523-3443, is the site of the original posting of American saint Elizabeth Ann Seton when she committed to the Catholic Church and began her teaching career (see Frederick, Western Maryland chapter). There is a small chapel and the dwelling house used by the Sisters of St. Joseph on the property. It's open Mar.–Oct. Sat.–Sun.

1–4 P.M.; Nov.–Feb. Sat.–Sun. 1–3 P.M. Donations accepted.

If a set painter were to design a church as background for a gothic romance, they would probably come up with something that looks like **Mount Vernon Place United Methodist Church,** 10 E. Mount Vernon Pl., 410/685-5290. This soaring green serpentine, gray stone, and red-painted church was built in 1874 on the spot where Francis Scott Key died some 30 years before. The inside is as ornate as the outside: the organ has nearly 4,000 pipes. Guided tours are available Mon.–Fri. 9 A.M.–3 P.M. Donations accepted.

SCIENCE AND NATURAL HISTORY SITES

By now, everyone has heard about the **National Aquarium in Baltimore,** Piers 3 and 4, 501 E. Pratt St., 410/576-3800, www.aqua.org. The project started in 1970 as part of the inner harbor redevelopment, and has become the crown jewel of the waterfront. The modern facility showcases sophisticated theme exhibits including an outdoor seal pool; aqua environments "Mountains to the Sea," "Surviving Through Adaptations," "North Atlantic to the Pacific," and "Open Ocean"; and a temperature-controlled "South American Rain Forest." There's been a lot of excitement over Spirit, Raven, and Maya, three dolphins born in 2001 and featured in performances of "Coastal Connections: Dolphins at Our Shores." There's a walkway over an extensive manta ray pool, and a spiraling path through a four-story aquarium, the "Atlantic Coral Reef." Wet-suited divers swim around the tank during feeding times, which are posted in the main lobby. The feeling inside the main building is of being underwater—a hypnotic effect guaranteed to leave you spacey (it has the same effect on the workers, so they tell me). The main facility is linked by a walkway to a Marine Mammal Pavilion with a 1,300-seat amphitheater and a 1.2 million–gallon pool that features 30-minute presentations starring the aquarium's talented team of dolphins. The entire aquarium is state-of-the-art and an amazing experience; don't miss it. It's also very crowded; the best times to visit are during the fall and winter, and before 11 A.M. and after 3 P.M. There are services available for visitors with vision, hearing, and mobility special needs. The aquarium is open July–Aug. daily 9 A.M.–8 P.M., hours extended to 10 P.M. Fri.–Sat.; Nov.–Feb. Sat.–Thurs. 10 A.M.–5 P.M.,

© JOANNE MILLER

National Aquarium

Friday 10 A.M.–8 P.M.; Mar.–June and Sept.–Oct. Sat.–Thurs. 9 A.M.–5 P.M., Friday 9 A.M.–8 P.M. Visitors may purchase advance tickets online or at the aquarium, and tickets are also available from TicketMaster for an additional charge (410/481-SEAT or 410/481-7328 in Baltimore, 800/551-SEAT or 800/551-7328 outside the region). Admission is $17.50 adults, $14.50 seniors, $9.50 children 3–11; the information line (above) gives advance warning on bargain days and hours.

The aquarium is spectacular, but one of my other favorites is the **Baltimore Zoo,** Druid Hill Park, 410/366-LION, www.baltimorezoo.org. This beautifully landscaped park features more than 2,000 animals, including many threatened and endangered species. Cages are few: many animals are kept in natural habitats such as the boardwalk through the African veldt, and the Maryland wilderness area. Healthy, active animals are showcased in numerous educational programs, and keepers hold regularly scheduled "encounters" to talk about everything from bees to polar bears throughout each day.

KidZone, an eight-acre children's zoo-within-a-zoo, has been rated number one in the nation by the American Zoo and Aquarium Association; it's open for face-to-face interaction during the summer. The zoo offers many special family-oriented events throughout the year, and camel rides, a climbing wall (the Siberian Summit), a little train (ZooChoo), and a carousel add extra fun for nominal charges. Kids receive a free Zoofari Adventure Guide, a brightly illustrated manual that turns learning about animals—with the help of Paco, the zoo's macaw mascot—into puzzles and games. The 180-acre grounds are extensive, and for those who would rather ride than walk, a tram is available. There are four refreshment stands on the grounds, and two gift shops—an opportunity to pick up hippo-shaped poo perchers (fertilizers) for your plants. The overall impression is one of a well-maintained, enlightened, happy place to visit. This is one of the best zoos I've seen. From May 1–Sept. 4, hours are Mon.–Fri., 10 A.M.–4 P.M., Saturday 10 A.M.–8 P.M., Sunday 10 A.M.–5:30 P.M. The rest of the year, hours are 10 A.M.–4 P.M. daily. Admission is $11 adults, $9 seniors, $7 children 2–11; between 10 A.M. and

noon on the first Tuesday of each month, children under 12 with a paying adult are admitted free.

The **Maryland Science Center,** 601 Light St., 410/685-5225, www.mdsci.org, is Maryland's oldest scientific institution and one of the oldest in the nation. Painter Charles Willson Peale and a group of friends who shared an interest in the natural world, including Charles Carroll of Carrollton and J. H. Latrobe, met informally in 1797 and opened a natural history museum—of sorts. Visitors could examine a live rattlesnake, stuffed birds, wax figures of famous people, a kitten with one head and two bodies, and an assortment of sea life. Over time, the organization developed into the Maryland Academy of Science, and the unprecedented growth in scientific and technical knowledge during the 20th century expanded the mission and resources of the organization into its current form. From asteroids in the atrium to a math exhibit titled "Beyond Numbers," from the hands-on science arcade to "The Visible Human," the Science Center seeks to stimulate and cultivate awareness, interest, and understanding of the sciences in its diverse programs. In addition to its regular and featured exhibits, the center offers planetarium shows, an antique telescope/observatory on the roof, and an IMAX theater. It's open Tues.–Fri. 10 A.M.–5 P.M., Saturday 10 A.M.–6 P.M., Sunday noon–5 P.M. Summer hours are late June–early Sept. Mon.–Fri. 10 A.M.–5 P.M., Sat.–Sun. 10 A.M.–6 P.M. Admission to the museum only is $12 adults, $8 children 3–12; tickets for the IMAX theater only are $7.50 for all. A combination ticket to the museum and theater is $15.50 adults, $10.50 children 3–12.

ESPECIALLY FOR KIDS

If the short set hasn't run off enough energy touring the inner harbor, make sure you stop by **Port Discovery,** 34 Market Place (also known as NationsBank Plaza, one block north of the aquarium), 410/727-8120, www.portdiscovery.org. If you go there first, you may never leave. This gigantic playroom was designed by Disney and offers hours of serious fun for all ages. Some of the exhibits, such as the three-story net/pipe/ramp climbing gym, are best left to kids and professional gymnasts. Other exhibits are meant to be shared by adults and kids: one shadowy and mysterious exhibit consists of figuring out a hieroglyphic message by putting together a puzzle of pot shards, pulling oneself across the "Nile" on a raft, and wandering around a dark maze inside a pyramid to find the secrets of the Pharaohs. Expect lots of creative learning, holograms, and other special effects—and lots of fun. There are play stations appropriate for all ages, including an area dedicated to international *Sesame Street* (Big Bird speaks Mandarin; Ernie sings to his rubber ducky in Spanish: "Pato de goma, yo soy l'uno!"). This is light-years away from plunking the kids down in front of a video terminal. Adventurous adults without accompanying children can sneak in and play the day away. Highly recommended.

One special attraction at Port Discovery is the HiFlyer, a helium-filled balloon with an enclosed gondola that holds 20–30 passengers and transports them 450 feet up the air for a real bird's-eye view of the harbor in the afternoons and evenings. No fear of blowing away and ending up in the bay, however—the balloon is tethered by a steel cable.

Port Discovery has different hours throughout the year. Summer hours are Memorial Day–Labor Day Mon.–Sat. 10 A.M.–5 P.M., Sunday noon–5 P.M. In July and August, enjoy special Friday Fun Nights—the museum is open until 8 P.M. September hours are Fri. 9:30 A.M.–4:30 P.M., Saturday 10 A.M.–5 P.M., Sunday noon–5 P.M. Oct.–May hours are Tues.–Fri. 9:30 A.M.–4:30 P.M., Saturday 10 A.M.–5 P.M., Sunday noon–5 P.M. The museum is closed on Thanksgiving and Christmas. Admission is $11 adults, $10 seniors, $8.50 for kids 3–12, and free for kids under three.

ART MUSEUMS AND GALLERIES

Baltimore is blessed with a variety of significant collections—art lovers could visit one a day and never tire of the variety and quality. In fact, two of the museums, the Walters and Baltimore Museum of Art, hold some of the finest collections in

© JOANNE MILLER

Walters Art Museum

the world. The Visionary Art Museum easily holds the most unusual.

When I first saw the name Walters Gallery, I pictured a little gallery with paintings for sale and wondered what all the hoopla was about. After my first visit, I could see the hoopla was well founded; the collections were expansive and outstanding. Now—after an extensive multimillion-dollar renovation that resulted in 39 newly configured and refurbished galleries, a new four-story glass entryway, more public spaces, and a new name, the **Walters Art Museum,** 600 N. Charles St., 410/547-9000, www.thewalters.org, the Walters is better than ever. Named for William Walters and his son Henry, the gallery is composed of three very large connected buildings, significant in themselves for their architecture. But what's in them—the fruit of a half-century of conscious acquisition, one of the most generous acts of cultural philanthropy in American history—is mind-boggling. The directors of major American museums collectively held their breath when Henry Walters's will was read, only to find that he left his entire bequest, including buildings, to the city where he was born, "for the benefit of the public." The original palazzo and the more modern 1974 building hold selections from the "main" collection, covering 55 centuries from antiquities to

BALTIMORE

THE FIRST (ART) FAMILIES OF BALTIMORE

William Walters, born in 1819, claimed that he spent his first five dollars on an artist's view of Napoleon crossing the Alps. When shrewd investments made him a rich man, he continued his love of art, first collecting works by American painters of the New York School and of the Chesapeake Bay. During the Civil War, Walters moved his family to Paris—his Southern loyalties made for an uncomfortable home and business life in Union Maryland. There, he discovered Corot, Daumier, and the sculptor A. L. Barye. He also developed an appetite for oriental porcelains and other Asiana. Upon his death in 1894, his son Henry expanded the collection; in 1902, he purchased the contents of the Accoramboni Palace in Rome, some 1,600 works, including dozens of sculptures from classical antiquity. Though Henry lived with his friends Pembroke and Sarah Jones in their residences in New York and Rhode Island—he married Sarah after her husband's death—Henry always shipped the goods to Baltimore. Henry Walters left the fabulous collection and its buildings to the city on his death in 1931. The Walters Art Museum remains one of the showplaces of Baltimore.

Dr. Claribel Cone and Miss Etta Cone were sisters, "spinsters," and members of a group of wealthy Jewish immigrant Baltimoreans who envisioned a museum of art for the city in 1914. Claribel Cone hosted Baltimore's leading salon in the family's Eutaw Street apartments, regularly attended by Gertrude Stein and her brother Leo, who had moved to Baltimore from San Francisco in 1892. The Cone sisters followed the Steins to Europe in 1903, and became acquainted with the avant-garde painters of the day. Thanks to Ms. Stein and her friends, their tastes were decidedly modern; they became major patrons of Picasso and Matisse, and collected Gauguin, Seurat, and others. Matisse became especially favored, and at the time of their deaths, the sisters owned 42 paintings, 18 sculptures, and dozens of works on paper, including 250 items that illustrated his first book, the *Poésies de Stéphane Mallarmé.* Picasso fell out of favor when he entered his cubist period. Etta, who survived her sister by 20 years, brought the collection up to 3,000 pieces, adding works by Cézanne and Van Gogh before her death in 1949. She bequeathed the entire collection, plus a substantial endowment for maintenance, to the Baltimore Museum of Art.

modern art, and the third building, the Hackerman House Asian Art Gallery, displays the Asian collection. A recent exhibition on 17th-century Dutch and Flemish paintings was titled "An Eye for Detail," a phrase that effectively sums up the ability of the Walters to pick the most astounding examples of period, style, and artwork. Absolutely everything in these galleries is the best example available—visitors can spend hours in a single gallery marveling at a Victorian brooch in the shape of a siren made from a single mabe pearl, a Fabergé egg with a golden palace inside it, or a jeweled Tiffany iris. A gold and red-enamel watch with pearls for hours (it was meant for a blind person) is near a box by Boucheron made from gold, rock crystal, and diamonds. The rich materials depict a bucolic scene on the box lid: a coach and horses speeding through the countryside.

It's almost beyond comprehension that items as diverse as the oldest surviving text by the mathematical genius Archimedes, Egyptian sculpture, Byzantine icons, paintings by Peter Paul Rubens, and Kabuki prints by Knish Horsed could be appreciated by, much less carefully collected by, a single father and son. Each item in this collection is to be savored and enjoyed. Don't miss it! The Walters Art Museum is open Tues.–Sun. 10 A.M.–5 P.M. and until 8 P.M. on the first Thursday of each month (when admission is free all day). Admission is $8 adults, $6 seniors; those 17 and under are admitted free. The gift shop is also a great place to browse.

The **Baltimore Museum of Art,** N. Charles and 31st Streets, 410/396-7100, www.artbma .org, is Maryland's largest art museum, and the home of several notable art collections given by philanthropic Baltimoreans including the Cone sisters. A major renovation has recently reframed (literally) the Cone collection, and the Matisses and other works presented to the city by Dr. Claribel Cone and Miss Etta Cone remain the heart of the museum's displays. In addition, the museum's west wing houses 16 galleries for the display of the permanent collection of post-1945 art (including a gallery of works by Andy Warhol). Two sculpture gardens showcase modern and contemporary sculpture, and three floors of the original building present American painting and sculpture prior to 1900, decorative arts of the 18th through the 20th centuries, and period rooms from six historic Maryland houses. Whew! Of course, that's in addition to the art from Africa, the Americas, and Oceania; the Chinese ceramics; paintings by European Old Masters; and collections of prints, drawings, and photographs. Whatever your interest, you'll find it here. Gertrude's, an attractive indoor/outdoor restaurant inside the museum (see Food, below) is an excellent spot for a meal. The museum is open Wed.–Fri. 11 A.M.–5 P.M., Sat.–Sun. 11 A.M.–6 P.M. Admission is $7 adults, $5 seniors; those 18 and under are admitted free. Admission to the museum is free on the first Thursday of the month 11 A.M.–8 P.M.; free first Thursday evenings feature tours, talks, live music, and hands-on workshops for kids.

The modern **American Visionary Art Museum,** 800 Key Hwy., 410/244-1900, www.avam.org, holds work "born of intuition and self-styled imagination . . . created by farmers, housewives, mechanics, retired folk, the disabled, the homeless, as well as the occasional neurosurgeon—all inspired by the fire within." You'll not find any formal "schools" of work here. A 12-foot-tall sculpture of Baltimore movie diva Divine welcomes visitors to view art cars, 20-foot-tall whirligigs, matchstick altars, crayon paintings, homemade air balloons, and hundreds of other wondrous objects created by self-taught artists. The galleries will leave you delighted, and with a new respect for art as a means to express the inner lives of everyday people. The featured artists' personal stories are as interesting as their work. Richard Saholt, a World

War II veteran diagnosed with schizophrenia, cured himself through his collages; Martin Ramirez's works on scraps of paper held together with spittle and mashed potatoes now sell in excess of $100,000; Frank Jones was a prisoner who drew visions of his own winged devils in houses to "contain them."

One recent exhibit featured the work of 73-year-old Paul Darmafall, the "Baltimore Glassman." His painting/mosaics are created on scrap doors and other bits of wood; millions of bits of broken glass are his medium. The paintings transform empty-lot litter into jeweled statements about the importance of fresh air, pride in America, and the evils of electricity. You may be inspired to create something of your own. Even the bathrooms are "done up," the ceilings covered with thousands of tissue roses.

The restaurant, the Joy America café (see Food, below), has its own following, and the gift shop is worth a stop. Parking is difficult; there's a pay lot across the Key Highway in front of the Rusty Scupper restaurant, but there are often cheap metered spaces on the street behind the museum. This unique and wonderful museum is open Tues.–Sun. 10 A.M.–6 P.M.; admission is $9 adults, $6 seniors and students.

Rotating exhibitions at the **Maryland Institute College of Art, Meyerhoff Gallery,** 1300 Mt. Royal Ave., 410/669-9200, provide a chance to look at the work of tomorrow's professional artists. Some of the work is extremely good, and the most varied show of the year, the Alumni Exhibition, features the work of hundreds of graduates of the school since its inception in the 1930s. The Alumni Exhibition is usually held in June. The Meyerhoff Gallery is open Mon.–Sat. 10 A.M.–5 P.M., Sunday noon–5 P.M. Free.

The **City Gallery,** 330 N. Charles St., 410/685-0300, www.mdfedart.org, like its sister facility, the Circle Gallery in Annapolis, is affiliated with the Maryland Federation of Art, a nonprofit organization that supports local artists. The small gallery features new exhibits monthly, in all types of work, from paintings to fine crafts.

BALTIMORE

PARKS AND SCENIC SPOTS

Harborwalk Promenade, a paved pathway ideal for a stroll or jog, is nearly eight miles long and extends all the way from Fort McHenry along Fort Avenue, then along the water all the way around the harbor past Fell's Point to Canton Waterfront Park. It's a spectacular way to get exercise and spend the day. Because of ongoing construction, the path may "disappear" at some points, but it's easy to find again.

At Johns Hopkins University, 3400 N. Charles St., in Dunning Park behind Mudd Hall, the **Bufano Sculpture Garden** will raise your spirits. Ten pieces of sculptor Benjamin Bufano's charming work sit along a meandering path under a grove of trees. Look for interpretations of animals in various types of stone, either singly or in groups, sometimes a mother and babies.

The Baltimore Conservatory, at Druid Hill Park, McCulloh Street and Gwynns Fall Parkway, 410/396-0180, is a soaring Victorian glass palace created in 1888. The original Palm Court now has four greenhouses attached, and all are surrounded by outdoor gardens. Neglected for years, the conservatory has been renovated and filled with all types of exotic plants. The parks department has developed a series of special events—call 410/396-6694 for more information. The conservatory is open Thurs.–Sun. 10 A.M.–4 P.M. Free.

Baltimore City Department of Recreation & Parks, 410/396-7900, is the place to call for information on the city's public parks. **Druid Hill Park,** Druid Park Lake Drive, is the second largest urban park in America (Central Park in New York City is larger). Like Central Park, Druid Hill is dandy in the daytime, iffy at night. **Patterson Park,** Eastern and Patterson Park Avenues, is a community park that covers several blocks in a residential neighborhood. This is where the baseball teams meet and kids make themselves dizzy on the merry-go-round. There's a covered ice rink in winter, too—the park is in such good shape thanks to the local community, who have made it a priority for all to enjoy. Local workers take a picnic lunch to **Federal Hill Park,** Key Highway and Battery Avenue, to catch a breeze off the harbor in warm weather and enjoy the spectacular views.

The mansion at **Cylburn Arboretum,** 4915 Greenspring Ave., 410/396-0180, www.cylburn association.org, houses a small nature museum and is surrounded by several gardens, including a heritage rose garden with species more than a century old. Jesse Tyson, a wealthy Baltimore industrialist, started to build Cylburn for his mother in 1863; her death and the Civil War delayed completion until the 1880s. Tyson, then in his 60s, married a 19-year-old debutante, moved into the house, threw lavish parties, and established the gardens. Ever modest, he's quoted as saying, "I have the fairest wife, the fastest horses, and the finest house in Maryland." You can see for yourself: The grounds are open daily 6 A.M.–9 P.M.; the mansion is open Mon.–Fri. 7:30 A.M.–3:30 P.M. and the museum is open Tuesday and Thursday 1–3 P.M. Free.

Recreation and Entertainment

The newest venue on the scene is the multimedia **Patterson Theater,** 3134 Eastern Ave., Highlandtown, 410/276-1651, www.creative alliance.org. This historic movie theater with a rare marquee (it's vertical with a five-part lighting sequence) closed in 1995 and reopened in 2003 as a "cultural factory," and home to the Creative Alliance, an eight-year-old community-based arts nonprofit. In its new incarnation, the brick structure houses a theater, two art galleries, eight live-work studios for artists, film and video making center, sidewalk café, and offices for the Creative Alliance. The Patterson offers workshops, life drawing sessions, critiques, and more for artists in all media. In addition, it presents exhibitions of contemporary art, and performances of theater, performance art, cabaret, and live music such as ethnic and experimental music, blues, and jazz, plus zydeco and tango dances with live bands. The theater will also be a locus for the screening of locally made film and video.

WALKS AND TOURS

The **Mount Vernon Cultural District,** 217 N. Charles St., 410/605-0462, sponsors free walks and historical talks throughout the year. In the past, visitors have been treated to a pre–Valentine's Day "Mt. Vernon's Romantic Legacy" walking tour, featuring tales of locals Jerome Bonaparte and Betsy Patterson, the Duke and Duchess of Windsor, H. L. Mencken's short-lived marriage, and George Peabody's bad luck with women. Another tour was titled "The Great Book Hoof," and included stops at the Peabody Institute and Library, and tidbits about Mencken, Francis Scott Key, Mark Twain, F. Scott and Zelda Fitzgerald, Robert Frost, and filmmaker John Waters. The district also publishes three self-guided walking tours of Mount Vernon, Belvedere, and Cathedral Hill that are fun and informative.

First Thursdays are often the time for festive events around town. Free concerts and art exhibits are among the varied offerings. Contact the Downtown Baltimore Association at 410/244-1030 or www.godowntownbaltimore.com to find out what's happening on First Thursday and all other local events.

The Maryland-based Discovery Channel gives tours aboard World War II–era amphibious vehicles, so visitors can see the city by land and by water. Built in 1945, the Army DUKW vehicles are big trucks with watertight hulls, which travel on six wheels, then navigate the wet stuff with a rudder and marine propeller. This is a good introductory tour, as it covers several neighborhoods and hotspots, such as the Babe Ruth Museum and Edgar Allan Poe's gravesite.

SPECTATOR SPORTS

Pimlico Race Course, Hayward and Winner Avenues, 410/542-9400, is home of the Preakness plus plenty of other racing action.

Oriole Park at Camden Yards, 333 W. Camden St., 410/685-9800, is the home park of the O's. The 2001 Super Bowl champions the Balti-

more Ravens, 410/261-7283, www.baltimoreravens.com, also play at Camden Yards in the newly named **PSINet Stadium.** The **Baltimore Arena,** 201 W. Baltimore St., 410/347-2020, is where to see the hometown NPSL soccer team, **Baltimore Blast;** the **Baltimore Bay Runners,** the IBL basketball team; and the **Baltimore Thunder** lacrosse team.

College lacrosse action is represented by the **Johns Hopkins Blue Jays,** who play at Homewood Field, Charles St. and University Pkwy., 410/235-6882.

If your dreams of recreation are filled with rows of numbers, try **Bingo World,** 4901 Belle Grove Rd., 800/992-9300. Games run seven nights a week, starting at 7:30 and 11 P.M., 1 A.M.

THE LITTLE BROTHER OF WAR

French Jesuit missionaries in Canada and upstate New York recorded accounts of lacrosse (loosely translated, "a game played with a curved stick and ball") being played by the Huron in the 1630s. Though different forms of the game existed at the time of European encroachment, lacrosse was played by indigenous peoples throughout the Great Lakes and eastern United States.

Lacrosse played a serious role in Native American culture. Its origins are rooted in legend, and the game itself was surrounded with ceremony. Equipment and players were ritualistically prepared by a shaman, and team selection and victory were often considered supernaturally controlled. The game was used to vent aggression and territorial disputes between tribes, and the rituals used to prepare the players were identical to those practiced in preparation for war; hence the Algonquin name, "Little Brother of War." Today, the game continues to be played by the Iroquois and tribes in the Southeast, and is often used for curative purposes.

The modern form of the game, using a three-foot-long shaft ending in a crook and large, flat, triangular surface of webbing, was adapted from the New England tribes. A ball is passed between team members (never touched by the hands) and moved toward a goal.

Fridays and Saturdays—only minutes from downtown. Call for free transportation.

PERFORMING ARTS

Baltimore Arena, 201 W. Baltimore St., 410/347-2020, hosts sporting events, Stars on Ice, Ringling Brothers and Barnum & Bailey Circus, WWE Wrestling, USHRA Motorsports events, and concerts.

Baltimore Center for the Performing Arts, 1 N. Charles St., 410/625-4230, is a nonprofit corporation dedicated to the presentation of theater, music, and dance in downtown Baltimore at the Morris A. Mechanic Theatre.

Music

The **Baltimore Opera Company,** 110 W. Mount Royal Ave., Ste. 306, 410/625-1600, produces fully staged grand operas featuring international singers, directors, and conductors at the **Lyric Opera House,** 128 W. Mount Royal Ave., a replica of Germany's Leipzig Music Hall. Operas are performed in the original language with English subtitles.

Meyerhoff Symphony Hall, 1212 Cathedral St., 410/783-8100, presents the internationally acclaimed **Baltimore Symphony Orchestra,** a world-renowned group of conductors and musicians. The orchestra offers a wide variety of classical, pops, and family concerts year-round.

Pier 6 Concert Pavilion, Pier 6, 410/625-3100, www.concerthotline.com, presents pop, jazz, and classical concerts out-of-doors.

Theater

The **Baltimore Theatre Alliance,** P.O. Box 5982, 410/342-4416, www.baltimoreperforms .org, is a nonprofit organization of more than 40 theaters, managers, producers, directors, artists, technicians, and theatergoers dedicated to supporting and promoting theater in the greater Baltimore area. They're a great resource for the latest theater news.

Center Stage, 700 N. Calvert St., 410/685-3200, is the State Theater of Maryland and considered one of the top 10 regional theaters in the country.

Maryland Stage Company, 1000 Hilltop Circle, 410/455-3529, is the city's premiere professional summer theater.

The Vagabond Players, 806 S. Broadway, 410/563-9135 presents Broadway plays such as *Death of a Salesman* and *Prelude to a Kiss* in Fell's Point.

NIGHTLIFE

Baltimore has an active party scene. The inner harbor hotels and bars are always hopping at night, and tend to be easy, safe destinations. Here are a few that stand out, plus some out-of-the-way places.

Pubs and Bars

The **Owl Bar** in the Belvedere Hotel, 1 E. Chase St., 410/347-0888, is a cool place to have a drink. The food's good too. **Capitol City Brewing Company,** 301 S. Light St., #93 Light Street Pavilion, 410/539-7468, has brews and food, and a great view of the harbor.

The Wharf Rat at Camden Yards, 206 W. Pratt St., 410/244-8900, is a friendly English-style pub with full-service dining and an exhibition brewery. The Rat offers tastings and tours daily until 7 P.M.

Buddie's Pub and Jazz Club, 313 N. Charles St., 410/332-4200, is a classic neighborhood pub, owned by the same family since 1986. They serve food, and offer jazz on the weekends.

White Cat Tavern, 110 S. Eutaw St., 410/962-0202, is a cozy bar/lounge. It's in the Marriott Inner Harbor across from Oriole Park at Pratt and Eutaw Streets.

Michener's, at the Sheraton, 7032 Elm Rd., 410/859-3300, serves pub food in an elegant atmosphere.

Three hotel bars offer quieter alternatives: **Celebrities Lounge,** Tremont Hotel, 8 E. Pleasant St., 410/576-1200; **The Lobby Bar,** Radisson Plaza Lord Baltimore, 20 W. Baltimore St., 410/539-8400; and my favorite, the **Explorer's Lounge,** in the Harbor Court Hotel, 550 Light St., 410/234-0550. It has hand-painted African murals, aged cognacs, and live jazz.

A couple of neighborhood bars offer different atmospheres. **Claddagh Pub,** 2918 O'Donnell St., Canton, 410/522-4220, is an occasionally rowdy neighborhood Irish bar.

Mother's, 1113 S. Charles St., Federal Hill, 410/244-8686, serves food as well as drink. It's open to the street, so the bar is a great place for people-watching and meeting.

The **Latin Palace,** 509 S. Broadway St., Fell's Point, 410/522-6700, plays hot rhythms from south of the border, plus a variety of other music.

The best dance club in town is reputed to be the **Paradox,** 1310 Russell St., 410/837-9110, www.thedox.com, not only for its roomy dance floors and retro look, but also for its mix of gay, straight, black, white, etc.

The small but mighty **Talking Head,** 917 Cathedral St., no phone, talkingheadclub@ yahoo.com, is gaining a reputation as a hip place to hear live rock and roll.

North of town, **The Martini Bar,** in the Holiday Inn, 2004 Greenspring Dr., Timonium, 410/252-7373, offers a suave piano player during its Friday happy hour.

Comedy

The **Comedy Factory,** 36 Light St., 410/752-4189, above Burke's Café, features shows on Thursday at 8:30 P.M., and Friday and Saturday at 8:30 and 10:30 P.M. There's a one-drink minimum; call for reservations and lineup. The **Improv Power Plant Live,** 34 Market Place, 410/727-8500, www.improv.com, showcases big names like Margaret Cho and Gary Owen.

SHOPPING

Antiques

Antique Row, 800 block of N. Howard Street, is a loose compendium of dealers with shops along the street. Most dealers carry an eclectic mix of goods, and many are of exceptional quality; this has been the center of Baltimore's antiques trade for a century. One, **Cross Keys Antiques,** 801 N. Howard, is a good (if somewhat pricey) resource for European furniture, paintings, chandeliers, accessories, and garden furniture from the 17th through the 20th centuries.

More than 40 dealers display their wares in

quaint antique shops and multi-dealer emporiums on the streets of **Fell's Point.**

The **Antique Center at Federal Hill,** Key Highway and E. Cross Street, is a renovated industrial building that houses 35 dealers of upscale antiques and fine art.

Antique Warehouse, 1300 Jackson St. at Key Highway, also shows the wares of 35 dealers.

Another Period in Time, 1708-1710 Fleet St., offers the collections of 14 dealers: clocks, lamps, jewelry, paintings, coins, furniture, advertising material, and collectibles.

Malls

Towson Town Center, 825 Dulaney Valley Rd., U.S. 695 exit 27A, is the biggest shopping destination close to the city. It has 200 retailers including Hecht's, Nordstrom, and Nordstrom Rack.

Harborplace and the Gallery at Harborplace are shopping/eating extravaganzas. Harborplace (www.harborplace.com) consists of a series of buildings on the water at Light and Pratt Streets, and the Gallery is on Pratt Street between Calvert and South Streets. The shopping areas are made up of more than 100 dealers such as Banana Republic, Coach Store, Godiva Chocolatier, and more, and there are dozens of eatery/snack shops (see Food, below) and 16 sit-down restaurants and cafés (Capitol City Brewing Co., J. Paul's, Phillips Seafood Buffet, and more). It is possible to spend an entire week in Baltimore and never leave this three-block area, but hey, is that what you came for?

Specialty Shops

A great "only in Baltimore," **Hometown Girl,** 1005 W. 36th St., 410/662-4438, in the Hampden neighborhood features all things Baltimorean, from videos to painted screens. One T-shirt is printed with Balmerese translations of ordinary English phrases. The store features a "Honfest" in June.

For unregenerate tobacco fans, **Fader's of Baltimore,** 12 S. Calvert St., www.faderstobac.com, is a necessary pleasure. It stocks premium cigars, pipes, tobacco, and accessories, and the downtown location has an English-style pub and a conference/reception area.

A People United, 516 N.Charles St., is Baltimore's favorite place to pick up global artifacts and Asian furniture. Nearby, **Nouveau,** 519 N. Charles St., www.nouveaubaltimore.com, features contemporary goods for the home (there's another, even larger shop in Canton, at 2400 Boston St.).

A fun place to shop for a unique gift, **2910 on the Square,** 2910 O'Donnel St., in Canton, has an ever-changing panoply of personal and home goods. While in Canton, stop at **Chesapeake Wine Company,** 2400 Boston St. in the Can Company, 410/522-4556, www.chesapeakewine.com. The tasting bar is the best in the city, and you can pick up snacks to enjoy at the deli in front.

For booklovers, the **Ivy Bookshop,** 6080 Falls Rd., www.ivybookshop.com, is an independent that offers staff recommendations with a literary bent, and **Normals,** 425 E. 31st, www.normals.com, has an exceptional collection of used books and music.

Food and Produce Markets

Baltimore has a long history of local public markets. The following are very visitor-friendly and are all good places to pick up fresh food or takeaway items.

The "World-Famous" **Lexington Market,** 400 W. Lexington St., www.lexingtonmarket.com, was established in 1782, and is America's oldest continuously operating market. There are at least 140 reasons to go there (there are that many shops and food stalls), not the least of which is **Faidley Seafood** (see Food, below).

Among the other produce and take-away stalls at the Lexington are purveyors of meats, fresh fruits and vegetables, candies, pastries—just about

anything you'd want to eat, and all at good prices. The market also features live entertainment on Saturdays—I saw *Part Harmony* when I was there, a local a cappella group sweeter than the cookies that surrounded them. The market is open Mon.–Sat. 8:30 A.M.–6 P.M.

The **Broadway Market,** Broadway and Fleet Streets, in Fell's Point, is nearly as old as Lexington, but much smaller, and more of a neighborhood place. There are about 20 food stalls, and a very popular diner counter where Fell's Point locals drop by for eggs and toast.

The **Cross Street Market** at Cross and Charles Streets in Federal Hill is another smaller neighborhood market with roughly 20 purveyors; the place really hops on Friday nights when locals gather at **Nichiban,** a sushi bar in the back (see Food, below).

Trinacria's Grocery, 406 N. Pace St., is one of those places that would be easy to overlook if you didn't know about it. This little store, packed full of fine Italian imported goods and wines, supplies a number of restaurants in Little Italy. It also have good, inexpensive deli items.

A true "open-air market," the **Baltimore Farmer's Market** operates on Sunday mornings early June–Dec. from 8 A.M. until everything is sold out; it's in the shadow of the Jones Falls Expressway at Holliday and Saratoga Streets. Call 410/837-4636 for specific days and times. The **32nd St. Farmer's Market,** 400 block of E. 32nd Street, is a local favorite; it's open Saturday 7 A.M.–noon June–November. The **Market at the Can,** at the renovated Can Company building (shops, restaurants, etc.), 2400 Boston St., Canton, 410/558-0525, www.thecancompany.com, takes place every Saturday 9 A.M.–1 P.M. June–December.

Accommodations and Food

ACCOMMODATIONS

Like most big cities, there are a few B&Bs, but lodgings in Baltimore tend to be hotels on the expensive side. Most lodgings, especially hotels, are flexible about rates—meaning if they have too many rooms available they may be willing to drop prices, and conversely, will raise prices if room space is at a premium. Prices seldom change if you've booked the room in advance, although last-minute arrivals can sometimes find bargains (or no room at the inn). Rates vary by season (usually higher in summer), capacity, and day of the week. The following are a sampling of what's available, with least expensive alternatives first.

Uptown

The **Peabody Court—A Clarion Hotel,** 612 Cathedral St., 410/727-7101 or 800/292-5500, www.peabodycourt.snbhotels.com, is in a great location, on the west side of Mt. Vernon Square park. The narrow park surrounds the original Washington Monument and abuts the Walters Museum and the Peabody Institute. The hotel—Baltimore's oldest and best known—has a small, elegant lobby with a six-foot Baccarat chandelier and an in-house restaurant and bar, George's on Mt. Vernon Square (see below). All of the 103 rooms and the Presidential Suite have been updated, and all have modern accoutrements and are very clean and pleasant. The Peabody Court has 24-hour valet parking for $18 for overnight guests and $10 for daily valet parking (the going rate). Standard room rates range $100–170; call for suite rates. For more information on the Mt. Vernon area, visit the Mt. Vernon Cultural District website at www.mvcd.org.

The **Inn at Government House,** 1125 N. Calvert, 410/539-0566, is a refurbished late-19th-century Victorian in the shabby-genteel Belvedere neighborhood. The inn is owned by the city of Baltimore. All 19 rooms have baths and small refrigerators. Rates range $125–145, and include a continental breakfast and free parking.

The **Inn at the Colonnade,** 4 W. University Pkwy., 410/235-5400, is an elegant hotel near Johns Hopkins. It looks like it would cost a great deal more, considering the neighborhood and the fact that it has all the amenities: indoor pool, sun decks, exercise room. The rates range $139–300.

Downtown

The **Radisson Plaza Lord Baltimore,** 20 W. Baltimore St. (at Hanover), 410/539-8400 or 800/333-3333 (reservations), www.radisson.com/lordbaltimore, is in the middle of downtown Baltimore and comes with an illustrious history. The Hilton was a makeover of one of Baltimore's most prestigious hotels, the Lord Baltimore, built in 1928 ("A Radio in Every Room," declared the *Baltimore Sun* newspaper). Over the years, the hotel enhanced its decor with a mural of the growth of the city of Baltimore in the main ballroom, and has hosted a raft of political leaders, including Reverend Martin Luther King Jr. In 1985, the hotel opened under the Hilton gravure, retaining the Italian Renaissance design, the immense lobby with more than 100 coffered plaster panels, and the murals. Mercifully, they scrapped the tiny rooms, making one out of every two. As a result, the airy, elegant rooms are more than comfortable ($135–235), and the largest suites have kitchenettes and two-plus bedrooms ($800–1,200). There's a concierge level available for an additional $30 that features continental breakfast and snacks. The Lord Baltimore Grill (see Food, below) is on the premises.

Canton

Debbie and David Schwartz renovated an old Canton bordello into the sleek and friendly **Inn at 2920,** 2920 Elliott St., 410/342-4450, www.theinnat2920.com. David, a former corporate chef for a major hotel chain, rustles up a spectacular breakfast from fresh local produce (special dietary needs are welcomed)—a perfect addition to the all-natural theme in decor and accoutrements. The inn was designed to be as allergen-free as possible, right down to

BALTIMORE

BALTIMORE

DOWNTOWN BALTIMORE FOOD AND LODGING

BRASS ELEPHANT ▼

▼AKBAR

DONNA'S HELMAND
▼ ▼| ST.

MADISON

MONUMENT ST.

PEABODY COURT
HOTEL/GEORGE'S
CENTRE   ST.

83

FRANKLIN

KAWASAKI
▼ ST.

40

▼ TRINACRIA'S
GROCERY

MULBERRY

BAN THAI   ST.

40

ST.   ST.   ST.   ST.

▼MARTICK'S

MASON MARCONI▼

SARATOGA

ST.   ST.   ST.

HOLLYWOOD
ST.   ▼

THE WOMAN'S INDUSTRIAL
EXCHANGE

BUDDIE'S PUB AND ▼
JAZZ CLUB

FAYETTE

ST.

BALTIMORE

LORD BALTIMORE
GRILL
▼   ST.

RADISSON PLAZA/LORD
BALTIMORE GRILL ●

BURKE'S CAFÉ/ ▼
THE COMEDY FACTORY

FADER'S OF BALTIMORE ▼
▼ WERNER'S DINER

GREENE   PACA   EUTAW   HOWARD

LOMBARD

SAINT PAUL   CALVERT

CAFÉ BOMBAY ▼

ST.

MARRIOTT/WHITE ●
CAT TAVERN

PRATT

LIGHT ST.

CHARLES

HARBORPLACE

▼ THE WHARF RAT AT
CAMDEN YARDS

CONWAY   ST.

Inner
Harbor

WASHINGTON   ST.

ORIOLE PARK AT
CAMDEN YARDS

HYATT REGENCY
ON THE INNER HARBOR/ ●
BISTRO 300/PISCES

LEE   ST.

395

HARBOUR COURT
HOTEL/BRIGHTON'S/ ●
HAMPTON'S

KEY

ONE WORLD CAFÉ ▼ ● SCARBOROUGH FAIR B&B

BANJARA▼

BANJARA

CAFÉ MANET/
BANDALOOPS▼

REGI'S
TEN OH
▼ SIX

Federal
Hill

To
Bicycle▼

BALTIMORE

45

147

MADISON

ST.

MONUMENT

ST.

ST.

ST.

40

ORLEANS

ST.

ST.

ST.

ALT 40

AVE.

FAYETTE

BALTIMORE

ST.

WEISS DELI

LOMBARD

ST.

ST.

ATTMAN'S AUTHENTIC
NEW YORK–STYLE DELI

ST.

PRATT

BALTIMORE
BREWING CO.

OBRYCKI'S

BROADWAY

WOLFE

WASHINGTON

GAY
PL.

MARKET

DA MIMMO

CAESAR'S DEN

To Greektown,
Highlandtown,
and Inn at 2920

ESPN ZONE

VACCARO'S
PASTRIES

HARD ROCK CAFÉ

RASOI

ALDO'S

EASTERN

ST.

SABATINO'S

LATIN PALACE

FLEET

ST.

DELLA
NOTTE

CENTRAL

EDEN

ALICEANNA

LIQUID
EARTH

PIERPOINT

ANN

ST.

Little Italy

THE NILE CAFÉ

CELIE'S WATERFRONT
B&B

Federal

JOHN STEVEN
LTD.

HWY.

RUSTY
SCUPPER

JOY AMERICA CAFÉ

DEAD END
SALOON

Hill

Northwest

Fell's Point

Park

Harbor

0   0.25 mi

0   0.25 km

© AVALON TRAVEL PUBLISHING, INC.

the filtered air—but the three guest rooms, all with private bath, are far from sterile. Vintage pieces mix with earth colors, contemporary furniture, and artwork from local artists. Guests do have to climb stairs, but parking is free and plentiful, and good restaurants and bars are within easy walking distance. Rates range $140–225 per night.

Fell's Point

It would be easy to miss the front door of **Celie's Waterfront Bed & Breakfast,** 1714 Thames St., 410/522-2323 or 800/432-0184, www.bbonline.com/md/celies, tucked as it is between shops, cafés, and watering holes on one of Fell's Point's main streets—it's actually across from the gloriously over-decorated police station that held a starring role on the television series *Homicide.* Celie's is notable for two things—heavy security (no surprise there), and access to a satellite system that will either have you bopping while you iron (audio music channels) or watching TV programs you never thought you'd see (*I Love Lucy* meets the pansexual channel). Fell's Point is a delightful little town, full of shops and cafés; and if you're into partying late, Fell's Point is the place—and Celie's is a grateful short stagger from anyplace in town. The seven guest rooms are fully equipped with all the amenities, and are decorated in Baltimore eclectic. Some of the guest rooms have fireplaces, others have whirlpool tubs, private balconies, or harbor views; one room is completely handicap-accessible. All have private baths. Overnight guests are treated to a continental breakfast in the morning, served in a dining room that opens onto a small garden. Rooms run $139–210.

Inner Harbor

Hyatt Regency on the Inner Harbor is the ideal location for visitors who plan to spend most of their time in the area. Its location, at 300 Light St., 410/528-1234 or 800/233-1234, makes it one of the primary hotels on the water. It offers plenty of amenities, including a fully equipped exercise facility, outdoor pool, sauna, tennis courts, and jogging path. It's big: 486 guest rooms, including 25 suites, two restaurants (see Food,

below), and two lounges, and it's popular, so book well ahead. Like most Hyatts, this one has a six-story glassed-in atrium and glass elevators. The views, even from the back rooms, are spectacular. The Hyatt has a club level, for an extra charge, that includes continental breakfast and evening hors d'oeuvres and cocktail service. Guest rooms range $170–300, and suites are in the $400–1,400 range.

Leave the cut-offs at home if you're planning on staying at the **Harbor Court Hotel,** 550 Light St., 410/234-0550 or 800/824-0076. This place exudes serious glamour. Besides being the venue for two of the best restaurants in town, Hampton's and Brighton's, this hotel has won so many awards, it's embarrassing: #11 Hotel in the United States and #75 Best Destination in the World, "The Gold List" Best Places to Stay (all from *Condé Nast Traveler*); Four Diamond Awards from AAA and Mobil Travel Guide; Best in Baltimore, Zagat, etc. But is it really that good? Oh, yes. Rumor has it that oil sheiks have been known to reserve entire floors for their families when coming for various treatments at Johns Hopkins—apparently the big and beautiful rooms just aren't big enough. The rumor is probably close to truth. Among the available TV channels is a very modest version of MTV in Arabic (and you can watch it in the bathroom—all the rooms are equipped with a TV set if bathing bores you).

Harbor Court aims for a grand English country house look, complete with swimming pool, tennis courts, a croquet court, and a state-of-the-art fitness center. Service is whisper-quiet and as charming as it gets; parking is available by valet. There's a large multilanguage library off the lobby, a café, and a lounge with an African explorer theme. Rooms with a city or courtyard view range $195–330, with a harbor view $210–360. Suites are far more (a harborview suite is around $655).

Federal Hill

Scarborough Fair B&B, 1 E. Montgomery St., 410/837-0010, www.scarborough-fair.com, is my favorite B&B in the harbor area, since it's near everything and the rooms in the Georgian-style brick building are a home-away-from-home. That's quite a statement considering the building was modified by innkeepers Ellen and Ashley Scarborough from offices into six tastefully furnished guest rooms (all have private baths). Four of the rooms have working fireplaces, and two have whirlpool tubs. In the dining room, a light tea is served in the afternoon, and a full breakfast in the morning; there's a library on all things Maryland, too. The Scarboroughs are experts on the local area (especially restaurants), and they offer the most precious of all commodities, parking, at no extra charge. Rates range $149–189.

FOOD

It won't take long to discover that Baltimore is Food Central. I ate my way through town, from stand-up counters to the last word in elegant. You can get very, very fat here; everybody serves crab cakes, which, to my infinite despair, are not a diet food. The following restaurants—a sampling of the extraordinary variety and price range available—are listed by neighborhood, then by type of food, with the least expensive first. Restaurants can come and go with the tide; most of these have had a little staying power.

Uptown

As one would expect of an area heavily populated by college students, the streets that surround the campus are a hotbed of international cheap eats, plus a couple of elegant places with exceptional food.

Café Hon, 1002 W. 36th St., 410/243-1230, is at a neighborhood crossroads and serves meatloaf, burgers, roast beef with mashed potatoes, and all the other comforts of home. It's open for breakfast and lunch Mon.–Fri., dinner every day, and brunch Sat.–Sun. Entrées average $9.

Tamber's, 3327 St. Paul St., 410/243-0383, is an old-fashioned diner with the usual burgers and malts, but the owners have snuck a few Indian items onto the menu to broaden your horizons—aficionados claim it's the best Indian food in town. It's open Mon.–Thurs. 9 A.M.–10 P.M., Fri.–Sat. 9 A.M.–11 P.M., Sunday 9 A.M.–9 P.M. Prices average $10.

Gertrude's, 10 Art Museum Dr., in the Baltimore Museum of Art, 410/889-3399, is the brainchild of TV celebrity John Shields, Mr. Maryland Cooking himself—in fact, you can catch him buzzing around the restaurant when off-duty from his TV show. The food can range from adequate to great (seafood is a specialty), and the setting couldn't be more beautiful—big windows face one of the museum's sculpture gardens, and patrons vie to dine alfresco in good weather. The restaurant's hours extend beyond the museum's; it's open for lunch and dinner Tues.–Sun. Sunday brunch is very popular, and reservations are recommended. Lunch entrées average $12, dinner about $22.

On any given day, **Polo Grill,** at the Colonnade Hotel, 4 W. University Pkwy., 410/235-5400, will be filled with well-dressed people, smacking their lips over meticulously prepared food. The menu, wine list, and service are all top-drawer, and the atmosphere is one of subdued privilege—it has the feel of a very genteel men's club, mercifully without the snobbery. There are a lot of father-son couples here (dads visiting the Johns Hopkins campus across the street). Wear your pearls, hon, and come for an always-elegant bit of lobster tail, boiled or fried; it's open for lunch and dinner Mon.–Sat., and Sunday brunch. Dinner entrées average $28.

The **Owl Bar** in the Belvedere Hotel, 1 E. Chase St., 410/347-0888, is a cool place to have lunch, a late dinner, or drinks any time. The bar has been around since the hotel opened in 1903, though the owls that are perched above the bar didn't appear until Colonel Consolvo, the bar's owner from 1917 to 1936, took over. Rumor was that the owl's eyes would blink when whiskey was available during Prohibition. These days, the fancy bar food (brick-oven pizzas, chicken Caesar, open-face prime rib sandwiches) are the draw, along with the romantic murals that grace the walls. Prices average $12 for lunch, $19 for dinner. The Owl is open every day for lunch, dinner, and late night (until midnight or 1 A.M.), plus brunch on Sunday.

Holy Frijoles!, 908 W. 36th St., 410/235-2326, does the Mexican thing in an informal and inexpensive (under $10) setting. Get lunch or dinner Tues.–Sun.

BALTIMORE

To Pimlico Race Course ↑

To Towson State University and Towson Town Center ↑

ROLAND AVE.

★ EVERGREEN

LN.

SPRING

COLD

▼ LOCO HOMBRE

KITTERY LN.

Hampden

FALLS

CHARLES ST.

ST. PAUL ST.

GREENMOUNT AVE.

UPTOWN BALTIMORE

To Cylburn Arboretum →

83

40TH ST.

41ST ST.

RD.

HICKORY

BEECH

UNIVERSITY

★ LACROSSE HALL OF FAME MUSEUM

● THE INN AT THE COLONNADE/ POLO GRILL

37TH ST.

■▼▲ HOMETOWN GIRL

CAFÉ HON ▼■

36TH ST.

▲ AMERICAN CAFE

JOHNS HOPKINS UNIVERSITY

AVE.

Roosevelt Park

▼ HOLY FRIJOLES

AVE.

Wyman

CHARLES ST.

PKWY.

34TH ST.

KESWICK RD.

WYMAN

Park

● HOMEWOOD HOUSE MUSEUM ★

TAMBER ▼

33RD ST.

ST.

→ THAI

45

Druid

33RD ST.

BALTIMORE MUSEUM OF ART ★ ▼ GERTRUDE'S

Hill

FALLS RD.

WYMAN

PARK DR.

31ST ST.

ST.

Park

29TH ST.

HUNTINGDON AVE.

28TH ST.

BARCLAY ST.

83

SISSON ST.

28TH

★ BALTIMORE ZOO

MARYLAND

CHARLES ST.

ST. PAUL

CALVERT

25TH ST.

NEW NO DA JI ■

■ CONSERVATORY

Druid Lake

24TH ST.

DRUID PARK LAKE DR.

23RD ST.

★ BALTIMORE STREETCAR MUSEUM

FALLS

21ST ST.

TERANGA ▼

AVE.

ST.

ST.

ST.

LOVELY LANE UNITED METHODIST CHURCH ■

ST.

1

NORTH AVE.

SWAN DR.

McCULLOH

DRUID HILL

1

RD.

MOUNT ROYAL AVE.

MONTREAL

83

LANVALE ST.

→ To Great Blacks in Wax

MARYLAND INSTITUTE COLLEGE OF ART ★

PENN STATION ■

45

ST. AVE.

LYRIC OPERA HOUSE ★

GREEK ORTHODOX CATHEDRAL OF THE ANNUNCIATION ★

PRESTON ST.

DOLPHIN ST.

MEYERHOFF SYMPHONY HALL ★

★ THE OWL BAR

BIDDLE ST.

SPIKE AND CHARLIE'S ▼

INN AT GOVERNMENT HALL ■

CHASE ST.

JUNIOR BLVD.

■ TALKING HEAD

■ CITY CAFÉ

BREWER'S ART

EAGER ST.

0 0.25 mi

0 0.25 km

MOON

© AVALON TRAVEL PUBLISHING, INC.

Loco Hombre, 413 W. Cold Spring Ln., 410/889-2233, is another place to roll your beans, though the menu offers a lot more than the usual tacos and burritos—they offer chicken mole plates and tapas, too. It's open Mon.–Thurs. and Sunday 11 A.M.–10 P.M., Fri.–Sat. 11 A.M.–11 P.M.; prices average $12.

New No Da Ji, 2501 N. Charles St., 410/235-4846, is best known for its huge buffet, and serves Chinese, Korean, and Japanese food. It's open Tues.–Sun. for lunch and dinner, and expect to pay around $12 for any entrée, cash only.

For something completely different, try **Teranga,** 20 W. 21st. St., 410/783-0780, a Senegalese restaurant. The national dish, baked bluefish, is a specialty, and prices average $10. It's open Tues.–Sat. 11:30 A.M.–3 P.M. and 5–9 P.M., Sunday 5–9 P.M.

Downtown/Charles Street

Many Baltimoreans refer to Charles Street as restaurant row, though some of the places mentioned here are a few blocks away. You can get anything you want, often at low prices. There are quite a few cafés—**City Café,** 1001 Cathedral St., **Donna's Coffee Bar and Café,** 2 W. Madison St., and **David & Dad's Café,** 334 N. Charles St., to name a few—that serve coffee and food, and an endless array of international restaurants. The following is a mere sampling of what's available.

Check out the Lexington Market for takeaway (see Shopping, above), especially **Faidley Seafood,** 410/727-4898. Several people told me that Faidley's had the best crab cakes in Baltimore (a pretty daunting challenge), but, after downing the backfin crab cake sandwich ($10), I'd have to say Faidley's has the best stand-up, take-out, and/or ship-anywhere crab cake in the city. And backfin is its second grade—all-lump, at $15, is the top of the line. They serve several kinds of seafood: crab, shrimp, trout, oysters, and more, in platters, assortments, and sandwiches, plus soups. The top price is $19; be prepared to wait in line. Faidley's is open Mon.–Wed. 9 A.M.–5 P.M., Thurs.–Sat. 9 A.M.–5:30 P.M.

George's on the Square, 101 W. Monument St. at the Peabody Court/Clarion Hotel, 410/727-1314, is making a comeback as a place to enjoy a good glass of wine, a grilled scallop salad ($10), or a sandwich (around $8). The setting is cozy; deep burgundy walls, hardwood floors, and original marble tabletops provide an elegant, casual dining experience. It's a taste of old Baltimore and is convenient to the Walters Art Museum. It's open daily for breakfast, lunch, and dinner.

One World Café, 904 S. Charles St., 410/234-0235, has coffees, teas, "small foods" (a bagel for less than $1), breakfast (waffles, eggs), "larger foods" (hummus, pasta salad, under $5), and big sandwiches, again under $5. It's open every day for breakfast, lunch, and dinner, and it's open until 1:30 A.M. Fri.–Sat.

There's always a diner, and the **Hollywood Diner,** 400 E. Saratoga St., 410/962-5379, caters to the breakfast and lunch crowd daily 6 A.M.–6 P.M. with a classic menu that includes some vegetarian dishes, all under $12. This is the place that was used in the 1982 film *Diner.*

Another diner of note is **Werner's,** 231 Redwood St., 410/752-3335, which also served as a backdrop for the Hollywood magic of *Tin Men* (1987) and *Liberty Heights* (1999). Breakfast, lunch, and dinner are served, Mon.–Fri. 7 A.M.–midnight; expect to pay less than $12.

Now here's a place! **The Woman's Industrial Exchange,** 333 N. Charles St., 410/685-4388, has a history as interesting as its name. After the Civil War, through the Depression, up to today, neighborhood ladies in need of a few dollars could sell their handiwork through the exchange without suffering the embarrassment of public penury. A shop still sells craftwork in the front (the hand-crocheted christening dresses and hand-sewn children's clothes are excellent buys both price- and quality-wise). In the back, a little restaurant serves chicken salad sandwiches, aspic, and bread pudding to generations of genteel ladies and neighborhood priests (expect to pay less than $10). The spic-and-span checkered-tile floor and blue-uniformed waitresses make this a Baltimore exclusive. It's open for breakfast and lunch Mon.–Fri.

Brewer's Art, 1106 N. Charles St., 410/547-6925, www.belgianbeer.com, draws a hip crowd to sample an international menu of beers along with grilled tuna salad and updated pub food. It's open for dinner ($18) Tues.–Sun.

Lord Baltimore Grill, in the Radisson Plaza Lord Baltimore, 20 W. Baltimore St., 410/539-8400, is cool and quiet, and just coming into its own as a fine restaurant. The menu is American, with an emphasis on steaks and chops for dinner. Breakfast, lunch ($9), and dinner (entrées $25) are available daily.

H. L. Mencken ate here (while grousing about Americans' lack of culture between bites): **Maison Marconi,** 106 W. Saratoga St., 410/727-9522, is often referred to as a "legendary local institution," a phrase that makes one question the good sense of eating there. Aw, put on your jacket (tie optional), and head for the black-and-white-striped awning; it's well worth it, especially considering the "old Baltimore" atmosphere and the reliable menu. Dinner entrées are around $26, lunch slightly less. A restaurant with rules is good for you. Lunch and dinner are served Tues.–Sat., no arrivals after 8 P.M. Tues.–Thurs., and 9 P.M. Fri.–Sat. No charge for the valet parking (a welcome touch in parking-challenged downtown).

The **Brass Elephant,** 924 N. Charles St., 410/547-8485, is another Baltimore favorite. Jack Elsby has been welcoming guests into his elegant townhouse since 1980. The food is contemporary Continental—duck farfalle, tea-smoked quail, filet mignon—and the wine list is quite good. The "tasting menu" is a satisfying choice if you can't decide on just one entrée. It's a bit dressy (jackets for gentlemen are appreciated, but not required). Prices hover in the $25 range.

Spike and Charlie's, corner of Preston and Cathedral Sts., 410/742-8144, was voted the "Best Place for Special Occasions" by *Baltimore Magazine* and has won *Wine Spectator*'s Award of Excellence in the past. Open for dinner Tues.–Sun.; prices average $29.

A hometown favorite with a French accent, **Martick's Restaurant Francais,** 214 Mulberry St., 410/752-5155, serves fabulous paté, bouillabaisse ($19), and chocolate bread pudding—it's a "Best Restaurant" winner from *City Paper,* citing consistently great food and reasonable prices. Martick's is open for dinner Tues.–Sat.

Akbar, 823 N. Charles St., 410/539-0944, serves an inexpensive north Indian lunch buffet and a full dinner daily; prices average $12 for entrées. It also features brunch on the weekends, and has another branch south of town in Columbia.

Ban Thai, 340 N. Charles St., 410/727-7971, is the place for Thai, with entrées around $10. It's open for lunch and dinner Mon.–Sat.

Helmand, 806 N. Charles St., 410/752-0311, created a market for Afghan cuisine, and remains popular, especially for its *kaddo borawni* (spiced pumpkin) and pastries. It's open for dinner daily, and entrées average $10.

One of my favorites, **Kawasaki,** 413 N. Charles St., 410/659-7600, offers wonderfully fresh sushi, plus a full Japanese menu. Traditional (floor) and Western seating is available. It's open for lunch Mon.–Fri. and dinner Mon.–Sat., and prices average $15 for a dinner selection. They have another location, the **Kawasaki Cafe,** 907 S. Ann St., 310/327-9400.

Inner Harbor

Stopping off for a snack or meal in the Inner Harbor poses no problem other than choice. All the restaurants listed are within a block or two of the water. There are several "name" chains in this area, and a few small but good surprises.

Looks like home to me: **Burke's Café,** 36 Light St., 410/752-4189, is an old-fashioned bar-restaurant that serves breakfast, lunch, and dinner every day—and it's open until 2 A.M. Think giant onion rings and pan-fried chicken ($10).

Bistro 300, on the mezzanine of the Hyatt, 300 Light St., 410/528-1234, serves breakfast, lunch, and dinner every day, with entrée prices ranging from under $13 up to $17. It also features "Cuisine Naturelle," a menu with calorie and nutritional breakdowns.

Harborplace on Light Street is a massive gathering of 40 eateries on two floors. The snack and take-away shops are open for lunch and dinner daily, and include the **Capitol City Brewing Company,** 410/539-7468, for brews and burgers ($14), and **Phillips,** 410/685-6600, an outpost of the Ocean City seafood restaurant ($15); there are places to sit, cafeteria-style. For a snack or light meal, there's enough variety here for everyone. Harborplace on Pratt Street has an assortment of sit-down restaurants; all are open daily for lunch and dinner.

The lights dim, and restaurant chatter ceases as the TV sets placed strategically throughout the **ESPN Zone,** 601 E. Pratt St., 410/685-3776, blare at eardrum-busting level with the intro to another "sports moment" (usually an interview with a power sports personality). This testosterone-drenched sports-theme restaurant caters to those who can't walk in the house without zapping on ESPN to check bowling scores. Mega-jocks and those who just like to watch will enjoy the constant sports reporting between the "moments"; it's possible to catch a soccer game in China, a tennis match at Wimbledon, and women's basketball from the local college simply by swiveling your head. The rest of us come for the great burgers and fries. The food is good, if the hyperactivity level doesn't bother you (kids *love* it). There's a floor full of video games upstairs (bring lots of change) and plenty of sports memorabilia to gawk at; it's open for lunch and dinner daily, and prices average $12.

If you'd rather boogie than bogey, there's always the **Hard Rock Café,** 410/347-7625, next door. Both of these places can be very busy, so make it an early lunch or dinner ($13–20).

Take the opportunity to try the seafood at **Pisces,** 300 Light St., 410/605-2835. You'll enjoy gazing out over the inner harbor while sipping an excellent martini and diving into your seared tuna. Fortunately, they've not gotten smug about the view and started serving mediocre food—the fresh seafood and service are both quite good. Pisces is open for dinner Tues.–Sun.; the lounge area features a raw bar and serves light fare 4–6 P.M. and 10 P.M.–midnight. Live jazz is played Fri.–Sat. 10 P.M.–1 A.M. Entrées average $28.

Brighton's, in the Harbor Court Hotel, 550 Light St., 410/234-0550, is the eatery that services hotel guests for daily breakfast, lunch, and dinner. Though this might relegate it to the ordinary in some hotels, expect a lot. The casual-dressy restaurant (a lot more relaxed than Hampton's, below) is four-star rated, and the food and service are excellent. Breakfast in this gracious room is especially pleasant—suited businesspeople take morning meetings here. Brighton's also serves a formal tea from 3–5 P.M. Breakfast and lunch can be had for $8–25, and dinner entrées average $29.

Hampton's, at the Harbor Court Hotel, 550 Light St., 410/234-0550, is a destination, four-star restaurant where the elite meet to sample innovative American cuisine and an extensive and sophisticated wine list. Elegant is the word. *Condé Nast Traveler* Reader's Poll named this restaurant number one in service and number two overall in the United States in the late '90s, and nothing has changed. They've won so many awards—from Mobil Travel Guide's Four-Star Distinction, *Traveler's* Top 50, AAA Four Diamond Award—it's a foregone conclusion that you will dine well. Specialties include lobster flamed in Laphroaig Scotch whiskey, and lamb with cilantro gremolata and Grand Marnier—each season brings a new menu. Main courses average $45, but the prix fixe is always popular; a four-course seafood menu is offered for $75–97, or a four-course vegetarian menu for $50–78 (the higher prices reflect wine selection). Hampton's is open for dinner Tues.–Sun. and serves Sunday brunch 10:30 A.M.–2:30 P.M.

If you're looking for something more exotic and less expensive, walk two blocks to 114 E. Lombard St.; **Café Bombay,** 410/539-2233, serves up Northern and Southern Indian dishes—its stuffed crepe-like *masala dosa* is a favorite. It's open for lunch and dinner daily ($8).

Little Italy

Baltimore has one of the most authentic and wonderful Italian districts of any American city. The neighborhood is delightful to walk around in, and the food is incredible! Little Italy is bordered on the north by the old Jewish district, so there are a few fine delis and a German hofbrau in the mix.

Sabatino's, 901 Fawn St., 410/727-9414, opened in 1955, and serves classic Italian dishes—spaghetti with meatballs, rigatoni with pesto—in massive quantities. Going away hungry is not an option. They make a side dish, spinach à la Ralph, that is a meal in itself, and so delicious you'll dream about it. Pastas average $13, meat and seafood entrées $18. Sabatino's has a huge menu and is open for lunch and dinner (until 3 A.M.) every day.

If Sabatino's is classic, **Aldo's,** 306 S. High St., 410/727-0700, is the Italy of Prada and Versace. The columned interior is as elegant as the tiny roast quail. The owner and executive chef, Aldo Vitale, designed much of the burnished, deeply carved woodwork in the foyer bar as well as the sophisticated menu. His handsome sons, Alessandro and Sergio, guide visitors through the wine list and suggest the freshest choices of the day. Aldo's is open for dinner daily, and the valet will park your car. Entrées average $25—have a little goat cheese salad (it's so fresh they must keep the goat in the cellar) and *limonata* (a potent lemon-flavored liqueur).

I'll admit it, I'm addicted to **Vaccaro's Pastries.** The original location, 222 Albemarle St., 410/685-4905, serves food as well as cakes, pies, cannoli (filled and unfilled), classic Italian pastries, and their own gelati (ice cream) and granita (sorbet). Vaccaro's makes serious, serious cookies, with enough almond paste to cause immediate girth expansion. They also have locations in Harborplace, Owings Mills, and the D.C. area.

Also recommended: **Caesar's Den,** 223 S. High St., 410/547-0820, for the black fettuccine with arugula, and grilled meats, open for lunch Mon.–Sat., dinner daily, $18; **Della Notte,** 801 Eastern Ave., 410/837-5500, for both innovative and traditional Italian (and parking!), lunch and dinner daily, $25; and **Da Mimmo,** 217 S. High St., 410/727-6876, famous for its three-hour-long dinners (lunch Mon.–Fri., dinner daily, $35). But it's impossible to get a bad meal anywhere in the area. . . .

Lombard Street, just north of Fell's Point, was the site of the first Jewish congregations in Baltimore well before the 1900s. Once a thriving neighborhood, the district has seen better times, but the two remaining delis keep the old food traditions alive.

Weiss Deli, 1127 E. Lombard St., 410/276-7910, "The Place with Real Good Taste," is a few feet away from the city's original temple. Fancy it's not, but piled-on pastrami doesn't get much cheaper. A butter-soaked bagel is less than a buck, and it's a good place to pick up cold cuts and picnic supplies ($6). It's open for breakfast and lunch, and has table seating and take-out.

Attman's Authentic New York–Style Delicatessen, 1019 E. Lombard St., 410/563-2666, has been around since 1915, and is still everyone's favorite place for corned beef, pastrami, and the infamous hot-dog-and-baloney sandwich. You can hang out in the kibbutz room over lunch and dinner every day; prices average $8.

Baltimore Brewing Company, 104 Albemarle St., 410/837-5000, is an unpretentious, spacious beer hall that serves German and pub-style food and award-winning house brews under the DeGroen's label. It's open for lunch and dinner every day. Expect to pay around $13 for an entrée.

Inexpensive and popular, **India Rasoi,** 411 S. High St., 410/385-4900, features a lunch buffet for $8 and dinner entrées that average $13 Mon.–Sat.

Fell's Point

This district is alive with pubs, bars, and small cafés in addition to some fancy restaurants.

A longtime resident of the city swore to me that **John Steven Ltd.,** 1800 Thames St., 410/327-5561, was the king of crab cakes. The menu is eclectic: Southwestern, sushi, and seafood. It's open daily for lunch and dinner, and keeps late hours for the Fell's Point party crowd. Lunch is around $25, dinner roughly $32.

Another established restaurant in the Point is Chef Nancy Longo's **Pierpoint,** 1822 Aliceanna St., 410/675-2080. The rumor is that she prepares James Beard's favorite bouillabaisse, and bends a few traditions by smoking her crab cakes (must be hard to keep lit) and serving barbecued duck egg rolls. The restaurant is open for lunch by reservation only Tues.–Fri. ($18), dinner Tues.–Sun. ($25 and up).

The **Dead End Saloon,** 935 Fell St., 410/732-3602, is a rock & roll sports bar; the testosterone gloom is tempered by cheerful plantings in front and bright light streaming in from the windows overlooking quiet Fell Street. It has a full bar, and lunch specials under $6 every day. It offers good pub food at reasonable prices, and a pleasant alternative to Fell's Point's more formal dining.

Obrycki's, 1727 E. Pratt St., 410/732-6399, www.obryckis.com, was recommended to me by the owner of an Italian restaurant as "the place we go when we don't want home cooking." A few blocks east of Little Italy and north of Fell's Point, it's a standard newsprint-on-the-tables crab house, serving steamed hardshells, crab cakes, crab soup, and crab marinara. Obrycki's is open for lunch and dinner daily in the summer; it's closed mid-November–mid-March, so call for hours. Prices are high, in the $28 range for dinner, and they have a kids' menu.

For something a touch more exotic, **The Nile Café Egyptian Kitchen & Oven,** 811 S. Broadway, 410/327-0005, offers Middle Eastern and Egyptian cuisine, and—for that Cleopatra/Marc Antony connection—a variety of pizzas. The prices are right, around $12. It serves lunch and dinner Mon.–Thurs. 11 A.M.–11 P.M., Fri.–Sat. 11 A.M.–midnight, Sunday noon–10 P.M.

Liquid Earth, 1626 Aliceanna St., 410/276-6606, is a deluxe juice bar that serves vegetarian and vegan sandwiches for lunch and dinner daily. Prices are all under $12.

East Baltimore/ Canton/Highlandtown

For Sunday brunch, a local favorite is **The Morning Edition Café,** 153 N. Patterson Park Ave., 410/732-5133. Cranberry-apple-walnut pancakes and strawberry-hazelnut French toast are a few examples of what's available. The café is open Friday 9 A.M.–2:30 P.M., Saturday 8 A.M.–3 P.M. and Sunday 9 A.M.–3 P.M.; prices range from $3–15.

Another brunch favorite is the **Blue Moon Café,** 1621 Aliceanna St., 410/522-3940. It serves big portions of the usual breakfast favorites, averaging $10—but try to come on a weekday, since this place is often packed on the weekends, with an hour wait.

Helen's Garden Restaurant, 2908 O'Donnell St., 410/276-2233, www.helensgarden.com, is a real neighborhood place, and you'll meet quite a few Cantonites over a bowl of fresh homemade

soup or a quesadilla platter if you sit at the friendly bar. The restaurant also has table seating, and an excellent wine selection. It's open for lunch and dinner Tuesday–Sunday, and prices average $12.

Nacho Mamas, 2940 O'Donnel St., 410/675-0898, is one of those bar/restaurants so full of character that it's both a nightlife spot and a place to chow down on Mexican fare. You can get Natty Boh here (National Bohemian—once made in Baltimore, now out of North Carolina, but the same fizzy, light brew), along with lunch and dinner daily. Entrées average $11; you can enjoy your tacos in the Elvis lounge, immersing yourself with images of the grand wiggler himself on the walls and overhead.

Tiburgi's, 900 S. Kenwood, 410/327-8100, is a sleek addition to the suburban side of Canton. The menu features pastas and other Italian favorites in the $8–25 range for dinner daily.

For a casual bar with great crack-'em-yourself crabs Thursday–Saturday, try **Kelly's,** 2106-08 Eastern Ave., 410/327-2312. Crabs run $27–40 a dozen.

Haussner's, 3242 Eastern Ave. (in Highlandtown), was a place everyone in Baltimore knew, and one of those restaurants that was so associated with the city, it's hard to believe that it's gone. William Haussner immigrated to America from Bavaria (where he trained as a master chef) and Frances Wilke came from Germany (where she studied voice and piano); they married in 1935, three weeks after they met. A year later, they moved William's thriving restaurant to Eastern Avenue. One of the most extraordinary things about Haussner's was its display of original art. The couple bought their first painting on their fifth wedding anniversary, and since then acquired nearly 500 paintings, including works by Rembrandt, Whistler, and Charlie Chaplin. Their taste ran strongly to romantic pictorials, so patrons were up to their eyeballs in puppies and rustic waifs. People used to say, "You haven't done Baltimore, hon, if you haven't eaten at Haussner's." It's sorely missed, right down to the giant ball of string in the basement.

But all is not lost in Highlandtown. **DiPasquale's Deli,** 3700 Gough St., 410/276-6787, serves up chicken parmesan, and hot and

FESTIVALS AND EVENTS

Baltimore's inner harbor (particularly Harborplace, 800/HARBOR-1) has continual entertainment and sponsors many events during the year. Since event contact numbers frequently change, get in touch with the city's tourism office at 410/837-4636, www.baltimore.org, for the latest, or try *Where Baltimore* magazine, www.where-baltimore.com, for their listings.

January
The **Masque Parade,** a New Year's spectacular, features giant papier-mâché puppets, marching bands, and dancers on the streets of downtown Baltimore. The harbor celebrates the winter season with an ice-carving competition, winter sports clinics, sled dog exhibitions, and children's carnival, among other activities. 800/282-6632.

March/April
First Thursdays on Charles Street (the 200–1300 blocks) features receptions from 5–8 P.M. in the area's many art galleries, plus art talks, events at the Walters Art Museum, outdoor music, and specials in the street's shops, restaurants, and theaters. March–June, 410/837-4636.

    Bunny Bonanzoo is one of the city's oldest and best-loved Eastertide traditions, featuring a bunny hop and egg hunt, among other activities, at the wonderful Baltimore Zoo. 410/366-5466.

    The **Harborplace Street Performers Auditions** take place mid- to late April in the Harborplace Amphitheatre—comedians, jugglers, and magicians perform to win a spot on the roster. 800/HARBOR-1.

May
The **Preakness,** second jewel in horse racing's Triple Crown, takes over the city in May. There's a parade with marching bands, floats, and equestrian units, and dozens of related events and parties. Call 410/837-3030 for information on the parade. The race is held at Pimlico Race Course, 410/542-9400.

    Another "only in Baltimore" event, the **Living American Flag Program,** features 4,000 grade-school kids who gather at Fort McHenry to re-create the first American flag with a huge mosaic of colored cards. A project of the National Flag Day Foundation, 410/563-3524, www.ubalt.edu/flagday.

cold subs that will take the chill off any winter day. Prices are around $8.

Greektown

This is the quintessential Greek neighborhood, with dozens of restaurants to prove it, in all price ranges. Not everything is Greek, however; one of the city's best Spanish restaurants is also in the neighborhood. The following are recommended: The **Acropolis,** 4718 Eastern Ave., 410/675-3384, serves lunch and dinner daily; dishes such as braised lamb and moussaka average $15.

    Ikaros, 4805 Eastern Ave., 410/633-3750, presents a mix of Greek and American dishes

for lunch and dinner, Wed.–Mon. Traditional dishes are served by a friendly staff; lunch averages $10, dinner $18. Just to give you some idea of Ikaros' staying power, it was voted Best Greek Restaurant for 18 consecutive years by the Baltimore *City Paper.*

    Samo's, 600 S. Oldham St., 410/675-5292, also in Greektown, is famous for its garlic-spiked leg of lamb ($15). Entrées average $11, cash and check only.

    Marbella, 4700 Eastern Ave., 410/522-5092, combines Spanish and Brazilian dishes with flair and occasionally provides a flamenco show on Saturday night. It's open for lunch Tues.–Fri., dinner Tues.–Sun. Prices average $13–25.

June/July

From June through September, the city hosts several weekend festivals celebrating its varied ethnic heritage. The festivals all feature food, music, and live entertainment, and include German, Ukrainian, Greek, and Latino cultures, among many others. 410/837-4636.

Artscape is Baltimore's annual festival of literary, performing, and visual arts, with readings and performances. Three stages showcase more than 150 performers, arts programs, and exhibitions. 410/396-4575.

September/October

The **Baltimore Book Festival** is held outdoors under tents in Mount Vernon Square. Browse among booksellers and publishers, attend storytelling and author signings, and enjoy crafts, refreshments, and entertainment. 800/282-6632.

Every year in October, the Lexington Market presents its **Chocolate Festival,** with the seductive bean in all forms. Tasting, music, games, and demonstrations round out the four-day celebration. 410/685-6169.

An event that sometimes also takes place in May, the **Blessing of Baltimore's Work Boats** features a boat parade on the inner harbor. 800/HARBOR-1.

November/December

The Cathedral of the Annunciation **Greek Festival** is a three-day celebration of all things Greek. The festival, held since 1972, is usually on a weekend in early November, and the food stalls are worth the trip. 410/727-1831.

The **Potters Guild of Baltimore** offers up wares from more than 40 potters in this annual November pre-holiday sale. 410/235-4884.

The city celebrates Turkey Day with a **Thanksgiving Day Parade** on Pratt Street with floats, marching bands, and good old Santa. 800/282-6632.

In December, another kind of procession takes place: the Baltimore **Lighted Boat Parade,** with more than 50 decorated boats and other pleasure craft participating. 800/HARBOR-1.

BALTIMORE

Federal Hill

Café Manet, 1020 S. Charles St., 410/837-7006, was named by several people as an excellent everyday restaurant, though one felt it was too brightly lit for a romantic tête-à-tête. The prices and variety might make up for romance: Chef Mario, who is rumored to have cooked for three years for Paul Prudhomme, creates Italian/French/Argentinean dishes that are under $14. Chicken Provençale, shepherd's pie, *pulpo à la gallega* (octopus), and a variety of pastas are on the menu. It's open for lunch and dinner, and desserts and a glass of house wine are both less than $5.

Bicycle, 1444 Light St., 410/234-1900, www .bicyclebistro.com, is one of the hottest restaurants in town, serving dinner Mon.–Sat. from a menu featuring squeaky-fresh seafood and vegetables. The Balinese mahi mahi and shrimp is seasoned in a garlic chile sauce, and comes with baby spinach baked in phyllo over shanghai noodles in creamy cilantro-walnut jalapeño pesto; complicated and delicious. Prices average $25 for entrées.

Regi's American Bistro, 1002 Light St., 410/ 539-7344, calls itself "your friendly neighborhood bistro" and serves a sophisticated menu of pastas, salads, soups, and sandwiches at decent prices (sandwiches average $10, entrées $19). This is the kind of place you could probably eat at every day and still like it—fortunately, they're open daily for lunch and dinner, and serve a popular brunch menu on Sat.–Sun. (call to make sure you can get in).

Banjara, 1019 S. Charles St., 410/752-1895, is a favorite among the locals for its excellent East Indian cuisine and reasonable prices. Curries, tandoori, and *biryanis* made with chicken, lamb, and seafood average $15, and there's an extensive vegetarian menu as well. In case none of those tempt you, they also serve pizza. Lunch and dinner Wed.–Mon.

Nichiban, in the Cross Street Market, Cross and Charles Streets, 410/837-0816, is a popular sushi bar that also serves full dinners. On weekend nights, this place is packed with locals kicking back with a tray of *tekka maki* and a cup of green tea. Lunch specials average $7, dinners $9–30, and rolls of sushi $4.

Ten Oh Six, 1006 Light St., 410/528-2146, is a popular hangout with a Thai-American menu. Dinners average $15.

Mother's Federal Hill Grille, 113 S. Charles St., 410/244-8686, is a hip bar with good, inexpensive breakfasts, sandwiches, soups, and salads. Entrées include pasta, beef, and, of course, crab and shrimp dishes. Sandwiches, etc., average $7, entrées $13. Mother's is known for its nightly specials, such as Thursday night steak and lobster for $21 (lobster for $12), and $10 entrees on Sunday. There's a small but good vegetarian selection, too. It's open Mon.–Fri. 11 A.M.–2 A.M., Sat.–Sun. 8 A.M.–2 A.M.

SoBo, 6-8 W. Cross St., 410/752-1518, is an informal place with informal food: chili, macaroni and cheese, burgers. The kids won't feel out of place here. It's open daily for lunch and dinner, and prices range $6–15.

The menu at **Corks,** 1026 S. Charles St., 410/752-3810, is designed from the wine up, according to chef Jerry Pellegrino. This upscale neighborhood restaurant features nouveau cuisine thoughtfully paired with one of the best wine lists in the city; all bottles are $11 over cost. The menu concentrates on seafood and meats, and entrées average $20–29. It's open daily for dinner only.

Also recommended: **Bandaloops,** 1024 S. Charles St., 410/727-1355, is where the beautiful people stop in for wine and cheese after work and a contemporary American menu for lunch and dinner. The bar is always open until 2 A.M., and the restaurant stays open late when the Ravens play; entrées average $16.

South Inner Harbor/Key Highway

The space that stretches from Federal Hill out to Fort McHenry offers an eclectic mix of eateries.

Rallo's, 838 E. Fort Ave. at Lawrence Street, 410/727-7067, is one of those places that's such a fixture that it's a water taxi stop. It's a tavern/diner that serves inexpensive breakfasts (under $5) and the kind of sandwiches that you can usually only get at home: braunschweiger, meatball, hot dogs, and Italian cold cuts, to name a few (around $4). Don't forget those vitamin-packed liver-and-onion entrées—as well as breaded pork chops, veal parmesan, and other old favorites ($9, includes two vegetables). It's open for breakfast, lunch, and dinner, daily.

One chain establishment that's very popular in the inner harbor is **Rusty Scupper,** 402 Key Hwy., 410/727-3678. The seafood is fresh, the wine list good (lots of California vintages), and the servings are reliably big (including the desserts— one helping of chocolate cake could serve five people). The view is one of the best in the inner harbor; happy hour is Mon.–Fri. 4–7 P.M., and the bar offers a beautiful view of lights around the water. It's open for lunch and dinner daily; lunch averages $14, dinners range $19–45.

The **Joy America Café,** 800 Key Hwy., in the American Visionary Art Museum (across from the Rusty Scupper), 410/244-6500, gives cuisine a new look, and an innovative twist on the ingredients, too. The silverware and plates are chosen for their amusement value, and the food pairings are fresh and unusual with a pan-Latin theme. The menu, written out in handmade "books," keeps with the museum's theme of enhancing the everyday with fun. It's open Tues.–Sun. for dinner, and prices average $21. Tapas are also available, from $9–15. Joy America is brought to you by the owners of Spike and Charlie's.

Walking into **Little Havana,** 1325 Key Hwy., 410/837-9903, www.littlehavana.com, is like stepping into an authentic Cuban restaurant nightclub. A bar in the middle of the large open room is surrounded by dark wood; immediately after entering, you're seized with the urge to light up a cigar and mambo over to one of the tall, dimly lit booths. Seafood, chicken, and other meats are prepared in the Cuban tropical manner: *pollo à la Castro,* chorizo Habana, and paella are on the menu. It's open for lunch and dinner, and has a late-night menu and open-air dining that overlooks the inner harbor when the weather is fine. Prices are in the $7–22 range.

Information and Services

INFORMATION

The **Baltimore Area Convention and Visitors Association,** 100 Light St., 12th Fl., Baltimore, MD 21202, 410/659-7300 or 800/282-6632 (General Visitor Information), www.baltimore .org, will send all the additional information you need and answer questions.

MEDIA

The daily newspaper in town is the ***Baltimore Sun,*** with day and evening editions. The ***Washington Post*** is also good for general news and information on the gateway area between Baltimore and the capital.

EW (Every Wednesday) and ***City Paper*** are free local entertainment and arts guides. The free ***Baltimore Alternative*** is aimed at gay and lesbian readers.

Baltimore Quickguide, www.cityspin.com/ baltimore, is a publication of the tourist bureau that gives pertinent visitor information in a nutshell. ***Where Baltimore*** is a competing publication that duplicates much of the basic information but also has interesting articles.

Radio station **WBAL** (1090 AM) is a news and weather station, and **WJHU** (88.1 FM) is an affiliate of National Public Radio.

PERSONAL SAFETY

Downtown Baltimore—a few blocks away from the inner harbor—can be raucous and a little scary for visitors at night (unless you're from New York City—in that case, you'll find it pretty tame). Paca and Howard Streets are filled with people hailing each other, laughter, and a nasty argument or two; chances are, if you're a stranger, it's probably a good idea to keep to the high-tourist-traffic areas. Though the downtown hotels encourage visitors to use their convenient (expensive) valet parking, street parking in well-lighted areas east of Charles Street remains reasonably safe (keep everything in the trunk).

Forty-five Downtown Public Safety Guides patrol the streets of Baltimore every day during daylight hours, serving as goodwill ambassadors and additional "eyes and ears" for the police. The guides are trained by representatives of the local hospitality industry to answer questions, give directions, and generally help visitors have a great experience while in town; they're also trained by the police to spot and report suspicious behavior. In addition, Baltimore offers local workers a Mon.–Fri. evening Safety Guide Escort Service in the 106-block core of downtown, Oct.–Apr. until 7:30 P.M. and May–Sept. until 10:30 P.M. If you would like someone to escort you to your car, bus, metro, or light rail stop, call a Downtown Safety Guide, 410/244-8778.

In other parts of the city that attract tourists, the worst you'll likely encounter is a panhandler. Much of Baltimore is residential, but the economic spread is vast—and it changes quickly. The west side especially has some pretty heavy neighborhoods. Baltimore has one of the lowest incidences of crimes against visitors in cities of similar size; however, if you feel uncomfortable, follow your instincts.

GETTING THERE

Baltimore/Washington Airport (BWI) is 10 miles south of town. Limousines, 410/859-7111 (about $28), and a somewhat unreliable shuttle (it sometimes takes an hour to make a 20-minute trip, and pickup at a specified time can be iffy),

800/258-3826 ($11–16), operate between the airport and downtown hotels. Taxis, 410/859-1100, are also available ($2.10 for the first mile, $1.20 for each additional mile—about $19 to the inner harbor).

The best deal by far from the airport to downtown is the **light rail**—only $1.35. Call 410/539-5000 or visit www.mtamaryland.com for schedules and stops.

The **Amtrak** train pulls into Baltimore at Penn Station from points east and west. Call 800/USA-RAIL (800/872-7725), or access the website at www.amtrak.com.

Greyhound Bus Terminals are at 210 W. Fayette St. and the intersection of I-95 and O'Donnell Street. Call 800/231-2222 for ticket and schedule information.

GETTING AROUND

On Land: BWI hosts most of the large rental car companies and a few smaller ones. Penn Station also has a few car rental booths, and some rental agencies will pick you up at other locations. Some of the companies available are Budget, 410/859-3820; Enterprise, 410/243-0252; Hertz, 410/850-7400 or 800/654-3131; and Thrifty, 410/859-4900.

Yellow Transportation, 410/727-7300, has been in charge of the city's taxicabs, buses, limousines, 21-passenger mini-coaches, vans, and trolleys since 1909. It also operates BWI's Shuttle Express transportation between BWI Airport and Baltimore's downtown area hotels.

In an effort to increase cabbies' knowledge of the city and personal service, each of Baltimore's 2,500 cabbies receives eight hours of hospitality training. Taxis charge $1.40 for the first .1 mile and $1 for each additional mile. Cab companies proliferate; some of the bigger ones are Diamond, 410/947-3333; Sun, 410/235-0300; and Yellow, 410/685-1212.

Baltimore's MTA (Mass Transit Administration) is responsible for buses, light rail, and the Metro subway system. Routes reach all parts of the town and outlying areas. Fares for each system are $1.35, exact change (commuter route fares depend on destination). A $3 one-day pass is good for unlimited use of all three systems. For route maps of all three systems, call 410/539-5000.

On Water: The Water Taxi, 410/563-3901 or 800/658-8947, is the best way to get around the inner harbor and places within walking distance of the bay. Parking fees downtown are stiff; a lot of people park in Fell's Point ($4 all day) or Canton Water Park (free) and take the water taxi from those stops downtown and back. The water taxi charges $5 for unlimited pick-ups all day; there are no tickets to carry. Captain Dennis, first mate Tom, or one of the other taxi pilots stamps your hand with a little picture of the boat. Thirteen boats serve 40 attractions. The fare also includes a Letter of Marque ticket that features dozens of discounts.

Central Maryland and the Capital Gateway

The new red houses spring like plants
In level rows
Of reddish herbage that bristles and slants
square shadows. . . .
Where hastening creatures pass intent
On their level way,
Threading like ants that can never relent
And have nothing to say.

D. H. Lawrence, "Flat Suburbs, S.W.,
In the Morning," 1916

Maryland's most populous area has more to offer the visitor than miles of suburbs. Much of the western part of this area—bordered by the meandering Potomac River—is rural. In the central and eastern portions, small towns are linked by high-speed freeways and narrow two-lane roads. Treasures dot this landscape like wildflowers in a field—easy to miss if you're not looking.

The state's capital, Annapolis, is one of the most historic and delightful political centers in America. The town has retained its Federal-era authenticity while enlarging its appeal through inviting shops, good restaurants, and the attractions of the U.S. Naval Academy. Another small town, Ellicott City, once a summer retreat for Baltimore's middle classes, remains a charming place for a getaway.

Of the counties that make up central Maryland—Anne Arundel, Howard, Montgomery, and Prince George's—only the latter two abut

© JOANNE MILLER

sailboat race on the Chesapeake

Washington, D.C. However, the history, energy, and wealth that radiate from the nation's capital spread far beyond its invisible borders. Fortunately for visitors, many government agencies do research and business in Maryland, providing low- or no-cost opportunities to see programs of national significance in action. The Beltsville Agricultural Research Center, NASA/Goddard Space Flight Visitor Center, and Patuxent Research Refuge/National Wildlife Visitor Center are among the facilities that offer information and activities for visitors. The U.S. government is the largest employer in Maryland, and Rockville and Bethesda are two of the most visited areas in the state. The road from Rockville to Washington, D.C., is heavily trafficked and lined with shopping centers and restaurants, suburban pleasures and pastimes. But there's history here as well, and within a short distance, the fields are heavy with winged creatures and delicate floating seeds in the summer, views of the broad Potomac in winter. Take time to explore.

Anne Arundel County

ANNAPOLIS AND ENVIRONS

Annapolis has the highest concentration of Georgian style buildings in the United States. In this "Athens of America," many of the homes were used in winter only—when government was in session. Largely responsible for the preservation of the town, the Historic Annapolis Foundation (HAF) began as an effort to stop developers from pulling down colonial era buildings in the 1950s. Properties were restored house-by-house with state and federal monies. The ongoing advisory group regulates everything visible from the street except the color of the houses (it's easy to pick out rebels in downtown Annapolis). In recent years, their function has shifted from regulation to education.

Don't expect a dour history tour—Annapolis, apart from being the state capital, is one of the liveliest cities around. Colonial buildings on the streets hold art galleries, fashionable shops, and dozens of restaurants. Two diverse seats of higher learning, the United States Naval Academy and St. John's College, provide more than a modicum of culture. The town's harbor and surrounding rivers teem with boats of all types. This is a fun place to visit, and a hard place to leave. The local free paper, *New Bay Times Weekly,* will keep you connected to the Chesapeake via the Web, www.bayweekly.com, long after you've left.

Historic Sites

Historic Annapolis Foundation (HAF), 410/267-7619, www.annapolis.org, maintains a number of properties, among them the **Shiplap House Museum,** 18 Pinkney St. Built in 1715, it's one of the oldest houses in Annapolis, and has been restored as an 18th-century house and inn. It's open Mon.–Fri. 2–4 P.M. Close by, the **Waterfront Warehouse,** 4 Pinkney St., displays a model of the Annapolis waterfront as it was in the 1750s, and is open 9 A.M.–5 P.M. Pinkney Street is a joy in itself—it takes little imagination to picture it as it was in its colonial days, since most of the row house fronts are reminiscent of the period.

The **William Paca House and Garden,** 186 Prince George St., 410/263-5553, completed in 1765, was the home of a three-term governor of Maryland and signer of the Declaration of Independence. The manor house and formal two-acre pleasure garden are restored and furnished to reflect the lives and interests of the attorney-patriot Paca, his family, his household (which included slaves), and his community. The house was all but obliterated when a hotel, Carvel Hall, was built around it and on top of the gardens in the early 20th century. After the hotel was dismantled, the original structure was lovingly restored. Only the stone boundaries of the gardens remained, under nine feet of landfill; they were brought back to life after restorers studied a portrait of Paca by Charles Willson Peale that detailed the garden and its two-story summerhouse in the background. The restoration with its Chinese Chippendale motifs inside and out is masterful, and the gardens are a period-authentic delight. The house is open

Pinkney Street, Annapolis

© JOANNE MILLER

to return freed slaves to Africa. The house features exhibits, tours, living history performances, and special events related to Maryland's 18th-century heritage. Hours vary; so call in advance, 410/269-1737. Admission is $5.

The **Hammond-Harwood House,** 19 Maryland Ave., 410/263-4683, built in 1774, retains more than 90 percent of its original building materials, and was considered the finest example of Georgian architecture in colonial America. This building is deemed to be the masterwork of architect William Buckland, notable for its level of detail and ornately carved interior and exterior moldings. The house is furnished with mid-18th-century pieces and fine art, including a collection of portraits by the Peale family. Hours are Jan.–Feb., Sat.–Sun. noon–4 P.M., Mar.–Apr. and Nov.–Dec., daily noon–4 P.M., May–Oct. daily noon–5 P.M. Guided tours take place on the hour. Admission is $6.

The **Maryland State House,** 91 State Circle, 410/974-3400, is the oldest state capitol in continuous legislative use. From November 26, 1782, to August 13, 1784, it served as the nation's capital and meeting place for the Continental Congress; the Treaty of Paris was ratified here in 1784, ending the Revolutionary War. Exhibits and displays chronicle Maryland history, and one room is devoted to a mural of General George Washington resigning his commission as Commander in Chief of the Continental Army. Hoping to retire from public life, he emerged six years later as president. The walls are hung with several portraits by Charles Willson Peale, including one of William Pitt, the English statesman who inspired early colonials to win back the forks of the Ohio (modern Pittsburgh) from the French during the French and Indian War. The State House is open daily 9 A.M.–5 P.M., with 30-minute tours at 11 A.M. and 3 P.M. Free. Photo ID is required to enter the State House, and all bags will be checked.

U.S. Naval Academy (USNA)

Established in 1845, the USNA, 52 King George St., 410/263-6933, www.navyonline.com, is the undergraduate college of the United States Navy. Like all top colleges, the USNA accepts only

Mon.–Sat. 10 A.M.–5 P.M., Sun. noon–4 P.M. The garden is open until 5 P.M. Apr.–Oct. Admission is $7.

The **Charles Carroll House,** 107 Duke of Gloucester St., 410/269-1737, is a restoration in progress, original home of three generations of Carrolls, including Charles Carroll the Settler, first Attorney General of Maryland, his son, Charles Carroll of Annapolis, and his grandson, Charles Carroll of Carrollton, signer of the Declaration of Independence (see the special topic "Those Confusing Carrolls" in the Baltimore chapter). Maryland is the only colonial state in America that has preserved all of the homes of its signers of the Declaration—and all four of them are in Annapolis. Three of them—the Chase-Lloyd House, William Paca House, and the Charles Carroll House—are open to the public for tours. Charles Carroll of Carrollton was considered the wealthiest man and the largest slaveholder in the colonies at the time of the Revolution; in 1828, he became president of the American Colonization Society, which sought

the academic cream of the crop of high school students, who must also demonstrate physical prowess—fitness activities take up a minimum of two hours every day, in addition to a full academic course load. Polar explorer Rear Admiral Richard Byrd (class of 1912) was captain of the 1910 men's gymnastic team, and football player Roger Staubach (class of 1965) was a Heisman trophy winner before he turned pro. The class of 1980 was the first to accept women, and by 1998, 55 had graduated. This four-year college offers 19 majors, covers all costs, and pays a stipend to students. Graduates become Navy Ensigns or Marine Corps second lieutenants, and are required to serve for five years.

Guided walking tours of the academy are offered June–Labor Day, Mon.–Sat. 9:30 A.M.–3 P.M. and Sunday 12:30–3 P.M.; spring and fall: Mon.–Fri. 10 A.M.–3 P.M., Saturday 9:30 A.M.–3 P.M., and Sunday 12:15–3 P.M.; Dec.–Mar. Mon.–Fri. 10 A.M.–2:30 P.M., Saturday 9:30 A.M.–2:30 P.M. and Sunday 12:30–2:30 P.M. Tours cost $6.50 for adults, less for seniors and students, and begin at the **Armel-Leftwich Visitor Center,** Gate 1, King George Street, 410/263-6933. The visitor center displays *Freedom 7,* the space capsule piloted by Rear Admiral Alan Shepard (class of 1945), and interactive exhibits that feature the history, requirements, and opportunities the academy offers. An excellent gift shop gives visitors the chance to purchase Navy- and Marine-logo-emblazoned merchandise while listening to tapes of the Navy band thumping out military marches.

Campus attractions include **Halsey Field House and Lejeune Physical Education Center,** two of several facilities used by midshipmen (students) for sports and physical training. Inside are an Olympic-size pool, diving complex, wrestling loft, and weight-training/conditioning area. The Athletic Hall of Fame, a collection of photographs of notable sportsmen and women, is on the second floor of Lejeune.

The Navy chapel and crypt of John Paul Jones, 410/263-3601, are must-sees. The chapel is more like a cathedral—soaring Tiffany windows soften the light, and the walls support carvings of ships, representing God watching over sailors. The public is invited to worship Sunday

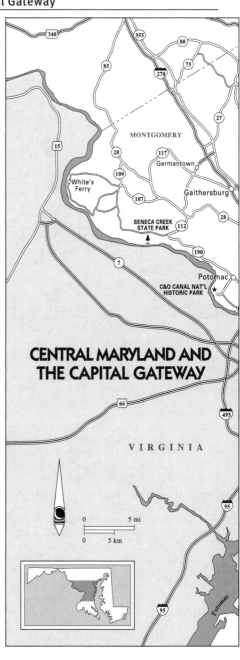

CENTRAL MARYLAND AND THE CAPITAL GATEWAY

CENTRAL MARYLAND

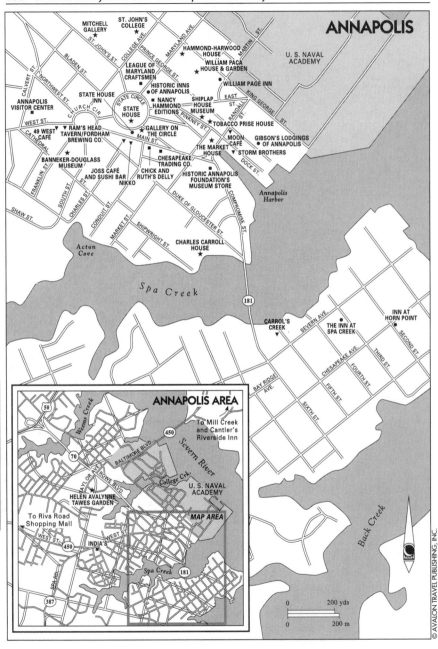

morning; Catholic services are held at 9 A.M., Protestant at 11 A.M.

The crypt of John Paul Jones lies underneath the chapel. In spite of popular sentiment, Jones did not found the Navy, though he was responsible for many of its traditions. His senior officer, John Barry, is the Navy's founding father, and is buried in Philadelphia, near Independence Hall. The crypt of John Paul Jones is meant to represent a burial at sea, and is one of the most beautiful funerary presentations in the world. The darkened room, guarded constantly by still-as-statues Marines, is dramatically lit, and the coffin rises beneath a dome on waves of bronze and marble. The church and crypt are open Mon.–Sat. 9 A.M.– 4 P.M., Sunday 1–4 P.M.

The **Statue of Tecumseh,** in Tecumseh Court, is a reproduction of the original ship figurehead that stands in the visitor center. Named in honor of the Shawnee chief, the statue represents the warrior spirit of midshipmen—during Commis-

© JOANNE MILLER

the Navy chapel and crypt of John Paul Jones

sioning Week (graduation), Alumni Weekend, and before all home football games (particularly the annual Army-Navy game), Tecumseh is painted and dressed in full war regalia.

In **Preble Hall,** the **U.S. Naval Academy Museum** contains more than 35,000 paintings, prints, and artifacts depicting naval history. The **Gallery of Ships** in the basement of Preble Hall is another exceptional attraction. The gallery contains dozens of pristine miniature reproductions of warships from the 17th, 18th, and 19th centuries—some more than 250 years old—and models crafted from the bones of beef rations allowed French prisoners-of-war during their incarceration in England from 1756 to 1815. Some of the bone carvers became so successful that they remained in England after their release. Henry Huddleston Rogers, an American industrialist, bequeathed most of the models to the academy in 1935. All are constructed with strict regard to scale, usually one quarter-inch to the foot. This is one of the best collections in the world, fascinating for kids and adults.

Also in Preble Hall, the **U.S. Naval Institute Bookstore,** 410/268-6110, offers a selection of books and other items about the Navy, ship modeling, and related subjects. Preble Hall is open Mon.–Sat. 9 A.M.–5 P.M., Sunday 11 A.M.–5 P.M.

In the entrance to **Bancroft Hall,** one of the largest single dormitories in the world, is **Memorial Hall,** a magnificent rotunda that honors graduates who were killed in action and midshipmen who died prior to graduation. Commodore Oliver Hazard Perry's famous "Don't Give Up the Ship" flag is displayed here.

Full dress parades are held in April, May, and September. Call 410/293-2611 for times and dates.

Other Sights

You wouldn't expect to find a garden featuring Maryland's natural environments in the middle of an office complex, but **Helen Avalynne Tawes Garden,** Tawes State Office Building, Taylor Avenue, 410/974-3717, is full of surprises. Park in the government building's visitors spaces and enter through the Tawes Building—there are a number of exhibits on wildlife, a small cafeteria,

CENTRAL MARYLAND

AGITATE

Frederick Douglass, born in rural Tuckahoe, Maryland, in 1817 or 1818, became the most famous of all black abolitionists as well as one of the greatest American orators of his day. Douglass's mother was a slave; his father is thought to have been his mother's owner.

As a toddler, Frederick was sent to live with his grandmother on a nearby plantation. While still a boy, he was hired out to the Auld family of Baltimore. Mrs. Auld taught Frederick how to read even though her husband objected, fearing that education might make the boy unhappy with his lot in life. After hearing what his master said, Frederick vowed he was going to learn as much as he could. He perfected his reading with discarded papers from the gutter, street signs, and posters. When he was 12, he saved up $.50 from shining shoes to buy his first book, *The Columbian Orator.* It was the story of a slave who argued so well with his master on the ills of slavery that he was set free.

When Frederick Douglass turned 16, Hugh Auld died and left Frederick to his brother, Thomas, in St. Michael's. Douglass was whipped, starved, and forced to do field work. He refused, and was sent to live with the famous slave breaker Edward Covey. Covey's beatings had little effect. Frederick Douglass planned a slave revolt, but it failed. He was sent back to Baltimore to learn shipbuilding.

While there, Douglass met some free African Americans who asked him to join a club called the East Baltimore Mutual Improvement Society. In 1838, with seaman's papers supplied by a free black, he escaped to New Bedford, Massachusetts. Five months later he came into contact with William Lloyd Garrison's antislavery weekly, the *Liberator,* and in 1841, after publicly speaking out against slavery, he was enlisted as an agent by the Massachusetts Anti-Slavery Society.

As his speeches became more polished, fewer people believed that he actually had been a slave. To dispel doubt, Douglass published his *Narrative of the Life of Frederick Douglass* (later titled *Life and Times of Frederick Douglass*) in 1845. Although this meant exposing himself to capture, Douglass became the most famous runaway slave in the country. His owner, Thomas Auld, sent bounty hunters after him. He escaped to England, where he spent the next two years making speeches against slavery. British abolitionists bought his freedom in 1847 for 150 pounds sterling.

He settled in Rochester, New York, where he founded his newspaper, the *North Star,* later renamed *Frederick Douglass' Paper.* His house became a stop on the Underground Railroad, and he counted prominent abolitionists William Lloyd Garrison and Harriet Tubman among his friends. During the Civil War, Douglass fought for the enlistment of black men in the Union army and assisted in recruiting the 54th and 55th Massachusetts Colored Regiments, which later won distinction in battle. As the war progressed, President Lincoln conferred with Douglass on African American issues.

During his last years Douglass served as assistant secretary of the Santo Domingo Commission (1871), marshal (1877–81) and recorder of deeds (1881–86) of the District of Columbia, and U.S. minister to Haiti (1889–91). He remained an active reformer, supporting women's suffrage and other human rights issues, until his death in February 1895. His home, Cedar Hill, in Anacostia, Washington, D.C., is now a monument maintained by the National Park Service. When a young student asked Frederick Douglass what advice he would give to young people, his reply was "Agitate."

and gift shop inside the Visitors Center. The center is open Mon.–Fri. 8 A.M.–5 P.M.; the garden itself, featuring every environment found in the state, is a fun place to wander. It's open daily from dawn to dusk. Free.

The **Banneker-Douglass Museum,** 84 Franklin St., 410/974-2893, features exhibits of black art, historical artifacts, archives, rare books, and special collections. Named for scientist Benjamin Banneker and abolitionist Frederick Douglass, it's housed in the 1876 Mt. Moriah AME Church building. It's open Tues.–Fri. 10 A.M.–3 P.M.; Saturday noon–4 P.M. Other times are available by appointment. Free.

Tours

Stop by the **Annapolis Visitor Center,** 26 West St., 410/280-0445, www.visit-annapolis.org, and take one of the $12 one-hour history tours to orient yourself to the town, and see some parts of it that you might miss. The tour ends up at the Governor Ritchie Overlook for panoramic views of the Naval Academy and city. Discover Annapolis Tours, www.discover-annapolis.com, 410/626-6000, also depart from the Visitors Center.

Historic Annapolis Foundation, 18 Pinkney St., 410/267-7619, www.annapolis.org, offers several audio walking tours. One, the African-American Heritage Audio Walking Tour, explores the city through the diverse experiences of slaves (Kunta Kinte, a real person and hero of Alex Haley's book *Roots,* first landed here) and freemen who played a large part in the everyday life of Annapolis. Newsman Walter Cronkite narrates another audio tour. The tours are available at HAF's Museum Store, 77 Main St., 410/268-5576. There is a charge to use the audio equipment.

Eastport, across the bridge, began as a small farming community, and became increasingly residential until, by 1868, the farms had all but disappeared. Boatyards were built in the late 19th century—John Trumpy & Sons moved to the town from New Jersey, and built some of the grandest luxury motor-yachts on the water for presidents and kings. Eastport retains its maritime flavor, and the close-knit community "seceded" from Annapolis to become the Maritime Republic of Eastport when faced with the closure

view of Annapolis from across the Severn River

© JOANNE MILLER

of the Spa Creek Bridge in 1998. The small **Annapolis Maritime Museum,** 133 Bay Shore Ave., 410/295-0104, gives out free walking tour brochures so visitors can roam and learn the history of Eastport.

Some say that the best way to see Annapolis is from the water, and **Watermark Cruises,** 410/268-7600, www.watermarkcruises.com, based at City Dock, offers several options. Visitors can enjoy narrated cruises focusing on the ecology and scenery of the Severn River, or travel out on the bay to the Thomas Point Lighthouse.

Arts and Crafts

The **League of Maryland Craftsmen,** 216 Main St., 410/626-1277, is one of two retail stores that feature the work of more than 140 league members (the other is at Savage Mill, in Savage, Maryland). The thorough jury process is evident in the quality of the merchandise—there's nothing made from kits or assembled from commercial components here. Wonderful glass, charming ceramics, and prints are a few of the finds. This is a good resource if you're looking for a special gift. The shop is open Mon.–Fri. 10 A.M.–5:30 P.M., Saturday 10 A.M.–6 P.M., Sunday 11 A.M.–5:30 P.M. Closed on Tuesday Jan.–Mar.

The **Mitchell Gallery,** Mellon Hall off St. John's Street on the campus of St. John's College, 410/626-2556, is open to the public, and often features museum-quality work by artists such as Rembrandt, Renoir, Calder, and Lipschitz. However, the gallery's purpose is to help students establish connections between the visual arts and liberal arts with exhibits of historical and regional interest, so exhibits are broad in scope, and often include works by students. It's open Tues.–Sun. noon–5 P.M., Friday 7–8 P.M. Free.

Gallery on the Circle, 18 State Circle, 410/268-4566, displays original fine art in all media by local and regional artists. Works featured are by members of the Maryland Federation of Art, and much of the work is visually stunning. The exhibits change monthly. It's open Tues.–Sun. 11 A.M.–5 P.M. Free.

Nancy Hammond Editions, 64 State Circle, 410/267-7711, www.nancyhammondeditions.com, is a gallery devoted to the graphic, colorful work of Maryland artist Nancy Hammond. Limited silkscreen editions of her works on paper can be found here, as well as note cards and other

ST. JOHN'S LIBERTY TREE

The style of St. John's College varies greatly from Annapolis's other font of higher learning, the U.S. Naval Academy. St. John's students study the "Great Books," beginning with Aristotle and ending with Nietzsche. Tuition is around $30,000 a year, and croquet is the only intercollegiate sport. Though both schools are steeped in tradition, St. John's recently lost one of its most prized, the Liberty Tree.

The 400-year-old tulip poplar that stood on St. John's campus in front of McDowell Hall was the last of the Liberty Trees, rallying points for the Sons of Liberty. Pre-revolutionary colonists used the poplar and trees like it as meeting places to foment rebellion against the British. There were once 13 liberty trees, one in each of the original colonies; the trees became a potent Revolutionary War symbol. At least two were destroyed by British forces, and others were cut down or lost to disease or old age.

Winds from Hurricane Floyd fractured the trunk of the St. John's tree, and the damaged tree endangered everything around it, according to a report from arborist Russell Carlson. It also suffered damage from lightning and earlier hurricanes over the years, and was largely held together by concrete and metal cables. In his report, Carlson said, "The entire tree now consists of a hollow shell of wood, sometimes only two or three inches thick." He estimated 85 percent of the wood was lost to decay, and rejected the use of extensive internal or external mechanical supports. "It would be an obtrusive and ignominious life-support system for this grand old champion. Campers and wanderers, children and philosophers, vagrants and presidents have all stood in the shade of this ancient giant. But finally, it is time to say goodbye to our old friend." The college, which held its commencement under the tree for 200 years, decided to remove the tree.

In the spring of 1999, state officials arranged for cuttings to be taken from the tree so clones could be produced and presented to the 49 other states. Several hundred people gathered in a solemn ceremony in late autumn as crews began cutting down the old poplar. Wreaths were laid at the base of the tree and at the base of a 100-year-old offspring that stands a hundred yards away. "We all feel a great sense of sadness over the duty we must perform today," said college president Christopher Nelson.

After a bell tolled 13 times for each of the original colonies, crews went to work with chain saws. It took several days to bring down the whole tree. Wood from the tree was used to make mementos for St. John's students and alumni.

screen-printed doodads. Hammond's work is highly evocative of the Chesapeake, and if you're looking for a meaningful souvenir to remind you of Annapolis, you might find it here.

Shopping

Main Street contains most of the trinket and clothing shops in Annapolis, including **Insight Concepts,** 155 Main St., and **Chesapeake Trading Company,** 147 Main St. One diverse and interesting shop is **Historic Annapolis Foundation's Museum Store,** 77 Main St. Maryland Avenue is also a fun place to stroll.

There is also a shopping mall at the intersection of Riva and Jennifer Roads.

Accommodations

Annapolis has dozens of B&Bs and historic inns in town as well as larger hotel chains. One unique option is to spend the night aboard a yacht in the harbor. The prices in Annapolis are not for the faint of heart. Here are a few select lodgings.

One of the least expensive lodgings in town, with the added benefit of being very close to breakfast, is the **Scotlaur Inn,** 165 Main St., 410/269-6738, www.scotlaurinn.com. Ten newly equipped and furnished guest rooms with private baths are owned and operated by "Uncle Teddy," the zippy proprietor of Chick & Ruth's Delly. The inn is above the restaurant, so nourishment is just a short tumble down the stairs, 24 hours a day. Rooms average $75–95.

Gibson's Lodgings of Annapolis, 110 Prince George St., 410/268-5555, http://avmcyber.com/gibson, are actually three separate homes surrounding a courtyard parking lot. The two-story stucco Berman House has eight guestrooms sharing four baths and one guestroom with a private bath; it's also wheelchair-accessible. The Lauer House combines modern architecture with the style of earlier times, and offers two suites plus four rooms with private baths. The Patterson House features six guestrooms sharing three baths, two parlors, and a formal dining room. This Georgian townhouse with a Victorian facade once served as home to Richard Hill, first naval officer of the port of Annapolis in 1681. All guests enjoy a full continental breakfast. Rates range $68–130.

The **State House Inn,** 25 State Circle, 410/990-0024, www.statehouseinn.com, is also across from the colonial-era capital building on State Circle—it sounds busy, but it's not, as everything in Annapolis remains on a horse-and-buggy scale. The completely renovated and updated inn is of the same period as the State House; each of the seven rooms has a private phone and TV, and a Jacuzzi, bath, or shower. Rooms are decorated in period style, and all have water views. Expect to pay between $110–150.

The **William Page Inn Bed & Breakfast,** 8 Martin St., 410/626-1506, ext. 10, or 800/364-4160, ext. 10, is just two blocks from the waterfront, right near the naval academy. The 1908 building has been cheerfully renovated, and three of the rooms have private baths, while two share a bath. Breakfast is included in the room rate: $125–215.

Historic Inns of Annapolis, 58 State Circle, 410/263-2641 or 800/847-8882, www.annapolisinns.com, is made up of three 18th-century buildings. The Governor Calvert House, 58 State Circle, is the check-in point for all the facilities. This 54-room lodging was built for a colonial governor who wanted a short commute (the state capital is across the street). He was also quite an innovator. Archaeological research on the site uncovered a hypocaust, a heating system of Roman origins: a fire built in one end of a series of brick channels heated air that flowed under the buildings, warming floors and greenhouses. Other lodgings include the 29-room Robert Johnson House, 23 State Circle, and the 44-room Maryland Inn, 16 Church Circle. "Elegant" best describes the accommodations; all rooms have been carefully refurbished and upgraded (cable TV, free movies, and private baths are standard) and are individually decorated with period antiques. The inns offer free access to data ports and health club privileges (the club is a few blocks away). Airport transportation, laundry, and valet parking are available for an extra fee; there is no overnight parking in the immediate area. The historic inns are in the middle of the action—everything in Annapolis is a short stroll away. The **Treaty of Paris Restaurant** continues the upscale 18th-century theme; it's in the Maryland Inn (the inns

I HEAR YOU CALLING ME

The Maryland Inn was built on the front part of a lot deeded to the Annapolis Town Drummer in 1772. The Town Drummer held a position that was unique to Maryland. His function was much like that of the Town Crier, except he conveyed public information through a complex variety of drumbeats. In Annapolis, one of his tasks was to call the General Assembly to session. If a member failed to appear by the third drumroll, he was fined 100 pounds of tobacco. William Butterfield, who performed the tasks of the Town Drummer during the 1750s, was paid five pounds sterling per year for his efforts.

also feature a pub, Drummer's Lot, and the King of France Tavern). Packages and discounts are available, and some rooms are equipped with kitchens and other long-term-stay facilities. Rates range from $150–215.

The Inn at Spa Creek, 417 Severn Ave., 410/263-8866, www.innatspacreek.com, is over the bridge in the Eastport section of town. If you're a walker, you'll find the distance to downtown just right; parking is available, a plus in a small town with few but expensive options. The inn itself is unusual; it's a very modern, airy, bright building in a colonial haven. The interior calls to mind a great ship on the sea, and it's easy to imagine standing at the bow from the railing on the upper deck (especially after a good strong cup of coffee served a few steps away in the open kitchen). Four rooms, all with private baths, range from spacious twins to luxurious suites. The Garden View has a private entrance, and the Upper Deck suite—frequently booked by honeymooners—has a private balcony with views of Spa Creek and Annapolis. Room rates include breakfast: $130–170.

Also in Eastport, the **Inn at Horn Point,** 100 Chesapeake Ave., 410/268-1126, www.inathornpoint.com, is a 1902 Victorian converted into a five-guestroom B&B. Each of the rooms—often named after famous yachts—has a private bath with clawfoot tub and shower, and Internet hookup. A full breakfast is served. With on-site parking, most attractions, restaurants, and nightlife are just a short stroll away. You will find a water taxi stand within three blocks. Rates vary depending on season and room: $119–199.

The **Schooner *Woodwind*** is a 74-foot wooden sailing schooner that offers four staterooms with two shared heads (toilets) plus an evening sail. The boat is available on weekends May 1 to the end of September. Docked near the Marriott in Annapolis, it can be reached at P.O. Box 3254, Annapolis, MD 21403, 410/263-8619, http://schooner-woodwind.com. Each stateroom is $235 per night.

Food

Annapolis has more places to eat than the food court at the Great Mall of America. Most are open every day, and some provide evening entertainment. Here are a few, tried and true:

Storm Brothers Ice Cream Factory, 130 Dock St., 410/263-3376, has been around since 1976, and though they no longer make their own brand, this is the place to stop for a cool cone of locally made Hershey's or Jack and Jill ice cream (or both, what the heck). Lick and look at the boats passing by.

49 West Café, 49 West St., 410/626-9796, offers breakfast, lunch, and dinner, plus live music—classical to jazz—Tues.–Sat. The light gourmet fare, full bar, and coffee and tea selection encourage lingering, as does the plethora of newspapers and books to enjoy. You can spend anywhere from $2 to $12.

Chick & Ruth's Delly, 165 Main St., 410/269-6737, is a local institution. Chick and Ruth Levitt started a sandwich shop in 1965, and expanded the menu over the years to include breakfast, lunch, and dinner, 24/7. Many local residents grew up on messy Delly pastrami sandwiches, and pictures of celebrities, local and national, decorate the walls. The specialty sandwiches are named for politicians—the George Bush (no "W." but this is the presidential nosh—it used to be named the Bill Clinton) combines a big turkey breast with lettuce and tomato on whole-wheat toast for $5.45. Traditional Jewish deli foods anchor the menu, along with everything else that can be cooked in a hurry—the milkshakes are excellent. If you're real good, you'll get a visit from "Uncle Teddy," Levitt family scion, who began working behind the counter at age 10. Prices start at $2 and go up to $16 for the crab cakes.

The Market House on City Dock, on the waterfront at the base of Main Street, offers a number of options, including the popular **City Dock Café** for coffee and baked goods. Though the market house isn't big, it holds a lot of variety: a delicatessen, sandwich shop, raw bar, fish market, poultry seller, pizza place, fruit market, and ice cream store are among the purveyors. The market is open May–Oct. Mon.–Thurs. 9 A.M.– 6 P.M., weekends 9 A.M.–7 P.M.; Nov.–Apr. daily 9 A.M.–6 P.M. except Tuesday 9 A.M.–3 P.M.

One of my favorite places in Annapolis, the **Rams Head Tavern/Fordham Brewing Co.,** 33 West St., 410/268-4545, www.ramsheadtavern.com, features great sophisticated pub food and brews. The shrimp dishes and hamburgers are equally good, and the dining area is divided into several rooms, so you never feel crowded (no matter how busy it gets). This is the home of the Fordham Brewing Co., and their excellent brews (produced with equipment imported from Germany) are featured among the 170 served. The tavern provides a full menu for lunch and dinner daily, plus brunch on Sunday. Prices range from $6–22. Part of the tavern is sectioned off for stage shows. Past performers include the Fabulous Thunderbirds blues band, the Dukes of Dixieland from New Orleans, and comedian Kevin Meaney; ticket prices range from $10 to $40.

For something a little more exotic, try **Nikko,** 189A Main St., 410/267-6688. It offers traditional dishes such as tempura and gyoza at good prices (under $5), but the main focus is on quick-grilled seafood and meats ($11–22). As you would expect, the sushi (under $5 each) is morning-port fresh. They offer good lunch specials under $9, and are open for lunch and dinner daily.

Joss Café and Sushi Bar, 195 Main St., 410/263-4688, also serves traditional dishes such as tempura, teriyaki, sukiyaki, sushi, and sashimi, and you can wash it all down with sake and beer. Lunch and dinner are served daily; prices range from $3.50 for individual sushi to $22.

Farther down the road, **India's,** 257 West St., 410/263-7900, serves tandoori (clay oven) specialties, curries, and a wide variety of East Indian foods. The $7.95 buffet lunch from 11:30 A.M.–2:30 P.M. is well attended, and dinner is also available daily. The food is both good and authentic.

The *Baltimore Sun, Baltimore Magazine,* and *Bon Appétit* all give **Carrol's Creek,** 410 Severn Ave., Eastport, 410/269-1406, high marks for seafood, grilled fish, steaks, and chops. In warm weather, the harbor view from the deck is peerless. The sea scallops in shredded phyllo dough on wilted spinach is especially good. It's open for lunch, dinner, and Sunday brunch. The restaurant has its own parking lot; prices average $25.

Though it's not in Annapolis proper—it's on the other side of the Naval Academy bridge on Mill Creek—**Cantler's Riverside Inn,** 458 Forest Beach Rd., 410/757-1311, is worthy of mention for the freshness and quality of their seafood. Since they bring it in daily on their own boats, this is not a surprise. Their hard-shell crabs compete with the view; you can try them for dinner seven days a week. Many of their patrons arrive by boat and berth for the evening in one of the local marinas. Prices range from $6–18. The main kitchen serves full meals until 11 P.M. weekdays, but continues to serve a limited menu until 1 A.M. Fri.–Sat.

Getting Around/Parking

Jiffy Water Taxi originates from the city dock and makes various stops in the harbor mid-May to Labor Day, Mon.–Thurs. 9:30 A.M.–midnight, Friday 9:30 A.M.–1 A.M., Saturday 9 A.M.–1 A.M., Sunday 9 A.M.–midnight.

Annapolis offers excellent public transit, by bus and trolley. Buses operate Mon.–Sat. 5:30 A.M.–7 P.M., and travel around old town and out to the Riva Road shopping mall and other outlying points. Base fare is $.75 (exact change) and transfers are free. Trolleys run Mon.–Fri. 6:30 A.M.–8 P.M., weekends 10 A.M.–8 P.M. from the Stadium Parking Lot on Rowe Boulevard, and from Gotts Court garage by the visitor center to downtown Annapolis. Bus and trolley fares and transfers are interchangeable.

Most parking meters in town accept coins for two hours, and meter maids are vigilant. City garages are open 24/7; the first hour is free, then $1 per hour up to eight hours, $8 for 8–24 hours or overnight. The special $2 flat rate (in by 4 P.M., out by 8 A.M.) is the best choice if you're staying at a parking-challenged downtown inn. The two largest garages are Gotts Court garage on Calvert Street between West and N. West Street, and Noah Hillman garage on Duke of Gloucester across from Market Street.

GREATER ANNE ARUNDEL COUNTY

Attractions

London Town, 839 Londontown Rd., Edgewater, 410/222-1919, was an important tobacco-shipping center and served as the county seat from 1684–1695. After the town reached its zenith in the 1730s, shipping and industry began to move elsewhere. By the end of that century, little remained of London Town. Today, it's the site of the largest archaeological investigation in the state. The site features the William Brown House, an elegant dwelling built in 1760 with an eight-acre woodland garden. It's open Mon.–Sat. 10 A.M.–4 P.M., Sun. noon–4 P.M.; house tours are given hourly, and there's a museum shop on the premises. Admission is $6.

If 1684 just isn't early enough for you, try the **Medieval Times Dinner & Tournament,** 7000 Arundel Mills Circle (Arundel Mills Mall), Hanover, 443/755-0011, www.medievaltimes .com, an entertainment/dinner concept venue. The setting is the 11th century, and m'lord and his lady are served a four-course meal while knights on horseback joust and whack each other with swords, all in good fun. It's open for dinner daily; reservations required.

Dust off those lederhosen and prepare for some frivolous footwork. **Blob's Park Biergarten,** 8024 Blob's Park Rd. (Route 175 and Washington Road), Jessup, 410/799-0155, is a fun place to spend an evening, especially on weekends, when singles and families hop and twirl to live polka bands (Fri.–Sat. 9 P.M.–1 A.M., Sunday 5–10 P.M.). Blob's began in 1933 when Max Blob built a beer

garden for his friends on his farm; family members continue to run the business, which expanded into a big new building in the mid-1970s. Blob's serves dinner nightly, and the fare is traditional German with great prices: sauerbraten and dumplings, $7.50, bockwurst, bratwurst, and knockwurst plates, $6.50 each, and sandwiches for under $3.50. Beer? Of course! The service isn't fancy, and the seating is family-style, but the crowd (with many people dressed in traditional outfits) is happy. Plan to eat early when the band is going to play—the kitchen closes around 7 P.M. to make way for some serious dancing.

Recreation

The **Baltimore-Annapolis Trail,** a 13.3-mile, 10-foot-wide paved trail, runs from Glen Burnie to Annapolis. Walkers, runners, bicyclists, and equestrians are all welcome to use the 2 percent grade trail. In Glen Burnie, the northern terminus, the trail is accessed off I-97 (exit 15 to Dorsey Road). Turn right onto Route 648 (Baltimore-Annapolis Boulevard); take the first right after the second traffic light. There is free parking in the garage above the theater. The southern terminus is in Arnold. Take Route 50 to exit 27 to the Naval Academy. Parking is one-tenth of a mile on the right, on Boulters Way. Call 410/222-6244 for a map and other access points on the trail.

Sandy Point State Park, 1100 East College Pkwy., 410/974-2149, is a day-use park, at the terminus of the Wm. Preston Lane Jr. Memorial Bridge (the Bay Bridge), seven miles east of Annapolis off U.S. 50/301. The park is surrounded on three sides by water. Swimming, fishing, crabbing, boating, and windsurfing are popular on the park's beaches, which have lifeguards on duty from Memorial Day to Labor Day. The park provides several launching ramps and a concession for bait and tackle; rowboats and motorboats are available for rent. Two trails and miles of waterfront are ideal for hiking and migratory bird viewing. There is a $4 charge for day use.

Thomas Point State Park, end of Thomas Point Rd., is almost like a private club. Closed gates bar the way at the entry point of the park (they look locked, but they're not). The signs that say "permit required" refer to an annual parking permit limited to 60 issued per year for repeat users—usually fishers who come for a few of the rockfish (striped bass) that begin life in one of the 150 tributaries of the Chesapeake Bay. However, occasional day users who wish to picnic and enjoy the park's short trails and a view of Thomas Point's eight-sided lighthouse one mile out in the bay are not charged. Be warned: there are only four parking spaces, and they are gone early in the day during the summer. The park closes at sunset. Free.

INFORMATION

For further information on activities and attractions in Annapolis and Anne Arundel County, contact their conference and visitors bureau at 26 West St., Annapolis, MD 21401, 410/280-0445, www.visit-annapolis.org.

Howard County

ELLICOTT CITY

Ellicott City is a charming small town that's busy with visitors seeking relief from the steamy city during the warm months—and has been since H. L. Mencken's time. New shops mix with good restaurants and historic attractions to provide an afternoon's entertainment. Most of the addresses listed are on Main Street, which is about five blocks long, starting at Thomas Isaac's Log Cabin on the west side—the oldest surviving structure in Ellicott City, circa 1780 (open weekends)—and ending at the B&O Railroad Station in the east. In spite of its size, the town has a parking fine system that can only be described as diligent. The Howard County Visitor Information Center, 8267 Main St., has an excellent flyer called "Smart Parking"—it might save you a buck or two.

Sights

The **B&O Railroad Station Museum,** Main Street (Route 144) at Maryland Avenue, 410/461-1944, www.ecbo.org, will delight history and rail fans with its sound and light show featuring a 40-foot-long HO scale model of the first 13 miles of passenger railroad in the United States (from Baltimore to Ellicott City—making this the oldest station in America). In addition, a living history program presented by costumed docents takes place in the restored rooms of the 1830 building and 1927 caboose. The museum presents varying programs throughout the year, such as the Holiday Model Train Ex-hibit, Dec.–Jan. The museum is open on weekends year-round, and admission is $3.

Patapsco Female Institute Historic Park, 3691 Sarah's Lane, 410/465-8500, is an active archaeological site, the remains of one of the nation's first women's facilities that educated girls age 12–18 in music, languages, history, and the sciences. The institute was founded in 1837 and became Maryland's most prestigious school for young ladies during the 1840s and 1850s. A key factor in the success of Patapsco was the appointment of Almira Hart Lincoln Phelps as principal. A liberated woman by the standards of any age, Ms. Phelps wrote textbooks on chemistry, biology, botany, physics, and geology for secondary schools and colleges, and turned a portion of the fortune she made back into the institute. She disdained an ordinary "finishing school" education and insisted that the institute prepare the girls to earn a living. The school continued until 1891, but competition from public schools, which were developed in the late 1860s, finally forced it to close.

Today, elevated walkways lead visitors through the 8,000-square-foot granite Greek Revival structure, and the grounds are being redesigned into 19th-century formal gardens. The school is a short (but very steep) walk from Main Street in Ellicott City. Take Church Road from Main Street to the dead-end at Sarah's Lane; autos may turn left and park in the courthouse parking lot. The visitor's center is in the pretty 1837 yellow building, Mount Ida, across from the courthouse. The institute is open seasonally, Apr. –Oct. Sun. 1–4 P.M.

CENTRAL MARYLAND

THE ROAD TO ELLICOTT CITY

Like other well-to-do Baltimoreans in the late 19th century, H. L. Mencken's family would spend the warm summer months in the vacation haven of Ellicott City—not only to escape the heat, but also to avoid the frequent infestations of yellow fever. Mencken remembers the journey to their holiday home in his childhood memoir, *Happy Days*:

From our house in Hollins street to Ellicott City was but ten miles by the old National Pike, but the road had no surface save bare rock and there were four or five toll-gates and six or seven immense hills along the way, so no one ever drove it if the business could be avoided. One of the hills was so steep and so full of hair-pin bends that it was called the Devil's Elbow. A hay-wagon coming up would take half a day to cover the mile and a half from bottom to top, and sometimes a Conestoga wagon from Western Maryland (there were still plenty of them left in the [18]80s) got stuck altogether, and had to be rescued by the plow-horses of the adjacent farmers. At intervals of a mile or so along the road there were old-time coaching inns, and they were still doing a brisk trade in 25-cent country dinners and 5-cent whiskey.

Two tours are available, 1:30 and 3 P.M. Admission is $4 and includes a video tour of historic Mount Ida and a guided tour of the site. Patapsco hosts several events throughout the year, such as "Ghosts" in October and "Victorian Christmas" in December. Call for more information.

Recreation

Guided walking tours of Ellicott City are given by reservation for groups only at the Howard County Tourism Council Visitor Information Center. Ghost tours are also available Friday and Saturday evenings Apr.–Nov.

The "man who wears the kilt," Phillip Krista, has shared his love of fishing—beginning fly-fishing, fly-fishing for the handicapped, pond and lake fishing, saltwater fishing on the Chesapeake, and guided wading trips—for 30 years. If you'd like to learn, or to learn where the best spots are, contact him at 730 Pleasant Hill Rd., Ellicott City, MD 21043, 410/461-3007.

Shopping

Ellicott City features dozens of shopping opportunities along Main Street, mainly for collectibles and antiques. **Starry Night Antiques,** 8006 Main, **Vintage Rose,** 8026 Main, **Ellicott's Country Store,** 8180 Main, and **Dust-Off Collectibles,** 8345 Main, are just a few. For multiple antique and collectible dealers, try **Antique Depot,** 3720 Maryland Ave.

Arts and entertainment aren't left behind with **I Love Theatre,** 8141 Main St., a gift shop for lovers of the performing arts, and **Margaret Smith Gallery,** 8090 Main St., which specializes in art from Walt Disney and Warner Bros. **Oh My Word,** 8191 Main St., is a shop that represents more than 42 calligraphers—visitors can have poems, sayings, and original writings custom designed.

Food and Nightlife

Main Street and the surrounding streets are lined with cafés and eateries. Here are a few:

A café with light meals, **Bean Hollow,** 8059 Main St., 410/465-0233, is a good place to stop downtown ($3–12). They roast their own coffee, and offer 30 varieties.

Tersiguel's, 8293 Main St., 410/465-4004, is a *rara avis*—an award-winning French country restaurant. They serve regular entrées (average $20) and two prix fixe menus for dinner each night.

The Tiber River Tavern, 3733 Old Columbia Pike, 410/750-2002, is in an old stable just a short walk away from Main (though it is uphill). The food is American, and the decor is charming; it's open daily for lunch ($15) and dinner ($21), and the bar is a popular spot at night.

Ellicott Mills Brewing Company, 8303 Main St., 410/313-8141, offers a spate of its own brews, strictly produced within the confines of the Bavarian purity law, *Reinheitsgebot,* established in 1516—the law states that all beer must be brewed from only four ingredients: water, malt, hops, and yeast. The brewmeister, Martin Virga, trained in Munich and attributes the quality of his brews to the low mineral content of local water. To accompany this excellent beer, chef Rick Winter creates an eclectic menu with such unique features as wild boar in beer sauce, buffalo strip steak, and venison sausage. Yes, they have chicken salad, too. Lunch averages $7, dinner $15. It's open every day for lunch and dinner until 2 A.M. Brewery tours are available by appointment.

Though it's a few miles west of Ellicott City off Frederick Road, **The Crab Shanty,** 3410 Plum Tree Dr., 410/465-9660, has remained a popular choice for seafood lovers for years. Meals average $9–33, and it's open daily for lunch and dinner.

Alexandra's, in Turf Valley Resort, 2700 Turf Valley Rd., 410/465-1500, is also some distance from downtown Ellicott City—a few miles west of the Crab Shanty off U.S. 40. But if elegant dining is what you're looking for, this is the place. American dishes with an international flair—steak, seafood, and poultry—are served along with a view of the landscaped grounds (dinner averages $21, and is served daily); Alexandra's also features a popular brunch on the weekends.

For a more casual atmosphere in the same location, try **Terrace on the Green** for big sandwiches, soups, salads, and really good burgers (breakfast, lunch, and dinner, $5–18).

GREATER HOWARD COUNTY

Sights

Still have that Captain Marvel decoder ring? Then the National Security Agency's **Cryptologic Museum,** Project 7 Road (intersection of Route 295 and Route 32, Fort Meade exit on Route 32), is for you. The museum is in a branch of the agency; inside are exhibits on cracking codes and creating them, too. It's open Mon.–Fri. 9 A.M.–3 P.M., Saturday 10 A.M.–2 P.M. Free.

Benjamin Banneker Historical Park, 300 Oella Ave., Oella, 410/887-1081, is located on the original homestead of "the first Negro Man of Science." Benjamin Banneker's grandmother was a maid in England who emigrated to Maryland as an indentured servant. When she finished her seven years of bondage, she bought a farm along with two slaves to help her work it; she eventually freed both slaves and married one, Robert Bannaky. They had several children, among them a daughter, Mary. When Mary Bannaky grew up, she bought a slave named Robert, married him, and had several children, including Benjamin in 1731. The family farm was known as "Bannaky Springs" due to the freshwater springs on the land. Robert Bannaky (he took her last name) used ditches and little dams to control the water from the springs for irrigation, so that crops flourished even in dry spells.

Benjamin's grandmother taught him and his brothers to read. There was no school in the area until a Quaker teacher came to live in the Patapsco Valley. He set up a school for boys that Benjamin attended (it was here that Benjamin changed the spelling of his name to Banneker). He learned to write and do simple arithmetic.

When Banneker was 21, he saw a patent watch for the first time; he took the watch apart and carved watch parts out of wood to make a clock of his own, the first striking clock to be made completely in America. Banneker's clock was so precise it struck every hour, on the hour, for 40 years. After Banneker's success with his wooden watch, he worked as a watch-and-clock repairman and helped Joseph Ellicott, one of the founders of Ellicott City, build a complex clock. They became friends. Joseph and his brother George lent Banneker books and scientific instruments, and Banneker taught himself astronomy and advanced mathematics.

After Banneker's parents died, they left him the family farm. He built a "work cabin" with a skylight on the property to study the stars and make calculations. He compiled information and published the results in six almanacs. In 1791, Major Andrew Ellicott, George Ellicott's cousin, asked Banneker to help him survey the "Federal Territory" (the section of Maryland proposed for Washington, D.C.). Banneker and Ellicott worked closely with the notoriously foul-tempered architect in charge, Pierre L'Enfant, until L'Enfant was suddenly dismissed from the project. When L'Enfant left, he took the partially finished plans with him. Banneker recreated the plans from memory, and expanded them to design the city. He continued to study and record his astronomical observations until he died on October 26, 1806.

The historical park is composed of a museum building with artifacts and biographical material and a main gallery with changing displays; in addition, trail guides lead walking tours in the park's wooded 142 acres. It's open Tues., Thurs., and Sat. 10 A.M.–4 P.M., though it's wise to call ahead, since most staff are volunteers. Admission by donation.

The **African Art Museum of Maryland,** 5430 Vantage Point Rd., Columbia, 410/730-7105, www.africanartmuseum.org, is dedicated to collecting, exhibiting, and preserving the art of Africa. This small museum/gallery offers an excellent opportunity to enjoy the diversity of African art and culture in a pleasant setting. Exhibits contain traditional art forms such as masks, carvings, and shell work, but Doris Ligon, the director, is equally interested in modern African artists. Recently, the museum featured the colorful and ornate tapestries of Abdoulaye Kasse, master weaver from Senegal, with a special appearance by the artist (and his loom). Works by contemporary artists reflect the sophistication and enormous variation found in one of the world's largest continents—a rare find. The museum is open Tues.–Fri. noon–5 P.M., Saturday noon–4 P.M., and Sunday 2–4 P.M. General admission is $2.50, children $1.50.

Shopping

Savage Mill, 8600 Foundry St., Savage, 800/788-MILL (800/788-6455), started out as a textile mill complex in 1820. Today, it consists of nine remaining buildings that are used as an upscale marketplace with more than 50 specialty shops, art and craft studios, and dealers of high-quality antiques and collectibles. In addition, the nearby Manor House (built in 1840 for the mill's first manager) is maintained as a permanent decorator's showplace, highlighting items from the market's merchants. Rams Head Tavern of Annapolis has a branch in the mill. Open Sun. 11 A.M.–

6 P.M., Mon.–Wed. 10 A.M.–6 P.M., Thurs.–Sat. 10 A.M.–9 P.M. While you're in the area, take a look at the **Bollman Truss Railroad Bridge,** right next to the mill. It's one of only two iron semi-suspension bridges in the world. Built in 1869, it's now used as a footbridge spanning the Little Patuxent River.

Columbia is a planned community made up of one very large shopping area, **Columbia Mall,** 10300 Little Patuxent Pkwy., 410/730-3300, and several "villages," each centered around a small shopping and restaurant complex. Columbia Mall has every major mall store, plus most of the smaller ones—there may be sales, but this isn't an outlet center. The area has plenty of restaurants, too.

Recreation

Patapsco Valley State Park is set in a largely undeveloped area along the Patapsco River. The park follows the narrow river valley a few miles west of Baltimore and runs the entire length of the city, from Liberty Heights Road in the north almost to the airport in the south. In an area that is one housing development after another, the relative wildness comes as a welcome surprise.

Because the park covers so much territory, there are several park entrances. The Avalon–Glen Artney–Orange Grove area, the oldest developed area in the park, offers hiking, picnicking, equestrian trails, fishing, canoeing, and ballfields. It's located off Route 1 (exit 3); drive toward Elkridge, and make a left on South Street, the first street after crossing the river. The park entrance is on the left. The Hilton area offers one of the park's camping facilities, in addition to hiking, picnicking, and a playfield; from I-695, take exit 13, Frederick Road, through Catonsville to S. Rolling Road. Turn left in 150 feet to Hilton Avenue, and follow Hilton Avenue 1.5 miles to the park entrance on the right. Hollofield (exit 15 off I-695, to U.S. 40 westbound, approximately 2 miles to the park entrance on right) features a scenic overlook, picnicking, fishing, and family camping. Additional camping may be found at the McKeldin area, along with hiking and equestrian trails, picnicking, fishing, and a ballfield. To get there, from I-695, take I-70 to Marriotsville

Road (exit 83). The park entrance is about 4 miles on the right. The Pickall area has eleven picnic pavilions, a scenic trail, ballfields, and a playground; to get there from I-695, take Security Boulevard (exit 17) one-half mile to N. Rolling Road, and turn left. The park entrance is approximately 1.5 miles on the left.

Overall, the park features six hiking trails, ranging in distance and difficulty from 1.2–3 miles and from mild to strenuous. Naturalists lead informative hikes for $2 per person during the warmer months, including an especially popular "light of the moon" walk several times a season. There is no charge for general park use, but the 73 campsites, operated from the first Friday in April to the last weekend in October, run $15–20 depending on amenities. Reservations may be made by calling 888/432-CAMP (888/432-2267), and an $8 service fee is charged for each reservation. For more information on the park and trails, contact Patapsco Valley State Park, 410/461-5005, Mon.–Fri. 8 A.M.–4 P.M., or write to 8020 Baltimore National Pike, Ellicott City, MD 21043.

Fairway Hills Golf Course, 5100 Columbia Rd., Columbia, 410/730-1112, and **Timbers at Troy,** 6100 Marshalee Dr., Eldridge, 410/313-GOLF (410/313-4653), are both 18-hole public courses.

Accommodations

Though **Turf Valley Resort and Conference Center,** 2700 Turf Valley Rd., 410/465-1500, www.turfvalley.com, is technically in Ellicott City, it's actually much closer to U.S. 40. It's an indulgence, and a great one. The elegantly landscaped property covers 1,000 acres and encompasses a hotel and spa, two restaurants, three superb golf courses (54 holes), a driving range, indoor and outdoor pools with whirlpool and steam room, tennis courts, volleyball, basketball and shuffleboard courts, and individual housing units. One luxury suite in the hotel could house an extended family in most third-world countries—they could probably all take a whirlpool in the tub at the same time, too. Less expansive rooms are available. One might feel guilty if the staff wasn't so pleasant and accommodating, the food in the restaurants so good, and the feeling of enjoyment so complete.

The spa uses Aveda natural personal products, and the staff is highly trained in technique. Herbal wraps, massages, and facials are among the simpler offerings. One of the most complex is the "Silk Body Polish," which consists of lying face-down on a table while an attendant rubs salt and pre-chosen aromatherapy oils into your skin, then operates a "Swiss hose" (essentially a hose full of holes) and a series of nozzles above you to swirl warm water continuously on your back and legs. The effect is of being able to breathe underwater while being carried through a whirlpool. Afterwards, you can hear the blood racing through your body for several minutes, and you have the sensation that you've never felt better in your life. Each service runs $45–70, and they offer packages.

Turf Valley is central Maryland's only getaway spa, and it's first-rate. Fortunately, the tariff for all this smooth fun is frequently made more accessible by packages and overnight specials, particularly in the off-season (Nov.–Mar.)—call the resort for details. Room prices normally range $100–450, and they offer AAA/AARP and other discounts.

In addition to camping at Patapsco Valley State Park, **Ramblin' Pines,** 801 Hoods Mill Rd., Woodbine, 410/795-5161 or 800/550-8733, offers a full-service campground with full hookup sites, 30- and 50-amp electric, pull-through, and tent sites. In addition, they have rustic cabin rentals, an activities building, game room, laundrette, dump station, and general store. On-site are a swimming pool, catch-and-return fishing pond, miniature golf course, and other recreational activities. There is a two-day minimum stay on weekends, and discounts are available for AARP, AAA, GoodSam, and other RV clubs.

Food

Cover-to-Cover Bookstore Café, Owen Brown Village Center, Owen Brown Road, Columbia, 410/381-9200, is a cozy and relaxed place for a cup and a light meal. Breakfast, lunch, and dinner are served daily ($9 for an entrée).

Bombay Peacock Grill, 10005 Old Columbia Rd., Columbia, 410/381-7111, features pan-Indian cuisine with many vegetarian choices. Tandoori mixed grill and chickpea curry are favorites. There's a daily luncheon buffet for $8, and dinner is served daily (average $12).

Columbia is home to another exceptional East Indian restaurant, **Mango Grove,** 6365 Dobbin Rd. (Dobbin Center), 410/884-3426; this one has the added quality of being exclusively vegetarian. It specializes in hearty South Indian dishes (characterized as meat-and-potatoes without the meat), and has gained such a reputation that Baltimoreans will make the trip down for a meal. It's open for lunch ($7) and dinner ($10) Wed.–Sun.

Hunan Manor, 7091 Deepage Dr., Columbia, 410/381-1134, features a lengthy menu and is reputed to have the best hot-and-sour soup in Maryland. It's open daily for dinner ($9).

Kings Contrivance Restaurant, 10150 Shaker Dr., 410/995-0500, serves a sophisticated American/Italian menu for lunch and dinner daily in a lovely historic manor house. Entrées run about $14–25, and prix fixe dinners are also offered.

History and elegance are inextricably bound in the **Elkridge Furnace Inn,** 5745 Furnace Ave., Elkridge, 410/379-9336. Nestled on the Patapsco River, the inn was first established as a tavern in 1744. An iron-smelting furnace was added around 1750, and in 1810, the Ellicott brothers, James and Andrew, modernized the iron-smelting furnace and constructed an elegant home next to the existing tavern. The house and inn are set on 16 acres graced by beautiful linden, holly, and magnolia trees. Chef/owner Dan Wecker has garnered a passel of awards for his menu, including *Wine Spectator's* Award of Excellence and a Zagat rating of "Extraordinary." Lunch, served Tues.–Fri., might include roast leg of lamb with scalloped potatoes Dauphinoise, or seafood crepes Nantua, shrimp, scallops, and crab meat in crepes topped with a lobster sauce (both $13; lunch prices average $12). Dinner, served Tues.–Sat., features supreme de volaille Micronesia, boneless, skinless breast of chicken stuffed with toasted macadamia nuts and arugula, served with a fresh fruit salsa and herbed risotto ($21), and filet de porc aux abricots, medallions of pork tenderloin with grilled apricots and a spiced rum demiglace ($24); dinner entrées average $24. The wine list is on a par with the food, and Sunday brunch has been added to the mix.

INFORMATION

For Howard County and Ellicott City, call or stop by the Howard County Tourism Council Visitor Information Center, 8267 Main St., Ellicott City, 410/313-1900 or 800/288-8747, www.VisitHowardCounty.com.

Montgomery County

Only in fetters is liberty.
Without its banks,
Can a river be?

> *Louis Ginsberg, in an address to*
> *the Poetry Society of America, 1966*

Starting with Takoma Park, the first Washington, D.C., "suburban development," the towns and villages around the capital city have expanded exponentially and grown together into a boundary-confused mega-suburb that surrounds the capital for nearly 20 miles in every direction. A few of the towns in this capital gateway area—chiefly Bethesda and Rockville—have identifiable centers, though the boundaries between Bethesda, Chevy Chase, and Silver Spring have long since disappeared. Beyond the farthest reaches of commuter growth, the county is dotted with pretty little towns and villages separated by green farmlands. The western section of Montgomery County along the Potomac is downright rural—something of a surprise after the upmarket sprawl of the capital gateway.

SIGHTS

Clara Barton National Historic Site

The world-renowned "Angel of the Battlefield" spent her last years here, 5801 Oxford Rd. at MacArthur Boulevard, Glen Echo, 301/492-6245. The home, converted from a Red Cross warehouse, is preserved much as it was in Barton's day, when simplicity and shared work were the ideal for Barton and her coworkers. A truly remarkable and courageous woman, Barton found her calling among the dying and wounded of the Civil War and went on to create the American branch of the Red Cross—an emergency care organization developed on the battlefields of Europe—to serve

in peacetime disasters such as the Johnstown, Pennsylvania, flood of 1889. The house is open for guided tours daily, every hour on the half hour, 10:30 A.M.–4:30 P.M. Admission is $3.

Glen Echo Park

Long a shadow of its former self, Glen Echo Park, MacArthur Boulevard and Goldsboro Road, Glen Echo, 301/492-6282, began as a Chautauqua, a center where people could participate in science, art, and literature. In 1899, it was converted to a full-scale amusement park with rides and a ballroom where Glenn Miller played. Few vestiges of the gaily colored amusement park remain in the peeling buildings and

THE PRICE OF BEING A HEROINE

Women who move beyond traditional roles—no matter how humanitarian—have always been treated schizophrenically by our ambivalent society. Clara Barton was born on Christmas day in 1821, and was brought up with a sense of duty to humanity, and, for the times, a liberal education. She worked as a teacher, starting one of the first free schools in New Jersey. During the Civil War, she felt compelled to join other members of the U.S. Sanitary Commission to work on the battlefields of Manassas, Antietam, Fredericksburg, and elsewhere, earning herself the sobriquet "Angel of the Battlefield." "Men have worshipped war till it has cost a million times more than the whole earth is worth," she said. "Deck it as you will, war is Hell. Only the desire to soften some of its hardships and allay some of its miseries ever induced me to face its pestilent and unholy breath."

After the war, Barton continued her charitable work, and began to speak out and express her opinions and convictions as to the enfranchisement of former slaves and her support for the growing feminist movement. "I must have been born believing in the full right of women to all privileges and positions which nature and justice accord her common with other human beings. Perfectly equal rights—human rights." In 1868, the conflict between her personal beliefs and her culture—coupled with her earnest, shy demeanor—lead to a bout of "hysteria." She traveled to Europe and heard of the Red Cross, established by the Treaty of Geneva some years before. She worked with the organization during the Franco-Prussian War, and determined to bring the Red Cross to the United States. She was confounded by 10 years of poor health and public and government apathy, but by 1882, the U.S. Senate ratified the Treaty of Geneva, establishing the Red Cross in the United States, with Clara Barton as its founder and president.

In the last 15 years of her life, she purchased a barn in then-rural Glen Echo and used the space for Red Cross personnel and storage. At the age of 76, she directed relief on the battlefields of Cuba during the Spanish-American War. At that time, a faction in the Red Cross pressed for her resignation—they considered her a charismatic figurehead when the changing world required hard business sense and organization. She retired under protest and converted the Glen Echo barn into a spartan home for herself. Though bitter about being ousted from the organization she worked so hard to create, she continued her life's work by establishing the National First Aid Association of America to bring about emergency preparedness on the community level. She died in the Glen Echo home, where "the moon seemed always to be shining," in 1912.

crumbling bumper car pavilion, but Glen Echo is on its way to becoming, once again, a center for learning and the arts, now that it's become part of the National Park System. Glen Echo's stunning 1921 Dentzel-carved wooden carousel has been refurbished by volunteers. Professionals in fields ranging from performing and visual arts to consumer-oriented topics are repairing and revitalizing the buildings and, in exchange, opening the facilities to the public for classes, demonstrations, and performances. The Crystal Studio houses an artisan glassblowing shop, **Glassworks** (301/229-4184), which produces exquisite bowls and goblets; visitors are afforded a rare opportunity to see glass blown directly from the furnace in time-honored tradition (definitely the place to be on a cold day). Shops and demonstration areas are open at different times; the park office is open 9 A.M.–5 P.M. daily, and the carousel operates May–Sept. noon–6 P.M. on weekends and Wed.–Thurs. 10 A.M.–2 P.M. Picnic areas are first-come, first-served. Free.

F. Scott and Zelda Fitzgerald Burial Place

Francis Scott Key Fitzgerald (so named for his illustrious ancestor) and his glamorous wife traveled the world while writing the books and stories that would make them both famous. He was an icon of the Jazz Age and died in Hollywood, California, in 1940—so why is he buried in Rockville? Fitzgerald's father's family had been residents of the Rockville area since the early 1800s, and he visited the area many times. His father and mother joined an assortment of ancestors buried in the cemetery of St. Mary's Catholic Church, the oldest in Rockville (1817). Fitzgerald chose the little burial ground as the final resting place for his wife and himself after attending his father's funeral in 1931. The grave is just behind the small church. In *Tender Is the Night* (1934), Fitzgerald described his protagonist's feelings at the burial of his own father: "It was very friendly leaving him there with all his relations around him. . . . Good-by my father—good-by all my fathers."

Once on the edge of town, St. Mary's is now in the midst of heavily traveled major roads. The

the grave of F. Scott and Zelda Fitzgerald

church and cemetery are at 500 Veirs Mill Rd. (Route 586), at the intersection of Rockville Pike (Route 355), which becomes Hungerford Drive at the intersection.

If you're in the mood to explore another interesting cemetery in the Rockville area, go to **Aspin Hill Pet Cemetery,** 13630 Georgia Ave. (entrance on Aspen Hill Rd.). One of the oldest in the country, it was founded in the 1920s; the circle-eyed pooch Jiggs from *Our Gang,* at least one dog owned by J. Edgar Hoover, and Lyndon B. Johnson's beagle were all buried or cremated here.

George Meany Center for Labor Studies and Memorial Archives Library

This center, 10000 New Hampshire Ave. (Route 650), Silver Spring, 301/431-5451, is a division of the AFL-CIO labor organization. It consists of a campus concentrating on the study of labor and a library open to the public. A big bronze sculpture portraying a beefy cigar-waving George Meany is in the library lobby—a powerful portrayal of the former plumber and leader of the American labor movement for 55 years. He was awarded the 1963 Presidential Medal of Freedom for his human rights work with "the people's lobby." The library features an exhibit on the history of the labor movement and the lives of working people, and, in addition, houses thousands of books, pamphlets, and other source materials that illuminate the history of every labor organization from Actors Equity to the United Textile Workers of America. The library periodically prepares special bibliographies for topics such as "Women at Work and in the Labor Movement." Anything you ever wanted to know about work in America and the world is here. The library is open Mon.–Fri. 9 A.M.–4:30 P.M. Materials may be borrowed through interlibrary loan.

Government Facilities
Both the **National Institutes of Health** (NIH), Cedar Lane, Bethesda, 301/496-1776, and nearby NIH **National Library of Medicine,** 8600 Rockville Pike, Bethesda, 301/496-6308, have something to offer visitors.

The NIH Visitor Information Center is in Building 45 (Natcher Conference Center), Room 1AS-13, 45 Center Dr., on the NIH campus; it's open Mon.–Fri. 8:30 A.M.–4:00 P.M., except federal holidays. The visitor center conducts a free general overview of the NIH on Monday, Wednesday, and Friday at 11:00 A.M. The overview consists of a videotape introduction to the NIH and a talk about the NIH's organization and programs. Tours of the NIH campus may be arranged by appointment; call 301/496-1776. "Science in the Cinema" is a free film festival held each summer at the National Institutes of Health. One evening a week for six weeks, a film with a medical science theme is screened.

The NIH **National Library of Medicine** features changing exhibits on medicine and conducts tours for the public Mon.–Fri. at 1:30 P.M. The library is open Mon.–Wed. and Friday 8:30 A.M.– 5 P.M., Thursday 8:30 A.M.–9 P.M., Saturday 8:30 A.M.–12:30 P.M. One recent exhibit focused

on asthma and included a stellar list of overachievers who suffered from the illness, among them Pliny the Elder (Roman historian), John Calvin (religious reformer), Ludwig van Beethoven (composer), Marcel Proust (author), Edith Wharton (author), and Che Guevara (revolutionary).

NIH visitors must park in designated areas only, and parking is available at a cost of $2 per hour for the first three hours or $12 per day. Be prepared to show two pieces of identification including a government-issued piece (driver's license, passport) to enter any building not explicitly for visitors. To reach NIH by the D.C. Metro, take the Red Line to the Medical Center station, located on the NIH campus. There is a free shuttle bus service from the Metro station to Building 45. The NIH Visitor Information Center and the library are both free.

C&O Canal National Historic Park, Great Falls
This park, 11710 MacArthur Blvd. near Falls Rd. (Route 189), Potomac, 301/299-3613, is part of the 184.5-mile Chesapeake & Ohio Canal National Historical Park trail. The canal officially begins at the tidewater lock near the Thompson Boat Center (by the intersection of Virginia Avenue and Rock Creek Parkway) in Washington, D.C. The trail meanders along and catches the towpath further on (for the best mile-marker-by-mile-marker description of the canal and its history, see *The C&O Canal Companion,* in the Suggested Reading section at the back of the book). Great Falls Park is between mile 14 and mile 15 of the canal. The Great Falls of the Potomac were the largest impediment to navigation on the river. The successful six-lock bypass (lock 15, at mile 13.6, is the first; lock 20, mile 14.4 at Great Falls, is the last) built there became a tourist attraction at the outset of construction in 1828. The Great Falls Tavern, built to house and feed visitors, still stands, and now serves to disseminate information on the canal and the area. There are several footpaths in the park: The path near lock 17 (mile 14.1) leads to Olmstead Island and the Great Falls Overlook; another, the Billy Goat trail (begins mile 12.7), runs between the canal

and river, and is an excellent way to see the geographical layout of the area. The locks and weirs are all operational at Great Falls, and it's a good place to see how the canal operated in its heyday. From Apr.–Nov. Wed.–Sun., a mule-drawn canal boat plies the waters, and visitors are welcome aboard for a half-hour ride; fares range from $5 to $8. A $5 fee is charged to enter the park by automobile; for cyclists, it's $3. Summer is a very busy time for this park, so plan accordingly; it's open daily 9 A.M.–5 P.M.

White's Ferry

White's Ferry, Route 107 to White's Ferry Road, Dickerson, 301/349-5200, has been in operation since the early 1800s, when it was the only ferry that crossed the Potomac. Today, the *Jubal Early* takes cars and visitors across the river 5 A.M.–11 P.M. for a small fee, much as the mule-driven barges did in the early days of the republic. During the Civil War, the ferry's namesake, General Jubal Early, along with Robert E. Lee and J. E. B. Stewart, used the ferry to clandestinely transport troops from Virginia. Today, a little provisions store operates on the Maryland side, and it rents canoes by the hour for a quiet trip up the Potomac. They'll arrange a shuttle pick-up with 48-hour notice; call 301/349-5200 for more information. The area is verdant, quiet, and isolated; a park with picnic area abuts the ferry slip. The day I visited, a church was holding services there: a single baritone led the group in Spanish hymns, and little boys in suits and girls with white kerchiefs on their hair played games on the grass.

PARKS, GARDENS, AND SCENIC SPOTS

McCrillis Gardens, 6910 Greentree Rd., Bethesda, 301/365-1657, is a small, beautifully landscaped public garden away from the suburban hustle of Bethesda. William McCrillis was special assistant to the Secretary of the Interior under three presidents starting with Franklin Delano Roosevelt, and as a hobby bred and developed an impressive array of azaleas and other shade plants. He and his wife donated their home

and the surrounding five acres to Maryland in 1978. The home/art gallery on the premises is open Tues.–Sun. noon–4 P.M., and the grounds are open 10 A.M.–sunset. On-street parking is limited, so get there early. Peak bloom is the first week of May. Free.

Brookside Gardens, 1800 Glenallan Ave., Wheaton, 301/949-8230, located in Wheaton Regional Park, consist of a 50-acre display garden and conservatory. The gardens are landscaped to offer horticultural interest throughout the year, with plants such as paperbark maple and Lenten rose in January, and hydrangeas and roses in June. The gardens are open daily (except Christmas Day) from sunrise–sunset. The conservatory is open 10 A.M.–5 P.M., and the visitor center 9 A.M.–5 P.M. Free.

Recognized as one of Maryland's springtime showplaces, the **Brighton Dam Azalea Garden** is on five acres next to the Tridelphia Reservoir and Brighton Dam, Brighton-Clarksville Road (off Route 650) on the Montgomery

the **Mormon temple in Kensington**

MONTGOMERY COUNTY PUBLIC GOLF COURSES

Tournament golf is one of the most popular pastimes in Montgomery County. Home to the annual Kemper Open, the county hosted the U.S. Open and the Kemper Open back-to-back in 1997. These courses are open to the public:

Falls Road—18 holes
10800 Falls Rd., Potomac
301/299-5156

Hampshire Greens—18 holes
616 Firestone Dr., Ashton/Sandy Spring
301/476-7999

Laytonsville—18 holes
7130 Dorsey Rd., Laytonsville
301/948-5288

Little Bennett—18 holes
25900 Prescott Rd., Clarksburg
301/253-1515

Needwood—19 holes/9 executive holes
6724 Needwood Rd., Derwood
301/948-1075

Northwest Park—27 holes
15701 Layhill Rd., Silver Spring
301/598-6100

Poolesville—18 holes
16601 W. Willard Rd., Poolesville
301/428-8143

Rattlewood—18 holes
13501 Penn Shop Rd., Mt. Airy
(Frederick County border)
301/607-9000

Sligo Creek Park—9 holes
9701 Sligo Creek Pkwy., Silver Spring
301/585-6006

White Oak Golf Course—9 holes
10911 New Hampshire Ave., Silver Spring
301/593-6910

County/Howard County border. The gardens began in 1949 as a labor of love by Raymond Bellamy, late chairman of the Washington Suburban Sanitary Commission (WSSC); maintenance and improvement has been provided over the years by WSSC personnel. Ten Oaks Nursery in Clarksville donated more than 300 plants to supplement cuttings, and the garden now contains 22,000 azaleas, hybrids, and other spring-blooming plants. The display is best in May and June. Free.

The soaring architecture of the Mormon **Washington D.C. Temple,** 9900 Stoneybrook Dr., Kensington, 301/588-0650, can be seen for miles in the lower county area. Though the temple is not open to the public, the extensive formal gardens are, and the grounds and building are especially festive during the Christmas holidays. Free.

Seneca Creek State Park, 11950 Clopper Rd., Gaithersburg, 301/924-2127, is a rural enclave on the west side of the county. Its 6,000-acre grounds and lake offer hiking, biking, fishing, and canoeing. Trails wind past a historic mill and stone quarry, and there's a Frisbee disc-golf course and playground. This is a day-use park, open Oct.–Apr. weekends and holidays ($2 per vehicle admission), daily May–Sept. ($2 per person admission).

Riley's Lockhouse, lock 24 (mile 22.7) in the park, is the only original one left on the canal. It's at the end of Riley's Lock Road (on the Potomac), off River Road in the southernmost part of Seneca Creek State Park. The lockhouse is open to the public for tours Mar.–Nov. Sat.–Sun. 1–4 P.M.

ENTERTAINMENT AND EVENTS

The hotspot for entertainment in the area is the recently built **American Film Institute (AFI) Silver Theatre and Cultural Center,** 8633 Colesville Rd., Silver Spring, 301/495-6776, www.afi.com. The three-screen film complex is anchored by the rehabilitation of the historic 1938 Silver Theatre, and offers a year-round program of American and international cinema, in addition to an eclectic mix of festivals, premieres, on-stage guest appearances, and educational programs. One festival, SILVER-DOCS, sponsored by AFI/Discovery Documentary, is an annual competition that selects and shows the best documentaries from all over the world.

The Montgomery County Dept. of Economic Development, Agricultural Services Division, sponsors an annual **Farm Tour Harvest Sale** in July. More than 20 farms open their doors to the public. Fresh produce is for sale, and other activities such as hayrides, demonstrations, and music are also planned. The tourism bureau and libraries in the county provide maps and brochures. Free.

SHOPPING

Judging from the number of options for shopping in Montgomery County, residents have a great deal of time and money on their hands. The 10-mile stretch of road between Bethesda and Rockville is known locally as the "miracle mile." It's lined with shopping centers for every taste and budget, from G Street Fabrics in the Mid-Pike Plaza, 11800 Rockville Pike, to Lord & Taylor and Bloomingdale's in the White Flint Center, 11301 Rockville Pike.

Similar to New York's Fifth Avenue, the shops in Chevy Chase on **Wisconsin Avenue** at Bradley Boulevard house the most sophisticated national and international purveyors of clothing, jewelry, and accessories (think Ralph Lauren and Armani).

Specialty shops can also be found in historic communities such as Burtonsville, Damascus, Germantown, Kensington, and Poolesville. These quaint towns have a corner on antiques, especially the community of Kensington.

ACCOMMODATIONS

The heavily urbanized zone of Montgomery County—Bethesda, Rockville, Silver Spring, Gaithersburg, and nearby College Park (just over the line in Prince George's County)—offers dozens of chain hotels. The outlying rural areas feature additional hotels and a few B&Bs. Here are a few lodgings of note.

Bethesda Marriott, 5151 Pooks Hill Rd.,

301/897-9400 or 800/228-9290, www.marriott.com, is a particularly fine example of the chain—not unexpected, since this area is Marriott's home base. This one offers all the usual amenities, including two restaurants, a lounge, health club, tennis courts, and indoor/outdoor pool. It's especially convenient, as Pooks Hill Road is right off Route 355, far enough away from the urban centers to be pleasant, but right in the middle of everything. Rates range from $79–170, depending on the season and room. They offer weekend packages and discounts.

Longwood Manor Bed & Breakfast, 2900 DuBarry Ln., Brookeville, 301/774-1002, www.erols.com/longwoodmanor, is a restored 1817 Georgian manor set in two acres of lush gardens. The building, six miles north of Washington, D.C., resembles Mt. Vernon—Thomas Jefferson was a houseguest. Rooms and suites have private baths, and there's a swimming pool. Rates range $95–150.

Cherry Hill Park, 9800 Cherry Hill Rd., College Park, 301/937-7116 or 800/801-6449, www.cherryhillpark.com, has campsites for tents and RVs. It's open year-round, and offers a pool, sauna, hot tub, and store in addition to electric, cable TV, water, and sewer hookups. Prices run $35–50 per night. Cherry Hill is at the junction of the U.S. 95/495 split. The Metro Bus stops by the campground to make getting around easy.

FOOD

Bethesda has a reputation for a plethora of exotic eateries mixed with mall quick-stops and high-end restaurants. Those in search of sophisticated menus and exotic settings can stroll down Bethesda's **Restaurant Row.** Tucked within this eight-block neighborhood between Route 355 (Rockville Pike/Wisconsin Avenue) and Old Georgetown Road is a mix of traditional, seafood, and ethnic restaurants; European, Asian, Middle Eastern, Caribbean, and South American fare are all available in the shifting kaleidoscope of eateries. Equally sophisticated are the many restaurants along **Connecticut Avenue** (Route 185) near Chevy Chase Circle (at the intersection of Western Avenue on the border of Washington, D.C.).

One of the local favorites in Restaurant Row is **Rock Bottom Brewery,** 7900 Norfolk Ave., 301/652-1311. It's a popular place to stop for well-made, sophisticated pub food and brews. Open for lunch and dinner, prices average $6–16.

At **BD's Mongolian Barbeque,** 7201 Wisconsin Ave., 301/657-1080, www.bdsmongolianbarbeque.com, you can create your own stir-fry from mounds of meats, poultry, seafood, and vegetables for a fixed price ($5–10 for lunch, $13 for dinner). It has a full bar, too.

One unusual place to pick up supplies in Bethesda is the **Montgomery Farms Women's Cooperative Market,** 7155 Wisconsin Ave. (across Willow Lane from BD's Mongolian Barbeque). An anachronism among downtown Bethesda's skyscrapers and modern development, this old wooden building houses a produce, meat, and poultry market Wed.–Sat. 7 A.M.–3 P.M. year-round, and a Sunday farmers market 9 A.M.–5 P.M.

Along the "miracle mile," the **Silver Diner,** 11806 Rockville Pike, Rockville, 301/770-2828, is a glorified version of the old-style diners made from converted dining cars. This oft-packed place is on the main road in front of a shopping center. Breakfast, lunch, and dinner are served daily, and prices average $6–12.

GETTING AROUND

Like most American counties, Montgomery is most conveniently traveled by automobile. However, the Washington Metropolitan Area Transit Authority (the Metro) does have service lines throughout the gateway portion of the county, radiating out of Washington, D.C. The west Red line crosses into the county at Friendship Heights and travels northwest through Bethesda past Rockville to Shady Grove; the east Red line travels up through Silver Spring through Wheaton to Glenmont. The Green line winds northeast through College Park and Greenbelt. All stations sell fare cards, and fares are based on when and where you travel. A $5 One-Day Pass (available at most stations) buys a full day of Metro rides and will get you most anywhere; it's also a great way to see all the attractions in D.C.

INFORMATION

Contact the Montgomery County Visitor Information Center, 12900 Middlebrook Road, Suite 1400, Germantown, MD 20874, 301/916-0698 or 800/925-0880, www.visitmontgomery.com.

Prince George's County

SIGHTS

Central Maryland offers a marvelous government-sponsored panoply of attractions that are free to the public: The Patuxent Research Refuge and National Wildlife Visitor Center, Beltsville Agricultural Research Center, and NASA/Goddard Space Flight Center.

Patuxent Research Refuge/ National Wildlife Visitor Center

This facility, 10901 Scarlet Tanager Loop off Powder Mill Road, Laurel, 301/497-5766, www.prr.r5.fws.gov, is so vast that airline pilots look for the pool of black that marks the unlighted refuge to sight their way to BWI Airport at night. Nearly 13,000 acres were carved from former military lands to create this sanctuary; Patuxent is the oldest and one of the largest wildlife research centers in the United States and the world.

Primarily used for wildlife and environmental research, the grounds include four miles of walking trails and half-hour guided electric tram tours through surrounding woods, fields, and wetlands on weekends from spring through fall (weekday tours may be arranged in advance). The visitor center is particularly worthwhile. Visually dramatic dioramas on global and environmental issues, habitats, endangered species, and the techniques and tools of research scientists make up the largest part of the center. Gray wolves, whooping cranes, sea otters, and other creatures are

THE NATIONAL WILDLIFE REFUGE SYSTEM

Sponsored by the U.S. Fish and Wildlife Service, the refuge system is a diverse network of national public lands set aside for conservation of fish, wildlife, and plants, a total of more than 92 million acres of land and water. Though President Theodore Roosevelt established the first national refuge in 1903 (Florida's Pelican Island) to protect egrets, herons, and other endangered birds, J. Clark Salyer, a government official, was considered "Father of the Refuge System." Representing the nascent refuge movement, Salyer began the process of placing land aside during the severe drought of the 1930s by driving around the country and buying critical wetland as waterfowl refuges. Several such refuges have been named for writers and artists associated with an appreciation of the natural world: Mark Twain, Rachel Carson, J. J. Audubon, and "Ding" Darling, originator of the duck stamp.

Of the 500 current refuges, nearly 400 protect or have reintroduced threatened and endangered species. Roughly 98 percent of the land in the refuge system is open to the public. Though the system is better funded now than at any time in the past, refuge personnel are calling for changes. Ninety percent of refuge managers who responded to a survey by Public Employees for Environmental Responsibility said refuges need more attention from the Fish and Wildlife Service. About 60 percent of the managers endorsed a 1997 proposal by more than 100 votes calling for a refuge "chief" in the Fish and Wildlife Service and a line of budgetary command flowing to regional refuges. Another 34 percent endorsed a National Audubon Society proposal to create a separate agency for refuges within the Department of the Interior.

In spite of being understaffed and underpublicized, refuges draw 34 million Americans each year to watch birds and other wildlife, and to hunt, fish, and go on interpretive hikes. Hundreds of national wildlife refuges are located along the major waterfowl flyways. Patuxent, on the Atlantic flyway, is one of these stepping-stones, preserving the Eastern U.S. corridor so hundreds of bird species may survive their annual migration.

frozen in time in their natural habitats. Another section of the center is set up as a viewing pod with spotting scopes, binoculars, and radio tracking equipment for visitors to observe wildlife through a large picture window overlooking part of the refuge. Free wildlife films are offered on weekends, and there's a gift shop on the premises. The staff is dedicated, knowledgeable, and unabashedly pro-wildlife. Considering the excellence of the displays and the opportunity for learning and appreciating the bounty of the planet alongside those who have made this study their lives, this is not a place one would expect to get in for free—but it is. There is a nominal charge to ride the tram: $2 for adults, and $1 for children (12 and under) and seniors. The visitor center and refuge are open 10 A.M.–5:30 P.M. daily.

Beltsville Agricultural Research Center

The purpose of this research center is similar to that of Patuxent—to use current resources in the best way possible. This 7,000-acre U.S. Department of Agriculture facility is made up of 47 laboratories and management units on a working/experimental farm, and includes the U.S. National Arboretum some distance away in northeast Washington, D.C. (3501 New York Ave. NE, 202/245-2726). The National Visitor Center, Log Lodge Road (follow signs on Powder Mill Road), 301/504-9403, www.barc.usda.gov, is housed in a magnificent log structure built by the Civilian Conservation Corps during the Depression. It features an overview of the research done at the facility and an apiary with the queen bee marked in blue among millions of her workers (searching for her among the horde is a busy, buzzy version of *Where's Waldo?*). Guided tours of the agricultural center field laboratories and buildings are available at no charge by appointment only through the visitor center (write or call ahead).

The scope of the research done on the premises is extensive. Livestock and poultry studies include development of natural products as diet additives to increase disease resistance (and eliminate dependence on antibiotics); research on the Chesapeake Bay ecosystem revealed significant amounts of pesticides returning to land in rain and dust. Scientists developed two new American elm varieties resistant to the fungus that nearly eliminated the species in the 1930s, and other researchers developed DEXA, a method to measure bone density and body composition via radiation equivalent to a fraction of a dental x-ray. Also under way are studies on the most effective ways to recycle nutrients in manure, sustainable plant production through cover crops, and 100 percent recyclable packing "peanuts" (made from corn byproducts).

The visitor center is open Mon.–Fri. 8 A.M.–4:30 P.M., and guided tours may be reserved during those hours. Admission and tours are free.

NASA/Goddard Space Flight Center

The home of acronyms! Goddard (GSFC), Soil Conservation Road, Greenbelt, 301/286-8981, http://pao.gsfc.nasa.gov/vc/vc.htm, was established in 1959 as the National Aeronautics and Space Administration's first center devoted to the exploration of space. Named for physicist Dr. Robert Goddard, the facility continues to seek answers about the formation and substance of the universe, but is also dedicated to the study of earth as an environmental system and the development and use of cutting-edge technologies that impact the world.

One of GSFC's first projects was OAO-2, the Orbiting Astronomical Observatory launched in 1968 to determine the properties of interstellar dust and hot stars in the Milky Way. Numerous other projects followed, including the Hubble Space Telescope (HST), the first observation device designed to be serviced in space. The successor to HST is the much more powerful NGST (Next Generation Space Telescope), with a launch date of 2007. Several NASA satellites have been launched to study the ozone layer and map weather patterns, useful for predicting environmental damage and storms. Goddard researchers developed a new nonsurgical technique for de-

NASA capsule at Goddard Space Flight Center

tecting breast cancer (BBS-Breast Biopsy System). And GSFC's Acousto-optic Imaging Spectrometer (AImS) was used by the Smithsonian in 1998 to identify and repair deterioration to the Star-Spangled Banner (the giant flag that flew over Fort McHenry in Baltimore in 1814, inspiring Francis Scott Key).

GSFC offers many programs to the public free of charge throughout the year. In the visitor center's 2,600-square-foot gallery, self-guided earth science exhibits, films, and hands-on activities are available to visitors by appointment Mon.–Fri. On the first and third Sunday of each month at 1 P.M., a host of model rockets are launched (visitors are welcome to bring their own). On second Saturdays, Oct.–Apr., 7–9 P.M., stargazers meet to explore the night skies followed by films and presentations on astronomy. One-hour tours of the research labs, including an opportunity to meet some of the scientists and staff, are available by appointment. The center also offers special programs for children, such as

© JOANNE MILLER

CENTRAL MARYLAND

ROCKET SCIENTIST

Robert H. Goddard's experiments in rocket propulsion first came to the notice of the public in 1907 when a powder rocket misfired, producing an acrid cloud of smoke in the basement of the physics building at Worcester Polytechnic Institute, where Goddard studied. Fortunately, he was not expelled. Goddard went on to teach physics at his alma mater, and later at Clark University, but his true life's work was invention.

He received two U.S. patents for rocket propulsion fuel and rocket structural developments, and, two days before the 1918 Armistice, created a prototype for the bazooka at the Aberdeen Proving Ground in Aberdeen, Maryland. His launching platform was a music rack. In 1926, Goddard built and tested the first rocket using liquid fuel in Auburn, Massachusetts. Though his discoveries at the time were as revolutionary as those of the Wright Brothers, they made little impression on government officials. Modest subsidies by the Smithsonian Institution and the Daniel Guggenheim Foundation made it possible for him to sustain a lifetime of research while teaching.

In 1920, when Goddard wrote of the possibility of a rocket reaching the moon, the press ridiculed his idea. After that incident, he was reported to have "reached firm convictions about the virtues of the press corps which he held for the rest of his life." During World War II, Goddard helped to develop practical jet-assisted takeoff and liquid propellant rocket motors capable of variable thrust. Goddard's achievements received little notice until the dawn of the space age, when many of his ideas were used as the basis for modern technology. In September 1959, the 86th Congress authorized the issuance of a Congressional gold medal to honor Professor Robert H. Goddard, space age pioneer.

"Rockets, Rockets, Rockets!" (basic rocketry, an alternative to blowing up the garage with the Jr. Science Lab Kit) and "Stars in the Sky" (create your own constellation). Children's programs must be booked at least two months in advance due to space limitations (or should I say mass/volume limitations?). Call to reserve and verify event schedules: 301/286-9041.

Started in response to the 1957 Soviet launch of *Sputnik*, GSFC grew from 160 researchers to nearly 12,000 in Greenbelt (there is another center in Wallops, Virginia). It's a thrilling way to introduce budding scientists to the real thing. The visitor center and neighboring gift shop are open by appointment 10 A.M.–4 P.M. except major holidays, and admission and all activities are free.

OTHER POINTS OF INTEREST
College Park Aviation Museum
This airy, modern museum, 1985 Corporal Frank Scott Dr. (off Paint Branch Parkway), College Park, 301/864-6029, is set on the world's oldest continuously operating airport. The airport was established in 1909 when Wilbur Wright came to train two military officers to fly the U.S. government's first airplane; in fact, an audio-animatronic Wright greets museum visitors. He stands next to the stopwatch and other artifacts Wright used and tells about the airfield's early years.

The 27,000-square-foot glass and brick museum was designed by the same architectural team that produced the Smithsonian's National Air and Space Museum. The display area features a rare 1911 Wright B Aeroplane, a 1918 Curtiss Jenny, and others suspended in midflight like insects in amber. Other rooms offer interactive exhibits: a wind tunnel, a map with headphones so visitors can hear local air traffic communication, a flight simulator, and more. An on-site aviation library offers research opportunities (call 301/864-6029 for more information). The museum sponsors many programs throughout the year, such as model-making workshops, Air Career Night (with speakers who examine the past, present, and future of aviation), and the annual AirFair held in September. It's open daily 10 A.M.–5 P.M.; admission is $4.

Surratt House Museum

Built on a crossroads and operated as a tavern before and during the Civil War, this is the home of Mary Elizabeth Surratt, convicted conspirator in the assassination of President Abraham Lincoln. The well-preserved house, 9118 Brandywine Rd., Clinton (formerly Surrattsville, the name was changed after Mrs. Surratt's death), 301/868-1121, looks much as it did during the 1860s, with the table set for visitors and the post office/tavern ready to dispense mail and whiskey. The upper floor remains open to show the concealment space that held the "shooting irons" used to confirm Mrs. Surratt's guilt and cause her to be the first woman executed by the federal government.

Though Prince George's County and Southern Maryland in general were pro-Confederacy, and the Surratt tavern a well-known meeting place for Southern sympathizers, historians continue to argue whether Mrs. Surratt was a pawn in a plot hatched by her son and his friend John Wilkes Booth. The house/museum features rotating period displays throughout the year, and is home base for the John Wilkes Booth Escape Route Tours in April and September of each year. The 12-hour bus tour visits the roads and houses used by Booth (most of which are intact). Call for current prices and reservations on the tour. The museum is open March 1–mid-Dec.; guided tours are conducted by costumed docents Thurs.–Fri. 11 A.M.–3 P.M. and Sat.–Sun. noon–4 P.M. Admission is $2.

Belair Mansion and Stable Museum

Built in 1745, the mansion, 12207 Tulip Grove Dr., Bowie, 301/809-3089, www.cityofbowie.org/comserv/museums.htm, was the Georgian plantation house of Samuel Ogle, Provincial Governor of Maryland. Enlarged in 1914 by the New York architectural firm of Delano and Aldrich, the mansion was also the home of William Woodward, famous horseman in the first half of the 20th century. Restored to its former glory, the house reflects its occupants in artwork and furnishings. Governor Samuel Ogle's paintings of the Four Seasons, a gift from Lord Baltimore, Proprietor of the Colony of Maryland, hang in the hall. Later works include privately issued prints of the famous Belair Stud Thoroughbred racehorses, and a 1932 bronze of Triple Crown winner Gallant Fox. The mansion is open Thurs.–Sun. 1–4 P.M.; admission is by donation.

Belair Stable, 2835 Belair Dr., 301/809-3088, was part of the famous "Belair Stud," one of America's premier racing stables from 1930 to 1960, home to Gallant Fox and Omaha, father-and-son winners of the Triple Crown; Nashua, "Horse of the Year" in 1955; and many other well-known racehorses. Until its closing in 1957, Belair was the oldest continually operated racing horse farm in the United States. The stable has been restored and is open as a museum, with displays on thoroughbred history and bloodlines, racing silks, and trophies, a carriage collection, and the 1923 stable master's apartment. It is open free of charge Thurs.–Sun. 1–4 P.M.

PARKS AND SCENIC SPOTS

The **Accokeek Foundation/National Colonial Farm,** 3400 Bryan Point Rd., Accokeek (uh-CO-keek), 301/283-2113, is a bit out of the way, but definitely worth it, both for the destination and the verdant farmland that surrounds it. The grounds are home to a living-history mid-18th-century farm with rebuilt structures, and the Ecosystem Farm, a modern experimental organic vegetable farm. Because of its isolation, it's possible to experience the drifting sunlit pollen, quiet waters, and peaceful surroundings that the earliest settlers took for granted (in between endless chores). Today, flyovers from BWI periodically violate the silence, but the occasional interference is a minor consideration. A solitary walk around the grounds will leave you enchanted. Piscataway Park, on the property, offers a variety of trails, meadows, a boardwalk, and a public fishing pier. The grounds are open dawn–dusk year-round. The visitor center is open March 15–Dec. 15 Tues.–Sun., Dec. 16–March 14 weekends only 10 A.M.–5 P.M. Admission is $2.

On weekends, from the end of May to early September, Accokeek Foundation offers boat rides to Mount Vernon, George Washington's plantation, across the Potomac in Virginia. The

DID SHE OR DIDN'T SHE?

Mary Elizabeth Surratt, a devout Catholic, had the unfortunate luck to be married to a wastrel alcoholic and fervent supporter of the secessionist cause. During the Civil War, the tavern and post office John Surratt Sr. operated in Surrattsville (now Clinton) became a hub of pro-South activities and a convenient stop for Confederate agents. In 1862, he died suddenly and left his wife with complicated debts, runaway slaves, and insistent creditors. Their youngest son, John Jr., had returned from college and replaced his father as postmaster, a position he was removed from for "disloyalty" to the Union. Mary, her son John, and daughter Anna were forced to move to a house they had previously leased out at 541 H St. in Washington, D.C. Her intentions were to rent out the extra rooms and thus support herself and her family. By March of 1865, seven boarders filled the H Street house.

Meanwhile, John Wilkes Booth, born in 1839 to an eminent British tragedian, Junius Brutus Booth, was developing an obsession with Abraham Lincoln. In a room of the McHenry House in Meadville, Pennsylvania, where Booth was staying, a pane of window glass bore the following inscription in Booth's handwriting: "Abe Lincoln departed this life, Aug. 13th, 1864, by the effects of poison." Whether Booth actually tried to poison the president is unknown, but he had long fomented a conspiracy to do the president harm. During the summer of 1864, Booth formulated a plan to hold Lincoln hostage in Richmond to force the exchange of Confederate prisoners. Booth traveled to Montreal, Canada (a meeting place for the Confederate underground), in October 1864 and was given a letter of introduction to sympathizers in Charles County, Maryland. He made two trips to the county in November and December, where he met Dr. Samuel A. Mudd and Thomas Harbin, a Confederate secret service agent. Harbin counted among his associates a courier for the Confederate government, John Surratt Jr.

Dr. Mudd met Booth in Washington in December 1864, a meeting that included John Surratt Jr. Surratt then deeded to his mother all of his worldly goods and proceeded to help Booth round up an active group of kidnap conspirators. All of the conspirators—Harbin, David E. Herrold (a.k.a. Herold), Lewis Powell, George Atzerodt, and others—met at Mrs. Surratt's H Street boarding house at one time or another, and many had "private" conversations with her, according to witnesses.

On March 15, 1865, Booth explored Ford's Theatre as a possible place for the abduction. On March 17, he heard that Lincoln was going to attend a play in another location just outside the city and mobilized his conspirators. In preparation for escape after the kidnapping, weapons had been taken to Surrattsville on the afternoon of the 17th. Since the tavern was searched regularly by Union troops, the carbines were hidden between the joists above the dining room, where they remained. Lincoln never showed up, and the conspirators, disgruntled and in disagreement over further action, split up.

Booth became more radical. He persuaded a few of his old cohorts to join him in his next scheme. Since it was obvious that the South was about to surrender, kidnapping would be futile; Booth insisted the only meaningful act would be the assassination of the president and his cabinet. John Surratt was not among the conspirators—he had left on assignment from Confederate General Edwin Lee to Elmira, New York.

On April 10, Booth came to Mrs. Surratt's H Street home. That evening, she asked Louis Weichmann, one of her boarders, to take her out to the Surrattsville tavern the next day in order to settle a debt. Before they reached Surrattsville, they met John Lloyd, keeper of the Surrattsville tavern. She asked him to "get [the shooting irons] out ready: they would be wanted soon," according to his testimony. On April 14, 1865, Mrs. Surratt again asked her boarder to drive her to the tavern, again to settle a debt. "Wait, Mr. Weichmann, I must get those things of Booth's," she told him as they were about to leave, and came back with a paper-wrapped package which she described as "glass." At the tavern, Mrs. Surratt gave John Lloyd the package and told him to have the package, weapons, and some whiskey ready, and to give them to "whoever would call for them that night."

On the morning of April 14, Abraham Lincoln learned the details of Lee's surrender from his son and, in a joyful mood, met with his cabinet. That evening, as planned, he attended a performance at Ford's Theatre with his wife. A well-dressed gentleman—Booth—entered the theater by the rear door. He went up the stairs and to the box occupied by the president. Taking out a card, he gave it to the president's messenger, and immediately followed him into the box. As he entered he fired, aiming at the president's head. One of the president's guests tried to stop Booth, but Booth stabbed him in the chest. Booth leaped down to the stage, shouting, "Sic semper tyrannis" (Thus be it ever to tyrants), the motto of Virginia. In a moment, he was gone.

As the president lay mortally wounded, one of Booth's co-conspirators appeared at the door of Secretary of State Seward's chamber and pretended he was a messenger. In the bloody melee that followed, several of Seward's attendants were wounded, though he himself survived.

Booth escaped with David Herrold. (For more on Booth's fate, see the special topic "Booth's Wild Ride" in the Southern Maryland chapter.) Police went to Mrs. Surratt's H Street house on a tip; on April 17, police arrested Mrs. Surratt, her daughter Anna, and several boarders. While the police were at the house, a young man dressed as a laborer came to the door—Mrs. Surratt denied knowing him. After being questioned by the police, he was arrested, and was later identified as Lewis "Paine" Powell, attacker of Secretary Seward and an occasional visitor at Mrs. Surratt's. Three days later, another conspirator, George Atzerodt, was captured near Middleburg, Maryland. On April 14, he had stayed at the Kirkwood House, Washington, where Vice President Johnson was staying. A revolver was found there, along with some bowie knives and evidence of his complicity with Booth. Apparently, he had lost his nerve.

The conspirators in custody were tried in Washington by a military court. Four of them—Herrold (captured in Virginia), Atzerodt, Powell, and Mrs. Surratt—were hung. Mrs. Surratt insisted on her innocence to the end, and Powell said, "She might have known something was going on, but did not know what."

Her defenders portrayed her as a religious woman, a good mother, a person who was in the wrong place at the wrong time, but her boarder Louis Weichmann wrote, "I don't believe that Mrs. Surratt was an innocent woman." Though Mrs. Surratt was reputed to have considered Weichmann as a son, his statements at the trial were the most damning.

Mrs. Surratt's son John escaped to Canada after the assassination and remained there until September 1865, when he sailed to Liverpool. In the spring of 1866, Surratt was arrested in Italy but escaped and fled to Egypt, where he was once again arrested. John Surratt was brought to trial in a civil court, and the proceedings ended with a hung jury. He was set free, and never indicted again.

boat ride is $5; a ride and combination Mount Vernon tour package is $13. The boats depart at 11 A.M., 1 P.M., 2:20 P.M., and 3:40 P.M. Reservations are encouraged; call 301/283-2113.

Montpelier Mansion and Cultural Arts Center, Muirkirk Road, Laurel, 301/953-1376 (mansion) and 301/953-1993 (cultural arts center), is a true Georgian beauty. The mansion, completed in 1783, hosted both George Washington and Abigail Adams, wife of President John Adams (traveling separately, we assume). Mrs. Adams described the estate as a "Large, Handsome, Elegant House, where I was received with what we might term true English Hospitality." Public tours are available Mar.–Nov., Sunday noon–4 P.M., and admission is $2. The nearby cultural arts center houses three galleries and studios with working artists. The arts center sponsors several events throughout the year, including a jazz series with artists such as Charlie Byrd and McCoy Tyner. It's open daily 10 A.M.–5 P.M., and entry is free. Also on the grounds is a charming gift shop, **The Little Teapot,** that features tea-related gifts, candies, and cookies. It's open Wednesday and Sat.–Sun. noon–4 P.M.

Fort Washington National Park, 13551 Fort Washington Rd., Fort Washington, 301/763-4600, is a pleasant park on the Potomac surrounding an authentic 19th-century fort. Fort Warburton, as it was originally known, was built in 1809 after the Treaty of Paris. British/American hostilities continued after the United States was formed, and the fort was built to protect the new nation's capital. Its effectiveness came into question, however, when the British sailed up the Patuxent River to the east and marched overland to Washington, D.C., sacking the city in 1814. Fort Warburton/Washington was blown up by the American commander to keep it from falling into enemy hands. In 1815, Secretary of War James Monroe hired the temperamental architect of Washington, Pierre L'Enfant, to redesign the fort. He was fired less than a year later (what a résumé he must have had), and the fort was periodically ignored and upgraded over the years, serving in some military capacity until 1939, when it was transferred to the Department of the Interior. After a short stint as a military facility during World War II, the fort was

converted into a public park in 1946. It's open daily 8 A.M.–dusk, and admission is $2.

Merkle Wildlife Sanctuary, 11704 Fenno Rd., Upper Marlboro, 301/888-1410, offers a visitors center with captive live animals, exhibits, and demonstration gardens, four hiking trails of varying difficulty (ranging from three-fourths of a mile to 2.8 miles), and a spectacular drive-through route.

Edgar Merkle, founder of Merkle Press, Washington, D.C., and an ardent conservationist, arranged to gift and sell portions of his 400-acre farm to the state of Maryland with the stipulation that the area would continue to be managed as a refuge. The refuge now encompasses more than 1,600 acres, and is one of several that are part of the Patuxent Agricultural Demonstration Project, created to improve water quality on the river.

One of the best features of the sanctuary is its Critical Area Driving Tour (CADT), a one-way, seven-mile loop with pullouts and observation towers. The road passes through several different ecosystems, with excellent opportunities to enjoy wildlife sightings. Fall highlights include Canada geese breeding season; midsummer is rife with riparian activity; and each spring, a bounty of colorful wildflowers bloom in fields and marshes. The CADT is open to autos Sunday 10 A.M.–3 P.M. Jan.–mid-Sept., every Saturday, it's open 10 A.M.–3 P.M. for hikers and bikers only—the best way to be part of the landscape. Those who wish to tour the CADT must register at the visitor center and pick up a map; it's open daily 10 A.M.–4 P.M. and the sanctuary trails are open 7 A.M.–sunset. Free.

OTHER RECREATION

Consider the **Old Town Laurel Walking Tour.** Established as a mill town in the mid-1800s, Laurel continues to be the hub of a busy, populous area. Unlike most towns, however, Laurel's Old Town, along Main Street from U.S. 1 (Baltimore Avenue) to 9th Street, retained many of its historic buildings, including the brick, stone, and stucco mill company workers' houses, an old electric car station made into a saloon (Oliver's), and the pharmacy, built in 1871. Stop by the Laurel Museum, 817 Main St.—the town's oldest mill worker's house, from 1840—for a map and schedule of tours. It's open Wednesday 10 A.M.–2 P.M. and Sunday noon–4 P.M., 301/725-7975. Free.

Six Flags America, Rte. 214, Largo, 301/249-1500, www.sixflags.com, is one of the more than 30 mega-theme parks owned by Premier Parks. The company poured in more than $40 million to develop the old Adventure World site in 1999. Much of the sweet, old, occasionally run-down amusement park feel has been exchanged for a slick, racy cartoon theme park that, judging from the crowd, appeals to urban teens and young families.

Premier managed to keep the best (two wooden roller coasters, one of which, the Wild One, is rated among the top five in the world by coaster aficionados) while adding high-speed thrill rides—The Joker's Jinx, The Bat Wing, Superman Ride of Steel, and Two-Face twister roller coasters among them. Also new is a revamped section for smaller kids, Looney Tunes Movie Town; several live musical entertainments (Bugs Bunny stars in one); and a stunt show, "Batman Thrill Spectacular." An elaborate water park, game arcade, and all the fair food you'd ever want are also on the premises. Day admission to the more than 100 rides, water park, shows, and play activities (excluding Go-Karts and the Rock Climbing Wall) is $35.99 for adults, $24.99 for kids 54 inches and under; kids three and under are free. Parking is an additional $9 per car. Six Flags is open April 12–Oct. 31 with some blackout dates; the water park is open third weekend in May–Labor Day weekend. Hours vary (as late as 10 P.M. on July and August weekends) but the park always opens at 10 A.M.

Prince George's Equestrian Center, 14900 Pennsylvania Ave., Upper Marlboro, 301/952-7900, features a heavy schedule of dressage, hunter/jumper, and breed horse shows from May through August. **Rosecroft Raceway,** 6336 Rosecroft Dr., Ft. Washington, 301/567-4000, features harness racing May–Aug. **Laurel Park Race Track,** Racetrack Road off Route 198, Laurel, 301/735-0400, www.marylandracing.com, features thoroughbred racing, including the historic half-million-dollar February sprint races.

ACCOMMODATIONS AND FOOD

Colony South Hotel, 7401 Surratt's Rd., Clinton, 301/856-4500 or 800/537-1147, is a good option for lodging in an area that's slim on options other than chain hotels. The Colony has been around awhile, a fact that's easy to discern if you wander onto one of the "smoking" floors; however, the entire hotel has been upgraded to attract a more distinguished clientele, and it does. The rooms are updated and attractive, and amenities include a fitness center, indoor pool, tennis courts, and an outdoor walking/jogging trail. There's a small takeout café near the lobby, and the **Wayfarer Restaurant** serves breakfast ($6), lunch ($9), and dinner ($19) daily, and brunch on Sunday. The **Decoy Lounge** is the local hotspot. Rooms start at $159; kitchenettes are also available. The hotel offers discounts for AAA, AARP, and military.

The **Bay 'n Surf,** 14411 Baltimore Ave. (U.S. 1), Laurel, 301/776-7021, is one of those places you'd whiz right by unless you knew how good the food was. Though it offers beef and chicken dishes, this restaurant is known for its fresh seafood platters. Lunch is served Mon.–Fri. ($7), dinner daily ($19). A good bet for lunch is the backfin crab cake quarter-pounder with french fries and cole slaw for $6.95. Everything on the menu is available for carryout.

94th Aero Squadron Restaurant, 5240 Paint Branch Pkwy., College Park, 301/699-9400, is a delightful theme restaurant overlooking the historic College Park Airport. With the atmosphere of a European WWII bistro, it features warm decor, artifacts, and a lawn full of vintage warplanes. Open daily for lunch and dinner, as well as Sunday brunch. Lunch averages $8, dinner $20.

INFORMATION

Prince George's County Conference & Visitors Bureau, 9200 Basil Ct., Ste. 101, Largo, MD 20774, 301/925-8300, www.visitprincegeorge.com, can fill you in on events and attractions in the area.

FESTIVALS AND EVENTS

Phone numbers for events change frequently. The best place to check for updated information is the county tourism bureaus; all are listed in the text.

January/February

January through April, **Spring Has Sprung** at Brookside Gardens Conservatory in Wheaton. Floral displays include dozens of snapdragon varieties developed by local breeder Fred Winkler. 301/949-8230.

March/April

Steeplechase and horse racing make for an exciting day at the **Marlborough Hunt Races,** at the Roedown Farm in Davidsonville, Anne Arundel County. 410/798-5040.

Gladiator meets *Private Ryan* in the annual **Marching Through Time** living history encampment in Glenn Dale (Prince George's County). More than 300 re-enactors represent soldiers and others from Roman times to World War II. Food, craft, and hobby vendors too. 301/464-5291.

Juried traditional, contemporary, and holiday handmade crafts from more than 200 artisans are the focal point of **Celebration of Crafts** at the Oella Mill in Ellicott City. 410/795-2021.

The annual **Maryland Sheep & Wool Festival** in late April or early May will instruct you in "Rug Braiding" and "Hands-on Beginning Shepherd Skills," among dozens of other classes, exhibits, and displays. It's held at the Howard County Fairgrounds in West Friendship. 410/531-3647, www.sheepandwoolfestival.org.

May/June

Columbia Festival of the Arts in June is 10 days of performing arts at Lake Kittamaqundi in Columbia, including two weekends of free performances in addition to ticketed performances, workshops, and master classes. Past years have featured Branford Marsalis, Rick Danko, and many others. 410/715-3044.

While you're in town for music, don't miss **Jazzfest,** presented in partnership with the Festival of the Arts. Jazz greats Jimmy McGriff and Hank Crawford have performed at prior festivals, and events include concerts, workshops, and the "House of Jazz"—dinner and continuous live entertainment. 410/730-7105 or 301/596-0051.

Summer Solstice is celebrated at Accokeek Foundation, 3400 Bryan Point Rd., 301/283-2113, with boat rides, demonstrations, lawn games, and walks along the river.

For more than 100 years, the **Baltimore Watercolor Society's Mid-Atlantic Regional Watercolor Exhibition** has drawn some of the best artists in the region. 301/854-6447.

The **Chesapeake Bay Bridge Walk** gives participants a chance to enjoy views from the bridge in a 4.3-mile-long stroll. 410/228-8405.

June is the month for Maryland's only PGA Tour golf event, the **Kemper Insurance Open,** held annually in Potomac. 301/469-3737.

July/August

John Paul Jones Day, held in July in Annapolis, is a time for flag-raising, presentations, special tours, and colonial period entertainment. 410/263-6933.

Butler's Orchard Peach Festival in Germantown, Montgomery County, offers hayrides, pony rides, a straw mountain, and plenty of peaches. This is one of many celebrations of orchard bounty throughout central, north, and western Maryland. 301/972-3299.

Kunta Kinte, hero of *Roots,* arrived on these shores on the auction block at Annapolis. Today, St. John's College and a host of performers celebrate the **Kunta Kinte Heritage Festival,** a weekend of dance, food, and music. 410/349-0338.

September/October

A benefit for Howard Community College, the **Columbia Classic Grand Prix** is a day of steeplechase, equestrian events, and parades with displays and a food court. 410/772-4828.

Western Regional Park in Columbia constructs a **Mammoth Maze** to "cornfuse" and delight participants during its Harvest Happening. 410/313-7275.

Ghosts of the Patapsco Female Institute is a popular 35-minute moderate walk from 6:30–8:30 P.M. that weaves through the spooky ruins of the old girls' school. Come in costume with a flashlight. Boo! 410/465-8500.

The nation's oldest and largest **Sailboat Show** takes place in Annapolis in October. New sailboats, sailing accessories, equipment, and services are on display. A **Powerboat Show** also takes place this month. 410/268-8828.

Germantown celebrates its heritage during **Oktoberfest;** authentic food, crafts, and games, all to the tunes of a German band. Other entertainment includes hot-air balloon races. 301/217-6798.

The **Maryland Million** is the state's celebration of a 250-year tradition of thoroughbred breeding and racing. A million dollars in purses is wagered on Maryland-sired horses, and other events such as a horse country tour, horse shows, and polo matches are on the roster. Festivities take place at Laurel Park track in Laurel. 410/252-2100.

November/December

Annapolis's justifiably famous historic district hosts **Annapolis by Candlelight** with more than a dozen private homes open for touring. 410/267-7619.

On a more electrified note, three areas in Central Maryland sponsor light displays. **Lights on the Bay** at Sandy Point State Park features a two-mile drive with 50 animated and stationary holiday displays—a benefit for the Anne Arundel Medical Center, 410/260-3161.

Another illuminating event, the **Symphony of Lights** in Columbia, is a spectacular drive-through display of holiday lights. 410/740-7666.

And Seneca Creek State Park near Gaithersburg offers a 3.5-mile drive, **Winter Lights.** 301/258-6310.

Southern Maryland

Southern Maryland used to be one of the least populated areas in the state. Though it still looks like wide-open spaces to visitors, Washingtonians in search of better housing are discovering this once-rural area. The slow development of the southern counties from colonial times to the present made superhighways unnecessary, however—so the suburbanization of southern Maryland is going to take awhile.

The south counties are the birthplace of Maryland as a Euro-American entity, but the area was populated by Native Americans and their predecessors for centuries. The earliest people came to southern Maryland's shores to harvest the natural abundance of the Patuxent River (also known as the "Pax" River) and Chesapeake Bay as early as 5000 B.C. Ample evidence of their lives—oyster shells and native species of corn in storage pits—has been found on the Jefferson Patterson Park archaeological site in Calvert County. Objects from the site have been carbon-dated to A.D. 1450, and other evidence places shore dwellers in the area from 600 B.C. to A.D. 1500. At St. Mary's City, archaeologists have found signs of occupation as early as 7000 B.C.; more recently (4000 B.C.) the area was home to a large

the beach at
Piney Point Park

© JOANNE MILLER

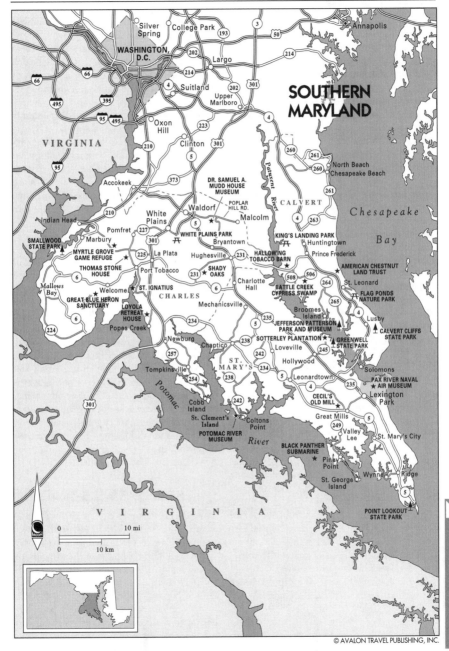

SOUTHERN MARYLAND

settlement, people who formed tribal groups named Piscataway, Yoacomoco, Mattaponi, Doegs, Choptank, and Patuxent.

Two small ships, the *Ark* and *Dove,* under the command of Leonard Calvert, landed in Maryland on March 25, 1634, on St. Clement's Island. The settlers had seen the fires of the native Yoacomoco on the shore, and feared a massacre if they landed there. However, the Indians proved friendly, and Calvert bartered land to build St. Mary's City, the first capital of the colony. In 1694, the capital was moved to Annapolis.

Originally established with religious tolerance in mind—especially for Catholics like the Calverts—the colony became a battleground as the European Reformation spread to the New World. Protestant Reformists sacked St. Mary's and other villages in 1658, capturing Father Andrew White—founder of St. Ignatius, the first Catholic church in Charles County—and another priest, and sent them back to England as prisoners. Even after the Reformation wound down, Catholics found it difficult to practice their religion openly.

During the Revolution, most colonists supported freedom—St. Mary's refused to allow a ship bearing British-taxed tea to land; however, many who depended on the area's chief cash crop, tobacco, held strong economic ties with the mother country.

During the Civil War, tobacco again played a major part in the divisiveness of the area. Though officially a Union state, southern Maryland was almost entirely in support of the Confederacy because of its heavy dependence on slave labor. Blockade runners from Charles and St. Mary's Counties routinely transported food and supplies to the Confederate army on the other side of the Potomac River. After assassinating President Lincoln in Washington, D.C., John Wilkes Booth and his companion David Herrold (or Herold—*Harper's Weekly,* during its Civil War reportage, used the double "R" version) escaped through the southern counties and on to Virginia.

After the Civil War until the 1930s, steamboats continued to be the main source of transportation. When the Potomac River Bridge opened in the late 1930s, the popular mode of travel changed to automobiles, their numbers increased by the building of highways through the counties. The U.S. military found several sites in the counties that suited it, and it became the major employers in both Charles and St. Mary's as tobacco cultivation lost ground in the modern age.

With its foundation of rich soil surrounded by water, the southland was and is a land of bounty. Today, farms separate the small housing divisions and highways, and watermen continue to make their living from the Chesapeake. Though the Potomac River has seen its share of misuse and pollution, even that waterway is making a comeback under the enlightened care of local government and those who dwell near it.

Today, the counties remain largely rural with small pockets of population concentration. It's a sportsman's paradise: 80 percent of all rockfish caught in the Potomac River are caught between the Route 301 bridge and St. Clements Island, and Charles County is known across the country as a world-class largemouth bass fishery. Several shady parks and scenic spots can be found on the serene, rippling waters of the Potomac. As the river widens into the Chesapeake Bay, visitors can view some of the state's most historic sites. On the eastern edge, in Calvert County, boaters, anglers, and beachgoers all have an opportunity to enjoy themselves in uncrowded resorts and villages. Until far more city dwellers from both Baltimore and Washington "discover" southern Maryland, this is a wonderful place to enjoy a quiet vacation. Y'all stay awhile.

ON THE ASSASSIN'S TRAIL

This 50-plus-mile road trip roughly follows the route of John Wilkes Booth's escape after he assassinated President Lincoln during the last days of the Civil War. (For more of the story, see the special topics "Did She or Didn't She?" in the Central Maryland and the Capital Gateway chapter and "Booth's Wild Ride" in this chapter.) New roads have covered the old, and paths have been altered, but with the exception of the dense urban sprawl reaching from Washington, D.C., to Clinton, much of the countryside is as it was in

1865. Some sites are privately owned—please don't disturb the residents—and are so noted. All distances are approximate.

John Wilkes Booth spent considerable time in two Washington, D.C., residences: the Pedersen House, 516 10th St. NW, and Mary Surratt's boarding house, 604 H St. NW. The tale of his escape begins at the Ford Theatre, 511 10th St. NW. Go south on 10th Avenue; turn left (east) on Pennsylvania Avenue across the John Philip Sousa Bridge. On the edge of Washington, D.C., Pennsylvania Avenue becomes Route 4.

Immediately after the assassination, Booth and Herrold crossed the Potomac River on horseback and rode 12 miles through Prince George's County, Maryland, to the Surratt house and tavern, 9110 Brandywine Rd., Clinton, to pick up guns and supplies. About one mile after crossing the Sousa Bridge, take Branch Avenue (Route 5) south. At 4.75 miles, look for Route 337 (Allentown Road), and turn left (west). After a few hundred yards, make a left (south) onto Old Branch Road, which parallels Route 5. Follow Old Branch for 2.66 miles until it crosses Woodyard Road in Clinton—the Surratt House is just south of the crossroads. After visiting the museum, continue south (Old Branch becomes Brandywine Road) for a little over four miles. The road branches to the left (east) and becomes Floral Park Road—it leads directly to U.S. 301/Route 5.

Suffering from a broken leg suffered during his escape from Ford Theater, Booth proceeded with his companion to Charles County. They crossed into Charles County on the Old Washington Road, and then proceeded to Dr. Samuel Mudd's house (about 12 miles). Continue south on U.S. 301 about three miles to Mattawoman/Beantown Road (Route 205), and continue south 2.5 miles until it dead-ends on Poplar Hill Road. Make a left (east) 2.3 miles on Poplar Hill Road to Dr. Samuel Mudd Road; the Mudd farm is less than one-half mile on the left. There, Dr. Mudd set Booth's leg and Booth and Herrold rested for several hours.

Before the assassination, Booth met with Southern sympathizers at Bryantown Tavern. After leaving the Mudd farm, turn right on Dr. Samuel Mudd Road, go 1.5 miles (south), turn right on Bryantown Road (Rte. 232). Go three miles, cross Rte. 5 (Leonardtown Road)—Bryantown Road becomes Oliver's Shop Road, Rte. 232—and immediately turn right onto Trotter Road (west). The tavern, second house on the right, is now privately owned. St. Mary's Catholic Church is one mile south of Trotter Road on Oliver's Shop Road, on the east side.

After leaving Dr. Mudd's home, Booth and Herrold tried to rent a carriage, but were unsuccessful. They continued on horseback and during the next week were seen in the vicinity of Zekiah Swamp. From St. Mary's Church, turn left (south) onto Oliver's Shop Road, and travel four miles to Rte. 6 (stay right at the Y). Turn right (west) on Rte. 6 (Charles Street/New Market Road). In a little less than a mile, you'll see the sign for Zekiah Swamp. (If you'd like to see the Zekiah Swamp Natural Environment Area, turn left on Penns Hill Road—it's 4.5 miles to the south, a 9-mile round-trip). Continue on Rte. 6 roughly three miles and turn left (south) on Bel Alton-Newtown Road). After two miles, you'll come to a plaque on the right for Rich Hill, the home of Samuel Cox, in Bel Alton (privately owned—the house can't be seen until you pass the plaque). Booth and Herrold hid in thick woods on Cox's farm for several days while Union Troops sought them nearby.

Continue on Bel Alton Road about one mile, crossing the railroad tracks; make an immediate left (south) onto Wills Street. Another Confederate sympathizer suspected of sheltering Booth and Herrold owned the Collis House (now private) at 9185 Wills St. At the southern end of the street is a pine thicket where the conspirators hid out.

Return to Bel Alton Road and turn left (west). It dead-ends at Crain Highway, U.S. 301. Take this road south about 1.33 miles to Pope's Creek Road. Turn right on Pope's Creek. On the right side of the road about a mile south is Huckleberry Cottage, home of a Confederate agent, Thomas A. Jones, who also helped to shelter Booth and Herrold. The cottage is on the grounds of the Loyola Retreat House. Jones supplied the boat that ferried the conspirators to Virginia from

Dent's Meadow (about 1.8 miles north of Pope's Creek) on the night of April 21, 1865. Follow Pope's Creek Road about three miles around until it dead-ends at Edgehill Road. Turn left on Edgehill for 1.3 miles to Crain Highway. Turn left on Crain and cross the Harry Nice Memorial Bridge ($1.50 toll) into Virginia.

After crossing the Potomac, you can drive by a couple of homes that sheltered Booth and Herrold. All are privately owned. Turn left at the first traffic light onto Potomac Drive (Rte. 614). Quesenberry house is at the end of Potomac Drive at Ferry Dock Road. Backtrack on Potomac Drive to Rte. 206 (Dahlgren Road) and turn left, eventually crossing U.S. 301 and driving past Rte. 218. Go about 1.5 miles and turn left into the newish Cleydael housing development; turn right at Old Peppermill Road and look for the Cleydael house, second house on the right (an old white frame house with a porch and black shutters). Backtrack out of the Cleydael development, turn left on Rte. 206 and go about a mile; turn left on Rte. 611 (Eden Drive) and go

about two miles, then turn right on U.S. 301 (known here as the James Madison Highway). In the village of Port Royal, turn left on Caroline Street; the Peyton House, now dilapidated, is on the right corner of Caroline and King Streets.

Leaving Port Royal, turn right on King Street, then right on Middle Street, then left on U.S. 301. The plaque for Garrett farm is only 2.5 miles south of Port Royal, but it's in the northbound lane of U.S. 301, so it's best to travel south to Bowling Green and double back. Continue south from Port Royal on U.S. 301 to the 301 South/Business exit into Bowling Green. Turn left at the light onto Main Street; go about .4 mile and stop when you see DeJarnette and Beale Insurance Agency on the left, the site of Star Hotel where Willie Jett stayed (he lead cavalry into Garrett farm). Backtrack to U.S. 301, and turn north toward Port Royal. Travel about nine miles (you'll pass a sign for Peumansend Creek), and look carefully on the right side of the road for the plaque designating the former site of Garrett farm.

Charles County

Charles County is not so much sprawling as diffused. The largest population concentration is around the county seat in La Plata. U.S. 301 runs through the town and leads up to it in either direction with a series of shopping centers and fast-food joints. The remainder of the county is doggedly rural. Long, flat two-lane roads make traveling the backcountry easy by auto or bike.

SIGHTS
Scenic Loop to Cobb Island
This approximately 24-mile round-trip leaves suburban congestion behind and coasts into the low country to Cobb Island; it's ideal for bicycles as well as autos. The lightly traveled paved roads reveal glimpses of plantation homes, many from the mid-18th century, and most privately owned. Start on Rte. 257 (Rock Point Road) past the intersection of U.S. 301 at Newburg. Follow Rte. 257 all the way down to Rte. 254, and then

to the island. Cobb Island itself is mainly residential, with a couple of older seafood restaurants. For the return trip, consider taking Mt. Victoria Road (the road branches off at Tompkinsville in the south and rejoins Rock Point Road at Newburg).

Dr. Samuel A. Mudd House Museum
The Mudd plantation is one of the few houses in Maryland that has remained in the family since original settlement by Thomas Mudd in the mid-1600s. The house and outbuildings are set on 10 acres on Dr. Samuel Mudd Road, La Plata, 301/645-6870. Dr. Samuel Mudd, born in 1833 to a wealthy, slave-owning family, took over the plantation upon his marriage. He was a 32-year-old country doctor, the father of four, when President Lincoln was assassinated. John Wilkes Booth and his companion David Herrold made their way to Mudd's home at 4 A.M. the morning after the assassination. Although he was reputed

© JOANNE MILLER

old plank barn, Charles County

to have met Booth on at least three prior occasions, Dr. Mudd said he did not recognize his patient, and that the two used the names "Tyson" and "Henston." Dr. Mudd set Booth's broken leg and sheltered them until 2 P.M. later in the day. They then left on their own horses after an unsuccessful attempt to rent a carriage. The two were later captured at Garrett farm in Virginia.

During the trial of the conspirators that followed, Dr. Mudd was indicted, although he continued to protest his innocence. One of the conspirators, Mr. O'Loughlin (suspected of an attempt on General Grant's life), Dr. Mudd, and two others who were implicated in helping Booth escape received life sentences. Mudd was sent to Fort Jefferson prison, Dry Tortugas Island, Florida, in 1865. An attempted escape that year failed, and Dr. Mudd was reassigned to the prison's carpentry shop. Another attempt was successful, but Mudd was recaptured and sent back to the prison. In the summer of 1867, yellow fever broke out on the island. After the prison's physician died, Mudd took a heroic role in caring for the sick and came down with the disease himself, though he survived. Because of his outstanding efforts, all noncommissioned of-

ficers and soldiers on the island signed a petition to the government in support of Dr. Mudd. His wife continually wrote letters to President Andrew Johnson seeking her husband's release. He was pardoned on February 8, 1869. He returned home, fathered five more children, partially regained his medical practice, and lived a quiet life on his farm until his death from pneumonia in 1883. He was buried in St. Mary's cemetery next to the Bryantown church where he reputedly first met Booth in 1864.

Proponents insist that Mudd was never an accomplice to Booth, though others—including several well-regarded historians—claim the two men had met some time before, and that Mudd knew exactly what he was doing. After the Civil War, journalist George Alfred Townsend interviewed Confederate secret agent Thomas Harbin, who confirmed meeting with Mudd and Booth at the Bryantown Tavern, a story never quoted by present-day defenders of Dr. Mudd. Dr. Mudd's grandson, Dr. Richard Mudd of Saginaw, Michigan, worked tirelessly to clear his name of any complicity; he filed a petition in the United States District Court for the District of Columbia bringing suit against the Secretary of the Army, Togo

Dr. Samuel A. Mudd House Museum

West, et al., ordering the Archivist of the United States to ". . . correct the records in his possession by showing that Dr. (Samuel A.) Mudd's conviction was set aside pursuant to action taken under 10 U.S.C. sec. 1552." In March 2000, Army Assistant Secretary Patrick T. Henry rejected an appeal to overturn the 1865 conviction. Henry said his decision was based on a narrow question—whether a military court had jurisdiction to try Samuel Mudd, who was a civilian. He stated, "I find that the charges against Dr. Mudd constituted a military offense, rendering Dr. Mudd accountable for his conduct to military authorities." Others, including a U.S. district judge, have ordered the army to reconsider the conviction, and Dr. Mudd's champions have included several former presidents, Jimmy Carter and Ronald Reagan among them.

In that light, visitors loudly proclaiming Dr. Mudd's conspiratorial guilt will get run out of the Mudd house on a splintered rail (wear thick pants if you plan to picket). The Samuel A. Mudd House Museum is open from the first weekend in Apr.–late Nov., weekends noon–4 P.M., Wednesday 11 A.M.–3 P.M. Admission is $5; there's also a gift shop on the property.

Smallwood State Park

General Smallwood Retreat House, U.S. 1, Marbury, 301/743-7613, is named for a Colonial Army general and former governor of Maryland. The original home of General Smallwood, decorated with 18th-century furniture, is open to the public, and a colonial tobacco barn has been re-created on the premises. The home is open daily Apr.–Oct., 1–5 P.M.

The house is part of Smallwood State Park, which features hiking trails in Mattawoman Natural Area (named for the Mattawoman Indians who had a fort and town in this area in 1670), picnic sites, and the 50-slip Sweden Point Marina. The concession store rents rowboats, motorboats, canoes, and paddleboats. Fishing is a popular pastime at the park, which hosts a number of bass fishing tournaments each year. The 300-foot fishing pier, shores of the Potomac River, and Mattawoman Creek are home to several varieties of catfish, herring, pickerel, bluegill, croaker, carp, pumpkinseed, rockfish, crappie, and perch. Wading and swimming are not permitted. Smallwood offers 16 camping sites and 4 mini-cabins by reservation, and is open to the public year-round. A $2 entrance fee is in effect May 1–Sept. 30 on weekends and holidays; the remainder of the year, park use is free.

A welcome recent addition to Smallwood State Park is **Mattawoman Creek Art Center,** 301/745-5159, a two-gallery space that presents changing exhibits of regional, national, and international art. The art center evolved from a virtually forgotten century-old farmhouse into a complex that combines art and nature. The studio spaces of several working artists are also on the premises, and the organization offers classes and workshops. Free.

Port Tobacco Historic District

The former town of Port Tobacco, Rte. 6 and Chapel Point Road, is the site of one of Maryland's oldest communities, originally an Indian village known as Potobac—Captain John Smith dropped by in 1608. Once a busy colonial shipping port, the settlement faded away as the land around it failed under the duress of tobacco farming, combined with the move of the county seat to nearby La Plata (la PLAY-ta). At the time, La Plata boasted a railroad siding, telegraph station, and little else. A special election was held in 1892 to determine whether the courthouse

BOOTH'S WILD RIDE

After he fatally wounded President Abraham Lincoln with a single gunshot and stabbed one of the Lincolns' companions, John Wilkes Booth leapt from the president's box at Ford's Theatre to the stage; his foot became entangled in the flag draped on the railing, and he broke his leg. He limped across the stage and mounted his horse, which was being held for him outside by one of the theater workers. Booth was joined by a cohort, David Herrold; they rode to Surrattsville (now Clinton), 10 miles away. There they obtained the paper-wrapped field glasses brought by Mrs. Surratt and carbines that had been held for them. From there, Booth and his companion hurried to the house of Dr. Samuel Mudd in Maryland.

Dr. Mudd set Booth's broken leg, and Booth and Herrold hid in the area for nearly a week. The two were sighted at Brice's Chapel off Piney Church Road and at Col. Samuel Cox's home in the village of Bel Alton. They then crossed the Potomac into Virginia. On the night of April 25, authorities found them hiding in a tobacco-curing barn on Garrett's farm, a short distance from Port Royal. Herrold surrendered, walking out to waiting authorities, but Booth refused to leave the barn. The building was set on fire, and Booth lunged out of the doorway. As he tried to escape, he was shot in the back of the head by Sergeant Boston Corbett, against orders. The wound he received was similar to the one he inflicted on President Lincoln. He was laid on the grass and he asked that his hands might be raised so that he could see them. As he looked at them he uttered his final words, "Useless! Useless!" Booth carried his diary, with some pages ripped out. What was left pertained solely to the assassination, and implicated no one else in the murder.

A letter of Booth's that was published after his death read, ". . . How I have loved the old [Union] flag can never now be known. A few years since, and the entire world could boast of none so pure and spotless. But I have of late been seeing and hearing of the bloody deeds of which she has been made the emblem and would shudder to think how changed she had grown . . . her once bright red stripes look like bloody gashes on the face of heaven. . . . My love is for the South alone. . . . If success attend me I go penniless to her side. [signed] A Confederate doing duty upon his own responsibility. J. Wilkes Booth."

As Lincoln's coffin was carried in state to his birthplace in Springfield, Illinois, a small rowboat on the Potomac carried the remains of John Wilkes Booth to an unmarked grave. The U.S. government decreed that the place and manner of his disposal were to be left unknown; perhaps because of this, some historians claim that Booth was never shot, but managed to escape, disappearing into the Southern countryside.

SOUTHERN MARYLAND

TOBACCO BURNS

Tobacco was a perilous way to make a living. Though it was the main commercial crop of colonial planters in Maryland, the financial risks were enormous. After the uncertainties of weather, soil depletion (tobacco leaches nutrients from the soil much more quickly than other crops), insects, and disease, the planter also had to pay for losses in transporting his crop by sea to the London market. If the tobacco was damaged by seawater, rotted from sitting in damp holds, or lost at sea, the planter took the full loss.

Tobacco stalks with attached leaves were harvested in autumn, and overwintered in a tobacco barn—allowed to cure, dry out, and mellow. The following spring, leaves were stripped from their stalks and gathered into a "hand," which was made up of eight or 10 leaves from one plant. Hands were then compressed into a straight-sided barrel-like container called a hogshead, between five and six feet tall and roughly five feet in diameter. A packed hogshead weighed around 950 pounds.

Most Maryland planters grew Oronoco, a variety that wasn't "stemmed," or heavily veined, like Sweet Scented, the main variety of Virginia. As a result, it was lighter by weight. Since English taxes were levied by hogshead rather than by weight, "Maryland" (Oronoco) tobacco was taxed more heavily than "Virginia" (Sweet Scented), a continual source of protest. Maryland planters remedied this discrepancy by making their hogsheads somewhat larger than the standard size. A number of planters also packed their hogsheads with "trash"—stems, leaves, and other unusable filler—giving Maryland tobacco a reputation for questionable quality.

After being sealed, a hogshead was turned on its side, attached by poles to a team of horses, and rolled down to the warehouse at the nearest wharf—these "rolling roads" were the origin of many of today's roads. The hogsheads were then packed into the holds of British ships (Maryland was forbidden to trade with any other country), along with smaller quantities of "loose leaf" from smaller growers, and shipped to England, where it was sold and distributed to other countries, particularly France and Holland, where Oronoco tobacco was popular. Consignment firms such as Bridges and Company that handled the transport of tobacco grew wealthy as agents for planters, shipping and selling the leaf (for a percentage) to the English market. After the crop was sold, the consignment firm would pick up items such as cloth and books ordered by the planter and ship them back by return vessel—charging the planter with freight expenses and another percentage for services rendered.

By the early part of the 18th century, the old consignment system was beginning to fail, and planters were able to take greater profits with less risk. However, European buyers were hesitant to purchase any colonial tobacco because so much trash was being shipped in the hogsheads. A severe depression in the tobacco market caused Virginia to enact an inspection law that raised both the quality and reputation of its leaf, but Maryland lagged behind for some years, losing much of its market.

In 1758, an agent named John Stevenson bought one thousand barrels of wheat and some flour and sent them to New York aboard the *Sharp*. The profits from this one voyage caused a farming revolution in parts of Maryland. Many planters on the Eastern Shore abandoned tobacco and planted wheat, and Maryland's agricultural future was set on a different course.

Today, however, tobacco remains a cash crop for many farmers in southern Maryland. Visitors may attend tobacco auctions held in the spring in Hughesville (see the special topic "Festivals and Events" in this chapter).

should remain at Port Tobacco or be moved to La Plata. Port Tobacco won; however, less than three months later, the Port Tobacco courthouse burned to the ground—but not before the county records had been carefully removed. No one was ever prosecuted, and the courthouse and county seat went to La Plata. Then the Port Tobacco River silted over, leaving the town high and dry. A few of the original buildings, including the old courthouse and schoolhouse, have been reconstructed; the courthouse and a small museum are open Wed.–Sun. noon–4 P.M., 301/934-4313.

Further down Chapel Point Road is **St. Ignatius,** the oldest Catholic Church in America. It sits high on a hill above Chapel Point, overlooking the confluence of the Port Tobacco River and the Potomac; the graveyard, dating from 1860, spills down the hill to the road below. The priests' cemetery alongside the church dates from 1794. The colonial cemetery was located near the river shore, but most of the tombstones were destroyed when Union soldiers camped there and used them for target practice. There is ongoing controversy over future use of the land below the church—the riverfront offers prime development property, but local interests have so far quashed the project. The church, founded in 1641 by Father Andrew White, continues to serve as a house of worship. If the church is open, go inside to see and appreciate the kneeling pads in the pews; parishioners have lovingly decorated many with crewelwork. The old wooden tabernacle on the altar is made of mahogany from Santo Domingo, and the needlework on and in it was done by Carmelite nuns before 1830. The window above the entrance of the church commemorates the baptism of the Piscataway chief and his wife, who were converted to Catholicism by Fr. White. When he sailed with Leonard Calvert aboard the *Ark,* Fr. White brought a relic of the True Cross with him—it is still kept in the church.

Not far west from old Port Tobacco is the **Thomas Stone House,** 6655 Rose Hill Rd., 301/392-1776, the country home of a lawyer and signer of the Declaration of Independence. Stone and his wife died within months of each

SLAVERY

In the early days of the colony, slave ships from England, Holland, and New England carried black Africans from the Ivory Coast to the Caribbean (the Middle Passage); the few slaves that were brought to Maryland came from ports there, in the West Indies. By 1700, slavery had become a way of life in Maryland; slave ships sailed directly up the Chesapeake to dozens of small ports.

Slavers picked up their human cargo from factors in Africa who kept barracoons, warehouses where prisoners were stored until sold. The barracoons were kept full by slatees, chiefs of inland tribes, who staged kidnapping raids on other tribes; the raids increased in frequency as the sale of captives proved more and more profitable. Their victims would be chained together and branded with the slaver's company symbol. Narrow, fast slave ships packed their unwilling passengers tightly, next to each other, or spoon fashion, one behind the other. Often, nearly half of the captives didn't survive the voyage.

Survival had value. Bought by a planter on consignment, a slave who survived three years in the fields was considered acclimatized, and brought three times his original price. At first, black Africans were on the same basis as indentured whites—released after a few years' service; but by 1663, slavery-for-life codes were recognized as law, and blacks were hanged for causing—or even being accused of—the death of their masters. Runaways were sometimes maimed, and often beaten.

In spite of the immoral and brutish aspects of keeping slaves, colonists continued to import them and profit from their unpaid labor. In 1712, estimates of the slave population were roughly 8,000 out of the total of 46,000 Maryland residents—sizable, though far less than neighboring Virginia. The percentage of slaves in the state actually dropped by the middle of the next century, but planters in southern Maryland and the Eastern Shore were entirely dependent on slave labor for economic survival; it was in their best interests to support the Confederacy during the Civil War.

other in 1787, leaving their children to be cared for elsewhere by his relatives. The mansion stayed in the family until 1936 and remained intact until swept by fire in 1977. The National Park Service restored the property, and now offers mansion tours, exhibits, an orientation video, picnic sites, and walking trails. The park is open Memorial Day–Labor Day daily 9 A.M.–5 P.M., and Wed.–Sun. the remainder of the year. Free.

The Stone House supports a number of special events throughout the year, such as an annual Southern Maryland Heritage Day in June, and outdoor concerts. Call the number above for specifics.

Pomfret

African Americans have a long—and not always willing—history in Charles County. Through the Civil War, the entire tobacco economy was made possible by slave labor. Segregation—voluntary and otherwise—caused African Americans to create their own communities. One that continues today is Pomfret, and the church that services the community there has achieved some recognition as a lively place of faith. The **African-American Heritage Society** operates a museum on Gwynn Road off Bumpy Oak Road that chronicles the black experience in southern Maryland. It's open mid-Apr.–Oct., Wed.–Sun. noon–4 P.M. Call 301/259-2328 for more information; admission is $2.

Pope's Creek

If your travels have left you ready for a quiet respite, try the **Loyola Retreat House,** Pope's Creek Road, Pope's Creek. This Jesuit retreat, on 235 acres of woodsy bluffs overlooking the Potomac, is no yuppie spa. The surroundings are lush, but the accommodations—with meal plans—are modest and inexpensive. There are 75 single rooms with half bath (toilet and sink) in the main building (showers down the hall) and a lounge with fireplace for conviviality. The premises are often used for silent retreats; the Catholic order of St. Ignatius Loyola focuses on deepening one's faith and commitment to justice. This is an excellent place to leave the world behind and spend time in renewal and introspection. Private

retreats (completely on your own) or directed retreats (that include a daily meeting for spiritual counseling) are available for varying lengths of time. Call 301/934-8862 for more information.

Waldorf

The **Piscataway Indian Museum,** 16816 Country Ln., Waldorf, 301/372-1932, is operated by the Maryland Indian Heritage Society. A modern take on the traditional longhouse, the museum displays replicas of living quarters and artifacts of the many tribes that flourished in the area, and features a gift shop/trading post with native-made crafts. The museum, dedicated to Native American ancestors and the retention of indigenous culture, is open Tues.–Thurs. 9 A.M.–3 P.M., Sunday noon–5 P.M.; however, it's a good idea to call ahead. One of the best times to visit is during the June Pow-Wow or during the Fall Festival, the third week in September.

RECREATION

Golf

In the southern part of the county, **Swan Point Golf Course,** Swan Point Road, 301/870-2971, offers the public a championship 18-hole course in a beautiful setting. Designed by Bob Cupp, senior designer for Jack Nicklaus, the course is tucked into a private 904-acre waterfront community where the focus is on appreciation of nature and golf, naturally. A clubhouse is open for dining Tues.–Sun. for breakfast and lunch, and dinner Fri.–Sat.

Part of the public White Plains Park in the northern part of the county, **White Plains Golf Course,** DeMarr Road and St. Charles Parkway, Waldorf, 310/645-1300, features an 18-hole course, putting green, and practice areas. The park also has six lighted tennis courts open Apr. 1–Oct. 31.

Biking

Charles County has at least three excellent **bicycle loop trips** that cover various types of scenery and terrain, from farmland to riverfront. See any county information source for a map of all southern Maryland routes.

Bird-Watching

Great blue herons—the county bird—return to pair up, reinforce their nests, and lay eggs during Valentine's Day week at **Nanjemoy Creek Great Blue Heron Sanctuary.** The herons have been returning to the site since the 1940s; the rookery grew from around 100 nests to more than 700 in 2003. The sheer volume of their droppings combined with beaver activity has thinned out enough trees to make the birds expand their nesting area beyond the 273-acre Nature Conservancy sanctuary. The conservancy is planning to expand its holdings to further protect the birds and the headwaters of Nanjemoy Creek. The birds stay on the sanctuary until the young are fledged in July. Good spotting places are at the ends of the roads that front the waters of Nanjemoy Creek: Benny Gray Pt. Road, Bluff Pt. Road, Tayloes Neck Road, and Walter's Landing Road.

Fishing and Hunting

Mallows Bay, on the western border of Charles County on the Potomac River, is a veritable graveyard of ships, with vessels dating from the American Revolution to 1920. The U.S. Shipping Board Emergency Fleet sent 235 wooden ships that had carried troops and supplies to Europe during World War I here to be salvaged and sunk. Many of them have literally become islands, and provide some of the best bass fishing grounds on the East Coast.

Myrtle Grove Game Refuge, one-half mile north of Ripley on Rte. 225, was developed for the purpose of propagating game, which it does very well. Anglers will appreciate the year-round bounty of Myrtle Grove Lake, and hunters can pursue a range of game from white-tailed deer to wild turkeys. An eight-station firearms shooting range is open for use by permit every day except during deer season. Permits can be obtained from the Myrtle Grove Work Center or any DNR Regional Service Center.

SHOPPING

Though each of the towns of any size in Charles County has one or two antique shops—Route 5, just north of Leonardtown, features the sprawl-

BOAT TRIP ON THE STYX

For more than two centuries, boats of all descriptions were the main—and often only—form of transportation that connected the widespread plantations and settlements of southern Maryland. All of the rivers of the southern counties and the Chesapeake itself were traversed by some sort of vessel. The *Express* was one of several packet boats—a vessel that made scheduled stops carrying passengers and mail—up the Potomac River from ports on Chesapeake Bay. One of the *Express*'s stops was Cross Manor, home of Captain Randolph Jones and his family. During a heavy storm, Capt. Jones sat in his parlor one evening entertaining friends when they heard a knock at the door. When the captain looked out the window to see who was there, he saw his wife motioning him toward the door. When he opened it, no one was there. Within a few hours, he learned that the *Express* had gone down in the Chesapeake, and his wife, a passenger aboard the vessel, had drowned at the time that he had seen her through the window of their home.

ing **Maryland Antiques Center**—the crossroads of Hughesville is a hub of collectible commerce. Don't be concerned about the lack of street numbers. Technically, all the shops listed are in the 8300s, but though few have addresses on them, the buildings are among the main features of Hughesville—there's no danger of zipping past. **Lost Horizons,** Rte. 5 (Leonardtown Road), north of the Rte. 231 traffic light, is a multidealer, as is **Southern Traditions,** across the road. The local favorite, **Hughesville Bargain Barn,** Rte. 5, is made up of two converted tobacco auction barns that house more than 70 shops each of permanent and transient dealers of antiques and collectibles. It features everything from local crafts to old farm tools, cast-offs, and treasures. **Everything Amish** ("If it ain't Dutch, it ain't much"), Rte. 5, Hughesville, specializes in wood furniture.

Waldorf, near the intersection of Rte. 5 and Rte. 925, is another antiques hotspot with **Mulberry Cottage, Heritage Designs,** and **Simpler Times,** among others.

SOUTHERN MARYLAND

The Indian Head Flea Market, Rte. 210, Indian Head, is held every Saturday Apr.–Oct. From July–Oct., local farmers stop by with pickup trucks of local produce.

ACCOMMODATIONS AND FOOD

You can find chain hotels such as Best Western, Days Inn, and Hojos (Howard Johnson's) in either La Plata or Waldorf. Here are a few alternatives:

Shady Oaks of Serenity, 7490 Serenity Dr., Bryantown, 301/932-8864 or 800/597-0924, is a modern adaptation of Georgian architecture, set in a development of stately homes. The peaceful country that surrounds this B&B offers visitors a pleasant alternative to the motels that line busy U.S. 301 near La Plata. Kathy and Gene Kazimer are wonderful hosts, and are really helpful referring visitors to needed services and giving directions in the vast rural spaces of this county. Each of the comfortable rooms has TV and bath, and a suite is available for larger families. Shady Oaks also has meeting space for groups up to 25. Room rates are $70–135 depending on the room; continental breakfast is included.

Goose Bay Marina and Campground, 9365 Goose Bay Ln., Welcome, 301/932-0885, offers RV sites, tent sites, and boat slip rentals.

Limited tent camping is also available at Smallwood State Park.

Capt. Billy's Crab House & Restaurant, Popes Creek Road, Popes Creek, 301/932-4323, has been in business since the end of World War II. The food is good and the prices can't be beat: the most expensive sandwich on the menu, the crab melt, is $8.75, and entrées—traditional Maryland fare such as crab meat in garlic butter, oysters casino, or fried chicken—run $9–20. Though the mailing address is in Port Tobacco, Popes Creek Road is off U.S. 301 roughly nine miles south of La Plata.

Capt. John's Crab House, Cobb Island, 301/259-2315, serves breakfast, lunch, and dinner daily, year-round. Breakfasts are simple and inexpensive (under $5), but entrées such as lobster tails, combo platters, and prime rib can run up to $30. It also features an extensive take-out menu for those who might not have the time to lounge around enjoying the great view from the dining room windows.

INFORMATION

For a packet of information and any questions you might have, contact Charles County Tourism, P.O. Box 2150, La Plata, MD 20646, 301/645-0558 or 800/766-3386, www.explore charlescomd.com.

St. Mary's County

The shoreline of St. Mary's County is as convoluted as the average primate brain. Narrow roads crisscross the land and terminate at points on the water—it's a great place to drive or bike with no destination in mind. Since there's so much farmland, people are used to driving distances to get a crab dinner or enjoy a little history. But the distances aren't intimidating, and the scenery is priceless.

SIGHTS

Historic St. Mary's City

This reconstructed town, Rosecroft Road off

Rte. 5, 301/862-0990 or 800/SMC-1634 (800/762-1634), www.stmaryscity.org, was the colonial capital of Maryland, the first permanent settlement established by Lord Baltimore in 1634, and the fourth English settlement in North America. Archaeologists are excavating more than 150 structures on 20 sites in an 832-acre area; meanwhile, the entire preserve is open to the public as an outdoor museum, complete with costumed interpreters. Much of the acreage is a rural preserve of shoreline, fields, forests, and wetlands, providing a variety of habitats for wildlife watchers. The effect is of a kinder, gentler—and authentically low-key—Williamsburg.

A VERY LITIGIOUS WOMAN

Margaret Brent emigrated from England with her sister Mary and two brothers in the last days of the Reformation. As Catholics, even the wealth of their family could not protect them from prejudice and harassment. In 1638, armed with a generous land grant from Lord Baltimore (Cecil Calvert), Margaret and her sister settled on St. Mary's town lands and named their 70-acre farm "Sister's Freehold." Both Margaret and Mary remained single, possibly because they had taken vows of chastity—and this proved to be extremely freeing, since married women were not allowed to own property or bring actions in court. Margaret frequently lent money to other colonists, readily going to court to collect overdue payments. In fact, her name appears so often in early court documents—124 times in eight years—that the American Bar Association's Commission on Women in the Profession named its Women Lawyers of Achievement Award after her. Most of Margaret's cases involved property disputes and debts. She had no formal legal training, but then there were no lawyers in Maryland—everyone argued their own cases before the provincial court or appointed "attorneys in fact" to act for them. Because of Margaret's success in her own cases, others probably asked that she speak on their behalf.

She became a close friend of the Catholic governor Leonard Calvert, Cecil's younger brother. As religious hostilities spilled over to the New World, Protestant renegades ransacked Maryland's few colonial outposts in 1645, including St. Mary's City. Leonard Calvert and many other settlers fled to Virginia; when the colony was retaken in 1647, Leonard Calvert, dying, appointed Thomas Greene as governor, but made Margaret sole executrix of his estate, bidding her to "Take all and pay all." Mercenaries hired by Calvert to retake the colony threatened to wreak havoc if not paid. Leonard Calvert's personal estate was poor in everything but land; he was also responsible for land and cattle belonging to his brother, Cecil. When Leonard died, the provincial court granted Margaret power of attorney over all properties until Cecil could name another. Margaret found herself in a bind; under English law, she could not sell anything but personal possessions, and therefore could not pay the soldiers. In 1648, in an effort to channel money from public coffers to pay the menacing soldiers, Margaret approached a meeting of the Assembly and asked for permission to vote twice as a member, not only for herself, but also as attorney for the Calvert estate. Since women were not allowed to vote in the Assembly at all, she probably expected to be turned down. From court records, "The Govr denyed that the sd Mrs Brent should have any vote in the howse. And the sd Mrs Brent protested agst all proceedings in this pnt Assembly, unless shee may have vote aforesd."

Historians suggest that Margaret's appeal to join the Assembly may have been in the hope to persuade them to tax tobacco to raise money or to endorse her next move—selling Lord Baltimore's cattle without his permission. Contacting Lord Baltimore in England would have taken months, and the mercenaries were threatening immediate action. Margaret sold the cattle, paid the mercenaries, and saved the colony from being overrun with British soldiers sent "for the colonists' protection." The colonists feared that once the British soldiers arrived, the Protestant government of Britain would revoke the Maryland charter and make the colony part of Virginia. Unfortunately, Lord Baltimore didn't see it that way. In Margaret's defense, the Assembly wrote, "We do Verily Believe and in Conscience report that it was better for the Collonys safety at that time in her hands then in any mans else in the whole Province after your Brothers death for the Soldiers would never have treated any other with that Civility and respect and though they were even ready at several times to run into mutiny yet she still pacified them."

Lord Baltimore refused to be mollified, and he continued to rail against Margaret and her siblings. Around 1650, the Brents bought extensive property in Virginia and moved there. Margaret led a quiet life in Virginia and died at her plantation, named "Peace," in 1671.

First stop is the visitor center, which features an exhibit titled "Once the Metropolis of Maryland." The exhibit traces the story of Maryland's first capital from its English roots in the 1630s through its demise at the end of the 17th century and subsequent rebirth as a major archaeological project and outdoor museum in the later 20th century. Significant artifacts found at the site are on display, coupled with stories of discovery and the interpretation of these finds and how the work of historians and archaeologists comes together to describe the past. While there, pick up a list of daily highlights to find when various demonstrations (17th-century navigation aboard the *Maryland Dove*, the plantation walking tour, etc.) are given.

A walking trail leads to the Woodland Indian Hamlet, an exhibit with re-created *witchotts* (wood and bark dwellings) that interprets 17th-century contact between European settlers and the Yoacomoco inhabitants. The founding site of the Roman Catholic Church in the English colonies can be seen in Chapel Field. Visitors can view the cross-shaped brick foundations where the 1667 Brick Chapel is being reconstructed using 17th-century materials and techniques. Town Center, the heart of the colonial capital, is being re-created as research on the original structures is completed. Visitors can explore an ordinary (a combined tavern/inn), learn about colonial commerce at Cordea's Hope, and see a mock trial at the State House of 1676. The State House of 1676 is a re-creation of an imposing brick structure, among the first public buildings in Maryland. Nearby is a plaque honoring Mathias de Sousa, the first Marylander of African descent, who came aboard the *Ark* when the ship explored St. Mary's River in 1634. The home of Maryland's first governor, Leonard Calvert, and other colonial buildings are marked with ghost frames today; in time they will be rebuilt. The Shop at Farthing's Ordinary, the museum shop, features unique items inspired by history and nature, and also serves refreshments. One of the most fascinating re-creations of the period is in the river below: an authentic working square-rigged ship, the *Maryland Dove*. Historic St. Mary's

City also has a working farm, the Godiah Spray Tobacco Plantation; costumed interpreters portray the Spray family and their indentured servants as they lived the everyday life of early Tidewater farmers. The Brome-Howard Inn is adjacent to the property.

Historic St. Mary's City sponsors special events throughout the season, including the Maritime Heritage Festival in June; the Tidewater Archaeology Dig in July, which encourages visitors to participate in archaeological excavations; and Woodland Indian Discovery Day in September, a hands-on exploration of Native American culture and skills. Interpretive signage and an audio tour are available in addition to costumed interpreters.

Hours for the living history exhibits are mid-March–mid-June Tues.–Sat. 10 A.M.–5 P.M., mid-June–mid-Sept. Wed.–Sun. 10 A.M.–5 P.M., mid-Sept.–Nov. Tues.–Sat. 10 A.M.–5 P.M. The museum grounds may be visited even when the living history exhibits are closed; call or check online for details. Admission is $7.50 for adults, $6 for seniors and students, and $3.50 for children age 6–12.

Point Lookout State Park

This scenic multiuse recreational area, end of Rte. 5, Scotland, 301/872-5688, was one of three manors owned by Leonard Calvert, first governor of Maryland. When the Civil War started, Point Lookout was a popular summer resort with a hotel, beach cottages, a wharf, and a lighthouse. As the war raged on, the resort failed; the Union leased the property for use as an army hospital. By 1863, the hospital was used to hold Confederate sympathizers from Maryland; soon after the Battle of Gettysburg, construction began on a camp capable of holding 10,000 prisoners of war, to be named Camp Hoffman. By 1864, more than 20,000 imprisoned enlisted men (officers were sent to Fort Delaware, in northern Delaware) crowded the camp. Disease, contamination, and freezing conditions killed nearly 4,000 prisoners out of the total of 52,000 held there over the years. Those who survived were sent home at war's end, and by 1865, the camp was deserted.

The state took over in 1965 and turned the 1,046-acre property into a park. The visitor center

St. Clement's Island

features exhibits on the area's Civil War past. The park contains the partially reconstructed remains of Fort Lincoln, the last of the Civil War structures. Boat trips to Smith Island are available June–Sept. Wed.–Sun., $20–35 per person. The park is open year-round 8 A.M.–sunset; the visitor center is open daily May–Sept., on weekends Apr.–May and Sept.–Oct. The park features a swimming beach, 400-foot fishing pier, boat ramp, and canoe, motorboat, and rowboat rentals, plus 150 RV and tent sites, a cottage, camp store, and self-service laundry. Reservations are recommended. Admission is $3 to enter the park May–Sept.

Visitors may drive to the end of the park's main road to see the fenced and gated Point Lookout lighthouse, but it's maintained by the Coast Guard and only open to the public on the first Saturday in November from noon–4 P.M. The light had three female keepers between 1830 and 1869. Perhaps it was their ghostly presence, among others, sensed by paranormal researchers during the 1990s when they claimed to have recorded 24 different "voices" in the lighthouse.

Other Sights

St. Clement's Island–Potomac River Museum,

Bayview Road, end of Rte. 242 (follow signs), Colton's Point, 301/769-2222, celebrates both the landing of the first Maryland colonists in 1634 and their Catholic faith. Though it's a bit out of the way, the museum itself is worth visiting for its interesting displays and murals on the history of Maryland. The setting is beautiful as well, with St. Clement's Island, the original landing place, not far offshore. The island has shrunk somewhat since Jesuit priest Andrew White first said mass there for the small, ocean-weary band that disembarked from the *Ark* and the *Dove;* wave action of the Chesapeake has eaten away at the shoreline for nearly 400 years, shaving 400 acres down to 40 acres. Today the island is a state park with hiking trails, exhibit panels, and picnic facilities. A water taxi departs from the museum to the island May–Oct. weekends at 12:30 P.M. and returns at 2 P.M. The museum is open Mar. 25–Sept. 30 weekdays 9 A.M.–5 P.M., weekends noon–5 P.M.; from Oct. 1–Mar. 24, it's open Wed.–Sun. noon–4 P.M. Admission is $1; there is an additional charge ($5 for adults) to take the water taxi to the island.

The **Pax River Naval Air Museum,** Rte. 235, Lexington Park, 301/863-7418, is the only museum in the country dedicated to naval aviation. The grounds feature aircraft from different eras, and exhibits inside the museum illustrate testing and evaluation of aircraft systems and components. The museum has a nifty model shop on the premises. It's just outside the main gate of the Patuxent River Naval Air Station, and is open year-round Tues.–Sun. 10 A.M.–5 P.M. Free. A guided tour may be arranged by calling the number above.

Parks and Scenic Spots

Piney Point Lighthouse and Park, Lighthouse Road, Piney Point, 301/994-1471, sits at the end of a road lined with beach houses; the colony, though not fancy, comes complete with highly individual private cabanas on the beach across the road from the homes. The area was a popular getaway for American presidents, beginning with James Madison.

The Piney Point Lighthouse, a classic light tower, was constructed in 1836; it held a fixed beacon light that was visible for more than 11 miles. Today, it's one of only four in existence on the Potomac River. A pleasant six-acre park with boardwalk and beach access surrounds the lighthouse, and a small separate museum that chronicles local history is nearby. The park was animated by a small group of squealing kids and their adult supervisor (and no one else) popping in and out of the water in mid-June. Piney Point Park is open daily year-round. Free.

A **"Black Panther" German submarine** lies one mile from the lighthouse; the U-boat, coated with black rubber that made it invisible to the sonar of the day, was captured at the end of World War II and intentionally sunk off the coast after being tested by the navy. It has become Maryland's first underwater park: the *U-1105* is accessible by boat and may be explored by divers; specific location and information are available from the lighthouse museum. It's open Memorial Day–Oct. weekends noon–6 P.M.

With a little imagination, it's easy to picture the view of the Patuxent River from the windows and gardens of **Sotterley Plantation,** Rte.

Piney Point Lighthouse

245 (Sotterley Road), Hollywood, 301/373-2280 or 800/681-0850, www.sotterley.com, as it was in 1710, the year this manor house was built. Sotterley was once a thriving tobacco plantation and colonial port of entry, and the house and adjacent outbuildings are superbly preserved. Older than Mount Vernon or Monticello, it has been home to governors and gamblers alike. There's an interpretive walking trail on the property, and the house may be toured every hour on the hour with a guide. The grounds and walking trail are open Nov.–Apr., Tues.–Sun. 10 A.M.–4 P.M. The manor house is open May–Oct. Tues.–Sun. 10 A.M.–4 P.M. A $2 fee is charged to use the grounds; for the house tour, admission is $7. Sotterley sponsors events throughout the year, including Ghost Tours in October, and an annual Southern Maryland Quilt and Needlework Show is held in May.

Not far from Sotterley is **Greenwell State Park,** Steerhorn Neck Road, Hollywood (for information, call Point Lookout State Park,

PRE–BLAIR WITCH

The Blair Witch Project, an independent film that swept America in 1999, was filmed near the town of Burkittsville, not far from South Mountain. However, Maryland has long had an interest in witches. The concept of ordinary people being "bewitched" began centuries ago, fueled by the words of Pope John XXII (1326), who ordained that penalties should be imposed on all "Who ally themselves with death and make a pact with hell—sacrifice to the demons—make or have images, rings, mirrors, phials—intended to serve as bonds to hold the demons—ask questions of the demons—and have recourse to the demons to satisfy their depraved desires." All it took to convict a neighbor of having unsavory friends was the testimony of two witnesses of "good and honest report." One suspicious activity might be witnessing the teen next door as she "entertained a familiar spirit and had conference with in the likeness of some visible creature" ("Here Spot, come get the stick. Don't you want the stick? Come and get it!").

In spite of the fantastic opportunity this presented to colonial misanthropes, Maryland remained relatively low on the point-and-burn scale, as compared to say, Salem, Massachusetts. Bad luck aboard the *Charity of London,* bound for St. Mary's City in 1654, was blamed on the demonic congress of one Mary Lee. The captain (perhaps fully aware that the boat's leakage problems were due to neglect) opted to put the ship ashore in Bermuda. On the way there, unfortunately, the crew tied Ms. Lee to the capstan, extracted a "confession," and promptly hung her.

Not all demon-lovers were women—John Cowman was convicted in 1674 for "enchantment upon the body of Elizabeth Goodale," but was granted a reprieve after a guided tour of the gallows. Rebecca Fowler of St. Mary's City wasn't so fortunate. Many Marylanders were accused of being accursed, but she retains the distinction of being the only one actually hung, in 1685. Apparently she and the "Divell" caused several people in the community to fall ill.

In 1702, Charles Kilburn complained that when he met one Katherine Prout on the path, she would abuse and threaten him, specifically stating that she hoped he would "languish to death." Though charges of witchcraft were dropped, the court fined Ms. Prout for "misbehavior in her Saucy Language and abusing this Court." Kilburn was back in court two months later, suing Prout for slander, for calling him a "foresworn rogue." Prout was ordered to pay the highly sensitive Kilburn a token sixpence, but then was forced to pay court costs of 1,101 pounds of tobacco. It would seem the judge was the real foresworn rogue. Ms. Prout, apparently finding court procedure to her liking, sued another woman for slander and theft of molasses and "New England Capons" (mackerel) from her cellar. Prout won this one (to the tune of three pounds sterling), and never ventured before the bench again.

The last formal witchcraft case was heard in Annapolis in 1712. Virtue Violl ("spinster") of Talbot County rendered her neighbor speechless after causing her to pine. Ms. Violl pleaded not guilty, and was excused.

301/872-5688). This 596-acre park is on the Patuxent River. The Greenwell family donated part of the property to the state for use as a public park, with particular emphasis on access for the disabled. The state bought the adjacent acreage, and the park now offers several miles of marked foot trails, fishing, picnicking, and swimming and boat launch from a beach. Greenwell is a day-use park, open from sunrise to sunset. Free.

RECREATION

Fishing Charters: The fishing season in St. Mary's starts in late April and runs through December. Bluefish, striped bass (rockfish), sea trout, flounder, white perch, hard head (croaker), Norfolk spot, Spanish mackerel, black sea bass, and channel bass are commonly caught. Most of the charter boats run out of Ridge; here is a sampling: Captains Stephen and Greg Madjeski,

48415 Wynne Rd., 301/872-4215; Capt. Greg Drury, 16390 Fishermen Wy., 301/872-4455; Capt. Gary Sacks, 48862 Curley's Rd., 301/872-5506; Capt. Bruce Scheible (who provides the raw material for Scheible's/Courtney's Restaurant in Ridge), 48342 Wynne Rd., 800/895-6132; Capt. Bob Holden, 43785 Blake Creek Rd., 301/994-0269, out of Leonardtown; Capt. Butch Cornelius, St. Georges Island, 301/944-0347; and Capt. Steve Owens, P.O. Box 176, 301/737-4286, out of St. Mary's City.

Speedways: Not all that moves is wet. **Maryland International Raceway,** 301/884-9833 (information line 301/449-RACE, website www.mirdrag.com), and **Potomac Speedway,** 301/884-4200, both on MD 234 in Budd's Creek, present drag racing and stock-car racing March–November.

Golf: Breton Bay, 21935 Society Hill Rd., Leonardtown, 301/475-2300, is a par-72 golf course reputed to be great for the long driver. **Wicomico Shores,** Wicomico Shores Subdivision, Chaptico, 301/934-8191, is the county municipal course, also par 72.

SHOPPING

Cecil's Old Mill, Indian Bridge Road off Rte. 5, Great Mills, 301/994-1510, is full of the work of local artists and craftspeople at great prices. Much of it is "country style" (cows and chickens are big), but this is really worth a stop. It's open Thurs.–Sun. year-round, and daily from Nov. 1–Dec. 24. An old barn with antiques and junque, **St. Mary's Antiques & Gifts,** 301/373-4721, is across the way; it's open Mon.–Sat. 10 A.M.–5 P.M., Sunday 11 A.M.–5 P.M.

Leonardtown has a number of antique shops on Fenwick Street and Washington Street, especially **Antiques on the Square,** on Washington Street, a multidealer shop with a bit of everything. Also check out **The Maryland Antiques Center,** Rte. 5, Leonardtown, which has more than 30 dealers and a tea shop inside. Both are open daily.

Deep in the heart of Mennonite farm country, the roads around **Loveville** are dotted with roadside stands and nurseries from June through November.

There's an **Amish Farmer's Market** every Mon.–Sat. May–Oct. during daylight hours in Charlotte Hall on old Rte. 5. A nearby farmers' market also on Rte. 5 features more than 100 stalls selling crafts, antiques, pastries, and produce.

ACCOMMODATIONS

The elegant **Brome-Howard House Inn,** 18281 Rosecroft Rd., St. Mary's City, 301/866-0656, once sat squarely in the middle of "downtown" St. Mary's City—it was built by a physician and tobacco plantation owner, John Brome, about 1840. The property passed through many hands until it became part of Historic St. Mary's City. Because the house was considerably newer than the period focused on by St. Mary's City (the 17th century), the commission in charge of the development decided to move the house and its outbuildings to a bluff overlooking the St. Mary's River, where it is today. A young couple from the Washington, D.C., area, Lisa and Michael Kelley, have made it their goal to turn the building into a world-class restaurant and lodging. The house features five large bedrooms, two with shared bath, three with private bath; three have fireplaces, and two have water views. A five-mile walking trail winds along river beaches and shady woods to St. Mary's City. An excellent full breakfast is included; rates run $65–160.

The restaurant at the Brome-Howard Inn is open to the public for dinner Thurs.–Sun., and brunch is also served on Sunday. Michael is professionally trained, and it shows; the food is innovative and sophisticated without being pretentious. The filet mignon and breast of duck are highly recommended, and the wine list features a number of good California wines; dinner entrées average $16.

Nap on the sofa and fish at the same time: **Cedar Cove Marina,** Rte. 249, Valley Lee, 301/994-1155 or 800/705-2628, rents houseboats, starting at $80 a day.

A fun place to get away from it all with the family, **Camp Merryelande Vacation Cottages,** Rte. 249, St. George Island, 800/383-1073, offers six fully furnished cottages and bunkhouses on the beach of St. Mary's River. There are also tent sites and showers on the property, and it's open year-round. Rates are $50–340, depending on cottage and number of nights. Tent sites are $15–20 per night, less for longer stays.

FOOD

The reputation of **Café des Artistes,** 41655 Fenwick St., Leonardtown, 301/997-0500, www.cafedesartistes.ws, has spread far and wide—a fellow airplane passenger told me about it. Karleen and Loic Jaffres have created a Continental atmosphere with menu to match—classic dishes such as chicken Cordon Bleu and beef Wellington share the spotlight with crab cakes and grilled Norwegian salmon (lunch is around $13, dinner entrées average $18). The food is exceptional, as are the prix fixe dinners ($19.95) and senior specials. Try to save room for dessert. There's often musical entertainment on the weekends. It's open for lunch Tues.–Fri., dinner Tues.–Sat., and Sunday noon–8 P.M. Definitely make reservations.

Locals swear that once you've tasted Julie's fried fish at **Scheible's/Courtney's Restaurant,** at Scheible's Motel, Wynne Road, Ridge, 301/872-5185, you'll be a deep-fried convert. It's a local "dive" with ultra-fresh seafood; Bruce Scheible and Tommy Courtney are both watermen and the fish are literally right off the boat. Lots of local color, all for under $15.

Evans Seafood, Rte. 249, St. George Island (south of Piney Point), 301/994-2299, is one of the county's premier restaurants. The menu includes seafood, steaks, and stuffed ham; the restaurant has pleasant water views. It's open April–Labor Day Tues.–Sun.; Sept.–Mar., weekends only. Prices average $8 for lunch, $18 for dinner.

Bert's Restaurant and '50s Drive In, Rte. 5, Mechanicsville, 301/884-3837, is a St. Mary's County landmark. The front door looks like a jukebox, and there's '50s memorabilia galore. The menu includes subs, sandwiches, pizza, full-course dinner entrées, soft and hand-dipped ice cream, sundaes, malts, floats, and milkshakes. It's open daily year-round ($6).

INFORMATION

For further information on St. Mary's destinations, contact St. Mary's Division of Tourism, P.O. Box 653, 23115 Leonard Hall Dr., Leonardtown, MD 20650, 301/475-4411, www.stmarysmd.com.

Calvert County

God bless y'all real good.

Louis Goldstein, former Maryland State Controller and resident of Calvert County

Calvert County combines ripe farmland with watery pleasures on its narrow peninsula. Solomons is the most developed town, though Prince Frederick is the county seat. Much of the county produces bountiful fruits and vegetables in season; the Calvert County Agriculture Commission publishes a farm directory that lists a wide variety of products from goats to gourds to daylilies, all for sale. Visit their website, www.co.cal.md.us/cced, or email them for a brochure: cced@co.cal .md.us. You can also get a brochure through the Calvert County Visitor Center, 410/257-5381 or 410/326-6027.

SIGHTS

Jefferson Patterson Park and Museum

This innovatively used property, 10515 Mackall Rd., St. Leonard, 410/586-8500, is named for one of its owners, a former ambassador and son of the founder of the National Cash Register Company. His wife, Mary "Marvin" Breckinridge Patterson, was the granddaughter of B. F. Goodrich, and prior to marrying the ambassador was a freelance photojournalist of some repute. She once rode a bicycle in northern Finland to capture pictures of an arctic Lapp colony, and was the first female CBS broadcaster in Europe, sharing the spotlight with her old friend Edward R. Murrow. The Pattersons used "Point Farm" as a retreat and laboratory for modern methods of agriculture. After Mr. Patterson's death in 1977, Mrs. Patterson continued to live occasionally at the farm; in 1983, she donated the property to the state of Maryland, under the stewardship of the Maryland Historical Trust.

The property is now home to the Maryland Archaeological Conservation Laboratory (MAC), a state-of-the-art research, conservation, and collections facility for archaeological finds from all over Maryland, and the Academy of Natural Sciences Estuarine Research Center. MAC's library is open to the public on a nonlending basis by reservation, 410/586-8550. Visitors can see archaeology in action on the property by strolling down the one-mile Riverside Trail. The .8-mile Woodland Trail affords the opportunity to enjoy local flora and fauna, and the .75-mile Shoreline Loop explores a section of the Patuxent River shoreline. The Academy of Natural Sciences offers a self-guided .25-mile BayScapes walk from the parking lot at 10454 Mackall Rd.

The visitor center houses a permanent exhibit, "12,000 Years in the Chesapeake." The park sponsors many special events throughout the year, including a Celtic Festival and Highland Gathering in April, an African American Family Community Day in May, a War of 1812 Tavern Night and Reenactment of the Battle of St. Leonard in September, and other events throughout the season; call 410/586-8501 for more information. The park is free, and is open Apr. 15–Oct. 15, Wed.–Sun. 10 A.M.–5 P.M. To get there, take Rte. 4 south, and turn right (west) on Rte. 264 three miles south of Prince Frederick. Follow Rte. 264 for two miles, then turn left on Rte. 265 (south) for six miles.

Other Parks and Scenic Spots

Southern Maryland has little "islands" of ecosystems, and **Battle Creek Cypress Swamp,** Gray's Road, Prince Frederick, 410/535-5327, is one of them. One of the northernmost stands of bald cypress trees in America, this swamp/sanctuary features a small interactive museum where visitors

can see a rare albino snapping turtle and wander on walkways above the water. Most of the bald cypress trees here are 75–100 years old, though the trees can live for 2,000 years. The trail can be walked in 15 minutes, and among the jutting "knees" (projections from the tree roots that help to anchor the conifers) are remnants of moonshine stills that operated during Prohibition. The Nature Conservancy acquired this unique property in 1957, and you'll feel you've stepped into a land far removed from the Chesapeake shore. To get there from Rte. 301, turn to Rte. 4 south and continue through Prince Frederick. Turn right (west) onto Sixes Road (Rte. 506), and look for the sign and left turn (south) on Gray's Road. The sanctuary is about one quarter mile south on the right (west) side of the road. It's open Apr.–Sept. Tues.–Sat. 10 A.M.–5 P.M., Sunday 1–5 P.M.; Oct.–Mar., it closes at 4:30 P.M. Admission is free.

If your taste runs to chestnut rather than cypress, take a walk around the **American Chestnut Land Trust,** Scientists Cliffs Road, Port Republic, 410/586-1570. The 790-acre ecological preserve is home to one of the state's largest living American chestnut trees; it's open dawn to dusk daily, all year. Leave your car at the gate and explore some or all of the eight miles of wooded trails.

The most prominent physical feature of the Chesapeake's western shore lies in **Calvert Cliffs State Park,** 14 miles south of Prince Frederick on Rte. 2/4, Lusby (contact Point Lookout State Park, P.O. Box 48, Scotland, 301/872-5688). Stretching 30 miles along the coast of Calvert County, the cliffs were formed more than 15 million years ago when a warm and shallow sea covered all of southern Maryland. The land became uplifted at the end of the last ice age, exposing more than 600 species of fossils in the cliffs, including calcified shark teeth and various mollusk shells.

This day-use (sunrise–sunset) park features 13 miles of foot trails; a two-mile hike from the parking lot leads visitors to the open beach and fossil hunting area (visitors may keep what they find). Because the cliffs are unstable, there is no fossil hunting permitted close to the cliff bot-

© JOANNE MILLER

Calvert Cliffs

toms. Bicycles and equestrians are restricted to specific trails, and some trails are closed during hunting season (hunting is permitted in the park). A one-acre pond is stocked with freshwater fish, and a playground is available. Camping is for youth groups only. There is a $3 charge for vehicles to enter the park. Follow signs from Rte. 2/4 to reach the park entrance.

One of the prettiest beaches around can be found at **Flag Ponds Nature Park,** 10 miles south of Prince Frederick, 410/586-1477. The park is named for the blue flag iris and other wildflowers that bloom from early spring to autumn. A half-mile trail leads to the boardwalk and beach; there is a parking area closer to the beach for those who might have difficulty walking. On the way to the white sands, visitors will pass an old fisherman's shanty, one of three left over from the days when the area supported a major fishing industry. There's a wide-open vista of Calvert Cliffs to the south. Visitors occasionally see one-inch blue balls wash up on the beach. They're used to clean the condenser tubes at Calvert Cliffs Nuclear Power Plant—most are trapped in the system, but a few escape into the bay, providing a strange juxtaposition with shark

vertebrae and other natural flotsam. Yucca, a plant most people associate with the desert, also blooms freely among the dunes and pines in May. Several short (under one mile) trails loop around three small ponds on the park property. The park is open daily Memorial Day–Labor Day 9 A.M.–8 P.M., weekends only the rest of the year. There is a fee to park: $4, or $6, if your plates are out of the county.

King's Landing Park, west of Huntingtown on the Patuxent River, 410/535-5327, features a 200-foot fishing pier and a great place for kayakers and canoeists to access the river. Walking trails lead through mature hardwood forests, and a boardwalk overlooks marshes along Cocktown Creek. The park is open in summer 8:30 A.M.–8 P.M. daily; Apr.–May and Sept.–Oct. Mon.–Fri. 8:30 A.M.–4:30 P.M., weekends 8:30 A.M.– 6 P.M.; Nov.–Mar. weekends only 8:30 A.M.–5 P.M.

The **Port Republic School Number 7** is a restored 19th-century one-room schoolhouse on the grounds of Christ Church on Broomes Island Road (Route 264). Schoolhouses like this one ordinarily held up to 30 students in grades ranging from kindergarten to 12th—all held in check by one harried teacher. It's open June–Aug.

SOUTHERN MARYLAND

HOW NUCLEAR PLANTS WORK

The fossil-filled bluffs of southern Maryland are home to both past and present. The state's one and only nuclear facility, Calvert Cliffs Nuclear Plant, lies just north of Calvert Cliffs State Park. Only 380 acres of the 2,100-acre site are used for the plant; the rest is maintained in a natural state.

Prior to September 11, 2001, the facility was open for tours and featured informative displays and a pleasant picnic area. Now, as with all U.S. plants, it's under heavy security and closed to the public until further notice. The plant was the first U.S. facility to have its license extended, in 1999, for another 20 years of use; it has one of the most outstanding safety and production records in the nation. Calvert Cliffs supplies much of the energy used in central Maryland.

In a simplified scenario of how nuclear power works, it's easiest to first picture the results. When a light switch is turned on in the home, electrical current is permitted to flow from the wall connector through the wire and into the light bulb. When the switch is turned off, the current remains (which is why it's a bad idea to stick your finger into a wall socket), pumped through miles of wires from the source, the energy plant. At the plant, electricity is produced and stored in a generator, which is powered by the spinning motion of giant fans, or turbines. The turbines may be driven by water (hydroelectric power), wind (windmills or wind turbines), or steam. Steam is produced by burning coal, natural gas, or oil, or by nuclear energy.

Though nuclear energy has significant pitfalls, there's no disputing that the original sources of heat used to generate steam power—burning wood, coal, oil, and gas—are major causes of pollution. And raw materials have limited renewability or are not renewable at all. When it was first developed in the 1950s, nuclear power was hailed as the solution to pollution; today, more than 100 nuclear power plants provide about 20 percent of all electricity used. Unlike the burning action necessary to convert carbon-based sources to heat to turn water into steam, nuclear energy relies on fission—the splitting of uranium atoms—to generate heat.

Uranium comes in the form of ceramic pellets, about the size of a fingertip. The pellets—made up of highly fissionable U-235 and other less reactive forms of uranium—are stacked inside 12-foot-long zirconium tubes, bundled together inside the plant reactor core. Water flows through the bundles, picking up heat and increasing the probability of fission. When a nuclear plant starts up, neutrons are released inside the reactor core, which starts the fission process. The speed of the chain reaction (atoms splitting, releasing more neutrons, which split other atoms) is mitigated by "control rods" that are inserted into the bundles to absorb excess neutrons. The fission process continues until all the atoms have split. The leftover "fission fragments," though still radioactive, slow the efficiency of the chain reaction, and must be removed to concrete pools lined with stainless steel, and eventually, to storage deep underground.

U.S. nuclear power plants come in two designs: pressurized water reactors and boiling water reactors. Calvert Cliffs is a pressurized reactor plant. The reactor, in which the nuclear core is seated, heats pressurized water (called primary coolant) in a closed system. Another closed system filled with water (secondary coolant) flows around the ultrahot primary coolant pipes and becomes steam, which then drives a turbine. The problems of Three Mile Island Nuclear Plant, in Pennsylvania (another pressurized reactor), stemmed from a design flaw, now addressed in other working reactors—an inability to read the levels of primary coolant in the core; a drop in the water levels caused the reactor to overheat dangerously.

Sundays 2–4 P.M.; call 410/486-0109 or 800/331-9771. Admission is free.

Hallowing Point Park Tobacco Barn, 4755 Hallowing Point Rd. (off Rte. 231), Prince Frederick, 410/535-1600, ext. 225, was built around the time of the Civil War, and now holds exhibits on the history of the Calvert County tobacco industry and the process of raising tobacco. The barn is set within the confines of a pretty park near the Patuxent River. It's open daily 9 A.M.–5 P.M.; admission is free.

Accommodations and Food

The Cliff House, 156 Windcliff Rd., Prince Frederick, 410/535-4839, www.bbonline.com/md/cliffhouse, is a private home overlooking the Chesapeake Bay, with water access for fishing. A single suite with queen-sized bed and full bath are available to guests with children older than 12. Breakfast is included in the $120 fee.

Tasty Kwik Diner, 1541 Solomons Island Rd. S. (Rte. 4), Prince Frederick, 410/535-3242, is straight out of the '50s, serving burgers, shakes, and ice cream, in addition to fresh fried haddock. Thursday night, hot rods and other classic cars fill the parking lot.

TWIN BEACHES

Today, the "Twin Beaches"—Chesapeake Beach and North Beach—are quiet waterfront residential communities that cater to boaters and bathers; but it was not always so. Chesapeake Beach was the terminus of the Chesapeake Beach Railway, and a grand resort and boardwalk opened there in 1900. Adjacent North Beach grew as a neighboring cottage community. In 1930, the railway closed operations, and the amusements were moved inland; the park was finally closed in 1972. A boardwalk runs along Rte. 261, paralleling the communities and offering a mile of beachfront to sun seekers. Parking is available all along the boardwalk on Bay Street.

Sights

The **Chesapeake Beach Railway Museum,** Mears Avenue and C Street, Chesapeake Beach, 410/257-3892, features memorabilia from the beaches' glorious past as a resort and amusement park. May–Sept. daily 1–4 P.M., Apr. and Oct. Sat–Sun. 1–4 P.M. Admission is free.

Chesapeake Beach Water Park, Rte. 261 and Gordon Stinnett Avenue, 410/257-1404, is a good place for kids to cool off on hot summer days. It features eight slides (including one with wheelchair access), lap lanes, a children's activity pool, and a separate "diaper" pool for the littlest swimmers, a 12-foot floating alligator, a 12-foot floating snake, a seashell slide, and a slow river. An adult must accompany children under 13. It's open Memorial Day–June 10, weekends 11 A.M.–8 P.M.; June 10–first day of school, daily 11 A.M.–8 P.M. Admission costs range from $4–14 depending on day, size, and residency (the closer your home address, the cheaper it is).

Food

Beach Cove, 8416 Bayside Rd., Chesapeake Beach, 301/855-0025, is a casual restaurant with outside deck that looks out over the bay and offers seafood and pasta. It's open daily for lunch and dinner, and features live music Fri.–Sat. Prices are around $9 for lunch and range $8–29 for dinner.

The **Rod 'N' Reel,** Rte. 261 and Mears Avenue, Chesapeake Beach, 877/763-6733, is a big seafood restaurant that serves up its own catch of the day for lunch and dinner ($12–20). Rod 'N' Reel also rents out space on its boats for fishing parties; call 800/233-2080 for more information.

Thursday's Bar & Grill, 7th Street and Bay Avenue at the end of the boardwalk, North Beach, 410/286-8695, looks a bit like a tavern, but offers a lively menu that includes seafood classics, prime rib, and chicken. It's open daily and prices average $7 for lunch, $14 for dinner.

SOLOMONS

Solomons, a tiny enclave of homes, restaurants, shops, and lodgings, was actually an island until about 1868. At that time, Isaac Solomon, who developed oyster canning in Baltimore, purchased "Sandy Island" and built a processing plant at the northern end. The channel that separated the mainland from the island was gradually filled in with oyster shells until only a ditch remained. A small bridge near the Waterman's Memorial Park connects the island to the mainland, and the area is known collectively as Solomons. A riverwalk along the water extends from the park to the island neck, affording strollers an opportunity to enjoy the bay and the shops and restaurants that line the principal street, Solomons Island Road (Rte. 2).

Sights

Calvert Marine Museum, 14200 Solomons Island Rd., 410/326-2042, www.calvertmarine-museum.com, is one of the most fun things to see in Solomons. The museum covers maritime history and life of the river and bay. One exhibit features the fossilized remains of local ancient inhabitants, including the extinct megatooth white shark of the Miocene age. There's an indoor 15-tank "estuarium" that displays local water creatures, and river otters to entertain adults and children alike. A boardwalk extends into the marsh for active exploration. Visitors may clamber up ladder-like stairs to an authentic screw-pile lighthouse, the Drum Point light. The inside is decorated as it would have been when a lighthouse keeper and family were in residence. The boathouse is full of log canoes, skiffs, scrapes, and other examples of small craft used on the Chesapeake.

On weekends in May and September, and June–Aug., the museum runs shuttle buses to the Cove Point Lighthouse at the end of Cove Point Road, which sits on a spot great for viewing the Chesapeake. Since it's still in use, access may be limited.

Museumgoers can also cruise around Solomons harbor and the Patuxent River aboard the *Wm. B. Tennison,* an 1899 nine-log bugeye, for an extra fee ($6). The museum also operates the J. C. Lore Oyster House, one-half mile south of the main museum, which is dedicated to information about the boom and decline of the region's commercial seafood industries.

Museum admission is $5, and it's open daily 10 A.M.–5 P.M. One-hour cruises aboard the *Tennison* are available May–Oct. Wed.–Sun. 2 P.M., and an additional 12:30 P.M. cruise is offered during July–Aug. weekends.

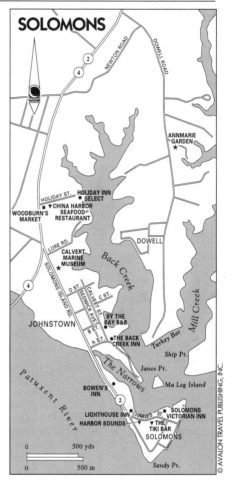

"Memory is a form of renewal. It offers a second chance," *A Survivor's Map,* Jane Rosen-Queralt, Annmarie Garden. Two miles north of Solomons on Dowell Road, 410/326-4640, **Annmarie Garden on St. John** is a magical combination of wilderness and sophisticated site-specific sculpture, including the lyrical quote above, which is part of an assembly on an elevated walkway. St. John refers to the creek that runs through the back of the property, and the shady green groves of trees that cover the land make for a peaceful commune with nature. Bought as an investment property in 1960, the owner, Francis Koenig, decided to keep the 30-acre parcel as it was and named it for his wife. "Everything I have built in my life will someday be taken down. The Annmarie Garden will always remain," he said.

You can't miss the entrance on Dowell Road; artists Peter King and Marni Jaime of Pensacola, Florida, built two enormous walls covered with eight tons of ceramics that bracket iron gates. The sculpture inside is as varied as one can imagine. The *Tribute to the Oyster Tonger* by Antonio Mendez is a formal fountain that is irresistible to children in the summer; in some seasons, you can glimpse giant tin fish floating through the trees. A pathway winds through the groves, with stops at various "rooms" containing works by select national sculptors. Two more installations of note are *The Council Ring* by B. Amore and Woody Dorsey, a beautifully constructed ring of granite council chairs, and the *Generations Room,* by Jerome Meadows, symbolizing the generational cycle of plants and man. Art exhibitions are held in the garden gallery, and the garden sponsors special events throughout the year, particularly Garden in Lights during the holiday season, and Artsfest, with more than 250 performing and visual artists, and food and spirits. Call the number above for dates. Make sure to stop in the restroom—it's a beautiful surprise, and all the work inside was donated. The garden is open daily 10 A.M.–4 P.M., and admission is free to the garden, though there is a charge for some special events.

Accommodations

There are several B&Bs on the island; a few are featured here. The Holiday Inn is on the mainland part of Solomons, just before the island bridge. All are within easy walking distance of attractions (except Annmarie Garden, which is a short drive out of town).

Holiday Inn Select, 155 Holiday Dr., P.O. Box 1099, Solomons, 410/326-6311 or 800/356-2009, might be just another Holiday Inn if it weren't for the spectacular views from the waterside rooms, the Hospitality Harbor Marina (where you can dock your boat for a fee), and the outdoor courtyard and bar, the Afterdeck. All the amenities are in place: rooms range from basic sleeping quarters with coffee maker, ironing board, and cable TV to suites with Jacuzzis and kitchenettes. There is a health club on the premises, tennis courts, and an outdoor pool. Since Holiday Inn offers many deals and packages, you'll see lots of kids here as well as businesspeople. Rooms average $130.

Solomons Victorian Inn, 125 Charles St., 410/326-4811, www.chesapeake.net/solomons victorianinn, looks out over Solomons Harbor from the southernmost part of the island. The inn features five rooms in the main house, all with private bath, plus a third-floor suite. In addition, the carriage house offers two rooms with private entrances, views, and whirlpool tubs. The decor reflects the era, and a full breakfast is served in a delightfully bright sunroom. Prices range $95–175.

The Back Creek Inn, Alexander Lane and Calvert Street, 410/326-2022, www.bbonline .com/md/backcreek, is in the residential section

Calvert Marine Museum

© JOANNE MILLER

KEEPER OF LIGHTS

One of the world's earliest warning lights was also one of the seven wonders of the ancient world: the lighthouse of Alexandria, Egypt. Built around 280 B.C., it towered 450 feet above the harbor—the light within was an open flame. At the time, bonfires on promontories were the rule, and were the only protection to be had by ship captains on stormy nights until the glass lantern room was invented and first installed in England's Eddystone Light. Candles replaced the open fires, and mirrors placed in huge wooden bowls served as crude reflectors.

Born near the cusp of the 18th and 19th centuries, Frenchman Augustin Fresnel grew to be a slow learner who could barely read by the age of eight. However, he led a secret life away from school—his friends called him "the genius" for his ability to modify their toys to go faster, higher, and longer. As a man, Fresnel applied his thought processes to optics, and produced the most important breakthrough in distance warning lights in 2,000 years.

In 1822, Fresnel worked out a number of formulas for light refraction through glass prisms. Working with several glassmakers, he produced a combination of prism shapes that could gather and intensify light and project it outward. The lens looked like a giant glass beehive, with a light at the center. The apparatus could be as tall as 12 feet, with concentric rings of glass prisms above and below to bend the light into a narrow beam. At the center, the lens was shaped like a magnifying glass, so the concentrated beam was even more powerful. Tests showed that while an open flame lost nearly 97 percent of its light, and a flame with reflectors behind it still lost 83 percent of its light, the Fresnel lens was able to capture all but 17 percent. The first Fresnel lens, installed in the Cardovan Tower lighthouse on the Gironde River in France, was visible a remarkable 20 miles away. Fresnel lenses quickly spread all over Europe.

Despite the clear superiority of Fresnel lenses, America clung to the weak lights that protected U.S. coasts; the French export was too expensive, the government declared. Finally, a reshuffling of the government's Lighthouse Board in 1852 brought in eminent scientists and mariners, who began distributing the Fresnel lens to lighthouses on this continent. By the Civil War, most U.S. lighthouses were equipped with the elegant and effective lenses. Fresnel's theories of light form the basis of modern optics: his lenses continue to be used in distance lights, and the principle behind his lighthouse lens is used in automobile headlights and the flashing lights on police and emergency vehicles.

of Solomons and looks out onto the tree-lined banks of Back Creek. The 1880 home is decorated in contemporary style, and offers a full country breakfast, four rooms, two suites, and a cottage, all with private bath and cable TV; it also has a private pier, and bicycles are available for guest use. Rates range $95–145.

By the Bay B&B, 14374 Calvert St., 410/326-3428, www.chesapeake.net/~bythebaybandb, is close to the Back Creek Inn and, though it was built at roughly the same time (1900), has a less modern flavor. Stenciling and flowered walls complement the Victorian decor of this expanded "waterman's house"—a one-story building with additions and a deep-water dock. Two rooms and one suite have private

baths; rates range $90–125 for the rooms, $110 for the suite.

Food and Nightlife

Woodburn's Market, Solomons Island Road (Rte. 2), Patuxent Plaza, 410/326-3284, is an upscale gourmet market that sells ingredients and take-out foods from a sushi bar, pizza bar, pastry shop, etc.

Also in Patuxent Plaza, **China Harbor Seafood Restaurant,** 13958 Solomons Island Rd., 410/326-6888, offers fresh seafood specialties as well as Cantonese style (mild) duck, pork, and vegetable dishes. It's open for lunch and dinner daily, and prices average $9.

The **Lighthouse Inn,** 14640 Solomons Island

Rd. (at the neck), 410/326-2444, www.light-house-inn.com, is easy to find. The main road runs north-south; when the road narrows so you can see the water within 50 feet on both sides, you've reached the neck. If you get lost (unlikely), ask anyone. The Lighthouse is the premier restaurant in town, not only for its excellent seafood, but also for its view of the water and dockage. It features a surf-and-turf buffet every Tuesday and Thursday that can't be beat. Dinner is served daily year-round, lunch only on weekends. An outside deck is available, weather permitting. Along with seafood dishes such as the mariner's platter ($27) and seafood Naples ($17), the menu also features Santa Fe chicken and mixed grill. Dinner prices average $20.

Bowen's Inn, 14630 Solomons Island Rd. S, 410/326-9880, is known for its crab cakes and the $5 all-you-can-eat specials: spaghetti Tuesday, fried chicken Wednesday, and taco Thursday. It's also a lively nightspot on Friday and Saturday, with music and dancing. Open for lunch and dinner Tues.–Sun. (lunch $7, dinner $16).

Harbor Sounds, 120 Charles St., Solomons, 410/326-9522, www.harborsounds.com, is Solomons' party place, with a Cajun menu, daily all-you-can-eat specials, and live music on weekends. There's a full bar, and prices average $10; it's open for dinner Tues.–Sun.

The **Tiki Bar,** Solomons Island Road past the neck, 410/326-4075, is a venerable nightspot, a little grass shack lit by tiki torches night and day. It's open spring–late fall. Polynesian themes are big in Solomons, and island fever has spread to nearby Lusby.

RECREATION

Did you say fishing? Calvert County is well equipped to furnish the visitor with anything that has to do with water sports. There are also two golf courses for those who prefer their water hazards in different form.

Fishing Charters: Solomons Charter Captains Association, 410/326-2670, will hook you up with a fishing charter. Solomons charter boats clean your fish and give B.Y.O.C. tickets (Bring Your Own Catch), good at several par-

ticipating restaurants that will cook it to order. Two other sources for head boats are **Chesapeake Beach Fishing Charters,** 301/855-4655, and **Rod 'N' Reel,** Chesapeake Beach, 800/233-2080, www.rodnreelinc.com.

Boat Rentals: Try **Solomons Boat Rental,** 410/326-4060 or 800/535-2628 (powerboats), or **Bills Boat Rental,** Broomes Island, 410/586-3599 (skiffs, canoes, sailboats, and windsurfers).

Golf: The **Chesapeake Hills Golf Club,** H. G. Truman Road, Lusby, 410/326-4653, is a traditional par-72 course, with putting green, practice sand trap, and driving range. **Twin Shields Golf Club,** 2425 Roarty Rd., Dunkirk, 410/257-7800 or 301/855-7670, is a par-70 golf course offering 18 holes, a driving range, and teaching and putting greens.

SHOPPING

Calvert Country Market, Rte. 4, Prince Frederick Shopping Center (between Church and Duke Streets), 800/331-9771, features locally grown fresh produce, area seafood, and local crafts.

The **Chesapeake Market Place,** .25 mile east on Calvert Beach Road from the intersection of Rte. 4 and Calvert Beach Road, St. Leonard, 410/586-3725, www.chesapeakemarketplace.com, is an indoor market open Wed.–Sun. with 100 antique and collectible shops. It hosts auctions on Wednesday and Friday nights. Its mailing address is P.O. Box 118, St. Leonard, MD 20685.

CAMPING

Breezy Point Beach, Breezy Point Road, Chesapeake Beach, 800/331-9771, is run by the county and is a combination public beach and campground. The beach features a swimming area, picnic facilities, a playground, bathhouses, and a 300-foot fishing and crabbing pier. It's open Memorial Day–Labor Day, 6 A.M.–sunset, and a fee of $5 per adult, $3 per child is charged. Camping facilities are available May 1–Oct. 31 and include water and sewage. Depending on the site, seasonal fees range from $1,850–2,550, but monthly camping ($380) and daily camping ($25) are also available. To get there, take

SOUTHERN MARYLAND

FESTIVALS AND EVENTS

Many states are issuing new area codes for growing counties, and southern Maryland is a prime example. If you reach a number that has been disconnected, try the local county tourism bureau; they often have up-to-the-minute information on festivals and events.

March/April/May

Three of Maryland's six tobacco warehouses are in Charles County, and mid-March–April is tobacco auction time in Hughesville. Visitors are welcome to watch the action as auctioneers, buyers, and sellers amble down the aisles of elbow-high tobacco. Call 800/766-3386 for specifics.

The **Southern Maryland Annual Spring Festival,** St. Mary's County Fairgrounds, Leonardtown, features an antique tractor pull, carnival, crafts, live entertainment, and rides. 301/994-0525.

The **John Wilkes Booth Escape Route Tour** gives participants the chance to follow the trail of the president's assassin in considerably more comfort than Booth himself. The tour is on an air-conditioned bus, sponsored by the Surratt House Museum. 301/868-1121.

Jefferson Patterson Park in St. Leonard is a lovely place to enjoy the **Celtic Festival of Southern Maryland.** Music and historic reenactments, bagpipes, highland dancing, and athletic competitions are among the entertainment. 410/257-9003.

June/July/August

Several tribes celebrate their heritage at the **American Indian Pow-Wow and Festival,** Waldorf; visitors can check out native regalia, crafts, food, drinks, songs, and dances. 301/373-1932.

Fireworks? The **Navy Surface Warfare Center** has a shell or two—some consider their Fourth of July celebration to be the best in southern Maryland. It's held in the Village Green Park, Indian Head. 301/743-5574.

North Beach celebrates **Bayfest** with 150 craft vendors, live music, antique cars, and kid's activities, all held on the town's beautiful beachfront. 301/855-6681.

Rte. 260 east toward Chesapeake Beach. Turn right (south) on Rte. 261. Go five miles and turn left (east) at the green sign for Breezy Point. Follow the road one mile to the campground.

Breezy Point Cabins, 5230 Breezy Point Rd., 410/535-4356, features seven cabins next to the beach.

Patuxent Camp Sites, 4770 Williams Wharf Rd., St. Leonard, 410/586-9880, is open year-round, but shuts down a few of its 100 campsites in winter. Water and electricity, full bath facilities, boat ramp, and a 100-foot pier are provided.

FOOD

One of my favorite places to eat in the county requires a drive out to the end of Broome's Island Road, to **Stoney's,** Broome's Island, 410/586-1888. Outdoor tables look out over the rural

harbor, filled with the comings and goings of small boats (there's indoor seating, too). It's a great place to enjoy crab cakes, chowder, and oyster sandwiches at good prices. The tables are set with the traditional newspaper, a roll of paper towels, and cracking implements if crabs are what you seek. Prices average $8–15, and it's open for lunch and dinner.

Vera's White Sands Restaurant, 1200 White Sands Dr., Lusby, 410/586-1182, is in a class by itself. The decor will have you humming "Bali Ha'i," but the menu isn't restricted to conch and blowfish—it's continental, and there's a mixed bag of entertainment on weekends. Bring the boat, Vera provides a dock. You won't be bored, but fantasy isn't cheap; expect to pay around $13–22 for dinner, and the place is closed during the winter months.

A popular hangout for local families is **Adam's,**

September/October

Spend a lyrical night in a splendid setting at **Concert Under the Stars,** Sotterley Plantation, Hollywood. Visitors will be serenaded with a live concert on the east lawn overlooking the Patuxent River, and food and drink are served. 301/475-8434.

A good old-fashioned family-oriented fair, the **Charles County Fair,** La Plata, features games, food, entertainment, produce, and livestock. 301/932-1234.

The **Blessing of the Fleet** takes place where it all started: St. Clements Island. Entertainment, food, exhibits, arts, crafts, and fireworks are part of the fun. Boat transportation to the island is available; sponsored by the Potomac River Museum, Colton's Point. 301/769-2222.

The **Grand Militia Muster** in Historic St. Mary's City is the largest gathering of 17th-century reenactment units in the United States. 800/SMC-1634.

The **Hot Air Balloon Festival,** La Plata, offers day and evening entertainment, food and craft booths, and early morning balloon launches. 800/766-3386, ext. 146.

Bivalves 'R' us: **St. Mary's County Oyster Festival** is home of the national oyster shucking championship and the national oyster cook-off; continuous entertainment. 301/863-5015.

December

Historic St. Mary's City presents a number of holiday events, including a Christmas concert in the Old State House and an evening of feasting and madrigals. 240/895-4991 or 800/762-1634.

Solomons Island is also done up for the holidays; during the second week in December, the streets are lit by candlelight, and the shops are open late; a lighted boat parade takes place on the weekend. 410/394-3029. Nearby Annmarie Garden is also festively lit. 410/326-4640.

Colonial Christmas at Smallwood State Park, features colonial decorations, costumed docents, and cooking demonstrations. 301/743-7613.

---

the Place for Ribs, 220 Solomons Island Rd., Prince Frederick, 410/586-0001. In addition to the barbecued ribs, chicken, and shrimp on the menu, there are also broiled steaks, sandwiches, salads, and a children's menu. It has a full bar, and there's often a wait on Saturday night. It serves lunch and dinner; sandwiches and salads average $6, entrées are around $12.

INFORMATION

Calvert County Dept. of Economic Development, Courthouse, Prince Frederick, MD 20678, 410/535-4583 or 800/331-9771, www.co.cal .md.us/cced, is the place to go for maps and more information on destinations in that area.

Southern Maryland is popular with bicycle riders—the land is flat, scenic, and not heavily traveled except on the major roads. The tourism divisions of the various counties have published a well-researched, award-winning map that features routes all over the three-county area, highlighting scenic spots and resources for cyclists. Ask for a free *Southern Maryland Bicycle Map* from any of the county information sources listed above.

Southern Maryland/This Is Living is a full-color glossy publication focusing on the southern Maryland region. Designed for residents as well as visitors to southern Maryland, this magazine features information on activities and sites in Calvert, Charles, and St. Mary's Counties. Emphasis is on new and historic homes, gardening, history, and historic sites in these three counties in addition to special editions on antiquing, dining out, and what to do and where to go. Write to P.O. Box 1213, Huntingtown, MD 20639, 410/414-9414, or check online at http://somdthisisliving.somd.com.

SOUTHERN MARYLAND

Western Maryland

When tillage begins, other arts follow. The farmers therefore are the founders of civilization.

Daniel Webster, On Agriculture, *1840*

One warm midsummer evening a few years ago, a small group gathered in front of the Piper farmhouse, on the edge of Antietam battlefield. As Venus pierced the fading sky, the nearby field of ripening corn blazed with lightning bugs, all rising at once to the heavens—"like the souls of all the boys who died here" said Ginnie Clark, innkeeper of Piper House B&B. The American Civil War is more than a memory to those who live in western Maryland; the area provides a landscape where the spirits of Native Americans, patriots, volunteers, pioneers, farmers, and industrialists reside, at peace among the villages and cornfields, tufted hills and black-water lakes. This long arm of land stretches out to those who seek a slower, more relaxed pace, with plenty of contemporary enticements such as shopping, antiquing, history quests, and outdoor recreation.

Man has been associated with this rich land for thousands of years. Prehistoric nomadic hunters and gatherers, followed by tribes of Native Americans, roamed through the western mountains but left little record of their presence. By the middle of the 17th century, the fierce Iroquois Confederacy (a six-tribe brotherhood consisting of the Cayuga, Mohawk, Oneida, Onondaga, Seneca, and Tuscarora nations) claimed western Pennsylvania and

Savage River State Forest

Maryland to the south, using the area to expand their hunting territory. They permitted Lenni Lenape (Delaware) and Shawnee—escaping European encroachment in Delaware and Maryland—to populate the then-empty territory. Beginning in the 1700s, European pioneers trickled into the region and eked out an existence using the area's abundant natural resources.

Hagerstown was settled in 1737, Frederick (named for the Prince of Wales) in 1745. About the same time, Thomas Cresap, a settler from Yorkshire, England, moved to the wild frontier west of Hagerstown to Shawnee Old Town (now Oldtown), where he built a fortified house and made a living farming, trading, and raising cattle. Though Cresap's name isn't widely known outside the state's history books, he was involved with every major event that shaped western Maryland and the young colonies, and his life is representative of those tough and resilient settlers of the west. Shawnee Old Town was on the Great War Road between the Iroquois Six Nations of New York and their enemies, the Cherokee of North Carolina. Passing white traders and Indian war parties alike stopped at Cresap's for food and rest; they dubbed him "Big Spoon." He was so familiar with the region that he was asked to determine a boundary dispute between Virginia and Maryland: the location of the "First Fountain" of the Potomac, the headwaters that would serve as the western boundary of Maryland.

West of Hagerstown, farmlands tended by descendants of the first Anabaptist settlers spread over ridges and valleys; the hilly terrain then convolutes into the peaks of the Allegheny Mountains. The forefathers of these toilers of the earth often used the alternative spelling "Allegany" in naming towns and counties along the way. The mountain range, which stretches diagonally east-to-west across Pennsylvania, continues south through western Maryland, and provides rugged forests, fast-moving streams, and wide lakes for lovers of outdoor recreation. This is wild Maryland, ideal for hikers, bikers, water sports enthusiasts, and those who enjoy winter sports, hunting, and fishing.

In 1750, Cumberland, west of Oldtown in the Allegheny Mountains, was nothing more than a storehouse and trading post for the Ohio Company, a group of wealthy Virginia planters and London merchants who wished to keep the Ohio Valley (present-day Pittsburgh and the convolution of the Allegheny, Monongahela, and Ohio Rivers) away from the French, who held Canada and northwestern Pennsylvania.

During the 18th century, European settlement was curtailed for many years west of Frederick due to the French and Indian War and Pontiac's Rebellion. After nearly 80 years of relative peace, however, the Civil War had a devastating effect within the triangle formed by Frederick, Harpers Ferry, and Hagerstown. Several sites—protected and without the plastic fanfare that sometimes surrounds such areas—allow visitors to contemplate the price exacted from this nation in its fight to determine the true meaning of individual rights. One angle of the triangle can be stretched out a few miles north past Frederick and Emmitsburg, Maryland, into Gettysburg, Pennsylvania—the northernmost point reached by the Confederate Army.

In 1859, native Marylander and radical abolitionist John Brown gathered a group of like-minded men around him in Kennedyville, Maryland, to plot the takeover of Harpers Ferry. His goal was to capture the military encampment there, free local slaves, and start his own revolutionary army. Though Brown ultimately failed, many saw him as a martyr to the cause of antislavery. As the controversy over personal and states' rights deepened, several Southern slaveholding states seceded from the Union, forming the Confederate States of America. Former Union general Robert E. Lee was chosen to command the outmanned, outgunned Confederate States Army and won several early victories against the Union. He moved his troops into Maryland, in the hopes of winning over the border state.

Lee's troops were overwhelmed by Union forces on South Mountain, and he commanded all troops to reassemble outside the village of Sharpsburg, near the Shepardstown crossing. During the next few days, troops from both sides sustained heavy casualties during the battle of Antietam; Lee withdrew across the Potomac.

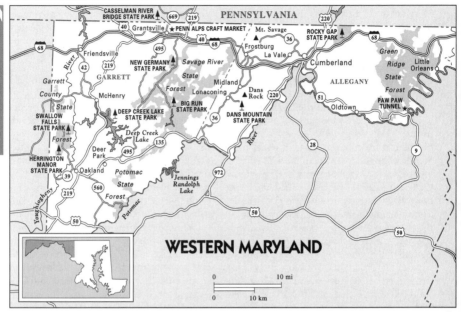

Within a year, he marched north again through Maryland to meet defeat at Gettysburg. Lee retreated to Virginia, then sent part of his army north toward Washington, D.C. They defeated Union recruits at Monocacy, but were unable to take the Union capital. Within a few months, Lee surrendered at the Appomattox courthouse, and the war was over.

Western Maryland, particularly Cumberland, was rich in the natural resources that powered the Industrial Revolution after the Civil War. Coal, iron, and glass were all manufactured with the assistance of the free-flowing Potomac River. Later, the C&O Canal ferried tons of coal to the mouth of the Chesapeake to be used to power oceangoing ships. But even while it was being built, the canal was overtaken by the swift railroad, rendering it obsolete. Cumberland remained a boomtown through the early part of the 20th century, when America's industrial base again changed. Coal, iron, and steel were either not in demand or more easily produced elsewhere. Western Maryland began to revert to its former forested glory, and the farms that had been the backbone of the economy for so long

continued to reap their bountiful harvests. Though agriculture remains the economic mainstay of western Maryland, tourism, with an emphasis on history and outdoor recreation, has become the new focus.

The ideal way to see western Maryland is on U.S. 40, the old national toll road. I-68 runs parallel with the old road, but whisks drivers along at subsonic speed, so that the heavy forest that lines the road becomes a purple-green blur. The old road, two-lane and often deserted, winds through the expansive farm country and gentle mountains, giving glimpses of businesses that started up during the "See the U.S.A. in your Chevrolet" era. It fits together beautifully.

Though western Maryland is the shy sister of the rest of the state, it's far from undiscovered. Frederick, a sophisticated and well-preserved colonial/Civil War–era town with upscale shops and restaurants, is western Maryland's gateway. After a day in Frederick, one is tempted to peruse the windows of real estate offices in hopes of snagging a trim brick row house at a good price—the city is a welcoming place to visit and to live. Deep Creek Lake, in the far south-

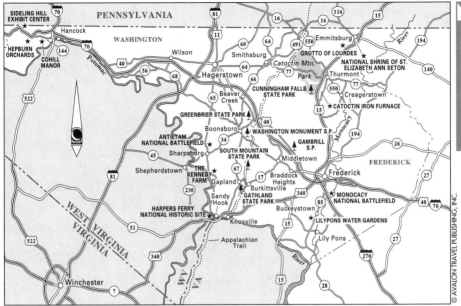

west, is surrounded by fancy vacation homes fronted by expensive watercraft. It's the getaway area of choice for many Washingtonians, Baltimoreans, and even Pittsburghers—the area's cool mountains and stunning water vistas are just isolated enough so that they'll never be overrun. Like the lake, western Maryland's still waters run deep.

Frederick and Environs

Frederick played a significant role in America's history, and the town continues to cherish and build on those memories. One Frederick resident, Dr. John Tyler, gained fame before the Civil War as the first American ophthalmologist to successfully perform cataract removal; the physician lived and worked at 108 W. Church St. In front of his home, he placed a statue of his faithful and beloved dog, Guess. In 1862, Confederate troops passing through the town commandeered Guess, apparently with the intention of melting him down into bullets. The dog of iron was found intact some time later near the battlefield at Antietam.

Today he continues to stand vigil at Dr. Tyler's former front door, a reminder of the town's active past. Frederick is a delight not only for its his-

torical value, but also for its excellent variety of contemporary shops, restaurants, and activities available to visitors.

Scenic Tour of Covered Bridges

The hunt for king-post trusses—covered bridges constructed with a sidewall consisting of a triangle reinforced with upright timbers—never ends! Maryland has considerably fewer covered bridges than Pennsylvania, but these three are beauties, and the roads through them are surrounded with green spears of corn and flowing wheat in summer, frost-cracked trees and long views in the winter. There's also an intimate and secluded park for a picnic, and this tour is suitable for both autos and reasonably fit bike riders: terrain consists of soft rolling hills and long

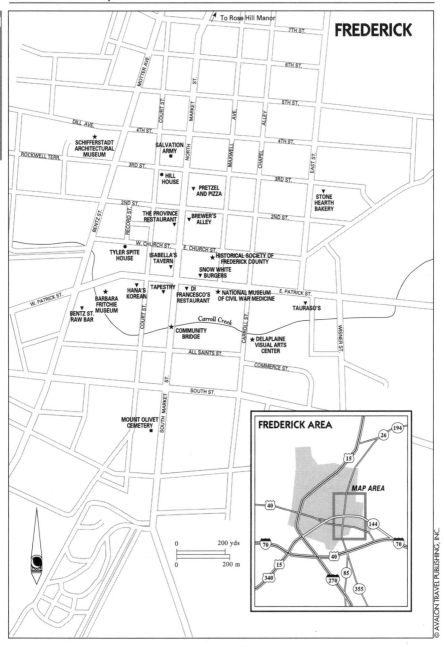

WESTERN MARYLAND

FREDERICK

To Rose Hill Manor

7TH ST.
6TH ST.
5TH ST.
4TH ST.

MOTTER AVE.
COURT ST.
MARKET ST.
MAXWELL AVE.
ALLEY
EAST ST.
CHAPEL ST.

DILL AVE.
ROCKWELL TERR.
4TH ST.

★ SCHIFFERSTADT ARCHITECTURAL MUSEUM

■ SALVATION ARMY

NORTH ST.

3RD ST.

● HILL HOUSE

▼ PRETZEL AND PIZZA

3RD ST.

▼ STONE HEARTH BAKERY

2ND ST.

BENTZ ST.
RECORD ST.

▼ THE PROVINCE RESTAURANT

▼ BREWER'S ALLEY

2ND ST.

● TYLER SPITE HOUSE

W. CHURCH ST.
E. CHURCH ST.

▼ ISABELLA'S TAVERN

★ HISTORICAL SOCIETY OF FREDERICK COUNTY

▼ SNOW WHITE BURGERS

W. PATRICK ST.

★ BARBARA FRITCHIE MUSEUM

▼ HANA'S KOREAN

▼ TAPESTRY

▼ DI FRANCESCO'S RESTAURANT

★ NATIONAL MUSEUM OF CIVIL WAR MEDICINE

E. PATRICK ST.

▼ BENTZ ST. RAW BAR

COURT ST.

▼ TAURASO'S

CARROLL ST.

Carroll Creek

★ COMMUNITY BRIDGE

● DELAPLAINE VISUAL ARTS CENTER

WISNER ST.

ALL SAINTS ST.
COMMERCE ST.

SOUTH MARKET ST.

SOUTH ST.

■ MOUNT OLIVET CEMETERY

FREDERICK AREA

194
26
15
40
144
70
15
340
270
85
355
70

MAP AREA

0   200 yds
0   200 m

MOON

© AVALON TRAVEL PUBLISHING, INC.

straightaways. The off-road loop from the Roddy Road exit off U.S. 15 is just under 22 miles. All distances are approximate.

From the junction of Route 140 and U.S. 15 in Emmitsburg, travel 3.9 miles south to the Roddy Road exit (bikers may want to start here). Turn left (east) on Roddy Road. One mile south, you'll pass through the Roddy Road covered bridge. Continue south 1.2 miles to the intersection with Route 77. Continue south on Route 77 for one-third mile; look for signs for Graceham. Turn left (east) on Route 77, passing through the lovely village of Graceham to Old Frederick Road (about two miles from the intersection). Turn right (south). Within a few hundred feet, you'll pass through Loy's Station covered bridge. The little park south of the bridge is an ideal place for a rest stop/picnic.

Continue south on Old Frederick Road to Creagerstown (2.3 miles from Route 77). At the intersection of Route 550 and Old Frederick Road in Creagerstown, continue on Old Frederick Road 4.1 miles south to Utica Road. Turn right on Utica Road (west), and pass through Utica Mills covered bridge within a few hundred feet. Utica Road, 1.25 miles long, dead-ends into Route 805. A left turn (south), one mile, leads back to U.S. 15—central Frederick is less than five miles south on U.S. 15, and Emmitsburg is 12.5 miles north.

To return to the Roddy Road exit off U.S. 15 without taking the highway, turn right (north) on Route 805 through Lewiston to Route 806/Black's Mill Road (two miles). Turn left on Route 806—you'll pass the Catoctin Furnace on your left—into the town of Thurmont (3.9 miles). In Thurmont, take Route 77 east (.8 miles) to Roddy Road and retrace your path back through the covered bridge to U.S. 15 (north, 2.2 miles).

HISTORICAL SITES

The **Schifferstadt Architectural Museum,** a simple sandstone-block building, 1110 Rosemont Ave., Frederick, 301/663-3885, sits at the end of the city park; in addition to the museum, the grounds afford excellent picnic sites and strolling paths. Inside the two-story structure,

wood, pottery, and iron implements illustrate the daily lives of the German immigrant farmers who populated the area in the early days of the colony. Schifferstadt is the oldest known house in Frederick still standing; the cast iron stove, dated 1756, is inscribed in German, "Where your treasure is, there is also your heart." In summer, the kitchen garden in back is fragrant with rosemary and other culinary herbs. There's a small gift shop off the main building. The museum is open Apr.–mid-Dec., Tues.–Sat., 10 A.M.–4 P.M., Sunday noon–4 P.M. Admission is charged to enter the building: $2.

The **Barbara Fritchie Museum,** 154 W. Patrick St., 301/698-0630, celebrates the life of that original assertive woman; Fritchie delivered a fiery fist-shaking to a column of Confederate troops when they tried to shoot out her 34-star Union flag on their way through Frederick. Whether the story is true or a bloom of a poet's imagination (see the special topic "Shoot If You Must" in this chapter), Barbara Fritchie herself was quite a gal. She married when she was 40—late in life for a woman of her time—settling down with (literally) the boy next door; he was 28, son of her saloonkeeper neighbors. She outlived him by 14 years, and was 95 when she defied Jackson's troops, proof that you can get away with almost anything if you live long enough. The cozy two-story house/museum contains many items owned or made by the Fritchie family, including doll clothes sewn by Barbara for her niece. The Fritchie Museum is open Apr.–Sept., Mon.–Sun. 10 A.M.–4 P.M.; Oct.–Nov., Saturday 10 A.M.–4 P.M., Sunday 1–4 P.M. Closed Dec.–Mar. Admission is $2.

Mount Olivet Cemetery, 515 S. Market St., 301/662-1164, is the resting place of several historical celebrities, including the first Gray Panther, Barbara Fritchie, and Francis Scott Key, who grew up in the area and penned "The Star-Spangled Banner." Key's memorial is the first thing a visitor sees when driving into Mount Olivet; his bronze likeness gestures limply toward Old Glory, flying a few feet away. (Shouldn't he be more excited? However, considering Key was held on a prison ship for some hours before he emerged into the rockets' red glare, perhaps the statue is

SHOOT IF YOU MUST

Barbara Fritchie's supposed outspokenness to armed Confederate soldiers in 1862 earned her a place in history, thanks to abolitionist poet John Greenleaf Whittier. Whittier, who lived in Massachusetts, heard Fritchie's story some months after the event took place, and wrote a piece on it, using lavish poetic license. It was published almost immediately, and became an instant hit. It was republished in *Harper's Weekly* in 1866. Whittier might have had a different impression if he had known that Fritchie owned two slaves.

In addition to becoming *the* choice for schoolchildren's recitals, the poem found favor in other places. In the 1930s, when Winston Churchill visited the area with President Franklin D. Roosevelt, he stood outside the Fritchie house and recited the entire poem:

Up from the meadows rich with corn,
Clear in the cool September morn,
The clustered spires of Frederick stand
Green-walled by the hills of Maryland.
Round about them orchards sweep,
Apple and peach tree fruited deep,
Fair as a garden of the Lord
To the eyes of the famished rebel horde.
On that pleasant morn of the early fall
When Lee marched over the
    mountain-wall
Over the mountains winding down,
Horse and foot, into Frederick-town.
Forty flags with their silver stars,
Forty flags with their crimson bars,
Flapped in the morning wind: the sun
Of noon looked down, and saw not one.
Up rose old Barbara Fritchie then,
Bowed with her four score years and ten
Bravest of all in Frederick-town
She took up the flag the men hauled down
In her attic window the staff she set,
To show that one heart was loyal yet.
Up the street came the rebel tread,
Stonewall Jackson riding ahead.
Under his slouched hat left and right
He glanced: the old flag met his sight.
"Halt"—the dust-brown ranks stood fast,
"Fire"—out blazed the rifle blast.
It shivered the window, pane and sash:
It rent the banner with seam and gash.

Quick as it fell, from the broken staff
Dame Barbara snatched the silken scarf.
She leaned far out on the window-sill,
And shook it forth with a royal will.
"Shoot if you must, this old gray head,
But spare your country's flag," she said.
A shade of sadness, a blush of shame,
Over the face of the leader came.
The nobler nature within him stirred
To life at that woman's deed and word;

"Who touches a hair on yon gray head
Dies like a dog! March on!" he said.
All day long through Frederick's streets,
Sounded the tread of marching feet.
All day long that free flag tost,
Over the heads of the rebel host.
Ever its torn folds rose and fell
On the loyal winds that loved it well.
And through the hill gaps sunset light,
Shone over it with a warm good-night.
Barbara Fritchie's work is o'er.
And the rebel rides on his raids no more.
Honor to her! and let a tear
Fall, for her sake, on Stonewall's bier.
Over Barbara Fritchie's grave,
Flag of freedom and Union, wave!
Peace and order and beauty draw
Round the symbol of light and law
And ever the stars above look down
On thy stars below in Frederick-town.

historically accurate.) Barbara Fritchie gets her own flag, and a triangular boulder. Thomas Johnson, the first governor of Maryland, is just west of Fritchie (follow the signs).

What may be most interesting, however, are the Civil War monuments and Confederate soldiers' graves created on the northwest side of the cemetery nearly 20 years after the Battle of Antietam. A small black granite stone under a willow memorializes children who died in the conflict: the nameless drummer boys and 13-year-olds who fought for both sides. The Confederate Soldier's Monument, a tall granite obelisk under a circle-of-13-stars flag, was erected by the Ladies Monumental Association of Frederick County in 1880. During the war, few Southern families had the ways or means to bring home the bodies of their loved ones. Consequently, rebel soldiers were often buried in mass graves. At the bequest of sympathetic Northerners like the Ladies of Frederick, Confederate soldiers' remains were extracted from common graves on the battlefields of Antietam, Monocacy, and elsewhere, identified as well as could be done, and properly buried. Along the fence near the monument, named and unknown soldiers are remembered with plain headstones. One of the graves belongs to George Boatwright, who is perhaps still waiting to hear a "Yes!" to his proposal of marriage from his beloved Mattie (see the special topic "The Ballad of George and Mattie" in this chapter). The Confederate Soldiers Monument bears these words: "Soldiers rest, thy sleep the sleep that knows no waking / Dream of battled fields no more / Days of danger, nights of waking / Their praises will be sung in some yet unmoulded tongue / Far on in summers that we shall not see. Honor to the Brave."

Mount Olivet is open daily, from dawn to dusk. Free.

The Catoctin Iron Furnace is part of Cunningham Falls State Park, and is three miles south of the town of Thurmont on Route 806. This intact iron furnace operated from 1776 until 1903, and was once part of a booming industrial complex and community. Before he was elected, Maryland's ubiquitous first governor, Thomas Johnson, owned and operated the furnace with his brothers; they supplied 100 tons of shells used by revolutionary forces at Yorktown. The small park that surrounds the furnace is open dawn to dusk. Free.

OTHER POINTS OF INTEREST

Frederick played a central role in the Civil War for more than four years: three Confederate invasions, 38 skirmishes, and three major battles (South Mountain, Antietam, and Monocacy). It's an appropriate home for the **National Museum of Civil War Medicine,** 48 E. Patrick St., 301/695-1864, www.CivilWarMed.org. The museum is dedicated to all the women and men who brought medicine out of the dark ages, fueled by the imperatives of the War Between the States.

Dental surgeon Dr. Gordon Damman began collecting Civil War memorabilia in high school. The 3,000 artifacts in his collection—including a medical chest made by Dr. E. R. Squibb, who invented numerous medical instruments and later founded Squibb Pharmaceuticals—became the basis for the museum. The historic building that houses the museum was an embalming station for the dead from Antietam in 1862.

The National Museum of Civil War Medicine does an admirable job of chronicling the lives of those who served in the war as soldiers, and those who healed them. The well-displayed collection features the Union coat of Louis Razinski, assistant surgeon of the 36th New York Volunteers, who later became surgeon to the 54th Massachusetts, the famous black regiment featured in the film *Glory.* Videos and displays tell of members of the fledgling nursing profession, such as Clara Barton, founder of the Red Cross: as she tended a man on the battlefield of Antietam, a bullet passed through her sleeve and killed the soldier she nursed. Author Louisa May Alcott also volunteered to help the wounded. She wrote: "The sight of several stretchers, each with the legless, armless, or desperately wounded occupants, admonished me that I was there to work, not to wonder or weep."

Because of the vast number of surviving disabled, the Civil War was responsible for many developments in prosthetic devices and plastic surgery. These treatments were in their infancy, and, as the museum's video illustrates, the end result was meant to replace function with little thought to aesthetics. Several fine videos, along with authentic medical and period paraphernalia and an interesting layout, make this small museum a must-see for medical professionals and anyone interested in the human side of the Civil War. The museum also offers Civil War walking tours of Frederick, from Apr. –Nov., Sat.–Sun. at 2 P.M. ($4.50). The National Museum of Civil War Medicine is open Mon.–Sat. 10 A.M.–5 P.M., Sun. 11 A.M.–5 P.M. From mid-Nov. to mid-Mar., the museum closes at 4 P.M., and it's closed Dec. 24–Jan. 2 and most national holidays. Admission is $6.50.

One of the oldest historical societies in Maryland, **The Historical Society of Frederick County,** 24 E. Church St., 301/663-1188, was founded in 1888 to commemorate native son Francis Scott Key and Key's brother-in-law, Roger Brooke Taney. Both men practiced law in Fred-

erick, and Taney went on to become Chief Justice of the U.S. Supreme Court; he handed down the unfortunate decision on the Dred Scott case prior to the Civil War (in short, "once a slave, always a slave"). Judge Taney's home on Bentz Street in Frederick is owned by the society and is open for tours by appointment.

Church Street, lined with genteel mansions, was the "millionaire's row" of Frederick. The current three-story home of the historical society was built in the 1820s by local physician Dr. John Baltzell; it later served as a home for female orphans. The building displays furnishings and art of the early 1800s, including portraits of prominent Frederick County residents, glassware, dolls, and an exceptional array of tall case clocks; Frederick was the clock capital of the colonies in the late 18th century. An excellent small shop is attached to the main building. Guided tours are available throughout the year. Admission is $2.

National and regional exhibitions encompassing all aspects of visual arts, including drawing, painting, crafts, photography, and large installations, are featured at the **Delaplaine Visual Arts Center,** 40 S. Carroll St. on Carroll Creek, 301/698-0656. The Mountain City Mill building that houses the center was once a whiskey rectifying house, then a flour mill. It's open Thurs.–Sat. 10 A.M.–5:00 P.M., and admission is free.

The bridge that crosses Carroll Creek next to the arts center is worth a moment. Visitors standing near the creek just outside the Barbara Fritchie house often look up and down Carroll Creek for the **Community Bridge,** an arts project sponsored by the citizens of Frederick. Most see an old stone bridge a block away on Carroll Street. "It must work," said one of the guides at the Fritchie house; "that's the bridge." The community bridge, which is made of solid concrete, has been masterfully painted by *trompe l'oeil* muralist William M. Cochran, whose angels appear on walls all around Frederick. The bridge has been painted to resemble ancient stonework, and features a number of sponsored "stones" with sheaves of wheat, angels, spirals, and other abstract designs, all of which appear to be carved in the rock. The

© JOANNE MILLER

caution sign in western farm country

website for this project, http://bridge.skyline.net, was named one of the top ten arts sites on the Web by America Online.

Rose Hill Manor Park, 1611 N. Market St., 301/694-1648, was the home of Thomas Johnson, first elected governor of Maryland, from 1794 until his death in 1819. Johnson nominated his good friend George Washington to be commander-in-chief of the Continental Army. Today, the 43-acre park and manor are a "touch and see" museum that provide glimpses into life in the 19th century.

The first floor of the manor houses the Children's Museum: guided by costumed docents, children can make stitches on a quilt, card wool, and play with replica toys, kitchen tools, and costumes. The upper floors of the manor exhibit historic furnishings, including a study where Governor Johnson might have worked.

The outlying structures include an icehouse with 13-foot stone walls, a log cabin with furnishings similar to the original, a blacksmith shop, and early American garden and orchard. Also on the grounds are a Carriage Museum with more than 25 restored vehicles ranging from an Amish-style buggy to an elaborate 12-passenger carriage, and a Farm Museum, featuring hundreds of farm implements, a bank barn and a dairy barn.

Tours are available to walk-in visitors from Apr. 1–Oct. 31, Mon.–Sat. 10 A.M.–4 P.M., Sunday 1–4 P.M. During November, tours are available on weekends, Saturday 10 A.M.–1 P.M., Sunday 1–4 P.M. Admission is $3.

Lilypons Water Gardens, 6800 Lilypons Rd., Buckeystown (eight miles south of Frederick off Route 85), 800/999-5459, features acres of lilies and lotus blossoms, fountains, and goldfish. This commercial enterprise is a fine place to walk even if you're not looking to furnish your own pond. The water gardens are in bloom Memorial Day–Labor Day, and the grounds are open Mar.–Oct. It's free to enter, and Lilypons sponsors several special events in season.

The **National Shrine of St. Elizabeth Ann Seton,** 333 S. Seton Ave., Emmitsburg, 301/447-6606, includes a museum, basilica, historic buildings, and the mortuary chapel where Elizabeth

THE AMERICAN LOOK

Back in the 1950s, *Life* magazine listed a Frederick woman, Claire McCardell, as one of the 100 most important Americans of the 20th century. Though her name may be unfamiliar now except to followers of fashion, McCardell was the clothing designer who radically altered the way American women dress, based on her own reaction to changes in lifestyle after World War I. What clothing manufacturers needed to do, she said, was to "make clothes a woman can get into without the help of a maid—care for without a laundress. Make independent clothes for independent working gals."

McCardell said, "[I've always] designed things I've needed myself. It just turns out that other people need them, too." She left Frederick in 1932 and went to work for Townley Frocks in New York City; she stayed with them until her death in 1958. In an era when clothing designers weren't "names," McCardell's ideas influenced every American designer who came after her. Leotards and ballet slippers for everyday wear, the "separates" concept, and wool jersey suits are a few of her innovations that turn up on fashion runways year after year.

Ann Seton was interred. Mother Seton, who converted to Catholicism and served as a teaching sister in the early 1800s, was recognized as America's first saint by that church in 1959. Catholic saints are required not only to have led virtuous lives, but to also have been responsible for four verifiable miracles (see the special topic "Becoming a Saint" in the Maryland Introduction chapter).

Mother Seton practiced her faith and educated local inhabitants in the Emmitsburg area. She also established Sisters of Charity, a community that later merged with a similar group of nuns in France to become Daughters of Charity, a communal religious order. Their informational brochure states, "We . . . pray, work, and live together in order to bear witness to Christ, and to strengthen one another for the service of the poor." Daughters of Charity dedicate their lives to the improvement of health care and education in severely depressed areas.

The museum presents a straightforward telling of how an ordinary widow with several children rediscovered her spirituality, acted upon her faith, and became revered. The basilica, a church that contains a saint's relics (mortal remains), demands a visit to view the beautiful statuary, stained glass, marble, and glasswork within. Worshipers are often in the basilica praying at all times of day, but it's permissible to quietly walk the perimeter of the church. (The urns on either side of the entry contain water that's been blessed by a priest. Catholics will touch it and make the sign of the cross on themselves to signify entry into a holy place.)

The parklike grounds contain historic buildings used by Mother Seton and her community, and the Mortuary Chapel where her remains were buried before she was canonized. The museum and historic buildings are open daily 10 A.M.–4:30 P.M.; closed Monday from Nov. 1–Apr. 1; closed New Year's Day, Easter, Thanksgiving, Christmas, and the last two weeks of January. The Basilica is open daily 10 A.M.–4:30 P.M. Admission is free.

Though the **Grotto of Lourdes** and its grounds may strike some as an affected manifestation of personal religious beliefs, many Catholic faithful make a pilgrimage to this spot, which grants indulgences. The Catholic Church recognizes heaven, hell, and purgatory; the last of these is a sort of pleasant waiting room for heaven, where one works off minor sins over time. A pilgrimage to the grotto, with appropriate prayers, grants an indulgence to the pilgrim: less time to serve in purgatory. The grotto is a simulacrum of the original in France, in which the Virgin Mary appeared to a young girl, Bernadette Soubirous, 18 times (Bernadette was later canonized).

The grotto is built near the site of old Mt. St. Mary's, the church in which Saint Elizabeth Ann Seton worshiped. The grounds also include a small chapel and beautifully crafted stations of the cross (the story of the end of Jesus of Nazareth's life from his condemnation to his being laid in the sepulchre), religious mosaics, and numerous sculptures of other Catholic saints. A campanile topped with an enormous gilded statue of the Virgin

Mary stands in place of the long-destroyed church. The statue is visible from Route 15 for several miles. The Grotto of Lourdes is west of Route 15 about two miles south of Emmitsburg; look for signs on the highway for the turnoff, and follow signs along the road. Admission is free.

PARKS AND SCENIC SPOTS

Most state parks, forests, and national parks offer some sort of overnight facility, though types and prices vary by park. Each park office will have current information and maps.

Cunningham Falls State Park

A popular 5,000-acre recreation area in the Catoctin Mountains, this park is the site of Cunningham Falls, Maryland's highest waterfall. The 78-foot cascade shoulders its way through a rocky gorge and may be reached from four of eight hiking trails. Cunningham Falls State Park is split into two parts: the Houck Area (where the falls are) and the Manor Area. The park office is at 14039 Catoctin Hollow Rd., Thurmont, 301/271-7574.

Because it's so close to Frederick, the park gets very crowded on warm weekends—camping reservations are a must. Hunting Creek Lake, at 44 acres, offers swimming, boating, and fishing. Picnicking and hiking are popular pastimes. Modern camping facilities are available in both areas of the park. There is a camp store, dump station, food and beverage outlet, and picnic shelters. Biking is prohibited on all trails, and pets on a leash are permitted only in the wildlands area of the park.

Hiking: Two of the park's eight trails are rated easy or easy-to-moderate: the quarter-mile Catoctin Furnace Trail and the half-mile Lower Trail (this is the shortest route to the falls). The 27-mile strenuous Catoctin Trail is the most challenging, though park personnel rate all the other trails (ranging in length from .75 mile to 7.5 miles) as strenuous. A wheelchair-accessible 300-yard trail to the falls may be accessed from Route 77 (opposite side of the road from the Falls Nature Trail).

Hunting and Fishing: Hunting is allowed on 3,500 acres of undeveloped wildlands within the forest. Call the main park number for a brochure with specifics. Disabled hunters can hunt in a special area by reservation. A current Maryland fishing license is required for all fishers over 15 years old. Little Hunting Creek in the Manor Area and Big Hunting Creek on Route 77 are catch-and-release trout streams limited to artificial fly-fishing only. In Hunting Creek Lake, anglers can fish for trout, bass, bluegill, sunfish, crappie, and catfish. Fishing facilities for wheelchair users include a fishing pier located by the boat ramp. The Maryland Freshwater Sportfishing Guide has information on applicable creel and size limits.

Swimming: Swimming is permitted in three designated areas of Hunting Creek Lake. Lifeguards are on duty Memorial Day to Labor Day.

Water Sports: The use of power boats, aquacycles, canoes, rowboats, and flat-water canoes (kayaks) are allowed on 44-acre Hunting Creek Lake during the summer. Private craft launching is available for a fee at Catoctin Hollow Road ramp for watercraft, including those with one-horsepower-or-less electric motors only (gasoline motors are prohibited). In the summer season, canoes and rowboats may be rented at the boathouse.

Overnight Facilities: The Houck Area has 149 sites, including four camper cabins and five camper-ready (with tents and some camping equipment provided) sites. The Manor Area has 31 campsites. Site reservations are necessary Memorial Day–Labor Day, and are available through the park office.

Getting There: The park is in the Catoctin Mountains, roughly 15 miles north of Frederick. The Manor Area is off U.S. 15, and the Houck Area is three miles west of Thurmont, off Route 77, on Catoctin Hollow Road. Follow signs to the parking areas.

Catoctin Mountain National Park

Operated by the National Park Service, this outdoor recreation area, 6602 Foxville Rd., Thurmont, 301/663-9388, is right across the road (Route 77) from the Houck Area of Cunningham Falls State Park. Catoctin has two family campgrounds, a group camping area, and cabins, plus hiking trails, a number of special programs including an orienteering overview, a cross-country skiing seminar, and nature walks. The Blue Blazes whiskey still, part of a larger Prohibition-era operation, is on the park grounds. Reminiscent of those used by farmers during the Whiskey Rebellion of the 1790s, the still offers information on whiskey-making.

Campsites and cabins are open mid-April to mid-November. The park begins taking reservations for the cabins in January (301/271-3140); campsites are first-come, first-served, and begin filling up by Friday afternoons during the warm months.

Gambrill State Park

Northwest of Frederick off U.S. 40 (c/o Cunningham Falls State Park, 301/271-7574), Gambrill is primarily a day-use park with some improved campsites. The main feature of this park is its scenic vistas of the Catoctin mountains and surrounding valleys. The 1,600-foot summit of High Knob offers panoramic views of the Frederick City Municipal Forest to the north; Crampton's Gap, Middletown, and Monocacy Valleys to the southwest; and South Mountain to the southeast. In the 1930s and 1940s, many of the park's structures were built of native timbers and stone by Civilian Conservation Corps members.

Picnicking: The High Knob Area offers three picnic shelters and a lodge-style stone shelter, the Tea Room. These units are available for rental from April through October (call the number listed above).

Overnight Facilities: The Rock Run Area has 32 campsites, available Memorial Day to Labor Day on a first-come, first-served basis. The day-use area is free.

Getting There: The park is six miles northwest of Frederick, south of Cunningham Falls State Park. The park is accessed from U.S. 40 via Gambrill Park Road.

SPORTS AND ENTERTAINMENT
Spectator Sports

The **Frederick Keys,** a farm team of the Baltimore Orioles, are big with baseball fans in Frederick and elsewhere. Not only do they hold the

"Oh" during the singing of "The Star-Spangled Banner" out of respect for the Orioles, during the seventh-inning stretch, the crowd "shakes its keys." The Keys play at Harry Grove Stadium, a small open-air field with stadium seating just beyond Olivet Cemetery on S. Market Street. Call 301/662-0013 for more information.

Entertainment

Weinberg Center, 20 W. Patrick, 301/228-2828 (the former Tivoli Theater), is now a center for all kinds of performing arts, such as musicals, musical performances, and children's theater.

SHOPPING

Downtown Frederick is made for strolling, and the intersection of Patrick and Market Streets is a good place to start. North Market is lined with collectibles shops, antique stores, galleries, and craft shops. A local candy maker, the **Candy Kitchen** (specializing in handmade chocolates), is on the east side of N. Market between Church and Patrick Streets. **3rd Street,** starting with the Salvation Army store at 301 W. 3rd St. and moving east, has a plethora of less-organized (often cheaper) shops.

Antiques: Frederick has dozens of antique dealers. **Cannon Hill Place,** on S. Carroll Street at Commerce Street (between South Street and E. All Saints), 301/663-8574, is an old warehouse with lots of antiques and collectibles for sale by multiple dealers; there's also a café inside. It's open daily 9 A.M.–5 P.M. **Antique Station,** 194 Thomas Johnson Dr. (north of downtown Frederick off Motter Avenue/Oppossumtown Pike), 301/695-0888, features more than 140 dealers, and is open Thurs.–Tues. 10 A.M.–6 P.M.

Malls: Everedy Square is the site of Talbots and other boutiques; **Shab Row,** a renovated group of row houses, features more shops and the **Frederick Coffee Company,** 100 East St., an espresso bar and café. Everedy Square was once the factory headquarters of the Everedy (battery) Company, and the brick paved buildings along Shab Row were the original homes of Frederick's earliest citizens. Both are on East Street between E. 2nd and E. Patrick Streets.

The 60-shop **Frederick Towne Mall** is home to the larger national retailers such as JCPenney and Bon-Ton, and a 10-screen cinema. It's on U.S. 40, just west of Frederick.

Country Markets and Orchards: McCutcheon Apple Products, 13 S. Wisner St., has a factory store at this location that sells sweet cider, apples, preserves, honey, pickles, and more. **Mr. Natural's,** a fruit stand and nursery on U.S. 15 at the intersection of Route 806, offers a variety of goods year-round, delivered with a dose of grinning sunshine from the curly-tressed Mr. Natural himself. **Pryor's Orchard,** 13841-B Pryor Rd. (one half-mile west of Thurmont on Route 77), is open mid-June to mid-November, and offers a variety of seasonal fruits (peaches, apples, pears, plums, cherries), vegetables, and nuts, honey, and other ready-made food goods.

ACCOMMODATIONS

At **Hill House,** 12 W. 3rd St., 301/682-4111, Mrs. Damian Branson makes the creamiest grits accompanied by the sweetest fried tomatoes on the planet. Of course, that's only one part of a stay (and part of a breakfast) at this charming B&B. Hill House is within convenient walking distance of downtown Frederick's shops and restaurants. Damian and her husband, Taylor, moved up from southern Maryland and bought and renovated this three-story row house in 1996. The unique decor of each guest room reflects their interests: Chesapeake, Victorian, Mexican folk-art modern, and Frederick Federal. There are three spacious guest rooms, each with private bath; in addition, the top floor is a suite of rooms, including a kitchen; it's ideal for longer stays, and guests can watch the fireworks after the local ballgame from the bathroom window (the Frederick Keys, a farm team of the Orioles, play at Harry Grove Stadium on the edge of town). The common rooms of the house are warm, welcoming, and especially pretty during the winter holidays. The Bransons are connected to Frederick's happenings, and give great information on places to go and things to do. Corporate clients and long stays receive discounts on room rates. Rates range $125–235.

Locals also recommend the **Tyler-Spite House,** 112 W. Church St., 301/831-4455, a former Georgian mansion remade into a gorgeous B&B. As the name implies, a neighbor's tiff caused the three-story house to be built out of spite. Rates range $120–250.

A large portion of the **Catoctin Inn**'s business is business—it's a popular spot for wedding parties, reunions, and corporate groups because of its capacity and location. The inn is south of Frederick in peaceful, rolling farmland, beyond Frederick's corporate industrial area (you'll pass English Muffin Way on the way to Buckeystown—Cadbury has a facility outside Frederick).

This rural historic inn, 3619 Buckeystown Pike (Route 85), Buckeystown, 301/874-5555, www.catoctininn.com, was built by George Buckey, who established a tannery around 1775. Terry and Sarah McGillivray, and Sarah's mother, Avadna Coghill, bought and began renovating the old mansion and outbuildings in 1990. The Catoctin Inn remains a family affair. In the main inn (the old mansion), rooms are decorated in traditional styles, often linked to family members or local memorabilia; all rooms have private baths. The mansion would be a wise choice for those seeking a more romantic experience. Outlying buildings, such as the former Stable Hands Quarters and the Carriage House, feature large (20-foot-square), modern rooms with up-to-the-minute amenities including whirlpool baths, room phones, and some gas fireplaces. Separate cottages offer whirlpool tubs, fireplaces, and refrigerators, and the Smokehouse has everything, including a small kitchen—a good choice for families. Rates range $99–159.

FOOD

Snacks and Delis

Pretzel and Pizza Creations, 210 N. Market St., proves that creativity and pretzel dough were made for each other—they have everything from sweet cinnamon to hot Cajun. Great cheap snacks under $5.

Cheeseburgers 'N Paradise, at the Frederick County airport on Bailes Lane, 301/631-0188, produces the ultimate sloppy burger, and great fries. It's open Wed.–Sat., after 1 P.M., Sunday after 2 P.M.

Snow White Grill is in central Frederick, 9 E. Patrick St. (also 12 S. Potomac St. in Hagerstown and another location in Virginia). Customers lurk about, peering out of their overcoats as if the lure of tiny burgers was somehow pornographic. Order two or three teensy "deluxes" (two inches square) with fried onion, tomato, lettuce, pickle, and mayo for $1 each; the burgers are really tasty and made fresh to order. Fries are $1.25.

The **Stone Hearth Bakery,** 138 East St., is the spot for fresh breads and other baked goods.

Italian

A classic spaghetti-and-meatballs Italian restaurant, **di Francesco's,** 26 N. Market St., 301/695-5499, has been a local favorite for years. Consistently delicious, dinner is served daily, and lunch is available Mon.–Sat. Pastas average $7, fish and meats, $10.

Tauraso's is a hip Italian restaurant, 6 East St. near E. Patrick in Everedy Square, 301/663-6600. The menu features seafood with a nouvelle twist and a wide variety of pizzas, served in both formal and casual dining areas, and a great fireplace to sit by in winter. This place attracts a fashionable crowd and those looking for a good, unique pizza. Lunch and dinner is served Fri.–Sun.; Mon.–Sat. 4–5 P.M. they serve pizzas only. Pizzas average $10, entrées $14.

International

Serving Spanish tapas (little dishes), **Isabella's Tavern & Tapas Bar,** is at 44 N. Market St., 301/698-8922. It has a good wine list and is open for lunch and dinner Tues.–Sun.

Hana's Korean Restaurant, 140-B W. Patrick St., 302/695-9150, features both authentic Korean (rice/meat/vegetable salad Bi-Bim-Bop) and Vietnamese specialties (noodle soups, grilled beef in grape leaves). This off-the-beaten-path eatery is a pleasant departure from the ubiquitous American-style menus. Hana's is right around the corner from the Barbara Fritchie house, next to Delphey's Sport Shop through the parking lot. Entrées average $8, and lunch specials are available.

Landmarks

The Shamrock mixes casual dining with goofy entertainment, such as potato-peeling contests for patrons. The restaurant is known for its excellent fried shad roe, a Maryland specialty. It's off Route 15, Thurmont, 301/271-2912, and is open daily for lunch and dinner until 10 P.M. It's near another local party spot: **The Cozy,** on Route 806 off Route 15 in Thurmont, 301/271-7373, which has fed visitors lunch and dinner seven days a week since 1929. In addition to an American menu and steam bar, the Cozy loads its service tables with more than 100 items during its Friday- and Saturday-night buffets. Entrées average $15.

Local Favorites

Hagan's Tavern, 5018 Old National Pike (Route 40A, Braddock Heights), 301/371-9189, is a restored 1790 stone tavern, featuring colonial atmosphere, artwork, and costumed workers. It's open for lunch and dinner Tues.–Sun. Entrées average $16.

Dutch's Daughter is reputed to have the best crab cakes in Frederick. The restaurant is at 581 Himes Ave., southwest of the main part of town off Route 15; call 301/663-0297 or 800/819-4040. Prices average $13.

Breweries and Nightlife

At **Brewer's Alley,** unique appetizers (wood-fired soft pretzels with spicy Creole cheese), a broad southwestern/Cajun pub menu with lots of lighter dishes, and a knockout beer sampler (excellent hefeweizen and pale gold ale) are crowd pleasers. In central Frederick, 124 N. Market St., 301/631-0089, Brewer's Alley also offers a children's menu and their own root beer on draft. Sandwiches and pizzas are priced $6–12 (for the large), dinner entrées average $15.

Bentz Street Raw Bar, a sassy, late-night (dinner only) seafood restaurant and raw bar, features live music seven nights a week in a casual atmosphere. It's one of the best nightlife hot spots, at 6 S. Bentz St., 301/694-9134.

INFORMATION

The **Tourism Council of Frederick County, Inc.,** 19 E. Church St., Frederick, MD 21701, 301/228-2888 or 800/999-3613, www.fredericktourism.org, has details on events and things to do in the area.

GETTING AROUND

Most of Frederick's attractions are within walking distance of the center of town, so it's easy to park your car along one of the residential streets and walk in. The town is laid out in a simple grid; the central intersection is at Market (north-south) and Patrick (east-west) Streets.

Crossroads of the Civil War

It is well that war is so terrible, or we should grow too fond of it.

Robert E. Lee, *after the battle of Fredericksburg, 1862*

CIVIL WAR HISTORY AND SITES

During the Civil War, the area of Maryland roughly between Hagerstown, Frederick, and Harpers Ferry was one of the most trafficked pieces of territory in the United States. Maryland, a deeply divided border state, vividly illustrated the phrase commonly associated with the Civil War—brother fighting against brother. Though the war ended with Lee's surrender at the Appomattox courthouse, it grew from a spark set in 1859.

In the summer of that year, radical abolitionist John Brown rented a small farmhouse north of Harpers Ferry, from which he rallied volunteers to his incendiary cause and planned a raid that would, he hoped, begin a slave revolution similar to the one that had recently taken place in Haiti.

© JOANNE MILLER

Kennedy Farm

The Kennedy Farm

This farm, also known as Samples Manor, 2406 Chestnut Grove Rd., Sharpsburg (in the area formerly known as Kennedyville), was the leased summer dwelling of "Isaac Smith and family"— John Brown, his two daughters, ages 16 and 17, and three of his sons. The farm was owned by one Robert F. Kennedy, who bought it in the 1850s and frequently leased it to a church group, the Brethren. The "Smiths" stayed in the small log-and-wattle structure from late spring to autumn of 1859, keeping to themselves, much to the chagrin of their curious neighbors. Though the two girls came and went frequently, the other dwellers within the house were well hidden during the day—twelve white men and five black men, in addition to John Brown and his sons. Brown sent his daughters home in early October, just before the planned raid on Harpers Ferry.

The grounds of the farmhouse are open May–Oct. Sat.–Sun. 9 A.M.–5 P.M. Tours at other times or for groups may be booked by calling 301/977-3599 and asking for the Kennedy Farm curator. There is also an automated information terminal on the upper balcony.

Harpers Ferry National Historical Park

Harpers Ferry National Park spans the Potomac and Shenandoah Rivers, and is shared by Maryland, West Virginia, and Virginia. The town of Harpers Ferry, at the confluence of the two rivers, is accessed via I-340, in West Virginia, and is definitely worth several hours of a visitor's time (contact the park directly: Superintendent, P.O. Box 65, Harpers Ferry, WV 25425, 304/535-6298, www.nps.gov/hafe).

In 1747, a Philadelphia millwright, Robert Harper, bought out the original German settler and established an improved ferry service and several local industries. By October 1859, Harpers Ferry was a bustling town of nearly 3,000, 150 of whom were free blacks, with an equal number of slaves. The town was accessed by both the Baltimore and Ohio Railroad and the Chesapeake and Ohio Canal. The town's major business—and the main interest of John Brown and his followers—was the U.S. Armory. The armory consisted of 20 brick structures along the Potomac River, two arsenal buildings where thousands of finished weapons were stored, and the U.S. Rifle Factory.

THE ADVERSARIES: ROBERT E. LEE

Robert E. Lee was the son of one of the founding families of Virginia; two of his forbears were among the signers of the Declaration of Independence. Lee's father, "Legion Harry," a celebrated cavalry commander, delivered George Washington's funeral oration, immortalizing the dead president as "First in war, first in peace, and first in the hearts of his countrymen."

Lee entered West Point in 1825, and graduated with the highest honors of his class. Shortly thereafter, he married the daughter of the adopted stepson of George Washington, and entered into the A-list social crowd in Washington. For the next 30 years, his military career was distinguished by honorable service for the United States. He captured John Brown at Harpers Ferry, and at the outbreak of the Civil War was serving as a colonel in Texas.

During the North-South controversy of the 1850s, Lee, a moderate, was dismayed by extremists on both sides, but his primary allegiance was to Virginia. The day after that state seceded in April 1861, Lee resigned his commission in the United States Army; at the age of 55, he chose to abandon the Union and thus everything he had worked for in his life—professional rank, private fortune, and, if secession failed, his family's good name. Refusing to accept the advice and admonitions of his old friend General Scott, commander of the Union Army, Lee replied, "I have felt that I ought not longer to retain my commission in the army. I therefore tender my resignation, which I request you will recommend for acceptance. It would have been presented at once but for the struggle it has cost me to separate myself from a service in which I have devoted all the best years of my life, and all the ability I possessed. . . . Save in defense of my native state, I never desire again to draw my sword." To his sister, Lee wrote, "The whole South is in a state of revolution, into which Virginia, after a long struggle, has been drawn; and though I recognize no necessity for this state of things . . . I had to meet the question whether I should take part against my native state." On June 3, Robert E. Lee accepted command of the Confederate States Army in Virginia, and held the position until the end of the conflict. Four years later, almost to the day that Lee resigned his commission, he surrendered the remnants of his army to Union Commander U. S. Grant, the successor of the man who urged him not to resign.

Critics of Lee complain that he was too genteel, that his politeness sometimes obscured the necessity for quick, total obedience to his orders; others felt he entrusted too much discretion to subordinates who, with the exception of Stonewall Jackson, were not up to the responsibility. Despite these weaknesses, many historians maintain that Lee was the most capable commander of the Civil War.

After the defeat of the South, Robert E. Lee served as a symbol of courage in defeat, embodying the finest elements of the Southern heritage. He became president of Washington College (now Washington and Lee University) in Lexington, Virginia, and devoted himself to education and to helping rebuild the South. Lee died on October 12, 1870.

It was Brown's intention to seize the 100,000 weapons at the arsenal and to flee to the nearby Blue Ridge Mountains, establishing a base for the slave-guerrilla war that he predicted would ensue. His 21-man "Provincial Army of the United States" crossed the railroad bridge from Maryland into Harpers Ferry on the evening of October 16, 1859, and seized the armory and several other buildings. Local militia and a contingent of marines under the command of Lt. Col. Robert E. Lee (among them Abraham Lincoln's future assassin, John Wilkes Booth) fought Brown's raiders for 36 hours, killing or capturing almost all the men, including Brown, who held out to the last in the armory fire-engine house. Found guilty of treason, Brown was hanged in December 1859. The attack on Harpers Ferry inflamed both North and South, and lead to secession of the Southern states over their right to allow slave ownership, followed by the bombing of Fort Sumter by Federal troops in 1861—the start of the Civil War.

Harpers Ferry continued to play a significant role for both sides for the duration of the Civil War; the town changed hands eight times between 1861 and 1865. On April 18, 1861, less than 24 hours after Virginia seceded from the Union, Federal soldiers set fire to the Harpers Ferry armory and arsenal to keep them out of Confederate hands. However, Confederate forces managed to douse the flames and send the remaining weapon-making machinery south to be used in their cause. When the Confederates abandoned the town two months later, they burned most of the factory buildings and blew up the railroad bridge that John Brown and his men had crossed in their failed attempt to capture arms. The ruins, however, became the foundation of a hopeful future. Storer College, an integrated school, was founded on the grounds of the armory just after the Civil War.

Harpers Ferry National Historical Park not only contains the town of Harpers Ferry, with its many restored buildings and cemetery, but also a number of hiking trails that trace paths taken by Union and Confederate troops: Maryland Heights, Loudoun Heights, Bolivar Heights, and Schoolhouse Ridge.

Crossroads

During the next four years, Union troops stationed within Maryland's borders repeatedly fought the Confederate Army in its attempts to capture Washington, D.C., and Philadelphia, the two Federal centers of power nearest Confederate territory. As a result, three major battles were fought in this triangle, the "crossroads of the Confederacy." The first two, South Mountain and Antietam, took place in 1862.

In his new role as leader of the Confederate forces, inspired by a series of victories over Union forces in Virginia, Major General Robert E. Lee wrote to rebel President Jefferson Davis in early August 1862: "The present seems to be the most propitious time since the commencement of the war for the Confederate Army to enter Maryland."

Lee knew that Maryland was deeply divided in its alliances. He figured Maryland was ripe for secession; once the state joined the Confederacy, Washington could no longer be held as the Federal capital. On September 2, Lee, Stonewall Jackson, and General D. H. Hill and their troops began a rapid march north to Frederick, Maryland's second-largest city, arriving about 60,000 strong a few days later. Lee exhorted the people of Frederick and all Marylanders to join his army, fully expecting their cooperation. According to the editors of *Harper's Weekly Magazine* (1866), "This prospect was not alluring to those to whom war had presented itself as a gay holiday show. When the theoretical secessionists of Maryland saw their liberators, officers as well as men, barefoot, ragged, and filthy, they looked upon them with hardly concealed aversion. Yet that ragged and begrimed army was as brave a body of soldiers as the world ever saw. The enthusiasm of the Maryland secessionists exhausted itself in a few women secretly sewing clothing for the army, and in presenting to Jackson a magnificent horse, which threw him the first time he mounted it."

The Northern general McClellan was by then aware of Lee's presence and was advancing his troops toward the threat. Characteristically, McClellan estimated Southern troops at twice their strength, while just as mistakenly, Lee estimated Northern troops to be many fewer than their actual number of nearly 120,000—three to one.

While in Frederick, Lee had decided that winning Harpers Ferry was crucial to Confederate victory; the Potomac crossing was necessary to keep his supply lines open. In a decision that altered the course of the battles that followed, Lee divided his forces; his plan was to capture the crossing at Harpers Ferry and heights on either side of the water by surrounding the force of 12,500 raw Union troops that held it. He sent his generals out from Frederick by different routes: Longstreet's troops first went northwest to Hagerstown for money and supplies, and D. H. Hill's men were ordered southwest to Boonsboro for the same purpose. A group of men, led by General Walker, was sent first to destroy the canal aqueduct at Monocacy Creek, then to Harpers Ferry. Troops led by Jackson, Franklin, McLaws, and Anderson were sent directly to Harpers Ferry and left Frederick in a fast march on September 10. They reached Harpers Ferry on the 12th; by the 15th, Federal forces surrendered with little resistance, an act later viewed with embarrassment by the Union government.

Meanwhile, Lee had left a rear guard in Frederick and began a leisurely march with the remaining half of his troops down the west side of South Mountain, planning to meet the others at the ferry crossing. South Mountain runs roughly north-south, starting in the vicinity of York, Pennsylvania, and ending at the Potomac River, not far from Harpers Ferry. It's crossed east-west by two large gaps (Turner's and Crampton's) and one small gap (Fox). Union general McClellan's men occupied and skirmished with Lee's rear-guard forces on September 12 in Frederick. By a stunning piece of luck—Lee's battle plans had been found wrapped around three tobacco butts left as trash in his encampment—McClellan anticipated that, by rapid march, he could throw the whole Union Army between Lee's divided forces and "cut the enemy in two, and beat him in detail." Lee learned that McClellan's men were moving to the narrow pass of South Mountain known as Turner's Gap, southeast of Boonsboro, on the 13th.

Lee, who barely had 28,000 troops with him spread over a distance of 25 miles, hurriedly recalled D. H. Hill from Boonsboro and Longstreet from Hagerstown. The Confederate objective was to delay the Union advance for a day or so while the scattered divisions of their army could reunite.

The Battle of South Mountain

Though no official battlefield exists to commemorate South Mountain, a detailed map of the battle sites and auto tour maps may be picked up at the visitors center at Gathland State Park.

Turner's Gap was the main Union objective because the National Road, which passed through it, led to Boonsboro and Hagerstown. Lee's lost orders indicated to McClellan that he would find pieces of the divided Confederate Army in those areas. Mountain House, a wayside tavern still in operation (now the South Mountain Inn), was a key landmark in the gap. The first action occurred at Fox's Gap, just south of Turner's Gap.

Union troops coming from the east tried to round the right flank of the main Confederate forces posted at Turner's Gap. General Hill, who commanded the troops at Turner's Gap, dispatched General Samuel Garland's brigade south to meet the Union flank attack. Garland's men fought with Jacob Cox's Kanawha Division of the Union IX Corps on the eastern slope. Two future U.S. presidents were with the Kanawha Division: Lieutenant-Colonel Rutherford B. Hayes (who was wounded) and Commissary Sergeant William B. McKinley (who went on to dish up chow at Antietam). Hill's rebel troops fought Union forces for most of the day of September 14, trying to secure Turner's Gap. His reinforcements, lead by Longstreet, arrived late in the afternoon.

Farther south, at Crampton's Gap, Confederate general Franklin's troops left Harpers Ferry to try to hold the pass, which was quickly overrun by Union forces. The main thrust of Franklin's assault on Crampton's Gap came from the fields east of Gathland State Park. The Confederates' initial defense position was on the west behind the stone walls. Confederate artillery at Brownsville Gap, a mile to the south, raked the Union ranks. The Union forces pushed the Confederates up the slope, through the gap, and into Pleasant Valley on the other side of the mountain.

The third phase of the battle began late in the day with a combined Union assault on both Fox's and Turner's Gaps. Union forces succeeded in securing Hagerstown Road north of Turner's Gap, but the determined Confederates held on to the main prize, Turner's Gap. It was only a matter of time before the superior number of Union troops succeeded in taking the gap; General Lee ordered Hill to withdraw late in the evening, ending the Battle of South Mountain.

By the night of September 14, McClellan's army had possession of the three passes. Had he pushed on quickly, the Union general might have attacked Lee's army before it was reunited. McClellan's failure to advance is considered to be one of the greatest missed opportunities in American history, and one of the leading causes of his eventual dismissal as leader of the Union Army. Lee sent word to his scattered troops to join him near the village of Sharpsburg.

THE ADVERSARIES: GEORGE B. McCLELLAN

After the decisive victory of Southern troops against great odds at the battle of Bull Run in Virginia, the Union began to examine its once confident forces. Who could transform these boys who volunteered on a lark into an army? President Lincoln singled out General George B. "Little Mack" McClellan, who had been leading troops with favorable results in West Virginia, winning a series of encounters in rapid succession, and as a result, becoming popular with the newspaper-reading public in the North. "Another quality, more characteristic of McClellan than of any other general, and one which was more than all others calculated to make him the centre of popular attraction," according to the editors of *Harper's Magazine*, "was his extraordinary capability of creating enthusiasm in his army. This enthusiasm was of no ordinary character, but rather a sort of inspiration, by which the troops became identified with their leader, a part and parcel of his personal ambition and destiny as well as of his military operations. It was not a simple frank outburst of admiration, but it was personal sympathy, fervent devotion."

President Lincoln saw McClellan as a political choice who would be likely to conciliate the South if it were possible, avoiding a long and bloody war; in addition, his popularity would unite the North. What Lincoln hadn't foreseen were the inevitable disagreements between McClellan and his administration: Lincoln's own sentiments and approaches to warfare differed radically from those of Little Mack. Upon his appointment, McClellan set about the overwhelming task of reorganizing the army, including troops, artillery, and supply systems. Lincoln and his cabinet, meanwhile, set out to micromanage McClellan's movements, creating a situation where McClellan's assessments of field maneuvers were frequently at odds with Lincoln's. Disagreements began almost immediately as to where to attack, how many men were needed to defend Washington, etc., and continued throughout McClellan's tenure as head of the Army of the Potomac.

While leading the Union forces, McClellan kept up a voluminous stream of correspondence with the president, often presenting his "victories" in a light so favorable that a modern publicity flack might blush. Mack relied on the Pinkerton Agency for his spy information, and they were frequently wrong. The 100,000 Confederates he was expecting at South Mountain turned out to be 19,000. Perhaps his continual overestimation of the size of Confederate forces, coupled with his overestimation of Confederate dead and wounded, was an attempt to loosen Lincoln's leash. However, his apparent inability to assess his enemy's potential would cause unnecessary troop losses more than once, including those at Antietam.

Another characteristic of McClellan, perhaps because he valued the welfare of his troops more than most, was his hesitancy to enter into battle without full planning and preparation. Delays sometimes cost him the battle, and eventually, his command. After Antietam, Abraham Lincoln heard that Lee's army was close to the Maryland border; he wrote to McClellan, insisting on pursuit and full destruction. McClellan demanded reinforcements and supplies. Lincoln countered that the Army of the South had few or none of the things McClellan requested, yet they continued to resist in an annoyingly adept fashion. On October 26, McClellan crossed the Potomac and pursued the rebels, with few results. On November 7, McClellan received these terse orders from the Secretary of War: "By direction of the President of the United States, it is ordered that Major General McClellan be relieved from the command of the Army of the Potomac, and Major General Burnside take command of the army." The command of the Northern forces would pass through many more hands before the war was over. In 1864, McClellan ran unsuccessfully against Lincoln for president of the United States.

Of the 28,000 Union soldiers engaged in the Battle of South Mountain, 1,800 were reported killed, wounded, or missing. Of the 18,000 Confederates, 2,800 were lost. The nearby hamlet of Burkittsville received and treated wounded troops from both sides at the two churches on Main Street after the battle.

Antietam National Battlefield

Antietam Battlefield, Route 65, .7 mile north of Sharpsburg (send inquiries to: Superintendent, Box 158, Sharpsburg, MD 21782, 301/432-5124), is preserved as a monument to those who died in the bloodiest day of fighting in the Civil War. During a single 20-minute segment of the battle, both sides suffered a total of 2,000 casualties. Six generals suffered mortal wounds.

Lee soon had news of victory at Harpers Ferry, but little had changed: the Union troops now camped in Pleasant Valley continued to present a barrier between him and his reinforcement troops at the crossing. Lee retreated the night of September 14 and took up positions between the Potomac and Antietam Creek in the small farming community of Sharpsburg. The scattered parts of his army joined him in Sharpsburg, taking a strong defensive position by the morning of September 17. Lee's forces numbered around 36,000 infantry and artillerymen—little more than half the original force.

Union general McClellan's plan was to strike north, middle, and south on the battlefield. The editors of *Harper's Weekly*, Guernsey and Alden, commented in 1866, "Every thing pointed to the one conclusion, that the whole Union force should be thrown at the earliest moment upon the Confederates. That this was to be done on the morning of the 17th was the decision, as understood by [Union general] Hooker, to whom the initiative was assigned." And so General Hooker's troops attacked Confederates in the woods near Dunker's Church, on the north end of the battlefield. Dunker is a corruption of the German word "tunker" or "tunken," to dip, denoting a full-immersion baptism. The Dunkers were a group of pacifists originally from Germantown, outside of Philadelphia; they were among the first settlers on Antietam Creek. The church that bears their name was built in 1853.

After several hours of fighting, General Hooker fell mortally wounded, and the battle turned, due to the Southern artillery's 80 large guns. Shattered, Hooker's troops fled, and the battle went to the Confederates. However, they were unaware of their own victory, and fell back.

Union forces pressed the Confederate center, and Lee threw the majority of his troops into that confrontation, withdrawing men from the woods to the north and south. The Confederate troops were overwhelmed by wave after wave of Union artillery, but managed to break the Union line. Two of General Hill's brigades clung desperately to a sunken road. By nightfall, troops of both sides occupied almost the same positions as they had that morning. One Union captain, Oliver Wendell Holmes, Jr., fought with the 20th Massachusetts Volunteer Infantry and was wounded in the neck during the battle. He survived, returned home, and became a renowned U.S. Supreme Court Justice.

Lee had fewer than 2,500 soldiers left to defend the southern portion of the battlefield, a stone bridge over Antietam Creek. Union general Burnside, with 14,000 men under his command, had been ordered to take the bridge at 8 A.M. that morning. For an unknown reason, he hesitated to attack until 4 P.M. that afternoon. By then, Confederate forces at the bridge had been relocated except for 500 Georgia riflemen under the command of an officer named Toombs. When Burnside did decide to take the bridge, he sent wave after wave of soldiers to their deaths—easy pickings for the Georgia riflemen who were hidden in the forested heights on the other side. After Toombs's men had withdrawn to the defense of the Confederate center, Burnside's men crossed the easily fordable stream without opposition. In one of those ironic twists of history, the bridge is named after the man who sent hundreds to their deaths.

Though Dunker's Church was damaged in the first day's battle, it still provided necessary shelter and a modicum of peace. During a brief truce on the 18th, soldiers from both armies used the church as a field hospital; they spoke freely of their homes and families, fully expecting to be sighting each other over rifles the next day. That battle never took place. In the darkness of night on September 18, the rebels slipped away, crossing the Potomac at Shepherdstown, foiling McClellan's plans to renew the battle on the 19th. After the battle damage was repaired, the Dunkers continued to hold services in the small white church for several more decades.

Total forces engaged by the Union numbered nearly 58,000; by the Confederacy, 38,000. Though losses to both sides were close to equal on the north and center battlegrounds, Burnside's excessive losses brought the total of Union dead and wounded (but not missing) to 14,200; that of the Confederates, about 12,500. The Battle of Antietam (or Sharpsburg, as it's known in the South) was considered a draw, but it put a temporary end to Lee's plans to invade the North. However, he would enter the Maryland crossroads once again in less than a year.

Antietam National Battlefield is open dawn to dusk, daily; closed Thanksgiving, Christmas, and New Year's Day. The visitor center on Route 65 displays Civil War relics and offers an interpretive film on the battle. A small store in the visitor center sells or rents an inexpensive and excellent audiotape auto tour of the battle. Since the battlefield is kept much as a shrine, auto touring, bicycling, and walking are allowed, but picnicking and other recreational activities are not. Monuments to various regiments are scattered throughout the area, including one to the Zouaves, French colonial soldiers who fought for the Federal Army. There is a $3 charge to enter the park.

The **Newcomer House Museum,** 18422 Shepardstown Pike, Sharpsburg, 301/432-0300, displays artifacts from the Civil War including the sword presented by General George McClellan when he stepped down from Union command, a letter written by General Stonewall Jackson in Sharpsburg, a lock of President Abraham Lincoln's hair, and a Confederate flag that flew at Burnside Bridge during the Battle of Antietam.

Antietam Cemetery

On Route 34 in the town of Sharpsburg, the cemetery is open dawn to dusk daily. Since so many soldiers died during the battle, burial was haphazard, often in shallow graves with little or no identification. By 1864, many of the graves surrounding Sharpsburg were becoming exposed. The state purchased an 11-acre burial site, and the arduous task of exhuming the dead began. In the years following the Battle of Antietam, two local men, Aaron Good and Joseph Gill, were instrumental in finding the old burial sites and helping to identify the dead through letters, receipts, diaries, photographs, and marks on belts or cartridge boxes. Despite their efforts, 38 percent remain unknown. Their graves comprise the greater part of Antietam Cemetery. There is no charge to walk about the grounds.

Because the South was unable to raise funds to exhume their dead, and because bitterness continued after the war's end, no Confederate soldiers are buried here. Charitable organizations—often made up of Northern women—paid to have remains of 2,800 rebels—60 percent unknown—buried in three cemeteries: Mount Olivet Cemetery in Frederick, Washington Confederate Cemetery in Hagerstown (now known as Mount Rose), and Elmwood Cemetery in Shepherdstown, West Virginia.

The Road to Gettysburg

Maryland was once again invaded in June 1863, prior to the Battle of Gettysburg. Lee's troops had been making raids into Pennsylvania, hoping unsuccessfully to draw and divide Union forces. He resolved to make a serious invasion by his whole army. His troops crossed the Potomac at Williamsport and Shepardstown; cut off from their supply system, they were ordered to live off the country. Lee ordered that supplies should be extorted in an orderly manner: first, upon formal requisitions, payment being tendered in Confederate notes; if these were declined, certificates were to be given showing the amount and value of the property taken—a sort of IOU; if these were refused, the required supplies were to be seized. This last was the most common form of acquisition. Towns with few assets were literally held hostage, and burned if they were unable to pay. The army marched on to Pennsylvania, engaged the Union Army during the three-day Battle of Gettysburg, and returned to Virginia once again.

Monocacy National Battlefield

Monocacy (send inquiries to: Monocacy National Battlefield, 4801 Urbana Pike, Frederick, MD 21701-7307, 301/662-3515) was the final attempt of Southern troops to bring the war to the North.

In June 1864, Robert E. Lee withdrew his Army of Northern Virginia from the Confederate capital at Richmond to Petersburg, pursued by Union general Ulysses S. Grant. Grant had pulled all able-bodied forces from Washington, D.C., in hopes of defeating Lee and ending the war. Lee, desperate to draw Federal forces away from his

army, ordered Lt. General Jubal Early to take one-third of the Confederate forces, raid Harpers Ferry for supplies, then cross the Potomac at Sharpsburg. Early's goal was a last-ditch attempt to invade Washington, D.C. His men advanced through Hagerstown and Frederick, extorting $20,000 from the former and $200,000 from the latter.

Grant dispatched troops to meet the Confederate forces well before they arrived at the capital, but until they could reach Early's troops, the only Federal soldiers available to engage the rebels were a group of 2,300 raw recruits quartered in Baltimore under Major General Lew Wallace. Wallace, who was to become famous in later years as the author of *Ben-Hur,* rushed his men

THE BALLAD OF GEORGE AND MATTIE

George Boatwright, a young man from Toombsboro, Georgia, enlisted in May 1862 as an artillery soldier in the Confederate Army. He left behind a 13-year-old girl of slight acquaintance, Miss Martha Jane Burrows. George began a hesitant correspondence with "Miss Mattie": "It is the case with a majority of soldiers, to have some one to correspond with them, and knowing no better subject I solicited yours." Miss Mattie responded by asking why he wasn't writing to his girlfriend instead, and George replied, "you accuse me of being in possession of that almost indispensable article—[a] sweetheart. For I was not aware that I had one, but if such is the case, I appeal to you to inform me who she is, who has condescended to allow me to claim her, or who has thought enough of me to claim me."

Over the next year, they continued to write to each other whenever the machinations of war permitted—often missing each other's replies. George suffered through bouts of the "chills" (dysentery), and reported in July 1863 that "The coast service is so monotonous that I have nothing of interest to write." The situation had changed by October of that year, however: "I have been disappointed in procuring a furlough. Some of our company have . . . went home and over stayed their time, and our officers are refusing to grant furloughs at all now." George finally secured one day's leave in November, and spent it with his family, returning to his battalion the next morning—his letters to Mattie begged her forgiveness for his inability to call on her. She assured him that she understood; by January 1864, he wrote, "I hope you will excuse my boldness; for I am prompted by the purest of motives to speak thus: love you know is the first law of our nature and . . . the assurance you have given me of your willingness to correspond with me has caused a new era to dawn upon me. . . . I feel that life possesses a charm worth living for." He proposed to run the blockade around Savannah the following Saturday in order to see her. He carried out his promise and found her absent from home (she never received his letter); he was arrested by his fellow soldiers for disobeying orders, and remained under guard for some months. He wrote, "This is the first time I have been arrested since the war begun, and had I have known the good of it . . . it is the easiest position I have found. . . . I think when I get out of this I will run the blockade again."

In his letter of April 30, 1864, both George and the war had changed. He had been moved from artillery to infantry: "In the whole of our tramp, according to my memorandum, we

west to Monocacy Junction, the meeting point of four major transportation routes: the Georgetown Pike to Washington, the National Road to Baltimore, the Monocacy River, and the Baltimore & Ohio Railroad. Wallace planned to stretch his little force along the river to protect as many of these transportation centers as possible. He knew he and his men would provide a delaying action at best; Confederate troops outnumbered him five to one.

On July 9, 5,800 of Grant's troops arrived to reinforce the battle, but by the afternoon, they were overrun by the superior Confederate forces. Roughly 1,300 Union troops were killed, captured, or wounded, while Early lost nearly 900 men.

Early continued his march to the capital and stood before the earthworks of Fort Stevens two days later, one day too late; Grant's reinforcements had already arrived there to defend it. Had Early not been forced to lose a day at Monocacy, the Union capital might have been in Confederate hands. Though Early was successful in drawing troops away from Lee's fleeing forces, the taking of Washington was not possible; the rebel army withdrew to Virginia. Though the Confederates returned to western Maryland for raiding skirmishes, Monocacy marked the last major C.S.A. offensive in the state.

The Gambrill Mill (4801 Urbana Pike/Route 355), which was used as a field hospital during the battle, houses a visitor center and is the base

marched upwards of one thousand miles. We captured and hung a great many deserters and bush-whackers and had a good time generaly." By the end of May, "we marched through Gen. Beauregards battlefield between Petersburg and Richmond, and from the appearence of it, the fight must have been a desperate one. There was an immens quantity of blood upon the field, though the bodies were all intered."

In late June 1864, George was dispatched under General Jubal Early in an attempt to draw Grant's troops away from the certain destruction of the remaining rebel army. Before he left Richmond, George wrote to Mattie: "Thees words are my hearts pure sentiments . . . they are words that I have longed to speak. I must say that you feel nearer to me than any one I have ever met with, and to seal what I am now saying, will you consent to be my Mattie? . . . Pleas answer my question in your next [letter], as my fate either for weal or woe depends on your answer." He added, "I scarcely have time to sleep at all. I have been on the front line for several days. . . . Our boys equiped themselves very well with blankets, oil clothes, and canteens [for our march to Maryland]."

General Early's troops crossed the Potomac, extorting money from Maryland towns whenever possible, moving toward Washington, D.C., the federal capital. On July 9, Union general Lew Wallace's raw recruits met the enemy at Monocacy Junction. Though the Union took the worst of it during several hours of fighting, George Boatwright was mortally wounded. He died four days later and was buried in a mass grave. Decades after the war's end, George's remains were identified and reinterred at Frederick's Mount Olivet cemetery, plot number 243, along the north wall.

It's unknown when Mattie learned of George's fate, but she kept his letters until her death in 1932. She remained unmarried for 30 years, and then wed a much older man; they were childless. Mattie helped raise her sister's children; one of them, Jane Lucille Pope, was given the letters. When she passed away, the letters were found by Ms. Pope's daughter, who recognized their significance; with her husband, she traced George Boatwright to Monocacy.

Many thanks to Cathy Beeler of the National Park Service for sharing George's letters and the bittersweet romance of George and Mattie.

of walking and driving tours of the battlefield. (Wallace's comment was, "the place appeared well-selected for the purpose, its one inconvenience being that it was under fire.") From Memorial Day to Labor Day, it's open daily 8 A.M.–4:30 P.M. From Labor Day to Memorial Day, it's open Wed.–Sun. 8 A.M.–4:30 P.M. Free.

OTHER POINTS OF INTEREST

Boonsboro Museum of History

This tiny, eclectic museum, 113 N. Main St., 301/432-6969, is a treasure trove not only of Civil War relics, but also of history in general. Owner Doug Bast started collecting historical memorabilia when he was eight years old, and never stopped. The museum contains numerous unusual Civil War artifacts, such as bullets carved by idle soldiers into tiny flowers, dice, buttons, and animals; a pike used by John Brown's raiders; an original order by Stonewall Jackson; and personal items of Confederate officer Henry Kydd Douglas. A diary written by the son of Harriet Beecher Stowe (author of *Uncle Tom's Cabin*) is also part of the museum collection: Stowe searched for her son and located him after the battle of Antietam. He survived, but later died mysteriously as he set out for California by ship.

Walls are covered with weaponry from around the world; cabinets burst with ceramics and glass, including China trade porcelain of 1790, Depression glass from the 1930s, and examples of local Bell pottery. There's even a copy of *Martyr's Mirror,* the first book printed in 1748 by members of the Ephrata Cloister in central Pennsylvania, and a mourning bouquet made from human hair. The museum's exhibits change according to what has been lent out to surrounding museums. The bountiful array of items in the rooms can be dazzling and bewildering. Tell Doug your interests when you go in, and he'll show you around. The museum is open May–Sept., Sunday 1–5 P.M., or by appointment. Admission is $3.

Crystal Grottoes Cavern

For those who need a troglodyte fix, Crystal Grottoes, 19821 Shepherdstown Pike, Boons-

boro, 301/432-6336, is the place to go. The limestone cavern features a large variety of formations and an easy set of dry walkways to follow. The tour is escorted, and takes about 40 minutes. Crystal Grottoes is about one mile west of Boonsboro, and is open Apr.–Oct. daily 9 A.M.–6 P.M., Nov.–Mar. Sat.–Sun. 11 A.M.–4 P.M. Admission is $8.50.

OTHER PARKS AND SCENIC SPOTS

Most state parks, forests, and national parks in greater Frederick County and adjoining Washington County offer some sort of overnight facility, though types and prices vary by park. Each park office will have current information and maps.

Gathland State Park/National War Correspondent's Memorial

This small park (c/o South Mountain Recreation Area, 21843 National Pike, Boonsboro, MD 21713, 301/791-4767) sits at the top of Crampton's Gap, straddling Washington and Frederick Counties. Volunteers work with visitors and give interpretive tours at a small museum, which includes information on the Battle of South Mountain.

Gathland was the home of George Alfred Townsend, one of the youngest journalists to work for the *New York Herald* during the Civil War, and later an important novelist and journalist during the Reconstruction era. Gathland is the site of a unique collection of restored buildings and structures that he designed. A soaring stone monument with Roman arches dedicated to war correspondents is the outstanding attraction at this 135-acre day-use park. The monument, erected in 1896, was paid for by funds donated by Thomas Edison, Joseph Pulitzer, and others. The Appalachian Trail traverses the park and passes the monument's base.

Picnicking is available year-round, and cross-country skiing is popular in winter. Park grounds are free and open year-round; the museum is open Apr.–Oct., weekends and holidays, noon–5 P.M.; donations requested.

Getting There: It's one mile east of Route 67, and two miles west of Burkittsville, off Route 17 (look for signs).

South Mountain State Park

An 8,039-acre site (c/o Greenbrier State Park, 21843 National Pike, Boonsboro, MD 21713, 301/791-4767), South Mountain attracts hikers year-round—40 miles of the Appalachian Trail pass through it. The park also features campfire programs, picnic shelters, and a playground. South Mountain, a ridge composed largely of quartzite, rises from 200 feet above sea level by the Potomac River to nearly 2,000 feet at Penn-Mar, almost 40 miles north. It posed a formidable obstacle to the early settlers until "Braddock's Road" was completed, thereby opening the west to settlement.

Hiking: The Appalachian Trail follows South Mountain with numerous side trails. There are scenic overlooks within a short hike of the trailheads on Route 40, Weverton Cliff, Gathland, Route 17, or at Penn-Mar and High Rock.

Winter Sports: Cross-country skiing is available on most trails.

Overnight Facilities: Backpackers are permitted to camp in any of the trail shelters or at the Dahlgren Backpackers' Camp.

Getting There: The South Mountain range and park covers considerable territory. Contact Greenbrier State Park for information on facility locations.

Greenbrier State Park

This Appalachian Mountain park (21843 National Pike, Boonsboro, MD 21713-9535, 301/791-4767) is a multiuse facility featuring a 42-acre man-made lake and beach. Hiking trails, including a portion of the Appalachian Trail, meander through a variety of wildlife habitats. The Appalachians are one of the earth's oldest mountain ranges; Greenbrier's rocky outcroppings show much of the earth's geologic history. Picnicking, two playgrounds, a visitors center, interpretive programs, and nature study are also available. Fees are charged for day use and overnight camping.

Water Sports: Swimming, canoeing, and boating are features of the park. Near the lake is a boat rental and boat launch area.

Fishing and Hunting: The freshwater lake is stocked with trout, largemouth bass, and bluegill. All Maryland fishing laws apply; a Maryland Angler's License is required for all fishers 16 years of age or older. Fishing with live minnow bait is not permitted. Hunting is permitted in designated areas of the park in season.

Winter Sports: Cross-country skiing on the park's hiking trails is permitted.

Overnight Facilities: There are 165 campsites offering conveniently located bathhouses with hot showers. Each campsite is equipped with a table, grill, and parking area. Forty sites have electric hookups. In addition, there is a camp store, dump station, and food and beverage concession. Reservations may be made through the park office.

Getting There: The park is approximately 10 miles east of Hagerstown on U.S. 40. The park is also accessible via I-70 from the Myersville, Beaver Creek, or Hagerstown exits.

Washington Monument State Park

Four miles east of Boonsboro and 1.5 miles north of Alternate Route 40 on Monument Road, this park is named for the first U.S. monument erected to George Washington (send inquiries to: Greenbrier State Park, 21843 National Pike, Boonsboro, MD 21713, 301/791-4767). In 1755, British general Edward Braddock traveled through western Maryland with young George, a surveyor. They laid out a road that could be used by British soldiers to advance to the forks of the Ohio and capture the territory from the French during the French and Indian War. In 1827, the citizens of Boonsboro dedicated a rugged stone tower to the first president. During the Civil War, the tower was used as a signal station.

The Appalachian Trail winds through the park and passes the base of the monument, and there are additional hiking trails on the property. The park offers a visitors center, picnic shelters, playing fields, a playground, and campfire programs. The Cumberland Valley is a migratory bird flyway, providing excellent opportunities for birders in the spring and autumn. An annual hawk and eagle count is made by ornithologists at the monument. Cross-country skiing is a popular winter activity. Camping is limited to organized youth groups by reservation only.

The Appalachian Trail

Conceived in 1921 by private citizens and maintained today by volunteers, the trail winds 2,167 miles through 14 states from Springer Mountain, Georgia, to Mount Katahdin, Maine. It consists of a well-marked, narrow path with occasional overnight shelters and privies. Maryland has 37.5 miles of the interstate hiking trail, much of which runs along the east side of South Mountain from Harpers Ferry northeast toward the Pennsylvania border. For specifics on Maryland's portion of the trail, contact The Appalachian Trail Conference, P.O. Box 807, Harpers Ferry, WV 25425, 304/535-6331.

SHOPPING

Route 65 Flea Market, a large livestock-shed-turned-collectibles-market, is on Route 65, about six miles north of Sharpsburg. Many dealers have booths there, and local farmers bring in their produce on the weekends. During the warm months, it's open Mon.–Fri. 10 A.M.–6 P.M., Sat.–Sun. 7 A.M.–6 P.M.

Though tiny, **Turn the Page Bookstore & Café,** 18 N. Main St., Boonsboro, will satisfy your needs for caffeine and information at the same time. You might spot romance maven Nora Roberts there, visiting with the owner, her husband. The celebrate author of dozens of romance novels and her family live nearby in rural Maryland.

Because of restrictions engendered by its proximity to the Antietam battlefield, the village of Sharpsburg has remained largely undeveloped. However, **Shepardstown,** on the West Virginia border (less than three miles west of Sharpsburg over the Potomac bridge on Route 34), has seen a renaissance, and is filled with interesting cafés, restaurants, and shops. Many visitors to Antietam cross the river to dine there.

ACCOMMODATIONS

AYH Harpers Ferry Lodge, 19123 Sandy Hook Rd., Knoxville, MD 21758, 301/834-7652, is the least expensive stay in this area. Private rooms and parking are available. Since the Harpers Ferry area is also a popular kayak, canoe, and tubing spot, make sure that you make reservations well in advance. The hostel is closed Nov. 15–Mar. 15, and lodging is around $12 per night.

On September 15, 1862, Confederate lieutenant general James Longstreet and members of his staff commandeered a farm just outside of Sharpsburg, and set about preparing for the Battle of Antietam. The farm's owners, the Pipers, a slave-owning family of Union sympathizers, wisely went to stay with nearby relatives. After the battle, Longstreet left campfires burning in the farmer's fields during the night of the 18th, while he and his men slipped across the Potomac at Shepardstown.

In 1962, the National Park Service purchased the site. Regina and Louis Clark leased it in 1994, respectfully maintaining the Piper farmhouse and slave quarters in its original simple style, renting out three rooms (including Longstreet's bedroom) as a bed-and-breakfast, **Piper House.** The Clarks keep an extensive Civil War library, and the rooms, with private baths, remain largely unadorned (bring your own toiletries). A stay at the Piper Farm, Route 65, one mile north of Sharpsburg (P.O. Box 100, Sharpsburg, MD 21782, 301/797-1862), must be booked several months in advance for special-event weekends and reenactments at Antietam. Rates are $95 per night.

Another option in the Antietam area is the **Jacob Rohrbach Inn,** 138 W. Main St., Sharpsburg, 301/432-5079 or 877/839-4242, www .jacob-rohrbach-inn.com. Built around 1800 by Capt. Joseph Chapline, Revolutionary War patriot, the inn is a shining example of Federal-period architecture updated with modern conveniences. Jacob Rohrbach lost his life defending the property against horse thieves claiming to be Mosby's men on July 4, 1864. The building was appropriated and used as a hospital to care for the wounded following the battle of Antietam. Four guest rooms, all with private bath, range in price from $109–129.

Turning into the driveway of **Stone Manor,** 5820 Carroll Boyer Rd., Middletown, 301/

473-5454, www.ourhome.net/stonemanor, one is immediately transported to the verdant countryside of late-19th-century English romantic novels. The massive stone manor house, begun in 1760, has seen centuries of additions and improvements, and today presents an elegant facade wrapped around the latest conveniences. Each of the six spacious guest rooms is decorated with period antiques and has a large whirlpool tub and thoroughly modern amenities; many have one or more fireplaces, and private porches with views of the woods. The manor's 114 acres contain a formal garden, park (acres of groomed lawn surrounded by large trees), and farmland framed by walking trails. On dark summer evenings, hundreds of lightning bugs provide a brief but flashy show. All guests are welcomed by a fruit and cheese plate in their rooms; an excellent continental breakfast is served in the morning (not a surprise, considering Stone Manor offers some of the best dining in the area). This is secluded luxury in a quiet country setting—an opportunity to play lady or lord of the manor. Rates range $125–250.

FOOD

Some sort of trading post has existed on the site of the **Old South Mountain Inn,** 6132 Old National Pike (U.S. 40A), 301/432-6155, Boonsboro, since 1732, but it wasn't until after 1765 that the stone house here was built as a family home by Robert Turner, the man for whom Turner's Gap is named. By 1790, it was a full-fledged inn, and remained so through the Civil War; it was the headquarters of Confederate officer D. H. Hill during the battle of South Mountain. In 1876, it was purchased by author, lecturer, and philanthropist Madeline Vinton Dahlgren, who built the stone chapel across the road. In 1925, the stone house was returned to its original purpose and renamed the Old South Mountain Inn. Today, the inn serves Saturday lunch, a Sunday buffet brunch, and dinner Tues.–Sun. The menu is American: prime rib, beef Wellington, chicken, and seafood; a cozy bar, the President's

Lounge, features signed pictures from Washington, D.C., bigwigs. The wine list offers California, French, German, and Italian wines, as well as products from local vineyards. Dinner averages $18, lunch $8, Sunday brunch $13.

Though it requires a drive deep into the country, **Stone Manor** draws people from Washington or Baltimore, with good reason. Dinner ($45–55 prix fixe, 4–5 courses, each with different breads, wine additional) is served Tues.–Sun., in addition to a Sunday brunch ($20, three courses). Each dinner course allows a choice between two or more items: for example, grilled breast of Magret duck with mango-papaya risotto, cumin oil, and plantain chips, *or* pan-seared sea scallops with angel-hair pasta with lemon, capers, and thyme (and that's the second course, not the entrée). Dinner starts with an "amusee"—the chef's welcoming gift. On the night I was there, it was cold gazpacho with crème fraîche in a demitasse. The food here is as good as it sounds—made even more delicious by the knowledge that the chef, Charles Zeran, left his former profession as a divorce lawyer to follow his passion for food. He shoved his law books aside one day, walked into a family-style restaurant in his hometown, and asked for a job. Stone Manor is light years away in both distance and style, but the legal profession's loss is everyone's gain.

Battleview Market, a combination convenience store and deli, 5331 Sharpsburg Pike, 301/432-2676, on Route 65 between Sharpsburg and Antietam battlefield, serves up the best breakfasts and hoagies around. Prices average less than $5, and the market is open for three meals daily.

INFORMATION

Since the battlefields are spread over two counties, information may be requested from the Tourism Council of Frederick County, Inc., 19 E. Church St., Frederick, MD 21701, 800/999-3613, and Hagerstown/Washington County Convention and Visitors Bureau, 16 Public Square, Hagerstown, MD 21740, 888/257-2600.

Hagerstown and Environs

As a slaveholding county in a Federally held state during the Civil War, this peaceful farming town became the scene of considerable strife between Southern and Northern sympathizers. Like Frederick, Hagerstown was also held for ransom by Confederate general Jubal Early; however, the demanded amount of $20,000 (not $200,000, as in Frederick) was suspected to be due to a clerk's error. The rebels got their $20,000 and didn't bombard the town.

Today, Hagerstown has returned to its quiet existence. The loudest roar to be heard is from stock cars at the Hagerstown Speedway, several miles west of the city. However, its heritage as a rich and long-established center between the Eastern cities and lands to the west is still demonstrated by its exceptional art museum and historical sites.

HISTORICAL SITES

Hager House

Jonathan Hager migrated from Germany in 1736, settling in the wilderness of western Maryland. In 1739, he built a three-and-a-half-story uncut fieldstone house for his new bride; the 22-inch-wide walls provided ample shelter from hostile elements, both natural and human. The home was taken over and restored inside and out to its colonial glory by the Washington County Historical Society. A museum featuring artifacts from the life of Jonathan Hager and his family is on the grounds next to the house. The immaculately preserved Hager House, 110 Key St., 301/739-8393, is adjacent to the Washington County Museum of Fine Arts in Hagerstown's beautiful city park, off Prospect Street (U.S. 11). It's open Tues.–Sat. 10 A.M.–4 P.M., Sunday 2–5 P.M.; closed Jan.–Mar. and the last week of Nov.–first week of Dec. (to prepare for the traditional German Christmas celebration). Admission is $4.

Rose Hill Cemetery

Rose Hill Cemetery, 600 S. Potomac St., 301/739-3630, is one of the sites where 2,447 unknown and 241 known rebel soldiers were reburied. The remains were gathered from mass graves at South Mountain, Antietam, Gettysburg, and Hagerstown. The large circular gravesite, known originally as Washington Cemetery, is surmounted by a granite monument; it's on the north side of Rose Hill Cemetery. When the gate is closed, Washington Cemetery is visible from S. Potomac Street. Free.

Miller House Museum

This two-story townhouse, 135 W. Washington St., 301/797-8782, was built in the early 1800s and serves as the headquarters and research library of the Washington County Historical Society. Once the home of a prosperous attorney, the Miller house is adorned with a "hanging staircase" (no visible support), and fireplace hearths made of local puddingstone marble; the home contains several excellent period collections. More than 260 dolls, representing all major doll manufacturers of 19th-century Europe, are on display, and more than 200 clocks, including Hagerstown- and Frederick-made tall case clocks may be seen. The rooms of the house are furnished in period style of the 1820s. The museum is open Apr.–Dec. Wed.–Fri. 1–4 P.M., Saturday 2–5 P.M. Admission is $5 for adults.

OTHER POINTS OF INTEREST

Sitting peacefully by the lake in Hagerstown's City Park, the small, graceful **Washington County Museum of Fine Arts,** Prospect Street (U.S. 11) and Memorial Boulevard, 301/739-5764, is a hidden gem in an unexpected setting. The museum maintains a remarkable collection of top-quality American paintings, drawings, prints, and sculpture from the 18th century to the present, as well as outstanding examples of glassware, ceramics, and furniture. Each intimate room is dedicated to a style or era, and the works in it are thoughtfully displayed. To stroll into the cool marble foyer on a hot day, then to take in each of the gallery

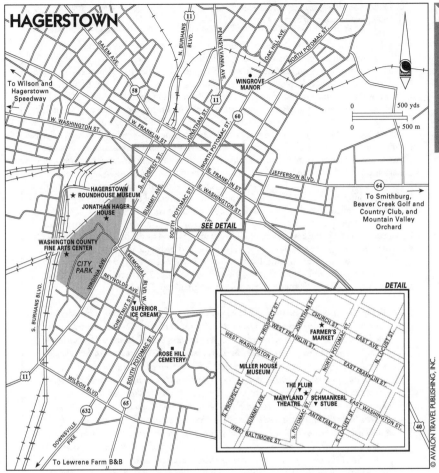

rooms, enjoying post-colonial-era portraits by members of the Peale family, *art moderne* sculpture from the 1920s, and contemporary photography and abstract works, is to enjoy a visual feast. The art is inspiring, and what's more, there's no cost to view it. This museum is so exceptional that it has earned a well-deserved accreditation from the American Association of Museums, an honor extended to fewer than 10 percent of museums in the United States. The museum is open Tues.–Sat. 10 A.M.–5 P.M., Sunday 1–5 P.M.

The **Hagerstown Roundhouse Museum,** 300 S. Burhans Blvd., 301/739-4665, www .roundhouse.org, documents the history of the Western Maryland Railroad and six others that made Hagerstown the "Hub City." Displays include pictures, lights, lanterns, bells, whistles, and tools; a railroad library; railroad layouts; and a gift shop with railroad-related items. It's open Fri.–Sun. 1–5 P.M.; admission is free. If you'd like to see a real steam locomotive, the museum sponsors a scenic train excursion to view the changing leaves every October. Or you could

A SEPARATE COUNTRY

Western Maryland, from Frederick County to the West Virginia border, makes up one-fifth of the landmass of the state; the territory is dramatically different from the coastal plains and Piedmont Plateau, and has remained scarcely populated and fiercely independent since colonial days. This is Appalachian mountain land, consisting of rugged peaks separated by fertile valleys. It was the promise of abundant crops, especially in the long valley that unrolls south from Hagerstown to the Potomac River, that attracted the first non-English settlers to Maryland. By the late 18th century, space was becoming increasingly rare in Pennsylvania and Virginia; the new settlers, Palatine Germans—Mennonites, Moravians, or Lutherans—seeking relief from religious intolerance, and Scotch-Irish, fleeing English persecution, recognized the possibilities of the mountain valleys. The west became the stronghold of independent freeholders, farmers who supported separation from Britain and worked the land with their families, remaining largely loyal to the North during the Civil War. Today, Frederick is one of the major areas of population growth in the state, but Hagerstown and the rest of the west retain much of their rural flavor; though according to Frances Trollope, quite pleasantly changed from colonial days.

Ms. Trollope spent three and a half years in America, ostensibly to escape financial embarrassment at home in England. She returned home in 1831, and by the next year had penned *Domestic Manners of the Americans*, a singularly snooty and bad-tempered look at the winners in the British-Colonial War. America-bashing was big in the old country; the book was a success and saved the Trollope family from economic ruin. Under "Western Maryland, Summer 1830, Family Life and Domestic Arrangements of Small Landowners," she wrote:

> *One of these families consisted of a young man, his wife, two children, a female slave, and two young lads, slaves also. The farm belonged to the wife, and, I was told, consisted of about three hundred acres of indifferent land, but all cleared. The house was built of wood, and looked as if the three slaves might have overturned it, had they pushed hard against the gable end. It contained one room, of about twelve feet square, and another adjoining it, hardly larger than the closet; this second chamber was the lodging-room of the white part of the family. Above these rooms was a loft, without windows, where I was told the 'staying company' who visited them, were lodged. Near this mansion was a 'shanty,' a black hole, without any window, which served as a kitchen and all other offices, and also as the lodging of the blacks.*

> *We were invited to take tea with this family, and readily consented to do so. The furniture of the room was one heavy huge table, and about six wooden chairs. When we arrived the lady . . . vehemently urged us to be seated, and then retired into the closet-chamber above mentioned, whence she continued to address to us from behind the door with all kinds of "genteel country visiting talk," and at length emerged upon us in a smart new dress.*

> *Her female slave set out the great table, and placed upon it cups of the very coarsest blue ware, a little brown sugar in one and a tiny drop of milk in another, no butter, though the lady assured us she had a 'deary' and two cows. Instead of butter, she 'hoped we would fix a little relish with our crackers,' in ancient English, eat salt meat and dry biscuits. Such was the fare, and for guests that certainly were intended to be honoured.*

> *I could not help recalling the delicious repasts which I remembered to have enjoyed at little dairy farms in England.*

drop by the City Park and see the engine 202 steam locomotive and several cabooses (cabeese?).

The Maryland Theatre, 21-27 S. Potomac St., 301/790-3500, www.mdtheatre.org, is a charming restored Victorian jewel of a performance space. The Maryland Symphony often plays here, and there are performances and theatrical productions every week of the year. Built in 1915, the theatre was destroyed in the late 1970s by fire, but is completely restored today. If you saw the Shirley Maclaine/Nicolas Cage film *Guarding Tess,* you'll recognize the ornate interior instantly.

The bustling **Hagerstown City Farmer's Market,** open Saturday from 5 A.M.–noon, features a large variety of local produce, baked goods, an Asian market, and meats from surrounding farms. There's also a crafts area. Many local Amish and Mennonite farmers sell here. Be aware that much of the produce is sold before 9:30 A.M., so it pays to get there early for the best selection. If you miss the market, there's always breakfast or a pork chop sandwich for a couple of bucks at Karen's Country Kitchen inside the market. Established in the late 1700s, the old Hagerstown Marketplace is on 25 W. Church St., 301/739-8577, ext. 183, www.hagerstownmarket.org.

RECREATION

Hagerstown Speedway caters to all types of auto racing, though stock cars are a specialty. Used primarily by local racers, the speedway began with a small track in the early 1950s, and has become a premier draw for dirt racing fans. You'll hear the roar emanating from 15112 National Pike (U.S. 40), about five miles west of Hagerstown. Call for scheduled events and tickets: 301/582-0640, or visit www.hagerstown-speedway.com.

Beaver Creek Golf & Country Club, 9535 Mapleville Rd. (Route 66), Hagerstown, 301/733-5152, six miles east of Hagerstown near the village of Beaver Creek, features a challenging 18 holes, driving range, and restaurant. A PGA pro is on duty.

SHOPPING

One hundred and fifty dealers show their antique and collectible wares at the massive, covered **Beaver Creek Antique Market,** 20202 National Pike (U.S. 40), 301/739-8075, www.beavercreekantiques.com. It's open Thurs.–Tues. 9 A.M.–5 P.M.

Mountain Valley Orchards is one of several farm stores on Route 64, east of Hagerstown, near the crossroads of Route 66 (Mapleville Road). During the summer, the area's abundant produce—peaches, apples, plums—is sold at tasty prices. Call 301/824-2089 for information.

Though **Wilson Bridge** over Conoccocheage Creek is a historical landmark, the real draw to the **Wilson Village** is the original country store, schoolhouse, and the women's clothing shop that's located upstairs. The country store and school are of historical interest, but the clothing at the **Upstairs Emporium** is contemporary, well chosen, and well priced. The village is at 14921 Rufus Wilson Rd., Clear Spring, 301/582-4718 (though its address is Clear Spring, it comprises the actual village of Wilson, marked on most maps; it's on U.S. 40, approximately 1.5 miles west of the Hagerstown Speedway).

ACCOMMODATIONS

Situated in an upscale section of Hagerstown, at 635 Oak Hill Ave., 301/797-7769, www.wingrovemanor.com, **Wingrove Manor** is gracefully decorated to reflect its Victorian-era Greek Revival origins. Close to central Hagerstown, the manor features five rooms, each with a large private bath; a home-cooked continental breakfast is served in the morning. Innkeeper Winnie Price also offers special golf packages. Rates range $135–150.

Lewrene Farm Bed and Breakfast, just south of the city at 9738 Downsville Pike, Hagerstown, 301/582-1735, lewrenebedandbreakfast@juno.com, is a 13-room colonial that treats guests to fresh air, crowing roosters, and a hearty breakfast, often made from ingredients found in the kitchen garden of this 125-acre working farm. Each of the four guest rooms (two with private bath, two share a bath) is decorated with handmade quilts and solid mahogany, canopied cherry wood, or iron-framed beds. The farm is open all year, and rates range $69–120.

FOOD

Schmankerl Stube, 58 S. Potomac St., Hagerstown, 301/797-3354, www.schmankerlstube.com, a Hagerstown favorite since 1988, is a Bavarian restaurant that serves specialties such as German meatballs and American meat and fish dishes. Prices average $17 for a dinner entrée; lunch and dinner Tues.–Sun.

An inexpensive ($4 average) café, **The Plum,** downtown on 6 Rochester Place, an alley off W. Washington between Summit and Potomac Streets, dishes up pastries, soups, salads, and sandwiches Mon.–Fri. 7:30 A.M. to 2:30 P.M.

On a hot night, the sidewalks surrounding **Superior Ice Cream,** 500 Chestnut St., 301/790-0650, are filled with happy lickers. A Hagerstown institution for many years, Superior offers a variety of ice cream flavors plus treats such as sundaes and dipped cones ($2).

Seven miles east of Hagerstown, **Clopper's Orchards,** 23334 Fruit Tree Dr., Smithsburg, 301/824-7106, sells fresh-picked fruit, and during the summer and fall sends their own strawberries, black cherries, and peaches to a small dairy in Waynesboro, Pennsylvania, where it's transformed into custom-made ice cream and delivered back to the farm for sale. This is ambrosia, and sells out quickly—but if they're temporarily out of stock, they have traditional ice cream in plenty of flavors.

INFORMATION

Hagerstown/Washington County Convention and Visitors Bureau, 16 Public Square, Hagerstown, MD 21740, 888/257-2600, is the place to contact for more information.

Orchard Country and the C&O Canal

Rocky farms and orchards spread benignly to the west in this, Maryland's former frontier. Many side roads offer verdant views of the land as it begins to roll toward the Allegheny Mountains. The 184.5-mile-long C&O Canal, which was reconstructed into a hiking/biking path along the Potomac River, is an extraordinary example of intelligent reuse of unproductive space. Best known in the western part of the state, its overnight parks, miles of well-maintained bikeways, and wildlife-rich scenery beckon a much wider audience of adventurers. The canal's eastern terminus is in Georgetown, north of Washington, D.C.; Williamsport is roughly halfway, and the western terminus (marked by a park and museums) is in Cumberland.

C&O Canal National Historical Park

The towpath of the former Chesapeake and Ohio Canal (contact C&O Canal NHP, 1850 Dual Highway, Suite 100, Hagerstown, MD 21740, 301/739-4200), this park features campgrounds roughly every 5–6 miles along its 184-mile length; towns, hotels, and places to stock up on food in the sparsely populated west are more erratic. *The C&O Travel Companion* by Mike High (see Suggested Reading, at the back of the book) is an indispensable tool for anyone planning to travel part or all of the canal. It lists all of the above, plus information on canal specifics, such as where the locks are and where to find canal boats.

The Chesapeake and Ohio Canal was the focal point of an apocalyptic dam proposal that would have flooded massive portions of the Potomac Valley after World War II. It was also considered for conversion to a driving parkway in the 1950s. In 1954, Supreme Court Justice William O. Douglas invited the editors of the pro-dam, pro-power-company *Washington Post* to join him on a walking tour of the towpath. A sizable group started out near Cumberland, but only nine hiked the whole way to Georgetown; nonetheless, it brought the need for conservation of the area to public attention. It wasn't until 1971 that Presi-

CANAL FEVER

The Chesapeake and Ohio Canal had its beginnings in the late 1700s, when the new nation sought pathways through the Alleghenies to the rich forks of the Ohio. Thomas Jefferson, among others, was convinced that the Potomac River was the route they sought. George Washington, who held land in the Ohio Valley, headed a group formed to navigate the river; the Patowmack Company sought to remove obstacles in the waterway and to skirt several of the falls that impeded navigation. Washington's tenure was interrupted by an eight-year stint as president of the fledgling United States. He died before the first leg of the canal, from Georgetown to Williamsport, was completed.

By 1825, canal fever had seized the eastern states. In New York, the Erie Canal was fast on its way to completion, and a group of Maryland influentials including Francis Scott Key and George C. Washington (grandnephew of the former president) pressed for government support for a canal from Georgetown to the rivers of Pittsburgh. In spite of its enormous cost of $22 million, the project was begun in 1828. Fourteen years later, the canal had reached the town of Hancock, roughly halfway, and funds had petered out. Worse, the Baltimore and Ohio Railroad had already bypassed the terminus of the canal and had reached the city of Cumberland. Maryland waived its lien on the canal and construction was completed in 1850. The canal was able to compete with the railroad due to its ability to ship coal from the fields west of Cumberland south to the nation's capital. The Civil War raised canal revenues significantly, and it continued to operate for an additional 15 years before it was finally made inoperative by two massive floods; it was then purchased and shut down by its rival, the B&O Railroad, around 1890.

Though the railroad kept the canal operating on a minor level, another flood in 1924 caused it to cease operations. During the Depression, the canal was sold to the U.S. government and turned into a Civilian Conservation Corps project. Another flood in 1942 destroyed all hope of restoring the canal to commercial usefulness. In 1954, under threat of turning the canal's towpaths into a highway, Supreme Court Justice William O. Douglas invited editors from the *Washington Post* to walk with him on the towpath, in the hopes of turning the canal site into a protected area. He succeeded in raising American consciousness to the value of the site, but it wasn't until 1971 that President Richard Nixon designated the C&O Canal a national park.

dent Nixon designated the entire length of the canal a national historic park. Today, the C&O Canal offers one of the greatest recreational opportunities in America.

One way to travel all or most of the canal (allow five days by bicycle, up to three weeks on foot) is to take Amtrak's Capitol Limited (from Pittsburgh, Philadelphia, Baltimore, Washington, D.C., or New York, 800/USA-RAIL or 800/872-7725) or a Greyhound bus to Cumberland, and begin the journey there, ending at either Hancock (50 miles), Williamsport (100 miles), or Georgetown (184 miles) and returning via public transportation. Amtrak does not have baggage handling in Cumberland and other quick stops, so bikers may need to look at alternatives to bringing bikes on Amtrak.

Visitor centers are in Georgetown, Washington, D.C.; Great Falls, Maryland (both offer canal boat rides); and in Williamsport, Hancock, and Cumberland, Maryland.

Traveling by Auto: Most of the canal is inaccessible to cars, though drive-in camping, picnic areas, and canoe launch sites along the canal are available at McCoy's Ferry, Fifteenmile Creek, Little Orleans, and Spring Gap. All campsites, including hiker/biker campsites, are primitive. There is a paved road to Little Orleans campground in Green Ridge State Park (I-68/U.S. 40, exit 68), but beware! State maps often show the road as completely paved from Little Orleans to Paw Paw Tunnel; in reality, it's a narrow, rutted, unmarked dirt road marked by occasional hunting camps manned by questionable quasi-military personnel. Not a great place to ask directions; stay on the asphalt.

A feat of industrial era engineering, **Paw Paw Tunnel** is a 3,118-foot-long brick-lined passage carrying the towpath through a mountain; it was constructed over a period of 14 years. The tunnel is accessible from Route 51 east from Cumberland. Auto parking is available one-half mile from the tunnel entrance; it's a short and pleasant walk to the tunnel. The Tunnel Hill trail, which rises 362 feet over the top of the tunnel, affords great views of Green Ridge State Park, one of the largest in Maryland. The Purslane Run overnight campground is roughly one-half mile south of the parking lot on the trail, south of Route 51 on the Maryland side of the Potomac. Route 51 parallels the Potomac River on its way to Cumberland, passing through historic Oldtown, the farthest outpost of the frontier during colonial days.

Traveling by Bicycle: This is the favorite method of transportation for many visitors to the canal, permitting relatively fast travel but affording opportunities to explore some of the canal's side interests as well. The road is mixed gravel, so hybrid- or off-road tires, a patch kit and inner tube, and panniers for supplies are necessary. If you'd rather go with a group, two resources are **Allegany Adventures, Inc.,** La Vale, Maryland, 301/729-9708, and **Potomac Pedalers Touring Club,** in McLean, Virginia, 202/363-TOUR.

Traveling on Foot: Though most campsites are placed conveniently, there are two expanses where the sites are farther apart than eight miles: Between Georgetown and Swain's Lock (17 miles) and Bald Eagle Island and Huckleberry Hill (12 miles, near Brunswick, Maryland). A sturdy backpack with supplies (including sufficient water for two days) is necessary. The **C&O Canal Association,** P.O. Box 366, Glen Echo, MD 20812, occasionally sponsors group hikes.

Traveling by Kayak or Canoe: Seeing the canal by water is limited to those areas that remain filled. The most popular of these is the 23-mile stretch between Georgetown and Seneca. There are also short segments at Big Pool, Little Pool (near Hancock), and a stretch between Old-

town and Town Creek. Boating on some sections of the Potomac River itself is considered hazardous, especially east of Harpers Ferry. Canoe launch sites on the Potomac are located throughout the park, with the westernmost site at Spring Gap. **Thompson's Boat Center,** Georgetown, D.C., 202/333-9543; **Blue Ridge Outfitters,** Harpers Ferry, West Virginia, 304/725-3444; and **Hancock Outfitters,** Hancock, Maryland, 301/678-5050, all offer rentals, advice, and some escorted trips.

Fort Frederick State Park

Fort Fred, as it's referred to locally (send inquiries to: 11100 Fort Frederick Rd., Big Pool, MD 21711, 301/842-2155), was the site of Maryland's major frontier defense during the French and Indian War, built after the defeat of British general Braddock (1754–1763). The diamond-shaped corners on the rectangular fort were engineered to permit crossfire against invaders. Families within a radius of 10 miles would flee to the fort during Indian attacks; those outside 10 miles would attempt to fortify a central home in their area—hence all the villages with "Fort" in front of their names. The fort was a prisoner-of-war camp during the Revolution, and the Union's defense against Confederate raiders during the Civil War. Fort Fred's massive stone surrounding walls and two barracks have been restored to their 1758 appearance; two-thirds of the fort's stone walls are original. History displays are set up in the fort, barracks, and nearby visitor center, and costumed interpreters are available for more information. Military reenactments, campfire programs, and other special events are held frequently. Fort Fred became Maryland's first state park in 1922. The grounds adjoin the Potomac River; the Chesapeake and Ohio Canal passes alongside. Big Pool, part of the original canal system, is a large body of captured water popular with canoeists and boaters. The serene setting is particularly pleasant for a picnic and a stroll. There are two museums on the property: the visitor center displays soldiers' regalia from different eras and related park history, and a Civilian Conservation Corps museum features the C.C.C.'s role in restoration. Captain Wort's Sutler Shop sells souvenirs and food. The fort's gates are open Apr.–Oct. daily 8 A.M.–sunset; Nov.–Mar., Mon.–Fri. 8 A.M.–sunset, weekends 10 A.M.–sunset. The grounds are free, but there is an admission charge to tour the fort: $3 for adults and $2 for kids 6–12.

Hiking: The park offers two short interpretive trails and the C&O Canal towpath for hikers and joggers.

Water Sports: There is no boat launch into the Potomac River at Fort Frederick, but boats may be launched at nearby McCoy's Ferry or Four Locks. There is a boat ramp for launch into Big Pool in the park; canoes and rowboats are available for rental from Captain Wort's Sutler Shop in the summer.

Fishing: Fishing is popular on both the Potomac River and Big Pool. A Maryland license is required for all anglers over 15 years of age.

Winter Sports: Cross-country skiing is allowed on the fort's extensive grounds.

Overnight Facilities: From the first Friday in April to the last Sunday in October, visitors may rent a tent site for a fee in the Riverfront campground; restrooms, picnic tables, and grills are nearby. Sites are first-come, first-served.

Getting There: Fort Frederick State Park is in the Cumberland Valley, 18 miles west of Hagerstown and one mile south of I-70 near Big Pool, Route 56, exit 12. Bear right at the Y for the visitors center; a 25-minute orientation film is shown on request. Bear left to get to the fort. Both U.S. 40 and Route 56 (exit 18 from I-70) are only slightly longer and much more scenic.

OTHER PARKS AND SCENIC SPOTS

Most state parks, forests, and national parks offer some sort of overnight facility, though types and prices vary by park. Each park office will have current information and maps.

Green Ridge State Forest

This expanse of pines and hardwoods (send inquiries to: Green Ridge State Forest, 28700 Headquarters Dr. NE, Flintstone, MD 21530-9525, 301/478-3124) stretches across the mountains of western Maryland and occupies 44,000 acres. The forest, once privately owned, cleared, and planted, was touted as "the largest apple orchard in the universe." When the orchard proprietor went bankrupt in 1918, the state Department of Forestry stepped in and began to restore Green Ridge to its original environment. Much of the forest remains wild, laced by dirt roads and trails, dotted with hunting lodges. Since conditions are primitive, stop by the forest headquarters, exit 64 south off U.S. 68, for a map of trails and campsites.

Fishing and Hunting: Popular fishing areas include the Potomac River, White Sulphur and Orchard Ponds, Town Creek, Fifteenmile Creek, and Sideling Hill Creek. Maryland Angler's License required. Hunting is the largest single recreational activity in the forest; wild turkey, grouse, squirrel, and deer are plentiful in the vast forest. All types of hunting are permitted during designated seasons.

Hiking: Twenty-seven miles of trails over narrow ridges and forest streams pass by several overlooks for spectacular views of the surrounding mountains. The trails connect with the C&O towpath for an extended hike of 43 miles.

Biking: Mountain biking is allowed on all roads, the designated bike trail, and most of the hiking trails.

Canoeing: Call the Green Ridge Headquarters for guided trip information on the Potomac River.

Horseback Riding: Equestrians are allowed in most areas of the forest. Two campsites are designated for horses, their riders, and their equipment.

Off-Road Vehicles: The forest has designated 20 miles of trail for unregistered motorcycles, four-wheelers, and snowmobiles; a permit is required (call the park number for more information).

Overnight Facilities: Green Ridge features 92 primitive single campsites and 8 primitive group sites. The sites are on a first-come, first-served basis, and there is a charge for their use.

Getting There: Green Ridge State Forest is in eastern Allegany County, about 22 miles east of Cumberland (exit 64 on I-68).

Sideling Hill Exhibit Center

The narrowest point in Maryland is roughly three miles west of Hancock on I-68. Until the 1980s, the only way around Sideling Hill, a massive stone conformation, was U.S. 40. Engineers blasted Sideling Hill to cut a straight path for I-68, exposing geological formations formed 360 million years ago. The visitor center features exhibits on geology, focusing on the three kinds of rock that make up our planet: igneous (formed from the cooling of molten material—granite is an example), metamorphic (formed by intense pressure, heat or chemical change, such as marble), and sedimentary (particles carried by wind or water that settle and become compacted). Sedimentary rock covers 80 percent of the earth's surface, and a bridge across the freeway outside the visitor center permits excellent views of the folded and twisted layers of sedimentary rock that make up Sideling Hill. A scope is available on the south side of the bridge; it may be focused on the nearby Mason-Dixon line as it marches east. The center is free; it's open year-round. Call 301/678-5442 for information.

ACCOMMODATIONS AND FOOD

In Hancock, east of Sideling Hill, **Cohill Manor,** 5102 Western Pike, 301/678-7573, www.nfis .com/~cohill, can actually brag with certainty that George Washington slept there—at least somewhere on the property, if not in the actual manor house. Washington's own diaries mention that he stayed with Joseph Flint, original owner of the site, an Indian trader. Flint's log cabin is on the property, and the newer white stucco manor house with its multi-arched porch and raised-seam tin roof was restored to its original beauty and now offers five rooms to guests. Visitors share the home with a herd of angora goats, a family of geese, mallard ducks, a cat, chickens, and three friendly basset hounds. February and March are "kidding" months at Cohill Manor, and guests can welcome the birth of baby angora kids. March and October are shearing times, and guests are invited to participate. Rates range $50–75 per night.

Weavers, a pleasant little restaurant, 77 W. Main St., Hancock, 301/678-6147, has been in business since the late 1950s, and is definitely worth a stop off the interstate. The Maryland crab soup (tomato-based, buttery, not spicy) was the best I've had, and they have their own salad bar and bakery with tempting pies and cookies. Lunch averages $7, and they're open 11 A.M.– 8 P.M. Mon.–Thurs. and 7 A.M.–8 P.M. Fri.–Sun.

Hepburn Orchards, a big warehouse at the Route 144 turnoff of I-68, sells plants and souvenirs, but the big draw is the produce (especially their peaches), and the homemade pies and cookies. Behind the register, you can see the bake room where pies are lined up to be wrapped for sale. Prices are inexpensive, and the baked goods are excellent.

INFORMATION

Maryland's wasp waist divides this area into two counties. Hagerstown/Washington County Convention & Visitors Bureau, 16 Public Square, Hagerstown, MD 21740, 301/791-3246 or 888/257-2600, has information on the eastern part, and Allegany County Visitors Bureau, 13 Canal St., Cumberland, MD 21502, 301/777-5132, can help you out with the west.

Cumberland and Environs

Cumberland, with 24,000 residents, is Maryland's largest city in the west, and was once its industrial epicenter. A 12-foot-wide seam of bituminous coal was discovered under Big Savage Mountain and Dan's Mountain in 1810, changing the area from a sleepy frontier town to a major player. Cunard Line steamships demanded high-quality Cumberland coal, and the C&O Canal and B&O Railroad became profitable hauling the fuel to market. The creeks ran yellow with sulfurous mining

byproducts until oil replaced coal in the early 1900s and Cumberland and its environs reverted to their green and settled heritage. Now, as the terminus of the C&O Canal and departure route for scenic trips through the Alleghenies, all of western Allegany County is finding new life through tourism.

On the county's farthest boundary, Frostburg, a quiet college town surrounded by farmland, already has its share of excitement: during July and August, Frostburg is overwhelmed by big

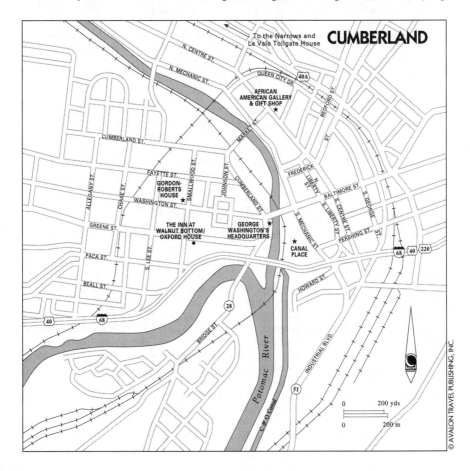

A WALKING TOUR OF GRAND HOMES

Washington Street was the street of realized dreams in Cumberland. Created by the city's wealthy and influential during its heyday, the structures are of a uniformly high architectural quality; all were constructed during the last half of the 19th century.

But the area now known as Washington Street had a much earlier use. Fort Cumberland, built by the British in the 1750s, was the last major outpost of civilization during the French and Indian War; the fort fell to ruin before the onset of the American Revolution. A century later, the massive Emmanuel Episcopal Church, 16 Washington St., was built on the site of the fort. The church features three Tiffany stained-glass windows in its English Country Gothic embrace. Nearby, at 30 Washington St., the Allegany County Court House, built in 1893, is in Richardsonian Romanesque style, patterned after the Allegheny Court House—one of H. H. Richardson's masterworks—in Pittsburgh.

Continuing up the hill, visitors can appreciate an architectural mélange of early Victorian styles such as Greek Revival (number 104, built in 1841 for Judge Thomas Perry, a member of the House of Representatives), numbers 110 and 112, Greek Revival–Italianate (originally occupied respectively by a coal magnate and a hardware and saddlery entrepreneur), and Second Empire (108 Washington St., built for William Walsh, who also served in the House of Representatives). Bishop James E. Walsh, who was held prisoner in Red China for 10 years, was born in this house. Number 201 was built in 1846 by Southern sympathizer and banker William Sprigg. During the Civil War, the family was taken into custody and the building was used to house Union officers.

Joseph Shriver, a local banker and engineer on the C&O Canal and National Road, advanced pay for a regiment of Union soldiers during the Civil War when it was not forthcoming from the government. He built his Italianate home, 300 Washington St., in the 1860s. Sargent Shriver, philanthropist and Kennedy in-law, is a descendant.

The Colonial Revival built in 1890 at 400 Washington St. was constructed for Bayse

guys in tights when the Washington Redskins come to town for training. Year-round, Frostburg is the home of one of the premier collections of horse-drawn carriages in the United States.

Scenic Drive: Little Erin

From Cumberland, take U.S. 40 through the narrows to Route 35/36. Head north on this road as the sparse suburbs give way to farmland. Turn west on Route 36 at Corriganville, and you'll follow the route of the Maryland Scenic Railroad through rolling hills reminiscent of Ireland and Scotland. At Mount Savage, turn south toward Frostburg. On the south side of Mount Savage, turn southeast on Route 638 toward Clarysville. When you reach U.S. 40, a right turn (west) leads to Frostburg, a right on U.S. 40 Alt. returns to Cumberland past the LaVale Tollgate House.

CANAL PLACE

Bordered by Baltimore Street, Mechanic Street, Route 51 (Industrial Boulevard S.) and the Potomac River, Canal Place, 301/724-3655 or 800/989-9394, www.canalplace.org, encompasses the terminus of the C&O Canal and much of downtown Cumberland, and features a number of attractions. Its development began in the mid-1990s, and culminates with the rewatering of the terminus of the canal in Cumberland.

Western Maryland Railway Station, a magnificent four-story 1913 brick and wood train station, has been restored to full use and serves as the departure point of the **Western Maryland Scenic Railroad**, 800/TRAIN-50 or 800/872-4650, www.wmsr.com. WMSR sightseeing trains leave for round-trips to Frostburg on a regular basis; the trips are especially popular in

Roberts, manager of the Electric Company and the Street Car Company of Cumberland in the early 1900s. One of the later owners of 403 Washington (built in 1862), was Mrs. Doub, wife of a local judge; she was remembered as "a quite colorful person" who would sit in the middle of Washington Street, easel poised and paints in hand, forcing cars to detour around her. The Doubs acquired the property in 1914. Number 408 was built in the 1870s for Daniel Annan, a descendant of the Revolutionary War general and member of the Continental Congress. A variation of Queen Anne and Colonial Revival, the home at 412 Washington St. was built for W. C. Devecmon, descendant of Pierre d'Evequemont, French aristocrat and cousin of Louis XVI. The five-story house has a 30- by 40-foot living room that was once the ballroom.

The house at 501 Washington St. was designed in the Queen Anne style and built in 1890 for Judge Hunter Boyd, chief judge of the Fourth Judicial Circuit of Maryland and an honorary pallbearer at Confederate general Robert E. Lee's funeral. Will Lowdermilk, the founder of the *Daily Transcript* (the first daily newspaper in Cumberland), built an Italianate home in 1860 at 527 Washington St. He was appointed postmaster of Cumberland by President Grant, served for eight years, then moved to Washington, D.C., in 1878 and opened the venerable Lowdermilk's Book Store. The McKaig Mansion, 528 Washington St., was built in Colonial Revival style in 1880 by Merwin McKaig, an industrialist with interests in the McKaig Foundry, Cumberland Steel, Liberty Trust, and other businesses. McKaig had only one descendant, William, who married but was childless. When William McKaig died, he left millions to a scholarship fund for promising students in the name of his wife, Lalitta Nash McKaig; he left the mansion and all his material possessions to his housekeeper. The property was never occupied again.

A pamphlet with descriptions of architectural details that includes several other houses on Washington Street is available from the Allegany County Convention & Visitors Bureau, Western Maryland Station Visitor Center, 13 Canal St., Cumberland, MD 21501, 301/777-5905. Ask for "Cumberland's Victorian District."

the autumn. The station also houses the C&O Canal National Historical Park's Cumberland Visitor Center, the Allegany County Convention & Visitors Bureau, several administrative offices, a gift shop, and a restaurant.

The Shops at Canal Place features a bike shop, fine arts gallery, seafood restaurant, a candy shop, coffee shop, ice cream parlor, toy shop, tour service, and gift shop.

A full-scale canal boat replica, *The Cumberland* offers guided tours of the living quarters, hay house, and stable aboard a typical canal barge. Tours are available on the weekends from May through October.

A walk through the **Allegany County Museum** is a passage through Cumberland's past and present: Kelly Springfield tires, Old German Beer, Westvaco Paper, and thriving coal and glass industries made Cumberland the queen city, the second-largest manufacturing city in Maryland, after Baltimore. Cumberland sits on a vein of high-quality quartz silica, and local glass factories produced a pure blue glass of the highest quality. Examples of housewares produced by a myriad of small glass manufacturers are displayed, along with other Cumberland memorabilia and industrial artifacts. The museum is located at 210 S. Mechanic St.; call 301/777-7200 for information.

The **Trestle Walk/Promenade and Crescent Lawn** are worth a stroll. Trestle Walk is a pedestrian walkway that links the railway station with the C&O Canal and the Potomac River. Crescent Lawn is a recreational area/public park on the canal boat basin.

The historic **Footer Dye Works** building has been refurbished into shops and restaurants. The dye works faces the Crescent Lawn.

A COACH AND FOUR

A century ago, the road was shared by horse-drawn vehicles that were equivalent to today's Mercedes, Porsches, Saabs, Mack trucks, and economy run-abouts—all priced accordingly. In the United States the horse-and-buggy days extended primarily from 1723 to 1920, with maximum use of the buggy for transportation between 1890 and 1910. However, horse-drawn carriages have existed since ancient times.

One of the earliest known horse-drawn vehicles, the chariot, was the forerunner of the road cart, the simplest form of buggy. Though first use of the wheeled cart is commonly credited to the Middle East, recent archaeological discoveries in Russia have caused scientists to reassess that theory. Traces of spoke wheels were found that were dated to 2000 B.C. Russians were the first to domesticate horses 6,000 years ago, and so may have also been responsible for the first horse-drawn vehicles. The lighter spoke wheel, developed from the old solid heavy wheel, was the breakthrough that led to the invention of the chariot.

The first horse-drawn coach—a completely enclosed vehicle—was said to have been made in 1564 for Queen Elizabeth I. Early coaches were ornately decorated but brutally uncomfortable—think ripe tomato in a dryer. During the 15th century, leather braces were first used to suspend the coach body and take some of the bruises out of the ride, and in Paris in 1671, laminated steel springs were added to further soften the road. In 1909, a single advancement, the elliptical spring, made carriages almost comfortable.

Though carriages were common in the wealthier regions of the American colonies, most carriages were made in Europe and imported at significant expense. Soon after independence, Congress banned the importation of completed carriages. American carriage building began to thrive in the 1790s. By the 1850s the carriage industry in America had grown into big business; in the year 1900 as many as 907,500 pleasure vehicles were built.

American design also came into its own: the Rockaway was the first model that covered the driver outside the carriage—in European models, driver-servants were subject to the vagaries of weather. Early carriages had candle lamps in the front, used to show the position of the car-

THRASHER CARRIAGE MUSEUM

I never thought I'd lust after horse-drawn conveyances, but the fabulously restored collection at this museum in the college town of Frostburg (about 10 miles west of Cumberland) changed my conception. One of the top five collections in the country, the carriages on display are upper-middle-class rigs built between 1880–1910. All types of carriages are represented, including sedate and elegant ladies' carriages, racing rigs, and passenger vehicles. The collection also displays several models of historic interest: Theodore Roosevelt's green landau (a five-glass model—five windows—made by Cunningham, a true luxury item at $2,000 when purchased new in 1850); the basket-seat park phaeton used to convey Gerald Ford's daughter in his inaugural parade, and winter sleighs owned by the Vanderbilt family. There's also an unusual Park Drag, a private coach almost as big as a stagecoach, used to chauffeur a host and his friends to picnic sites and events, and to serve as a grandstand for the guests.

Several of the vehicles have been used in period films, including *Harry and Walter Go to New York* and *Puddin' Head Wilson*. The museum is across from the Western Maryland Scenic Railroad Depot (tour trains stop here) on Depot Street in Frostburg, 301/689-3380, www.thrashercarriage.com. Hours are March–Dec. Wed.–Sun. 10 A.M.–3 P.M.; it's open by appointment only Jan.–Feb. Admission is $3.

OTHER POINTS OF INTEREST

Gordon-Roberts House

Built in 1867 for Judge Josiah Gordon, this handsome brick townhouse was rescued from disrepair

riage on the road rather than for the purpose of lighting the way, and dozens of models were available, including sleek racing rigs (very much like today's racing sulkies); wicker, tub-shaped "governess" carts for driving the children about (as seen in *Gone with the Wind*); and lower, slower ladies' carriages with high fronts. It was considered unseemly for ladies to view a horse's natural functions, and totally out of the question for them to drive behind stallions (perhaps Victorian gentlemen chafed at the comparison).

Sensitivity aside, carriages were expensive. A custom-made Brewster was the equivalent of a Mercedes today; in fact, the Mercedes Motor Company eventually bought Brewster. An average model carriage cost $1,250 in 1906, and the price rose with added amenities and size.

One popular larger model, the buckboard, might be thought of as the first pickup truck. The term "buckboard," used so generically in movie westerns, actually refers to a type of suspension system that was invented to stabilize the carriage. The wide-bodied wagons named for their suspension system were widely used by most farm families in the years prior to the 20th century.

Some elements of carriage design survived unchanged: wheels remained "dished"—slightly concave—for stability, a style directly descended from predecessors in ancient China. The width of the wheel had much to do with the load carried; the wheels of delivery wagons were considerably wider than those of two-seater carriages. The Kelly Springfield Company invented the rubber tire, a major advancement in comfort and durability, in the 1890s.

Carriage driving is an acquired skill, especially when handling teams of two, four (the famous "four-in-hand"), and up to eight horses. Some of the nation's most prestigious horse shows, such as the Devon horse show in southeast Pennsylvania, have display and competitive carriage driving events. Two publications list upcoming events, and are a font of information on carriages and driving. The first is *The Carriage Journal*, official publication of The Carriage Association of America, 177 Pointers-Auburn Rd., Salem, NJ 08079, 609/935-1616, carrassc@jaguarsystems.com. The other is *The Whip*, official publication of The American Driving Society, P.O. Box 160, Metamora, MI 48455, 810/664-8666, AmDriveSo@aol.com.

by the Allegany Historical Society and turned into a fine example of period architecture and furnishings. Collections include clothing, hats, and fans; Civil War relics; B&O Railroad china; hand-blown Allegany County glass, and some unusual pieces of furniture, such as the courting sofa in the parlor (two seats facing each other side-by-side) and the "hunter's cabinet" in the hallway (decorated with life-size wooden carvings of captured game). An oil painting of Lover's Leap, in the narrows west of Cumberland, hangs near the dining room. All the rooms of the house display regularly rotated collections.

The Gordon-Roberts House features a Victorian gift shop and candlelight tours in December. The house is at 218 Washington St., Cumberland, 301/777-8678. Tours of the house are given on the hour, Tues.–Sat. 10 A.M.–4 P.M. Admission is $4 for adults.

George Washington's Headquarters

In 1755, as a young colonel attached to General Braddock's troops, George Washington began his active military career in this one-room cabin. The cabin, in Riverside Park on Greene Street, Cumberland, is the only remaining structure left of Fort Cumberland, a depot and rallying point of the French and Indian War and later Indian hostilities. Washington returned many times to Fort Cumberland, including a visit in 1794 to inspect troops gathered to suppress the Whiskey Rebellion (the first tax revolt in the new nation) in Pennsylvania. At one time, Cumberland was named "Washington Town," the primary city in "Washington County" (now Allegany County). For those interested in the history and dimensions of the old fort, a walking trail that includes 28 narrative plaques begins in the tiny Heritage Park on the corner of Canal and Baltimore Streets.

African American Gallery & Gift Shop

Cumberland's African American Gallery & Gift Shop, 183 N. Centre St., 301/777-7785, seeks to document the role African Americans played in the settlement and development of the region.

PARKS AND SCENIC SPOTS

Rocky Gap State Park, I-68, six miles east of Cumberland, was once a little-used state park; a portion of it has undergone a glamorous facelift to become a fancy golf resort for business meetings and vacationers.

The state park portion of Rocky Gap features amenities similar to Maryland's other parks. A large camping area with 278 campsites is equipped with electricity and showers and some electric hookups. There are also camper cabins. Camping reservations must be made by calling 888/432-2267 (all other inquiries: Rocky Gap State Park, 12500 Pleasant Valley Rd., Flintstone, MD 21530, 301/777-2139). The park's main attraction is 243-acre Lake Habeeb, with three swimming areas, bathhouses, boat launch, boat rental and launch, and other concessions.

Dan's Mountain State Park, approximately nine miles south of Frostburg on Route 36, 301/777-2139, is a day-use facility offering 481 acres of rugged terrain, fishing pond, hiking, picnicking, and swimming in an Olympic-size pool with a water slide. There's also a recycled tire playground.

Dan's Rock Overlook affords a panoramic view of the surrounding region from a height of 2,898 feet, and is well worth the three-mile detour from the main road. Though it's still an infamous party place for Frostburg State students (the graffiti may teach you a few new tricks), the view is too good not to share. The county has built a series of steps to the top, for those who find the charms of bouldering less than obvious. To get there, look for Paradise Avenue on the east side of the road, 1,000 feet north on Route 36 from the intersection of Route 936 and Route 36, north of the village of Midland. Once on Paradise Avenue, follow signs to

Dan's Rock Overlook; in summer, the sides of the road are lined with blue chicory.

While visiting Dan's Mountain or the Overlook, take a few minutes to head south on Route 36 to the small town of **Lonaconing.** The town park has a well-preserved iron furnace, the first successful coke-fired furnace in America, in operation from 1839 to 1856. A bronze marker honors a local hero: one of the greatest left-handed pitchers of all time, Robert Moses (Lefty) Grove. A member of the Baseball Hall of Fame, Lefty Grove was born in Lonaconing in 1900, and pitched for Philadelphia and Boston from 1925–1941. In his six years as a player for Baltimore in the International League, he won 108 games and lost only 36. Lefty, where are you when we need you?!

The **Narrows**—discovered after the road over Wills Mountain had been built by General Braddock—became the route of the National Toll Road (U.S. 40A) in 1833. The Narrows is a scenic pass that twists its way through 1,000-foot-high rock walls west of Cumberland. On the north side of the road, looming over the Fruit Bowl farm stand, is the surreally high granite outface of **Lover's Leap.** Many places claim to be the original Lover's Leap, right down to the story of the Indian maiden and young settler who were not allowed to marry; one glance up at this craggy jumping spot, though, and you just might believe.

For a weird juxtaposition of the old and new, pay a visit to the **La Vale Tollgate House,** 14302 National Highway (U.S. 40A), La Vale, 301/729-3047. This toll collector's booth was the first to operate daily on the nation's first road to the west; a horse and rider had to spend $.04 to pass through, and another $.06 if he was accompanied by a score of sheep or hogs. The tollgate house is easy to miss among the plastic signs, auto lots, and modern boxy buildings on the highway; it's .1 mile west of the intersection of U.S. 40 and Route 53 on the south side of the road. The tollbooth is open May–Aug., Sat.–Sun. 1:30–4:30 P.M., Sunday only in September. Free.

SHOPPING

Downtown Cumberland

The four-block area roughly bordered by Frederick, S. Mechanic, Pershing/W. Union, and S. George Streets has been reborn into a comfortable stroll for shoppers, dotted with fountains and pedestrian walkways. The area, particularly along the Baltimore Street promenade, features many fine examples of late-19th-century commercial architecture. The former Lazarus department store (55 Baltimore St.) now contains antique and collectible wares from 100 dealers, and similar shops are interspersed with alfresco cafés, hot dog shops, bookstores, and a C. G. Murphy Variety Store (138 Baltimore St.). The latter is surfaced with "secret recipe" white enameled brick manufactured in nearby Mount Savage.

A detailed walking tour of downtown Cumberland, which has been designated an Arts and Entertainment District by the state of Maryland, is available courtesy of the Downtown Cumberland Business Association from the Allegany County Convention & Visitors Bureau. The tour also includes adjacent historic residential areas.

ACCOMMODATIONS

Rocky Gap Lodge & Golf Resort, P.O. Box 1199, Cumberland, MD 21501, 301/784-8400, sits on Lake Habeeb, which offers swimming, boating, snorkeling, and fishing; the 18-hole Jack Nicklaus Signature golf course is also a big draw. The six-story modern lodge (described by Jim Yenckel in his *Great Getaways* newsletter as "sleek . . . bedecked in rustic-looking wood and stone like a Marriott in a coonskin hat") is reminiscent of lodges at the Grand Canyon or Yosemite. It offers a variety of rooms and a spate of activities for all members of the family, from an indoor/outdoor swimming pool to campfire programs to rappelling to scuba diving. The resort also features a Bar & Grill and a formal dining room, the Lakeside (dinner entrées average $15). Room rates are lower in the off-season (Nov. 2– Apr. 1), and vary from $89–325.

The Inn at Walnut Bottom, 120 Greene St., Cumberland, 301/777-0003, links two houses— the 1820 Cowden House and the 1890 Dent House (Julia Dent was the bride of President U. S. Grant)—that were built on the site of a grove of wild walnut trees. The current setting,

though still on the outskirts of Cumberland, is distinctly urban, and innkeepers Grant Irvin and Kirsten Hansen have modernized eight rooms to provide spacious accommodations with private baths, telephones, televisions, and all the other comforts of home; two additional rooms share a bath, and two-bedroom family suites are available. The inn offers mountain bikes at no charge for guests who wish to explore the city and the C&O Canal towpath. Kirsten, who is a native of Denmark, trained for three years in Copenhagen and is certified in relaxation therapy; guests have the opportunity to experience *Afspaending,* a combination of massage, stretches, and mild exercise. Rates range $89–198.

Around 1840, the Union Mining Company, based in Mount Savage, wanted to attract a medical doctor to the town; the solution was to build a fine home and invite a physician to nest in it. According to records, one Doctor Thompson took over **The Castle,** an American Gothic fantasy made of local limestone, and served the miners of the company and their families for the next 30 years.

Early in the 20th century, an eccentric inventor from Scotland, Andrew Ramsey, purchased the home and modified some of its architectural features. Perhaps because of the area's similarities to his birthplace, Ramsey altered the structure to resemble Castle Craig. Ramsey's trump card had been his invention of a one-step (normally a two- or three-step) process for glazing brick; he set up a kiln in Mount Savage. The company prospered, and Ramsey's work is in evidence all over the surrounding area, including commercial buildings on Baltimore Street and the train depot in Cumberland. Ramsey's glazed bricks still shine in the courtyard of his castle. The root cellar is lined with another of Ramsey's products: porcelain toilet bowls and tanks, which make excellent storage bins.

The Scotsman jealously guarded his secret process, but though he was an exceptional inventor, his business skills were no match for the Great Depression. He declared bankruptcy in 1929 and left the area. His secret glazing process died with him some years later. The castle became, briefly, a dance hall, a casino, and, possibly, a brothel. As the countryside healed from the ravages of industry and became as lush as the highlands, the castle fell into disrepair.

In 1984, the building was revamped into a bed-and-breakfast. Lavishly decorated, four of the six bedrooms have a private bath. A full breakfast is served in the dining room or on the porches in good weather, and the property itself is surrounded by 1.5 acres of landscaped gardens. The castle, designated a National Historic Landmark, is a favorite for weddings and special events. It's less than a mile south of the village of Mount Savage on Route 36, a scenic eight-mile drive from Frostburg, 301/264-4645. Rates range $115–150, with midweek and corporate discounts.

Failingers Hotel Gunter, 11 W. Main St., Frostburg, 301/689-6511, was opened originally as the Hotel Gladstone in 1896. William Gunter took over in 1903, and turned the marginally successful resort hotel into a hotel/jail/game cockfighting arena/speakeasy. In 1986, the Failinger family renovated the dilapidated building (all those irritable chickens!), turning the basement into a historical mini-museum and the floors above into small, functional hotel rooms. Rates range $64–90.

FOOD

Ms. Jaye Miller, former chef at the Swedish Embassy in Washington, D.C., makes the **The Oxford House Restaurant,** 129 Baltimore St., Cumberland, 301/777-7101, one of the best places to eat in the area. Crab Remick (crab, bacon, and tarragon served in an artichoke bottom) is a unique appetizer, and the entrées, averaging $15, are equally delicious. The salads are perfectly balanced, and the desserts (like crushed meringues in frozen cream with lingonberries) leave happy memories. The Oxford House serves dinner Mon.–Sat. 5–9 P.M. (service until 9:30 P.M. Fri.–Sat.).

Though **Au Petit Paris,** on Main Street is rumored to be the best restaurant in Frostburg, the **Princess Restaurant,** 12 W. Main St., 301/689-1680, is the best casual place to eat in town. George Pappas Sr. began the business in 1939, and his family continues to run it. In the 1950s, President Harry Truman and his wife Bess passed through and sat in the third mirrored booth from the door. There still are Seeburg Consolettes at each booth. Good diner food, cheery service, and great prices ($8.25 average dinner entrée, $3.95 sandwich platters).

Cafés and Takeouts

Coney Island Wieners, 15 N. Liberty St., 301/759-9707, and its rival in the weenie wars, **Curtis' Famous Wieners,** 35 N. Liberty St., Cumberland, both put on the dog: it's all a matter of style.

The **Tombstone Café,** 60 E. Main St., Frostburg, has coffee your way, plus salads and sandwiches (food is priced around $5).

Eastern Express, 109-111 E. Main St., Frostburg, 301/689-5370 (they deliver), satisfies that occasional need for something different with Americanized Chinese food ($4–10).

INFORMATION

Contact the Allegany County Convention & Visitors Bureau, Western Maryland Station, 13 Canal St., Cumberland, MD 21502, 301/777-5132, for more information.

Far West: Garrett County

Garrett County is justifiably famous for its recreational opportunities; more than 80,000 acres of the county's 648 square miles are dedicated to public parks, state forests, and open space. In fact, Garrett Community College and the Department of Natural Resources offer a two-year Adventuresports Degree with more than 50 courses in camping, mountain biking, rock-climbing, skiing, whitewater paddling, orienteering, swift water rescue, and many other activities tied to the great outdoors (for more information, call 301/387-3330).

The northern part of the county provides farmland for Amish and Mennonite settlers. The Grantsville area offers a quiet alternative to active outdoor recreation; a bulk store and crafts village provide a peaceful afternoon's diversion.

STATE PARKS

Garrett County's state parks are usually equipped with picnic shelters and playgrounds, a variety of day- and extended-use recreational facilities, and overnight facilities. Some, such as Herrington Manor, have furnished cabins that are available year-round.

Because so much public land stretches over the county, hiking and other trails often stretch beyond the boundaries of parks. Though specific information may be had by contacting individual parks, a comprehensive guide to all trails in Garrett County is available from the Deep Creek Lake–Garrett County Chamber of Commerce (see Information, later; ask for the *Garrett County, Maryland, Trail Guide*). The guide also features information on biking the county roads.

Casselman River Bridge State Park

Casselman Bridge (c/o New Germany State Park, 349 Headquarters Lane, Grantsville, MD 21536, 301/895-5453) is east of Grantsville on U.S. 40. The 80-foot stone arch bridge was constructed in 1813 as part of the old National Road. At the time, it was the largest of its kind in the world. The bridge is open to foot traffic and anglers but offers no other recreation or overnight facilities.

New Germany State Park

A small park with a 13-acre lake, New Germany (send inquiries to: New Germany State Park, 349 Headquarters Ln., Grantsville, MD 21536, 301/895-5453, www.dnr.state.md.us/public lands/western/newgermany.html. Call 888/432-2267 or click on the website for camping reservations) is popular during summer, offering a multiuse beach, picnicking, and camping. There is a $3 per person service charge for the day-use area. Visitors enjoy hiking and campfire programs in the warmer months and cross-country skiing in the winter.

This park lies within the boundaries of Savage River State Forest. The lake was formed in the mid-19th century when Poplar Lick Run was dammed for sawmill and gristmill operation.

Hiking: Approximately four miles of the Meadow Mountain trail (the entire trail is 11 miles) run through the park. The trail is accessible from the parking lot.

Water Sports: A boat launch and rowboat rental are available on the lake.

Overnight Facilities: There is a camp store and dump station, and 37 individual campsites close to modern bathhouses with hot-water showers. Tent campsites are available Memorial Day–Labor Day. The park offers 11 full-service cabins by reservation; all are furnished and equipped with electricity, bathrooms with showers, bedding, fireplaces, and kitchens. One cabin is equipped for the handicapped. The cabins are available year-round.

Getting There: The park is five miles southeast of Grantsville. Take exit 24 off I-68 on New Germany Road.

Big Run State Park

Big Run is a popular base camp for outdoor-lovers intent on fishing, camping, hiking, or hunting. Picnicking and a playground are also available; the day-use area is free. The park (c/o

New Germany State Park, 349 Headquarters Ln., Grantsville, MD 21536, 301/895-5453, www.dnr.state.md.us/publiclands/western/big run.html) covers 300 acres at the mouth of the Savage River Reservoir, and is surrounded by the acreage of Savage River State Forest.

Hiking: Big Run is the trailhead for the six-mile Monroe Run hiking trail.

Water Sports: The park offers a boat launch, fishing, and flat-water canoeing.

Overnight Facilities: Big Run State Park offers rustic camping year-round with 30 unimproved campsites and a youth group camping area.

Getting There: The park is 16 miles from exit 24 off I-68, south of New Germany State Park on New Germany Road.

Swallow Falls State Park

One of the most popular recreational areas in Garrett County due to its breathtaking scenery and swimming/sunbathing opportunities, Swallow Falls (c/o Herrington Manor State Park, 222 Herrington Ln., Oakland, MD 21550, 301/387-6938, www.dnr.state.md.us/publiclands/western/swallowfalls.html; call 888/432-2267 or click on their website for camping reservations) was named for the great flocks of cliff swallows that nested in the surrounding rock faces during pioneer days. The Youghiogheny (yuk-a-GAY-nee) River flows along the park's borders, passing through shaded rocky gorges and creating waterfalls, rippling rapids, and many sun-and-swim spots where visitors can play turtle. Picnic shelters and a playground are located near the parking lot; a day-use fee of $3 is collected during the summer season.

One of the features of the park is Muddy Creek Falls, a crashing 63-foot waterfall a short hike away from the parking lot. Swallow Falls is also home to an ancient stand of tall native hemlocks.

Hiking: The park contains a 1.5-mile loop trail that parallels the river, and is also part of the Garrett Trail System that starts north of Herrington Manor State Park and ends nine miles later at the Snaggy Mountain Road multiuse trail.

Overnight Facilities: The park features 65 campsites equipped with modern washhouses, laundry tubs, showers, and sanitary facilities.

Campsites for those who wish to bring their pets are available, but pets must remain at the site (call for details). Pets are permitted in the surrounding areas of Potomac/Garrett State Forests; during the off-season (Labor Day–Memorial Day), pets are allowed in the day-use areas of Swallow Falls as long as they are on a leash.

Getting There: The park is nine miles northwest of Oakland, on the Herrington Manor–Swallow Falls Road. It is four miles beyond the entrance to Herrington Manor State Park and three miles east of the West Virginia state line.

Herrington Manor State Park

This recreational area (222 Herrington Ln., Oakland, MD 21550, 301/334-9180, www.dnr.state .md.us/publiclands/western/herrington-manor.html) features a 53-acre lake, tennis courts, a ballfield, a volleyball area, picnic shelters, and a food and gift concession. The park's cabins make it a year-round destination, but be sure to make reservations well in advance by calling 888/432-2267 or clicking on their website.

Hiking: The park offers 10 miles of looped trails of varying difficulty. The park office on Herrington Lane distributes trail maps.

Water Sports: The lake is stocked with trout. A swimming beach and boat rental concession operate in the summer.

Winter Sports: The boat rental concession rents cross-country skis during the winter for use on the park's trail system.

Overnight Facilities: Twenty furnished cabins, complete with electricity, bathrooms, kitchens, bedding, and tableware, are available by reservation from Memorial Day–Labor Day on a weekly basis. For the rest of the year, the cabins are available on a one- and two-day basis.

Getting There: The park is five miles northwest of Oakland on Route 20.

Deep Creek Lake State Park

Maryland's largest lake is the biggest draw in Garrett County. Most of the land around Deep Creek Lake was privately owned until 2000, when much of the buffer area was purchased by the state. For information on the park, contact Deep Creek Lake State Park, 898 State Park Rd.,

Swanton, MD 21561, 301/387-4111, www.dnr
.state.md.us/publiclands/western/deepcreek
lake.html. Call 888/432-2267 or click on their
website for camping reservations.

Deep Creek Lake lies west of the Allegheny
Front and the Eastern Continental Divide on a
large plateau known as the Tablelands or Allegheny Highlands. Because of its mountainous
setting, the region experiences unique weather.
Long winters may bring more than 200 inches of
snow, and the greening of spring sometimes does
not occur until mid-May. Summer brings warm
days and cool nights, and autumn comes alive
with blasts of color in early October with clear,
crisp days and cold evenings.

Deep Creek Lake came into being as part of a
hydroelectric project constructed on Deep Creek
in the 1920s by the Youghiogheny Hydroelectric
Company. The park is the site of the historic
Brant coal mine and homesite, where a restored
mine entrance preserves a typical drift, or adit,
mine. The mine was worked for several years by
the Brant family and supplied bituminous coal
for local heating and blacksmithing.

Once the site of massive deforesting, more
than 95 percent of the park has been regenerated
into a mature northern hardwood forest. Oaks
and hickories are now the dominant species. Black
bear, wild turkey, bobcat, and white-tailed deer
have grown in numbers over the past decades as
habitat has been preserved and managed; squirrel,
chipmunk, raccoon, skunk, and opossum are frequently seen. The park is also home to numerous
plant species, some rare, found on the forest floor.

Park headquarters is at the intersection of
Brant and State Park Roads; it's open Mon.–Fri.
during business hours. Several picnic areas offer
excellent views of the lake with easy access to the
beach and other facilities, and evening campfire
programs, talks on the natural and cultural resources of the park, and ranger-led hikes are available throughout the year.

Hiking: The Meadow Mountain section of
the park offers opportunities for hiking. Trails
range from moderate to difficult. A trail guide is
available at Park Headquarters and at the various
trailheads for a small donation. Pets are allowed
on trails and must be kept on a leash.

Fishing and Hunting: Fishing for trout, walleye, bass, and yellow perch is generally good on
the lake (trout is stocked). Two wheelchair-accessible fishing docks are available at the park's
boating facility.

Hunting is permitted in the park's backcountry areas during regular hunting seasons. The
hunting areas are posted, and applicable regulations, including license requirements, apply.

Water Sports: The park includes approximately one mile of shoreline on the lake, and offers swimming, fishing, and boat launching.
Lifeguards are on duty at the park's beach during the summer months. The boat launch facility is open most of the year except when
weather or ice prohibit access. A limited number
of rowboats are available for rental through the
campground office.

Overnight Facilities: Meadow Mountain
campground has 112 campsites that are available by reservation from spring through fall.
Each site is located near heated restroom facilities
complete with hot showers. Several disabled-ac-
cess campsites are available by reservation. Electric hookups are available at 25 sites, and a dump
station is on-site for self-contained units. The
maximum length of stay is two weeks. Pets are
permitted in certain designated loops.

Getting There: The park is 10 miles northeast
of Oakland on the east side of Deep Creek Lake,
two miles east of Thayerville, off U.S. 219.

STATE FORESTS

Many state parks are within state forests, land
set aside for both recreational and commercial
use. State forests differ from parks in that they
cover territory that is privately owned, and they
usually offer primitive camping sites but very
few other amenities. Trails and roads in the state
forests are often, but not always, multiuse.

Garrett County State Forest

Acquired by the state of Maryland in 1906, Garrett Forest, 222 Herrington Ln., Oakland, MD
21550, 301/334-2038, www.dnr.state.md.us/
publiclands/western/garrett.html, was the first
site in the present public lands system. The

FESTIVALS AND EVENTS

The Tourism Council of Frederick, 800/999-3613, www.co.frederick.md.us, has additional information on upcoming events. Schifferstadt Architectural Museum (301-663-3885) and Rose Hill Manor Park (301/694-1650) sponsor numerous events throughout the year. Some of their activities are listed below, in addition to others.

February

Take time out from winter sports to participate in **Cabin Fever Weekend** at Spruce Forest Artisan Village. Artisans create crafts for sale in the log village; entertainment and refreshments are available. 301/895-3332.

April

The **Children's Festival** takes place in Baker Park, with free hands-on activities for children. Call 301/662-4549 for date and times.

The **Fruehlings Fest** celebrates the spring opening of Schifferstadt Museum with cooking demonstrations and a Civil War reenactment.

The **Farm and Family Festival** is a fun activity featuring hay rides, craft demonstrations, and children's activities at Rose Hill Manor.

Fort Frederick State Park sponsors a public competitive black powder shoot for muzzleloaders only. 301/842-2155.

May

Frederick's **Annual Art & Craft Festival** takes place at the Frederick Fairgrounds and showcases the work of more than 300 artists and craftspeople. Find out more by calling 717/369-4810.

Beyond the Garden Gates is a self-guided tour of historic and contemporary gardens in downtown Frederick. Call the Tourism Council at 800/999-3613 for dates and times.

Sharpsburg (Washington County) is home to the oldest **Memorial Day parade** in America, a tradition started after the Civil War to honor returning veterans. The parade is followed by a ceremony in the National Cemetery. 301/432-8410.

June/July/August

Baker Park is the site of Frederick's **Summer Concert Series,** which features a wide variety of performers: reggae bands, pop groups, and musicians from nationally known bands such as Scott Ambush from Spyro Gyra. Call the Tourism Council of Frederick for a brochure.

The **Lotus Blossom Festival** stars acres of lily and lotus blossoms; it's held in mid-July at Lilypons Water Gardens in Buckeystown. Call 800/999-5459 for dates and times.

8,000-acre terrain consists of mountain forests—red oak, white oak, scarlet oak, black cherry, hickory, red maple, white pine, and hemlock—streams, and valleys. Visitors can glimpse beaver ponds and cranberry bogs along the streams, as well as many other wildlife species. Additional information and a map of the forest may be obtained by calling the headquarters.

Hiking: Garrett State Forest and Potomac State Forest share the Potomac River Trail System (10.5 miles), the Garrett Trail System (nine miles), and Backbone Mountain Trail System (eight miles).

Overnight Facilities: Garrett State Forest and Potomac State Forest share four campgrounds: Piney Mountain Campground (Piney Mountain Road, near Friendsville), Wallman Campground (Wallman Road, near Oakland), Lost Land Run (Lost Land Road), and Snaggy Mountain Camping Area (Snaggy Mountain Road).

The **American Indian Inter-Tribal Cultural Organization Pow-Wow** is held annually in Frederick, featuring traditional singing, dancing, crafts, and food. 301/869-9381.

Traditional country and bluegrass music fills the air at the **Fiddler's and Banjo Contests,** Friendsville (Garrett County). Spontaneous clogging appreciated! 301/746-8194.

September

Also at Lilypons, early September brings the koi (Japanese decorative carp) festival and crafts fair.

Nearly three centuries of history march down the street in Frederick's **Grand Parade.** Floats, bands, and marching groups compete for attention on Patrick and Market Streets. Call 301/694-1100 for date and rain date.

The Great Frederick Fair features livestock, exhibits, entertainment, and a carnival. For information, call 301/663-5895.

The **Western Maryland Street Rod Round-up,** in Cumberland, features more than 1,000 pre-1949 cars and trucks. 301/777-3456.

October

Schifferstadt celebrates **Oktoberfest** with oompah bands, food, and crafts.

During the Frederick **House Pilgrimage,** more than 40 historical homes open their doors to the public. To find out more, call 301/694-1100.

One of the best places to enjoy fall color in Maryland is on a **Fall Color Hayride** in Herrington Manor State Park near Oakland. The wagons take in the state forest and adjoining country roads. 301/334-9180.

Cakewalkin' in Western Maryland! Hagerstown hosts its own version of the **Alsatia Mummer's Parade,** an event with 150 units, bands, and floats. 301/733-0033.

November/December

In late November, Schifferstadt offers a **Christkindelsmarkt** for those seeking Christmas crafts and gifts.

A very popular **Candlelight House Tour** is given in early December. Visitors have the opportunity to see historic and contemporary homes beautifully decorated for the holidays. Contact the Tourism Council of Frederick for dates and times.

Antietam National Battlefield, Sharpsburg, sets out 23,110 luminaries along a 4.5-mile route to honor Civil War soldiers killed and wounded during the three days of battle there. The **Memorial Illumination** has been an annual event for more than a decade. 301/733-7373.

Most sites are first-come, first-served; primitive shelter sites and group sites may be reserved. Call the park office or click on the website for detailed information on campsites.

Getting There: The forest is five miles northwest of Oakland, off U.S. 219.

Potomac State Forest

The highest point in any Maryland State Forest—Backbone Mountain, 3,220 feet—is within the boundaries of this 12,000-acre forest, 222 Herrington Ln. Oakland, MD 21550, 301/334-2038, www.dnr.state.md.us/publiclands/western/potomacforest.html. Another high point in the forest is the rock outcropping near the intersection of Route 135 and Walnut Bottom Road, which overlooks a portion of Potomac State Forest, Savage River State Forest, and Crabtree Creek. The headwaters of the Potomac River are also on state forest land. Additional information and a map of the forest can be obtained by calling the headquarters or visiting the website. Potomac State Forest is known for its excellent trout fishing.

Hiking: Potomac River State Forest and Garrett State Forest share three trail systems, listed under Garrett County State Forest.

Overnight Facilities: Potomac State Forest and Garrett State Forest share four campgrounds. Call the park office or click on the website for detailed information.

Getting There: The forest is in southeastern Garrett County, off Route 135, between the towns of Oakland and Westernport, bordering the Potomac River.

Savage River State Forest

At 52,812 acres, this wilderness area, 349 Headquarters Ln., Grantsville, MD 21536, 301/895-5759, or 301/895-5453, www.dnr.state.md.us/publiclands/western/savageriver.html, is the largest facility in the state forest and park system. Its northern hardwood forest preserves a strategic watershed in Garrett County. About 2,700 acres of the forest have been designated as Big Savage Wildland, an unimproved area.

Hiking: The forest encompasses all or part of Meadow Mountain Trail System (11 miles), Margroff Plantation Trail System (7.5 miles), Negro Mountain Trail System (eight miles), Monroe Run (six miles), and Big Savage Mountain Trail System (17 miles). A backpacking permit may be obtained at the Savage River office to backpack and camp in the state forest.

Biking: Mountain bikes are allowed on all hiking trails except for Monroe Run and Big Savage. Visitors can ride nonmotorized bikes on many of the trails and roads in the state forest but are asked to exercise extreme caution, especially on blind curves.

Hunting: Hunting is allowed in most areas of the state forest in season. Hunters must be licensed. The state forest offers two miles of handicapped hunter access roads that are open throughout the hunting season. These roads can be distinguished by the "Vehicle Access by Special Permit Only" sign at the road entrance. To use these roads, hunters must have a valid permit in their possession and a Permit Display Card on

their vehicle. Permit applications may be obtained from the Wildlife Regional Service Center, 301/777-2136, at 3 Pershing St., Room 110, Cumberland, MD 21502.

Water Sports: A boat launch is available, and the waterways offer both flat-water and white-water canoeing. Anglers must have a current license.

Winter Sports: The forest offers cross-country skiing and snowmobiling. Snowmobile and off-road vehicle (ORV) operators must have a current Department of Natural Resources (DNR) ORV sticker, available at the state forest headquarters. Trail maps are available at the park office for all trails, including 10 miles of cross-country ski trails.

Overnight Facilities: The forest offers 52 primitive sites on a first-come, first-served basis.

Getting There: The state forest is in central and eastern Garrett County, off I-68.

OTHER RECREATION
Skiing

Wisp Resort, 290 Marsh Hill Rd., McHenry, MD 21541, 301/387-4911 or 800/462-WISP (800/462-9477), www.skiwisp.com, is a four-season vacation destination on Deep Creek Lake. In winter, 90 percent of the resort's skiable terrain is equipped for snowmaking and night skiing. Slopes are 20 percent beginner, 50 percent intermediate, and 30 percent advanced, and two triple and three double chairlifts carry skiers and snowboarders to 23 slopes totaling 14 miles of runs. Rentals, lessons, and programs for children are available. A tubing park features seven tubing lanes with two surface tows—it allows non-skiers to enjoy schussing down the slopes, albeit from a lower perspective.

During the warm months, the ski trails are used for hiking and mountain biking. Wisp also features an 18-hole terraced golf course and a resort hotel with pool and restaurants.

Golf

In addition to Wisp's golf course, the **Oakland Golf Club,** Bradley Lane, Oakland, 301/334-2444, offers an 18-hole course in a country club setting complete with restaurant and lounge.

Horseback Riding

There are several stables in the Deep Creek Lake area. One that offers hayrides and camping as well as horseback riding is **Western Trails Riding Stables,** Mayhew Inn Road off Route 219, Oakland, 301/387-6155.

White-Water Rafting

The Allegheny Mountains that uplift southwest Pennsylvania, western Maryland, and West Virginia are home to challenging white-water rafting. Two companies, both out of Ohiopyle (uh-HI-a-pile), Pennsylvania, offer raft trips in the area: **Mountain Streams & Trails,** 800/723-8669, www.mtstreams.com; and **White Water Adventurers, Inc.,** 800/992-7238, www.wwaraft.com. **Precision Rafting,** in Friendsville, MD, 800/477-3723, www.precisionrafting.com, teaches kayaking in addition to leading white-water float trips.

Watercraft on Deep Creek Lake

Boat and watercraft rental places abound around the lake. The **Aquatic Center,** 634 Deep Creek Dr., McHenry, 301/387-8233, www.aquatic-center.com, rents water motorcycles and jet boats. **Crystal Waters,** at Will O' the Wisp Resort, 20160 Garrett Hwy. (Route 219), 301/387-5515, rents ski boats, pontoon boats, fishing boats, pedal boats, canoes, and water-ski equipment.

OTHER POINTS OF INTEREST

Spruce Forest Artisan Village is the realized dream of local resident Alta Schrock, who, while working as a teacher several decades ago, wanted to showcase crafts made by people in the surrounding mountains. At first, she drove from place to place in the area to pick up the handwork, then sold the goods in a small shop. Today, Spruce Forest Village, 177 Casselman Rd., 301/895-3332, www.spruceforest.org, is made up of a group of historic buildings, some original to the site, others brought from as far away as Salisbury, Pennsylvania, and reconstructed on the property. The buildings are set up as historical displays with interpreters (such as Compton School and Miller House), or house a select group of artisans demonstrating their crafts.

At various times, visitors can see working black-smiths, soapmakers, weavers, potters, woodcarvers, and others. Lynn Lais, whose subtle glazed ceramics are sold all over the United States, is based here, as is Gary Yoder, three-time winner of the World Champion Award for his radiantly alive and beautifully composed carved wooden birds. Yoder carved his first bird at Penn Alps as an 11-year-old, and continues to teach classes as artist-in-residence there during the summer. These days, his work is in such demand that he works by commission only, and the wait is one year. Many of the artisans sell their work on the premises. The village is open mid-May–Oct. 31, 10 A.M.–5 P.M.

The tiny **Garrett County Historical Museum,** 107 S. 2nd St., Oakland, 301/334-3226, chronicles the history of Garrett County through its artifacts. There are several pictures of those famous outdoorsmen and fishing buddies Henry Ford, Thomas Edison, Harvey Firestone, and President Warren G. Harding during one of their camping trips to Swallow Falls in 1919. So much for the separation of government and industry. The museum is open May 1–Dec. 31 Mon.–Sat. 10 A.M.–4 P.M., Jan. 1–Apr. 30 Thurs.–Sat. 11 A.M.–4 P.M., weather permitting. Donations are accepted.

SHOPPING

Though you won't be swept off your feet by volume ("Ten Antique Dealers Under One Roof"), the **Grantsville Antique Center** is a fun place to wander while in Grantsville. The building also contains a gift shop, quilt materials store, and thrift shop. The Antique Center is on Main Street, Grantsville, 301/895-5737, across from the Casselman Motel—you can't miss it. It's closed on Sunday.

The **Penn Alps Craft Shop,** inside the Penn Alps restaurant, 125 Casselman Rd., Grantsville, www.pennalps.com, features the cream of handmade goods from artists and craftspeople associated with Spruce Forest, plus a small amount of work of equal quality from other areas. This is a spectacular place to buy one-of-a-kind gifts. Handmade quilts, tiny blown-glass birds, silk-screened paper goods, honey from local apiaries,

DEER PARK

Well before the Civil War, executives from the Baltimore and Ohio Railroad dreamed up a luxury resort where they and their friends could meet and relax. The war delayed construction, but the site—Deer Park—was completed in 1873. It had everything a wealthy patron would want: bucolic surroundings, an elegant hotel featuring rooms with baths and electric lights, an elevator, Turkish baths, separate bathing pools for men and women, an 18-hole golf course, tennis courts, bowling alleys, a complete livery service, and of course, separate quarters for the servants. Guests were driven the short distance to the hotel from the depot by carriage.

By 1881, the resort was so popular that additional "cottages" (two- and three-story vacation homes) were added for the use of guests. Other cottages were privately built and owned by employees and associates of the railroad, including the elegant three-story Victorian that is now the Deer Park Inn. Its architect, Josiah Pennington, designed several local homes. His style was unusual for the time, incorporating tile fireplaces, large airy rooms with many windows, and wide verandas; all were innovative considering the prevailing dark, velvet-draped style of decoration.

President Grover Cleveland and his bride, Frances Folsom, spent their honeymoon in another of Deer Park's cottages—it's still standing, but is privately owned, as are the few remnants of the grand vacation destination. With the advent of the automobile, the hotel lost its exclusivity and fell out of fashion. In the 1940s, the grounds were purchased and the hotel and several outbuildings were torn down and sold for lumber.

Today, Deer Park exists as a small residential village—but the name maintains a national presence. One of the draws of the original resort was its water, sourced in nearby Boiling Spring. The spring supplied the water for the hotel, and was bottled and served in the dining cars of the B&O Railroad. Boiling Spring has stayed in commercial operation and is now owned by Perrier of America. Flying Scot Sailboats, nationally distributed 19-foot daysailers, are manufactured on the dry land of Deer Park. A family-owned business since its inception, Flying Scots are not only popular on Deep Creek Lake (there are roughly 200 of them plying the dark waters) but may be seen in waterways around the world—more than 5,000 of the lightweight watercraft have been distributed.

Deer Park Spring Water and Flying Scot continue to make the name of Deer Park known. But the once-elegant Victorian playground that was Deer Park lies within the memories of its villagers and beneath the wildflowers that blanket the open fields around the remaining cottages.

wooden furniture, and metal chimes are but a few of the offerings.

People drive 50 miles to shop at **Yoder's Market,** a plentifully stocked bulk market attached to Yoder's butchery, about one mile north of the intersection of U.S. 40 and Springs Road (Route 669). Cereals, candy, flour, pastas, dairy (butter in blocks), produce—everything you'd expect from a good Amish/Mennonite market. They sell quality meats, as you'd expect, and the prices are good on everything. Closed on Sunday.

Since it serves a large influx of seasonal visitors, **Book Mark'et,** 111 S. 2nd St., Oakland, 301/334-8778, stocks many of the latest popular titles

plus regional information. It's a comfortable place to browse, sit, and read, too.

ACCOMMODATIONS
Amish Country

The Casselman Hotel and Motor Inn, Main Street, Grantsville, 301/895-5055, www.thecasselman.com, was built in 1824 to serve travelers on the National Road, and the local handmade bricks and hand-hewn timbers and boards that are evident all over the hotel attest to the origins of the former Drover's Inn. The Casselman is now owned by a Mennonite family, the Millers, who comment in their brochure, "we believe that the finer things of life just dare not be lost in the rush of our modern day." The rooms in both the hotel and modern motor inn are simple, with much of the furniture handcrafted by members of the local community and by the Millers themselves.

For those who are looking for an inexpensive stay in the area, the Casselman is the best choice. The historic hotel features five rooms with private baths ($48–75); all 40 of the modern motor inn's rooms have a private bath, television, and telephone ($30–48). The Casselman also has a restaurant.

Elliot House Victorian Inn, an adjunct to the art and crafts colony of Spruce Village, 146 Casselman Rd., Grantsville, 301/895-4250 or 800/ 272-4090, www.elliotthouse.com, is an elegant Victorian B&B with additional guest quarters in its outbuildings. The home was built in 1870 by the Stantons, who owned and operated the nearby mill for five generations. Each of the inn's seven spacious rooms is uniquely decorated and has all modern amenities, including thick terrycloth robes, a private bath, cable television, and access to a sauna; an old-fashioned rear porch looks over several acres of riverfront paths. Bicycles are available for guests to explore the surrounding Amish farmlands. Spruce Village is literally a few steps away, as is the Penn Alps restaurant and crafts store, where a complimentary breakfast is served to guests of the Elliot House in the morning. Rates range $77–150, depending on room, day and season.

By the Lake

In addition to the hotel on resort property, Wisp owns three attractive modern properties on the lake, 20160 Garrett Hwy., Oakland, 301/387-5503, most with water views. **Will O' the Wisp** is a condominium with accommodations ranging from simple rooms to kitchen suites ($72–327 per day, $552–1,962 per week); there are also rustic cottages available in the same price range. **Lake Breez Motel** and **Lake Side Motor Court,** 20050 Garrett Hwy., 301/387-5503 x2206, www.deepcreeklakebrez.com, offer rooms with lake or garden views, indoor pool, whirlpools and sauna, exercise room and game room, and a sandy beach with docking facilities ($56–72 per

day, $350–495 per week). The Motor Court also features connecting units (two bedrooms, one bath; $68–95 per day, $375–693 per week).

Few trappings remain to let guests know that **Carmel Cove Bed & Breakfast** was once a Carmelite monastery. A short walk through the woods leads to Carmel Cove's dock, where guests may use a canoe to paddle out into the black waters of Deep Creek Lake. A tennis court, hot tub, billiards, bicycles, and sundeck add to the options. A full and delicious breakfast is served in the sky-lighted dining room, and a large common room stocked with snacks and the daily papers is a pleasant diversion. All rooms have private baths; some have decks and/or fireplaces. Carmel Cove is set among tranquil woods on Glendale Road, 301/387-0067. Rates range $95–120 per night.

Deer Park Inn, a beautiful 1889 17-room Victorian "cottage," 65 Hotel Rd., Deer Park, 301/334-2308, www.deerparkinn.com, was once part of the extensive Deer Park Resort. Built by prominent Baltimore architect Josiah Pennington, the home is now on the National Register of Historic Places. Deer Park's three spacious guest rooms will pull visitors back into the leisurely

Deer Park Inn

days of carriage rides and "taking the waters." The authentic decor is enhanced by Sandy Fontaine's beautiful arrangements of local wildflowers: bee balm, goldenrod, and Queen Anne's lace brighten every room in midsummer. Sandy's husband, Pascal, works his inimitable magic with breakfast; the omelettes, Cointreau and fruit in a melon shell basket, and plum preserves the color and clarity of garnets are almost worth the trip by themselves. Two rooms have private baths, and one room has a bath down the hall. Rates range $115–135 per night, and drop $15 for a two-day stay; all weekend reservations during the summer months must be for a minimum of two days.

FOOD

Diners and Family-Style Restaurants/Amish Country

Casselman Restaurant, located in the hotel on Main Street, Grantsville, 301/895-5266, serves simple American meat-and-potatoes dishes (breakfast, lunch, and dinner) and excellent baked goods at very reasonable prices ($7 average).

Next to Spruce Village, **Penn Alps,** 125 Casselman Rd., 301/895-5985, features an all-American menu with a few German specialties such as pork loin and sauerkraut. Breakfast ($6), lunch ($8), and dinner ($12) are served all day. May through August, Penn Alps sponsors concerts of both classical and traditional American music.

Diners and Family-Style Restaurants/The Lake

Canoe on the Run, 2622 Deep Creek Dr., McHenry, 301/387-5933, is an upscale cafe that offers casual indoor/outdoor dining. It's open early for coffee drinks and morning treats, and midday and early evening for panini/sandwiches, soups, simple entrées, and salads ($5–12).

Open seven days a week at 7 A.M., the hardworking folks at **Josie's Family Restaurant** dish up big home cooking for small prices (roast beef smothered in gravy is $9—prices average $6). This is a real family/local place; they serve until 7 P.M. on Sun. and 8 P.M. or later during the week. Josie's is on Route 135 across from the 84 Lumber Yard, 301/334-6500.

Lakeside Creamery, 20282 Garrett Hwy, Oakland, 301/387-2580, www.lakesidecreamery.com, is home to award-winning specialty flavors such as chocolate raspberry truffle, apple pie, and even vanilla—cited by the National Ice Cream and Yogurt Retailers Association. Their fudge and chocolate Muddy Creek Sundae will power a few trips around the lake, freestyle.

Continental/The Lake

Deer Park Inn, 65 Hotel Rd., Deer Park, 301/334-2308, www.deerparkinn.com, is the best place to eat dinner in Garrett County, bar none. This is not a well-kept secret, however; in spite of an 11-mile drive from Deep Creek Lake or Oakland, the small dining room was full of neatly casual diners on a Thursday night. Don't worry about not being seated; they have another dining room. However, reservations are a good idea on weekends. Charging prices ($18 average) that challenge the steak and seafood restaurants *ordinaire* around Deep Creek Lake, Chef Pascal Fontaine, formerly executive chef at the Westin Washington, D.C., trained at the Culinary Institute of Paris. He starts with locally grown and raised ingredients, and produces marvelous food with a French accent: warm Vidalia onion tart on greens; homemade pâté with port sauce; honey-glazed braised duck legs with orange, and green peppercorn sauce; rabbit with basil and tomato confit (very popular); topped off with peach crisp with vanilla ice cream.

Cornish Manor, a pleasantly revamped Victorian home, is a lovely stop for lunch, dinner, or a drink. The intimate bar is cozy and casual with a European feel, and the screened porch with a view of the surrounding old trees is a favorite on summer days. The Manor is at 830 Memorial Dr., Oakland, 301/334-6499. Prices average $6 for lunch, $18 for dinner; it's open Wednesday–Saturday.

INFORMATION

Find out everything you need to know about Garrett County by contacting Garrett County Chamber of Commerce, 15 Visitors Center Dr., McHenry, MD 21541, 301/387-4386, www.garrettchamber.com.

GETTING THERE

By Auto

The main east-west arteries that run through western Maryland are I-70 from Baltimore to Hancockm or, from Hancock to the Maryland border, I-68. Both of these four-lane speedways roughly parallel the old National Road, U.S. 40, a much slower, smaller (two-lane), and more scenic Route In Frederick County, I-270 runs north from Washington, D.C., to Frederick; in Garrett County, U.S. 219 is the main north-south Route Auto travel is by far the easiest way to get around, especially when touring the Civil War battle sites. Most of the state parks and forests in Garrett County are only accessible by auto.

By Bus

Greyhound buses run to Frederick, Hagerstown, Cumberland, Oakland, and points in between from many major cities. Routes, scheduling information, and prices can be obtained by calling 800/231-2222.

By Train

The only passenger train that touches the western region is Amtrak's Capitol Limited out of Washington, D.C. It stops in Rockville, Maryland; Harpers Ferry; and Martinsburg (on the West Virginia side of the Potomac); then arrives in Cumberland on its way to Pittsburgh. Call 800/USA-RAIL (800/872-7725) for timetables and prices, or visit Amtrak on the Web at www.amtrak.com.

North-Central Maryland

Heaven and earth never agreed better to frame a place for man's habitation.

Capt. John Smith on the Chesapeake Bay, 1608

North-central Maryland lies languidly over the top of the Chesapeake Bay like a cat in the sun. Carroll County in the west is a golden spread of farms, carrying out the legacy of the German settlers who brought their hopes packed in solid chests from the old country during the first years of the colony. During the Civil War, Confederate raiding parties periodically resupplied themselves at the expense of local towns. A small skirmish at the town of Westminster yielded a major result: rebel troops were delayed on their journey to Gettysburg, perhaps changing the outcome of that pivotal battle.

The most infamous man of that time—John Wilkes Booth—grew up in a pleasant manor house in Bel Air, about 20 miles north of Baltimore. His father, famed British actor Junius Brutus Booth, built the tree-shaded property to raise his two sons. He staged Shakespeare's plays in the manor hall.

Baltimore County continues to be an eclectic mix of upscale rural country manors and small towns, largely residential. The majority of

Chesapeake & Delaware Bridge, Chesapeake City

NORTH-CENTRAL MARYLAND

DELAWARE

PENNSYLVANIA

QUEEN ANNE'S

N. CENTRAL MARYLAND

Newark
Elkton
Chesapeake City
Cecilton
Galena
Crumpton
FAIR HILL
TAILWINDS
North East
ELK NECK STATE PARK
MOUNT HARMON PLANTATION
Georgetown
Still Pond
Kennedyville
Chestertown
CONOWINGO DAM
Port Deposit
Perryville
Havre de Grace
TURKEY POINT LIGHTHOUSE
Betterton
Fairlee
Pomona
KENT
CECIL
Conowingo
SUSQUEHANNA STATE PARK
Aberdeen Proving Ground U.S.A.
CHESAPEAKE FARMS
Rock Hall
Gratitude
Bel Air
Aberdeen
ROCKS STATE PARK
BE MY GUEST B&B
Eastern Neck Island National Wildlife Refuge
Jarrettsville
HARFORD
Hydes
Chesapeake Bay
Annapolis
LADEW TOPIARY GARDENS
Monkton
Parkton
Long Green
Lutherville
Towson
BALTIMORE
Prettyboy Reservoir
Timonium
Loch Raven Reservoir
BALTIMORE
Union Mills
PENNSYLVANIA DUTCH FARMERS MARKET
Liberty Reservoir
CARROLL
Columbia
Taneytown
Westminster
CARROLL COMMUNITY COLLEGE
Sykesville
Aspen Hill
College Park
WASHINGTON, D.C.
CARROLL COUNTY FARM MUSEUM

10 mi
10 km

VIRGINIA

© AVALON TRAVEL PUBLISHING, INC.

FOR SALE: ASSASSIN'S HOUSE, NEEDS TLC

Tudor Hall, childhood home of John Wilkes Booth, assassin of Abraham Lincoln, is a graceful Gothic-style house at the end of a tree-shaded cul-de-sac in Bel Air, Maryland. Also famous as the birthplace of Shakespearean theater in the United States, the home sits on eight acres, surrounded by hickory, beech, spruce, oak, and magnolia trees.

The house was built in 1847 by Junius Brutus Booth, a renowned Shakespearean actor who moved to Maryland from his native England. Both his sons, John and Edwin, became noted actors. After John assassinated President Lincoln in 1865, Junius Booth lost the property. Ownership changed hands over the years; Howard and Dorothy Fox purchased Tudor Hall in 1968.

The Foxes played host to small theatrical productions and converted the home into a museum, but were forced to let the property run down because of mounting financial trouble. The Foxes died within weeks of each other in 1999, each without a will. Their heirs decided to sell Tudor Hall.

Harford Community College trustees and others keen on preserving Tudor Hall worried that it would be torn down. The home is listed on the National Register of Historic Places, but there is no legal prohibition against razing it.

Tudor Hall's fate attracted interest from Hollywood: Actors Hal Holbrook and Stacy Keach joined a nonprofit group called the Preservation Association for Tudor Hall, and both pledged to help restore the property if Harford Community College bought it. Keach performed at the college to raise money to preserve the Booth property. "Are we going to allow it to become a condominium? It's sacrilege," he said.

The college, the only buyer to emerge publicly after the death of the former owners, offered to pay $293,000, which included about $50,000 each from the state and county. The college's offer was $68,000 more than the property was worth under an appraisal by an expert the college hired. The 11-room, two-story brick house badly needed fresh paint, roof repairs, and other restoration that could run as high as $850,000. The college wanted to transform Tudor Hall into a museum and center for theater lovers.

A lawyer for the estate of Tudor Hall's owners said $400,000 was a fair price, and that he was all for conservation, but the college's offer was too low. "This is not a trailer park stuck in the middle of nowhere. This is a darn fine piece of land," he said. "If this county is interested in historical preservation, they ought to be fair to the people who own it and pay fair market value."

In October 1999, the property was sold at auction for $415,000 to a local couple who planned to make it their residence. "We're disappointed that the Shakespearean history programs cannot be built at the home site," Harford College president Claudia Chiesi said after the auction. Stacy Keach added, "Hopefully, this wonderful couple will have an interest in preserving the legacy of the Booth family."

Tudor Hall has taken on a new life as Tudor Hall Museum Bed and Breakfast (410/838-0466).

Maryland's wineries are here in the sunny north, in addition to many of the state's top horse-breeding farms.

Harford and Cecil Counties combine bucolic scenery with high-speed highways; dreamlike parks embrace the area's major waterway, the Susquehanna River. The Susquehanna River/Chesapeake Bay confluence was a crucial transport area during colonial times—the British destroyed Havre de Grace, the town at the river's mouth, during the War of 1812. Colonial ports, both sleepy and active, provide plenty of attractions for visitors. Chesapeake City is, after all, the western terminus of the busiest canal in America. This gentle countryside is spiced with a pinch of ballplayer (Aberdeen is Cal Ripken's hometown) and a pound of heavy metal (the U.S. Government Ordnance Museum, also in Aberdeen).

Kent County is an in-crowd destination for sailors, boaters, and watermen. Rock Hall and Chestertown offer historic charm and plenty of good places to eat. This is also an area that begs the participation of cyclists—long, narrow, mostly untrammeled roads slice through whispering wheat fields to weave along miles of glittering bay and marshland.

In addition to cycling, north-central Maryland is the place to come for freshwater and bay fishing. The neat, quiet towns could have inspired Norman Rockwell.

Westminster and Carroll County

Carroll County remains determinedly untouched by urban encroachment. Westminster is the largest town, distinguished by a college and a healthy helping of history. The rolling hills of the Piedmont glow green in the evening light, much as they did when this area served as a crossroads for movement of both Northern and Southern troops during the Civil War.

SIGHTS

Carroll County Farm Museum

In 1837, Carroll County built an almshouse that provided work and shelter for indigent men and women; they lived in separate quarters in the main house and an adjoining building. The almshouse stayed in operation as a self-sufficient working farm until 1965. The original almshouse building has been remade into a typical 19th-century farmer's home, and the property has been reborn as the Carroll County Farm Museum, 500 S. Center St., Westminster, 410/848-7775.

The farmhouse offers a treasure trove of Victorian antiques, many of which were donated by Carroll County families. One of the most interesting aspects of the farmhouse was the pioneering use of power generated by gas from fecal matter—a form of recycling that we could probably benefit from today. Workers filled the 1,000-gallon metal tank on the north side of the building approximately 90 percent full of water. To this they added manure—chicken, pig, human, and cow. This was mixed to a consistency of pea soup with about 7 percent solid to 93 percent water. The tank was tightly closed. In a couple of days, gas was formed by the action of bacteria. The gas was roughly 60 percent methane and 35 percent carbon dioxide. Very little pressure was built up, so the gas had to be pumped to the light fixture system in the house. There was enough gas to operate several gas fixtures for nearly a week. Additional gas was produced by adding more manure to the top of the tank and drawing away the liquid from the bottom of the tank—the liquid was used for fertilizer. This simple system was used between 1850 and 1900.

The museum shows the self-sufficiency that was necessary for survival during the days when farm families worked their land, produced their own food, soap, and household goods, and spun wool into yarn for clothing and house linens. On the farm, visitors can watch artisans demonstrate period crafts; children will want to pay their respects to the ducks, horses, chickens, turkeys, pigs, goats, and lambs on the surrounding grounds. The museum tells the story of each farm animal and the purpose it served during the 19th century, whether for field labor, food, or clothing. Another kid-pleaser is the two-headed calf in the veterinarian's room, though adults might prefer the display of "tramp art," constructed from tiny bits of wood and glue by transients passing through the almshouse.

The County Farm Museum has numerous outbuildings beyond the farmhouse. There's a one-room schoolhouse, a springhouse where jars of food were kept cool, a general store, smokehouse, broom shop, garden, saddlery, blacksmith shop, and wagon shed, among others. The general store, reminiscent of the 1800s, sells items made by museum craftspeople, souvenirs, and old-fashioned candies. Among the carriages and sleighs in the wagon shed is the buggy that made the rounds for the first rural mail delivery service in America, begun in

N. CENTRAL MARYLAND

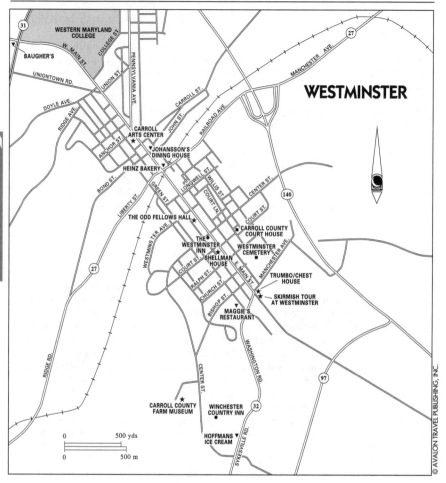

N. CENTRAL MARYLAND

Carroll County. On the original route between Westminster and Uniontown, 2,700 pieces of mail were delivered, in addition to a pig and two live chickens, over the years. Though we take mail service for granted, many of the locals objected to rural mail delivery because it interfered with regular trips to town to pick up mail and socialize. Another fascinating piece of Americana in the carriage shed is an 18-foot bobsled; when launched from the hill on the west side of town, the sled could reach a velocity of 70 mph on its way to the east side of town.

The Carroll County Farm Museum has several events during the year. In June, the Deer Creek Fiddlers' Convention features a day of dobros and banjos; a guitarist and bluegrass competition draws some of the best musicians in the region. Antique cars, steam engines, and home-cooked food star in early September during Steam Show Days. The third weekend of September is reserved for the Maryland Wine Festival. Maryland's wineries offer tasting of their vintages and provide a variety of cuisines to sample.

The museum is open July–Aug. Tues.–Fri. 10 A.M.–4 P.M.; from the first weekend in May through October 29, it's open weekends noon–5 P.M. Admission is $3.

The **Esther Prangley Rice Gallery** in Peterson Hall on the campus of McDaniel College is a free fine-art museum open Mon.–Fri. noon–4 P.M.

The **Carroll Arts Center,** 91 W. Main St., 410/848-7272, is in a newly renovated 1937 art deco theater. It includes a 263-seat audience hall where concerts, lectures, films, and plays are presented, as well as a large art gallery.

More art is on display at the **Scott Center for Fine and Performing Arts** at Carroll Community College, 1601 Washington Rd., 410/386-8000. Exhibits generally focus on county and state artists.

Skirmish at Westminster Tour

On June 27, 1863, General J. E. B. Stuart crossed the Potomac into Maryland with three brigades of Confederate cavalry, numbering nearly 6,000 men. He was on his way north to rendezvous with General Jubal Early. The next day, Stuart learned of the approach from Washington of a large Union wagon train. He succeeded in intercepting 125 supply wagons and their contents south of Carroll County. The poorly equipped Confederate forces welcomed the supplies; however, the wagon train and prisoners slowed the marching pace of the cavalry to a shuffle.

Moving on a parallel path west of the Confederates, Union major general John Sedgwick's Sixth Corps (a total of 18,000 men) marched north through Carroll County towns, passing

N. CENTRAL MARYLAND

SPOOKY CARROLL COUNTY

Carroll County—and Westminster in particular—is so pretty, many visitors are loath to leave. Sometimes, however, their extended stays aren't brought about by a love of the rolling farm country. The old Odd Fellows Hall, 140 East Main St., which served as a barracks during the Civil War, had one such resident. During the 1800s, the hall served as a local theater and venue for traveling performers. The town's businesspeople, farmers, and their families would gather on Saturday night to enjoy an evening of comedy, music, or drama. One traveling jokester was Marshall Buell of Alabama. Dressed in a shabby outfit, Buell kept up a topical monologue, liberally laced with jokes about President Grant and other government officials. Some Grant supporters were not amused, and expressed their displeasure by throwing a rock onto the stage. A second rock struck Buell in the neck. Shaken, Buell quickly finished his performance and exited the stage. Refusing the sheriff's offer of protection in the jail overnight, Buell explained he'd be on his way to Hagerstown for his next performance. As he saddled his horse in the darkness behind the hall, Marshall Buell was attacked. He was discovered lifeless, his throat slit ear to ear. Soon after, the town drunk reported seeing a "spirit-like" figure gesturing dramatically and mouthing a wordless monologue in back of the hall. No one believed him— except those who visited the theater the following Saturday night. There, they witnessed the ghost of Marshall Buell, still expounding—silently—on the defects of the president and his cabinet. Wonder what he'd have to say about the current administration?

The Carroll County Historical Society and Visitors Center now occupies 210 East Main St., the Kimmey House. During the mid-1800s, it was the home of Dr. George Collgate, who expanded his home to create office space for his medical practice. This small-town doctor had many a loyal patient, and it was not uncommon for his waiting room to be full to overflowing. Though most of the visitors to the house these days come to the historical society's administrative offices or library, occasionally personnel meet up with one of Dr. Collgate's patients, still waiting to see the doctor after 150 years. And you thought your insurance program was bad!

Stop by the visitor center for a copy of the "Ghost Walk" brochure, which features many more haunts in town (one of several walking tours offered). The Carroll County Public Library offers guided "Ghost Walks" in the fall; for more information, call 410/848-4250.

through New Windsor and Uniontown, a few miles west of Westminster, on June 29 and 30. There, some of the men, including Captain David Acheson, wrote to their families: "All look anxiously for news from Pennsylvania. I hope this is but the beginning of the final defeat of the rebs." Acheson died in Gettysburg, three days later.

Continuing on his way north, Stuart moved to cut off communications between Washington and the Army of the Potomac; his men tore up tracks of the B&O Railroad at Hoods Mill and Sykesville and set fire to two small bridges, one of them at Piney Run, all in the southern part of Carroll County. A cotton factory was raided, and the Confederate soldiers used the belts from the factory's machinery to replace the soles of their boots.

Stuart approached Westminster on June 29. Shortly before noon, units of the First Delaware Cavalry, commanded by Major Napoleon B. Knight, with Captain Charles Corbit and Lieutenant Caleb Churchman as company commanders, arrived in Westminster to guard the rail and road junction in the town. They numbered less than 100 men. They joined a detachment of the 150th New York Infantry—numbering fewer than 20—who had already occupied Westminster as a provost guard for several months. **The Odd Fellows Hall,** 140 E. Main St. (built in 1854, now the Opera Printing Company), was headquarters for the 16-man detachment of the New York Infantry.

Reports of approaching Confederates were brought to the Union troops by a doctor visiting a patient in the country. Union major Knight was incapacitated—rumored to be drunk. In his absence, Captain Corbit immediately gathered his men and led a charge through the streets of Westminster toward the Washington Road. They expected to meet a small unit of Confederates, but instead found themselves confronting the front ranks of Stuart's veteran cavalry. A fierce skirmish ensued, and the little unit of Union forces was quickly overpowered; many were captured, including Corbit and Churchman. Knight escaped to Baltimore to give a stirring account of an encounter he had never seen.

The historical marker commemorating **Corbit's Charge** is on the corner of E. Main Street and Washington Road. The **Trumbo/Chest House,** circa 1830, 297 E. Main St., was in the line of fire of the charging Confederate cavalrymen on the Washington Road to E. Main Street. The side of this home has bullet marks from the battle. **Carol County Court House,** built in 1838, had a large Union flag flying from the cupola. The flag was torn down and carried away by Stuart's men following the engagement. Thirteen ladies of the town of Westminster had sewn the flag and signed their names on the stars. As Stuart's men marched through the town, they passed the **Shellman House,** 206 E. Main St. There, little Mary Shellman shouted "Johnny Red Coat" as General Stuart passed by; he dismounted, and told her that her punishment for allegiance to the Union would be a kiss—he pecked her cheek, remounted, and rode on.

During the skirmish, two were killed, 11 were wounded, and a few managed to make their escape down the Reisterstown Road, pursued by Confederates. Local physicians and citizens cared for the wounded on both sides in improvised hospitals in Westminster. The **Crouse House,** built in 1850, 325 E. Main St., was used as a temporary hospital. The Westminster Cemetery on North Church Street was the site of the Union Meeting House used as a hospital. Local physicians treated the wounded of both sides here. The site is marked by an iron urn near the flagpole.

That night Stuart's five-mile-long column bivouacked along the Littlestown Pike between Westminster and Union Mills. The clash on the edge of town between General J. E. B. Stuart's cavalry and a small unit of the Delaware cavalry slowed the progress of the advancing Confederates. Instead of proceeding immediately into Pennsylvania to warn General Robert E. Lee about advancing Union troops, Stuart's cavalry was delayed long enough to spend the night in the Westminster area. Confederate brigadier general Fitz Lee spent the night sleeping in the orchard at the Shriver Homestead; men and horses rested for the first time since crossing into Maryland on June 27. General Stuart spent the night in Westminster and joined his troops in Union Mills early the next morning. The outcome of Gettysburg might have been different if Stuart had arrived before July 2.

Union Mills Homestead

The homestead, 3111 Littlestown Pike, Union Mills, 410/848-2288, is the family home of the Shrivers (Sargent Shriver, philanthropist, politician, and Kennedy in-law, is a prominent member, as is Maria Shriver, journalist and wife of Arnold Schwarzenegger), and both house and mill are open to the public for guided tours. The homestead was first claimed in 1797 when brothers David and Andrew Shriver purchased a large tract of land along Big Pipe Creek. The waterway provided an excellent source of power for milling, the valley was good, fertile farmland, and the surrounding rolling hills contained heavy stands of black oak that could furnish tanbark for processing hides.

Soon the brothers constructed a gristmill, tannery, and sawmill. The businesses took the name Union Mills because of the partnership of the two brothers and their various enterprises. Andrew's strong support of Thomas Jefferson earned the homestead a post office; later, a general store was added, and the homestead became a thriving crossroads settlement. For a time, the original house was opened as a stagecoach inn, which accommodated both Washington Irving and John James Audubon as overnight guests.

The original double house built for David and Andrew Shriver is now the center of the present-day main house. As Andrew's family expanded, so did the house, growing from six rooms to 23.

Until the mid-1960s, the homestead was continuously occupied by different generations of Andrew Shriver's descendants. The house is filled with a wide range of original family furnishings from the 1700s to the 1900s; a room will often blend the styles of Federal, antebellum, and late Victorian periods. Andrew Shriver was a great admirer of Thomas Jefferson and copied his front balcony from Jefferson's home at Monticello; Supreme Court Justice Roger Brooke Taney and attorney/poet Francis Scott Key both delivered speeches from this "Jefferson balcony."

SPURNING "NORTHERN SCUM"

In summer of 1862, the South was energized by its many victories over the superior numbers and weaponry of the North. Having freed Virginia from Northern troops, and more significantly, once again having acquired the productive Valley of the Shenandoah for Confederate supplies, Lee turned his campaign northward to the border state of Maryland. At that time, Richmond, Virginia, was being flooded with refugees and Southern sympathizers from Maryland who claimed that they were being held in the Union by force, and that most citizens of that state were waiting for an opportunity to be free to join the South. A popular song at the time (and now the Maryland anthem) stated this position:

The despots heel is on thy shore
Maryland! My Maryland!
His touch is on thy temple door,
Maryland! My Maryland!
Avenge the patriotic gore
That flecked the streets of Baltimore,
And be the Battle-queen of yore,
Maryland! My Maryland!

I hear the distant thunder hum,
Maryland! My Maryland!
The Old Line's bugle, fife, and drum,
Maryland! My Maryland!

She is not dead, nor deaf, nor dumb,
Huzzah! she spurns the Northern scum,
She breathes, she burns, she'll come,
she'll come,
Maryland! My Maryland!

Union Mills's most fascinating piece of history takes place during the Civil War. The Shriver family—much like the rest of the state of Maryland—suffered divided loyalties. Andrew K. Shriver's family supported the Union, while directly across the road, his brother William Shriver's family supported the Confederacy. Each family had sons in the respective armies. Just before the battle of Gettysburg, on June 29, 1863, J. E. B.

N. CENTRAL MARYLAND

Stuart's Confederate cavalry rode into the homestead orchard around midnight. The family awoke to the sight of horses and soldiers filling the yard and surrounding the house. William Shriver's family fed the hungry soldiers flapjacks; the young men grabbed them off the griddle before they were cooked. When morning broke, the rebel cavalry departed toward Hanover, Pennsylvania, with T. Herbert Shriver as their guide. William Shriver entertained the Confederate officers at breakfast and J. E. B. Stuart charmed the gathered Shriver family by singing, "if you want to be a bully boy, jine the cavalry." Shortly after the Confederates left, the Union soldiers arrived. Major General George Syke's Fifth Infantry Corps camped in the surrounding fields, and Andrew K. Shriver's main house became headquarters for the Union division commander. The daughters sang and danced with Union soldiers in a room off the front hall that has been referred to ever since as the "dancing hall." These soldiers also departed for Gettysburg. For the next four days the windows rattled from the cannon fire of the Battle of Gettysburg while the families awaited the outcome.

After the war, the homestead returned to its prosperous business enterprises. As time passed, modern factories replaced small family businesses and the Shriver family moved on. Today, the gristmill represents an excellent example of a working mill, with the wooden water wheel, gears, parts, and frame painstakingly re-created. Rye, whole wheat, buckwheat, and two kinds of cornmeal are ground in the mill and offered for sale. Union Mills Homestead has several special events throughout the year, chiefly the Annual Flower and Plant Market on the first weekend in May, and the Corn Roast Festival the first Saturday in August, which features a fried chicken dinner and all the roasted corn you can eat. The house and mill are open June 1–Sept. 1, Tues.–Fri. 10 A.M.–4 P.M., Sat.–Sun. noon–4 P.M. During May and September, the house and mill are open Sat.–Sun. noon–4 P.M. only. A donation is requested.

Backcountry Driving/Biking Tour

This 24-mile round-trip route takes you past a variety of terrains common to Carroll County. The route is moderately hilly, and has a short stretch of dirt road that may be difficult for both cars and bikes in wet weather. Fourteen miles of the trip—the first and last segments—are on main roads, though traffic is light. The Carroll County Visitors Center, listed under Information, offers a variety of bike routes that cover the county. All distances are approximate in the following tour.

The route starts at the juncture of Main Street and Pennsylvania Avenue in downtown Westminster. Head directly north on Pennsylvania Avenue (which becomes Littlestown Pike) for seven miles until you reach the settlement of Union Mills. Continue on the Pike for .6 miles, then turn left (south) on Murkle Road for two miles. Turn right (west) on Stone Road, continue for 3.3 miles. Turn left (south) on Robert Arthur Road (this .9-mile connector road is gravel-covered but in good shape). It dead-ends on Mayberry Road. Drive south on Mayberry Road 1.5 miles to Old Taneytown Road; jog to the left on Taneytown Road and continue south on Clear View Road for 1.6 miles. Turn left (south) on Trevanion Road for 1.5 miles to Uniontown. Uniontown remains much as it was at the beginning of the 20th century. Turn left (east) on Uniontown Road and return six miles to downtown Westminster.

SHOPPING

Carroll County has two farm markets of note. The **Carroll County Farmers Market** originated in 1971 as an outlet for farmers to sell locally grown produce. Free weekly demonstrations—including cooking, basketry, flower arranging, craft lessons, and selling tips—are scheduled each Saturday throughout the summer. The market is free and operates in enclosed buildings in a smoke-free environment. Fresh produce, baked goods, crafts, ceramics, baskets, jewelry, tole-painted items, wood items, furniture, quilts, and more are for sale. Special markets are planned for Easter and Christmas. The farmers market is held at the Agricultural Center on Smith Avenue overlooking the Carroll

County Farm Museum, and is open Saturdays, mid-June–early Sept., and mid-Nov.–mid-Dec. For more information call 410/848-7748.

The **Pennsylvania Dutch Farmers Market of Westminster** is held year-round on Thursday 10 A.M.–6 P.M., Friday 10 A.M.–8 P.M., and Saturday 9 A.M.–4 P.M. The information number is 410/876-8100; the market is located at the intersection of Route 140 and Route 97 south, near the Crossroads Square shopping center. Old Order Amish, Mennonites, and other local vendors display their produce and products including fresh meats, seafood, baked goods, and soft pretzels, and crafts such as stained glass, handmade jewelry, clothing, handmade quilts, oak furniture, and other items.

ACCOMMODATIONS

It's difficult to recognize **The Westminster Inn,** 5 S. Center St., Westminster, 410/876-2893, for the schoolhouse it once was. The building went up in 1899, and though memories of chalk dust may still cling to some corners, it has been transformed into one of Maryland's most elegant and romantic bed-and-breakfast inns. Each of the guest rooms is decorated in traditional style, with a queen-size bed and private hot tub. Guests of the inn also have complimentary use of a fitness club with pool, aerobics classes, and weight equipment next door. The Westminster Inn offers 13 guest rooms at rates ranging $95–195.

Deluxe in every way, **Antrim 1844 Country Inn,** 30 Trevanion Rd., Taneytown, 410/756-6812 or 800/858-1844, www.antrim1844.com, is one of the county's most beautiful getaways. In the main house (the mansion), nine guest rooms have been restored and redone with antiques, fireplaces, canopy feather beds, and marble baths or double Jacuzzis with panoramic views of the surrounding countryside. Thirteen additional guestrooms are located in the outbuildings, and each has its own fireplace and is furnished with a different theme, such as "The Ice House," with the atmosphere of an English cottage set in formal gardens, and "The Barn" with two rooms, each with its own private deck overlooking woods and a brook.

A formal breakfast is served around 9:30, often featuring the house specialty, Belgian waffles. Antrim also offers a dinner menu and special events throughout the year. Rates range $160–300.

FOOD

Winchester Country Inn, 111 Stoner Ave., Westminster, 410/857-0058, www.winchesterinn.freeservers.com, was built on the county's original land grant during the 1760s by the founder of Westminster town and is one of Carroll County's oldest buildings. The pine boards on the floors were polished by the comings and goings of the builder's 10 children. The inn serves afternoon tea—scones and bottomless pots of tea—in the Gypsy's Tea Room.

Though the tract was initially named Winchester, there was much confusion in the early days between Winchester, Maryland, and Winchester, Virginia; the town solved the problem by renaming itself Westminster. In 1986, the Winchester Country Inn and grounds were completely restored, combining the area's rich natural beauty with present-day comforts, such as private baths. The home, however, retains its rustic and somewhat rough charm.

The interior has been refurbished with period antiques; many pieces were donated by prominent Carroll County families or are on loan from the Winchester Historical Society. The Winchester Country Inn is one of the most authentic and refreshing country inns open to the public; in addition, it serves the community. In 1983, a professor at Western Maryland College recognized a need to educate and train developmentally disabled people in the area. He started an organization, which he named Target, with $500 from his savings account. Target owns the Winchester Country Inn and uses it as a training facility for jobs in the hospitality industry (it also owns the Inn at Sawmill Creek near Deep Creek Lake). It's open Tues.–Sat. 11 A.M.–4 P.M.

Heinz Bakery, 42 N. Main St., Westminster, is highly recommended for baked goods of all types. There's a parking lot next to the building for quick stops.

A great place for home-style cooking, **Baugher's Country Restaurant,** 289 W. Main St., Westminster, 410/848-5541, www.baughers.com, offers produce in the front (there's a U-pick orchard, too), country breakfasts and dinners such as turkey and stuffing and meatloaf and mashed potatoes inside, and fresh fruit pies topped with ice cream. It's open for breakfast, lunch, and dinner daily. Prices range $1–12.

Johansson's Dining House, 4 W. Main St., Westminster, 410/876-0101, is the kind of place where a diner can sink into a big leather chair and watch the world go by. The restaurant serves a tasty, sophisticated menu of soups and salads, big burgers, and specials such as veal Oscar, chicken marsala, and a variety of fresh seafood. Lunch entrées average $8, with burgers, salads, and sandwiches slightly less. Dinner entrées average $14. It's open Sun.–Thurs. 11 A.M.–10 P.M., Fri.–Sat. 11 A.M.–midnight. The large dining room is accessed through the bar, which may be packed and smoky at happy hour and beyond, but don't miss the chance to see the old-fashioned paddle fan whirling away above the heads of the crowd.

Maggie's Restaurant, 310 E. Green St., Westminster, 410/848-1441, is open seven days a week. Mon.–Sat., hours are 11:30 A.M.–11 P.M. (the bar stays open until 2 A.M.). On Sunday, the restaurant hours are 11:30 A.M.–10 P.M. (the bar is open until midnight). An average price for lunch is $9 and an average price for dinner is $15. This is a popular local place, and the casual American menu is well prepared.

For dessert, head out to **Hoffmans' Ice Cream,** 934 Washington Rd., Westminster, 410/857-0824, www.hoffmansicecream.com, for some strawberry cheesecake, peanut butter ripple, or one of a dozen other flavors of handmade ice cream.

INFORMATION

The Carroll County Visitors Center has a wealth of information on the area, including a fine series of walking tours of the various towns, driving tours of Civil War sites, and an excellent series of bike tours for all levels of fitness. The office is at 210 E. Main St., Westminster, 410/848-1388 or 800/272-1933, www.carr.org/tourism.

Baltimore County

Baltimore is moving north—of that there is no doubt. Boundaries between the towns that once surrounded the city are disappearing, but the northern part of the county remains wooded, softened with open farmland. The winery business is still being fledged in Maryland, though this area boasts one of America's pioneer vintners. Almost all of Maryland's wineries are clustered in the north-central counties.

SIGHTS

Wineries

At **Boordy Vineyards,** 12820 Long Green Pike, Hydes, 410/592-5015, www.boordy.com, 85 percent of all wines produced are crushed from their own grapes—a rarity in this area. In addition to the northern Maryland property, Boordy also owns vineyards on South Mountain in west-ern Maryland near Burkittsville. Boordy is one of America's pioneer vineyards, and its founder, Philip Wagner, is credited as one of a handful of vintners who revived a crippled industry.

During Prohibition, 1917–1933, untended vineyards and the loss of knowledge of high-quality winemaking came close to destroying America's wine industry. When Wagner published *American Wines and How to Make Them* in 1933, it was thought to be the only available book of its kind in the English language. During Prohibition, Phillip Wagner learned of the vidal blanc grape, which was the basis for a significant portion of the wines of France, yet was largely unknown to the American public. On a tour of duty in Europe as a war correspondent for the *Baltimore Sun* a few years later, he and his wife, Jocelyn, collected vines and brought them back to Maryland. The first vidal blanc vine in the United States was

HORSE COUNTRY

The Preakness is part of a long equine tradition in the mid-Atlantic. From colonial days, Marylanders have always appreciated fine horseflesh in motion.

Modern fox hunting is thought to have originated in Maryland. Early-17th-century settlers were more involved in the necessities of hunting for food, but as they came to be more comfortable with their new home, necessity evolved into sport. Foxhounds—dogs specially bred for a speedy run over rough terrain—became a valuable commodity in the state. Riders followed the baying hounds and fox, testing their horsemanship and mounts to the utmost; a good long run was the goal. A hunter's horse was prized for stamina rather than great jumping ability, though leaping rooks and rail fences was expected. Early hunts easily lasted a week, spaced out by overnight visits to the homes of friends and participants. Fox hunting was considered a sport for gentlemen. Horse racing, on the other hand, was for everyone.

Returning tobacco ships brought Arabians and Near Eastern horses, imported to be interbred with English and European stock already in the colonies. Race meets were established on the peninsulas between rivers, and began to attract the elite, including Colonel George Washington of the Virginia militia. Jockey clubs—exclusive groups of breeders and bettors—were formed at Marlboro, Chestertown, Annapolis, Port Tobacco, Leonardtown, and other ports on both shores of the state. Many towns have a Race Street—either the location of the actual track, or the road to it.

brought wrapped in a wet towel in Jocelyn's toilet case. This variety, which had superior disease resistance, made a well-balanced wine; it's now widely planted throughout the eastern United States. The Wagners set out their vines and began making wine in quantity. In 1965, Boordy Vineyards pioneered the *sur lie* process in America, where wine is "left on the lees" (the crushed grapes and seeds—lees—remain in the wine tank) for a brief period to add flavor, aroma, and complexity. The practice is common in California wineries today. Boordy's fame was greatly enhanced by Philip Wagner's reputation as an author on the subject of American winemaking. His classic, *Grapes Into Wine,* has been repeatedly revised and reprinted over the decades.

The R. B. Deford family, longtime friends of the Wagners and grape growers for Boordy Vineyards for many years, took over the Boordy name in 1980 and moved operations to their farm north of Baltimore. Rob Deford, who received formal training in enology at the University of California, Davis, set a new course for Boordy. He updated much of the equipment, adding new French and American oak barrels for aging. With the introduction of the three-time gold-medal-winning Boordy Nouveau in 1981, Rob Deford became the first Maryland vintner to produce and market quality early-release wines.

Today the winery continues to garner the accolades of the wine world: Eisling 2000 was named dessert wine of the year, and Tom Burns was named Winemaker of the Year by Maryland's Wineries. Boordy's original three standard table wines—a white, red, and rosé—have expanded to include varietals, port, and champagne.

One of Boordy's most interesting outreach programs is One Straw Farm, a community-supported organic farm that provides fresh vegetables for each participant who buys a share. Shares, sold around the beginning of May, cost $500, and the farm provides each shareholder with 25 weeks of fresh, in-season, organic produce. In addition, Boordy offers shareholders a 15 percent discount on wines.

Special events and concerts are held frequently on the property; call for details. The winery is open Mon.–Sat. 10 A.M.–5 P.M., and Sunday 1–5 P.M. throughout the year. Tours are given on the hour daily 1–4 P.M.

Woodhall Wine Cellars, 17912 York Rd., Parkton, 410/357-8644, is another ambitious winery north of Baltimore. Like many French wines, all Woodhall wines (with one exception) are blends from different sources or different varietals. The single exception is a Vineyard Reserve cabernet sauvignon from Copernica Vineyards in northern Maryland.

Boordy and Woodhall are the two oldest wineries in Maryland. Founded in 1983, Woodhall is a small family-owned operation; it produces a full range of table wines, including dry, sweet, and dessert styles. Wines are further segmented into three groups: inexpensive everyday wines, midpriced premium wines, and complex "super varietals." In the last few years, three Woodhall wines, Seyval, Riesling, and Copernica Reserve cabernet sauvignon, have been selected as Best-of-Show wines at the Maryland Governor's Cup Wine Judging. Woodhall Riesling was selected by the Goddard Space Center as one of three 40th Anniversary wines. Maryland Public Television selected Woodhall's cabernet sauvignon as its 30th Anniversary wine. And Woodhall Seyval was the "Aquarium White" of the National Aquarium in Baltimore.

The annual Harvest Winefest weekend draws more than 1,000 people during October to watch and participate in the Woodhall harvest, in addition to enjoying an afternoon of music, crafts, food, and wine. Woodhall features other special events throughout the year. On a daily basis, tours and tastings include barrel samples of various wines on request. The winery is open Tues.–Sun. noon–5 P.M.

The Fire Museum of Maryland

This large building, though a bit hard to find at the back of a parking lot, 1301 York Rd., Lutherville, 410/321-7500, warehouses and displays a spiffy restored collection of more than 50 hand-drawn, horse-drawn, and self-propelled fire engines and other fire-fighting apparatus. The collection represents manufacturers as early as 1822 up to 1957 from several states, Massachusetts to Tennessee.

The museum was opened in 1971 as a private, nonprofit corporation by Stephen Heaver and his eldest son, Stephen Jr. The quality and breadth of the collection makes this one of the finest fire-fighting equipment museums in the United States. The rigs are spit-shined by a staff of dedicated volunteers. Special exhibits include a fire alarm telegraph network, a display of fire company badges, a uniform collection, and information about Baltimore's high-pressure pumping system. This collection is an excellent opportunity for those who enjoy fire-fighting memorabilia and who appreciate technological design and development.

The museum is behind the multistory Heaver Plaza Office Building, one block north of exit 26 B (Lutherville) on I-695 (the Baltimore Beltway). It's open May–Oct., Sunday 1–5 P.M.; weekday tours are available by appointment. Admission is $2.

Harford County

Though some visitors to Harford County never get beyond the boundaries of I-95 on their way to Philadelphia or Baltimore, this area is home to several scenic small towns with plenty of amenities, several verdant parks, and the busiest canal in America—the Chesapeake & Delaware Canal, stretching from the Delaware River below Wilmington to pretty Chesapeake City. Ladew Topiary Gardens is legendary among those who appreciate fine gardens—a little bit of England in the Maryland countryside—and for a unique experience, stop by the U.S. Army Ordnance Museum in Aberdeen.

HAVRE DE GRACE

"Graceful Harbor" sits at the mouth of the Susquehanna River, a location that was explored by Captain John Smith in the mid-17th century; however, recent sources claim that Victor Hernandez, a Spaniard, beat John Smith by a good 75 years, exploring the upper bay in 1588. A ferry crossing was established at the mouth of the Susquehanna in 1695. The area was not chartered as a city until 1783, when it was a bustling town of seven houses. The city grew, and the old Post Road—now U.S. 40—was alive with stagecoaches traveling between Baltimore and Philadelphia; Havre de Grace narrowly missed (by one vote) becoming the nation's capital. The small port continued to grow, but in 1813, the British attacked the town and most of the structures were destroyed or damaged.

The Susquehanna and Tidewater Canal was completed in 1840, and opened all of central Pennsylvania to two-way trade between Philadelphia and Baltimore. The 45-mile canal ran from Havre de Grace to Wrightsville, Pennsylvania; the mule-drawn canal boats had to be raised a total of 233 feet through the use of 29 lift walks. The canal boats moved about 3 mph, and a trip took two days. The Susquehanna and Tidewater Canal enjoyed its most profitable years around 1870. It shut down, a victim of railroad competition, in 1900.

Fishing and boat-building added to the transport of grain and lumber as sources of income.

After the Civil War, coal and the canning industry brought new money into the economy. In the 20th century, tourism accounted for the city's continued growth. A thoroughbred racetrack opened in 1912; direct trains from Philadelphia and New York to the Havre de Grace track were filled with racing fans who had come to see Whirlaway and other major competitors in the 1940s. The track closed in the 1950s, a victim of political maneuvering. By that time, the commercial market for waterfowl was long gone as well, though sport waterfowl hunting continued to be an attraction that lured many to the city.

Though the canal and racetrack are memories, there are more than 130 structures within the city limits that are of historic significance, and the town is deemed a National Historic District. Havre de Grace is a popular overnight destination for a quiet getaway from Baltimore or Philadelphia.

Sights

The **Havre de Grace Decoy Museum,** 215 Giles St., 410/939-3739, documents and interprets waterfowl decoys as an art form and chronicles the art and use of decoys on the upper Chesapeake Bay. The museum houses one of the finest collections of working decoys ever assembled. An extensive research library complete with works on types of decoys, carving, waterfowl, and the environment is available by appointment. There's a fine museum gift shop with a selection of working and art decoys, reference books, and other waterfowl-related items. On many weekends, contemporary decoy carvers from the Chesapeake Bay exhibit and demonstrate their craft.

Decoys were originally made for one purpose: to lure waterfowl for hunters. The early decoys were not fancy—sometimes little more than crudely carved blocks of wood. Each maker had his own ideas of what ducks and other waterfowl looked like and made his decoys accordingly. The museum follows the development of decoy carving from a purely practical endeavor to a form of American folk art. In addition, the museum chronicles the history of waterfowl hunting in the upper Chesapeake. An abundance of ducks during spring and fall migrations was the

© JOANNE MILLER

skipjack *Martha Lewis*, Havre de Grace

N. CENTRAL MARYLAND

primary draw for visitors into the area in the early 20th century. Overhunting and changing environments eventually caused the duck population to fall off radically, which led to a ban on hunting; the museum's display on the development of boats, guns, duck calls, a re-creation of a carving shop, and related items recalls an earlier time.

Annual special events include the Decoy, Wildlife Art and Sports Festival, held the first weekend of May. The museum is open daily 11 A.M.–4 P.M. Admission is $5.

The **Susquehanna Museum of Havre de Grace at the Lockhouse** is in a small park at the end of Conesteo Street, 410/939-5780. The museum contains the locktender's house, constructed about 1840, which served as both the office for the Susquehanna and Tidewater Canal and the home of the lock-tender and his family—a portrait of the last lock-tender, painted in 1889, hangs in the parlor. The lower floor consists of a restored office, parlor, rear office, kitchen, and gift shop. The second floor features a historical display room; a short video on the history of the canal is available for viewing. Just in front of the house is the outlet lock, and over it is a reconstruc-

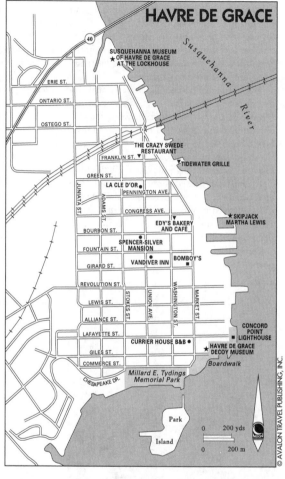

HAVRE DE GRACE

SUSQUEHANNA MUSEUM
★ OF HAVRE DE GRACE
AT THE LOCKHOUSE

ERIE ST.
ONTARIO ST.
OSTEGO ST.
FRANKLIN ST. ▼
GREEN ST.
JUNIATA ST.
ADAMS ST.
LA CLE D'OR ●
PENNINGTON AVE.
CONGRESS AVE.
BOURBON ST.
EDY'S BAKERY AND CAFÉ
FOUNTAIN ST.
SPENCER-SILVER MANSION
GIRARD ST.
VANDIVER INN
BOMBOY'S
REVOLUTION ST.
LEWIS ST.
STOKES ST.
UNION AVE.
WASHINGTON ST.
MARKET ST.
ALLIANCE ST.
LAFAYETTE ST.
CURRIER HOUSE B&B ●
CONCORD POINT LIGHTHOUSE
GILES ST.
HAVRE DE GRACE
★ DECOY MUSEUM
COMMERCE ST.
Boardwalk
CHESAPEAKE DR.
Millard E. Tydings Memorial Park

THE CRAZY SWEDE RESTAURANT
▼ TIDEWATER GRILLE
★ SKIPJACK MARTHA LEWIS

Susquehanna River

40

Park

Island

0   200 yds
0   200 m

© AVALON TRAVEL PUBLISHING, INC.

tion of the original pivot bridge that was opened and closed by hand to permit the passage of boats. The lockhouse is open weekends 1–5 P.M., May–Oct. Admission is $2.

The **Concord Point Lighthouse,** at the foot of Lafayette Street, is the most photographed and painted subject in the city. Built in 1827, it was one of eight lighthouses in the northern bay, and was part of an effort to improve the flow of goods down the Susquehanna River from Philadelphia to Baltimore. The construction of these structures coincided with the opening of the Chesa-

peake & Delaware Canal. The Concord Point lighthouse, at the juncture of the Susquehanna River and Chesapeake Bay, was in continuous operation for more than 150 years. The interior of the lighthouse is open to the public 1–5 P.M. on weekends May–Oct. There is no charge for admission. Near the lighthouse is a small cannon used in the defense of Havre de Grace when the British burned and sacked the town in 1813.

Early in the 20th century, V-bottom, double-sail boats known as skipjacks were a common sight on the Chesapeake Bay. Today, these work-

Susquehanna Museum of Havre de Grace at the Lockhouse

ing dredge boats that once made up the Chesapeake Bay oyster fleet are few. The *Martha Lewis,* docked at the end of Congress Avenue, is one of the last to fish commercially under sail in the United States. The skipjack, which is maintained by the Chesapeake Heritage Conservancy, offers several opportunities to come aboard, including a five-hour discovery classroom; a five-day Chesapeake Heritage Adventure that includes collecting and recording estuarine data; sailing classes; and an opportunity to work with a dredge crew hauling oysters. The *Martha Lewis* also offers 90-minute cultural explorations of the Susquehanna flats, the area where the Susquehanna River meets the Chesapeake Bay, on Thursdays and weekends Apr.–Oct., weather permitting (always check for hours of operation). For reservations and information, call 800/406-0766 or contact the Conservancy on the Internet at www.newmc.com/martha_lewis.

Shopping

The first few blocks of Washington Street and St. John Street offer a variety of low-key boutiques and antique shops. Book lovers will enjoy **Washington Street Books and Antiques,** 131 N. Washington St., 410/939-6215, a compendium of new and used books, crystals, incense, et al. **Courtyard Bookshop** specializes in used, out-of-print, and antiquarian books; it's at 313 St. John St., 410/939-5150. **Antique Mart,** 232 Washington St., houses dealers specializing in furniture, jewelry, and glassware.

The least-formal antique stores are on Market Street between Bourbon and Congress Streets.

Accommodations

The **Vandiver Inn,** 301 S. Union Ave., 410/939-5200 or 800/245-1655, is one of the most extensively restored buildings in Havre de Grace. Dating from 1886, the building had fallen into disrepair; the current owners found, repurchased, and reinstalled the original stained-glass windows that had been removed from the house. The Vandiver Inn also offers a candlelit dinner by reservation on Friday and Saturday evenings in addition to overnight accommodations. All eight guest rooms have private baths (though one is not in the room), and all are furnished in an understated Victorian style. Room rates range $75–105.

The **Spencer-Silver Mansion,** 200 S. Union

Ave., 410/939-1485 or 800/780-1485, www .spencersilvermansion.com, is another of Havre de Grace's large historic houses, and is the only Victorian stone mansion in the city. The structure was embellished with a two-story bay window, tower, gables, a dormer, and a variety of other architectural effects when it was built in 1896 for merchant and foundry owner John Spencer. Later, Charles Silver, a local cannery owner, purchased the house. The Mansion offers two rooms with private baths, two rooms that share a bath, and a carriage house with whirlpool bath and working fireplace. Children are welcome. Expect to pay $70–140 per night.

Also recommended: **Currier House Bed and Breakfast,** 800 S. Market St., 410/939-7886, janec@currier-bb.com. Members of the Currier family had lived in Cecil and Kent Counties since 1648, and Matthew Currier moved into the house named after him in 1861. The house has been modified since then, and now offers four guest rooms, all with private bath. Rates range $85–95.

La Cle d'Or Guesthouse, 226 N. Union Ave., Havre de Grace, 888/HUG-GUEST (888/484-4837), www.lacledorguesthouse.com, is housed in the historic 1868 Henry Harrison Hopkins House (the family home of Johns Hopkins of medical fame), and decorated in post–Civil War period style. Rates start at $110.

And another, out of town in nearby Forest Hill, **Be My Guest B & B,** 2414 Rocks Rd., 410/838-8943, is surrounded by gardens and features made-to-order breakfasts and massage by appointment. The Victorian house has two rooms, but only one is rented at a time, as there's one bath between them ($100). One room is available in the former blacksmith's shop next door with full bath ($125).

Food

One of my favorite places in Havre de Grace is **Bomboy's,** 322 Market St., 410/939-2924. This little shop makes a celebrated brand of homemade ice cream, and has a steady flow of local traffic through its old-fashioned ice cream parlor. They keep 28 flavors in stock at all times, and develop their own specialties, such as "Hokey-Pokey," chocolate malt ice cream with chunks of chocolate fudge. Across the street at 329 Market St., a new Bomboy's facility showcases amazing homemade chocolates and gives tours of the chocolate-making process upon request.

Edy's Bakery and Café, on the corner of Washington and Congress Streets, is a popular place to stop for coffee and a light snack.

The **Tidewater Grille,** on the water, 300 Franklin St., 410/939-3313, is appreciated by visitors and locals alike. The menu features the ubiquitous crab cakes plus filet mignon, prime rib, pastas, and chicken. It's open daily for lunch and dinner; lunch entrées average $10, dinner is slightly higher.

The **Crazy Swede Restaurant,** 400 North Union Ave., 410/939-5440, is part bar, part eating establishment. As the evening wears on, the dining room may get a little smoky. It serves American pub food, lunch and dinner, and Sunday brunch. Lunch fare includes tuna steak sandwiches, fried oyster sandwiches, and burgers and salads. The pub menu averages $6. Dinner entrées such as beef, veal, lamb, seafood, and pasta average $16 or $17. It serves breakfast only on Sunday from 10 A.M.–2 P.M., with a variety of egg dishes and pancakes.

OTHER SIGHTS

Ladew Topiary Gardens

This manor house with extensive formal landscaping, 3535 Jarrettsville Pike, Monkton, 410/557-9466, was created by Harvey S. Ladew, who had two abiding interests: fox hunting and gardening. The small piece of Eden he created has been deemed by the Garden Club of America as "the most outstanding topiary garden in America," and his home charmingly reflects his interests in horses and hounds.

Though many visitors are drawn to the outstanding topiary displays, especially the bounding fox and hounds on the front lawn and the swan hedge in back of the manor house, the house itself is not to be missed. Mr. Ladew's collection of ceramics, silver, and paintings portray clever foxes, noble horses, and eager hounds—and the framed photographs that decorate the house testify to his friendships with American and British notables, including the Duke and Duchess of Windsor. The rooms are elegant but comfortable, and the oval library, which has been highlighted in several architectural publications, has a secret swinging panel that leads to a card room in a separate building nearby.

The gardens are laid out in more than 20 separate areas with different themes, sometimes based on color, such as the pink garden or the yellow garden with its pagoda, or built around a sculpture like the Temple of Venus or a unique horticultural item such as the golden rain tree. Some part of the garden is in bloom spring through fall; azaleas and tulips are followed by irises, hydrangea, and chrysanthemums. Though the gardens and house require a special trip, this is a destination not to be missed for anyone who admires a casual country-gentry style and a thoughtfully designed garden that reflects years of planning and care.

The house and gardens are open from mid-Apr.–Oct., Mon.–Fri. 10 A.M.–4 P.M., Sat.–Sun. 10:30 A.M.–5 P.M. From Memorial Day to Labor Day, they're open Thursday evenings until 8 P.M. Visitors can tour both house and gardens ($10) or the garden only ($5).

Ripken Museum

This museum, adjacent to the visitor center, 8 Ripken Plaza, Aberdeen, 410/273-2525, is the embodiment of Ripken mania—for Orioles fanatics, this is a tiny slice of baseball heaven. Photographs, World Series memorabilia, and artifacts tell the story of the Ripken empire, beginning with father Cal Sr. and continuing with his two sons, Cal Jr. and Billy. All three played in 1987 for the Orioles: Cal Sr. managed the team and his sons were the team's heavy hitters. The museum brings the whole family into the act, though; according to one of the photographs, the boys' sister Elly had the best batting average of them all in adolescence. The museum also features a film about Cal Jr.'s life and a video on his famous consecutive-game streak that broke Lou Gehrig's record in 1995. The museum is in the old City Hall building in downtown Aberdeen, one block north of U.S. 40. In summer, it's open Friday

and Monday 11 A.M.–3 P.M.; Saturday 11 A.M.–4 P.M.; Sunday 11 A.M.–3:30 P.M. The rest of the year, weekday hours are 11 A.M.–3 P.M. with weekend hours the same as during the summer. Admission is $5.

U.S. Army Ordnance Museum

Attention combat fans: This weapons warehouse, Aberdeen Proving Ground, Aberdeen, 410/278-3602, contains enough cannons, machine guns, fuses, bombs, and handguns (all inactive and under glass) to arm the most violent Hollywood film. Among the thousands of pieces of ordnance on display are a veritable Divided Nations of weapons from Japan, Russia, and Vietnam, among others. Oddly, the overall impression is not of mass destruction, but rather a fascination with the technical aspects and machined precision of each piece. There is a beauty in these dormant weapons. On the mezzanine, a 58-pound body armor suit worn by EOD (Explosive Ordnance Disposal) personnel is on display next to a panel explaining bomb disarmament via fuse removal—not a career for the wimpy.

One less aggressive display asks the question "What has the Ordnance Corps done for you?" and provides several answers. ENIAC, the Electronic Numerical Integrator and Computer, developed by the Ordnance Corps, is the great-granddaddy of all modern computers. The Ordnance Corps also developed miniaturization by creating a tiny radio transmitter that would fit into the fuse of an artillery projectile—the forerunner of today's portable radios and hearing aids. America's ubiquitous sport-utility vehicles developed from the Ordnance Corps' World War II Jeep. The U.S. Army Ordnance Corps dates to the early days of the American Revolution when, in 1775, the Continental Congress appointed a "Commissary General of the artillery stores" to provide necessary ordnance material. The Ordnance Corps' "Flaming Bomb" insignia, adopted in 1832, is the oldest military insignia in the U.S. Army.

The U.S. Army Ordnance collection came into being in 1918 when the Westervelt Board met in France and determined a need to evaluate the use of artillery during World War I in order to

© JOANNE MILLER

U.S. Army Ordnance Museum

make recommendations concerning future policies. The Ordnance Corps collected all types of artillery, bullets, and gas masks to study and evaluate. Over time, the museum's collection expanded from artillery equipment to include small arms, military vehicles, aircraft bombs, fire-control equipment, and armored fighting vehicles. In 1942, a foreign material section was established.

Though the collection was nearly liquidated after the Vietnam War, a group of local citizens formed a foundation to save it, and built and donated the museum's current home. Its mission now is to collect, preserve, and account for historically significant weapons that relate to the history of the U.S. Army Ordnance Corps and the evolution and development of American military ordnance material from the colonial period in America to the present.

The Ordnance Museum is surrounded by a large park filled with more than 225 tanks and assault vehicles. It's a great place for a stroll and to exercise your imagination, whether it is in the form of memories or thankful thoughts that these behemoths are at rest.

Whatever your feelings about weapons, the U.S. Army Ordnance Museum offers a unique opportunity to view a collection that can be found nowhere else in the world. The museum is open daily 10 A.M.–4:45 P.M. The Mile of Tanks and the park are open every day during daylight hours. Admission is free, donations requested. You must stop at the Guard Gate on Route 40 to show your identification and car registration, which gets you a pass to enter the museum.

Susquehanna State Park and Rocks State Park

A woodsy getaway, these parks, adjacent to each other and accessed at 3318 Rocks Chrome Rd., Jarrettsville, 410/557-7994, offer 3,600 acres of activities for the visitor. The parks are in the Susquehanna River Valley, and have considerable river frontage on the Susquehanna River and Deer Creek. Susquehanna State Park encompasses two smaller recreational areas: Palmer State Park, a 486-acre primitive area, runs along Deer Creek off Forge Hill Road; and a timber management area, the Stony Demonstration Forest, has several miles of primitive hiking trails (call the park office for more information). Rocks State Park maintains the park office for both Rocks and Susquehanna State Parks. Both are open year-round from 9 A.M.–sunset. The campground is open May 1–Sept. 30. Some portions of the parks are closed in the winter months. Call the park office for specifics.

Fishing: The Susquehanna River offers excellent fishing opportunities for striped bass, large- and smallmouth bass, perch, catfish, shad, walleye, carp, and bluegill. This portion of the Susquehanna River is a saltwater fishing area, and a bass sport license is needed.

Boating: A boat launch facility is accessible 24 hours every day at Lapidum landing, at the south end of the park off Lapidum Road. There is a fee to use the boat launch, and the area is equipped with restrooms and boat-trailer parking.

Historic Area Walking Tour: The visitor center at the end of Rock Run Road contains several historic buildings. The Rock Run Gristmill was built in 1794; it's open weekends May 1–Oct. 31 10 A.M.–6 P.M. Grinding demonstrations are 1–4 P.M. The Rock Run House is a stone manor built by James Archer before the Civil War. Archer was a brigadier general in the U.S. Army who resigned to join the Confederacy. He was wounded and captured at Gettysburg July 1, 1863, and died shortly after being exchanged. The house is partially restored and contains furnishings and antiques from the era. The Toll House was built for the toll collector who annexed fees to use the bridge that crossed the Susquehanna River at Rock Run. The bridge was destroyed in 1856 by ice floes during the great freeze that year. The Toll House now displays information on forestry and is the main information center at Susquehanna State Park.

The privately owned and operated **Steppingstone Museum** features rural farm exhibits dating 1880–1920, and is open weekends May–Sept., 1–5 P.M. Admission is $5. Call 410/939-2299 for more information.

Hiking: The parks have nine marked trails ranging from .9 miles to three miles in length. Difficulties vary, and each trail offers a unique view of the terrain. The Ivy Branch trail, an easy-to-moderate two-mile trail, crosses farm fields, while the Deer Creek trail, a moderate-to-difficult 2.1-mile trail, has magnificent views of giant trees.

A BRIDGE OF ICE

For some years, the Philadelphia, Wilmington & Baltimore Railroad had tried to get permission from Maryland's State Legislature to build a bridge across the mouth of the Susquehanna River. The bridge would not only extend the railroad's reach, but would release it from financial dependence on ferries and riverboats. Politics were not the only obstacle; swirling currents, unpredictable depths, and winter ice all made the project a risky one. "The big freeze" in the winter of 1853 provided a perfect solution to the PW&B's problems. The mouth of the Susquehanna and much of northern Chesapeake Bay froze solid. Boat traffic was at a standstill, and the railroad attempted to push its bridge once more through the legislature. Sole opposition came from the village of Port Deposit, which claimed a structure across the mouth of the river would not only hinder navigation when the ice finally dissipated, but would obstruct the passage of broken ice into the Chesapeake, causing water to back up and flood the town. A compromise was finally reached, with the railroad agreeing to build a branch line into Port Deposit. Yard by yard, a wooden bridge was built, using the ice as a base. When the $1.5 million project was nearing completion, a tornado struck on July 25, 1866, blowing most of "the great engineering feat" into the bay. Rebuilding started immediately, and the completed bridge spanned the distance between Havre de Grace and Perryville. In November 1866 the bridge opened to traffic, making the route from Philadelphia to Washington by train uninterrupted for the first time in history.

Picnicking and Swimming: The Deer Creek picnic area is on Deer Creek at the northern end of the park and may be reached from the historic area by Stafford Road, which runs parallel to the Susquehanna River. Deer Creek is popular for tubing, swimming, and canoeing, though there are no lifeguards. Deer Creek is also a freshwater fishing area.

Overnight Facilities: Restrooms and hot showers are available at each of the two campground loops. The park offers 74 campsites, and a fee is charged on a per-night/per-site basis. Reservations can be made by calling the park office.

Getting There: Susquehanna Park is three miles northwest of Havre de Grace. From I-95, take exit 89 for Route 155. Proceed west on Route 155 to Route 161. Turn right (north) on Route 161, then right (east) on Rock Run Road. Follow Rock Run Road to the park office.

Conowingo Dam Driving Tour

This approximately 38-mile tour begins at the intersection of Route 22 and I-95 north of Aberdeen, passing through farm country, forest, and river towns. The Conowingo Dam was built as a W.P.A. project during the Depression, and it's easy to see the art deco roots of its design when approaching it on old U.S. 1. The dam is open for tours on the first Saturday of each month or by appointment; the visitor center is open weekdays 10 A.M.–4 P.M., 410/457-5011.

Drive north on Route 22 for approximately five miles to the village of Churchville. Turn right (east) on Route 155 and continue through wooded and rolling farmland to Route 161. Turn left on Route 161 (north); you'll pass one of the entrances to Susquehanna State Park on this road, so if you'd like to stop for a picnic, this would be a good place to do it. Otherwise, continue north on Route 161 to the village of Darlington. At the intersection of U.S. 1, turn right (east) and cross the Susquehanna River on the Conowingo Dam. On the other side of the dam (you're now in Cecil County), turn right on Route 222 (south) and drive through Port Deposit, a working-class village that grew from a mill and ferry built around 1725. In the 1800s, Port Deposit was a booming shipping center, and plans are afoot to revitalize it. There is a casual little museum here, with household items and letters from the Civil War, but hours are intermittent—if you're interested, make sure to call ahead (**Paw Paw Museum,** 98 N. Main, 410/378-3086). Continue to follow Route 222 south to I-95. From here, you can return west to your original starting point, or continue on to the village of North East.

ACCOMMODATIONS

Havre de Grace has a number of graceful Victorian inns on its tree-lined streets. In addition, the **Four Points Sheraton Hotel,** 980 Hospitality Wy., Aberdeen, 410/273-6300 or 800/346-3612, is a safe bet for a clean, modern lodging. Rooms and suites range between $89–169.

INFORMATION

Harford County information is available from the Harford County Tourism Council, Inc., 3 W. Belair Ave., Aberdeen, MD 21001, 410/272-2325 or 800/597-2649, harfordmdtourism@msn.com, www.harfordmd.com. Havre de Grace also has its own visitor center and tourism commission, 450 Pennington Ave. (P.O. Box 339), Havre de Grace, MD 21078, 410/939-3303 or 800/851-7756, www.hdgtourism.com.

Cecil County

The land/water connection deepens in Cecil County. Two villages whose livelihood was indelibly linked to the north bay marshes and the flora and fauna of the area are the main attraction here, in addition to two exceptionally beautiful parks.

VILLAGE OF NORTH EAST

North East is a charming village that once had a very tough reputation. However, the rowdies have been gone for more than a decade; nowadays visitors come to North East to enjoy its excellent restaurants, its variety of shops, and its proximity to Elk Neck State Park and Turkey Point Lighthouse.

North East has a number of historic buildings, including St. Mary Anne's Episcopal Church, first built in 1706, destroyed by fire, and rebuilt during the colonial era. The church retains much of its original exterior, and for special services continues to use a Bible and Book of Common Prayer presented in 1718 by Queen Anne of England. Another historic building houses the Upper Bay Museum.

Upper Bay Museum

This collection, at the end of Walnut Street in the town park, 410/287-2675, is sheltered in a structure built in 1880, originally a fish house, where the daily catch was stored and sold. The Upper Chesapeake Bay enjoys a rich history of water-related industry and commerce. It's the site of the famed Susquehanna flats, one of the nation's finest hunting spots for waterfowl; in the past the area attracted such highly visible sportsmen as J. P. Morgan and Grover Cleveland. Wildfowl hunting was once primarily a commercial venture; now it is exclusively a recreational sport.

The heritage of both the commercial and recreational hunter is preserved by the Upper Bay Museum. It features an extensive collection of hunting, boating, and fishing artifacts native to the Upper Chesapeake. Commercial hunting was outlawed at the beginning of the 20th century due to diminishing populations of waterfowl; however, many watermen continued to make their living by attracting waterfowl within the range of their guns. Of particular interest are the outlawed gunning rigs and sculling oars used by bushwhackers to ensure near-soundless movement of the hunter's skiff. The museum exhibits a rare punt gun, which was outlawed in 1918. The massive shotgun, primarily a tool of market hunters, often weighed more than 100 pounds and measured 12 feet in length, nearly as long as the boat that held it; a hunter didn't aim the gun, he aimed the boat.

In spite of what may look like a waterfowl wipe-out celebration, the museum is dedicated to the propagation and conservation of waterfowl and upland game, and to the improvement of their environments. It only makes sense; without prey, there are no hunters. The museum also features a fine collection of carved decoys, antique marine engines, and miniatures depicting the vessels of the Chesapeake Bay.

The Upper Bay Museum is open Memorial Day–Labor Day, weekends 11 A.M.–4 P.M. Admission is $4.

Shopping

Route 272 runs through the center of town, and most of the shops and restaurants are on the southern side, a.k.a. Main Street. A few of the shops of note are **Charing Cross Books,** 32 S. Main St., 410/287-0022, an eclectic bookstore; a tiny shop called **Schoolhouse Gifts,** 122 S. Main St., "gifts for the young at heart"; and **England's Colony on the Bay,** 505 S. Main St., 410/287-5575, which features locally carved decoys, models, and other crafts, as well as books, tapes, and CDs. England's Colony on the Bay is located in one of several refurbished century-old buildings in town.

One of North East's unusual shops is the **Day Basket Factory,** 714 S. Main St., 410/287-6100, www.daybasketfactory.com. The factory was started shortly after the end of the Civil War in 1876, when brothers Edward and Samuel Day came to North East from Massachusetts. They had been supplying the Southern market with baskets for picking cotton, and decided to ply their trade in North East both to save on shipping costs and because of the abundant supply of white oak, the best wood for basketmaking. Baskets are still made in back of the factory by local craftsmen, and a large variety of shapes and sizes are available for sale. In addition, the front of the factory rents stalls to individual sellers of antiques and collectibles.

Accommodations

Tailwinds Farm, 41 Tailwinds Lane, North East, 410/658-8187, www.fairwindsstables.com, offers guests canopied beds in a Victorian home on a working horse farm. Kids can visit the farm animals and help gather the eggs from the henhouse; after a hearty breakfast, guests may choose to take a riding lesson, or travel 10 minutes down the road to Fair Hill Natural Resources Management Area for a trail ride or a carriage ride with the innkeepers, the Dawsons. Stall rentals are available for horse owners who prefer to bring their own. Tailwinds offers many programs for children and families during the year, and this is a particularly beautiful setting. Rooms are $75 per night, and stall rentals are $25 (no canopied beds, but a lovely bag of oats makes up for it).

A hybrid of a country inn and a standard hotel, the **Crystal Inn,** 1 Center Dr. (exit 100 off Route 272), 410/287-7100 or 800/631-3803, offers the amenities of a hotel, such as a pool, fitness center, and cable TV, combined with the smaller size, free local telephone calls, and continental breakfast of an inn. The Crystal Inn is quiet and clean, and popular with families; it offers a number of specials throughout the year. Rates range $89–169, with discounts for AAA and AARP cardholders.

Sunset at the **North Bay Bed and Breakfast,** 9 Sunset Dr., 410/287-5948, is the best time of day—unless you count breakfast. Guests often take a bottle of wine and two borrowed wine glasses down to the Adirondack chairs at the end of the lawn to watch the Chesapeake turn gold. This beautiful and stylish home, a long green lawn away from the headwaters of the Chesapeake Bay, is popular with visitors year-round. All of the guest rooms offer a view of the bird-filled forest or the Chesapeake; the guest rooms are on the upper floor, and four rooms share two baths, unless only two rooms are booked. Hosts Bob and Pam Appleton also offer custom packages that include a half- or full-day sail on their beautiful 50-foot Gulfstar yacht, *Journey.* Pam, a former customer service manager, creates a formidable breakfast, and Bob, in addition to being a Coast Guard–licensed captain and sailing instructor, still works as a corporate trainer and motivator. A few miles south of North East off Hances Point Road, quiet country surroundings and warm hospitality make this B&B a special place to stay with reasonable rates. Children are welcome with forewarning, but Dusty, the resident kitty, requests no pets. Overnight accommodations plus a custom sailing package range from $145–650. Visitors may also charter the boat.

Food

Woody's Crab House, 29 S. Main St., 410/287-3541, is definitely the hot spot in North East for lunch and dinner. The restaurant offers every kind of sea creature that can be found in the Chesapeake, and a few more from out-of-town, like Alaskan king crab legs and Prince Edward Island mussels. Where else can you find a steamed sack of 50 shrimp for $15? They even have a vegetarian sack with steamed carrots, broccoli, corn on the cob, etc., for $9. Meat-eaters need not fear: there are also burgers and chicken, plus a good selection of draft and bottled beers and wines. Lunch averages $7, dinner about $15. Kids will love the roasted peanuts served as appetizers; shells just get swept away on the floor along with errant bits of crab shell. Woody's also owns the ice cream shop next door, for a sweet finish.

Just down the street from Woody's, **Windows on Main** in **Moore's Tavern,** 107 S. Main St., 410/287-3512, offers a similar menu and prices. Lunch is served Wed.–Mon., dinner Thurs.–Sun.

VILLAGE OF CHESAPEAKE CITY

This small town packs some serious appeal. Crossing over the massive and graceful Chesapeake & Delaware Bridge that spans the mouth of the C&D Canal, the rooftops appear much as they did 100 years ago when the village grew to serve the needs of the busy canal. The canal is still in operation today, and Chesapeake City has become a "boutique town," with inviting shops and excellent restaurants. Attractions are located in the historic district of South Chesapeake City, on the south side of the bridge, unless indicated.

Chesapeake & Delaware Canal Museum

The C&D Canal Museum is set in the canal's original pumphouse in a park next to a public marina. There are picnic tables available to enjoy the beautiful view of the canal, bridge, and 30-foot replica of the Bethel Bridge Lighthouse, one of many wooden lighthouses in use before 1927. The museum tells the story of the C&D canal from its beginnings in the 17th century to its present use as the busiest canal in the United States. Working models of locks, and the original power plant for the giant water wheel that pumped water to raise water levels in the canal locks, are on display. Follow Second Street south of town until you see a sign on the left for U.S. Army Corps of Engineers; follow that road to the parking lot. The museum is open year-round, Mon.–Sat. 8 A.M.–4 P.M. Free.

Shopping

The two "downtown" blocks of Bohemia Avenue are where you'll find the **Back Creek General Store,** a place for antiques and cards, **Horn & Hound Art Gallery, McKeown Art Gallery,** and other shops offering a day's diversion. The street ends in the Pell Garden, a small public space with a beautiful view of the canal. The **Bohemia Café & Bakery,** a block away at 2nd and George Streets, is a good stop for breakfast treats or just a cup of coffee.

Accommodations

The following inns are open year-round.

The **Ship Watch Inn** is right on the water, 401 1st St., 410/885-5300. It offers eight rooms with private baths, $90–115 during the week; $105–140 on the weekend.

The **Inn on the Canal,** 104 Bohemia Ave., 410/885-5995, has a view of the water and features six guest rooms, all with private bath, for $75–130.

The appropriately named **Blue Max Inn** is a big blue Victorian a block up from the water at 300 Bohemia Ave., 410/885-2781. It offers seven rooms with private baths, $95–135.

Food

The Bayard House, 11 Bohemia Ave., S. Chesapeake City, 410/885-5040, www.bayardhouse .com, serves sophisticated cuisine that would knock the socks off any gourmet. The ingredients aren't unusual—crab, rockfish, breast of duck— but the treatment and presentation are top-notch. The view helps too; windows open out onto the busy and varied boat traffic of the canal; it's especially beautiful at sunset, when the boats are lit and the water becomes blue-purple. In warm weather, the patio outside is open to guests. I tried a dish unique to Maryland here: cooked fish roe. Nothing like caviar, it had the taste and texture of a pork/fresh fish sausage—I'm a lifelong fan. The Bayard House is open daily year-round

for lunch and dinner. Lunch averages $15, dinner is around $22.

Schaefer's Canal House, Bank Street, 410/885-2200, is an old fixture of North Chesapeake City, on the north side of the C&D bridge. It features an Eastern Shore menu, with plenty of seafood, chicken, and beef choices, as well as Austrian specialties. Weather permitting, there's an outdoor deck. It's open 7 days a week; during the summer it opens at 8 A.M. for breakfast and the kitchen closes down at 10 P.M. (9 P.M. on Sundays). The average lunch prices are $10–14, and dinner entrées are $20–26. There's a seafood buffet for dinner on Thursday; Sunday, brunch is served 10 A.M.–3 P.M.

OTHER SIGHTS

Fair Hill Nature and Environmental Center

If you've seen the film *Beloved,* starring Oprah Winfrey and Thandie Newton, you'll know why this 5,600-acre partially developed park is so popular with area residents. Besides providing ethereal scenery for that film, which was set in the mid-19th century, Fair Hill features 40 miles of trails winding among woods, rolling hills, and streams; the routes are shared by bikers, hikers, and equestrians. It is unspoiled and uncrowded. Many of the county's outdoor events take place here, such as the annual steeplechase races, Highland Gathering Scottish Games, and the Cecil County Fair. Fair Hill is at the intersection of Route 273 and Route 213, 410/398-1246. A stable that offers trail rides, carriage rides, hayrides, and pony rides is inside the entrance to the park on Route 273; it may be reached directly by calling 410/620-3883.

Both of Cecil County's covered bridges are near Fair Hill. Gilpin's Falls bridge is alongside Route 272 north of I-95, and Big Elk Creek bridge is in the park itself.

Elk Neck State Park and Turkey Point Lighthouse

Lush forest covers 2,200 acres at the tip of a peninsula crowned by **Turkey Point Lighthouse,** one of the bay's oldest in continuous operation.

AMERICA'S BUSIEST CANAL

America's busiest canal and the third busiest in the world, the Chesapeake and Delaware Canal is 14 miles long, 450 feet wide, and 35 feet deep, and connects the Delaware River with the Chesapeake Bay and the Port of Baltimore. The eastern terminus is at Reedy Point in Delaware.

In the mid-1600s, a Dutch envoy and mapmaker, Augustine Herman, proposed that a waterway be built to connect the two bodies of water. The canal would reduce the water route between Philadelphia and Baltimore by nearly 300 miles. More than a century passed; in the mid-1760s, surveys were taken, but construction on a waterway was not begun until 1804. Over the next 20 years, the canal suffered a number of setbacks, and construction waxed and waned with the amount of available money. In 1824, canal construction resumed, using the labor of more than 2,000 men who dug and hauled dirt from

© JOANNE MILLER

The park, at the end of Route 272, offers a sandy beach for swimming, boat rentals, a snack bar, gift shop, miniature golf, and 10 miles of hiking trails. The lighthouse can be reached by one of the trails; it stands on a bluff 100 feet above the Northeast River and Elk River, which flow together to form the Upper Chesapeake Bay. There are facilities for trailers and motorhomes, tent sites, and rustic cabins for rent. For more information, call 410/287-5333.

The state park is set in the **Elk Neck Forest,** 3,500 acres that feature hiking, and shooting and archery ranges. Seasonal primitive camping is also available. For information, call 410/287-5675.

Mount Harmon Plantation

This beautiful plantation may be out of the way, sitting as it does on an inlet of the Sassafras River on the southern border of Cecil County, but if your time and its hours coincide, it's worth the effort. From a historical point of view, this 1730 manor house and outbuildings atop an isolated knoll give a genuine picture of country life in colonial times. The house is on Mount Harmon Road, off Grove Neck Road (Route 282) and hours vary, but visitors may be able to make an appointment to tour the manor house, outside kitchen, and tobacco prize house by calling 410/275-8819.

Cecil County Driving Tour

Cecil County offers visitors an audiotape that focuses on the history of the area starting in the town of Elkton and ending in Frederick-the ditch by hand, working with picks and shovels for an average daily wage of $.75. The waterway was finally open for business in 1829, one of the most expensive canal projects of its time (though not because of workers' wages).

Mule and horse teams pulled freight and passenger barges, schooners, and sloops through the canal. Lumber, grain, farm products, fish—everything needed for daily life—made its way between the big cities.

Loss of water from the locks was a problem early on. As boats passed through at Chesapeake City, the equivalent of a full lock of water drained into the lower-lying portion of the canal. This made it necessary to devise a means of uplifting water back into the upper part of the project. A steam pump was purchased in 1837 to raise water from Back Creek, and a steam engine and large water wheel were installed at the pump house in Chesapeake City (now the C&D Canal Museum). The water wheel, powered by steam, remained in continuous use through the mid-1920s.

In 1919, the canal was purchased by the federal government and designated part of the Intra-Coastal Waterway. The eastern entrance, originally at Delaware City, Delaware, was relocated south to Reedy Point, and all locks were removed as the waterway was converted to a sea-level operation at 12 feet deep and 90 feet wide. In the years since then, ships collided with bridges and traffic strained the canal's capacity, necessitating constant improvements; the canal has been periodically widened and deepened.

Today's canal is electronically controlled, and carries 40 percent of all ship traffic in and out of the Port of Baltimore. A U.S. Coast Guard–certified pilot—a sailor with special knowledge of the areas he or she covers—steers vessels engaged in foreign trade through the canal, Delaware River, and Chesapeake Bay. Traveling east to west, a Delaware River and Bay pilot boards the ship as it passes through Lewes, Delaware, and guides the vessel up the Bay and into the canal through to Chesapeake City. The changing of the pilots takes place at Chesapeake City, as a private launch maneuvers alongside the vessel and a Maryland pilot climbs aboard via the ship's gangway, Jacob's ladder, or port entrance. The new pilot takes over and continues the ship's transit into the Chesapeake Bay to Baltimore or Annapolis.

town and Georgetown, on the border of Kent County. The complete tour takes about two hours. One fascinating tidbit revolves around Elkton's famous marriage industry, which flourished in the 1920s and '30s. Unlike the surrounding areas, Elkton demanded no waiting period and no blood tests for prospective brides and grooms—sort of an eastern Las Vegas. Though the law changed in 1938, ballplayers Babe Ruth and Willie Mays, singer Billie Holiday, Bert Lahr (the cowardly lion in *The Wizard of Oz*), and John and Martha Mitchell of Watergate fame were all married in this small town (though not to each other). One wedding chapel still remains open for business in case you have the urge to merge.

The audiotape is available at shops around the county or may be ordered directly from the county for $6 by calling 800/CECIL-95 (800/232-4595).

Elk River Tours

Captain David B. Gulick runs charter cruises on the upper Chesapeake and rents canoes and kayaks. His boats dock in Chesapeake City next to the Chesapeake Inn; call 443/466-3237 or email Captaindavid@elkrivertours.com.

INFORMATION

Cecil County's office for tourism is at One Seahawk Drive, Suite 114, North East, MD. For information, call 800/CECIL-95 (800/232-4595), or surf to at www.seececil.org.

GETTING AROUND

Cecil County has a public water taxi service, the **Dreams Float Water Taxi,** which travels the shores of North East and Charlestown on weekend evenings. The taxi runs from 5 P.M. on Fridays, from 3 P.M. on Saturdays and from 1 P.M. on Sundays; fare is $5. Call 443/350-3431.

Kent County

The word "typical," as in "Kent is a typical tidewater county," implies ordinary, and Kent County is anything but. In fact, many of the roads traveled in Kent County, called Chesapeake Country, are part of a recent designation as a National Scenic Byway. This is the only National Scenic Byway in the state of Maryland. Kent County's portion of this Byway is Route 213 from the Chester River Bridge to Georgetown and the Sassafras River. Route 20 from Chestertown to Rock Hall also shares this honor, as well as Route 445 from Rock Hall to Eastern Neck National Wildlife Refuge.

The long, flat roads invite cyclists, the marshes are exceptional bird-watching territory, and the towns of Chestertown and Rock Hall each offer visitors unique charm. This is a very beautiful place—it's no wonder so many visitors come here and decide to stay.

CHESTERTOWN

People come to Chestertown to attend Washington College, a four-year institution that once had the reputation of being a major party school, and many never leave. As a result, Chestertown has all the attractions of a big college town, in a verdant rural setting.

Chestertown was founded in 1706 and became an important port of entry in colonial times. Merchants who made their fortunes in foreign trade in the 18th and 19th centuries built several of the stately homes on Water Street. A driving/walking tour that details the history of Kent County and Chestertown may be picked up at the Kent County Visitor Center.

The Schooner Sultana

The *Sultana* is an exact replica of a 1767 cargo schooner that was later used by the British Royal Navy to patrol the Chesapeake, Delaware, and Narrangansett Bays. *Sultana* is one of the most thoroughly documented American-built vessels from the colonial period. Her lines, logbooks, crew lists, and correspondence have all survived intact. *Sultana's* home port is Chestertown, but she may be found in sister ports on the Chesapeake Bay in thespring through fall. Her mission is to provide hands-on educational experiences in colonial history and environmental science. Opened in late 2002, the Sultana Center is at 105 S. Cross St. in downtown Chestertown and is an interactive educational center open to the public. Contact the offices at 410/778-5954, or write to P.O. Box 524, Chestertown, MD 21620, www.SchoonerSultana.com.

Tours

Cruising Chestertown by foot is a popular endeavor. If you'd prefer to go on your own, ask for the Walking Tour of Historic Chestertown from the Kent County Visitor Center. Guided options include the **Annual Candlelight Walking Tour,** held in September by the Historical Society of Kent County, 410/778-3499, www.kentcounty.com/historicalsociety, and the year-round **Historic Chestertown Tours,** 410/778-2829, and **New Yarmouth Tours of Chestertown and Kent County,** 410/778-3221. There is a charge for guided tours.

Entertainment

The **Prince Theatre,** 210 High St., 410/810-2060, www.princetheatre.org, was built in 1926 as a vaudeville theater and movie house. The theater has been carefully restored and now presents an exciting range of musical acts, films, and many other events; Wednesday is classic movie night.

BAD LUCK LOYALISTS

By the time the British engaged the Continental Army outside Philadelphia in 1776, scores of pro-British loyalists had been driven from their homes by colonial revolutionaries. A group of loyalists on the Eastern Shore of Maryland fled to British-occupied Philadelphia. Commissioned in 1777 as the First Battalion of Maryland Loyalists, led by former Kent County plantation owner Lieutenant Colonel James Chalmers, the soldiers evacuated the city in June 1778 ahead of the British army. While the British rear guard clashed with Washington's army in the Battle of Monmouth a short time later, the Marylanders were a full day's march in front. No military glory awaited them; as part of the advance guard, they had little to do except wait for the rear guard to finish battling the rebels and catch up.

After a short stint on Long Island, they were shipped off to Pensacola, Florida, to fight the Spanish. After a five-week siege by Spanish forces in the spring of 1781 (and an equally grueling siege of smallpox), the British and Provincial regiments at Fort George were forced to surrender. The Marylanders had proven courageous, executing a successful bayonet charge on one of the Spanish redoubts. This brief encounter would be their last taste of battle.

They sat out the rest of the war in New York. As with most loyalists, the United States offered no place for them, and they were forced to pack up and leave for Nova Scotia. When their transport ship set out for Saint John in September 1783, less than 100 of the original 300 members of the regiment were aboard. The rest had deserted or died of smallpox.

The transport ship struck a reef near the shore of Nova Scotia. Half the Maryland Loyalists and their families drowned. The survivors were brought to Saint John to face the approaching Canadian winter without clothing, blankets, or weapons. The tiny group of 50 Marylanders received their land grants (known as Block 1) along the northern shore of the St. John River. Some, like Captain Caleb Jones, former county sheriff of Somerset County, Maryland, did quite well for themselves; within four years, he purchased several adjoining lots from men who had been soldiers in his company. The rest faded into history.

Shopping

High Street between Mill and Queen Streets, and Cannon Street between Cross and Mill Streets, are the main shopping areas in town. Antique stores, art galleries, handmade furniture studios, and handmade sweater shops are found among the kind of service businesses that make this area a true downtown. Goods for sale include everything from whole foods (**Chestertown Natural Foods,** next to the free parking lot on Cannon Street between Queen and Cross) to literature (**The Compleat Bookseller,** corner of High and Cross Streets). A few other favorites are **Twigs & Teacups,** 111 S. Cross St., a sort of hip general store and contemporary emporium, and **Cornucopia,** across the way at 112 Cross St., a shop filled with luxurious bath items and housewares.

Accommodations

Built in 1860 as a plantation house, the **Brampton Inn,** 25227 Chestertown Rd., 410/778-1860, www.bramptoninn.com, still retains nearly all of its original details, including plaster ceiling medallions and a three-and-a-half-story walnut and ash central staircase that wends among floors made of Georgia pine. Brampton has 10 large rooms, all with private baths. Most have a woodburning fireplace ready to be lit during cold winter days. The manor house features a formal guest parlor and a family room with TV, VCR, and games. The 35 acres of grounds just outside of town provide a quiet place to stroll, and when the grove of Princess Pawlinia trees are in full purple bloom, it's hard to imagine a more beautiful setting. A full breakfast is served in the dining room, and afternoon tea with fresh coffee, tea, homemade muffins, cakes, and cookies is offered to each guest. The surroundings are elegant yet comfortable; innkeepers Michael and Danielle Hanscom and their friendly, helpful staff make this a very special place to stay. The guest book is filled with glowing comments from couples who honeymooned here and returned year after year. Rates range $135–225.

In downtown Chestertown, the **White Swan Tavern,** 231 High St., 410/778-2300, offers a very different lodging experience. The restoration of the building began in 1978 with an archaeological dig, uncovering the site's use as a tannery prior to 1733 and as a tavern after 1793. The property was restored to its late-1800s appearance, and the four rooms and two suites are decorated in a simple colonial style with full baths; $120–200.

Food

Play It Again Sam, 108 S. Cross St., 410/778-2688, is the place for morning coffee, a light lunch, or something sweet any time of day. It's open Mon.–Sat. 7 A.M.–5:30 P.M., Sunday 9 A.M.–3 p.m.

For a casual meal for lunch or dinner (great burgers), try **Andy's,** 337 ½ High St., 410/778-6779. Visitors walk through a tavern to a large dining room in back filled with living room furniture. Andy's features live music after 9 P.M., a good pub menu, and prices that average $6.

Blue Heron Café, 236 Cannon St., 410/778-0188, is acknowledged as the best in town by many locals. The menu features crabs, chicken, rack of lamb, and jambalaya; lunch averages $8, dinner $18. It's closed on Sunday.

Another favorite is the **Imperial Hotel,** 208 High St., 410/778-5000, featuring a similar menu, hours, and pricing.

VILLAGE OF ROCK HALL

Rock Hall is one of the last watermen's villages along the north Eastern Shore. In the summer, its streets are crowded with boaters who've stopped off for a meal and the lively social life that the little town offers. The big annual event in Rock Hall is the Rockfish Tournament in June, and festivities continue through July

"THERE WAS SO MANY, THE SKY TURNED DARK"

That quote, ascribed to a waterman during the heyday of wildfowl hunting, describes the incredible bounty of ducks and other water birds that drew hunters to the marshes of the Chesapeake during the latter part of the 19th century. The upper bay and Susquehanna flats have evolved from a major waterfowl center for the commercial trade—Philadelphia restaurants and hotels were a major market—to their current roles as playgrounds for private hunters. Decoy carvers such as P. Madison Mitchell, who plied his trade during the 1940s, have become celebrities.

By 1900, duck populations were decimated and the first national laws were established. Duck stamps, beautiful works of art in and of themselves, were sold as hunter's permits in an attempt to limit their numbers; this worked to some extent but not entirely. Laws were difficult to enforce, and market hunters largely ignored them. Prior to 1935, hunters scattered corn as bait and tied live geese and ducks near their blinds to draw wild birds; this was outlawed, as were sink boxes, bathtub-like boats in which the hunter sat, camouflaged. The sink box had wood-and-canvas panels fixed to each side, studded with decoys. Commercial hunters then used bushwhack boats, propelled by a single oar in the back to make as little noise as possible in the water. They often traveled in darkness (night hunting has been illegal since 1930). Today hunters use duck calls and body booting, a method suitable only for the rugged—a hunter sits on a decoy rig in the water in a wet suit behind a one-dimensional painted decoy big enough to hide him.

Though overhunting depleted the waterfowl population prior to the 20th century, today's greatest threat to wildlife is depletion of wetlands habitat due to overpopulation in all areas of the Chesapeake Bay.

Fourth to the **Party on the Bay** in August and FallFest in September.

Museums

The **Waterman's Museum** is dedicated to preserving the history of Chesapeake Bay watermen; a two-room collection of models, equipment, and photographs tells a sweet history of a hard industry. Entry to the museum is free, but you must stop in next door at the Haven Harbor Marina Office, 20880 Rock Hall Ave., 410/778-6697, to get the key.

Tolchester Beach Revisited Museum, tucked away in Oyster Court, off Main Street in Rock Hall, presents and preserves the history of the Tolchester Beach Amusement Park, 1877–1962. Tolchester Beach was once one of the most popular resorts along the shores of the Chesapeake Bay, drawing hundreds of vacationers by steamboat. The museum contains more than 300 photos, relics, and memorabilia recalling the bygone era of the popular bayside park.

Recreation

Sailing and Powerboat Cruises: Sunrise, sunset, half-day, full-day, weekend, and longer cruises are available from several locations in Rock Hall: **Gratitude Yachting Center,** 410/639-7111, and **The Kathryn,** 410/639-9902, are two.

Fishing Charters: Several boats are available for charter. Four sources to contact are Captain Manley (410/639-7420), Captain Jetton (410/639-7127), Captain Ritchie (410/639-7063), and Captain Simns (410/639-2966).

Kayak, Boating, and Fishing Equipment Rentals: Bob's Jet Ski Rentals, 410/639-7307, **Swan Haven,** 410/639-2527, and **Chester River Kayak Adventures,** 410/639-2001, are local resources.

Shopping

Sharp and Main Streets are the shopping stroll in Rock Hall: **Fishbone Antiques,** 21326 Sharp St., is a multidealer marketplace. **Oyster Court,** a little village of craft shops off Main Street behind the Mainstay Theatre, contains a natural scent and soap shop, wood carver's shop, gift shops, and others.

Accommodations

Swan Haven, 20950 Rock Hall Ave., 410/639-2527, overlooks Swan Creek and Rock Hall's many marinas. This Victorian "cottage" was built in 1898 and served at various times as a hospital and a private home. Visitors can enjoy a nap in the hammock, or spend the evening relaxing on the bench out on the pier. Swan Haven offers bicycle, boat, and windsurfer rentals to its guests; sailing, fishing, and crabbing can be done nearby. Each of the seven rooms has a private bath and cable TV. Rates range $98–138.

The Bay Breeze Inn, 5758 Main St., 410/639-2061, dates from the 1920s, and is in the middle of Rock Hall's revitalized Main Street area. Two of the five rooms share a bath, the other three have private baths, and a separate carriage house is available. Expect to pay $85–140 for a room, $140 for the carriage house.

Moonlight Bay Inn & Marina, 6002 Lawton Ave., 410/639-2660, not only offers 10 rooms, all with private bath, but also a 50-slip marina with bathrooms, picnic area, and barbecues. Dorothy and Bob Santangelo renovated the 150-year-old house from a deteriorated wreck in 1992, and now offer one of the prettiest lodgings around, with a great view of the sunset. Rates range $116–152.

Food

Durding's Ice Cream, Sharp and Main Streets, 410/639-7957, is the ultimate old-fashioned soda fountain and corner store. The original store was built just after the Civil War by the founder of Sharp and Dohme Pharmaceuticals (now Merck Pharmaceuticals). Mr. Alpheus Phineas Sharp and his wife retired to Rock Hall and eventually sold the shop to the Durdings. The pressed-tin ceiling, brass lamps, and wooden telephone booth complement the marble and stainless-steel soda fountain counter—you don't see many of these around anymore.

The Bay Wolf, 21270 Rock Hall Ave., 410/639-2000, serves Austrian and Eastern Shore cuisine such as sauerbraten and oyster stew. Lunch averages $7, dinner is around $15.

P. E. Pruitt's Waterfront Restaurant, 20899 Bayside Ave., 410/639-7454, is named after one of the few remaining oyster buy boats on the Chesapeake Bay. With its screened porch, deck, and tiki bar, dining is enjoyed overlooking Rock Hall Harbor. Lunch averages $8, dinner is around $19.

Getting Around

Transportation has never been easier or more fun (especially for those who come by water) thanks to the **Rock Hall Trolley Company,** offering regular trolley runs to and from and within Rock Hall and Chestertown: 410/639-7996 or 866/RHTROLY (866/748-7659). Trolley stops and times may be found at the Kent County Visitor Center or at www.rockhalltrolleys.com. Fares within towns are $2; Rock Hall and Chestertown run is $4; babes in arms are free—unlimited daily use.

GREATER KENT COUNTY

Chesapeake Farms Agricultural and Wildlife Management Area

The 3,300 acres of Chesapeake Farms are dedicated to the development, evaluation, and demonstration of advanced agricultural practices and wildlife management techniques. The farms are owned by a subsidiary of the DuPont Co., and are open to the public from Feb. 1– Oct. 10. A brochure that directs visitors through the area is available at the Kent County Visitor Center in Chestertown and at the headquarters just inside the entrance to Chesapeake Farms. The brochure discusses the use of various types of plantings and terrain that are demonstrated on the property; one of the fields is heavily planted in sunflowers, reminiscent of a Van Gogh painting, in full bloom during July and August. Though visitors may spend as much time as they like touring the farms, they must remain in their cars, as their presence disturbs the natural movement of wildlife.

Chesapeake Farms experiments with various types of integrated pest management, as-needed pesticide use, and balanced wildlife/crop ratios. Birds and mammals are abundant on the property, and the migratory waterfowl rest area near the farm headquarters is a popular spot in the spring and fall.

Eastern Neck National Wildlife Refuge

Europeans settled Eastern Neck Island in the 1660s; Joseph Wickes built a mansion on the island, raised tobacco and other crops, and exported them on ships built at the family shipyard. Between 1800 and 1900, the original parcels of land were divided up into small family farms and a fishing village. The Chester River Steam Boat Company operated a wharf that was served by steamships from Baltimore and other ports. During and after the 1920s, wealthy hunters were attracted to the area's concentration of waterfowl and bought portions of the island for hunting retreats. In the 1950s, a developer acquired a large tract and was preparing to turn it into 293 small houses when the U.S. Fish and Wildlife Service responded to the local outcry and purchased the entire island.

Eastern Neck provides a variety of habitats, including 1,000 acres of brackish tidal marsh, 600 acres of cropland, 500 acres of forest, 100 acres of grassland, and 40 acres of open water impoundments. Three threatened and/or endangered species, 243 species of birds, and a variety of mammals, amphibians, and reptiles inhabit the island. October through mid-March is the best time for migratory waterfowl; the refuge staff has documented 40,000 waterfowl during peak periods, and 32 different species have been reported, including Canada geese, tundra swans, and several species of ducks, including mallards, black ducks, and buffleheads. Songbird northern migration peaks in late April–early May, and many species such as woodcocks, eagles, and bluebirds fledge during this period.

In addition to providing a sanctuary for the threatened southern bald eagle, the refuge is home to the endangered Delmarva fox squirrel. This species once lived throughout the Delmarva Peninsula and into southern Pennsylvania and New Jersey, though now it exists only in portions of four counties on the Eastern Shore of Maryland.

Six miles of roads and trails, including three wildlife trails and a butterfly trail with a handicap-accessible observation deck featuring a panoramic view of the Chesapeake Bay, may be reached from Route 445 in Rock Hall. At the Ingleside Recreation area on the west side of the refuge, there are facilities for crabbing and car-top boat launching from May 1–Sept. 30. Picnic tables and grills are nearby. Bogle's Wharf is on the east side of the refuge and offers trailer boat-launching facilities for those with county permits (not available at the refuge office). Anglers like to cast from the bridge that spans that Eastern Neck Narrows.

If you're going to hike the trails in this area, make sure you are tick-protected (see the special topic "Lyme Disease Lookout" in the Maryland On the Road chapter). During a bad infestation year, the grasses along the wooded marsh trails are perfect tick hangouts.

Kent County Driving Tour

This more-than-100-mile drive covers Kent County from one end to the other, and can be easily broken up into shorter segments, using Chestertown as a pivot point. Distances are roughly approximated, though the roads are easy to see and clearly marked. Kent County's back roads are quite flat and seldom traveled—ideal for bikers and leisurely drivers.

The tour starts in Chestertown; take Route 289 (Quaker Neck Road) five miles south from the city of Chestertown to the village of Pomona. In Pomona, turn north on Brices Mill Road—in about one mile, it becomes Ricauds Branch–Langford Road. This road was one of the nation's first turnpikes. In a little over two miles, you'll see St. Paul's Episcopal Church on the right, erected in 1713—it's the oldest Episcopal church in Maryland, and contains the grave of actress Tallulah Bankhead, as well as that of colonial settler Daniel Coley, whose footstone admonishes, "Behold & see now here I lye; As you are so once was I; As I am now so must you be; Therefore prepare to follow me." During the War of 1812, the church became a barracks for British troops.

Return to Ricauds Branch–Langford Road and continue west to Route 20. You'll pass Chesapeake Farms on the left, a wildlife management demonstration area open to the public. Turn left (south) on Route 20 for six miles; continue on to the town of Rock Hall. This scenic little village offers a number of attractions; you might also want to take Route 445 south approximately 10 miles to Eastern Neck Island National Wildlife Refuge.

After exploring Rock Hall, head north on Route 445 about 10 miles to the intersection of Route 21. Continue nearly straight across the intersection; you're now on Bayshore Road, which curves around east to the village of Fairlee (10 miles). Turn north on Route 298, travel 10 miles; look for Cooper's Road on the left (north). Take this small two-lane road a little over six miles until it dead-ends, then turn right (east) to intercept Route 292. Turn left (north) to reach Betterton and Betterton Beach. You can see Aberdeen Proving Grounds across Chesapeake Bay from here.

Drive south five miles from Betterton on Route 292 to the town of Still Pond; the contemporary name is a corruption of "Steele's Pone," Steele being an early settler, and "pone" meaning "favorite" in Elizabethan English. In 1908, the first women in Maryland allowed to vote exercised that right in Still Pond. Continue east about a mile on Route 566; keep an eye out for Bloomfield Road on the left. Take this small two-lane road north four miles to the intersection of Route 448. Turn left (north); Turner's Creek Wilderness Area is on the left.

Turn around and take Route 448 south five miles to the intersection of U.S. 213 in Kennedyville. Turn right on U.S. 213 to return to Chestertown (11 miles).

Another way to tour the county is via the "Driving Tour of the Kent County Peninsula," which may be picked up at the Kent County Visitor Center in Chestertown. It is also online at www.kentcounty.com.

Recreation

Kent County, flat as morning toast and liberally spread with a rich jam of quiet, scenic two-lane roads, is modestly famous for its bicycle touring. To celebrate this bounty, the Kent County Tourism Development Office, 410/778-0416 or tourism@kentcounty.com, offers several bike tours of varying length and complexity. The office can also give information on other popular dry-land entertainments such as hunting and sporting clays.

Since the county is famed for its waterways as well as its roadways, boat charters and rentals abound, along with kayaks and other water toys.

FESTIVALS AND EVENTS

January/February

Ephemera such as antique books, advertising, postcards, photographs, and other perishables are the subject of the **Paper Americana Show** in Elkton. 410/398-7735.

April/May

Carroll Carvers Annual Festival of Carving is an international competition that takes place in the county Agricultural Center. 410/374-6521.

Ladew Topiary Gardens sponsors **My Lady's Manor Steeplechase Races,** two races, three miles over timber. This event has been taking place since 1911. 410/557-9466.

The **Upper Bay Skipjack Invitational Races** are sometimes combined with an Earth Day celebration in April. Visitors may sign on the racing skipjacks as passengers for a fee. It's held at the lighthouse in Havre de Grace. 800/406-0766.

Considered the oldest and most difficult steeplechase race in the country, the **Maryland Hunt Cup Race** takes place in Glyndon, north of Baltimore. 410/833-4188.

In sympathy with Boston, Chestertown residents boarded the British brigantine *Geddes* in 1774 and dumped its tea shipment into the Chester River. The **Chestertown Tea Party Festival** features a colonial parade, music, food, boat rides, and historical reenactments. 410/778-0416.

June/July/August

Once known as the marriage capital of the world for its lack of barriers to getting hitched in a hurry, Elkton celebrates **National Marriage Day** with an outdoor wedding and opportunities to take and renew vows. 410/398-7007.

No fish story, Rock Hall's annual **Rockfish Tournament** offers a $10,000 first prize for the best striper. 410/778-0416.

The Carroll County Farm Museum sponsors the **Deep Creek Fiddlers' Convention** with a bluegrass competition, food, crafts, farmhouse tours, and more. 410/876-2667.

More than 300 juried artists and craftspeople will display their wares at the **Havre de Grace Art Show** at Tydings Memorial Park. 410/939-9342.

September/October

The Decoy Museum in Havre de Grace hosts the annual **Duck Fair,** with carvers, retriever demonstrations, a duck-calling contest, whittling, food, and an auction. 410/939-3739.

Port Deposit Heritage Day is an excellent opportunity to visit the quaint river town as it comes alive with arts, crafts, music, and house tours. 410/378-2121.

For a spooky tour of Chesapeake City, try the **Ghost Walk,** a house-to-house storytelling party with hayrides and food. 410/885-2025.

November/December

Forty thousand holiday lights star on a 1.5-mile eye-popping drive through Fort Howard Park, late November–New Year's Day. 410/887-3873.

The small town of North East lights up Main Street for **Dickens' Christmas Weekend;** shopkeepers don Victorian costume, and carolers and other entertainers fill the streets with cheer. 410/287-2658.

The manor house is lavishly decorated for the holidays in **Christmas at Ladew Topiary Gardens.** Fresh greens and decorations are on sale. 410/557-9466.

Many charters and equipment rental companies are in Rock Hall, but others exist as well; the tourism development office can provide an up-to-date list of all charters available and their points of origin.

Shopping

Chestertown Antique & Furniture Center, 6612 Church Hill Rd. (Route 213 south of the Chester River Bridge), is a browser's treasure trove; it also contains thousands of used books.

One of the most mind-blowing sales in the world takes place in the vicinity of Kent County. **Dixon's Furniture Auction,** intersection of Route 544 and Route 290, Crumpton (on the border of Queen Anne's County), 410/928-3006, occurs every Wednesday, every week but Christmas week. It offers a mountain of goods of every quality and description in three "areas"—good, better, best—with base prices gauged accordingly, from $15 up. A real live auctioneer goes over the merchandise piece by piece (better not be in a hurry if the plates you plan to bid on are on table #60).

Galena, Rt. 213 north of Chestertown, is home to several antique, gift, and collectible shops. Galena Antiques Center on N. Main Street, 410/648-5781, is a multidealer coop.

Accommodations

The **Kitty Knight House,** Route 213, Georgetown, on the Sassafras River, 410/648-5200, offers a healthy helping of history alongside its dinners and lodgings. Kitty Knight moved away from her prominent Cecil County family and in 1775 purchased the brick home that became the basis of the Kitty Knight House Inn. In May 1813, the British were burning and shelling agricultural ports that supported the American cause along the Eastern Chesapeake. Admiral Sir George Cockburn led British troops up the Sassafras River to set Georgetown aflame. Kitty, determined to defy the British and save her house, sat on the doorstep in spite of threats, orders to leave, and several attempts to set fire to the house. In the end she prevailed and her house was one of few spared. Forty years later, she was buried at the old Bohemia Church in

Cecil County, and, proud of her single status to the end, insisted that her tombstone read "Miss Catherine Knight."

The Kitty Knight House prides itself on serving fresh local meat, seafood, and vegetables, and will cook to order. The inn features a main dining room with a view of Georgetown Harbor, and the Admiral Cockburn Tavern. Dinner entrées average $17. For overnight guests, each of the 11 rooms is equipped with a private bath and cable TV; the rooms vary in size and view. Expect to pay $50–100 for single rooms, $125 for suites.

Great Oak Manor, 10568 Cliff Rd., 410/778-5943 or 800/504-3098, www.covesoft.com/Great_Oak, is a large manor house eight miles from downtown Chestertown. It has 11 guest rooms with phones and private baths. Five of the rooms have working fireplaces, and the manor is next to a nine-hole golf course at Great Oak Landing. Rates ranges $95–160.

Food

For an inexpensive snack, lunch, or light dinner ($10), try **Procolinos Pizza,** 410/778-5900 in Kent Plaza shopping center on Route 213, just north of downtown.

Dublin Dock, Betterton Beach, 410/348-5896, offers a regular pub menu, but regulars say their Irish food is the best. They feature Irish music on weekends. Prices average $8.

The Kennedyville Inn, 1198 Augustine Herman Hwy. (Route 213), Kennedyville, 410/348-2400, has a reputation for innovation and excellent food. Its menu features emu with orange and ginger, and chicken breast with scallion pancakes and curry sauce. It's open for dinner Wed.–Sun., and dinner entrées are in the $12–$18 range.

INFORMATION

Stop by the Kent County Visitor Center at 122 North Cross St. in Chestertown for information and local brochures. For a free information packet, contact the Kent County Tourism Development Office at 410/778-0416 or email tourism@kentcounty.com. For an inside view of Kent County, visit www.kentcounty.com.

The Eastern Shore

We're two hours and thirty years from Washington.

Eastern Shore saying

The Delmarva Peninsula is bordered on the east by the Atlantic Ocean and Delaware Bay and on the west by the mighty Chesapeake. If water views are what you're after, you have just achieved Nirvana. The peninsula has thousands of miles of shoreline, hundreds of rivers, and thousands of acres of salt marshes—the Chesapeake is, after all, the largest inland estuary in the world.

For 11,000 years, the Eastern Shore had been home to those who quietly farmed, hunted, and lived off the rich resources of the Chesapeake. Captain John Smith met the peaceful Algonquin-speaking Ozinies in what was to become Queen Anne's County in 1608 or 1609. Some 25 years later, William Claiborne established a trading fort on Kent Island—the first settlement in the state. Claiborne claimed that the territory belonged to Virginia; Lord Calvert insisted it was his, and the Ozinies and other natives left the area to escape the din of battle. Calvert won out, and British settlers followed

Easton Courthouse

© JOANNE MILLER

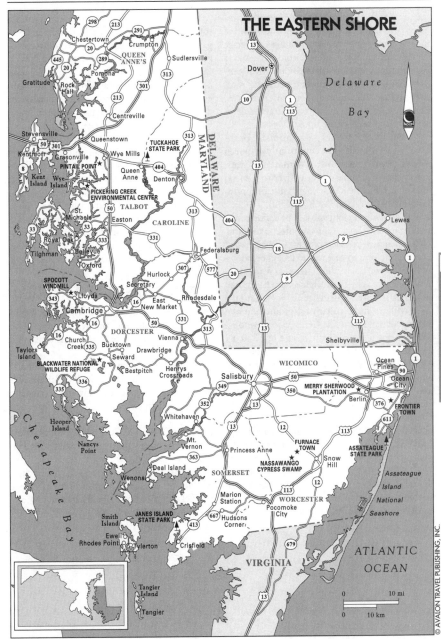

THE EASTERN SHORE

the rivers and shorelines to clear the land for tobacco planting. In the early 1600s, one pound of the leaf could fetch more than double an average English sharecropper's annual income. Tobacco as a cash crop was so prevalent by the 18th century that it was used as money; prices for most commodities were quoted in pounds of tobacco. Plantations grew along the rivers, and the rivers were the highways of the time.

Queen Anne's County was formally established in 1708, with the county seat at Queen Anne's Town (Queenstown). Within a few years, it was moved up the Corsica River to Centreville, which has the oldest courthouse in continuous use in Maryland (built in 1792).

By 1760, transatlantic tobacco prices were fluctuating wildly; many planters shifted to the blue-chip agricultural products of grain. The haphazard plantings of tobacco gave way to today's broad, orderly fields and linked the Eastern Shore to northern markets, chiefly Philadelphia. Merchants from that area invested in local mills, including the Wye Mill, in order to control production and prices. Market towns like Centreville grew to reflect the bustling trade activity, and by 1820, 80 percent of arable land was under cultivation.

The Industrial Revolution brought steam power, and farm machinery increased productivity. At the same time, steam replaced sail and opened regional markets on the Chesapeake and Delaware Bays for produce, oysters, and fish. Steamboats plied the rivers of the Eastern Shore, and linked small towns with the outside world. Railroad lines were built throughout the region in the 1870s, and fishing and oystering boomed. Kent Narrows and Kent Island became important seafood processing centers, with as many as 12 packing houses operating at one time.

By the 1920s, steamboats themselves were obsolete, replaced by railroads. And the iron horse gave way to iron horsepower—automobiles—by the 1950s. Lifestyles continued to be slow on the Eastern Shore until 1952, when the completion of the first Chesapeake Bay Bridge ushered in rapid business, industrial, and real estate development. The northern part of Queen Anne's County and much of the central and southern peninsula that comprise the Eastern Shore continue to be a place of small communities and vast farmland. A few cities—primarily Salisbury—have become more urbanized, though the population remains small.

Ocean City is a state unto itself. Once a spit of farmland, the area is now a playground for beach lovers, more like Miami than Maryland. However, there's plenty of fun to be found, whether you're seeking a quiet getaway or a social whirl.

GETTING THERE AND AROUND

By Air: Commuter airlines service the Salisbury airport from Baltimore and Washington, D.C., but that remains the only air access other than small planes.

By Auto: Main auto access to the Delmarva Peninsula from the west is the Bay Bridge, U.S. 50, which reaches all the way to Ocean City. The area is very spread out; for sightseeing, an auto is really the only option. U.S. 13, which begins in Delaware, is the main north-south route. Other roads are generally well-maintained two-lane blacktop.

By Bus: Greyhound services the major cities: Easton, St. Michaels, Cambridge, Salisbury, Crisfield, and Ocean City. Its telephone number is 800/229-9424.

Queen Anne's County

This area, which includes the Bay Bridge, Kent Island, and the gateway to the Eastern Shore, remains largely farmland, with a few small towns and commercial centers.

SIGHTS

The **Horsehead Wetlands Center,** administered by the Wildfowl Trust of North America, Perry Corner Road, Grasonville, 410/827-6694, is composed of six distinct wetland habitats in 500 acres. The trust was established in 1979 by a group of conservationists who modeled it after similar organizations in the United Kingdom. The Grasonville property's original purpose was waterfowl research, though it's now used to study migratory behavior and patterns, and as an education and information center. Migrating birds pass through the property seasonally, and a captive population of waterfowl and raptors is kept on the property—many are birds that were injured in the wild and were unable to survive on their own, such as a blind owl and an eagle with an injured wing. The center offers an environmental science camp and other educational programs throughout the year. Four easy trails, all less than a mile long, lead visitors through the habitats and gardens. Several ponds and lakes are home to turtles and other amphibians, and the surrounding marshes support wildflowers and butterflies. A visitors center offers information on the wide variety of birds that pass through the area, and also has a small, well-stocked gift shop. The center is open daily except major holidays, 9 A.M.–5 P.M. Admission is $5.

Queen Anne's Museum of Eastern Shore Life, 126 Dulin Clark Rd., Centreville, 410/758-8641, displays artifacts, household furnishings, and farmers' and watermen's gear from the past and present. Exhibits focus on rural life on the Eastern Shore. This is one of several historic sites administered by the Historic Sites Consortium of Queen Anne's County, 888/400-RSVP (888/400-7787). Others include the Tucker House, Wright's Chance, and the county courthouse in Centreville; the Cray House, old post office, and train depot in Stevensville; the colonial courthouse in Queenstown; Dudley's chapel and the train station in Sudlersville; Wye grist mill; and the Church Hill theatre. If local history is of interest, call for the consortium's excellent free brochure, "Explore Our History and Heritage," or pick one up from the Queen Anne's County Office of Tourism. All sites are open on the third Saturday of each month, May–Oct., and admission is free.

Kent Fort Farm, 135 Eastern Ln., Stevensville, 410/643-1650, is a great place to take the kids early summer–fall. It offers a variety of U-pick fruit Wed.–Sat. 9 A.M.–7 P.M. and Sunday 10 A.M.–6 P.M.; there's an annual peach festival the first Saturday in August, and a pumpkin patch on October weekends.

Tuckahoe State Park

Tuckahoe Creek runs the length of this park, 13070 Crouse Mill Rd., Queen Anne, 410/820-1668. A lake offers boating and fishing, and the Adkins Arboretum encompasses 500 acres of parkland and almost three miles of surfaced walkways leading through tagged native species of trees and shrubs. The park offers scenic hiking, biking, and equestrian trails, and flat-water canoeing. Visitors may take advantage of numerous seasonal activities, such as bird watching and guided walks. Pets are allowed in the family camping area and most of the park, except the lake area, as long as they remain on a leash.

Boating and Canoeing: Canoeing at Tuckahoe is a popular activity on both the 60-acre lake and the creek because of the park's abundant wildlife. Visitors share space with bald eagles, ospreys, and great blue herons; beavers and muskrats have surprised visitors by swimming past their canoes. Tuckahoe is full of pockets of secluded beauty, some only accessible by canoe. Canoes, kayaks, and paddle boats may be rented for a daily fee. Guided canoe trips on both the lake and the Tuckahoe Creek are offered throughout the year by the park naturalist. Gasoline motor use is prohibited.

Hiking, Biking and Horses: Tuckahoe boasts 20 miles of excellent hiking, biking, and equestrian trails, such as the Tuckahoe Valley Trail, a self-guided Natural Trail, the Physical Fitness Trail, and the Lake Trail.

Camping: The park offers 51 single-family sites, 33 with electric hookups, and a central bathhouse. In addition, there's a youth group camping area with four sites, each accommodating up to 30 people with a central bathhouse with showers and toilet facilities. Four camper (rustic) cabins are available; each cabin sleeps four and is equipped with ceiling fan, electricity, and air conditioning, but no running water. Call 888/432-2267 for reservations.

Getting There: Tuckahoe State Park is located approximately 35 miles east of the Bay Bridge, just off Route 404. Travel east on Route 50/301 across the Bay Bridge. Where Route 50/301 splits, bear to the right on Route 50. Make a left at the intersection of Route 50 and Route 404. Go approximately eight miles to the intersection of Route 404 and Route 480. Make a left on Route 480. Eveland Road is on your immediate left. Once on Eveland Road, follow the directional signs.

WYE AND ENVIRONS

The area around the Wye River came to the attention of many Americans in the 1990s as the site of a series of peace talks between Israeli and Palestinian leaders hosted by President Clinton. The talks took place in a private plantation home on **Wye Island.** The entire island is designated a Natural Resource Management Area. The island, at the end of Carmichael Road, consists of a number of private homes in a scenic jewel of a rustic setting. There are turnoffs on the single road where visitors may park their cars and walk tree-lined lanes filled with songbirds, including the rare indigo bunting. The state of Maryland purchased the 2,450-acre island in the 1970s, when the original 13 farms were in danger of being broken up for development.

On the way to Wye Island is **Pintail Point,** 511 Pintail Point Ln., Queenstown, 410/827-7029, www.pintailpoint.com, a sort of Disneyland for sporty types. The property has the look of a very wealthy private retreat; it offers deluxe lodging and extensive fishing, hunting, and sporting clay activities. Guests may take any of a num-

A LONG WAY FROM HAVANA

In April 2000, Wye Island became another sort of refuge. Elian Gonzalez, along with his father, stepmother, and baby half-brother, moved to a two-story, white farmhouse on the grounds of the secluded Wye River Conference Center, the 1,100-acre estate that was the home of one of the state's first governors, William Paca. The conference center, 70 miles east of Washington, is perhaps best known as the site of the Middle East peace negotiations in 1996 and 1998. The Gonzalez family was awaiting court action on whether the 6-year-old boy should be granted an asylum hearing or be allowed to return with his father to his birthplace.

Elian was a survivor of a shipload of Cuban refugees that sank off the coast of Florida, and became a cause célèbre when relatives in the Miami Cuban community insisted that he stay in the United States rather than return home to his father and Castro's Cuba.

Before being moved to Wye Island, Elian's Cuban family had been staying at Andrews Air Force Base upon arrival in the United States. To reunite the family, Elian was forcibly removed from the home of his Miami relatives.

One neighbor said he didn't think Elian's visit caused nearly the commotion of the 1998 peace talks, when Secret Service agents shut down the road leading to the estate. "That's the only time we had security that high, when the president was here," said Kevin Compton, operations manager at Pintail Point Farm. "There's constantly stuff going on down there that requires security, but we don't ever feel it."

Elian returned to Cuba with his father at the end of June 2000.

ber of fly-fishing classes, from casting to fly-tying, and may fish in the freshwater ponds on the property or take one of several charters out on the Chesapeake. Hunters can pursue deer, wild duck, sea duck, and doves in season, or take advantage of Pintail's hunting preserve. Guests may bring their own dogs, or select one from the facility's kennels. Those more interested in sport shooting—golf with a gun—may enjoy Pintail's 22-station shooting clay range. The "Cast and Blast" features a half-day of charter boat fishing, lunch, and a round of 50 targets on the sporting clay course. All equipment may be rented.

The village of **Wye,** Route 662, is home to the **Wye Grist Mill,** one of the earliest and most authentic industrial sites in Maryland. A mill has been operating on the site for more than 300 years. In fact, the milling operations were significant enough that the Maryland General Assembly of 1706 created Queen Anne's County using the mill as a reference point. In 1956, the mill and one acre was deeded by the state to Preservation Maryland. Today, the mill grinds Eastern Shore corn and wheat and Pennsylvania buckwheat by the traditional stone method using water power only, and visitors may purchase the flours. The small mill is a perfectly preserved example of colonial-era technology, right down to the conduit pipes made of boards battened together. A video and exhibit chronicle the Eastern Shore's role in the 19th-century agricultural boom. The mill is open daily mid-Apr.–early Nov., weekdays 10 A.M.–1 P.M., weekends 10 A.M.–4 P.M. On the first and third Sat. of the month, volunteers demonstrate the traditional stone grinding process. Admission is free, but a $2 donation is appreciated. Each year, on the Saturday nearest June 26, Wye Mill hosts a harvest craft fair.

The 96-foot tall **Wye Oak,** south of the grist mill in the village, is a sight to behold. The tree has been around since 1540—it pushed up out of the ground barely 50 years after Columbus reputedly set foot on American soil; when Europeans first explored the upper regions of the Chesapeake Bay, this white oak was already fully mature. In 1909, the tree was recorded as the largest white oak specimen in the eastern United States—it's 32 feet in circumference, with a crown

spread of 119 feet. Windfall is a continual threat to the large tree; more than 100 cables intertwine throughout the crown to prevent the stiff limbs from snapping during high winds. New growth is pruned to reduce wind resistance. The spreading giant fronts a 29-acre park. Behind it is **Wye School,** a small brick building that may have also been used as a plantation office or dwelling. Just down the road is the still-active **Old Wye Church,** built in 1717 and restored in the 1940s.

A visit to Wye wouldn't be complete without a stop at **Orrell's Maryland Beaten Biscuits,** Route 662 next to the Old Wye Church. If you've never had a beaten biscuit, the first bite might be a shock—even fresh out of the oven, the exterior is more reminiscent of granite than flour and water. The inside, however, is as tender and light as goose down. "Beaten," to me, means pummeled with a spoon—these biscuits date back to the plantation era, when leavening was in short supply and the term "beaten" was literal. Some cooks used a hammer, some the back of an axe—at Orrell's, the preferred instrument is a baseball bat. One old recipe states "beat thirty minutes for family and forty-five for company." As you might expect, everyone at Orrell's is very mellow. Ruth Orrell began the biscuit business in 1935, using her mother's recipe, and the little bakery employs many of the neighboring women, who sit around the table in flowered aprons chatting and pinching off dough into biscuit-sized balls. Nothing settles an upset stomach faster, and odd as they may seem at first bite ("Should I eat it or skip it across the lake?"), they definitely grow on you. Ruth has a hefty business shipping biscuits all over the country. Call her at 410/827-6244, or visit www.beatenbiscuits.com, and she'll send you a dozen or more, regular, honey, cheese, or flat.

SHOPPING

Chesapeake Outlet Village, Route 301, Queenstown, will satisfy your needs for a quick outlet-shopping fix on the Eastern Shore. All the standard outlet shops are there: Mikasa, Jones New York, Dansk, and more. Most shops are open daily.

THE EASTERN SHORE

Chesapeake Antique Center, Inc., adjacent to the Chesapeake Outlet Village on Route 301, is a multidealer antiques marketplace with a little of everything. It's open daily. For more information visit www.chesapeakeantiques.com.

Though it's on the border of Queen Anne's County and Kent County, **Dixon's Furniture Auction,** intersection of Route 544 and Route 290, Crumpton, 410/928-3006, is worth a special trip. A public auction takes place every Wednesday. It offers a mountain of goods of every quality and description in three "areas"— good, better, best, with base prices gauged accordingly, from $15 up. A live auctioneer goes over the merchandise piece by piece; he/she moves fast, but be prepared to wait if the merchandise you want sits on the tables farthest from the front.

ACCOMMODATIONS

Kent Manor Inn, 500 Kent Manor Dr., Route 8 South, Stevensville, Kent Island, 410/643-7716 or 800/820-4511, www.kentmanor.com, was established on one of the oldest tracts of land in Maryland, dating back to 1651. The main section of the current hotel was built in 1820. More than 226 acres of the original farm surround the manor house, and all rooms in the gracious (and completely modernized) inn have a water view, private bath, and telephone. Kent Manor Inn is designated a "Historic Hotel of America" by the National Trust for Historic Preservation. The elegant building, with its expansive lawns and gardens, is frequently a site for weddings. The inn also offers formal lunch and dinner in its first-floor dining room; in summer, the windows look out on the lawns and inlet, and in winter, the Victorian fireplaces fill the space with warmth and light. The dining room is open to the public. Weekdays, rooms range $130–190; weekends, $170–235.

Stillwater Inn Bed & Breakfast, 7109 2nd Ave., Queenstown, 410/827-9362, is a stroll away from Queenstown Creek. This charming, airy, country-style B&B was built in 1904 for a local doctor, and sometimes served as the vestry of Wye parish before becoming a B&B. Both guest rooms have a private bath. The innkeepers, Kevin and Linda Vasbinder, serve a full country breakfast in the morning; Kevin's library may contain every fantasy book ever written, and it's tempting to sink into a world of swords and sorcery. Guests will enjoy the lovely private garden in the warmer months. It's a good idea to get directions from the innkeepers, as many of the streets of Queenstown were modified from narrow alleys, and don't necessarily connect in a logical way. The old town area seems a million miles away from busy Route 301, though it's less than one. A room and breakfast is $125.

Pintail Point, 511 Pintail Point Ln., Queenstown, 410/827-7029, offers guests several sporting activities and beautiful accommodations. Because of the isolated rural setting, visitors who have no interest in sporting activities could still enjoy a quiet retreat. There are two bed-and-breakfast locations on the property. A 1936 English Tudor, the Manor House, is surrounded by gardens and walking paths along the Wye River. Two rooms, one suite, and a cottage, all with private bath, are available ($185–350 per night). Irishtown is an early-1900s farmhouse with three bedrooms and two baths, $500 per night for the entire house.

FOOD
Quick and Cheap

Though the Kent Narrows and surrounding area is famous for big seafood restaurants, there are a few inexpensive places to eat that are quite good. Anyone who's crossed the bridge more than once knows about **Holly's,** five miles east of the bridge on Route 50 in Grasonville, 410/827-8711. It's a restaurant and motel, opened by the Ewing family in 1955; and judging from the decor and the prices, Holly's remains firmly in the '50s; you'll barely have time to name more than a few states and their capitals (the placemats quiz your geographical knowledge) before your fried chicken special arrives ($7.50). Even if your U.S. geography is rusty (where exactly is Missouri?), the food will make you feel smart. Real milkshakes and whole apple dumplings star on the diner-style menu, and most salads and sandwiches run

blue crabs packed for shipping

under $6. This Eastern Shore institution is open every day, 7 A.M.–9:30 P.M.

Chesapeake Chicken & Rockin' Ribs, on the north side of Route 50 at Hissey Road (seven miles east of the bridge), 410/827-0030, is a locally owned barbecue joint with tasty platters. Chicken with two sides is under $9, ribs and two sides are $13. You can eat in the cheerful dining room or get everything to go—party platters that serve up to 40 people are a specialty. It also offers excellent chicken soup and salads. Open daily for lunch and dinner.

Bob's Mini Mart & Deli, corner of Route 301 and Del Rhodes Ave., Queenstown, 410/827-8280, isn't fancy, but the sandwiches, subs, and salads are good and everything is prepared to order; the prices rival fast food (less than $5). Yes, it's in a gas station, but there's a separate sit-down dining area. This is the place the locals eat, and it's often very crowded around lunchtime. It's open Mon.–Sat. 5:30 A.M.–8 P.M.

Seafood

The large seafood eateries on Kent Island on the east end of the bridge range in quality and price. **Annie's,** 500 Kent Narrows Way, 410/827-7103, doesn't specialize—the menu is several pages long and includes all the local seafood dishes (steamed clams, crab cakes), Angus beef, sandwiches, salads, and Italian specialties (a local favorite). This is a big, casual place, with big plates—not gourmet, but perfect for the hearty eater who wants a lot of choices. Salads and sandwiches average $8, dinners around $19. It's open daily for lunch and dinner; reservations are accepted.

The Narrows, 3023 Kent Narrows Way S., Grasonville, 410/827-8113, is also open for lunch and dinner daily, and reservations are a good idea. The feel is elegant without being stuffy, and the menu is sophisticated and well prepared. Lunch features items such as a steak-and-brie sandwich and pecan-crusted catfish (average $10), and dinner offers grilled chicken Oscar and filet mignon with broiled crab cake ($26.75), among other dishes. It also serves light suppers—a petite version of regular menu items—for around $15.

Drive a few miles down Kent Island on Route 8, and you'll come to Kentmoor Road, which leads to a planned development built around a private airport. Many of the homes have airplanes parked nearby, and at the end of the road,

910 Kentmorr, Stevensville, 410/643-2263, you'll find **Kentmorr,** www.kentmorr.com, an upscale neighborhood restaurant with spectacular views and a broad menu. Though the place is out of the way, it's very popular. The menu features steamed crabs, a raw bar, seafood, chicken, and beef, and soups, pasta, and salads. The chef will barbecue your choice of meat, and prime rib is a specialty. The Sunday breakfast buffet is a local favorite. Kentmorr serves lunch and dinner Mon.–Sat., dinner daily, and is open 11:30 A.M.– 9 P.M. Dinner prices run from $9 for chicken

to $25 for steak with crab cake. Steamed crabs are market price.

INFORMATION

Questions on Queen Anne's can be directed to Queen Anne's County Office of Tourism, 425 Piney Narrows Rd., Chester, MD 21619, 410/604-2100 or 888/400-7787, www.qac.org. The visitors center there offers interactive, hands-on exhibits that tell the story of the Chesapeake Bay and the Eastern Shore.

Talbot County

The flotilla of pleasure boats that ply the 600-plus miles of Talbot County's coastline might fool visitors into thinking that maritime-related tourism is the county's most important product—it's not. Though Talbot County has the longest shoreline of any county in the United States, agriculture still ranks number one as its largest local commercial industry, a fact easily proven by a short drive away from the haunts of captains and crews. Soybeans, corn, and wheat make up the bulk of the produce that is the backbone of Talbot's economy; all told, farms gross more than $40 million a year. However, the waters—including the Tred Avon, Tuckahoe, Wye, Miles, and Choptank Rivers—produce their own riches, from seafood to dockage. This is an difficult place to visit on a tight budget, so be prepared.

ST. MICHAELS

St. Michaels, founded in 1677, was once a haven for ship builders, privateers, and blockade-runners. It prides itself on civic cooperation during the War of 1812. When British marines converged for a night attack against the town's shipyards in 1813, the forewarned residents doused their lights and hung lanterns in trees and masts, drawing fire away from the town—only one house was hit.

Shortly afterward, Frederick Douglass—born near Tuckahoe Creek—lived as a slave in St.

Michaels in 1830. He taught a clandestine school for blacks there, and escaped to freedom in 1836.

These days, the town is a destination for pleasure boaters and yachts flying international colors. *Power & Motoryacht Magazine* named St. Michael's one of America's favorite anchorages, out of 12 including Desolation Sound in British Columbia and Bimini in the Bahamas. During the summer, the town is bustling, though the action slows down markedly by October.

Sights

Chesapeake Bay Maritime Museum, a sprawling enterprise, end of Mill Street, Navy Point, 410/745-2916, www.cbmm.org, is one of Maryland's top cultural attractions, and a major attraction on the Eastern Shore. Twenty-three buildings contain interactive exhibits on boat building, historic boats, decoys, and Chesapeake Bay life. The museum spreads over 18 acres, and several historic vessels, such as the skipjack *Rosie Parks* and the log-bottom bugeye *Edna E. Lockwood,* are docked on the waterfront. The Hooper Strait Lighthouse, a fully restored 1879 screwpile wooden structure, is one of the most popular exhibits. Visitors can climb the narrow stairs to visit the living quarters and see the Fresnel lens that surrounds the light on the top deck—it's the second—largest size ever made. The octagonal lighthouse was moved from its first location several miles out in Chesapeake Bay when it was scheduled for destruction in the mid-1960s. The

THE EASTERN SHORE

LOG CANOES AND SKIPJACKS

Water transport on the Chesapeake was developed to meet a number of needs, from swift transportation to food gathering. Most of the bay and the many rivers that feed it are quite shallow (less than 10 feet). Wind-powered watercraft with shallow drafts were a necessity; working boats also needed to be speed-controlled. The typical Chesapeake working vessel is wide, shallow, and heavy.

Log canoes were modified from the common form of Native American transportation, logs that were burned and hollowed out. Basically, several of these were lashed together to form a hull. Decking was placed over the logs, and planks were built up from the sides. Three- and five-log canoes were common. An unusual nine-log canoe is restored at the Maritime Museum in St. Michaels; the museum sponsors log canoe races throughout the summer. Log canoes built for working watermen were sometimes referred to as bugeyes, thought to be a corruption of "buckie" or "pungie," the Scottish word for oyster in colonial times.

Skipjacks are broad, shallow-draft sailing vessels made especially for oystering. Their slow and steady pace permitted watermen to drag a 12- to 15-foot-long set of "tongs" behind the boat and pull the mollusks off the bottom.

museum offers families overnight stays in the lighthouse during the summer.

On Tuesdays and Thursdays, the workshops are busy with the sounds of volunteers (more than 300) repairing and maintaining the museum's all-wood boat collection. Much of the wood—mostly white cedar—is donated.

The museum sponsors a number of special events throughout the year. Of note are the Arts Festival, Antique and Classic Boat Festival, and a Wooden Boat Show in June, the largest of its kind. This event displays boats from 80-foot yachts to 15-foot working skiffs, plus models, books, and boat races. The museum shop is well stocked with books about boats and Chesapeake Bay life, toys, and souvenirs. It's open daily 9 A.M.–5 P.M. in spring and autumn (till 6 P.M. in summer, 4 P.M. in winter). Admission is $8.50.

Dockside Express Land & Sea Tours of St. Michaels, P.O. Box 122, Tilghman, 410/886-2643, www.cruisinthebay.com, features costumed guides who escort visitors from the information booth on Mill Street daily at 1 P.M. for a one-and-a-half-hour walking and boat cruise around St. Michaels. The tours focus on local history, and operate daily between Memorial Day and Labor Day; cost is $10 per person.

Recreation

Landlubbers can get two-wheel transportation courtesy of **St. Michaels Town Dock Marina,** 305 Mulberry St., 410/745-2400. The marina rents single bicycles.

Tours

The glass-enclosed 65-foot *Patriot* cruises the Miles River and, during the one-hour outing, covers Talbot County history and Chesapeake lore. There's a snack and booze bar on board. You can catch the boat at 11 A.M., 12:30 P.M., 2:30 P.M., and 4 P.M. daily, Apr.–Nov. Captain Dave points out clammers, crabbers, and stately homes. It's docked next to the Maritime Museum, and ticket prices are $10 for adults, $4.50 for kids under 12; for information, call 410/745-3100 or click on www.patriotcruises.com.

Ed Farley welcomes visitors aboard his skipjack *H. M. Krentz* for a two-hour sail mid-Apr.–Oct. ($30). Captain Farley, a working waterman, gives a lively commentary of life in and around the Chesapeake. Call 410/745-6080 or visit www.oystercatcher.com for more information.

Dockside Express, 410/886-2643, www.docksideexpress.com, offers boat charters and scheduled 90-minute environmental tours. They also command a fleet of autos and vans available for shuttles and dry-land tours.

And if a steady equestrian pace is appealing, try a horse-drawn carriage ride from **Chesapeake Carriage Company,** 9072 New Rd., 410/745-4011; reservations are required.

Shopping

Talbot Street, the main street in town, is lined

LEGAL PIRACY

Too small and poor to equip a proper navy that could seriously threaten the Royal Navy during the War of 1812, the U.S. government relied on Yankee ingenuity. Congress encouraged ship owners to enlist their assets in the fight. American merchant vessels built in the colonies were designed to be fast and maneuverable on American waterways. Ships built in Fell's Point, Baltimore, were especially suitable—topsail schooners later dubbed Baltimore clippers. The seamen who sailed them were experienced and not at all interested in giving up their lucrative positions to become government employees.

In order to ensure the participation of these merchant seamen, Congress gave private ships the legal right to attack and seize enemy vessels, and to keep a percentage of the spoils. There were two types of commissions authorized: the first was for privateers, whose sole mission was to seize enemy shipping; the other was letters of marque, which permitted the ship's captain to engage in trade when possible and privateering when the opportunity arose. The authorizations stated that vessels were to "subdue seize and take any British vessel her appurtenances and goods and all the British persons and others who shall be found acting on board." During the 30 months that followed, hundreds of civilian-owned American vessels harassed British trade, capturing so many ships and valuable cargo in the Americas and Atlantic that British merchants brought pressure on their government to end the war. Baltimore alone docked 122 private armed vessels, and St. Michaels was another popular berth for privateers.

Each privateer captain was required to keep a journal and turn it over to the customs collector at his U.S. port of entry. Failure to do so resulted in a $1,000 fine and revocation of commission. In spite of the danger to their livelihood, some crossed the line into piracy. Captain Alexander Thompson of the *Midas* burned and sacked a plantation in Royal Island, Bahamas. Not long after the *Midas* put into port in North Carolina, a Baltimore newspaper printed an account of Thompson's raid, which quickly reached the eyes of President Monroe. Thompson was censured and lost his commission, to which he replied, in part:

> *To lend a hand in time of need*
> *When Britain she did burn*
> *Our Towns in every Part with speed.*
> *Determined to avenge the Cause*
> *I thought I would support the Laws*
> *And pay him [the British King] in his Kind.*
>
> *—The subject of the foregoing nonsense you may find at the sign of the 3 Living Squirrels, Fells Point Baltimore*

A peace treaty signed on Christmas Eve 1814 ended Captain Thompson's censure; privateering was no longer allowed. He received his share of the considerable spoils he brought in and went on to command several trading vessels. He continued to live at the Three Living Squirrels until his death in 1829.

with antique and collectible shops, clothing stores, bookstores, and every imaginable outlet for spending money. Many of the shops are open only during the high season, roughly mid-April to November. Of note is the **Mind's Eye,** 201 S. Talbot, 410/748-2023, a contemporary crafts gallery.

Accommodations

St. Michaels has dozens of inns and B&Bs, as might be expected of a summer tourist mecca. Lodgings on the main street, Talbot, cost less but experience fairly constant traffic until the wee hours during the summer.

Two historic properties were restored and joined to create **Five Gables Inn & Spa,** 202 N. Talbot St., 410/745-0100 or 877/466-0100, www.fivegables.com. It offers lodging and Aveda spa treatments, including herbal baths and massage. Rooms range from $150 to $375, and spa services are additional. Spa package specials are available throughout the year.

The Parsonage Inn suffers slightly from a location problem, 210 N. Talbot St., 410/745-5519 or 800/394-5519, www.inntravels.com/usa/md/parsonage.html, but makes up for it with lovely brick Victorian architecture and pretty rooms. The former owner, Dr. Henry Dodson, established the local brickyard in 1877 and built the house to show off different patterns in 1883. The eight rooms, all with private bath and breakfast, vary in price from midweek, off-season lows of $100–195.

Hambleton Inn, 202 Cherry St., 410/745-3350 or 866/745-3350, www.hambletoninn.com, offers five rooms with private bath in a lovely 1860 Victorian. The inn is in the middle of St. Michaels, but is a quiet two blocks away from the main street, on the water. It's open year-round, and a dock slip is available for a nominal fee. Enclosed porches decorated with seasoned wicker furniture look out on the harbor. Room rates change with the season. From Apr.–Nov., expect to pay $145–275; from Dec.–Mar., $125–195.

The Victoriana Inn, 205 Cherry St., 410/745-3368 or 888/316-1282, www.victorianainn.com, is across the street from the Hambleton, and very similar in ambiance and facilities. It offers seven rooms with full bath, and prices range from $125 (weekday, Jan. 6–Mar. 16) to $299 (weekend, Mar. 17–Jan. 5).

The **George Brooks House,** 24500 Rolles Range Rd., St. Michaels, 410/745-0999, www.georgebrookshouse.com, earned the Historical Society of Talbot County's Heritage Award for best historic renovation. This 1908 Gothic Revival Victorian is named for its builder, an African-American entrepreneur and author on race relations whose successful business ventures provided this home and care for his 11 orphaned nieces and nephews. Each of six bedrooms features a private bath and hand-carved mahogany furniture. The seven-acre property also has formal gardens and an outdoor pool. Rooms, which include a gourmet breakfast, run $95–225.

The fanciest place in town, the **Inn at Perry Cabin,** 308 Watkins Lane, 410/745-2200 or 800/722-2949, www.perrycabin.com, was originally the dwelling place of Samuel Hambleton, aide-de-camp to Commodore Oliver Hazard Perry in the War of 1812. When Hambleton retired to St. Michaels in 1816, he designed the north wing of the manor house to resemble Perry's cabin on the flagship *Niagara*—the ship that won the Battle of Lake Erie. The property changed hands several times, and in 1989, the Greek Revival–style inn and surrounding property was bought and renovated by Sir Bernard Ashley (husband of Laura Ashley of chintz and prints fame). The inn features 41 guest rooms, dockage, a heated indoor pool, health complex, helicopter access, and conference center, all set in protected wetlands and carefully tended gardens; the ambience is a cross between an upper-crust English country house and a top-level American hotel. There's even a secret passage in the library, and a snooker room. Each of the rooms is spacious and varied in layout and feeling, individually decorated with antiques and Ashley prints. Many have fireplaces and telescopes for viewing marsh wildlife. Expensive? Oh yes. Prices run from $195 to $575, including a full breakfast and afternoon tea in the inn's exceptional restaurant. But guests receive full value—the rooms and service are superb, and the inn is far enough from downtown St. Michael's to be a peaceful retreat, yet close enough to be easily accessible. It has received numerous awards over the years, including Fifth Best Resort Hotel in the United States from *Condé Nast Traveler.*

Food

Chesapeake Trading Co., 102 S. Talbot, 410/745-9797, has an espresso bar and fountain inside the store—a good place to browse while picking up a caffeine jolt. It carries a little bit of everything, including books with a local bent, clothing, CDs, and jewelry.

An inexpensive place for breakfast, lunch, and dinner ($4–8), **Chesapeake Cove,** 204 S. Talbot, 410/745-3300, is often crowded with locals.

The **Acme Grocery,** 114 S. Talbot, 410/745-9819, is a good place to pick up picnic fixings and household items.

The **Crab Claw,** Navy Point (next to the Maritime Museum), 410/745-2900, is reputed to have the best steamed crab around. It's open daily Mar.–Nov. for lunch and dinner ($19).

The **Inn at Perry Cabin,** 308 Watkins Ln., St. Michaels, is a wonderful splurge. The menu and wine list reflect the continental leanings of chef Mark Salter, who trained in Germany, Switzerland, and France before coming to Sir Bernard Ashley's Llangoed Hall Inn in Wales. The food is sophisticated and delicious—how about a French bean salad with dried cherries, pickled wild mushrooms, and golden beets ($14.50), followed by pan-seared wild rockfish with roasted garlic polenta and balsamic glazed peppers ($32)? Lunch (average price $23) and dinner ($69 and up) are served daily in the chandelier-lit dining room.

TILGHMAN ISLAND

Pittsburgh Post-Gazette writer Jayne Clark once wrote, "If St. Michaels appears perfectly coiffed, then its neighboring community of Tilghman Island hasn't shaved in a few days." Eighty percent of the 750 people who call Tilghman (TIL-man) home make their living as watermen. Of the 10–15 working skipjacks that remain in service on the Chesapeake, eight are moored on the island, in Dogwood Harbor. Several of these, along with larger boats, are available for charter.

Charter Boats

Wade Murphy takes guests for two-hour pleasure cruises aboard the oldest skipjack under sail, the *Rebecca T. Ruark* ($30). The *Rebecca* was built in 1886 and refuses to give in to age; she's won local skipjack races nine out of ten times. Captain Murphy also operates *Miss Kim,* a crabbing boat; a six-hour trip is $60 per person and includes a bushel of crabs (depending on the catch availability). If you'd prefer not to crab, it's $30. Call him at 410/886-2176 or 410/829-3976.

Captain Mike Richards takes visitors out for a two-hour sail on the Chesapeake Bay and Choptank River ($30) or a champagne sunset cruise ($35) on the 45-foot 1935 bay ketch *Lady Patty.* Longer trips are available by reservation. The captain also offers full- and half-day Chesapeake Lights Tours (www.chesapeakelights.com), a look at some or all of the bay's 12 lighthouses. Call 410/886-2215 or 800/690-5080 for more information.

Other Recreation

Sea kayaking is an excellent way to explore the shoreline and wild waterfowl of Tilghman Island. **Harris Creek Kayak,** 7857 Tilghman Island Rd., 410/886-2083, is a small operation that rents equipment, offers advice, and leads guided tours.

If it has to do with ships and sailing, you'll find it at the **Book Bank,** Tilghman Island Road, an old bank that's stuffed its vaults with sea lore. It's open weekends 10 A.M.–6 P.M.; call 410/886-2230 to special-order hard-to-find materials.

Accommodations and Food

The **Lazyjack Inn,** Dogwood Harbor, 410/886-2215 or 800/690-5080, www.lazyjackinn, is as quiet and tranquil as it gets. The 160-year-old house offers four rooms, each with private bath, and each with a special feature, such as a water view, fireplace, or private entrance. Mike and Carol Richards make a sumptuous breakfast to greet you in the sunny dining room overlooking the harbor. Rates range $140–230 per night. Mike also operates the ketch *Lady Patty.*

Black Walnut Point Inn, end of Black Walnut Road, 410/886-2452, www.tilghmanisland.com/blackwalnut, has seven rooms with private baths, tennis courts, and a pool on 57 acres.

Rates at this upscale private resort on the tip of Tilghman Island are $120–150 per night, with a two-night minimum on weekends.

Originally constructed in the 1920s as a fishing camp for vacationing anglers trying their luck at the Eastern Shore, the two-story **Sinclair House,** 5718 Black Walnut Point Rd., 410/886-2147, www.sinclairhouse.biz, was converted into the island's first B&B and remains a historic landmark on Tilghman Island. Sinclair House's innkeepers have lived and worked around the world. Monica, who is from Peru, met Jake in Guinea-Bissau, West Africa, where she served as an international officer with UNICEF and he was on diplomatic assignment to the U.S. Embassy. During their travels, both innkeepers were avid collectors of local art and handicrafts. Sinclair House now displays these individual treasures, including intricate inlaid and gilded mirrors from Asia, North Africa, and South America. Each of the four guest rooms (all have private baths) has a theme: African, Indonesian, Moroccan, and Peruvian. Prices range $109–119.

The **Bay Hundred,** 6178 Tilghman Rd., 410/886-2126, just north of the Knapps Narrows Bridge, is a casual place with great views and good food. They serve brunch Fri.–Sun. ($8) and lunch ($13) and dinner ($19) daily. Owner Fanoula Sullivan has brought sophistication to the usual seafood-restaurant menu, featuring filet Chesapeake (beef mignon in bacon, topped with crabmeat, $16–20) and salmon Rockefeller (grilled, topped with fresh sautéed spinach, $17). The menu is broad and eclectic; reservations are essential. The Bay Hundred also offers lodging—20 new rooms in a conference center, and charter boats; call to find out more.

OXFORD

Once you cross that Bay Bridge, there are no fast moves, no fast decisions, and no stress. Life is too short not to enjoy every moment.

Joe Waters, former bank executive, currently a charter boat captain, Oxford, Maryland

Judging strictly from its decelerated pace of life, it's hard to peg Oxford as one of two ports of entry for all of colonial Maryland (the other was Anne Arundel, later known as Annapolis). Before the Revolution, Oxford was a booming shipping and trade town; after, with the loss of British ships and the subsequent trade, the town dwindled. After the Civil War, Oxford entered into a new period of prosperity thanks to the railroad and increasing national markets for local oysters. With the diminution of the oyster beds in the early 1900s, Oxford once again tightened down. Today, the town is mainly a home for watermen and a sleepy getaway for visitors—there's not a lot to do in Oxford, and most people like it that way.

Sights

The Oxford Bellevue Ferry, 410/745-9023, has been in business since 1683, making it the oldest privately run ferry service in America. It crosses the Tred Avon River (.75 mile), making 25–30 trips a day, and has counted Paul Newman and the prime minister of Madagascar among its passengers. The ferry runs daily Mar. 1–Nov., weekdays 7 A.M.–sunset, weekends 9 A.M.–sunset. Summer hours are weekdays 7 A.M.–9 P.M., weekends 9 A.M.–9 P.M. Drive or walk aboard; walk-on passengers pay $1.25; car and driver pay $6 one-way, $10 round-trip.

There's a 25-mile **Scenic Loop** ideal for autos or bicyclists from St. Michaels: drive east on Route 33 to Bellevue Road, make a left (south) on Bellevue to the ferry. Float across to Oxford, then take Route 333 (Almshouse Road) east, then north, connecting with Route 322 to Easton. Return on Route 33 to St. Michaels.

The Oxford Museum, Morris and Market Streets, 410/226-0191, has mementos of the town's past—everything from 6,000-year-old Seneca arrowheads and stone tools to an oyster-shucking stand that resembles a pulpit. It's open Fri.–Sun. 2–5 P.M., admission by donation. Oxford started out as a land grant to Robert Morris in 1797—he paid representatives of the local tribes the princely sum of $1 for the use of a million acres, making this the best deal since Nieu Amsterdam. The best way to get a taste of Oxford's history is to either get a copy of Skipper Marquess's walking tour at the museum or schedule a tour around town with Skipper when he's available. He can be reached at La Motte Properties, 410/820-8000.

One of the stops on Skipper's tour is **Cutts & Case,** 306 Tilghman St., a family-owned business that's world-renowned for classic yacht design, construction, and restoration. Even those unfamiliar with wooden boats will recognize its crossed-flags logo. The smell of shaved cedar fills the workshops; boats in all stages of restoration line the pier behind the buildings. Recently, it worked on **Foto,** the wooden boat once owned by photographer Morris Rosenfeld.

Accommodations and Food

Combsberry, 4837 Evergreen Rd., 410/226-5353, www.combsberry.com, is just plain gorgeous, one of the premier historic homes on the Eastern Shore. The land was purchased in 1718 for 21,000 pounds of tobacco and 50 pounds of silver; the plantation's whitewashed brick manor house was built in 1730. After years of desultory care, the property was purchased by a group of investors for quick turnaround. Fortunately for visitors, the real estate market took a dive, and two of the partners, Mahmood and Ann Shariff, were reluctant to part with the property. They bought out their associates and restored the crumbling relic into an elegant, artistic guest inn. B&B veteran Cathy Magrogan manages the place—and whips up a masterful breakfast. It's served in either the formal dining room or the country kitchen that overlooks the nine-acre grounds dotted with majestic magnolia and willow trees and informal gardens. Four guest rooms are in the main house, and two more are in a newly built carriage house. All have private baths and water views, and are decorated in English country style. Prices run from $250–395.

The Robert Morris Inn, Morris Street and The Strand, 410/226-5111 or 888/823-4012, www.robertmorrisinn.com, dates back to 1710, when it was put together by ships' carpenters—evident in the wooden pegged paneling in the formal dining room. Robert Morris Jr. ran the Oxford-based shipping business started by his father; the endeavor was so successful, Morris was

able to lend large sums of money to finance the colonies' fight against Britain. He counted George Washington as a friend, and, after warming up his pen hand writing checks to the Continental Congress, became a signer of the Declaration of Independence, the Articles of Confederation, and the U.S. Constitution.

From Apr.–Nov. (and some winter weekends), the inn offers simply decorated bed-and-breakfast rooms in the main building (private baths, $110–220; $20 off if you dine at the inn). The establishment is celebrated for its traditional Chesapeake seafood and fine dining—more casual in the back tavern, formal in the front dining room ($25). Author James Michener, who spent considerable time here researching his book *Chesapeake,* claims their crab cakes are the best: "Raise a glass of beer in memory of an old-timer who enjoyed the place very much," he said. The restaurant is open daily for breakfast, lunch, and dinner April–Nov.

Robert Morris Inn also owns the **Sandaway Lodge,** a rambling Victorian a half-block away on a private beach (many rooms have enclosed porches, $180–280). Since the Sandaway is frequently used for weddings, the leafy interior of the gigantic weeping beech tree on the grounds has seen its share of tipsy wedding guests.

Also recommended in Oxford: the **Pier St. Marina and Restaurant,** W. Pier Street, 410/226-5171.

EASTON

Easton almost has the look of a movie set—a handsome little town with unique, locally owned shops, an exceptional art museum, and carefully maintained homes. The county seat, it was chosen as one of the 10 best American small towns in which to live several years ago by *Money* magazine, and as one of the top three "art" towns in Maryland in 1998 and 1999. In addition, Easton was awarded the ongoing "Main Street" designation and in 2000 received recognition for excellence in the area of downtown revitalization set by the Maryland Main Street Program and the National Trust for Historic Preservation's National Main Street Center. The message board at St. Andrew's Anglican Church in town advertises "Broken hearts mended." What more could you ask?

Sights

The **Academy of the Arts,** 106 South St., 410/822-2787, www.art-academy.org, is a modern space in an old building. The facade is a restored 1820s schoolhouse, but the inside is all space and light. The academy serves two main purposes: a public arts program with sunny well-equipped workshops, and a display space for professionally curated exhibits. The quality of any display space reflects its curators, and the hardworking staff at the academy (26 exhibitions a year!) chooses extremely well. Though the emphasis is on Eastern Shore artists, exhibitions include works by internationally acclaimed artists. A recent exhibit focused on the master Russian Impressionists Nikolai Timkov and his contemporaries. This work, though not widely known, was exceptional in every way. The permanent collection includes works by James McNeill Whistler, Grant Wood, Leonard Basking, and other notables. It's open Mon.–Sat. 10 A.M.–4 P.M., Wednesday 10 A.M.–9 P.M. Admission is $2; free on Wednesday. Closed August.

EASTON

THE EASTERN SHORE

© AVALON TRAVEL PUBLISHING, INC.

The **Avalon Theatre,** 40 East Dover St., 410/822-0345, www.avalontheatre.com, presents a lively year-round entertainment repertoire, including movies, choirs, musicians from the Caribbean and New Orleans, and ornate displays (one year, model trains and railroad lore filled the space at Christmas). The real star, though, is the restored art deco theater with its state-of-the-art sound and lighting systems. Call for schedule.

The **Historical Society of Talbot County,** 25 S. Washington St., 410/822-0773, www.hstc.org, offers several walking tours of the town to acquaint visitors with its many historic buildings. The Three Centuries Tour is a 45-minute guided tour of three houses that represent each of the three centuries since the founding of Talbot County in 1662—"Ending of Controversie" is a faithful reproduction of the 1670 home of Quaker Wenlock Christison; the Joseph Neall House was the residence and shop of a Quaker craftsman of the late 18th century; and the James Neall House (1810) was built in the Federal style for a family of 11, plus retainers.

The historical society also offers a **Frederick Douglass Driving Tour** that includes 14 sites connected to the abolitionist, including his birthplace. Ask for the brochure at the office or by phone. The S. Washington Street office houses a permanent exhibit of local history; it's open Tues.–Fri. 11 A.M.–3 P.M., Saturday 10 A.M.–4 P.M., and operates Tharpe Antiques & Decorative Arts, 30 S. Washington St., as a museum shop.

In 1682, a small group of Quakers took two years to build what is now known as the **Old Third Haven Meeting House,** 405 S. Washington St., 410/822-0293. The white clapboard building, still in use, is the oldest religious structure in the United States and the earliest dated building in Maryland. The meetinghouse stands in an open grove of trees at the end of a lane (look for the small sign on the west side of the street). It's almost always open, and in summer, you may see the resident family of fat woodchucks scurrying about. William Penn was among the prominent Quakers who sat in the simple wooden pews to worship; George Fox, founder of the Religious Society of Friends

(Quakers), sent books here, establishing the first public library in the province. All are welcome to attend a meeting any Sunday at 10 A.M. (the brick building next to the meeting house is used in the winter).

Pickering Creek Audubon Center, 11450 Audubon Ln., 410/822-4903, www.pickering creek.org, is a private sanctuary operated by the Audubon Society. The property—the home of a Matapeake Indian village prior to European colonization—features more than 100 acres of hardwood forest, including old-growth oak, beech, and hickory, and 270 acres under low-impact cultivation (an organic community garden). Additional acreage is in conservation easements, buffer strips, wildlife plantings (where local farmers plant a certain portion of the land in feed for wildlife), and a nature preserve. There's a mile of shoreline, and fresh and brackish marshes on the Wye River. The thrust here is on education, and the center offers numerous opportunities to enjoy the outdoors and learn. Evening canoe trips, forest ecology walks, herb workshops, and sea kayaking are a few of the one- and two-day programs that take place throughout the warmer months.

The center is open Mon.–Fri. 8:30 A.M.–5 P.M., Saturday 10 A.M.–4 P.M. The buildings are closed Sunday, but the grounds are open to visitors— there's a nature walk, and the sanctuary is studded with more than 40 bluebird boxes—as one would expect of the Audubon Society, this is an excellent bird-watching location. To get there, take Route 662 north from Easton (this runs parallel with U.S. 50) past the Easton Airport. Follow the signs: turn left at Sharp Road (west), and veer right at the Y; turn right (north) to Presquille Road, then right on Audubon Lane.

Shopping

Harrison Street in Easton is the site of several antique and collectibles shops. Contemporary crafts and clothing shops also line the street. **Talbot Town,** 218 N. Washington St., a small in-town mall, features a **Talbot's** (no relation) and several upscale home decorating shops. **Courthouse Square Shops** line a pass-through from

the Historical Society of Talbot County, Easton

Harrison Street to Washington Street; of note is **Rowens Stationery Store,** featuring local-interest books as well as best-sellers.

There are several antique shops and multiple-dealer shops in the 7700 and 7800 blocks of Ocean Gateway (Route 50). **Foxwell's,** 7793 Ocean Gateway, and **Camelot Antiques, Ltd.,** 7871 Ocean Gateway, are representative. **The Wood Duck,** 8374 Ocean Gateway, is a gallery featuring decoys, carvings, limited editions, and original artwork.

Also check out **Sullivan's Antiques Warehouse,** 28272 St. Michaels Rd. (Route 33).

A favorite "nameless" store is at the intersection of Royal Oak Road and Bellevue Ferry Road. Two old buildings stand across from one another—one has furniture piled end over end, and the other has everything else. Great prices and great fun.

Accommodations

The **Tidewater Inn,** 101 E. Dover St., 410/822-1300 or 800/237-8775, www.tidewaterinn.com, combines the intimate feel of a B&B with the amenities of a large hotel. Once a haunt of camouflage-coated goose hunters, the inn now caters to upscale customers (the goose hunters are still there, but now they dress for dinner). It's not as formal as it sounds, but leave the muddy boots and dogs outside; they're tough on the carpet and mahogany antiques in the lobby—and they'll wreak havoc in the pool. This is the best "modern" hotel in the area. A restaurant on the premises serves breakfast ($8), lunch, and dinner ($9–20). The Hemingway-esque **Decoy Bar** is heavy on Eastern Shore atmosphere, and a fun place to stop for a drink. You'll be in good company—actor Harrison Ford pulled a few off the top there when his small plane was grounded during a storm.

Room rates start at $75 for a single with twin bed, and go up to $300 for the executive suite. It offers special-rate packages throughout the year.

If an 1893 Queen Anne Victorian is more to your taste, try **Chaffinch House,** 132 S. Harrison St., 410/822-5074 or 800/861-5074. All of the rooms have a private bath and all are decorated in period style. Rates range from $110–130. Also recommended: the **Bishop's House B&B,** 214 Goldsborough St., 410/820-7290 or 800/223-7290, www.bishophouse.com; rates are $100–120.

Food

Mason's Café, 22 S. Harrison St., 410/822-3204, is a charming place to stop for coffee, and to enjoy the colorful pottery that's for sale along with handmade chocolates.

Hill's Soda Fountain, in Hill's Drug Stores, 32 E. Dover St., 410/822-2666, is the real thing. You'll find malts and burgers, tuna sandwiches and chips—all around $5.

Café 25, 25 Goldsborough St., 410/822-9360, is a light-hearted restaurant ("If you like us, send your friends. If not, send your enemies, or better yet, tell us") with an eclectic, well-prepared menu. It serves breakfast ($4), lunch, and dinner ($11) seven days a week. The menu features pizzas, pierogies (meat pies of Polish origin), and fresh fish, an extensive wine list from all over the world, and, to finish, tortoni and baklava to die for. Good attitude, good food, good prices.

Legal Spirits Tavern, 42 E. Dover St., 410/820-0765, offers Eastern Shore cuisine (cream of crab soup is a specialty) complete with bountiful desserts. Prices average $9 for lunch, $17 for dinner. Open daily for lunch and dinner.

One of the local happening hot spots at night is the **Washington Street Pub,** across from the courthouse, 20 N. Washington, 410/822-9011, www.wstpub.com. It has a raw bar and 19 beers on tap; open daily for lunch and dinner ($7–18).

INFORMATION

Most Talbot County destinations have their own contact numbers: St. Michaels, 800/808-7622, www.stmichaelsmd.org; Tilghman Island, 410/770-8000, www.tilghmanisland.com; Oxford, Oxford Business Association, 410/226-5730, www.oxfordmd.com/oba; and Easton, 410/822-0065, www.eastonmd.org.

Dorchester County

Dorchester is largely rural, threaded by rivers, including the 68-mile-long Choptank, immortalized by authors James Michener (*Chesapeake*) and John Barth (*Tidewater Tales* and *Floating Opera*). **Cambridge,** the largest town in the county, is one of the oldest in the state, settled in 1684. Tobacco built the local economy, on the backs of slaves. As trading ships from Europe began to dock in Cambridge during the 1700s (the unusable harbor had been dredged out to create a deep-water port), seafood and muskrat pelts joined tobacco as the major exports. The Industrial Revolution brought lumber mills and flour mills to Cambridge, and in the late 1800s, oyster packing became the major source of employment; the local industry was second only to Baltimore. In 1911, Phillips Packing Company took over the oyster packing plant and drove the town to new heights of prosperity, earning the name "Queen City." Phillips folded in the 1950s, and Cambridge was left to struggle.

Tourism is breathing new life into the city and the county; besides time-honored boating recreation, **Sailwinds Park,** a $30 million waterfront multiuse facility for concerts, fairs, festivals, and trade shows is under development in Cambridge; a beautifully designed Hyatt golf resort and spa has opened, a Holiday Inn Express has set down roots, and other major players in the hospitality industry will surely follow.

ISLANDS AND TOWNS TOUR

This 85-mile road trip begins and ends in Cambridge. The route makes a big loop around Dorchester County, swinging past several historic towns, crossing a large wildlife refuge, and wandering into two island communities. None of these "attractions" are developed, in the tourist sense, so be prepared for some serene country vistas and great history. Since some of the route is on major highways, it's not recommended for cyclists, though parts of it would be ideal. All distances are approximate.

Leave Cambridge heading east on U.S. 50, and turn left (north) on Route 16 (three miles east of town). Follow Route 16 five miles to the village of **East New Market,** settled in the mid-1600s. Most of the extant colonial-era houses are along Route 16 (which veers to the left at Linkwood Road) and the intersection of Route 14. (Route 14 loops around to the town of **Secretary** and the Suicide Bridge Restaurant.) The village that makes up the historic district is bounded on the south and east by Route 392 and on the west by Creamery Road. It features 75 buildings representing architecture from the 18th, 19th, and 20th centuries. The buildings are privately owned, and most look nearly new. For detailed information on some of the more prominent houses, contact Dorchester County Tourism and ask for the "East New Market" brochure.

Take Route 14 east and south out of town for five miles to Route 331, and follow it for six miles to **Vienna,** one-half mile below the intersection of U.S. 50. Settled about the same time as East New Market, Vienna's original name was "Vinnacokasimmon," after a native chief. It was also named Baltimore for a short period, at the request of the Calverts. Vienna prospered in the early years as a center for the tobacco trade and shipbuilding. As technology changed (and the river silted up), the town turned its focus away from industry and became a quiet residential village. It supports a B&B or two and a few antique stores. As with East New Market, details on the town's architectural treasures (mostly on Water Street on the Nanticoke River, and on Church Street at the south end of Water Street) are in a brochure available from Dorchester County Tourism.

Leave Vienna and travel south on Crossroads Road six miles to Henry's Crossroads. Go right on Henry's Crossroads (west) to the end (two miles), and turn left (south) onto Griffith Neck Road, which turns into Bestpitch Ferry Road, to **Bucktown** (10 miles). Bucktown is the home of the former Brodess Plantation, birthplace of Harriet Tubman. Take Greenbrier Road three miles west to Maple Dam Road. Make a left (south) to Key Wallace Drive and the settlement of Seward.

Continue west on Key Wallace Drive through the top of Blackwater National Wildlife Refuge, three miles. As an alternative route,

consider taking the refuge's driving tour, also great for cycling. Both routes dead-end on Church Creek Road.

Turn left on Church Creek/Golden Hill Road (south) until it dead-ends in Route 335/336, four miles. Turn right on Route 335, Hooper Island Road, and follow it as far down into Hooper Island as you'd like (2–14 miles). You'll pass the diminutive Star of the Sea Chapel on the north side of the road; it was built before 1767 as a place of worship for local Roman Catholics. **Hooper Island** is actually a chain of islands named for the family that settled there in the late 1600s; Colonel Henry Hooper and his son, Brigadier General Henry Hooper, commanded local militias against the British during the Revolution. Nearly 75 years later, Ella Carroll, feminist, friend of Abraham Lincoln, and Northern spy, called the island home. Today, the dwellings are almost entirely made up of the homes of watermen, set among marshes—a surreal, floating landscape. Sandy's is a good place to stop for a snack and an opportunity to pick up a locally made souvenir.

Return on Route 335 to Smithville Road and make a left (north) for seven miles until it dead-ends at Taylors Island Road (Route 16). Make a left, and within a mile, you'll be in the community of **Taylors Island.** This quiet village was settled in the 1650s. Along with late-18th-century churches and schools, it boasts a British ship's cannon captured by local militia during the War of 1812.

Return on Taylors Island Road east to Church Creek, five miles. **Old Trinity Church,** 1716 Taylors Island Road, is worth a look. The chapel was built between 1675 and 1690 and refurbished to its original state. The floor tiles (laid with a mortar of burnt oyster shells), altar table, and exterior brick walls are all original. Fifteen high-backed, gated pews made of beeswax-rubbed heart of pine, finished with handmade H-hinges, are faithful representations of the period. The loft in back was for slaves and servants, who were locked in during the service. The church still maintains an active (voluntary) congregation; services are at 11 A.M. on Sunday. Call the rectory, 410/228-3583, to set up a tour of the

Old Trinity Church

church, or wander about the old graveyard. A church regular commented that the headstones reflect the leading preoccupations of many Eastern Shore dwellers: boats, booze, and broads. You'll find history here, all kinds.

Route 16 will take you east and north back to Cambridge, five miles.

BLACKWATER NATIONAL WILDLIFE REFUGE

Once a farm used by muskrat trappers for the fur trade, the refuge was established in 1933 to provide sanctuary for migrating waterfowl. Geese number approximately 35,000 and ducks exceed 15,000 at the peak of fall migration, usually in November. October through March is the best time to visit to see migratory birds, though many songbirds, reptiles, and mammals stay year-round. Blackwater is also a haven for three endangered or threatened species: the bald eagle (largest nesting population north of Florida), peregrine falcon, and Delmarva fox squirrel. The refuge is stunningly beautiful, particularly in the late afternoon when the setting sun reflects off the mirrored ponds and birds swoop to feed on the plentiful insects.

Blackwater may be seen in several different ways. The visitors center offers exhibits, naturalist talks, and films. From there, several walking trails, including a wheelchair-accessible loop, meander through different habitats. A Wildlife Drive of either a 6.5-mile loop or a 3.5-mile all-weather road winds along through ponds, woods, fields, and marshes; walking and biking on the Wildlife Drive is permitted. Cyclists may choose from a 20-mile loop or a 25-mile loop. Boaters may enter the refuge via one of the surrounding waterways Apr. 1–Sept. 30, but may not launch within the refuge (there is a public boat launch on Shorters Wharf Road on the southern boundary of the refuge).

The visitors center is open Mon.–Fri. 8 A.M.– 4 P.M., Sat.–Sun. 9 A.M.–5 P.M. year-round. A daily permit is required: private vehicles, $3; pedestrian or bicyclist, $1. Golden Eagle passes are accepted. For more information, contact Blackwater National Wildlife Refuge, 2145 Key Wallace Dr., Cambridge, MD 21613, 410/228-2677, or the Fish and Wildlife Service, 800/344-WILD (800/344-9453), www.fws.gov.

OTHER SIGHTS

Attractions in Dorchester County are low-key. The **Underground Railroad Gift Shop,** 424 Race St., Cambridge, 410/228-0401, stocks a few items, but more significantly houses a "learning center" focusing on the life of Dorchester-born national heroine Harriet Tubman. Storyboards line the walls, illuminating the life of Tubman and other famous black Americans, the Underground Railroad, and other topics of interest. Admission is free, but donations are appreciated. **Hometown Tours** works out of the gift shop, and offers a tour of the county centered on the life and times of Ms. Tubman ($10 for adults, $7 for kids). Other tours—with a black viewpoint—can be tailored to individual interests, and may include historic buildings and churches.

Dorchester Arts Center, 120 High St., 410/228-7782, offers classes in artistic disciplines and exhibits local artwork. The gift shop is inspired, and well worth a stop. Admission is free. The location, in a stately Victorian, is another reason to visit High Street.

During Cambridge's wealthiest periods, **High Street** was *the* address, and a stroll from the long wharf up to Poplar Street provides the evidence. Several Maryland governors had homes on High, and the properties have been cherished and kept up over the years. Homes range in age from the late 18th century to the early 20th, most built from 1850–1880. A few of note are 200 High St., home of Governor Charles Goldsborough, built in 1790; it's one of the best-preserved Federal-style houses on the Eastern Shore. The Sulivane House, 205 High St., was built in 1763 and was home to generations of Sulivanes, including Colonel Clement Sulivane, a Confederate solider who participated in the burning of Richmond. The Bayly House, 207 High St., was built in 1755 in Annapolis and barged across the bay in 1760—still in the Bayly family, the white-columned porches recall the old South. Christ Episcopal Church, on the corner of High and Church Streets, was built from stones shipped over as ballast—there's no natural stone in the area. The graveyard was established before the Revolutionary War; Civil War–era graves of both Confederate and Union boys lie next to one another. The Dorchester County Department of Tourism publishes an excellent free guide to historic homes in Cambridge, including those on High Street. Visitors can pick one up at the Arts Center. For an interesting contrast, you might want to walk up Water Street and stroll on Vue de Leau Street, one block away from High Street; these were the homes of local watermen.

Cambridge has two small museums focusing on different aspects of maritime history. The **Brannock Maritime Museum,** 210 Talbot St., 410/228-6938, is dedicated to preserving artifacts from Dorchester County and boating life in general; the **James B. Richardson Maritime Museum,** 401 High St., 410/221-1871, concentrates on the art and craft of wooden boats, and displays examples of wooden craft. Visiting hours at both museums can be capricious—it's best to call first. Admission to the Brannock is by donation; the Richardson charges $1 for admission.

The **Meredith House and Nield Museum,** 902 LaGrange Ave. at Maryland Avenue, 410/228-7953, is the 1760 Georgian home of a former Maryland governor. The museum displays antique toys, agricultural and maritime artifacts, Native American handiwork, a blacksmith shop, and gardens. It's open Thurs.–Sat. 10 A.M.–3 P.M.; admission is $2.

Those interested in machines and history will want to stop by the **Spocott Windmill,** Route 343, six miles west of Cambridge in the vicinity of Lloyds. This is a rare post-style mill (it literally sits aloft a four-foot-diameter 200-year-old stripped white oak tree like a lollipop on a stick). Though the interior is seldom open to the public, it's worth a look. At one time, 18 post windmills operated in Dorchester County—all were eventually destroyed by forces of nature. The Spocott was destroyed in the blizzard of 1880 and rebuilt in 1971, using the original millstones, interior stairs, and much of the original timber.

RECREATION

Boat tours are a popular way to see the area. The *Cambridge Lady,* 410/221-0776, is a classic wooden yacht that offers several tours, including

"Michener's Chesapeake Tour" that visits Oxford and Cambridge by water and includes narration that brings the times and places of the novel to life. Combination walking and boat tours, a nautical history tour, and eco-tours are also offered, along with cruise-and-dine (you're ferried to a local restaurant) or dine-aboard buffets. Co-captains Frank and Sherri Herbert are locals who love the area and freely share their enthusiasm. The *Lady* sails daily, May–Oct. If a skipjack is more your style, the *Nathan of Dorchester,* 410/228-7141, www.skipjack-nathan.org, is the boat for you. The *Nathan* is newish—built in 1994—but has all the fine features of traditional skipjacks. Trips include narration on the lives of Chesapeake Bay watermen. The *Nathan* sails daily, April–Oct. Both boats are docked in Cambridge.

Let's say you were deeply influenced by *Show-boat* in your youth. The *Dorothy-Megan,* 410/943-4775, docked in Hurlock, is an 80-foot paddle wheeler that offers sightseeing and lunch and dinner cruises.

Sportfishing Charters: Sawyer Fishing Charters, 1345 Hoopers Island Rd., Church Creek, 410/397-3743, www.shorenet.net/sawyer, will take you out into the bay to reel in the striped bass of your dreams. It offers full- and half-day trips, and special rates during the summer. The *Joint Venture,* 410/228-7837, Cambridge, under Captain Ben Parks, provides a variety of bottom fishing, trolling, and casting day trips, from Tilghman Island to the Virginia line.

Bicycling: Dorchester County, like much of the Eastern Shore, is great bike territory. Along with the scenic loops in the Blackwater Refuge, an additional 32-mile back-road loop begins in Vienna. It covers part of the driving tour, but spends far more time on little-used roads. Take Crossroads Road south out of Vienna, and turn right (west) on Steels Neck Road. Continue to go straight when the road becomes New Bridge Road. It will dead-end at Ravenwood Road. Turn left (south). Turn right at Drawbridge Road, then left (west) on Decoursey Bridge Road. It dead-ends at Bucktown Road/Bestpitch Ferry Road. Turn left (south). The turnoff for Greenbrier Road and Blackwater Refuge comes up about a mile down the road—if you take the short refuge loop on Key Wallace Drive, it will add another 12 miles to the trip. If you choose to continue south on Bucktown Road/Bestpitch Ferry Road, it will turn into Griffith Neck Road (east), and turn sharply north (you'll cross the drawbridge). Continue on Drawbridge Road north to Steels Neck Road, and make a right (east) to retrace your path to Vienna.

Shopping: Cambridge has a dandy antiques center, **The Packing House,** and, next door, **Artwells's Bargain Center.** Both renovated warehouses offer miles of aisles and multiple dealers; both can be found at Dorchester and Washington Streets.

ACCOMMODATIONS

The Tavern House, 111 Water St., Vienna, 410/376-3347, was built on the Nanticoke River during colonial times. Today it offers four bedrooms, all with shared bath; two of the bedrooms have fireplaces. Rates are $75 per night.

The **Cambridge House,** 112 High St., Cambridge, 410/221-7700, www.cambridgehouse-bandb.com, is an elegant Queen Anne–style Victorian that was built for a wealthy sea captain. It was a peeling wreck when innkeeper Stuart Schefers took over in 1996; the meticulously renovated rooms are decorated in period antiques and all have fireplaces, private baths, air-conditioning, and TV. Schefers, a professional restaurateur, opened 37 restaurants in New York City before retiring to Cambridge. The breakfasts are spectacular, as you might expect. It's open year-round, and a room for two is $120.

Luxury, thy name is **Hyatt Regency Chesapeake Bay,** 100 Heron Blvd., 410/901-1234—this painstakingly designed and landscaped resort is a feast for the eye (and stomach). Perched like a castle on the shores of the Choptank River, it offers a par-71 18-hole golf course (The River Marsh Golf Club, created by Keith Foster), a full-service, top-flight spa (The Stillwater), tennis courts, a small private beach with paddleboats, a marina (with a provisions store), an exercise facility with classes, and three swimming pools, one of which appears to merge with the river below it. Visitors pull up to the grand circular arrival court via a private entry road that winds through natural plantings and the golf course. Every room has a view—of the river, of fountains, of the golf course. It's truly a beautiful place. Guests who choose not to dawdle in their airy and spacious rooms can mingle with others in the handsome glass-enclosed bar, Michener's Library, or shoot a game of snooker, or just sit by the big outdoor fireplace at night and grill a s'more. Though the resort appears to be a playground for adults, families are equally welcome; Hyatt offers Camp Hyatt at Pirate's Cove, activities for children ages 4–12 (half-day sessions are $28, full days are $52).

Luxury has its price—rooms start at $350. Use of the beach, pools, and tennis courts is included with the room, but exercise classes, golf, and spa treatments are extra: for example, expect to pay between $100 and $200 for spa services.

FOOD

The **Portside,** 201 Trenton St., Cambridge, 410/228-9007, is the sort of ultracasual place where locals come for a bite. The focus is on seafood, as entrées, sandwiches, and in baskets with fries. It's open for lunch and dinner Tues.–Sun.; prices range $5–20. There's a good view of the boats plying the river below. Also recommended in Cambridge: **Snappers,** 112 Commerce St., 410/228-0112, another local favorite for seafood.

The soaring ceiling and subtle lighting of **Water's Edge Grill,** 100 Heron Blvd., 410/901-1234 (in the Hyatt Chesapeake), reflect the lofty aims of the chefs at what is undoubtedly the most elegant restaurant in this part of the bay. Sophisticated variations of regional specialties such as crab cakes and roast duck are well prepared and beautifully presented. It's open for breakfast, lunch, and dinner daily; entrées range $16–35.

Also in the Hyatt Chesapeake, the **Eagle's Nest Bar and Grille,** 100 Heron Blvd., 410/901-1234, may be the most exquisitely male golf club restaurant and bar ever conceived. Large bronze sculptures of Chesapeake wildlife by William Turner stand guard over a long dark-toned wood room with enormous windows and imposing wrought-iron chandeliers. It's open 11 A.M.–3:30 P.M. for beer, cocktails, and sandwiches (around $9).

SUICIDE BRIDGE

In case you're wondering why they call the short span that crosses a tributary of the Choptank River "Suicide Bridge," here's the story. Apparently, this bit of wood and concrete has all the allure of San Francisco's Golden Gate Bridge. What it lacks is height, being only 10–15 feet above the water. That didn't stop the bridge's first victim, a postmaster from Hurlock, who shot himself and fell into the creek. The second victim, a local farmer, followed suit. The third victim either jumped off the bridge and struck his head on a piling, or was a victim of foul play—it was never determined.

The original structure was built in 1888; it was replaced in 1910 and once again in 1968. Less than six months after the newest bridge was built, a longtime employee of Continental Can in Hurlock chose to end his life rather than return to work from his vacation. He jumped off the bridge and drowned. Not long after, another man who was born and raised within half a mile of the bridge and who had moved away for several years came back and shot himself—on Suicide Bridge.

Things may be looking up for the unfortunate span—one woman who had jumped into the icy waters recently changed her mind and began calling for help; she was rescued by Dave Nickerson, who lives next to the creek (and owns the nearby restaurant). Local resident Pete Moxey says, "I don't think the bridge is jinxed. Maybe it's just the name that brings them here." The only way to guarantee peace on Suicide Bridge may be to rename it—how about "Second Thoughts Bridge"?

Suicide Bridge Restaurant, 6304 Suicide Bridge Rd., Hurlock, 410/943-4689, is the most popular eatery around, with both locals and visitors. It's about 10 miles out of Cambridge, on the Choptank River. Again, the focus is on seafood, baked, boiled, broiled, or fried, but they also have a complete beef/chicken/veal selection. Sandwiches are around $7, entrées $11–27. The atmosphere is boating casual (*good* shorts and collared knit shirt). It serves dinner daily.

Old Salty's, Hoopers Island Road, Hoopers Island, 410/397-3752, is an inexpensive place to stop for a sandwich (under $2–7) or an entrée ($5–15). The crab sandwiches and fresh fish sandwiches are quite good. Old Salty's has gained quite a reputation with visitors over the past few years, and not just for the cheap snacks. A big room next to the restaurant sells craft items made by local people. How could you resist a gold-painted crab shell filled with cotton snow, a glittering miniature Christmas tree and bear—especially when the bear is hoisting a jug to his snout? I couldn't—it has a place of honor on my tree. The woven potholders are also irresistible; anything for sale there shames made-in-Honduras-just-for-tourists merchandise.

INFORMATION

If you're on the Eastern Shore, keep an eye out for the *Tidewater Times,* a little (3.5 inches by 5 inches) powerhouse of a monthly publication that has lots of great information and articles about the Eastern Shore, especially Talbot and Dorchester Counties. You can also reach them on the Web: www.tidewatertimes.com.

For brochures and information updates, contact the Dorchester County Department of Tourism, 2 Rose Hill Pl., Cambridge, MD 21613, 800/522-TOUR (800/522-8687), www.tourdorchester.org.

Salisbury and Wicomico County

Salisbury, the largest city on the Eastern Shore (granting that Ocean City's population waxes and wanes seasonally), began as a mill community in the center of dense woods in 1732. The Wicomico River provided critical water access to the Chesapeake, and Salisbury grew as the principal crossroads of the southern Delmarva Peninsula. The importance of water travel during colonial times was emphasized by the prevalence of ferries; one that survives today is the Whitehaven Ferry, on the very southern end of the county.

The town of Salisbury burned to the ground in 1860, and was entirely rebuilt. Today, the town continues to thrive as a center of commerce, and offers major historical and recreational activities for visitors (and the restaurants are good, too).

Whitehaven Loop

This 38-mile round-trip from Salisbury is ideal for a leisurely two-day bike trip or a one-day auto trip. It travels along straight two-lane roads through marshes, open fields, and "telephone pole farms"—groves of commercially grown tall pines.

Begin on U.S. 50 in Salisbury, heading east. Make a left on Nanticoke Road, then take the first left on Pemberton Drive (south). Follow Pemberton as it angles sharply right, then left. You'll pass historic **Pemberton Hall** on the left, and the **Rockawalkin schoolhouse** near Rockawalkin Creek. It was built in 1872 and is typical of one-room schoolhouses of the period. At one time, it housed 35 students in grades one through seven. It's open by appointment (call the Wicomico Historical Society, 410/860-0447).

Pemberton Drive ends at Route 349. Turn left (west) and, in less than a mile, make the next left (south) on Route 352 (Whitehaven Road). This will take you all the way down to the **Whitehaven Ferry.**

To get some idea of how old the settlement of Whitehaven is, consider the fact that one of the first residents was Colonel George Gale, whose first wife was George Washington's grandmother. The free ferry has been operating over the narrow stretch of the Wicomico River since 1692; it was once a link on the old colonial road between the thriving seaports of Vienna and Princess Anne. The ferry can take a car or several bicycles, and operates year-round, though hours change with the seasons: Mar. 1–May 15, 7 A.M.–6 P.M.; May 16–Sept. 15, 6 A.M.–7:30 P.M.; Sept. 16–Sept. 30, 7 A.M.–6 P.M.; and Oct. 1–Feb. 28, 7 A.M.–5:30 P.M. It's part of the Maryland Highway System, and information is available at 410/334-2798. Unless you're eating or staying in the area, take the ferry across to Whitehaven Ferry Road.

Whitehaven Ferry Road dead-ends on Polks Road. Turn left (east) and continue for about five miles to Loretto-Allen Road; turn left (north). Cross Wicomico Creek and enter the village of Allen. At the stop sign, turn right (north) and go up Allen Road, which turns into South Camden Avenue. You'll return to Salisbury on this road, passing the outlying residential areas and the pretty campus of Salisbury State University.

SALISBURY
Sights

What was once necessity has become art, and that is nowhere better demonstrated than the **Ward Museum of Wildfowl Art,** 909 S. Schumaker Dr., Salisbury, 410/742-4988, www.wardmuseum.org. You will have to remind yourself that you are looking at carved and painted wood, and not wild birds in flight. The work is extraordinary, as you might expect from the premier collection of wildfowl art in the world. The museum looks at the history and heritage of the art, from antique working decoys to contemporary carvings, and two additional galleries feature changing exhibits. Winners in all categories from the annual world competition are displayed, including Shootin' Stool (active decoys), Miniatures, and Decorative Lifesize. Among the winners of past Decorative Lifesize awards were "Road Kill Pheasant" (Winner, Best in the World—not only for the outrageously beautiful carving, but also for the sly humor), a pair of fighting cocks, and courting kestrels in midflight. Wow. Admission is $7, and it's open Mon.–Sat. 10 A.M.–5 P.M., Sunday noon–5 P.M.

The **Salisbury Zoo,** 5 Park Dr. (Salisbury City Park), Salisbury, 410/548-3188, www.salisburyzoo.org, is a zoo-hater's zoo. Dr. Theodore Reed, Director Emeritus for the National Zoo, called it "one of the finest small zoos in North America," and so it is. Nearly 400 species—all native to the Americas—inhabit a compact and neatly landscaped 12 acres. One thing that makes this zoo unique is the preponderance of natural habitats—cages are few. Bright colored macaws zoom around the tall trees, unhampered by wire; ducks and other waterfowl come and go at will on the stretch of Wicomico River that borders the zoo; prairie dogs tumble around their specially built enclosure. Another unique aspect: the zoo charges no admission. It's open daily, year-round. From Memorial Day–Labor Day, hours are 8 A.M.–7:30 P.M.; the rest of the year, the zoo closes at 4:30 P.M. It's a peaceful place for a stroll, and a special place for children.

Historic Sights

Salisbury has a major force for historical preservation in the Wicomico Historical Society, 410/860-0447. It maintains a small museum

art deco doorway in Salisbury's city center

SALISBURY

To Salisbury Pewter and
The Centre at Salisbury

CHESAPEAKE EAST

POPLAR HILL MANSION

GOIN' NUTS CAFE

THE COUNTRY HOUSE

LEGENDS

CITY CENTER

RAMADA

SALISBURY ZOO

WATERMEN'S COVE

Municipal Park

WARD MUSEUM OF WILDFOWL ART

SALISBURY STATE UNIVERSITY

0   200 yds
0   200 m

© AVALON TRAVEL PUBLISHING, INC.

and store at **Pemberton Historical Park,** site of Pemberton Hall, built in 1741 for Colonel Isaac Handy. The grounds are threaded by 4.5 miles of self-guided nature trails, and the manor house may be toured by arrangement (call 410/742-1741). The museum and store are open by appointment; admission is $2. Pemberton Historical Park hosts a number of special events during the year, notably the Colonial Fair. To get there from U.S. 50 east of Salisbury, turn left on Nanticoke Road, then take the first left on Pemberton Drive (south). Follow Pemberton two miles; the park is on the left.

The historical society also publishes a walking tour of "Newtown"—now the oldest neighbor-hood in Salisbury—the area that was built after the great fires of 1860 and 1886 destroyed much of the city (call for the brochure). One of the homes spared by the fires welcomes visitors: **Poplar Hill Mansion,** 117 Elizabeth St., 410/749-1776, built in 1799. It's open to the public by appointment and is a popular site for meetings and events; donations are appreciated. If a house imparts its history in spirit to those who love it, then Robert Shourds Withey, the "Curator-in-Residence," surely embodies Poplar Hill's past. He answers questions and guides vis-itors with an added fillip of affection for the house and history of Salisbury.

The **Mason-Dixon Marker** lies north of Salisbury on the Delaware border, U.S. 13 just past Route 54 on the west side of the road. Charles Mason and Jeremiah Dixon surveyed the line between 1763 and 1767, and it was used as the formal dividing line between slave and free states. Maryland—below the Mason-Dixon Line—chose to be a free state, at least technically. One deciding factor was that the Emancipation Proclamation freed slaves only in those states that seceded from the Union. Therefore, slave owners in Maryland were not obligated by law to manumit their slaves.

Recreation

Shopping: Between Division and Main Street, Salisbury has closed traffic and created a pedestrian mall (City Center) surrounded by pretty historic buildings. The area includes sophisticated women's clothing stores, several antique shops, among them **Parker Place Antiques,** and a few galleries, including the **Salisbury Art Institute and Gallery,** and **Westbrooke Cottage,** which offers folk art, soaps, candles, and more. On Division Street, **Under the Rainbow** has a stunning collection of dolls, and next door, **Aesop's Fable Café** is a good place to stop for coffee and gaze at the Tiffany windows in Trinity Church across the street.

Several folks mentioned **The Country House,** 805 E. Main St., Salisbury, 410/749-1959, www .thecountryhouse.com, as being a great place to look for casual items for house and garden. The building is big—16,000 square feet—so you'll probably find more than you were looking for.

Salisbury Pewter, 2611 N. Salisbury Blvd., Salisbury, 410/546-1188, is the "home store" of the international company, and visitors have a chance to see the artisans at work while picking up some good buys. Pewter is a mixture of tin, copper, and antimony; during fabrication, lead is removed, making the pewter safe for food. Those who work forming the flat pewter discs into cups and trays are called spinners (a 10-year apprenticeship is the norm); the Salisbury Pewter trademark is applied by hand. Tiffany, the largest buyer, sells Salisbury pewter under its own trademark; the second biggest consumer of engraved pewter is the U.S. government. Check out the

STOOL PIGEONS AND GUNNERS

In the 19th century, hunters considered themselves successful according to quantity of kills. The term "stool pigeon," which today alludes to one who informs on his associates, originally referred to live passenger pigeons tethered to a tree-like post. Pigeons on the wing, being social creatures, would spiral down to land beside their brother and be picked off by the hunter's guns. A good hunter with a repeating rifle could bring down 100 birds a day.

Once copious enough to darken the sky, the passenger pigeon population was endangered by the 1890s and extinct by 1914. Though it was too late for the gregarious passenger pigeon, the Migratory Bird Laws began to be passed in 1914, outlawing specific types of hunting. In 1918, the Migratory Bird Treaty prohibited commercial sale of game birds.

Chesapeake Bay Gunning Clubs, which have been in existence from the 1850s, popularized the sport-hunting lifestyle, along with working companion dogs such as the Chesapeake Bay retriever and the Labrador and golden retrievers. Today, the clubs work actively to make sure the fate of the passenger pigeon isn't repeated. Through financial support and environmental lobbying, the clubs are largely responsible for the resurgence of waterfowl populations and habitat preservation on the Chesapeake.

THE EASTERN SHORE

samples on display, and you'll see the names of several presidents.

The Centre at Salisbury, U.S. 13 at the bypass (north of town on U.S. 13), will fulfill all mall fantasies. It offers more than 90 stores, and is anchored by Boscov's, Hecht's, and other major retailers.

An unusual shop, **Chesapeake East,** corner of Parsons and Lake Streets, is definitely worth a stop. It's full of bright and amusing made-in-Salisbury ceramics and other local goods.

Outdoor Recreation/Golf: The Salisbury area is home to a number of golf courses, including **Horse Bridge,** 32418 Mt. Hermon Rd. (one mile past Walston Switch Road),

410/543-4446; it's open year-round. **Green Hill,** 410/749-1605, www.greenhill.com, is the local country club, in operation since 1927. This beautiful 18-hole championship golf course, ranked #2 in the state by the *Washington Times,* is open for limited public play.

Nutters Crossing, 30287 Southampton Bridge Rd., Salisbury, 410/860-GOLF, is another popular semi-private club. The Ramada Inn offers a number of golf packages that include play at any or all of eight local courses, including those mentioned.

Accommodations

Salisbury tends to attract businesspeople, and therefore has a number of chain hotels. One of the most attractive is the **Ramada,** 300 S. Salisbury Blvd., 410/546-4400 or 888/800-7617. It's in a quiet south-of-downtown location and has a restaurant and indoor pool. A number of packages are available; one combines a stay with a round at local golf courses. Rates run $75–145.

If a quiet country place overlooking the river is more your style, try the **Whitehaven Bed & Breakfast,** 23844-48 River St., Whitehaven, 410/873-3294 or 888/205-5921, www.white-

haven.com. Two spotless Victorian homes, side by side, offer spacious and sunny bedrooms with private bath or shared bath. Enclosed porches make for a delightful (and bug-free) view of the Wicomico River, across the street, and the ferry just a half-block away. Whitehaven retains much of its colonial ambience, and the village itself consists of a triangle of three peaceful streets, no stores, no gas. Fortunately, your hosts, Maryen and Carlton Herrett, cook up a wonderful breakfast, and have everything that you need. The B&B is open all year. Rates drop to $75–85 per room Jan.–Mar. (the fireplace in the parlor will keep you warm, along with the Herrett's collection of classical CDs) and rise to $80–100 the rest of the year.

Food

Watermen's Cove, 925 Snow Hill Rd., Salisbury, 410/546-1400, is a cheery place for lunch or dinner—it attracts a casual business lunch crowd. The menu features shrimp scampi ($7–14), a seafood platter ($9), and other seafood, chicken, and beef dishes, plus salads and sandwiches. It's open daily for lunch ($7) and dinner ($16). Readers of *Metropolitan Magazine,* a Salisbury publi-

Whitehaven Bed & Breakfast

WORLD'S BEST RECIPE FOR STALE BREAD

Maryen Herrett, innkeeper at the Whitehaven Bed & Breakfast, passes on this recipe from her grandmother's Household Book. The book was a collection of recipes, started around 1900—it survived the 1906 San Francisco earthquake, along with Maryen's family.

Whitehaven B&B Bread Crumb Pancakes

1 ½ cups milk
2 tbsp. butter
1 ½ cups white bread crumbs (Maryen uses Pepperidge Farm Old Fashioned White)
½ cup sifted flour
4 tsp. baking powder
2 large eggs, lightly beaten

Scald milk, adding the butter until it melts. Stir into crumbs and let stand overnight. When ready to serve, add flour, baking powder, and eggs. Stir to combine and cook on buttered griddle. (Maryen likes to add a few fresh or frozen blueberries or raspberries to each pancake.) Serve with warm, buttered maple syrup.

cation that serves the eastern Delmarva, voted Watermen's Cove the best place for seafood five years in a row.

Goin' Nuts Café, 947 Mt. Hermon Rd., Salisbury, 410/860-1164, is a one-stop world food shop. It has a complete Italian menu, plus Thai seafood, quesadillas, bratwurst, Jamaican jerk chicken, Greek salad, Caribbean salad, broccoli tempura, and other vegetarian dishes. It's open for lunch and dinner daily, and prices range from $4 to $17.

Legends, City Center on Main Street, Salisbury, 410/749-7717, is an exceptional fine dining restaurant—the best in town. Charcoal-grilled filet mignon, Louisiana pasta with andouille sausage, a variety of large salads (the chicken salad has half a roasted chicken, fresh corn, and pine nuts), and the usual fresh fish dishes grace the menu. Dinner salads are around $10, entrées $15–22. It serves lunch Mon.–Fri. and dinner Mon.–Sat.; reservations recommended.

It's hard not to wax rhapsodic about the **Red Roost,** off Route 352 (follow the signs), Whitehaven, 410/546-5443. In the late 1940s, the roost was just that—a chicken house. Chickenmeister Frank Perdue stopped by to unload feed (he still lives in Salisbury). After a series of high tides floated away the last of the poultry in the 1960s, the place was abandoned until Frank Palmer, a car

dealer from Hyattsville, attempted to turn it into a campground. The 1970s oil embargo (and the fact that the roost was out in the middle of nowhere) kept customers away in droves. Mr. Palmer decided to experiment in the restaurant business by steaming up a few crabs and local corn. Word spread, and in 1978, when the all-you-can-eat feast was instituted, the Red Roost became an official Eastern Shore experience. Alas, the all-you-can-eat menu is restricted to fried chicken, steamed crabs, BBQ ribs, steamed shrimp, or Alaskan snow crab legs (there are dinner platters on the menu, but why would you pass up this amazing opportunity to see just how much you can stuff down your gullet?). To loosen you up before the feast begins, the kitchen sends out platters of perfect fried chicken, corn-on-the-cob, fried shrimp, clam strips, french fries, and homemade hushpuppies—all come with dinner. You will eat too much, guaranteed—especially if you're lubing up at the full bar. Then, if it's one of the entertainment nights (banjo, piano, Irish bands), you'll probably get up and dance and sing, too. Welcome to the Eats-tern Shore.

The Red Roost is open for dinner Mar.–Oct. Platters, such as steamed shrimp ($14), Red Roost chicken ($10), and New York strip steak ($17) are available. The all-you-can-eat specials range $12–35. If you can get there, go!

INFORMATION

Sandy Fulton at the Wicomico County Convention & Visitors Bureau, 8480 Ocean Hwy., Delmar, MD 21875, 410/548-4914 or 800/ 332-TOUR (800/332-8687), is a real county booster and source of information. Call the visitors bureau office, visit the website www.wicomicotourism.org, or email wicotour@shore.intercom.net.

Somerset County

It seems the farther south one travels on the Delmarva, the more things slow down. Driving through this rich farming region, you'll pass seemingly endless fields of sorghum and soy. Princess Anne, the county seat of Somerset County, is a sunny, one-main-street municipality with centuries of well-preserved architecture and a well-attended house and garden tour in October that focuses on the town's historic past. It's also the site of the University of Maryland, Eastern Shore, a modern college campus that offers a diverse curriculum. It was founded in 1886 under the auspices of the Methodist Episcopal Church and Centenary Biblical Institute of Baltimore as a school of higher learning for black Americans; today, its student body has an international profile.

Crisfield is a busy fishing and commercial seafood port that supports a bustling tourist industry during the warm months, but quiets down the rest of the year. Mid-May, the fish are running, and autumn is hurricane season—and they do blow through here. Deal Island, Smith Island, and Tangier Island all offer mellow getaways and a pace reminiscent of the Deep South.

SIGHTS

Princess Anne, founded in 1733, was named in honor of the 24-year-old daughter of King George II of England. The town is distinguished by many colonial-era Federal-style dwellings and mid-to-late-19th-century Victorian homes. One of these, the **Teackle Mansion,** 11736 Mansion St., 410/651-2238, www.teacklemansion.org, is open Apr.–mid-Dec., Wednesday and Sat.–Sun. 1–3 P.M.; and mid-Dec.–Mar., Sunday 1–3 P.M. for tours. Littleton and Elizabeth Teackle built the symmetrical and elegant mansion shortly after their marriage in 1800. Mr. Teackle had diverse interests as a merchant, statesman, and entrepreneur, but suffered from financial instability and sold the mansion in 1839. The mansion was divided into rental properties over the years and was purchased by a local group of residents determined to preserve it in the 1950s. Admission is $4. The "Historic Princess Anne" self-guided walking tour, which covers 37 other significant buildings, is available at the mansion or through the county's tourism board.

The Accohannock Tribe (ah-CON-ick), one of the original populations on the Eastern Shore, has built a Native American Living Village in Marion, 14 miles north of Crisfield. The village is very much like an early Algonquin-speaking Eastern Woodlands Indian village, with longhouses, wickiups, and gardens surrounded by a palisade fence. Demonstrations of basketweaving, cooking, dancing, gardening, hunting, and fishing are featured. A museum building houses artifacts collected and owned by the tribe, and is the site of classes in native arts and crafts. A snack bar serves native foods such as corn, squash, wild rice, wild game, fish, oysters, and crab. The tribe also hosts powwows and special events throughout the year, including Thanksgiving and Christmas dinners. The village (which is also the tribal home) provides easy access to Pocomoke Sound, either by canoe or pontoon boat; tours of the local bird sanctuary, wildlife refuge, and Pocomoke Sound are offered. Contact the tribe Mon.–Fri. at 410/623-2007 or 410/623-2660, www.skipjack.net/le_shore/accohannock.

DEAL ISLAND

This three-mile-long spit of land is accessible by auto at the end of Route 363. Ancestors of some of the current 350 inhabitants began to make a living from the sea here in 1675. **Arby & Deb's Sea Rations** is a combination fisherman's supply store/restaurant you'll encounter when first crossing the bridge. The food is local and fresh, in spite of the sign that advertises the mouthwatering duo of bloodworms and cheese steak.

The island has two churches, St. John's Methodist Episcopal and John Wesley United Methodist, each with its own cemetery. The epitaphs tell the story of life in a watermen's community. Graves are covered with concrete slabs; because of the high water table, they cannot be dug to the standard depth.

The island's 20-vessel skipjack contingent—the last of the 19th-century oyster fleet—is docked at the end of the road, in the village of Wenona. To see them, it's best to come late in the day, when they return from harvesting on the bay.

SMITH ISLAND

Accessible only by boat, Smith Island was chartered by Captain John Smith in 1608 and settled by dissenters from St. Clements Island in 1657. Many of the former Catholics converted to Methodism, which is now the only religion officially practiced here. Smith Island is made up of three bodies of land; the two southernmost are inhabited, and the northern island is the Martin National Wildlife Refuge.

Current denizens of Smith Island live in three small communities: Tylerton, Rhodes Point (formerly Rogue's Point, after the local pirates), and Ewell, the island's largest town. **Tylerton** is accessible by packet boat from Crisfield, and among the residences are a post office, a one-room schoolhouse, a church, and a market. **Rhodes Point** is connected to Ewell by road through the salt marsh and a wooden bridge; the only boat repair facility on Smith Island is in this tiny community. **Ewell** is the "big city," the place where the ferry boats dock, and where most of the island's residents can be found. The majority of the 380 Smith Islanders descended from the original colonists, cattlemen who turned to fishing by necessity. Some visitors claim that the heavy southern Maryland accent you'll hear spoken locally is reminiscent of the Elizabethan/Cornwall dialect brought here in the 18th century. The isolation of the island is highlighted by the fact that phone service wasn't available on and to the island until 1940, and electricity was nonexistent until 1949.

If you've got energy to burn, you've come to the wrong place. Smith Island will remind you that at one nearly mythical time, life wasn't lived by a clock. A walk around the streets will take about 15 minutes. A bike ride will take five minutes: you can rent bikes for $5 an hour at the booth next to the ferry dock, or you can go in style with a golf cart for $10 an hour. During your tour, you can count the multitude of shy feral cats that live off the seafood bounty (they have their very own spay and neuter charity: www.members.tripod.com/abcowebdesign). You can shop. **Ruke's Store,** corner of Jones and Smith Island Roads, is a combination flea-market jumble and country store, and **Driftwood General Store,** Jones Road, offers groceries and video rentals. When you're done shopping you can learn something: The **Middleton House,** Jones Road, is an interpretive center for the Martin

Smith Island shanty

A VICTORY FOR TEMPERANCE?

In 1999, the Associated Press reported that a Smith Island shopkeeper's attempt to end a 300-year ban on alcohol sales on the island ended in failure. About one-third of the island's 350 or so residents headed to the mainland to encourage the Somerset County liquor board to turn the liquor down; the board voted 2-1 to deny.

The shopkeeper's request was opposed by long-time residents, many of whom are Methodists with a strong bent for temperance. The shopkeeper, who moved to Smith Island in 1997, maintained that times have changed since the island was settled in 1657 and that the sale of alcohol is a sign of progress. Some locals apparently feared the availability of alcohol would lead to fighting (those wild tourists!). The nearest police officer is a 40-minute boat ride away.

National Wildlife Refuge, and the **Smith Island Center,** Jones and Smith Island Roads, is an information and heritage museum. You can eat. The **Bayside Inn,** 410/425-2771, has a package deal with groups that arrive on the Tyler boats from Crisfield that includes transportation and lunch (lunch alone runs $4–9 for a sandwich to $12.50 for the all-you-can-eat buffet). If you're diabetic, pack your own food—Smith Island cuisine is heavy on nonperishable ingredients, especially sugar. It's a prominent additive to everything from stewed tomatoes to corn fritters, but you won't go away hungry. The crab soup is quite good.

Boat-watching is a big activity here, as is sitting. Watching people sitting in their living rooms is frowned upon.

There are two places to stay in Ewell, and one in nearby Tylerton. The **Smith Island Motel,** Smith Island Road, Ewell, 410/425-4441, is away from the harbor (by about 100 feet), and the **Ewell Tide Inn,** 410/425-2141, www.smith island.net, is the local B&B ($75–85 per night for a double). Both offer simple accommodations. If you really want to get away from it all ("it" being roads, cars, people, and noise), take the

non-vehicular ferry *Captain Jason II* from Crisfield to Tylerton. It runs at 12:30 and 5 P.M. The fare is $20 per person, round-trip, and you may leave your car at the adjacent J. P. Tawes & Bro. Hardware parking lot in Crisfield. Tylerton, made up of 70 residents separated by water from the rest of Smith, is the remote place you didn't think existed anymore, the community Tom Horton celebrated in his *An Island Out of Time.* Surrounded on three sides by water, **The Inn of Silent Music,** 2955 Tylerton Rd., 410/425-3541, www.innofsilentmusic.com, offers stunning views, charming rooms decorated in an eclectic style, and good food. A full breakfast is included, and you may order dinner for an additional $15. Rooms all come with bath and refrigerator; rates range $105–125. The inn closes for the season mid-November and reopens mid-March.

The **Martin Wildlife Refuge** is almost entirely salt marsh, broken up by a maze of tidal creeks and freshwater potholes. Visiting species change with the seasons, though winter brings the heaviest populations of ducks (roughly 10,000), Canada geese (4,000), and tundra swans (1,500). Though you can cruise around the perimeter of the refuge, the interior is closed to the public.

From Memorial Day through October, you can reach the island daily via the passenger cruisers **Captain Tyler II,** Somer's Cove Marina, Crisfield, 410/425-2771, and the *Island Belle II* and the *Island Princess,* Crisfield City Dock, 410/968-3206. All year long, the smaller mail boats **Captain Jason I** and **Captain Jason II,** Crisfield, 410/425-5931, also ferry passengers to the island. The big boats cruise in style—the trip takes about an hour, and the gentle movement of the boat is very relaxing. The mail boats are speedier and choppier; the trip takes about 35 minutes.

Mail boats and the passenger cruisers mentioned above also sail to Tangier Island, Virginia, from Crisfield. Another vessel that offers transportation is the *Steven Thomas,* City Dock, 410/968-2338 or 800/863-2338. Tangier Island is about the same distance from Crisfield as Smith Island, and offers the same amenities, though slightly more developed. The romance film *Message in a Bottle* was supposed to be filmed on Tangier Island, but the local powers turned it down—too much disruption.

CRISFIELD

The biggest (five stoplights!) and best-known town in Somerset County, Crisfield has long been a destination for anglers and seafood lovers. Local Native Americans—Pokomoke, Annamessex, Minokan, Nessawattex, and Acqintica—lived comfortably in the area, and in 1677, the largest Native American town in Maryland, Askiminokonson, existed nearby at what is now the intersection of Route 364 and U.S. 13. The first English settlers adopted the Indian name Annamessex for the little fishing village that was to become Somers Cove. When the railroad was extended to the harbor in 1867, the town was renamed for the man whose efforts made it all possible: John Woodland Crisfield. By 1910, the Crisfield Customs House (now a marine supplies store) boasted the largest registry of sailing vessels in the nation, and Crisfield was a boomtown. Nearby Marion may have been the strawberry capital of Maryland, but the seafood industry was always Crisfield's ace; that main-stay of 1950s Catholic Friday-night dinners, Mrs. Paul's, was based in Crisfield, churning out fishstick after fishstick. Oysters were literally the foundation on which Crisfield was built: from the water tower on 8th Street to the City Dock, the streets are laid atop billions of oyster shells. Though crabbing and commercial fishing has replaced the moribund oyster industry, Crisfield remains on top of it all.

Sights

The **Gov. J. Millard Tawes Historical Museum,** Somers Cove Marina (end of 9th Street), 410/968-2501, is named after a local resident and 54th governor of Maryland. Governor Tawes was responsible for the creation of the Center for Public Broadcasting and the second span of the Chesapeake Bay Bridge, among other achievements. The museum features a well-put-together display on local marine life and its care and harvesting, as well as a section on the history of the area beginning with the native inhabitants. Rotating exhibits add interest; recently, the gallery exhibited "woolies," the embroidered renderings (usually depicting ships under full sail) of 19th-century sailors. One of the most interesting offerings of

© JOANNE MILLER

Crisfield from the water

the museum is the **Port of Crisfield Escorted Walking Tour.** Guides take visitors through town, revealing bits of history (for instance, the fact that Charlie Adams Corner is named for an eccentric local who used to sell newspapers there) and illuminating hidden corners of commerce that the average visitor would miss. Goode's Boat Yard (GOOD-ez) has several examples of different watermen's craft in dry dock; a walk through the Metompkin Soft Shell Crab processing plant and Metompkin Bay Oyster Co. is like slipping into another era. Everything, from sorting to picking, is done by hand. Soft-shell crabs were the first aquaculture industry in the United States, and a mainstay of the economy here. This is an informative and fun introduction to Crisfield; the museum also offers this tour via trolley for $2.50. Another tour offered by the museum is the Ward Brothers Heritage Tour; it explores the workshop of the famous brothers who pioneered the art form of decoy carving and painting, and the Jenkins Creek area.

The museum is open Memorial Day–Oct. 30 weekdays 9 A.M.–4:30 P.M., weekends 10 A.M.–3 P.M.; from Nov. 1–Memorial Day, it's open weekdays 9 A.M.–4:30 P.M., closed weekends. Admission is $2.50. The Port of Crisfield walking tour leaves from the front of the museum Memorial Day–Labor Day Mon.–Sat. 10 A.M. and costs $2.50. Call the museum for information on the Ward Brothers tour.

In the early part of the 20th century, brothers Lem and Steve Ward, residents of Crisfield, carved some of the most sought-after duck decoys on the Chesapeake. The **Ward Brothers Workshop,** 3195 Sackertown Rd., has been restored and is open by appointment; regular tour hours are in the works. Call 410/968-2501 for more information.

Cedar Island Marsh Sanctuary

Covering nearly 3,000 acres of tidal marsh, ponds, and creeks, this sanctuary in Tangier Sound near Crisfield attracts millions of black ducks in winter. In the 1960s, the black duck was declining in numbers due to loss of habitat. Today, black duck populations are on the mend, and Cedar Island is one of Maryland's best places to see the birds. Other tidal wetland wildlife

species are also attracted to the area; barn owls use nest boxes in the marsh to raise their young, typically between April and September. Trapping is offered by yearly lease, and crabbing, as well as fishing for sea trout, rockfish, bluefish and spot, are additional activities enjoyed by visitors. The island can only be reached by boat. The Crisfield Heritage Foundation, 9th Street and Somers Cove Marina, Crisfield, 410/968-2501, offers guided kayak tours for individuals, children, and families, plus photography classes. It's open daily year-round; call for tour schedule and reservations.

Jane's Island State Park

This is really a beautiful public space. The park's 3,100 acres include pristine beaches, wetlands, and abundant wildlife. Eight miles of sandy beaches invite nature walks, beachcombing, picnicking, and swimming. Fifteen miles of canoe/kayak trails offer protected paddling. There are two mile-long walking trails, one with 12 exercise stations. The mainland portion of the island is accessible by auto, but part of the park is accessible only by boat.

The original inhabitants, a tribe of Native Americans, left artifacts and shell mounds on the island. The latecomer Europeans used high ground for farming, and a fish processing plant operated on the south end of the island from 1877 to 1908, when fishing for menhaden (now an endangered species) was outlawed in Maryland. Though the plant returned and processed other fish after World War I, the stock market crash of 1929 made it unprofitable. Its 50-foot brick chimney remains.

The park has 104 campsites, 20 of which are waterfront. Five rustic mini-cabins are available during the warmer months, and four fully equipped, full-size cabins are available year-round. The cabins all have spectacular views of the sunset, so plan to book a year in advance. There are also accommodations at the island's Daugherty Creek Conference Center (sleeps 16—the entire center must be rented). Transient berths with hookups are available for visitors who arrive by boat. Motorboats, canoes, and kayaks may be rented at the Eagle's Nest park store. A softball field, volleyball courts, horseshoe pit, and shuffleboard area are also available.

To get there, take Route 358 west from Route 413. For information and reservations, call 410/968-1565.

Recreation

Fishing: Tangier Sound is one of the best places on the East Coast to catch fish: trout, flounder, drum, croaker, rockfish, and perch are abundant. Aspiring fishers with their own fishing licenses may rent 16-foot fiberglass boats hourly or by the half- and full day, from **Croaker Boat Rentals,** Somers Cove Marina, 410/968-3644. It also offers rods and reels and ring traps for crabbing.

Head boats are a big business in Crisfield; for a complete list, contact the tourism board. Visitors who choose the head boat option don't need their own licenses, as the boat captain's license covers everyone on the boat. Two speedy party boats that take visitors out for bottom fishing are *Barbara Ann II* and *Barbara Ann III,* Somers Cove Marina, Pier N, 410/957-2562. Also out of Crisfield, the *Prime Time II,* 800/791-1470.

Tours: Captain Larry Laird Jr. invites visitors aboard his Chesapeake Bay workboat on the waters around Crisfield for a **Learn-it Eco-Tour,** 1021 W. Main St., Crisfield, 410/968-9870. Visitors can see and hear about wildlife above the water such as ducks, geese, and osprey, and below the water: terrapins, eels, and those fast-moving, elusive oysters. Tours depart daily during the summer. Call for hours and reservations.

Shopping: Bargain alert! The **Carvel Hall Factory Outlet,** one mile north of Crisfield on Route 413, 410/968-0500, www.crisfield.com/carvel-hall, is a *real* outlet store that not only stocks great prices on Carvel Hall brand cutlery and seafood tools but a superb selection of housewares from big-name manufacturers like Lenox and Towle. Cut crystal goblets for $7 each, soup bowls in current china patterns for $3; let the guys go fishing! They also offer silverplate and seasonal gifts. They will ship UPS for you, so don't worry about hauling the champagne bucket home in your suitcase.

Another "out of town" treasure, **Kings Creek Antiques & Design Center,** Route 13 and Perry Road, Princess Anne, 410/651-2776, is one of those warehouse-like multidealer shops that provide hours of amusement for those who love to look (and buy). You'll find lots of American/nautical antiques, and varied collectibles.

The last five blocks of Main Street leading to the City Dock in Crisfield are dotted with boutiques and gift shops. Two of note are **Jane's Accents,** 907 W. Main, which carries new and consignment household items, and **Just Ducky,** 821 W. Main, 2nd floor, a gallery/shop with emphasis on wildfowl paintings and carvings.

Accommodations

The **Pines Motel,** 127 N. Somerset St., Crisfield, 410/968-0900, offers clean, comfortable lodging in town. It's away from the summer chatter on Main Street, and there's a pool and picnic area. Depending on the season, rates range $45–65 per night, $80–90 during festivals.

Bea's B&B, 10 S. Somerset Ave., Crisfield, 410/968-0423, www.innsandouts.com, is a nice little Victorian that's been simply restored. Three rooms either share a bath or have individual baths. Rates are $85 during the week, $95 on weekends, breakfast included.

Waterloo Country Inn, 28822 Mt. Vernon Rd., Princess Anne, 410/651-0883, is the place to go for a romantic getaway in elegant surroundings. Henry Waggaman, a wealthy local landowner, built the house in 1750 as a showplace residence. Like many properties that lie some distance from an urban center, the manor suffered years of neglect before being lovingly restored by Theresa and Erwin Kraemer, who emigrated from Switzerland in 1995. They came upon the crumbling edifice while visiting friends in the area, fell in love with it, and took the necessary actions to refurbish it and turn it into a wonderful B&B. Rooms are tastefully decorated in the Victorian style.

Canoes are available for guest use, and the nearby waterways are a haven for migrating Canada geese and other waterfowl. Paddling along during the late afternoon is an almost surreal experience. The inn also has a swimming pool and bicycles for guests.

Waterloo serves dinner on the weekend in its small (36-seat) dining room. The menu is a sophisticated blend of American and Swiss entrées.

Dining is over before 10 P.M., so houseguests are not disturbed. However, the inn occasionally hosts special events that may last longer—if you'd prefer peace and quiet, make sure your visit doesn't coincide with one of these. Breakfast is included with an overnight stay.

Main season rates (Apr. 1–Oct. 31) run $125–235, and off-season rates are $125–225.

Food

If you're looking for a quick inexpensive sandwich or supplies for several days, go to the **Sysco Systems Canning Plant** at the intersection of Route 667 and U.S. 13. The company store there has a deli and a grocery and produce store. Though you may not need a 20-pound bag of ginger snaps, even small items here are priced reasonably.

Allegro Coffee & Tea Salon, 11775 Somerset Ave., 6A, Princess Anne, 410/651-4520, is a homey stop for a quick cup and a leisurely browse among the gift items for sale.

In the film *Star Wars,* Luke was misdirected when he was told to beware **The Dockside.** This friendly casual restaurant, 1003 W. Main, Crisfield, 410/968-3464, is a good place for inexpensive meals from breakfast ($5) through dinner ($6–9) every day. Lots of Crisfield watermen eat here.

Peaky's, 30361 Mt. Vernon Rd., Princess Anne, 410/651-1950, is owned, as you might expect, by the Peacocks—Greg and Anne. It's the hot spot in town; everybody seems to eat there, all at once. The good news is there's plenty of room. The menu is classic American diner: grilled ham-and-cheese sandwiches, fried chicken, rack of pork ribs. The prices are classic, too; Peaky's is open for lunch ($5 average) and dinner ($13 average). And the pies are homemade.

Four days before my dinner at **The Captain's Galley,** 1021 W. Main St., Crisfield, 410/968-3313, workers were casually squeegeeing seawater from the carpet after a recent hurricane. They're used to this, since the restaurant is right on the city dock (great sunset views) and bears the brunt of hurricane season on occasion. At those times, the business card should read "In the water" instead of "On the water." Fortunately, the food is more dependable than the weather. The Galley serves a little bit of everything: lunch and dinner seafood specialties ($12), beef and chicken dishes ($10), and sandwiches ($5). All of it is available to go.

Also recommended: the **Side Street Seafood Market and Restaurant,** 204 S. 10th St., 410/968-2442, which has a nice outdoor dining area and serves lunch and dinner ($5–21), and the **Watermen's Inn,** in an old blacksmith's shop, 901 W. Main, 410/968-2119, open Wed.–Fri. 11 A.M.–9 P.M., Saturday 8 A.M.–9 P.M., and Sunday 8 A.M.–8 P.M. Prices range $4–20. Both restaurants are in Crisfield.

INFORMATION

Contact Somerset County Tourism, P.O. Box 243, Princess Anne, ROUTE21853, 410/651-2968 or 800/521-9189, http://skipjack.net/le_shore/somerset.

Worcester County

SNOW HILL AND ENVIRONS

Snow Hill, the county seat of Worcester, was settled in 1642 and made its mark as a trading port for schooners and steamboats. Today, the sedate river town offers a quiet getaway with stately B&Bs, a fine small museum, a historic village built around a peat-fired furnace, and canoe trips on the mirror-like Pocomoke River.

The **Julia A. Purnell Museum,** 208 W. Market St., 410/632-0515, www.purnellmuseum.com, is named in honor of the mother of a local resident. At the age of 85, a fall confined Mrs. Purnell to a wheelchair; she took up folk art needlework and completed more than 1,000 pictures before her death in 1943—two months after her 100th birthday, and two years after she was inducted into the National Hobby Hall of Fame. Many of her pictures depict historic buildings and scenes from Snow Hill, and the museum continues to focus on

© JOANNE MILLER

Furnace Town

local history. Tools, toys, machines, curios, and clothing are exhibited, along with their stories. Though many small museums fall into the dusty-cabinet category, this one makes the displays lively and colorful. In keeping with Mrs. Purnell's love of needlework, the museum holds the Delmarva Needleart Show and Competition in September. If you're expecting Grandma's embroidered linens, you're in for a surprise. Submissions include cross-stitch, embroidery, tatting, lace, quilting, and ap-pliqué, all expertly done and some so fantastically modern that the old techniques seem new again. One recent award winner was a portrait done in sepia-toned yarns that was indistinguishable from a photograph. This has to be seen to be appreci-ated. The museum is open Apr.–Oct., Tues.–Sat. 10 A.M.–4 P.M. Admission is $2.

While walking around the historic homes of Snow Hill (a walking tour brochure is available at the Purnell museum or from Worcester County Tourism), you might come across the **Mt. Zion One Room School Museum,** Church and Iron-shire Streets, www.octhebeach.com/Museum/Zion.html, which was moved to Snow Hill from the countryside and opened to the public in 1964. The school contains 19th-century texts

and furnishings; admission is $2. It's open mid-June–Sept. 7, Tues.–Sat., 1–4 P.M. One of the lovliest of the area's public historic homes is **Costen House,** 206 Market St., 410/957-3110, a Queen Anne Victorian with extensive gardens that once was home to the mayor of Pocomoke. It's open May–Oct., Wed.–Sat. 1–4 P.M.; admis-sion is $2.

Furnace Town, 410/632-2032, www.furnace-town.com, is a small restored village built around an iron furnace once fueled by bog-ore; in the 1840s, this furnace was a feat of mechanical engi-neering unmatched in the state. During its nearly 80 years of operation, it was converted from the standard cold-blast method to the high-tech (for the 19th century) hot-blast method using an in-novative system of recirculated heated air.

The village includes artisan shops such as a broom-making house, blacksmith shop, print shop, weaving house, and woodworkers shop, plus a museum and the Old Nazareth Church. Off the main parking lot, the Nature Conser-vancy maintains an easy mile-long trail through the Pocomoke Forest and over the **Nassawango Cypress Swamp**. The preserve is open year-round, and Nassawango Creek is banked by centuries-old bald cypress and black gum trees. One way to appreciate the serene beauty of the area is by canoe, between Nassawango Road and Red House Road (this is a two-mile route, and canoes may be launched on Red House Road, or it can be reached from Snow Hill via the Pocomoke River—about three miles away).

To get to Furnace Town by auto from Snow Hill, take Route 12 north five miles. Turn left (west) on Old Furnace Road, and proceed for one mile. Furnace Town is on the left. The buildings and grounds are open Apr.–Oct., 11 A.M.–5 P.M. and admission is $4. Various artisans demonstrate 19th-century crafts from 11:30 A.M.–4:30 P.M. Furnace Town often holds special events, such as a 19th-century Christmas church service in December and the Worcester County Fair in August.

Recreation: The Pocomoke is an exceptionally beautiful and uncrowded black-water river. The most fun way to see it is by canoe or kayak. The **Pocomoke River Canoe Co.,** 312 N. Washington St., 410/632-3971, rents both (and 14-foot aluminum boats) by the hour, day, or weekend. It also offers trips that include portage to the put-in and take-out sites.

Accommodations and Food

Two grand Victorians stand across from each other on E. Market Street in Snow Hill. The larger and more elegant of the two, the **River House Inn,** 201 E. Market, 410/632-2722, www.bbonline.com/md/riverhouse, has four guest buildings on more than two acres of rolling lawns that lead down to the Pocomoke River. The Little House is two suites, one with kitchen ($150–170); the River Cottage ($250) carriage barn has a microwave, fridge, and coffeemaker; the Ivy Cottage features all the comforts of home: fireplace, hot tub, TV, dining area, 1.5 baths, a full kitchen, and a bedroom upstairs ($250); and the Riverview Hideaway offers all the amenities of the carriage barn ($250). Larry and Susanne Knudsen have restored the house and outbuildings to their former Greek Revival glory, and have furnished everything in period style. The covered porches provide space for luxurious naps on hot summer afternoons, and the Adirondack chairs on the river's edge have armrests big enough for a wineglass. Larry, a Coast Guard–licensed captain, will take guests out on a pontoon riverboat tour by request.

Atlantic Hotel, Berlin

© JOANNE MILLER

THE EASTERN SHORE

Merry Sherwood Plantation, Berlin

The **Snow Hill Inn,** 104 E. Market St., 410/632-2102, www.bnbinns.com/snowhill.inn, is smaller (three rooms with private baths) and not quite as elegant as its neighbor, but still very pleasant. Overnight rates are $75–95. In addition, the inn's lower floor—with a view of the lush garden—serves lunch and dinner Tues.–Sun. ($9–20), offering a good wine list and sophisticated American food with thoughtfully prepared fresh veggies. The kitchen will also make box lunches and picnic baskets.

BERLIN

Colonial travelers once looked forward to this stop on the old Philadelphia Post Road, mainly due to the Burleigh Inn. In fact, the village name is thought to be a contraction of Burleigh Inn, hence the emphasis on the first syllable (BUR-lin, as in "I was burlin' through town when I saw the police car"). The inn is no more, but this pretty little town has a wonderful hotel and a number of historic homes among its tree-lined streets. If you saw the film *Runaway Bride,* with Richard Gere and Julia Roberts, you got an eyeful of Berlin. Besides being Hollywood's version

of a small Midwest town, it's a popular place to stop on the way to or from Ocean City.

One of Berlin's historic homes is open to the public. The **Calvin B. Taylor House Museum,** Main and Baker Sts., 410/641-1019, www.octhe beach.com/Museum/Taylor.html, gives visitors an inside look at 19th-century decorative arts, and also features a collection of local memorabilia. It's open Memorial Day–Sept., Monday, Wednesday, and Fri.–Sat. 1–4 P.M. Free.

Accommodations and Food: Mr. Gere himself slept at the **Atlantic Hotel,** 2 N. Main St., 410/641-3589 or 800/814-7672, www.atlantic hotel.com, and the hotel staff found him "real nice and down to earth" and "good looking in person, but shorter than I thought."

The hotel is so modern and meticulous, you wouldn't know that it's been around since 1895. Much of that Victorian flavor is retained; the rooms are spacious, with all amenities, and the hotel has an elevator, a rarity in vintage buildings. This is a pleasant, well-run hotel. Room rates vary from $65 up to $180, depending on season and day of the week (weekends are always a little higher).

The hotel has a formal dining room with a

nouveau American menu, featuring items such as grilled marinated tuna in tamari, garlic, and star anise with mango chantilly sauce, purple sticky rice, and bok choy. Dinner entrées range from $25–33. A less formal venue, the **Drummer's Café** is open daily for lunch and dinner; salads and sandwiches are around $8, entrées $13–24.

Merry Sherwood Plantation, 8909 Worcester Hwy., 410/641-2112 or 800/660-0358, www.merrysherwood.com, was built in 1859, the result of a union between a wealthy Philadelphian, Henry Johnson, and a local girl, Elizabeth Henry. Ms. Henry's father requested that a suitable house be built for his daughter on the property given as her dowry. The 8,500-square-foot Italianate/Greek Revival structure

was designed for lavish parties, with enough bedrooms to put guests up for long periods of time. It's fitting, then, that it's become an elegant country inn. The building and grounds are popular for weddings and receptions, so call ahead to see if a room is available. There are five rooms with private bath, two rooms with a shared bath, and a honeymoon suite. Rates range $125–150 mid-Oct.–mid-May, $150–175 mid-May–mid-Oct.

The **Neon Moon Café,** 9913 Old Ocean City Blvd., 410/641-3250, serves French and Northern Italian specialties in an upscale, brightly lit, plant-filled room. Lunch ranges $5–12, and dinner entrées range $15–28. It's open daily, and there are lots of specials.

Ocean City

The biggest destination in Worcester County and Maryland's Eastern Shore is Ocean City, "Miami of the North"—so nicknamed because of the 10-mile strip of fancy resort hotels and condos that line the beach and bay. Yet it's not nearly as tacky as its southern namesake or even nearby Atlantic City, saved by a lack of casinos, limited development space, and an emphasis on the beach. And what a beach it is. A seemingly endless swath of soft beige sand extends along most of the peninsula, and the wide boardwalk itself is several miles long. In the summer, brightly colored umbrellas (for rent on the beach) provide shade and color in the white-hot sun, and at night, the boardwalk is merry with strolling couples, singles, and families. Getting around is easy; there are two main north-south streets (Philadelphia heading south and Baltimore heading north—both turn into Coastal Highway above 33rd Street). Addresses are sometimes indicated as "oceanside" (closer to the Atlantic), "oceanfront" (on the beach), or "bayside" (closer to Isle of Wight Bay).

For a spot with so many part-time residents and visitors, you'd expect everything from wax museums to shell collections—not here. A few attractions aimed at tourists have been around for a while and have somehow managed to escape the oily, worn funkiness of such places. Newer at-

tractions are squeaky clean. The city refers to itself as "The East Coast's Number One Family Resort" and it's easy to see why.

There's enough to do in town to satisfy every taste and time limit. You could spend two weeks on the miniature golf courses alone, and several standard-size courses are within easy driving distance. The beaches of southern Delaware are all within an hour by auto. Atlantic fishing is a major pastime, as is horse racing. And Ocean City has its quirks: along the boardwalk, there's an artist who makes sand sculptures by moonlight; his creations are there to greet beachgoers the next day. Incredibly detailed, the sculptures all have religious themes, often illustrating a quote from the Bible.

If refueling is what you need after all the sights and activities, Ocean City is famous for its "beach food": the ultimate munchie triumvirate of Thrasher's french fries, Dumser's ice cream, and Fisher's caramel corn. There are cheap places to eat and expensive places to eat, classic and avant-garde menus. You won't be bored, guaranteed.

SIGHTS

The Boardwalk

Stretching from the inlet north past 27th Street, the boardwalk functions as a chronological history of this fishing village/resort. During the day, trams run nearly the full length of the boardwalk; tickets are $3, and include two stops. The oldest and most active part of the boardwalk is between the inlet on S. 1st Street and 8th Street. The inlet itself didn't exist until a 1933 storm removed a swath of land that connected Assateague Island with Ocean City. Locals liked the new bay access so much, they continued to dredge the inlet to keep it open.

In 1976, sculptor Peter Toth placed his 21st carving at the base of the inlet. The artist had vowed to create works that would honor Native Americans, one for each state. He dedicated the 30-foot-tall, 100-year-old oak carving to the local Choptanks, Nacotchtanks, Chapticons, and Nanticokes. The sculpture, dubbed the *Inlet Indian,* serves as his memorial to the first people.

The **Ocean City Life-Saving Station Museum** sits on the location of a U.S. Coast Guard lifesaving station designated by the federal government in 1878. Surfmen patrolled the beach on foot and horseback, watching for foundering vessels. The station was in use until 1964, when a new station was built on the bayside.

Trimper's Rides began in 1902 with the installation of a steam-powered 45-animal carousel, and has been expanded since. Grandparents now bring their grandchildren to ride their favorite steeds or sit on the carousel's rocking chair.

Taylor's Ocean Pier was completed in 1907, offering visitors a place for line fishing and trapshooting. Destroyed by fire in 1925, the city built a larger pier, complete with a frame building used as a convention hall and teen center. The building has been remodeled to hold souvenir shops and concessions.

In 1905, Rudolph Dolle, a candymaker from New York, began his candy business on the boardwalk. He lived over the store and handpulled his most famous creation: salt-water taffy. **Dolle's Candyland** has been owned and operated by generations of the same family.

Women played a major role in the development of Ocean City as a resort destination. Lizzie Hearne turned her eight-room beach house off Dorchester Street into a hotel in 1905. A nearby cottage, the Belmont, was joined to the Hearne

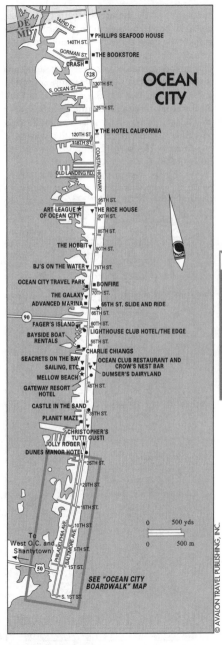

THE EASTERN SHORE

property, and the **Belmont-Hearn Hotel** continues to be run by the fourth and fifth generations of the original family. The **Lankford Hotel** is another example. Several hotels still in operation a block from the boardwalk were also built around this time: Josephine Hastings converted her house and two adjacent cottages into the **Avelon Inn,** 1st and N. Baltimore Streets (note that S. 1st Street is on the inlet, and 1st Street is several blocks north). Ms. Hastings also built the **Atlantic House,** N. Baltimore between 5th and 6th Streets.

Two blocks west of the boardwalk at 502 S.

Philadelphia Ave., **Dumser's** has built a replica of its original pier building that stood on the boardwalk, Inside, a full-scale manufacturing plant is on view, and visitors can enjoy a sundae in the adjacent ice cream parlor.

The remainder of the boardwalk contains the usual compendium of souvenir shops and T-shirt emporiums, and a smattering of restaurants and fast-food places. Their doors blow open with the late spring winds and slam shut with the arrival of autumn. But Ocean City will continue on, with the boardwalk as its backbone.

Amusement Parks

Probably the oldest ongoing attraction in Ocean City is **Trimper's Rides and Amusements,** Baltimore and 1st Street on the boardwalk and Fishing Pier, which has been around since the early 1900s. But the whirling rides, brightly lit games, and mechanical fortune-tellers are so well maintained that the only real reference to Coney Island is an antique Coney Island–style Herschel-Spellman merry-go-round, glittering with jewels and fantasy animals. Daniel Trimper bought the massive carousel in 1902—the only other carousel similar to this one, incidentally at Coney Island, was destroyed by fire. There's plenty of neon, skill games, Ferris wheels, merry-go-rounds, and bumper rides—more than 100 in all—so the kids won't be at all disappointed. It's open year-round; during the warm months, the hours are noon–midnight on weekends, 1 P.M.–midnight during the week. As the weather cools down, the hours become shorter and some rides are shut down. Tickets may be purchased in blocks or by single ride.

Jolly Roger, 30th Street and Coastal Highway, 410/289-3477, www.jollyrogerpark.com, is the city's largest family entertainment center, with a water park, car racing, miniature golf, rides, games, and concessions. It's open April–Memorial Day 9 A.M.–6 P.M.; Memorial Day–Labor Day 9 A.M.–midnight (not all amusements in the park are open at all hours); Labor Day–Oct. 9 A.M.–6 P.M. Rates are based on individual amusements.

One of the newer mini-amusement parks in

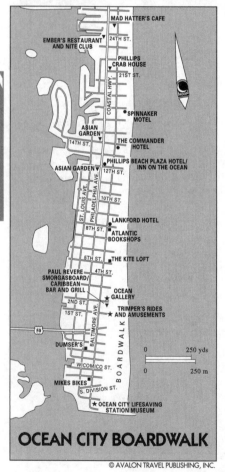

MAD HATTER'S CAFE
24TH ST.
EMBER'S RESTAURANT AND NITE CLUB
PHILLIPS CRAB HOUSE
21ST ST.
SPINNAKER MOTEL
ASIAN GARDEN
THE COMMANDER HOTEL
14TH ST.
ASIAN GARDEN
PHILLIPS BEACH PLAZA HOTEL/ INN ON THE OCEAN
12TH ST.
10TH ST.
LANKFORD HOTEL
8TH ST.
ATLANTIC BOOKSHOPS
5TH ST.
THE KITE LOFT
PAUL REVERE SMORGASBOARD/ CARIBBEAN BAR AND GRILL
4TH ST.
OCEAN GALLERY
2ND ST.
TRIMPER'S RIDES AND AMUSEMENTS
1ST ST.
50
DUMSER'S
WICOMICO ST.
MIKES BIKES
S. DIVISION ST.
OCEAN CITY LIFESAVING STATION MUSEUM
COASTAL HWY.
ST. LOUIS AVE.
PHILADELPHIA AVE.
BALTIMORE AVE.
BOARDWALK
0   250 yds
0   250 m

OCEAN CITY BOARDWALK

© JOANNE MILLER

relaxing at the beach in Ocean City

town is **65th St. Slide & Ride,** bayside at 65th Street, 410/524-5270, www.slidenride.com, with water slides, miniature golf, batting cages, bumper boats, and more. May–June and Sept., it's open 11 A.M.–7 P.M., July–Aug., 10 A.M.–11 P.M.

Planet Maze, 33rd Street and Coastal Highway, 410/524-4FUN, is open year-round, offering water play such as indoor and outdoor tubes and slides, tunnels, and a misty maze for hot days. There's a video arcade for the less active. It's open weekdays 9 A.M.–6 P.M., weekends 9 A.M.–9 P.M.; in winter, it's open weekends only.

There are two laser-tag places in town, both with high-tech arcades. **Laser Storm,** 33rd Street and Coastal Highway (part of Planet Maze), offers a "Stargate" arena. **Q-Zar,** 401 S. Boardwalk, 410/289-2266, is right off the beach. Both are open year-round.

Frontier Town Western Theme Park, Route 611, West Ocean City, 410/641-0880 or 800/228-5590, has developed the Disney concept of Frontierland into an entire park. Wild West shows, gunfights, paddle boats, trail rides, Indian dancing—one admission covers all. It's open mid-June–Labor Day, 10 A.M.–6 P.M.

Baja Amusements, 12639 Ocean Gateway (U.S. 50), West Ocean City, 410/213-2252, www.bajaoc.com, offers a large go-kart track, just west of the city. During the warm months, it's open 9 A.M.–midnight, and from Oct. 1–Nov. 15, 9 A.M.–11 P.M.

Sportland Arcade, 506 S. Atlantic Ave. (on the boardwalk at Worcester Street), 410/289-4987, offers the latest electronic games along with virtual reality theater: Up to 20 people can participate together, competing with each other to play out scenes. There's also a section of "Las Vegas–style" games with the opportunity to win tickets that can be coverted to prizes. Call for hours.

Museums and Galleries

Ocean City Life-Saving Station Museum, Boardwalk at the Inlet, 410/289-4991, www.oc-museum.org, is a fascinating small museum that preserves the history of the U.S. Life-Saving Service, telling the story of the heroes who were always at the ready to rescue passengers and crew from downed ships. The museum also focuses on Ocean City and its past. Exhibits change regularly; a recent one displayed delightfully kitschy shell-covered souvenirs from the town's past—jewel boxes and mermaids, mirrors and salt shakers. The museum's displays are both informative and charming; who could resist a collection of sand from around the world and dollhouse-sized models of local hotels and businesses? It's a fond look at a resort that's been functioning for more than a century. During May and Oct., it's open daily 11 A.M.–4 P.M.; June–Sept., daily 11 A.M.–10 P.M.; winter Sat.–Sun. 11 A.M.–4 P.M. Admission is $2.

Wheels of Yesterday, 12708 Ocean Gateway, West Ocean City, 410/213-7329, www.wheelsofyesterday.com, is a must-see for auto buffs, especially those with an eye for classic models. The 1928 Lincoln Overland touring car used in Jack Benny's TV program during the 1950s is here, as is an 1830 rural mail delivery wagon and a 1934 racing car, all in prime condition. There's an early version of a recreational vehicle, and an intact 1950s service station. Open Oct.–May 9 A.M.–5 P.M. and June–Sept. 9 A.M.–9 P.M. Admission is $4.

THE EASTERN SHORE

KRAZY GOLF

Ocean City is Fantasy Island when it comes to miniature golf. Local course owners try to outdo each other with themes, exemplified by figures and settings created out of chicken wire and plaster, enhanced by imagination and a creative sense of geography. Ice Land Golf, at the south end of the peninsula, is notable for oversized polar bears and frolicking penguins; Hawaiian Gardens relies on the tiki torch, as does the Polynesian section of the 136th Street triple course. The other two courses on the property are Pirate (masted ships, peg legs, and parrots) and Safari (elephants, lions, and giraffes). Viewed from the street, this one presents a very confused cultural picture.

While our imaginations are primed, it would be a fantasy violation to leave out Medieval Castle & Big Top Circus, and Dinosaurs! & Indoor Underwater. Somewhere, people are making big bucks creating giant clown heads and life-size rubber pterodactyls. Meanwhile, right here in Ocean City, visitors can spend many a lazy evening swinging miniature putters over a gargling sea monster, or aiming between the legs of a dancing suit of armor. If all else fails, return to the Garden of Eden. You can go home again.

Ice Land Golf, 400 S. Philadelphia St., 410/289-0443
Bamboo Golf, 3rd and Philadelphia, 410/289-3374
Old Pro Golf Hawaiian Gardens, 18th Street, 410/524-2645
Garden of Eden, 19th and Philadelphia, 410/289-5495
Old Pro Golf, 23rd Street and Coastal Highway, 410/289-6501
Old Pro Golf Medieval Castle & Big Top Circus, 28th Street, 410/289-9286
Jolly Roger Jungle Golf, 30th and Philadelphia, 410/289-3477
Doughroller Bamboo Golf, 41st and Philadelphia, 410/524-2476
Maui Golf, 57th and Philadelphia, 410/424-8804
Old Pro Golf Dinosaurs! & Indoor Underwater, 68th Street, 410/524-2645
Old Pro Golf Pirate, Safari, & Polynesian, 136th Street, 410/524-2645

And on the Delaware border above 145th Street:
Golf Down Under, Route 54 and Coastal Highway, 302/539-1199
Viking Golf, Route 54 and Coastal Highway, 302/539-1644
Fen-Tiki Golf, Fenwick Avenue and Coastal Highway, 302/537-9779

Other Sights

Ocean Gallery, 2nd Street at the boardwalk, 410/289-5300, isn't really an art gallery unless you're seriously looking for paint-by-numbers seascapes, those big rolling ocean pictures of the sort that decorate motels located several hundred miles from saltwater. The real art here is the building itself, which is made up of nailed-and pasted-together bits of wood, parts of torn paintings, signs, and other flotsam. Once in a while, an equally flamboyant art car encrusted with leftovers from the building's exterior is parked on the street outside.

The **Art League of Ocean City,** 516 94th St., 410/524-9433, www.artleagueofoceancity.org, is a community-oriented organization that sponsors classes, workshops, and a public art exhibit (no paint-by-numbers here). The gallery is open year-round except January, Tues.–Sat. 1–5 P.M.; admission is free. Meet the artists at a reception, held the first Friday of each month, 5–7 P.M.

ACCOMMODATIONS

Lodging in Ocean City can be broken down into five subsections: big hotels, small hotels, B&Bs and inns, condo rentals, camping, and for the truly budget-minded, sleeping in doorways. The last is recommended for those traveling close to the bone, as it's difficult to get a roof over the old noggin for less than $90 a night in season (weekdays in winter are a different story). To complicate matters, each lodging's "season"—and the higher prices associated with it—is slightly different. Many accommodations are on the boardwalk—the advantage being instant access to the beach, disadvantage being (below 8th Street) crowds and noise, more during the day than at night. Quite a few apartments are on the main streets—Baltimore heading north and Philadelphia heading south, and the cross streets. Prices are better, but traffic is heavy all the way up the peninsula during the day, somewhat less at night. The cross streets are slightly better, but since the blocks are so narrow, the improvement is slight. Best bet for a quiet night is the boardwalk above 8th Street or cross streets right off the boardwalk. The following are representative of what's available.

Big Hotels

Many hotels have been in operation for several years, and like all big hotels, some portion is usually being renovated. These are the rooms to ask for; the older rooms are sometimes comically small, with mattresses that offer support equivalent to stale marshmallows.

The **Commander Hotel,** oceanfront at 14th and the boardwalk, Ocean City, 410/289-6166 or 888/289-6166, www.commanderhotel.com, was called the "Grand Lady" and "Jewel of the Boardwalk" when it was built in 1930 by Mrs. Minnie Lynch. Innovations included an elevator and a telephone switchboard. It continues to be owned by fourth-generation members of the Lynch family, and has been completely modernized over the years. Rates range from a rock-bottom $52 weekday ocean-view efficiency Oct. 25–Nov. 29 to $255 a weekend night for an oceanfront suite July 2–Aug. 29. Weekly rates are slightly lower.

Lowest rates are for efficiencies with a water view (though not facing the ocean), one double bed and a small refrigerator. Higher rates reflect oceanfront views, large suites with refrigerator and microwave, two double beds, and a private balcony. Cabanas have private balconies, full-size refrigerators, and microwaves; they're located in the back section of the building away from the ocean and run $69–231 depending on the season. The Commander also rents two-bedroom apartments that range from $762–1,475 per week. Parking is free (a major advantage), and the hotel features indoor and outdoor pools, and a guest laundry. It also offers golf packages.

Phillips Beach Plaza Hotel, 1301 Atlantic Ave., 410/289-9121 or 800/492-5834, www.phillipsbeachplaza.com, opens onto a side street but is actually on the beach, near 13th Street. This is the place to indulge your Victorian fantasies, right down to the heavy ruby-colored velvet draperies and crystal chandeliers. The hotel features a cozy bar and fancy restaurant (below). Rooms range $40–164 per day and $250–1,095 per week, depending on season, view, and amenities (high season is June 25–Aug. 22). The hotel also offers lodgings ranging from small efficiencies to three-bedroom apartments, all with full kitchens, from $50–250 per day to $300–1,600 per week. Golf packages and three-day/two-night specials with breakfast and dinner are available.

The **Dunes Manor Hotel,** boardwalk and 28th Street, 410/289-1100 or 800/523-2888, www.dunesmanor.com, continues the Victorian theme. The hotel was built in 1987, and features an indoor-outdoor pool, fitness room, and a restaurant and lounge. Word has gotten out about the free afternoon tea 3–4 P.M., so the number of "guests" in the hotel seems to double during that hour. Parking is free for one car per room. All rooms have an oceanfront view and private balcony, and rates run $39–274 per day and $264–1,195 per week. High season is June 28–Sept. 1. Two types of efficiency apartments are offered, with rates ranging $85–370 per day, $477–1,682 per week. Packages are available.

Castle in the Sand, oceanfront at 37th Street, 410/289-6846 or 800/552-SAND (800/522-7263), www.castleinthesand.com, is close to the

Ocean City Convention Center and boasts a wide array of lodgings, from standard hotel rooms to two-bedroom cottage apartments. A 25-meter Olympic-size pool is nestled among the hotel's buildings. Some rooms feature a glass wall to take in the ocean view, others have balconies. Not all rooms have an ocean view. Rates range $59–259 per day, $345–1,550 per week for rooms and suites. Efficiency apartments range from $69–235 per day, $395–1,420 per week. The high season is roughly June 11–Sept. 5. The Castle offers good packages, and substantial discounts for seniors Sun.–Thurs. during the off-season.

Small Hotels/B&Bs and Inns

The **Lankford Hotel,** boardwalk at 8th Street, 800/282-9709 (reservations only), www.oceancity.com/lankfordhotel, is a sedate and slightly creaky three-story lodging right on the boardwalk. Built in 1924, it was one of the original boardwalk hotels, and is still run by relatives of the builder, Mary Quillen. The hotel welcomes guests with reasonable rates—though if you're

the historic Lankford Hotel

© JOANNE MILLER

under 21, you'd better bring mom or dad (a rule set up to keep out the party-all-night crowd). The rooms have private baths and air-conditioning. An ocean view ($67–95) isn't much more than a side room ($61–89). Side suites of two rooms and a bath are ideal for families ($102–150). Apartments feature one to three bedrooms with one or two baths; prices range from $129–515 daily to $464–1,582 per week. Keep in mind that the less expensive boardwalk hotels are often booked far in advance by regulars who come back every year.

The **Lankford Lodge,** just around the corner on 8th Street, 100 feet from the boardwalk, has rooms and apartment units, again with private baths and air-conditioning. Rooms run $78–102, two-room suites (one bath) are $102–150, and the apartments are two-bed/two-bath and kitchen for $206–412 per day to $644–1,320 per week.

The **Inn on the Ocean,** 1001 Atlantic Ave., 410/289-8894 or 877/466-6662, www.bbonline.com/md/ontheocean, is one of the prettiest renovated Victorian hotels on the beach. Attractively decorated rooms, all with private baths and air-conditioning and breakfast, range $125–195 Jan 1–May 2 and Nov. 3–Dec. 31; $140–240 May 3–June 15 and Sept. 3–Nov. 2; and $200–300 June 16–Sept. 2 and Memorial Day weekend.

The **Spinnaker Motel,** 18th Street at the Boardwalk, 410/289-5444 or 800/638-3244, www.ocmotels.com, offers kitchenettes, cable TV, and two double beds in all units. It's open March–Oct.; rates start out in May between $55–87, go up in June to $145–170, peak in July and August at $195, then drop down again to a low of $39–65 from Sept. 21 until October.

The **Lighthouse Club Hotel,** 201 60th St. (56th Street bayside), 410/524-5400 or 888/371-5400, www.fagers.com, is one of the most romantic places to stay in Ocean City. Built like an octagonal lighthouse (similar to the Thomas Point Lighthouse in the Chesapeake), the structure encloses 23 luxurious suites. Marble baths, hot tubs, Caribbean-style custom decor, wet bars, and refrigerators are in each suite (some have fireplaces); most have views of Isle of Wight Bay.

Though "in town," the hotel is built on the wetlands of Fager's Island, and the feel is of being much more secluded than the location would suggest. Fager's Island restaurant is connected to the hotel by a footbridge, and guests receive passes for Ocean City Health & Racquet Club a short drive away. When I stayed there, the weather was dark and sultry, but the building seemed like a safe haven in any storm, and the rooms are more like apartments. Ask about getaway specials throughout the year that include all meals. High-season rates, June 15–Oct. 4, range from $184–295 per night; the lowest prices are $79–259, in effect Jan. 2–March 31. Breakfast is included, and the hotel offers specials throughout the year.

The Edge, 56th Street on the bay, 410/524-5400 Ext. 4021 or 888/371-5400, www.fagers .com, is the Fager empire's newest hotel, built for luxury. Twelve suites with panoramic water views, Jacuzzis, feather beds, and natural soaps and lotions are named according to decor: South Beach, Left Bank, The Jungle, and so on. Tariffs range $209–419 per night.

Condos and Apartments

These are ideal for larger groups and longer stays. Most services, such as **Ocean City Weekly Rentals,** 410/289-7888 or 800/851-8909, www .ocwr.com, and **Summer Beach Condos,** 410/ 289-0727 or 800/537-7876, www.seagateoc.com, only handle weekly rentals in season with a few off-season properties. **O'Connor Piper and Flynn** will send a rental catalog; contact them at 800/633-1000, www.opf.com/beach (they also offer lodging-and-golf packages).

The **Gateway Resort Hotel,** 4800 Coastal Hwy., 410/524-6500 or 800/382-2582, www .gatewayoc.com, features efficiencies, condos, and three-bedroom apartments with oceanfront and ocean-view rooms. It has an Olympic-size pool and children's wading pool and is next to the popular restaurant/nightclub Mellow Beach. Rates run $39–289 per night, $240–1,595 per week. High season is May 14–Sept. 26. The Gateway offers several good package plans that include food and use of the nearby Clarion's indoor pool and health spa.

The same people who manage the Lankford Hotel mentioned above also caretake the **Sea Robin Apartments** on 8th Street and **The Anchor Inn** on 10th Street; both are 100 feet away from the boardwalk on Baltimore Street, the main route through town. The Sea Robin offers two and three bedrooms, living and dining room, bath, and kitchen, $206–412 daily, $644–1,320 weekly.

The Commander Hotel rents apartments, as does Phillips Beach Plaza, Dunes Manor, and Castle in the Sand. The **Sovereign Seas Condominiums** and **Condesa Condominium,** both close to and managed by Castle in the Sand, rent out weekly for $1,550–1,580 and $970 respectively. The Castle also manages a number of cottage apartments and townhouses in the vicinity of 37th Street; all are rented by the week, and prices range $840–1,550. Rates on these drop 25 percent before June 5, and 50 percent after Labor Day. Call 410/289-6846 or 800/552-SAND (800/552-7263) for availability.

Camping

Ocean City Travel Park, 105 70th St., 410/524-7601, is the only campground in Ocean City, and is open year-round. It's one block from the beach, and near the local bus service. It features all hookups, a laundry, and a camp store, and welcomes both RVs (no dump station) and tents.

Frontier Town, Route 611 and Stephen Decatur Highway, 410/641-0880 or 800/228-5590, the Western theme park mentioned above, has all facilities for RVs and tents, and is open Apr.–mid-Oct.

Additional camping is available at Assateague National Park and Assateague State Park.

FOOD AND NIGHTLIFE

Cafés and Light Fare

Mad Hatter's Cafe, 25th Street between Baltimore and Philadelphia Avenues, 410/289-6267, serves deli fare (including vegetarian items) to eat in or take out—they also offer free delivery. Prices average $8.

Beach Food

For the best in sand-and-sea cuisine, look

to Ocean City's holy triumvirate: Dumser's, Thrasher's, and Fisher's.

Dumser's Dairyland, 49th Street and Coastal Highway, 410/250-5543, has been around since 1939. The restaurant is justifiably famous for its homemade ice creams, serving up big milkshakes, floats, sodas, sundaes, and cones. For lunch and dinner, there's a malt-shop menu with sandwiches and subs (average $6).

Thrasher's, several locations on the boardwalk, is known for its french fries. Other beach eats such as corn dogs on a stick are also available (under $5).

Fisher's, also on the boardwalk in several locations, is the place for caramel corn and sweets (under $5).

There's an outlet for everything these days. The **Jerky Outlet,** U.S. 50, just over the bridge in West Ocean City, features Polish sausage as well as a plethora of dried meats and a deli.

Buffets

The **Paul Revere Smorgasbord,** 2nd and boardwalk, 410/524-1776, is a cherished hangout for the college crowd and families on a budget. The all-you-can-eat colonial feast Fri.–Sat. is $9 for adults, less for kids, and it's even cheaper if you get there between 4 and 4:30 P.M. There's plenty of meat, plenty of fish, and lots of carbs—gourmet it's not, but you'll be fortified for several busy days.

Though it can't match the prices at Paul Revere's, **Embers Restaurant & Nite Club,** 24th Street and Coastal Highway, 410/289-3322, is a huge place with an all-you-can-eat seafood buffet with prime rib bar and breakfast buffet plus à la carte dishes ($10–30). It's open 2–11 P.M. Mar.–Nov.

Jonah & the Whale Seafood Buffet, boardwalk and 26th Street, 410/524-CRAB, is another big place with an all-you-can-eat seafood buffet including a raw bar, dessert and salad bars, and a prime rib carving station. Prices are similar to Embers. It's open mid-May–mid-Sept. 4–9 P.M. and offers early-bird specials.

Asian

Charlie Chiangs, 5401 Coastal Hwy., 410/723-4600, advertises Hunan and Szechwan cuisine,

but the menu concentrates on Mandarin-style favorites—General Tso's chicken, kung pao trio (chicken, beef, and shrimp), and O.C. specialties such as golden soft-shell crabs. It's open for lunch and dinner every day, and entrées average $14.

The Rice House, Teal Marsh Shopping Center, 410/213-8388, serves a full Chinese menu ($9) in addition to sushi. It's open for lunch and dinner daily.

Asian Garden, 1509 Philadelphia, 410/289-7423, covers a lot of bases. Its menu features Chinese, Nepalese, and Indian dishes. It's open for dinner daily, and entrées average $11.

Italian

Christopher's Tutti Gusti, 3324 Coastal Hwy., 410/289-3318, www.ocean-city.com/tuttigusti .htm, gets my vote for the best food in town. Whole roasted garlic and olive oil accompanies fresh bread, and the house-made pappardelle pasta bathed in fresh tomato sauce Bolognese is excellent. It features a full range of Italian specialties and desserts. Entrées range from $10–24. Tutti Gusti is open for dinner Wed.–Mon. during the summer high season (until Oct. 15). Reservations recommended.

O.C. Traditional

The restaurant most people associate with Ocean City is **Phillips Crab House,** 21st and Coastal Hwy., 410/289-6821. Other locations are Phillips by the Sea, boardwalk and 13th (in Phillips Beach Plaza Hotel), 410/289-9121, and Phillips Seafood House, 141st Street and Coastal Highway, 410/250-1200. You'll see the Phillips name around a lot in Maryland. The restaurants employ so many people that the company imports help from overseas and provides inexpensive housing for them in Ocean City. The empire started with A. E. Phillips, a waterman from Fishing Creek on Hooper's Island. His grandson Brice moved to Ocean City in 1956 and opened a fresh crab takeout on 21st and Coastal Highway. It's still in operation, filling a corner of the larger restaurant, which is decorated in what the employees call "early Shirley"—Shirley being Mrs. Phillips: carousel horses and Victorian stained-glass windows. Phillips serves a full menu (entrées average

$16), but they're known for their buffet. It features snow crab, steamed blue crab, raw clams and oysters, cooked shrimp, and lots more, for around $28—it's open mid-May–mid-Oct., though the 21st Street restaurant is open Apr.–first week of November, for lunch and dinner. You might want to wash it all down with an Eastern Shore Lemonade: citron vodka, triple sec, sour mix, and 7-Up.

You'll find many more locals than tourists at **The Hobbit,** 101 81st St., 410/524-8100. It's the kind of dark wood/oak tables/big plates place that has kept people coming back for 20 years. Dinner is served daily, and entrées average $25.

Crab Alley Restaurant and Seafood Market, Golf Course Road and Sunset Ave., West Ocean City, 410/213-7800, is another eatery that's popular with locals. It's off the beaten path—on the west side, a few blocks south of Route 50. Though the restaurant serves a typical seafood menu, the ultra-fresh seafood is brought in by local watermen. Dinner entrées average $20.

Nouvelle Cuisine

The Galaxy, 6601 Coastal Hwy., 410/723-6762, could be set in a major city; its sharply designed blue-and-gold astronomically correct interior looks as if it's been plucked out of New York or San Francisco. The food tastes as good as it looks, and the wine list is sophisticated. It's open daily for lunch and dinner; entrées average $28.

Nightlife

O.C. has a major bar scene at night. The acknowledged premier spot in town, and the one that many other night spots are modeled after, is **Seacrets on the Bay,** 49th Street and bayside, 410/524-7777, www.seacrets.com. It serves lunch and dinner on a year-round artificial beach that is so Jamaican in execution that you'd be hard-pressed to remember you're in Maryland after a couple of rum drinks. The owner was the first to bring in palm trees and keep them alive by heroic measures during the intemperate winters. Seacrets is definitely still the hippest place in town, and it features live entertainment nearly every night. Get ready to shuffle to reggae; don't worry, be irie, and don't call the bartender "Ay, mon."

The **Caribbean Bar & Grill,** 2nd and boardwalk, 410/289-0837, is definitely an imitation, but has the advantage of being on the boards and next to Revere's Smorgasbord, so finding large quantities of food won't be a challenge. Live entertainment on the weekends.

Mellow Beach, 46th St. and the bay, 410/524-7421, www.mellowbeach.net, features lunch and dinner as well as cocktails and live entertainment on the weekends; dine on the deck or at tables in the jungle. The owners replace all the tropical plants that don't make it through the winter every year, so it's pretty lush.

Fager's Island, 60th on the bay, 410/524-5400, www.fagers.com, is also a popular restaurant, with Pacific Rim cuisine for dinner daily, half-price specials, and Sunday brunch. It's open year-round and has a variety of live entertainment (soul, rock, Top 40) and late-night action every night. Fager's has nine brews on draft and a tequila bar. Try to make it for the sunset; the restaurant pipes in Tchaikovsky's *1812 Overture* as the bay turns bright orange.

The **Ocean Club Restaurant & Crow's Nest Bar,** 49th at the beach, 410/524-7500, serves lunch and dinner daily, but it's the live entertainment and dancing most nights that

NOT SO KRAZY GOLF

Worcester County has dozens of challenging courses, among them:

Winter Quarters Golf Course, Winter Quarters Drive, on the river near Pocomoke City, 410/957-1171.

Deer Run, 8804 Logtown Rd., Berlin, 410/629-0060 or 888/790-4GOLF (800/790-4465).

River Run, Beauchamp Road off Rte. 589, Ocean City, 410/641-7200 or 800/733-RRUN (800/733-7786), www.riverrungolf.com (designed by Gary Player).

Rum Pointe, 7000 Rum Pointe Ln., Berlin, 410/629-1414 or 888/809-4653.

Nutters Crossing, 30287 Southampton Bridge Rd., Salisbury, 410/860-4653 or 800/61-LINKS (800/615-4657), www.nutterscrossing.com.

FESTIVALS AND EVENTS

Ocean City holds events year-round in its convention center, including a big boat show in February. Many O.C. events are handled by individuals, so the listed phone numbers may not be accurate; call the local convention and visitor's bureau, 800/OC-OCEAN, for an updated list. St. Michaels Business Association, 800/808-7622, www.stmichaelsmd.org, sponsors events around all major holidays, especially Halloween and Christmas.

March/April

The prestigious **Ward World Championship Wildfowl Carving Competition,** held since 1970, includes a weekend of activities. In Salisbury, 410/742-4988.

Ocean City knows how to celebrate, and proves it with a **St. Patrick's Day Parade and Irish Festival.** 410/289-6156.

Get those arms in shape for the **Nanticoke River Canoe and Kayak Race,** an 8.1-mile course from Mardela Springs to Vienna. 410/543-1244.

May/June

The first week in May is time for the **Salisbury Dogwood Festival,** when the town is covered in bloom and hosts special events. 410/749-0144.

Spring fest is the "official" opening weekend of Ocean City. Four days of activities. 410/250-0125.

The three-day **Mid-Atlantic Maritime Arts Festival** features ship models, maritime paintings, crafts, music, seafood, and more. It's on the grounds of the Chesapeake Bay Maritime Museum, St. Michaels, and is free with admission. 410/745-2916.

Janes Island State Park hosts the **Native American Indian Festival and Pow Wow** with traditional singing, dancing, food, arts, and crafts. 410/623-2660.

The **Annual Antique & Classic Boat Festival,** held at the Chesapeake Bay Maritime Museum, St. Michaels, features more than 100 classic boats and automobiles in a judged show. There are also seminars and special exhibits. Free with admission. 410/745-2916.

July/August

The **Tuckahoe Steam and Gas Show** in Easton features the huffing and puffing of a variety of antique steam engines, gas engines, and blacksmith displays, a museum, horse pull, and auction. 410/822-9868.

The annual **Thunder on the Narrows,** Kent Narrows, features hydroplane and speed skiff racing. 410/643-5764.

Ocean City's **White Marlin Open** offers cash prizes of $850,000 with more than 250 boats competing for record-setting catches of white marlin, blue marlin, wahoo, tuna, and shark. 800/OC-OCEAN, www.whitemarlinopen.com.

September

The Annual Skipjack Races & Festival is held early in September on Deal Island. Food, arts and crafts, and family activities are offered. 410/784-2811 or 800/521-9189, www.skipjack.net.

The **Pemberton Colonial Fair,** held outside Salisbury, combines 18th-century games, performances (including period dancing, and dressage and other horse events), and booths in an authentic country manor house and grounds. Call the Wicomico Historical Society for more information, 410/548-4914.

Polka lives! **Polkamotion by the Ocean** is four days of nonstop continuous polka boogie to live bands in Ocean City. 410/787-8675.

Also in Ocean City, the **Maryland State Surfing Championships** features top amateur surfers competing for the title. 410/213-0646. The end of September or beginning of October is also the official "closing" of the beach, and **Sunfest** is the four-day party that sees out the summer with a bang. 410/250-0125.

October

On **Tilghman Island Day,** the village is filled with exhibits and seafood. Visitors can watch skipjack and workboat races, listen to music, and participate in an auction. 410/822-4606, www.tilghmanisland.com.

Olde Princess Anne Days has been going on since the late 1950s, and is as popular as ever. The historic house and garden tour and colonial fair takes place over two days. 800/521-9189, http://skipjack.net/le_shore/visitsomerset.

The Historical Society of Talbot County in Easton holds **Heritage Weekend,** an antique show and sale that includes appraisals. 410/822-0773.

Furnace Town, near Snow Hill, hosts the **Chesapeake Celtic Festival,** which features music, dancing, sheep-herding, a medieval encampment, and food and crafts vendors. 410/632-2032.

November/December

Celebrate mollusk madness at **Oysterfest,** and learn to shuck, tong, and nipper from local watermen. Prepared oysters for sale, along with live music and boat rides. It's on the grounds of the Chesapeake Bay Maritime Museum, St. Michaels, and is free with admission. 410/745-2916.

The **Waterfowl Festival** takes over the town of Easton (literally—the streets are closed and decorated). This is one of the biggest events on the Eastern Shore, featuring art, sculpture, duck stamps, crafts, demonstrations, food, music, and more. 410/822-4567, www.waterfowlfestival.org.

Ocean City sponsors a big **Christmas Parade** each year, featuring floats, bands, motorcycles, and all revelant Clauses. 410/524-9000.

THE EASTERN SHORE

bring 'em in. The restaurant is all wood and arched windows, with a view of the "tropical" beach, and the bar is open-air and on the second floor. Both facilities are attached to a resort hotel, the Gateway.

BJ's on the Water, 75th Street at the bay, 410/524-7575, is another restaurant that offers entertainment nearly every night; bands range from blues to zydeco, hard rock to jazz.

The **Bonfire,** 71st Street and Coastal Highway, 410/524-7171, is more hard-rock-oriented, with live bands nearly every night.

RECREATION

Mikes Bikes, N. Division Street and Baltimore Avenue, 410/289-5404, rents bikes year-round. **Sailing, Etc.,** 46th Street at the bay, 410/723-1144, rents in-line skates, Windsurfers, sailboats, and kayaks and includes lessons on the use of each. **Bayside Boat Rentals,** 54th Street at the bay, 410/524-1948, is the place for jet boats and pontoon boats. **Advanced Marina,** 66th Street at the bay, 410/723-2124, is a complete marine store with fishing equipment and waverunners, water skis, and ski tubes for rent. The closest golf courses to Ocean City are in Berlin. Here are a few of many choices, all open year-round: **Rum Pointe Seaside Golf Links,** 410/629-1414 or 888/809-4653; **Ocean City Golf & Yacht Club,** 410/641-1779 or 800/422-3570; and **Eagle's Landing,** 410/213-7277 or 800/2-TEE-TIME (800/283-3846).

The yacht **O.C. Princess,** Shantytown lighthouse pier, 410/213-0489, www.ocfishing.com, conducts dolphin-, bird-, and whale-watching expeditions that sometimes include a cruise by Assateague Island to spot wild ponies. The **O.C. Rocket,** Talbot Street pier, 410/289-3500, a speedboat, covers some of the same sightseeing territory as the *Princess,* and also offers a cruise to Assateague. **Bally's at Ocean Downs,** U.S. 50 and Route 589, 410/641-0600, www.ocean downs.com, features live harness racing during the warmer months and simulcasts the rest of the year. The track restaurant offers specials on Friday and Sunday.

SHOPPING

One of the most popular shops in Ocean City is **The Kite Loft,** 5th Street at the boardwalk, 45th Street Village, and 131st Street and Coastal Highway. As you might expect, kite flying is a big pastime on the beach, and this shop has a wide variety. Another smaller retailer worth noting is **Crash,** 137th St.; it stocks lots of name-brand discounted clothing and accessories—mostly women's sportswear, but some men's stuff too. **Shantytown,** just west of the bridge on U.S. 50, West Ocean City, is where the fishing boats depart. It's an interesting little village made up of individual shops. Of course, Ocean City has a big **Factory Outlet** mall, with Bass, Ann Taylor, Haggar, Reebok, etc. It's at U.S. 50 and Golf Course Road, one-half mile west of the U.S. 50 bridge in West Ocean City.

Antiques and Collectibles: The **Route 54 Antiques Center,** six miles west of Ocean City on Route 54 (it's actually in tax-free Delaware), features 25 dealers and a variety of merchandise. It's open daily, year-round. **Ocean Downs Flea Market,** at Bally's racetrack, U.S. 50 and Route 589, takes place every weekend in September.

Books: The **Mason Collection,** Shantytown Village, is a book lover's paradise, with thousands of used books for sale. **The Bookstore,** 138th Street and Coastal Highway, specializes in mysteries, but features all sorts of new and used books. **Atlantic Bookshops,** 8th Street and boardwalk, is the place to go for new and shiny volumes; they have outlets in Rehoboth Beach and Bethany Beach, Delaware, too.

INFORMATION

Ocean City does a good job at promotion. For an information packet, contact the Ocean City Department of Tourism, 4001 Coastal Hwy, Ocean City, MD 21842, 800/626-2326, www.ocean-city.com or www.ococean.com.

GETTING THERE AND AROUND

The most common way to get to Ocean City is by auto, though the area is serviced by a municipal airport three miles west. Taxi service and car rentals are available at the airport. Call 410/213-2471 for more information.

Ocean City has wisely instituted a public transportation system that operates late May–late Sept., 24 hours a day. **The BUS** runs every 10 minutes 6 A.M.–noon, every 5–7 minutes noon–3 A.M., and every 20 minutes 3–6 A.M. You can catch it every other block from S. 1st to 141st Street on Philadelphia Ave. (which becomes the Coastal Highway as it proceeds north) and Baltimore Avenue. Two dollars (exact change) buys unlimited use within a 24-hour period. Call 410/723-1606 for more information. A handicapped bus is also available 24 hours a day; call 410/723-1607 2–3 hours ahead of pickup time.

ASSATEAGUE ISLAND

Assateague is a 33-mile-long sandy barrier island, originally created by glacial movements at the end of the last ice age, and continually recreated by wave and wind action. Before 1933, Assateague was connected to Ocean City, part of the peninsula that extended from Fenwick Island in Delaware. During that year, a powerful storm removed a shallow sand spit, and might have replaced it if it weren't for human efforts to deepen and widen the subsequent channel.

It's doubtful that the island was a place of permanent habitation by the local Assateague Indians, though the first European to report on it in 1524, Giovanni da Verrazano, found it "very beautiful." He promptly kidnapped an Indian boy who was attempting to hide, but gave up on a young girl of 18 "because of the loud shrieks she uttered as we attempted to lead her away." Welcome to the New World.

Over the years, small settlements grew on the island, but most faded away before 1900. As early as 1935, the federal government surveyed the island as a possible park, but no action was taken. Developers began building dwellings on the island in the 1950s, leveling the dunes for road access. Thanks to the lack of impediments, another storm literally floated the houses away in 1962.

At that point, the government did step in. Today, the island consists of three major public areas: Assateague Island National Seashore, managed by the National Park Service (the entire island); Assateague State Park, managed by the

© JOANNE MILLER

Assateague ponies

Maryland Department of Natural Resources (the northern end); and Chincoteague National Wildlife Refuge, managed by the U.S. Fish and Wildlife Service (the southern end). There is no access from the northern end of the island to the southern end: the Maryland side is accessed via Route 611 on the mainland, the Virginia side by Route 175.

Many visitors come to see the island's large herds of wild horses. The origin of the sturdy little animals has been disputed, though it's agreed that they roamed the island as early as the 17th century. Some say a Spanish or English ship floundered off the southern end of the island and the animals swam ashore; others claim that the horses are descended from domesticated stock that was grazed on the island (a handy way for local planters to avoid mainland taxes and fencing requirements). Today, a fence separates the herds across the state line. The Maryland herd is protected by the state and roams freely throughout the park, though they stay well away from groups of people on foot. The Chincoteague Volunteer Fire Company owns the Virginia herd; each year, horses are rounded up and many of the foals are sold at the Pony Penning and auction, held on the last Wed.–Thurs. of July. The funds support the fire company, and the animals are prized for their strength and longevity.

Recreation

Water Sports: Assateague State Park provides lifeguards throughout the summer on its **swimming** beaches. Both visitors centers present **surf fishing** demonstrations during the summer; no saltwater license is required. Fishing is prohibited on lifeguarded beaches, and an after-hours fishing permit is required on the Virginia end of the island. **Crabbing, clamming,** and **shell collecting** are popular pastimes; clamming is especially good on Maryland's bay side. **Canoes** may be rented from a concession at the end of Bayside Drive on the Maryland side. The bay is quite shallow, and canoeists and boaters may not land anywhere on the island's Virginia end other than Fishing Point Sept. 1–Mar. 14.

Hiking and Biking: On the Maryland side, hikers may use several short self-guided nature trails, or trek on the beach to Ocean City or south on the ORV trail to the Virginia border. Cyclists can enjoy three miles of paved bike path along Bayberry Drive; bike rentals are available from a concession at the end of Bayside Drive. In Virginia, 15 miles of trails wind through marshes and forests, and include a path to the Assateague Lighthouse. Hikers may also enjoy miles of undisturbed beach north of the Toms Cove Visitor Center. Half the trails are paved for cyclists, and a bike path leads from the town of Chincoteague to the refuge. In fact, bicycling is encouraged in the refuge during the busy summer weekends.

Off-Road Vehicles: ORV zones are posted and maps are available at the visitors centers and refuge headquarters. The National Seashore requires permits and strict specifications for ORVs. Contact them at 410/641-3030 or write to Assateague Island National Seashore, 7206 National Seashore Ln., Berlin, MD 21811.

Camping: The Maryland side features the **Barrier Island Visitor Center,** maintained by the Assateague Island National Seashore. A live touch tank, exhibits, guided walks, and other programs are available to visitors. This is also the place to inquire about backcountry camping: two oceanside sites and four bayside camps are backpack- and canoe-accessible. They have chemical toilets but no drinking water, and are free with a parking and backcountry use permit. The nearest is four miles from parking. For more information, stop by the visitors center or contact Assateague Island National Seashore, 7206 National Seashore Ln., Berlin, MD 21811, 410/641-1441. In addition, two car campgrounds, Oceanside and Bayside, are equipped with chemical toilets, drinking water, and cold showers. There is a dump station, but no hookups, and a few sites are for tents only. Some are open year-round. Reservations are necessary; call 800/365-CAMP (800/365-2267) April 15–Oct. 15 to secure a spot (book well ahead).

The 680-acre State Park offers swimming, surf fishing, surf boarding, bathhouses with hot showers, a bait and tackle shop, and a snack bar. The campground can accommodate any size camping unit (dump station only, no hookups) but may be closed during the winter. Reservations may be made for a full week only during the summer. For more information and reservations, contact Assateague State Park, 7307 Stephen Decatur Hwy., Berlin, MD 21811, 410/641-2120.

Chincoteague Island does not allow camping in the wildlife refuge, though it's an excellent birding and wildlife spotting area. The refuge was purchased with duck stamp revenues in 1943 to provide a protected environment for migrating waterfowl. The **Chincoteague Refuge Visitor Center** off Maddox Boulevard (follow signs from Route 175) offers guided walks and programs; a tour bus is available. Contact the Refuge Manager, Chincoteague National Wildlife Refuge, P.O. Box 62, Chincoteague, VA 23336, 757/336-6122, for more information.

Assateague National Seashore is open year-round. Some hunting is allowed on the Virginia side during September. Because of the wildlife population, pets are not permitted on most of the island.

THE EASTERN SHORE

Delaware

Introduction to Delaware

Delaware is the quiet, skinny girl in the back of the schoolroom who goes on to become class valedictorian, moves to the big city, becomes a supermodel, and makes a zillion dollars before she retires at 30 to start her own bank. Though Delaware is the next-to-smallest state (Rhode Island is the smallest), its importance in industry, banking, and technology far exceeds its size. Chances are, your credit cards are based in Delaware, thanks to its liberal interest-charge laws. Wilmington is called the "Corporate Capital of the World" because half of the Fortune 500 companies are based there. Another

interesting money fact about Delaware: there's no sales tax, so all purchases (with the exception of an 8 percent hotel room tax) are tax-free.

Delaware is flanked by Maryland to the south and west, Delaware Bay, the Delaware River, and Atlantic Ocean on the east, and Pennsylvania to the north. The new colony was named because of its proximity to the river, which in turn was named for Thomas West, Baron De La Warr, first governor of Virginia. The state itself combines two radically different elements: urban industrialization and rural agriculture. It's a rich, fascinating, underappreciated place, which makes it all the more appealing. Besides, how can you hate a place where the state bird is a chicken; not just any chicken, of course, but a tough and

view of New Castle

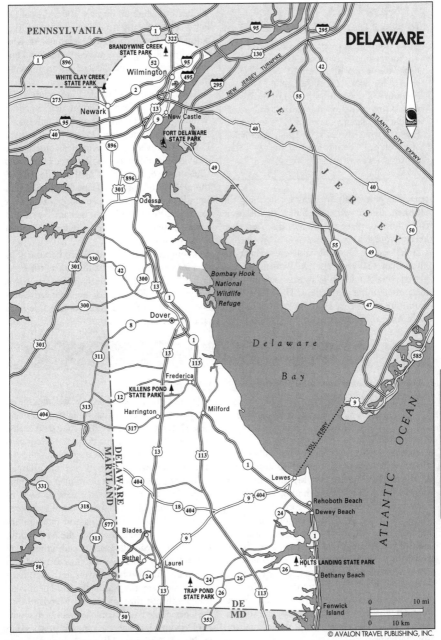

PENNSYLVANIA

DELAWARE

BRANDYWINE CREEK
STATE PARK

WHITE CLAY CREEK
STATE PARK

Wilmington

NEW JERSEY TURNPIKE

ATLANTIC CITY EXPWY

Newark

New Castle

FORT DELAWARE
STATE PARK

N E W

Odessa

J E R S E Y

Bombay Hook
National
Wildlife
Refuge

Dover

D e l a w a r e

B a y

Frederica

KILLENS POND
STATE PARK

Milford

Harrington

TOLL FERRY

MARYLAND
DELAWARE

Lewes

Rehoboth Beach
Dewey Beach

ATLANTIC   OCEAN

Blades

Bethel

Laurel

HOLTS LANDING STATE PARK

Bethany Beach

TRAP POND
STATE PARK

DE
MD

Fenwick Island

0   10 mi

0   10 km

© AVALON TRAVEL PUBLISHING, INC.

BIG D OR LITTLE D?

It's a proofreader's nightmare. É. I. du Pont, founder of the Du Pont dynasty, always signed his name with a small "d" out of deference to his father, Pierre-Samuel du Pont de Nemours. The tradition has continued, and when using names of individual members of the Du Pont family, the small "d" is still used. However, when discussing the family as a whole, or any of the DuPont companies, the big "D" is correct usage.

tenacious type bred especially for fighting: the blue hen, also known as the blue rock. Delaware is the kind of place you like to discover, then keep to yourself.

You'll see the Du Pont name everywhere: for more than 150 years the Du Pont family has played a major role in Delaware's economy, politics, and cultural institutions. The Hagley Museum, site of the first Du Pont factory, features early American industrial history collections; Winterthur Museum displays 100 rooms of Du Pont–collected early American furniture. Other cultural centers include the Delaware Art Museum in Wilmington, a museum of natural history in Greenville, and the state history museum in Dover.

Among Delaware's historical sites are the colonial capital, New Castle; "Old Swedes" church in Wilmington; Fort Delaware on Pea Patch Island; Dickinson House near Dover; and the State House in Dover, one of America's oldest state capitals. The Bombay Hook, Prime Hook, and Chesapeake & Delaware Canal wildlife refuges, the Delaware Seashore, Cape Henlopen, and Brandywine Creek offer a panoply of outdoor recreation. Rehoboth Beach, Bethany Beach, and Fenwick Island each offer a different version of ocean resorts.

Though sometimes overlooked because of its size, it's unwise to underestimate this little powerhouse of a state. Within its three counties is everything a visitor could desire, from active outdoor recreation to the pleasures of a fine meal and luxurious guest quarters.

The Land

Most of Delaware is too thick to drink and too thin to plow.

guide at the Dickinson Plantation, Dover

Delaware's tiny patch of rolling hills in the Brandywine Valley, part of the Piedmont region in the extreme north, provide the only variation in the state's terrain; the highest point in Delaware is there: 442 feet. From that dizzying elevation, a low, gently undulating plain slopes down to the Atlantic Ocean. The lowland is part of the Atlantic coastal plain; a northeast-southwest fall line separates the two regions. Most of Delaware is characterized by two types of soils built on clay accumulation (ultisols): humults, with a high organic carbon content, found in northern and central areas; and aquults, with a higher clay content, found in coastal and southern areas.

Waterways

For all of Delaware's early peoples, wealth came on the water, and the state has more than its share. The Delaware Bay provided food and transportation for generations of Native Americans and the settlers who came after them. The Atlantic Ocean provided speedy access to Europe.

Among the state's most prominent geographic features are salt and freshwater marshes, both inland and along Delaware Bay. Most of Delaware's rivers, such as the Christina and its tributary Brandywine Creek, as well as the Murderkill, Mispillion, Broadkill, Leipsic, and Smyrna, are relatively short waterways that flow eastward into Delaware Bay. Two larger rivers in the southern part of the state, the Nanticoke and Pocomoke, flow southwest through eastern Maryland into the Chesapeake Bay. Pocomoke Swamp, in southern Delaware, is the northernmost cypress swamp in North America. All ponds and lakes in

© JOANNE MILLER

enjoying the beach at Cape Henlopen

Delaware are captured water—there are no natural springs. Groundwater is held in permeable marine deposits atop crystalline bedrock.

The Chesapeake & Delaware Canal, an artificial waterway, links Delaware and Chesapeake Bays (its western terminus is Chesapeake City, Maryland) as well as the Delaware River and the port of Wilmington (the eastern terminus is just south of Delaware City). It's one of the busiest canals in America, accommodating most oceangoing vessels and smaller craft.

CLIMATE

Expect long, warm, and humid summers and relatively mild winters. Wilmington temperatures dip down to freezing (32°F) in January and average 75°F in July. There is some snow in the northern part of the state, less in the south; the average is 15 inches a year, overall. Meteorologists characterize the climate as humid-continental. The Atlantic Ocean and Chesapeake Bay combine to temper storms coming in from the Gulf of Mexico and continental weather systems from the west. Rainfall averages 44 inches a year.

Best Times to Visit

During most of the year, the temperature is rarely unpleasant, so any season is a good one—just bring an umbrella. In winter, dress in layers. Most of the state's attractions are outside the urban area of Wilmington, and even there casual clothing is *de rigueur*. As summer humidity builds, it's a good idea to protect yourself from biting insects with lightweight long pants and shirts. Mosquitoes are particularly pestiferous due to the preponderance of groundwater and marshes, but don't let the threat of a few bites stop you from enjoying Delaware's truly extraordinary out-of-doors.

FLORA

Native Trees

Forest covers roughly 622 square miles of the state. Oak, beech, walnut, maple, and dogwood are the prevalent species in northern Delaware. In the south, loblolly and Virginia pines are mixed with sweet and black gums, oaks, maples, yellow poplars, and hollies. Wild persimmons are an important food source for wildlife. Both Maryland and Delaware claim the country's northernmost stand of bald cypress; Delaware wins, by a few miles.

Shrubs and Flowers

Delaware's freshwater marshes are living wildflower garlands throughout spring, summer, and fall. Red bergamot, wild valerian, wild geranium, chicory, wild rose, daisy, goldenrod, wild iris, and dozens of other roadside species brighten up native grasses and tint the edges of fields. Shade is the ideal foil for jack-in-the-pulpit, trillium, trout-lily, and wood anemone. Moist areas shelter flowerless plants such as royal, cinnamon, New York, sensitive, and marsh ferns.

In the northern part of the state, azalea, rhododendron, redbud, mountain laurel, and magnolia are present as cultivars and naturalized plantings. The public Du Pont properties are especially notable for their beautiful gardens. Many sections of Wilmington are dreamy pink with flowering cherry in the spring.

As in Maryland, freshwater native grasses such as cattail, pond lily, bulrushes, and smartweed and well-adapted sea grasses like cordgrass wave

HARBOR LIGHTS

These lighthouses are all in Delaware Bay, and are accessible only by boat:

Miah Maull—18 miles north of Cape Henlopen State Park in Lewes.

Brandywine Shoal—seven miles north of Cape Henlopen.

Fourteen Foot Bank—13 miles north of Cape Henlopen.

Harbor of Refuge—visible from Cape Henlopen State Park.

Delaware Breakwater—about 1.5 miles from Harbor of Refuge.

Ship John Shoal—27 to 28 miles north of Cape Henlopen State Park.

Fisherman's Wharf in Lewes does an evening tour and a dolphin tour that pass by the two closest, the Delaware Breakwater and Harbor of Refuge. A six-hour narrated cruise with lunch passes by all the Delaware Bay lighthouses. For additional information, call 302/645-8862.

along the state's shorelines, sometimes supplanted by the ivory plumes of phragmites, a nuisance plant introduced from Eurasia.

FAUNA

Mammals

With few exceptions, the state is marsh or open farmland with a few wild forested areas; large mammals are rare-to-nonexistent. Deer and small game—river otter, raccoon, opossum, red and gray fox, striped skunks, gray and black squirrels, marsh rabbit, and muskrat—are present in the more rural areas of the state. Several species of bats, the little brown myotis, silver-haired bat, eastern pipistrel, big brown bat, red bat, and hoary bat, inhabit the state year-round. Harbor seals form nursery colonies on the shore.

Birds

The state is on the Atlantic migratory bird flyway, and the marshy Delaware Bay shore is a refuge for both migrating and local birds. Canada geese, wood ducks, and tundra swans gather in massive flocks on the edges of ponds and lakes (and in public and private parks, much to the annoyance of groundskeepers and owners) during migratory seasons. Some have found Delaware so inviting that they've established year-round residency, as at Hagley Mills. Shorebirds such as the long-legged killdeer, the endangered piping plover, and willits, avocets, seagulls, terns, and dozens of varieties of sandpiper search the shorelines for food. Ospreys, peregrine falcons, eagles, and other raptors nest on telephone poles and park structures; on the inland marshes and Pea Patch Island, great blue herons, egrets, cranes, and other wading birds ply the shallow waters.

Along the shore, loons, grebes, gannets, pelicans, and cormorants take to the air. Nonmigratory birds are similar to those in Maryland. Doves and

migratory bird-spotting station, central Delaware

© JOANNE MILLER

BIRD CITY

One of the nation's greatest heronries is nestled among the smokestacks of an industrial complex and the lanes of a major shipping channel at Pea Patch Island in the Delaware River near Wilmington. In late spring, the trees of Pea Patch are festooned with thousands of nesting egrets, ibis, and herons, including great blues.

The island was little more than a mud bank in the late 1700s. In 1859, Fort Delaware was built here, first as a military installation, then as a prison. The island doubled in size in the early 1900s after it became a channel-dredging depository. During the 1950s, as the spoil mounds on the island's northern tip grew increasingly forested, herons began moving in. By the early 1990s, it had become the second largest "city" in Delaware by sheer population numbers (bested only by the human population of Wilmington), hosting some 36,000 herons (adults and young) of more than half a dozen species. Egrets, cattle egrets, little blue herons, glossy ibis, and black-crowned night herons made up about 80 percent of the colony.

Most herons go through considerable comparison-shopping before forming short-lived mating pairs, so large groups are necessary for survival. Nests are built high in the trees, and by midsummer, blue heron chicks are almost as large as adults—and they require a daily caloric intake equivalent to the need of a grown human. The parents may range a dozen miles or more from the colony to forage. Only one in five juvenile great blues survives to its third year to become a breeding adult, largely because of the difficulty in learning to catch large prey. A bird will often stab at its catch for several minutes to subdue it; then the heron must position the fish to slide headfirst down its throat. A stiff-spined fish going down the wrong way can mean a slow, painful death for the heron. The relatively few juveniles that do master the difficult feeding techniques can look forward to a long life of 20 years or more.

In recent years, despite adequate food supplies, Pea Patch Island's bird colony population has been in decline, falling from about 12,500 nesting pairs to fewer than 7,000. Some species were raising young in lower-than-expected numbers. Rather than blame the obvious—the surrounding industrial complexes—researchers familiar with urban industrial heronries suspected the answer might lie in whatever was causing an unusually large number of lesions on the abdomens of young birds in many of the Pea Patch nests. The cause of the lesions appeared to be nest beetles that lived on scraps of regurgitated foods that the adults fed to their young. The beetles are in nests everywhere, but on Pea Patch, they seem to be causing lesions, most severely among those species that foraged heavily in nearby farm fields and other upland areas. After years of analysis, it was found that the lesions were related to lowered levels of cholinesterase, an enzyme that transmits nerve impulses in all animals; affected birds appeared to be too lethargic to avoid beetle bites. The lowered cholinesterase was linked to adult birds feeding where organophosphate pesticides, successors to DDT, were used. The study has important implications for SAMP—a Special Area Management Plan developed by New Jersey, Delaware, the federal government, and private environmental, business, and agricultural interests. The SAMP plans to build consensus for environmentally sound land uses, and for wetlands protection and restoration across thousands of acres, using the Pea Patch herons as a focal point.

Canada geese at Eleutherian Mills

cuckoos; owls and nightjars; swifts, humming-birds, kingfishers, and woodpeckers; flycatchers; larks and swallows; jays and crows; chickadees, titmice, nuthatches, and creepers; wrens; kinglets, gnatcatchers, and thrushes; mimics, pipits, waxwings, and starlings; vireos and warblers; tanagers, sparrows, finches, ravens, orioles, and blue-birds are found throughout the state.

Reptiles

Delaware has more than a dozen varieties of non-poisonous snake, including rough green, northern black racer, black rat, eastern king, eastern garter, and eastern milk snakes.

Several varieties of turtle, including the diamondback terrapin, eastern box turtle, musk turtle (stinkpot), and eastern painted turtle, sun themselves along freshwater ponds.

Amphibians

Frogs, newts, and salamanders—particularly the redback, marbled, and spotted varieties—inhabit the banks of streams, rivers, and catch basins.

Freshwater Fish

Black crappie, white crappie, rock bass, white bass, walleye pike, pickerel, trout, muskel-lunge, sunfish, bluegill, pumpkinseed, and perch are all found in freshwater streams, lakes, and impoundments.

Saltwater Species

From Lewes south, the Atlantic abounds in tuna, bluefish, dolphin, and occasionally marlin. Dolphin can be spotted from the shore, and whale-watching boats leave from all the major resort towns. Numerous ocean-based species including mako, blue, great hammerhead, tiger sharks, and smaller coastal species such as the finetooth shark and porbeagle are common.

As the blue crab is the symbol of Maryland, the horseshoe crab, which is more closely related to the spider, is the symbol of Delaware. Shellfish, hermit crabs, and other small varieties of crustaceans are found on the shore.

Insects

Though the ladybug is the state insect, the common mosquito wins the prize for sheer numbers and annoyance factor. Delaware's wonderful state parks and resource areas are most seductive in summer, when the little buzzers are at their peak.

CRABS CROON, FULL MOON, MAY AND JUNE

Is there ever a sight or sound more romantic than the scuttling of thousands of tiny tank-like creatures assailing the moonlit beaches of central Delaware, dragging their males behind them? It all begins in the depths of the Atlantic Ocean and Delaware Bay each March, when the water begins to warm. Horseshoe crabs—which aren't really crabs at all, but are related to spiders and scorpions—are stirred by the warming waters into a spawning frenzy that culminates in the appearance of millions of the creatures on the beaches of Delaware during May and June.

Females, which can grow up to two feet long and weigh up to 10 pounds, clamber onto the beaches with the much smaller males clinging to their spiky tails; there the females dig shallow nests and lay up to 20,000 small, olive-green eggs. The female then drags the male over the eggs to fertilize them; together, they cover the eggs with sand and head back to the water. After two weeks, the crablets scuttle to the water themselves, to feed on worms, clams, and dead fish, and spend the next nine or ten years molting to maturity and their own chance to mate in the moonlight.

Delaware Bay is home to the largest population in the world of the four remaining species of this trilobite-like creature. Though some may find the armored shuffler frightening (though the long, hard tail, the telson, is only used to maneuver into more favorable positions), horseshoe crabs are not prone to aggressive behavior of any kind. In fact, the peaceful little beasts that resemble wind-up toys are responsible for three Nobel Prizes in medical research. Much of our knowledge about the human eye was based on studies of the crab's compound eye; the crab's pure chitin shell has led to chitin-coated sutures and burn dressings that promote healing with less pain; and its copper-based blue blood contains a clotting agent called lysate that attaches to bacterial toxins. Modern pharmaceutical firms test their products for purity with lysate drawn from crab's blood; the crabs are captured, bled, and released.

Unfortunately, the commercial demand for horseshoe crabs has increased, as they are the preferred bait for eels and conchs, popular in European and Asian markets. Coupled with the fact that horseshoe crab eggs are the main food of many of the western hemisphere's migrating birds, the crab population had declined, prompting the Atlantic States Marine Fisheries Commission to develop a management plan to ensure an enduring population of the ancient sea dweller. At midnight, by the light of the full June moon, it will continue to appear that the rocks are dancing.

Bring plenty of insect repellent, and go boldly into that marsh.

ENVIRONMENTAL CONCERNS

Recent years have seen significant declines in numbers of horseshoe crabs and shorebirds. The usual suspects are pesticides in bird wintering grounds, overharvesting of horseshoe crabs for bait and scientific purposes, and loss of coastal wetlands along migration routes. New regulations in Delaware, New Jersey, and Maryland have reduced the legal harvest of horseshoe crabs.

The greatest environmental concern in the state has been preservation of wetlands. The Coastal Zone Act, passed in 1971, was a major step in balancing development with the natural environment; it threw a protective net around the coastal marshes. However, it continues to be challenged by economic interests. The state has few natural resources to exploit: mineral resources are located in the north, with kaolin the most significant, followed by construction granite, gravels, and clay (used to make bricks and tiles). No hydroelectric power has been developed in Delaware.

History

Precolonial Delaware

Lenni Lenape, called "Delaware" by European settlers due to their encampments on the Delaware River, were the state's original inhabitants, along with the Nanticoke, Pocomoke-Assateague, and Nause. Lenni Lenape were actually an Algonquian-speaking confederacy made up of three major tribes: the Munsee, Unalachtigo, and Unami. Tribal units would cultivate land near the rivers during the spring and summer, then depart to gather syrup and hunt during the winter, returning to the old encampments in the spring. They didn't farm,because foraging was excellent. Broadly speaking, both group leadership and territory were ill-defined, and political organization was kept on a small scale. Algonquian groups were among the first native North Americans to suffer destruction at the hands of Europeans; the cultures of many ended before the 18th century.

In 1609, Henry Hudson, an Englishman in the employ of the Dutch West India Company, sailed into Delaware Bay and noted the favorable conditions. In 1631, a small group of Dutch West India traders established a tobacco-growing and whaling industry at Zwaanendael (Lewes). They were there less than a year; the local Indians became frustrated with the settlers' apparent lack of cultural understanding and wiped out the entire camp.

Our Delaware

In 1634, Lord Baltimore sent his representatives to Maryland and took possession of a land grant that had been awarded to him by the British Crown—a territory that included all of Delaware. Four years later, the New Sweden Company built a fort and trading post in the vicinity of modern Wilmington, but Lord Baltimore, involved in affairs within Maryland, did nothing to remove them. The Dutch attempted to reclaim the Delaware River and its territories; they sent Peter Stuyvesant to oust the Swedes and claim the land as part of Nieuw Netherland. Lord Baltimore didn't protest the presence of either the Swedes or

the Dutch until 1659. In 1661, Charles Calvert, the son of Cecil, Lord Baltimore, ostensibly took over the governorship of the colony, and laid out the city of New Castle (in modern Delaware) as an outpost of Maryland.

The Swedes surrendered the territory to the Dutch, but the Dutch refused to move until the British bested them in a European-based trade war. Dutch influence remains in the names of rivers; "kill" is the Dutch term for waterway. The Dutch turned the colony over to the British in 1664, and Delaware officially became part of Maryland.

In England in 1680, the rebel Quaker son of an aristocratic family, William Penn, agreed to exchange a debt owed his family by King Charles for land in the new world. He planned to name it for his father: Pennsylvania, or Penn's woods. Penn was determined to have access to the Atlantic Ocean, even though his land grant clearly placed him out of reach, above the point where the Delaware River met Delaware Bay. In fact, New Castle, Lord Baltimore's settlement, was considered to be the mouth of the bay, and was 20 miles south of Penn's legal border. Penn persuaded the Duke of York to issue him a grant to New Castle plus a circle of territory 12 miles in radius (hence the odd bulge at the top of the state), plus a piece of land from this circle down to Cape Henlopen—almost all of the current state of Delaware. Penn was well aware that his claim to the territory was fictitious; he sailed to the New World and met with Lord Baltimore several times, trying to persuade him to deliver New Castle into his hands. Both men returned to England to plead their case. The king favored Penn: In 1682, Delaware came under the proprietorship of William Penn, but was administered separately from Pennsylvania as a distinct entity called the "three counties of Delaware" or "the three lower counties." At that time, the counties were named New Castle, St. Jones (now Kent County), and Whorekill (Sussex County—no need to question the name change).

Early Expansion

The first settlements were small, largely concentrated in New Castle and Wilington (Wilmington). However, from the 1730s on, the confluence of the Christina and Delaware Rivers positioned Wilmington as a major grain port and ship-building center. The Christina gave Wilmington access to its hinterland, and nearby Brandywine Creek provided excellent mill sites. Thus one of America's most intensive manufacturing districts came into being.

By 1720 the Five Nations Iroquois League, a confederation of Iroquois-speaking tribes based in northern New York and Ontario, dominated much of the remaining Lenni Lenape homeland by war or treaty. As European settlers moved in, the majority of the Lenni Lenape and other indigenous tribes moved west, away from the colonies, eventually establishing villages in eastern Ohio. Today, small Nanticoke colonies exist in Kent and Sussex Counties.

The Revolution

Though there were plenty of loyalists among early colonial inhabitants, the Delaware territory settlers proved to be fervent supporters of colonial autonomy. Three weeks before the signing of the Declaration of Independence, Delaware's assembly voted to not only separate from the British, but also from Pennsylvania. Caesar Rodney, a resident of New Castle, rode through the night to Philadelphia and cast the deciding vote for independence.

During the Revolutionary War, the British seized Wilmington after defeating George Washington at the Battle of Brandywine in 1777. The nearby colonial state capital, New Castle, was threatened, and the government was moved to the safer inland location of Dover, where it remained. Delaware was the first state to ratify the U.S. Constitution in 1787, thus earning the sobriquet "The First State." This is a point of pride for Delawareans; you'll often see the phrase "Delaware First" on businesses and license plates, as well as on the back of the 1999 state quarter (the first one issued), which bears the image of Caesar Rodney on horseback. Delaware troops in the Continental Army were nicknamed "Blue

MASON AND DIXON

British surveyors and astronomers Charles Mason and Jeremiah Dixon sailed from Britain to Philadelphia in 1763, expressly hired by the British crown to settle the boundary disputes that plagued Delaware, Maryland, and Pennsylvania. By comparing old deeds and hearing testimony, they decided that the north wall of a house on the south side of Cedar Street (now South Street) in Philadelphia was the proper southern limit of the city. Maryland's northern boundary was to follow a line parallel to the southern limit of Philadelphia and 15 miles south of it. So as to avoid the Delaware "bulge," they moved due west for 31 miles, and set up a marker, the Stargazers' Stone (in Chester County, Pennsylvania), which set the Maryland boundary. A Transpeninsular Marker near the site of the Fenwick Island Lighthouse indicated the southern boundary between Pennsylvania's "three lower counties" and Maryland. In April 1765, Mason and Dixon began to move west. Sighting was done from horizon to horizon, and as each mile was measured off, workmen piled up a rough heap of stones, later to be replaced with milestones that carried an "M" on the southern side, a "P" on the northern. Crown stones marked every fifth mile, with the Penn coat of arms on the north, and Lord Baltimore's on the south. By November 1766, Mason and Dixon entered hostile Six Nation Iroquois territory to the west. The party was allowed to continue with an Indian deputation, but when they reached the Monongahela River, a party of native guides and workmen refused to go on into Shawnee territory. Two weeks later, the chief Iroquois delegate announced that he would go no further, and advised the British surveyors to follow his example. They took his advice, and marked the end of the Pennsylvania border.

Hen's Chickens" for the tenacious fighting cocks they brought with them from Kent County, all from the brood of a single blue hen. Today, the name lives on in the University of Delaware football team (Go Blues!).

Wilmington Works

Delaware's booming (pun unintended) chemical industry was born in 1802 when a French immigrant, Éleuthère Irénée du Pont, established a black powder mill near Wilmington. The site is now a public park, Hagley Mills. By the mid-19th century the Delaware landscape had been made over. In northern Delaware, industry had expanded from simple tanning, grain milling, and paper making to sophisticated gunpowder and textile manufacturing. Entrepreneurs and citizens alike benefited from improved turnpikes, the construction of the Chesapeake & Delaware Canal (1829), and the completion of the Philadelphia, Wilmington, and Baltimore Railroad. By 1856, railroad lines extended the length of the state, bringing the economic boom to the agriculture-based businesses in southern Delaware.

Civil War

New Castle County in the north, where Wilmington is located, grew in response to urban-industrial developments in nearby Philadelphia; Kent and Sussex Counties to the south remained rural and culturally a part of the American South. This duality extended to the role Delaware played in the Civil War.

Delaware was divided over the slavery issue during the conflict. The state's original constitution in 1776 forbade the further importation of slaves, and abolition bills narrowly failed in the 1790s and 1847. Less than 2,000 slaves and about 20,000 free blacks were part of the total population of 112,000 in 1860. Though technically a slave state (slaveholding was legal and binding), Delaware did not secede; the majority of Delawareans took a moderate stance and supported the Union with labor and troops. After the Civil War, however, black rights were vigorously opposed. In 1873, blacks were effectively disenfranchised by poll taxes and corrupt politics. In 1897, the poll tax was replaced by a literacy test. Racial issues continued to plague Delawareans into modern times.

After the Civil War, the state's economic growth continued. Wealth and power was concentrated in Wilmington; tax laws instituted in 1899 encouraged corporations to locate their headquarters there. By 1920 the city contained almost half of Delaware's population.

The Last Century

Delaware's more liberal urbanized north and conservative rural south continued to battle over the state's social services and other public sector issues. As a result of legislative conflict between northern and southern factions, state unemployment insurance was withdrawn at the height of the Great Depression in 1934. Legislative districts that had long benefited the rural south were not redrawn until the 1960s in favor of the more populous Wilmington suburbs.

In 1968, the assassination of the great humanitarian leader Dr. Martin Luther King Jr. ignited a long-burning fuse. Blacks rioted in the streets of Wilmington. The National Guard was called in, and the city was placed under martial law. Today, Wilmington is peaceful, though it continues to be highly segregated.

Modern Delaware faces problems common to much of the United States—rapid development, suburban crowding, and economic growth versus environmental preservation. Delaware's economic growth was fueled in the 1980s by the passage of laws favorable to banking and corporate interests. By the 1990s more than 183,000 corporations had headquarters in the state, largely in the Wilmington area. The city is directing much of its wealth into a revitalized downtown area with tourist attractions that will rival those of Baltimore.

The fabulous beaches of southern Delaware remain destinations for thousands of visitors each year, and deservedly so. The last 30 years have seen a revitalization of the once run-down, sleepy beach areas. New hotels, restaurants, and amusements draw (they claim) more visitors than Hawaii. However, the entire state sparkles with interesting places to go and things to see. Delaware is our secret.

GOVERNMENT

Delaware continues to abide by a constitution created in 1897. An earlier version was presented to the people of Delaware, who voted it down;

HORSEMAN ON THE QUARTER

When the U.S. government decided to issue quarters with a design chosen by each state on the back, Delaware was, naturally, first. But a lot of people were confused by the charging horseman chosen as the First State's symbol; the name Caesar Rodney stamped below didn't help (many thought it was Paul Revere—oops, different state). Actually, Mr. Rodney was instrumental in making the First State first. Unfortunately, there are no true representations of Rodney; apparently, his face was deformed by disease or injury, and he never allowed himself to be portrayed for posterity.

Caesar Rodney inherited his father's large Delaware estate, and had been a member of the colonial legislature for 17 years, rising to the position of Speaker of the Assembly. He was an organizer of the Continental Congress, and served in it for two years.

On July 2, 1776, the gathered delegates to the Continental Congress were locked in controversy as to whether to create the United States and break with Britain or remain loyal. As the vote neared, key Delaware players Thomas McKean and George Read stood on opposite sides of the issue; McKean favored independence, while Read didn't. Though desperately ill and unable to attend the initial debates in Philadelphia, Caesar Rodney rode from his home in Sussex Country through "thunder and rain," as the legend goes, all the way to the City of Brotherly Love to cast the deciding vote for independence and statehood. As a result of his speedy return to Congress, the Delaware delegation was able to vote two to one for the adoption of the Declaration of Independence, thus making adoption by the 13 colonies unanimous. Rodney signed the Declaration and was commander of the Delaware militia when British troops marched through Delaware and occupied Wilmington in late 1777. He was elected president (governor) of Delaware the following year, serving until 1781. He died three years later.

To impress your friends while examining your quarter collection, you might want to reel off the original 13 colonies in order of statehood: Delaware, Pennsylvania, New Jersey, Georgia, Connecticut, Massachusetts, Maryland, South Carolina, New Hampshire, Virginia, New York, North Carolina, and Rhode Island. By the war of 1812, Vermont and Kentucky had been admitted to the Union, and the flag that inspired Francis Scott Key was emblazoned with 15 stars.

the current constitution was adopted without a popular vote. Since Delaware consists of only three counties, the state government provides many of the functions normally served by local leadership, though incorporated towns handle their own tax issues, and individual counties largely manage tourism.

State government consists of three bodies: executive, legislative, and judicial. As head of the executive branch, a governor is elected for four years and a maximum of two terms. The legislature (General Assembly) consists of a 21-member Senate and a 41-member House of Representatives; senators serve four-year terms and representatives serve two-year terms. The governor has veto power, although a three-fifths vote in each house will override it.

The judiciary consists of a supreme court, superior courts, courts of common pleas, family courts for juveniles, and a court of chancery for corporate matters. The Republican Party has dominated the state's politics in recent years, though registered Republicans and Democrats are evenly matched.

ECONOMY

Industry is Delaware's mainstay. Wilmington has been the state's industrial center since the colonial period, though space and price considerations have caused industries to spread downstate. Top-grossing industries include chemicals, food processing, primary metals, machinery, printing and publishing, leather goods, fabricated metals, transportation equipment, and textiles. If the vision of a smoking, chugging juggernaut comes to mind, it's useful to remember that a considerable amount of the output of these industries isn't produced in Wilmington—the income is based on the fact that the city is home to the corporate headquarters of these companies.

Prior to 1900, Delaware was known as the "Peach State," but repeated blights wiped out most of the orchards. Peach growing was replaced by the chicken industry; poultry plays such a large part in Delaware's current economics, it's hard to believe that it started by accident. In 1923, a resident of Ocean View, Cecile Steele, received 500 chickens instead of the 50 she ordered. She raised the birds to eating size and sold them in one large lot. Prior to that time, chickens were eaten when their egg-laying days were over, and stewing was the primary cooking option. The new "broilers" caught on, and now more than half of Delaware's agricultural income is derived from the production of broiler chickens. The remainder is spread out among variety of items, including soybeans, greenhouse products, milk, and corn.

EDUCATION

The oldest school in Delaware is the Wilmington Friends School, founded by Quakers in the early colonial days. The state established a public education system in 1829, but funding was erratic, quality of teaching was uneven, and blacks were excluded. This was partially remedied in 1907 when compulsory education was instituted. It took nearly 20 more years and considerable voter pressure (and outright financing by Pierre du Pont) for an administrative and taxation system capable of supporting modern educational facilities to be created. Du Pont insisted that relatively poor areas should not be forced to put up with inferior schools simply because of poverty. Schools were desegregated in 1954, and in 1978 court-ordered busing mixed students from white suburban schools with those of the predominantly black schools of Wilmington.

The University of Delaware at Newark (pronounced as two words: NEW ARK), which evolved from an academy in existence since 1743, and Delaware State College, in Dover, are the two public four-year institutions of higher learning in the state.

The People

Delaware has a population density well above the national average, due mainly to its position; the northern section of the state is part of the megalopolis between Philadelphia and Baltimore/Washington, D.C. Most of Delaware's residents are in this urban region and outlying suburbs.

ETHNOGRAPHY

The 19th century saw major migration into the Wilmington area by Germans and Irish, followed by Italians, Poles, and pan-European Jews. The early 20th century brought Greeks and Ukrainians. Today, Asians and Hispanics are the fastest-growing groups of new settlers.

At the time of the American Revolution, blacks made up one-fifth of the total population. In 1990, the population was about 80 percent white and 17 percent black.

The ethnic mix of southern Delaware has changed little over the years. Composed primarily of German and Scotch-Irish peoples, the area received an influx of Germanic Amish and Mennonite settlers during the Great Depression of the 1930s. Today, an enclave of one of Delmarva's indigenous tribes, the Nanticoke, has been established in southern Delaware near the town of Millsboro.

RELIGION

Roman Catholics make up the single largest denomination, though all Protestants taken together—Methodists, Presbyterians, and Episcopalians—outnumber them. The state also has significant numbers of Jews and Orthodox Christians.

CONDUCT AND CUSTOMS

Liquor Laws

Beer and alcohol are sold only in privately owned liquor stores, not in groceries or convenience stores. Beer and alcohol are not sold on Sundays, and Delaware has an open container law (you can't drink on the street like you can in New Orleans). You have to be 21 to drink.

Legal Gambling

Delaware has slots (video lottery terminals similar to Las Vegas's one-armed bandits) and simulcast racing only, no table games. Slot machines are only permitted in areas that had existing horse racing facilities when the law was passed to allow gambling. There are three slots locations: Dover Downs International Speedway and Slots, U.S. 13, one mile north of Dover, 302/674-4600 (also home to two annual NASCAR races and harness racing); Midway Slots and Simulcast, Delaware State Fair Grounds, U.S. 13, Harrington, 888/88-SLOTS (888/887-5687) (harness racing); and Delaware Park Racetrack and Slots, 777 Delaware Park Blvd., Wilmington, 302/994-2521 (thoroughbred racing).

Police

Wilmington has a large municipal police force, including beat cops, who cover the downtown area on foot. Most of the city is totally carefree, but some neighborhoods are iffy, and others

---

MOVING WITH THE EARTH

In Native American culture, dances are a way of bringing people together to consolidate energy toward a single purpose. All dances are performed to the varied beats of drum groups; the drumbeat is considered the heartbeat of Mother Earth. The Nanticoke tribe of southern Delaware holds a powwow each September that features the dances of many different tribes. Though a few of the dances at the Nanticoke Powwow are open to visitors (when in doubt, ask), most are traditional, such as the grass dance, or specialty dances, which honor certain attendees or a special event. Pecita Lonewolf, who regularly writes about tribal activities, describes several traditional dances: the grass dance, which originated in North Dakota in the early 1900s, is performed by dancers in fringed regalia, usually the first dancers at the powwow; their task was to prepare the grass for other dancers, while swaying gracefully to intricate dance steps.

Another traditional dance is the chicken dance, which also originated among the plains Indians. Performed by young men in fancy headgear and bustles bristling with plumage, the energetic movements imitate the mating dance of the prairie chicken, complete with running, leaping, and ducking. One dance that originated with the Algonquin tribes, the Woodland Snake Dance, tells the story of the cycle of life from its beginning through four stages, then into the spirit world.

One specialty dance recently performed was to honor attendees of Haskell Indian Nations University, a former federal U.S. Indian boarding school in Lawrence, Kansas, that educated many Native Americans until the early 1960s. Though some who left never returned, the dance was performed by at least 20 Haskell attendees from the Nanticoke and other tribes. Many Native Americans feared that attending a school so far from home would destroy both their culture and their family-based social structure; instead, the school provided a fertile ground for members of many tribes to intermingle and share their native heritage. Perhaps it is as Nanticoke Assistant Chief Charles C. Clark IV says: "[The] key to . . . survival is the memory of our intimate connection to this World and the Creator's promise that everything we would need to survive would be provided to us."

downright dangerous. Make sure you know where you're going, particularly at night; the downtown area used to look like a ghost town after dark, but that's changing.

The rest of the state has a small municipal police force in each town or village. The highways are regularly patrolled. Southern Delaware, particularly away from the beaches, has a reputation for conservatism, but generally, the whole state has a laid-back, mind-your-own-business attitude.

On the Road in Delaware

As Maryland is big, Delaware is small—but it's mighty. The First State packs a lot of fun into three counties: everything from scenic hikes to sugary beaches to mansions of the wealthiest families in America. You can drive from one end of Delaware to the other in about three hours, and accessibility is just one of its draws. Depending on the amount of time you have to spend and your interests, it's possible to admire the cupids at the Nemours Mansion in the morning, count birds at Bombay Hook Wildlife Refuge after lunch, and arrive at the beach by nightfall.

The Delaware chapters are arranged north-south, by county. The northernmost county contains the major urban area in Delaware: Wilmington, an up-and-coming city with a small-town feel. The countryside surrounding Wilmington—the Brandywine Valley—is home to most of the northern area's attractions. Here you'll find three Dupont properties, all stunning, and a must-see for those interested in decorative arts and crafts.

Those looking for outdoor recreation won't be disappointed; this little state is packed with parks, refuges and greenways—if you're a birder or a cyclist, you've found paradise. The pretty state capital, Dover, is surrounded by Amish farms in central Delaware; the coastline in both central and southern Delaware feature large wildlife refuges. In fact, southern Delaware's beaches—from jumping Rehoboth Beach to

a sunny wait north of Dover

peaceful Bethany Beach—are some of the best in the mid-Atlantic. This area offers nightlife aplenty, two state parks (Delaware Seashore State Park and Cape Henlopen State Park) for campers, and a fabulous tax-free group of malls for those who just can't stop shopping.

This chapter will give you a broad idea of what's available in the state, including specific destinations and festivals and events that take place throughout the year. Delaware as a destination is a well-kept secret; this book will help you join the in-crowd.

Outdoor Recreation

STATE PARKS AND WILDLIFE REFUGES

Delaware features 14 state parks, and a park is within two hours of any point in the state. The parks offer a surprising variety of natural areas: ocean beaches, inland ponds, forests, rolling hills, or piedmont streams. Pea Patch is an island with Civil War significance; Cape Henlopen, Delaware Seashore, and Fenwick Island State Parks are all on the ocean; Killens Pond, Lums Pond, and Trap Pond State Parks are all freshwater impoundments. In addition, Killens Pond has a water park. The parks offer a number of activities including camping, boat rentals, educational programs, hiking, surf fishing, sun bathing, clamming, crabbing, surfing, and swimming.

Delaware State Parks are largely self-funded and rely on user fees for about 75 percent of the operating and maintenance budget. Fees vary from park to park. Daily entrance fees are in effect on weekends in May, daily from Memorial Day to Labor Day, and weekends in September and October; season passes are available. For more information, contact the Delaware Division of Parks and Recreation at 302/739-4702, www.destateparks.com.

In 1994, the Delaware State Parks established the Carry In—Carry Out Trash-Free Parks Program. Trash cans were removed from most areas, and visitors now take their trash with them when they leave, reducing the strain on limited resources and increasing the beauty of the parks.

Wildlife Refuges: Bombay Hook National Wildlife Refuge and Prime Hook National Wildlife Refuge are bayfront areas administered by the U.S. Fish & Wildlife Service expressly for the preservation of native flora and fauna. Both provide ample opportunities for naturalists, birdwatchers, photographers, and casual observers to enjoy the unique beauty of Delaware's coastline. For further information, contact the U.S. Fish & Wildlife Service, Bombay Hook NWR, 2591 Whitehall Neck Rd., Smyrna, DE 19977, 302/653-9345.

GREENWAYS

Delaware's Greenway and Trail Program, administered by the Division of Parks and Recreation, is a statewide initiative to preserve and protect corridors of open space. A greenway is a natural area of unbroken vegetation where recreation and conservation are the primary goals. Greenways wind along rivers and streams, skirt wetlands, and cross barrier beaches, hilltops, abandoned rail lines, fields, and forests. Some greenways are publicly owned; others are private. Some are for recreation, containing biking and hiking trails; others protect a scenic view or wildlife habitat.

In spring 1996, Delaware's extensive Greenway and Trail Program was awarded the American Greenways DuPont Government Award, established by the DuPont Company in partnership with the National Geographic Society and the Conservation Fund to recognize businesses, nonprofit organizations, and government agencies that have been successful in creating greenways. Today, the state continues to add and enhance greenways, keeping the urban areas green and the countryside open. These projects are either completed or in the works:

Northern Delaware

In 1990 the Delaware Nature Society began a **Stream Corridor Greenways** protection pro-

GREENWAYS GUIDES AND INFORMATION

To obtain a trail guide and/or brochure, click on the Greenway and Trail Program at www.destateparks.com/greenway or call the Division of Parks and Recreation, 302/739-5285.

Delaware Greenways & Trails, a statewide map brochure, highlights parks, trails, museums, and other cultural and recreational sites along greenway corridors.

The *Coastal Heritage Greenway Auto Tour* highlights the cultural and natural resources of Delaware's coast from Fox Point to Cape Henlopen. View it on the Web at www .destateparks.com/greenway/trailguides/autotour/chgauto.htm, or call the Division of Parks and Recreation.

Coast Quest provides kids with a fun way to learn about Delaware's Coastal Heritage Greenway through puzzles, activities, and games.

The *Prison Camp Trail: Fort Delaware, Pea Patch Island* trail brochure guides Fort Delaware visitors along a three-quarter-mile Prison Camp Trail through Civil War prison grounds.

Fort DuPont: Defending the Delaware guides visitors along a one-mile trail where they will be able to see the remains of the three major periods of coastal fortification, dating from the Civil War to the First World War.

The Wetlands of Port Penn Interpretive Trail follows a 1.5-mile trail, providing a closer look at the relationships that existed between Port Penners and the wetlands in the past and recognizing its continuing influence on the lives of people here today.

The Historic Homes of Port Penn brochure highlights the historic buildings of Port Penn, interpreting the village's history through its architecture.

The *St. Jones River Trail Guide* takes visitors along a two-mile trail that passes through marsh, woodlands, and farmlands, focusing on the historical interaction of people and their environment.

The Pinelands Trail will guide visitors to Cape Henlopen State Park through a living example of natural and man-made change in a maritime forest. Along this trail, visitors will travel through an ever-changing environment of old bogs, drained wetlands, and maturing pine woods.

Southern Delaware Heritage Trail explores southern Delaware's hidden treasures by bike, canoe, or car. This guide takes you to the towns of Seaford, Laurel, Milton, Millsboro, and Milford.

---

gram as a means of improving water quality and protecting animal migration corridors along waterways in Northern Delaware and Chester County, Pennsylvania. Riparian landowners are contacted and encouraged to become stewards of the greenway corridor by managing their lands in an environmentally sensitive manner.

The **Upper Christina River Greenway,** a joint project of the Christina Conservancy and the Delaware Nature Society, strives to improve water quality through education of private landowners in the upper reaches of the Christina River in northwestern Castle County, Delaware; Cecil County, Maryland; and Chester County, Pennsylvania.

The **White Clay/Middle Run (Northern Delaware Greenway—West Link)** begins at the western terminus of the Mill Creek Greenway near the Middle Run Natural Area northeast of Newark. Several trails have been constructed throughout the Middle Run Natural Area County Park that continue westward to the Possum Hill Area of White Clay Creek State Park. The Hopkins Trail, a multiuse trail, continues over the "Land Bridge" in White Clay Creek State Park linking the Mason-Dixon trail, the White Clay Creek Preserve, the city of Newark and University of Delaware, and the Fairhill Natural Area near Elkton, Maryland.

New Castle County Department of Parks &

ON THE ROAD/DELAWARE

Recreation, Christina River Development Corporation, City of Wilmington, Christina Conservancy, Delaware Department of Natural Resources, and Kalmar Nyckel Foundation are all contributing to protection of the **Lower Christina River Greenway.** These efforts include creating pathways and revitalizing the Christina Riverfront in Wilmington.

Brandywine Nature Trail, Marketplace Trail, Swedes Landing Trail, the Historic Trail, the Brandywine Riverwalk, and the Christina Riverwalk are six **Wilmington Walkways** and driving tours that provide opportunities to enjoy the historic, cultural, and architectural amenities of Wilmington's past and present. These amenities range from serene, pastoral settings to active recreational areas. Bicycle routes have been designated and marked on Kennett Pike, Route 141, Faulkland Road, Route 9 to New Castle, and Route 7.

The 6,000-foot-long **Elsmere** pathway goes through the town park to link Centerville Road with Du Pont Road on the north side of the railroad tracks.

The urban trail, **Northern Delaware Greenway—East Link,** spans 10 miles of northern New Castle County from Fox Point State Park on the Delaware River to Brandywine Creek State Park. It connects with Wilmington Walkways and links together residential communities, schools, businesses, parks, and cultural sites. Eventually, the Northern Delaware Greenway will stretch across New Castle County and will connect with greenways in Middle Run Natural Area and White Clay Creek State Park near Newark. Fox Point State Park is the northern end of the Coastal Heritage Greenway.

The path of the **East Coast Greenway** in Delaware is still under construction. It's planned to be an 80 percent off-road route for cyclists, hikers, and other users, a more urban alternative to the Appalachian Trail. When completed, the East Coast Greenway will connect existing and planned trails with new corridors using waterfronts, park paths, rail trails, canal towpaths, and parkway corridors.

A greenway corridor and trail development from Beck's Pond to Lums Pond State Park, New

Castle County, the **Pencader Hundred** will include a new regional park near Glasgow, former Frenchtown Railroad lands, suburban streets through the Mansion Farms area, and a new district park.

Mill Creek Hundred trail winds through a combination of public lands, suburban streets, and lands held by community associations in the Mill Creek and Pike Creek areas of New Castle County. A trail crosses the wooded open space behind the North Pointe Town homes on Stoney Batter Road extending to Delcastle Recreation Area.

Central Delaware

Smyrna Trails, a paved bicycle/pedestrian trail along Green's Branch in northern Smyrna, connects three major thoroughfares: Glenwood Avenue, Duck Creek Parkway, and N. Main Street. The trail provides off-road access for pedestrians and cyclists to numerous residential and commercial areas. The trail will also provide access to two scenic overlooks of Duck Creek. This project represents the first phase of implementation of a town-wide system of trails.

The **St. Jones River Greenway Commission** was created as an umbrella organization to coordinate greenway efforts in the capital city of Dover, working to preserve and enhance the cultural, historic, and recreational resources of the area. As part of the overall plan, the city of Dover is planning a one-mile pathway from Silver Lake Park to the Legislative Complex; Kent County is creating a third landing at the midpoint of the St. Jones River at Lebanon Landing; and 431 acres along the St. Jones River are being protected as part of the National Estuarine Research Reserve system. In this preserve, an interpretive center and one-mile self-guided trail focus on the historical interaction of people and their environment.

For the **Murderkill River Greenway,** more than 2,028 acres and three miles of river corridor have been protected at Killens Pond State Park and the Murderkill River Nature Preserve stretching from Route 13 to Frederica. A one-half-mile pathway runs from the park entrance on Route 384 to the U.S. 13 intersection. The pathway is part of State Bicycle Route 1 and links Lake Forest High School and Killens Pond State Park. A 3.5-mile canoe trail was established from U.S. 13 to the Coursey Pond spillway.

The **Mispillion Riverwalk** in the city of Milford connects the downtown business area, library, amphitheater, community theater, University of Delaware Milford Campus building, and recreational areas. Plans are under way to link the Riverwalk via a pedestrian bridge to a long-established park on the river's north bank.

For the **Mispillion River Greenway,** The Nature Conservancy, Delaware Wildlands, and U.S. Fish & Wildlife Service have preserved 2,600 acres at Milford Neck. The greenway extends north from Abbotts Pond to Blairs Pond and will eventually connect the Milford chain of lakes.

Southern Delaware

The town of Milton has undertaken an ambitious plan to create Governor's Walk along the **Broadkill River,** commemorating the birthplace of four Delaware governors and a Wyoming governor. The Nature Conservancy has begun a new effort to protect land both upstream and downstream of the town. In addition, Milton has made outstanding efforts to preserve its historic town center.

The **Lewes Greenway** Committee is building a network of protected open space and pedestrian and bicycle pathways that link parks, natural areas, and historic sites throughout the town.

On the **Nanticoke River,** the city of Seaford is planning a riverfront walkway, and the town of Blades is working to create open space and new recreational opportunities.

The center of the **Broad Creek Greenway** is in the heart of Laurel. The greenway begins at Records Pond and extends west to Riverfront Park, linking the downtown area and the river.

The Division of Parks & Recreation holds 66 acres paralleling the **Assawoman Canal;** a master plan includes a pathway with connections to residential developments along the canal, water access points, and other amenities. The town of Bethany Beach has planned a system of pathways for pedestrians and bicyclists that will provide recreation and transportation and link with the Assawoman Canal lands.

A new long-distance trail, the **American Discovery Trail (ADT),** www.discoverytrail.org, is a continuous multiuse hiking path extending across the United States from one coast to another. The ADT eastern trailhead is in Cape Henlopen State Park. The route of the ADT through Delaware travels about 45 miles of sidewalks and rural roads, most with paved shoulders. The trail passes through Redden State Forest and the towns of Lewes, Milton, and Bridgeville, but it mostly follows open farmland. A principal goal of the ADT has been to connect as many of the National Trail System trails and local and regional trails as possible in order to complete a system of trails. Reaching across 15 states, the ADT connects six national scenic trails, 10 national historic trails, and 23 national recreational trails and leads to 14 national parks and 16 national forests.

The **Coastal Heritage Greenway** is the most comprehensive in the Greenway Program, spanning a corridor of open space along more than 90 miles of Delaware's coast between Fox Point State Park and the state line at Fenwick Island. Focus areas along the Coastal Heritage Greenway include: Fox Point, New Castle, Delaware City, and Port Penn in New Castle County; Woodland Beach Wildlife Area, Lower St. Jones River, and Milford Neck in Kent County; and the Cape Henlopen Focus Area in Sussex County.

ACTIVITIES
On Land

Hiking: Ten state parks contain more than 80 miles of scenic trails. Delaware has also come up with an ingenious and fun hiking program called the Trail Challenge. Hikers who take the Trail Challenge cover almost 40 miles in 15 designated state park trails in a 12-month period. Those who complete the challenge win the Golden Boot Award, a distinctive patch, and a certificate. Hikers can acquire a Trail Challenge card through any Delaware State Park Office, or from Cultural and Recreational Services, 89 Kings Hwy., Dover, 302/739-4143. While on the trail, participants locate the trail punch station along each trail, and use the coded punch to mark the appropriate space on

DELAWARE STATE PARK CAMPING RATES

STATE PARK	FACILITIES	RESIDENT FEE	NONRESIDENT FEE
Cape Henlopen	139 sites with water hookups	$24/night	$28/night
	17 sites without hookups	$22/night	$26/night
Delaware Seashore	145 sites with water, electric, sewer	$30/night	$34/night
	133 sites without hookups	$22/night	$26/night
	156 overflow sites (self-contained units only)	$22/night	$26/night
Killens Pond	59 sites with water, electric hookups	$21/night	$25/night
	17 secluded primitive tent camp sites	$15/night	$19/night
	10 camping cabins (Apr.–Oct.)	$57/night, $342/week	$70/night, $420/week
	(Nov.–March)	$51/night, $306/week	$64/night, $384/week
	1 pond view cottage (Apr.–Oct.)	$68/night, $408/week	$81/night, $486/week
	(Nov.–March)	$62/night, $360/week	$74/night, $432/week
Lums Pond	66 sites with no hookups	$17/night	$21/night
	6 sites with hookups	$20/night	$24/night
	2 yurts	$37/night, $222/week	$46/night, $276/week
Trap Pond	130 sites with water, electric	$20/night	$24/night
	2 island sites with no hookups	$20/night	$24/night
	10 secluded primitive tent sites	$15/night	$19/night
	2 yurts	$32/night, $192/week	$36/night, $216/week
	8 cabins	$45/night, $270/week	$54/night, $324/week

the card. If you miss the marker at any park, the park office can help out. State park trails in the Trail Challenge program are in Brandywine Creek, Fort Delaware/Port Penn, Lums Pond, White Clay Creek (all New Castle County); Killens Pond (Kent County); and Cape Henlopen, Delaware Seashore, Holts Landing, and Trap Pond (Sussex County).

Biking: Multi-use trails are available for biking in most state parks. This information can be found in the park map legends. Outside the park system, Delaware has many bicycle-friendly routes. The state publishes maps and information; contact the DELDOT Division of Planning, Bicycle/Pedestrian Coordinator, P.O. Box 778, Dover, DE 19903, 302/739-BIKE (302/739-2453). For a free brochure of the Southern Delaware Heritage Trail, which includes historic towns, greenways, parks, rivers, shops, and lodging, contact 800/357-1818, or email southdel@amv.com.

Camping: Five state parks permit camping: Cape Henlopen, Delaware Seashore, Lums Pond, Trap Pond, and Killens Pond (which also has cabins). All campgrounds provide drinking water outlets, showers, sanitary facilities, and sewage dumping stations. Campsites also include a picnic table and fire ring, and many have electric and water hookups. Two parks, Lums Pond (302/368-6989) and Trap Pond (302/875-5153), offer yurts, round stationary structures with canvas walls that feature a single and double bed, a double-bed futon, an outdoor seating area, and outdoor deck. These two parks take reservations for yurts, but campsites at other parks are on a first-come, first-serve basis. You can make a reservation online at www.destateparks.com or call 877/98-PARKS (877/987-2757).

In the summer season and in high-use areas like Delaware Seashore and Cape Henlopen State Parks, the parks can be quite crowded. Dogs are permitted in campsites as long as they are on a leash, except in the cabins at Killens Pond.

In the Water
Delaware's beach dunes are a fragile and constantly endangered ecostructure. Except for designated crossing areas, people, pets, and vehicles

boat to Fort Delaware on Pea Patch Island

are to keep off dunes. Foot or vehicular traffic quickly kills the fragile dune grasses that stabilize the shifting sand.

Swimming and Surfing: Fourteen miles of ocean beaches at Cape Henlopen, Delaware Seashore, and Fenwick Island State Parks offer guarded swimming and surfing away from the crowds of resort beaches. The ponds at Killens Pond, Trap Pond, and Lums Pond State Parks provide warm sand and beautiful scenery in a bucolic setting. The Water Park at Killens Pond State Park gives visitors a chance to slide down the tallest water slides in Kent County.

Boating and Sailing: Boat rentals are available at Lums Pond, Killens Pond, Trap Pond, and Fenwick Island State Parks during the summer and on weekends in May and September (weather permitting). A variety of vessels are available: rowboats, $4 per hour or $20 for an eight-hour period; canoes, $5 per hour; sailboats, $12 per hour; paddle boats, $5 per half-hour or $7 per hour; water bikes, $4 per half-hour or $6 per hour; and kayaks, $5 per hour/one person, or $7 per hour/tandem.

The Indian River Marina, part of Delaware

ON THE ROAD/DELAWARE

National Seashore, is a state-owned facility that permits dockage for fees ranging from $25 per day to $3,360 per year. Call 302/227-3071 for information.

Fishing

License Requirements: Anyone who is between 16 and 65 years of age is required to have a license to fish in tidal and/or nontidal waters—lakes, ponds, impoundments, and streams—in Delaware. A license may be obtained from the Delaware office of the Division of Fish and Wildlife, 89 Kings Hwy., P.O. Box 1401, Dover, DE 19903, 302/739-3441, www.dnrec.state.de.us/fw/index.htm, or from more than 100 license agents (mostly sporting goods and hardware stores) throughout the state. All funds derived from the issuance of fishing licenses are dedicated to the purpose of matching and securing federal money allotted to Delaware under the provisions of the Federal Aid in Sport Fish Restoration Act. Together, these funds support projects for restoration, conservation, management, and enhancement of sport fish and the provisions for public use and benefit from these resources.

Freshwater Fishing: Freshwater species include four varieties of bass, two types of crappie, and two varieties each of pike, pickerel, salmon, muskellunge, sunfish, bluegill, perch, and pumpkinseed. Delaware's freshwater trout program is a self-supporting put-and-take fishery in selected streams in northern New Castle County. The fees paid for trout stamps are used to purchase trout from commercial hatcheries. Rainbow, brown, and/or brook trout are stocked in selected streams within two weeks of the spring opening date and for an additional period of time into the season. No fishing is permitted in any designated trout stream within two weeks of the opening day of spring trout season, which is the first Saturday in April. Trout stamps are available from license agents.

Surf Fishing: Most of Delaware's bay communities have beaches suitable for surf fishing, with proper state licensing. State park fishing beaches are available at Cape Henlopen, Fenwick Island, and Delaware Seashore; surf-fishing licenses are $50 for Delaware res-

crab baskets

idents and $100 for nonresidents. Atlantic croaker, Atlantic sturgeon, bluefish, black sea bass, red drum, and scup are a few of the fish commonly caught.

Delaware State Parks also allow the use of licensed beach vehicles in strictly limited areas. Surf fishing vehicle permits are issued for the calendar year. These permits allow four-wheeled vehicle access to designated areas for the purpose of surf fishing. The permits cost $50 for residents and $100 for nonresidents.

Ocean Fishing: Lewes is a center for sportfishing. Migratory oceanic species such as bluefin tuna, bigeye tuna, yellowfin tuna, true albacore, blackfin tuna, swordfish, billfish, and certain shark species, when caught in waters outside Delaware's jurisdiction (ocean waters farther than three miles offshore), are subject to federal regulations. For further information on federal regulations, call the National Marine Fisheries Service at 301/713-2347 or 508/281-9260. In addition, a 24-hour information line is available at 301/713-1279 or 508/281-9305.

Crabbing and Clamming: Blue crab, soft

shells, conch, lobster, oysters, and clams are available for the taking at public beach areas from May to December. The Division of Fish and Wildlife, 301/739-3441, www.nmfs.gov, has regulations regarding minimum size, daily limits, and locations of approved areas; no license is required. The shores of Indian River and Rehoboth Bay are popular locations.

Hunting

The Delaware Division of Fish and Wildlife (see Fishing) also administers hunting in the two national refuges and several private tracts. A state license is required for all hunters; nonresident deer hunters must also purchase a permit, and all waterfowl hunters need state and federal duck stamps. Contract the DFW for current seasons and regulations.

Winter Sports

Snowmobiling: Snowmobiles are permitted on designated state park trails with proper registration (the fee is $10 for two years). Snowmobiles owned by nonresidents and covered by a valid registration in another county or state are exempt from this requirement. Registration does not grant permission for operation on any highway or on private property.

Entertainment and Events

SHOPPING

The Rehoboth Beach outlets, which are three mega-malls surrounded by smaller shopping centers between Lewes and Rehoboth Beach, are about as close as a bargain hunter can come to shopping paradise. Every outlet store in creation is there, which might draw a yawn from those familiar with outlet malls across the nation, except for the fact that these shops charge no taxes.

Delaware is also home to a couple of excellent auction/flea markets, Spence's Bazaar in Dover and Bargain Bill's in Laurel, as well as antique shops in every small town. Winterthur has a wonderful home shop featuring both upscale taste and prices.

ARTS AND ENTERTAINMENT

Performing Arts: Performances of symphonic music, opera, dance, and popular entertainment are centered in Wilmington and northern Delaware, and Wilmington is in the midst of developing a major cultural center on the Christina River. All the resort towns feature a multiplicity of art galleries. The capital, Dover, features a free Spring and Summer Performing Arts Series on the Green, 302/736-7050.

Gambling: Slot (one-armed bandit) gambling is legal in Delaware, and there are several state-owned locations.

Spectator Sports: Stock car racing, drag racing, and NASCAR competition are available at locations around the state. Harness racing takes place at several tracks, including the Harrington Raceway, one of America's oldest harness tracks.

FESTIVALS AND EVENTS

The Delaware State Fair takes place in the mid-state farm community of Harrington in late July–early August (call 302/398-3269 for specifics). From June through September, Wilmington is home to a number of ethnic celebrations, including the Greek Festival, St. Anthony's Italian Festival, St. Hedwig's Polish Festival, and the Caribbean Festival.

January/February

The **Wilmington International Exhibition of Photography,** often held on the university grounds in Newark, has been an annual event since the early 1930s. The annual **Delaware Antiquarian Book Show/Sale,** sponsored by the Wilmington Lion's Club, is a good place to scout for those rare first editions.

March/April

The tiny town of Delaware City holds a **Town-wide Yard Sale** for those who just can't resist a bargain. Fly high at the **Great Delaware Kite Festival** in Cape Henlopen State Park.

May/June

Separation Day in old New Castle celebrates Delaware's separation from Pennsylvania with a fair and fireworks. Blue hens welcome: the annual **Delmarva Chicken Festival** has been held since 1938 in Millsboro.

July/August

Celebrate independence on the beach at **Rehoboth's Beach Fireworks.** Also in Rehoboth Beach, the *Delaware State News* sponsors the annual **Sandcastle Contest.** For a wonderful cross-cultural experience, try the **Nanticoke Indian Pow Wow,** in Millsboro (great fry bread).

September/October

The artists' community of Arden in northern Delaware has held its annual **Arden Fair** since 1907. The Delaware Agricultural Museum and Village present the **1890s Great Country Fair,** just outside Dover. The scenic town of Laurel hosts an annual **Antique Show and Sale.** In Rehoboth, the annual **Sea Witch Halloween & Fiddler's Festival** includes creative parades, contests, and lots of great fiddle music. Costumed kids can trick-or-treat at many of the shops in town. The general revelry around **World Championship Punkin' Chunkin',** Harbeson, is something a few locals would rather forget—but it's impossible to ignore giant squash flying over fields of stubble, powered by homemade catapults. Distance matters.

November/December

Yuletide at Winterthur fulfills the fussiest decorating fantasy. Lewes celebrates the holidays with an annual **Christmas Parade, Tree Lighting and Caroling.** Rehoboth Beach sponsors a **Hometown Christmas Parade,** and **Caroling on the Green** and a **Candlelight Tour of Homes** are wonderful ways to celebrate the season in Dover.

Accommodations and Food

ACCOMMODATIONS

Delaware has fewer towns oriented toward visitors; that, and the compact resort areas, make for more limited lodging options and price ranges.

Under $50

The few hotel/motel rooms in the state that are under $50 are offered by chains and a few independents, usually on the "strip" outside of towns. One college in Wilmington offers inexpensive summer dorm rooms, but there were no youth hostels as of this writing. The least expensive option is camping, and several state parks and a few private campgrounds offer space year round.

$50–100

Most hotel rooms and B&Bs are in the $75–100 price range—usually hovering around the $100 mark. In Wilmington, there are several fine chain hotels but only one good B&B in the city limits. The resorts also have wallet-conscious motels and guesthouses, and the bigger resort hotels offer off-season packages that are priced well. Bed-and-breakfasts are sprinkled throughout the countryside.

Over $100

The Hotel du Pont in Wilmington is where the "price is no object" visitors go—it's historic and beautiful. In the Brandywine Valley, there are several gorgeous inns and B&Bs, as there are in the beach resorts, all in the luxury category.

FOOD AND BREWERIES

The quality and variety of restaurants in a place is a good indicator of how much money lives there—and if that's the case in Delaware, this is one very wealthy place. The good news is, most of the restaurant tariffs won't break the bank. There are excellent restaurants all over the state, almost all with standard American menus featuring plenty of—what else—chicken and seafood.

STATEWIDE HOTEL AND MOTEL CHAINS

The following chains have facilities throughout the state, usually in the larger towns. The beach resorts and smaller scenic towns also offer inexpensive locally owned motels. For specific locations or to book rooms, call the 800 numbers below for each chain directly. Hilton and Radisson hotel reservations are available through city listings. All rooms may also be booked through a travel agent.

HOTEL/MOTEL	TELEPHONE	WEBSITE
Best Western	800/528-1234	www.bestwestern.com
Comfort Inn	800/221-2222	www.comfortinn.com
Days Inn	800/325-2525	www.daysinn.com
Econolodge	800/553-2666	www.econolodge.com
Holiday Inn	800/HOLIDAY (800/465-4329)	www.holiday-inn.com
Howard Johnson	800/446-4656	www.hojo.com
Marriott	800/228-9290	www.marriott.com
Quality Inn	800/228-5151	www.qualityinn.com
Red Roof Inn	800/THE ROOF (800/843-7663)	www.redroof.com
Sheraton	800/325-3535	www.sheraton.com

Wilmington has several upscale restaurants, and many more of the midprice, great-food type in surrounding neighborhoods. U.S. 13 outside of New Castle may be a strip, but it's loaded with unusual eateries and some real finds. Rehoboth Beach has so many palaces devoted to gastronomic pleasure that it appears to be cobbled together out of restaurant fronts—there are also a few ethnic eateries there. Dover and central Delaware tend more toward home cooking, with notable exceptions. Little cafés in little towns on the coast are hidden treasures, brimming with crunchy-tender crab cakes and seafood.

Microbreweries are big business in Delaware. Newark and Rehoboth Beach both have brewpubs of exceptional quality—in beer and food.

Transportation

GETTING THERE

For general information, including travel advisories, contact the Delaware Department of Transportation (delDOT) during the week at 800/652-5600 (in-state) or 302/739-4313.

By Air

Philadelphia International Airport, 215/937-6937, and Baltimore/Washington International Airport, 410/859-7111, are the closest full-service airports to Delaware. Wilmington is about 45 minutes by auto from Philadelphia, and 1.5 hours from Baltimore; add another hour if your destination is Dover. The state also has a network of public and private airports, most of which can accommodate commercial and corporate aircraft. Limited commercial airline service is available through the New Castle County Airport, 302/571-6300, located on U.S. 13, just south of Wilmington. There are 12 other public airports in Delaware. For further information, call the Delaware Department of Transportation, 302/739-3264.

By Rail

This is the easiest way to get to Wilmington from New York, Philadelphia, or Washington, D.C., and stops in between. Amtrak (800/872-7245) serves Wilmington on the Northeast Corridor Line with 76 trains a day. Two trains per day also run to Newark.

By Bus

Greyhound, Carolina Coach Trailways, and Peter Pan Trailways serve Wilmington and the state. For information, call the Wilmington Transportation Center, 302/652-7391. SCOT (Salem County Transit) provides bus service between Salem County, New Jersey, and Wilmington. Contact them through New Jersey Transit, 215/569-3752.

By Car

The main access roads north-south are U.S. 113 and U.S. 13, which switch between four-lane and two-lane stoplight roads. In the northern part of the state, I-95 is the high-speed access road.

By Water

The Cape May–Lewes Ferry (800/64-FERRY, or 800/643-3779) operates vehicle and passenger service daily from Cape May, New Jersey, though schedules vary by season. The crossing takes one hour and 15 minutes.

GETTING AROUND

By Bus

Greater Wilmington, Dover, and Sussex Counties all have municipal bus systems. For detailed information and route maps, contact DTC, 400 S. Madison St., Wilmington, DE 19801, 800/652-DART (800/652-3278). Paratransit services are available for disabled, elderly, and special-needs customers; call 800/553-3278 for more information.

By Rail

SEPTA runs commute trains Mon.–Sat. between Wilmington and Philadelphia, and Wilmington and Newark.

By Car

U.S. 13 and U.S. 113 are the major routes, though progress can sometimes be agonizingly slow, especially between Wilmington and New Castle. U.S. 40 (the National Road) runs through the top of the state and crosses over to New Jersey. Delaware is full of lovely two-laners; considering the drive from the northern border to the southmost point, Fenwick Island, takes around three hours, it would behoove the interested visitor to wander off on a few of them. It's hard to get lost, thanks to a simple and well-maintained road and signage system and accurate maps, available from the state tourism board by calling 800/441-8846.

Information and Services

Visa requirements, money and banking information, what to take, and weights and measures are the same as for Maryland (see the Maryland On the Road chapter).

HEALTH AND SAFETY

Wilmington, Dover, and the Rehoboth area all have large, well-equipped hospitals. The rest of the state, depending on the population in the area, either has small hospitals or clinics.

With the exception of Wilmington, Delaware is supremely safe for visitors. Wilmington suffers from the usual woes of a big city, but crime against visitors is still a nonissue. The old rules still apply: know where you're going, how to get there and back, and leave the Hope diamond in the safe.

In a medical, police, or fire emergency, dial 911 toll-free on any public phone. In addition, many police departments monitor CB Emergency Channel 9 in case you're on the road and have citizens band radio.

SIGHTSEEING HIGHLIGHTS

Delaware is an unbeatable combination of urban sophistication, rural delights, and magnificent beaches. The really great thing is that all of these can be sampled in a fairly short period of time, thanks to the small size of the state. Here are a few must-sees:

Northern Delaware and Wilmington

The Du Pont properties are exceptional. **Hagley Museum/Eleutherian Mills, Nemours Mansion and Gardens,** and **Winterthur:** you won't find collections of fine American decorative arts combined with superb gardens like these anywhere else in the world. The **Delaware Museum of Natural History** is a little beauty, informative and fun. The **Delaware History Center,** in downtown Wilmington, is one of the best history museums around.

Central Delaware

Entire towns are one of the draws here. **New Castle** and **Odessa** both have different and special historic districts. The capital of Dover has several interesting attractions, including the **Sewell C. Biggs Museum of American Art** (fine and decorative arts), the **Johnson Victrola Museum** (celebrates the first musical recordings), **Delaware Agricultural Museum and Village** (a comprehensive collection of farm machinery and lore, with a few surprises), and **The Air Mobility Command Museum** (airplanes, in the air and on the ground—great World War II history). For those seeking the great outdoors, **Fort Delaware** is not only a unique and beautiful park, but the Civil War prison on the grounds is a rare bit of well-preserved history. Birders and other wildlife enthusiasts shouldn't miss **Bombay Hook National Wildlife Refuge.**

Southern Delaware

The beaches! **Delaware Seashore** and **Cape Henlopen State Parks** offer wonderful spots to hike, swim, camp, and enjoy summer at its finest. Beach resorts such as **Lewes** and **Rehoboth Beach** add fine restaurants and shopping to the mix. **Prime Hook National Wildlife Refuge** offers outdoor enthusiasts another opportunity to commune with nature and observe wildlife up close. The **Nanticoke Pow Wow** is a cultural celebration everyone can share. The south is also notable for its quaint river towns, **Seaford, Laurel, and Blades,** in addition to some fine antique shopping.

COMMUNICATIONS AND MEDIA

Delaware has several local newspapers and two daily newspapers: the *Delaware State News,* published in Dover, the state capital, and *The News-Journal,* published in Wilmington. Newspapers and broadcast media are limited to local news, with the exception of a public television channel based in Wilmington.

TOURIST INFORMATION

The **Delaware Tourism Office,** 99 Kings Hwy., P.O. Box 1401, Dover, DE 19903, 302/739-4271 or 866/284-7483, www.visitdelaware.com,

will send out a comprehensive travel packet and answer your general questions. Call them or visit one of the many walking information centers: Delaware Memorial Bridge (I-295), Greater Wilmington Convention & Visitors Bureau Center (100 S. 10 St., Ste. 20, Wilmington), I-95 Visitor Center (I-95, between Exit 1 and Exit 3), or the New Castle Court House (Delaware Street, Old New Castle). Three regional offices serve different parts of the state: Northern Delaware information is found at Greater Wilmington Convention & Visitors Bureau, 302/652-4088 or 800/422-1181; Central Delaware, Kent County Convention & Visitors Bureau, 302/734-1736 or 800/233-KENT

(800/233-5368), and southern Delaware, Sussex County Convention & Tourism Commission, 302/856-1818 or 800/357-1818.

International visitors may want to contact the **Delaware Council for International Visitors,** 910 Gilpin Ave., P.O. Box 831, Wilmington, DE 19899, 302/656-9928, with additional questions. Each county has its own tourism office (listed under each county).

State Park information is available from the **Delaware Division of Parks and Recreation,** 302/739-4702, www.destateparks.com.

Northern Delaware and Wilmington

Northern Delaware seems fated to be either ignored or flambéed by the press and the world at large. Yes, Wilmington has had problems (long since quelled), and Delawareans have rightfully had it up to here with people saying "Dela-WHERE?" In spite of it all, the area continues to offer a trove of cultural treasures and American history for willing seekers.

The Brandywine Valley between Wilmington and the Pennsylvania border (and beyond, if you count Longwood Gardens in Kennett Square, just over the border, and the Historic Homes of Odessa, in central Delaware) is Du Pont land;

the name is everywhere. Former Du Pont properties gifted or sold to the state offer the ultimate opportunity to see how the upper 1 percent lives. The Du Ponts who remain live elsewhere—the properties they've bequeathed to the public are rich in history, landscape lore, and just plain what-money-can-buy. Fortunately for the hordes of visitors that swarm over Du Pont land every year, individual family members were blessed with superb taste, a refined interest in horticulture, and a generous hand. Every one of the varied properties that is open to the public is a gem, for one reason or another.

Du Pont family home, Eleutherian Mills

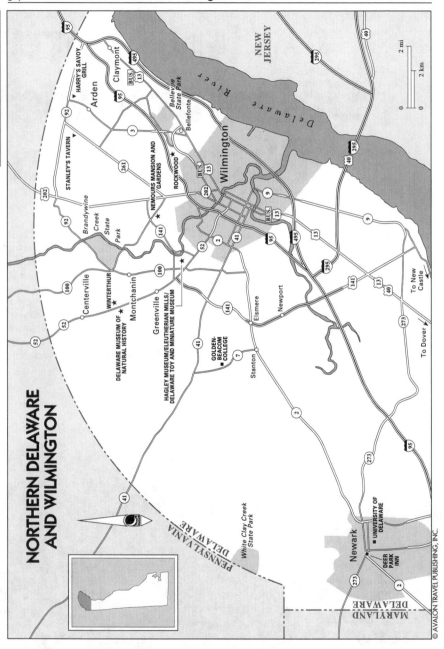

NORTHERN DELAWARE AND WILMINGTON

N. DELAWARE/WILMINGTON

NEW JERSEY

Delaware River

HARRY'S SAVOY GRILL
Claymont
Arden
Bellevue State Park
Bellefonte

STANLEY'S TAVERN
Wilmington

NEMOURS MANSION AND GARDENS
ROCKWOOD

Brandywine Creek State Park

Centerville
WINTERTHUR
Montchanin
Greenville

DELAWARE MUSEUM OF NATURAL HISTORY

HAGLEY MUSEUM/ELEUTHERIAN MILLS/
DELAWARE TOY AND MINIATURE MUSEUM

GOLDEN-BEACOM COLLEGE

Elsmere
Newport
Stanton

To New Castle

To Dover

White Clay Creek State Park

PENNSYLVANIA
DELAWARE

UNIVERSITY OF DELAWARE

Newark

DEER PARK INN

MARYLAND
DELAWARE

2 mi
2 km

© AVALON TRAVEL PUBLISHING, INC.

Though the Philadelphia-Wilmington corridor can truly be called a megalopolis, there are plenty of pockets of green west of the Delaware River, including two public parks bequeathed by . . . who else? The University of Delaware anchors the lively town of Newark, a hot spot for late night music and entertainment.

As one of the wealthiest cities in the nation—thanks to the clustering of Fortune 500 companies—Wilmington is experiencing a renaissance reminiscent of Pittsburgh and Baltimore. The Riverfront Development Corporation (RDC) is a state-funded organization that's transforming Wilmington's Christina riverfront into a center for arts, entertainment, dining, and shopping. The area is turning into a destination that offers a combination of attractions with changing events and exhibitions. The Delaware Theatre Company pioneered the revitalization of this area when it built its marvelous 400-seat theater along the riverfront in 1985.

Tubman-Garrett Riverfront Park (named for the famed Underground Railroad conductor Harriett Tubman and her Quaker cohort Thomas Garrett) and the Bank One Center at the Riverfront anchor the two ends of a beautifully landscaped and lighted 1.2-mile Riverwalk. The Delaware Theatre Company, the Delaware Center for the Contemporary Arts, The Riverfront Market, and a variety of plain and fancy eateries are found along the Riverwalk, along with Frawley Stadium, home of the Blue Rocks Baseball Team (a Kansas City Royals franchise). The Shipyard Shops, including L.L. Bean, Nautica, Coldwater Creek, and other catalog retailers and outlet shops, give visitors an opportunity to enjoy Delaware's famous tax-free shopping. Development on the Christina River is becoming a world-class draw, equal to the area's restaurants and hostelries. It's happening now—don't miss it.

Brandywine Valley

SIGHTS

Hagley Museum/Eleutherian Mills

Of the Du Pont properties in Delaware, Hagley is my favorite; it describes the origin of the Du Pont fortune and has little of the rampant conspicuous consumption of the other properties. In addition, the setting is serene, blooming with natural and planned beauty. Set in a narrow gorge, the Brandywine River flows through the property, dropping 160 feet on its journey to the coastal plain. In the early spring, the mist on the river makes the fiery purples and pinks of the rhododendrons and azaleas even brighter. Just the place for a black powder factory.

The powder yards are just one part of the property, though all facets of the business are included: rolling mills, machine shops, storehouses and drying tables, and the workers' village. Also on the grounds are the Hagley Museum and Library, the Du Pont family home, barn, and business office—all in the setting of natural greenery and formal gardens.

All tours start at the Henry Clay Mill, originally a cotton-spinning mill built in 1814. The DuPont Company acquired the mill in 1884 and converted it to the production of powder containers. Today, visitors view exhibits, dioramas, and models that give the history of the site, as well as two special exhibitions on the second floor, installed in 2002 to celebrate the company's 200th anniversary. They include hands-on science projects, an actual space suit, one of Jeff Gordon's NASCAR racers, and more. The small stone building next to the mill, a former cotton picking house, is now the Hagley Store, a gift shop. The property is large, 230 acres; visitors may either walk or take vans that leave every few minutes from the Henry Clay Mill and make regular stops along the road. Each of the buildings has its own costumed interpreter, all of whom are extremely well informed.

On Blacksmith Hill, the remaining buildings of one of several workers' communities contains a blacksmith shop (not open to the public), carriage house, and springhouse; the Gibbons

BOOM

Explosive black powder, composed of 75 percent saltpeter (potassium nitrate), 12.5 percent sulfur, and 12.5 percent charcoal, originated in China centuries ago. É. I. du Pont imported most of his materials: naturally occurring saltpeter was brought from the Bengal region of India; sulfur was imported from Sicily until sources were found in Louisiana and Mexico; and charcoal was produced on-site from burnt willow branches. Purity was important. Sulfur was boiled into a liquid, then vaporized and condensed. Saltpeter was boiled in kettles with water and a little glue, poured into cooling vats, and crystallized. It was then washed several times, dried, and pulverized.

All the ingredients were ground and sifted separately, then mixed with water proportionally. Water cooled and diluted the mixture, as it needed to be thoroughly mixed. Initially, a dangerous hours-long mortar/pestle process was used; in later years the mixture was rolled in a circular trough under massive stone wheels, called a rolling mill.

After mixing and drying, the powder was pressed into cakes, then broken into chips, which were sieved and separated according to size and need: cannon powder was large, while guns and fireworks required a much finer grain. The sorted powders were dried on racks; certain grades were then glazed with graphite for easier pouring.

From 1822 on, DuPont workers used rolling mills instead of the mortar/pestle process, which made the process somewhat safer. Considering that one ounce of black powder could send an object a distance of 20 yards, and each rolling mill processed 600 pounds of powder at once, it's no surprise that nothing but wooden nails were used to construct the rolling mill rooms, and that workers were routinely inspected for metal objects—a dropped belt buckle and a single spark could, and did, blow wheel and workers to their final reward.

House, a restored foreman's house; and the Brandywine Manufacturers' Sunday School, where workers' children received a serviceable, if limited, education. The Belin House, former home of the company's bookkeepers, is now a seasonal restaurant.

The Hagley Yard, the black powder manufactory, is on the main road near the river. An exhibit of working models in the millwright shop illustrates the powder-making process. The Eagle Roll Mill, with its multiple "rooms" featuring massive eight-ton rolling wheels and five-foot-thick walls, faces the river, where blow-outs—powder explosions—could do the least damage. In the 120-year period that powder was processed here, the yard experienced 288 explosions and 258 fatalities—dangerous business. The yard area also contains a press house with a hydraulic press used to compact the powder; dry tables to dry it; and a graining mill, where powder was ground, sifted, and sorted according to size. Using artifacts, the yard traces America's expansion from small water-powered mills through the In-

dustrial Revolution. Upstream from Hagley Yard are the remains of the Birkenhead Mills, the oldest roll mills in the yard, and their reconstructed waterwheel. The engine house at the farthest end of the yard features a working 1870s steam engine, used to supplement waterpower. In contrast to the yard's utilitarian stone buildings, three remarkable native trees stand on the grounds: a 300-year-old, 85-foot bald cypress and a 121-foot butternut (the second largest in Delaware) among the rolling mills, and a 200-year-old, 135-foot green ash near the quarry.

The Du Pont family home—Eleutherian Mills—overlooks the powder works. Built in 1803, the home contains many of the original furnishings. The second floor reflects the earlier generations of Du Ponts, while the first floor remains much as Éleuthère du Pont's great-granddaughter, Louise du Pont Crowninshield, left it. Nearby, the first office used by the DuPont Company is still set up for business; the barn displays carriages, wagons, and weathervanes. The front yard of the house is a restored 19th-century French garden as planted by Éleuthère du Pont, and the backyard of the house, which faces the creek, is a classical "ruins" garden planted by Ms. Crowninshield. The Hagley Library, a modern center for research in business and technological history, is open to the public Mon.–Fri. 8:30 A.M.–4:30 P.M., and the second Saturday of every month.

Hagley is on Rte. 141, just north of the intersection of Rte. 100, on the east side of the road. For more information, call 302/658-2400 during the week, or visit www.hagley.lib.de.us. The museum is open daily March 15–Dec. 30, 9:30 A.M.–4:30 P.M. From Jan.–March, the site is open weekends, 9:30 A.M.–4:30 P.M., and offers one guided tour by bus on weekdays, at 1:30 P.M. (Henry Clay Mill opens at 1 P.M. for ticket sales). A $10 admission is charged.

The **Delaware Toy & Miniature Museum,** just inside the entrance to the Hagley Museum on Rte. 141, 302/427-8697, www.thomes.net/toys, is one of only three such museums in the United States. It's a mélange of antique and contemporary dollhouses, miniatures, furniture, dolls, toys, trains, lead soldiers, boats, and planes, of both European and American origin. In addition to more than 100 furnished dollhouses, the museum features a permanent collection of more than 700 miniature vases dating from 700 B.C. that includes works by Tiffany, Fabergé, and Satsuma, as well as carved crystal, jade, and amethyst pieces. Though the main focus of the museum is on dollhouse miniatures, it offers several special exhibits throughout the year, such as "A Century of Dolls" and "Trains of Yesteryear." One advantage of visiting this museum first is that it frequently offers discount tickets to Hagley. Delaware Toy & Miniature Museum is open Tues.–Sat. 10 A.M.–4 P.M., Sunday noon–4 P.M. Admission is $5.

Nemours Mansion and Gardens

For Alfred I. du Pont, price was no object. This Du Pont heir built a 102-room Louis XVI–style château in 1909–1910 and named it after the town in North-Central France that Mr. du Pont's great-great-grandfather, Pierre-Samuel du Pont de Nemours, represented as a member of the French Estates General in 1789. The mansion itself contains furniture, Oriental rugs, tapestries, and paintings dating back to the 15th century. Three hundred acres of gardens surround the mansion and extend for one-third of a mile along the main vista from the house. The gardens are classic French style, very formal, and exceedingly beautiful—especially if you like cherubs.

Mr. du Pont put the considerable unspent portion of his fortune into a trust; his will stated, "It has been my firm conviction throughout life that it is the duty of everyone in the world to do what is within his power to alleviate human suffering. It is, therefore, natural that I should desire, after having made provision for the immediate members of my family and others whom I have seen fit to remember, that the remaining portion of my estate be utilized for charitable needs." His widow, Jessie Ball du Pont, was given control of the trust, and with her brother Edward proceeded to establish a number of medical facilities in Delaware and Florida. One of the best known is on the Nemours premises: the A. I. du Pont Institute, a hospital facility that specializes in children's medicine.

To get to Nemours mansion, take exit 8 (Rte. 202) on I-95, and head north to Rte. 141. Make a right (west) on Rte. 141 to Children's Dr.; left on Children's Dr. (second traffic light); then left on Rockland Rd. The parking lot is approximately one-eighth of a mile on the right. Follow the signs to mansion parking and the reception center. Guided tours are given May–Nov., Tues.–Sat. at 9 A.M., 11 A.M., 1 P.M., and 3 P.M., and Sunday at 11 A.M., 1 P.M., and 3 P.M. Holiday tours are available from mid-November until after Christmas. Tour groups are limited in size, so visitors are strongly encouraged to make reservations: call 302/651-6912 during regular business hours, or write to Nemours Mansion and Gardens, P.O. Box 109, Wilmington, DE 19899, or email sjelinek@nemours.org.

Visitors must be at least 12 years of age, and no food is allowed on the premises, though the hospital cafeteria is open to visitors. The tour involves climbing several staircases. A $10 admission is charged.

Winterthur

Perhaps the best-known property in the Du Pont constellation, Winterthur (WIN-tur-toor) continues the family fascination with horticulture combined with American decorative arts. The site was originally the home of Evelina Gabrielle du Pont (Éleuthère's daughter) and her husband, James Bidermann, who named Winterthur after the Bidermann ancestral home in Switzerland. The original house on the site was a fairly modest three-story Greek Revival, built in 1839; it was enlarged and renovated several times before passing into the hands of Henry Francis du Pont, great-nephew of the Bidermanns, in 1927.

Like his ancestors before him, Henry du Pont appreciated and collected fine European furniture and antiques. After World War I, a new wave of nationalistic sentiment caused collectors to look with a fresh eye at American objects. That great arbiter of taste, the Metropolitan Museum of Art in New York, opened an American Wing in 1924, and America's wealthy collectors followed suit. Henry Ford announced his plans to build a museum celebrating American ingenuity; John D. Rockefeller reconstructed the colonial capital, Williamsburg; and Henry Francis du Pont started collecting American furniture with moneyed enthusiasm.

Henry du Pont's collection quickly surpassed personal decorating needs and grew to museum size. He moved the best of his items to Winterthur, doubled the size of the existing house, and converted his home to a showplace for what many consider the most important assemblage of early American decorative arts in the world. In 1951, the Du Pont family created a nonprofit

DU PONT DYNASTY

In the mid-1700s, Louis XV was king of France, and Pierre-Samuel du Pont was a relatively unknown writer of plays. Pierre's mother arranged for him to be introduced to a group of wealthy capitalists, and he was immediately impressed with the power of the new merchant middle class. He abandoned the plays he had been writing and began to compose pamphlets on the fashionable topic of bourgeois economics. One of these pamphlets found its way to Jacques Turgot, a financier and capitalist leader, who became his mentor. Du Pont was given the job of editing Turgot's new *Journal of Agriculture, Commerce, and Finance*. At 26 Pierre married his childhood sweetheart, and by 1770 had fathered two sons. Du Pont asked Jacques Turgot to act as godfather to his second child; Turgot requested that the boy be named in honor of Liberty and Peace: Éleuthère Irénée.

Pierre was involved in negotiations that led to the peace treaty of 1783 between France's new ally, the United States, and her archenemy, Britain. In return for his service, Pierre was rewarded with nobility; he chose a coat of arms emblazoned with ostrich feathers, a lion, an eagle, and the motto "By Uprightness I Stand."

Pierre's new status proved to be a handicap during the French Revolution. He and his son Éleuthère, royalists to the end, were constantly in and out of jail. Finally, with the help of a friendly government official, Pierre pleaded senility and managed to get himself and his family exported to the New World along with millions of francs of investment money. The family traveled to America under the noble banner of Du Pont de Nemours aboard the *American Eagle*. The journey was rough; the family survived at one point on a soup made from rats. Upon arrival, the Du Ponts immediately established themselves in New Jersey, and went into business in New York City. Because of his prior negotiations, Pierre had a powerful political connection in the New World with Vice President Thomas Jefferson. The family used the investment capital from France to go into a number of businesses. After a long search, É. I. purchased land along the Brandywine River in Wilmington and established his black powder mill there on April 27, 1802. He was so successful (and unscrupulous, by some accounts) that he financed many of the other Du Pont undertakings—while managing to avoid paying off his French creditors.

institution to manage Winterthur and opened it to the public.

The public part of the museum consists of two buildings, one with 175 period rooms and another with three exhibition galleries. The period rooms contain more than 89,000 objects made or used in America between 1640 and 1860, including silver tankards made by Paul Revere and a 66-piece dinner service made for George Washington. The exhibition galleries feature both interactive displays focusing on American decorative arts and changing exhibitions. There's also a Touch-It Room, featuring a child-size period room, and a small general store with activities geared toward children. Don't miss the Campbell Collection of Soup Tureens in the "Glass Corridor" near the gallery wing.

The Louise du Pont Crowninshield Research Building, attached to the main house, holds the Winterthur Library, a research center for the study of American decorative and fine arts. The collection of more than 500,000 books, manuscripts, and visual images is open to the public Mon.–Fri., 8:30 A.M.–4:30 P.M.; visitors may copy individual pages but borrowing of books is limited to Winterthur staff and decorative arts students of the University of Delaware. A variety of short- and long-term fellowships, which support undergraduate and postdoctoral study, exhibition, and publication research, are available, and may include on-site housing. For details, contact the Advanced Studies Division, 302/888-4649.

Winterthur's buildings are surrounded by 966 acres, 60 of which are part of Henry du Pont's naturalistic landscaping. Miles of surfaced paths and woodland trails crisscross the estate, and

---

Pierre du Pont longed to return to France, and did so. He remained there until Napoleon's return to Paris, at which point Pierre sailed speedily back to the New World, where he died, buried in the family plot near Wilmington. Meanwhile, É. I. rescued his older brother Victor from numerous failed schemes and bought his way into a variety of businesses and banks. Never too busy for family life, É. I. and his wife, Sophie, had seven children along the way.

On March 19, 1818, five powder rooms at the factory near the family's home exploded (the ruins are still visible at Eleutherian Mills), killing 36 workers and permanently wounding É. I.'s wife. However, É. I. rebuilt and continued to expand his businesses and political connections (Victor was already a member of Delaware's House of Representatives in 1815). É. I. du Pont died of a heart attack in 1863, in the same city—and in the same hotel—as his brother Victor, seven years before. He was buried to the right of Victor and their father, Pierre, in the family plot on Buck Road in Greenville.

More than seven generations of Du Ponts have been born in the New World, and the family's wealth has increased exponentially. Black powder was a source of profit for many years, but the family's wealth expanded into banking, chemicals, and other industries—family members are major shareholders or own large blocks in more than 100 national corporations. With little fanfare, the Du Ponts have become the wealthiest family in America.

The fifth and final Du Pont resident of Eleutherian Mills, Louise du Pont, visited the home often as a guest of her grandparents. She married shipping magnate F. B. Crowninshield in 1920, and in 1923, Mrs. Crowninshield's father gave her Eleutherian Mills under the condition that she spend part of each year there. So, after renovating the home, the Crowninshields and their staff of nine—personal maid, parlor maid, chambermaid, cook, kitchen helper, waitress, laundress, and two chauffeurs—traveled to Delaware during the spring and fall of each year, spending winter in Florida and summer in Massachusetts. Eleutherian Mills, the seat of the family fortune, opened to the public after her death.

visitors are welcome to stroll the gardens or ride the tram. The garden is of interest starting in February, when snowdrops, crocus, and other early spring flowers announce themselves on the March Bank, followed by the huge saucer-shaped plantings of flowers in Magnolia Bend in April; in May, the eight-acre Azalea Woods is in full bloom, as is the Peony Garden. The Enchanted Woods, a special three-acre garden was installed in 2001. The gardens continue to produce well into the fall. The paths are open Mon.–Sat., 9 A.M.–dusk, Sunday noon–dusk.

Informal dining is available at the Crossroads Café in the visitor pavilion, the Cappuccino Café in the main building, or at the fancier Garden Restaurant. There are two museum stores: books and inexpensive items are in the visitor pavilion, and another shop on the grounds at Clenny Run offers more expensive, high-quality reproductions and decorative items (this is a great store).

Winterthur is on Rte. 52, six miles northwest of Wilmington. It's open Mon.–Sat. 9 A.M.–5 P.M., Sunday noon–5 P.M. Winterthur offers a variety of tours for all tastes and budgets, including introduction tours, one- and two-hour decorative arts tours, and a garden walk (visitors must be escorted in the main house). For information and to book tours, call 800/448-3883, TTY 302/888-4907, or click on the website www.winterthur.org. Admission starts at $10 and goes up depending on which tour you choose.

Delaware Museum of Natural History

The original designers of this small museum, across from Winterthur on Rte. 52, five miles northwest of Wilmington, 302/652-7600 or 302/658-9111, were artists in the finest sense of the word. The visual beauty of the dark interior is dreamlike: half-domed dioramas glow like jewels against a curved wall; a few feet away, a five-foot-diameter clear globe surrounds a star-like object, each of its hundreds of projections ending in a different exotic shell. The museum rightfully prides itself on its collections of shells (the 10th largest in the country), re-creation of a section of the Great Barrier Reef set into the floor (visitors must walk across it, akin to walking on water), and children's interactive room. The H. Lawrence du Pont (that

name again!) Discovery Room offers science-related activities for children of all ages, including a Discovery Box Station, with its series of single-themed, self-contained kits with fossils, shells, and skeletons, magnifying glasses, scales, and activity cards. Little ones will love the large Puzzler, where they can match magnetic animals to their habitats. Every member of the family will appreciate the care taken in display; one seldom thinks of a natural history museum in the same terms as fine art, but these displays break all the rules.

A relative newcomer to the Brandywine Valley, the museum opened in 1972; it's also the only place in Delaware with *real* dinosaur skeletons. In addition to its regularly changing exhibits—a recent one was on sounds that dinosaurs might have made—the museum is home to a set of animal models created by artist Carl Akley. The models were created as scale references for an exhibit at the Museum of Natural History of New York, and depict a herd of elephants—bulls, cows, and babies—in perfect, enchanting miniature. It's open Mon.–Sat. 9:30 A.M.–4:30 P.M., Sunday noon–4:30 P.M. Admission is $4.

Rockwood Mansion

A 19th-century country estate, Rockwood, 610 Shipley Rd., Wilmington, 302/761-4340, was built in the Rural Gothic style. The mansion, conservatory, and assorted outbuildings sit on 70 acres of wooded trails. The main building is lavishly decorated with 17th- through 19th-century pieces, and tours of the house and gardens are available along with use of the trails. Rockwood mansion has been intermittently under renovation for some time, though the grounds continue to be open to the public; be sure to call for current hours and tour availability. The Butler's Pantry tearoom offers light refreshments. Rockwood is the site of the enormously popular Ice Cream Festival in July, which usually includes a performance by the Delaware Symphony Orchestra. During the winter holiday season, tall trees on the estate are wrapped with more than 900,000 lights and the mansion is open in the evening. Normal hours of operation for the mansion are 10 A.M.–3 P.M. daily, and the park 6 A.M.–10 P.M. daily; admission to the house and gardens is $5.

A MAKER OF PICTURES

Felix Octavius Carr Darley was the best-known and most popular artist/illustrator of the mid-19th century—in fact, scholars laud him as the father of American illustration, predating Howard Pyle by nearly 50 years. Darley illustrated books by many well-known authors, including Charles Dickens, Edgar Allan Poe, James Fenimore Cooper (the complete works), Washington Irving, Longfellow, and Alfred Lord Tennyson. Our contemporary images of Rip Van Winkle, Natty Bumpo, and Ichabod Crane were creations of Darley's descriptive pen-and-ink drawings. He was also a sought-after magazine illustrator and bank note artist (before the federal government standardized paper money, individual banks commissioned and issued their own notes).

Darley was born in Philadelphia in 1821; his parents were entertainers on the theater circuit. He began his illustration career in New York, and quickly rose to international fame. Darley moved to the town of Claymont, Delaware, in 1859—the area offered a quiet country retreat with the convenience of a train station a few blocks away, a short journey to the cities that supported his work.

Many of the writers Darley worked with visited his home. Charles Dickens stayed for two weeks during his 1867 travels through America; "I never needed rest so much in my life as when I came to visit Felix at his lovely home, which stands on a hill overlooking a great river [the Delaware]. . . ." said Dickens.

Darley purchased a manor house in Claymont, "The Chimneys," and renamed it the "Wren's Nest" in honor of his wife, whom he affectionately called Jenny Wren. During Darley's ownership, the house was a center for community entertaining: a women's club met there to read Shakespeare, and the Darley family regularly put on plays for area children, neighbors, and household staff.

Darley continued to work and live at the Wren's Nest until his death in 1888. Over the years, his rural retreat became surrounded by the trappings of industry, and his view of ships on the Delaware River was obscured by trees and buildings, but his work continues to be recognized. Exhibits of Darley's work have appeared at the New York Public Library and the Brandywine River Museum in Chadds Ford, among other venues. In 1842, Edgar Allan Poe said of Darley, "His art is more truthful and full of character than anything of a similar kind which we have seen. There can be no doubt that the name of young Mr. Darley will soon rise to an enviable notoriety among artists of real genius."

RECREATION

Parks

The Du Ponts turned over their 850-acre dairy farm to the state for conversion into a park in 1965. **Brandywine Creek State Park** was one of the first parks in America to be purchased with Land and Water Conservation Funds. Two nature preserves are located within the park: Tulip Tree Woods, a stand of 190-year-old tulip poplar, and Freshwater Marsh, a conservation area for the Muhlenberg bog turtle. In addition, the park features an active bluebird population program and a variety of habitats for year-round wildlife observation.

The park maintains 12 miles of hiking trails and several open fields for both summer and winter use. The Brandywine Creek offers a site for fishing, canoeing, and tubing.

Open daily from 8 A.M.–sunset, the park is three miles north of Wilmington at the intersection of Rte. 100 and Rte. 92. The entrance is on Adams Dam Road. Call the park office at 302/577-3534 for more information and a calendar of special events. A $5 entrance fee is charged during the summer months.

Bellevue State Park offers another sterling opportunity to sample a former Du Pont property. Once the country estate of William H. du

Pont Jr., the 271-acre park is home to a mansion (no tours), two indoor and eight outdoor clay tennis courts, stables, a band shell, gardens, and a 1.33-mile fitness track.

Equestrian facilities are for boarding horses and riding lessons only—no trail rides (302/798-2407). The tennis courts are open to the public, and a pro is on duty for lessons (call 302/798-6686 for reservations). All facilities are run by private concessionaires, and require additional fees.

The fitness track, and the walking and biking trails that wind through the entire estate, are free. The band shell offers evening concerts June through August, and each season brings different recreational activities, such as hayrides in autumn and ice-skating in winter.

Bellevue State Park is in north Wilmington on Carr Rd., the frontage road off I-95. Take exit 9, Marsh Rd., then turn left on Carr Road; the park drive address is 800 Carr Rd. For general information, call 302/577-3390. The park is open 8 A.M.–sunset, year-round. An entrance fee of $5 is charged during the summer months.

Shopping

Last chance to shop tax-free, the Christiana Mall, Rte. 7 and I-95, exit 4 south, 302/731-9815, near Newark, has four main anchor stores plus more than 130 mall shops.

ACCOMMODATIONS

The Darley Manor Inn, 3701 Philadelphia Pike, Claymont, 302/792-2127 or 800/824-4703 (reservations only), www.dca.net/darley, is located in the area between Philadelphia and Wilmington, which is basically one long, extended commercial/industrial strip. Though the way to the inn—past a major industrial site—is a little jarring, the inn itself is on a main road that quiets down at night. The warmly decorated little manor house is a pleasant anomaly.

The house is dated from 1713, when the property was on an original 160-acre lot sold by William Penn. The main house was built as four rooms and an attic in the late 1700s; it was expanded in 1810 and 1842. The house, known at that time as "the Chimneys," was one of 103

homes featured in "Homes of America," compiled in 1879. Former owner Felix Darley was the mid-19th century's most popular book illustrator. He lived in the house from 1859 until his death in 1888.

After changing hands for decades and sitting empty with only a bag lady as resident, the house was saved from being sold as commercial lots thanks to community intervention and the purchase in October 1991 by Ray and Judith Hester. Extensive restoration and renovation have been done since then, and the inn opened in 1993.

The inn features five rooms and suites, all with private baths. Some have large tile baths, others have fireplaces—decor hovers between functional and fancy. The inn features a small exercise room with stationary bike, treadmill, and other exercise equipment. Darley Manor caters to businesspeople with in-room telephones, free local calls, computer ports, and a fax and copier on-site. In the foyer, guests may look over art prints by Darley and immerse themselves in a brief history of his work, the house, and the community. Though the gas station across the street is part of a radically different view from the one Mr. Darley enjoyed, the Darley Manor is a homey alternative for travelers on their way between cities. Rates range $80–100.

The Inn at Montchanin Village, Rte. 100 and Kirk Rd., Montchanin, 302/888-2133 or 800/COWBIRD (800/269-2473), www.montchanin.com, was once a crossroads settlement consisting of employees of the nearby DuPont powder mills and factories on the Brandywine River. It became a stop of the Wilmington & Northern Railroad between 1870 and 1910, but faded into memory when the economy of the area shifted. Now, the remaining buildings have been renovated into luxury accommodations linked by paths and gardens, a first-class restaurant, and a charming take-out deli. The setting is bucolic and peaceful, surrounded by farms and avenues of old trees.

All 33 guest rooms and suites have been restored with the sophisticated traveler in mind. The suites are more like condominiums—each sitting room has a bar and refrigerator, a large tiled bath, and private garden. This is a lovely place to get away from the city overnight or longer. Prices are high, but worth it; rooms run $160–180 and suites are $190–500.

FOOD

East End of the County

Harry's Savoy Grill, 2020 Naaman's Rd. (Rte. 92), 302/475-3000, is a deservedly popular restaurant north of I-95, near the Pennsylvania border. It's open for lunch and dinner daily, and offers a broad menu of standard American fare (Caesar salad, crab cakes, pasta, steaks, burgers, etc.). The food and service are both excellent, and there's a cozy full bar on the premises. Prices average $7 for lunch, $16 for dinner.

Also recommended: **Stanley's Tavern,** 2038 Foulk Rd. (near Harry's), 302/475-1887, a casual sports bar with beer and great sandwiches, $6.

Central County

Krazy Kat's Restaurant at the Inn at Montchanin Village, Rte. 100 and Kirk Rd., Montchanin, 302/888-4200, has wacky decor but serious Mobil four-star/AAA four-diamond dining. The contemporary decor is feline-based: portraits of cats in full formal dress reflect the leopards leaping on place settings. The food is fresh and sophisticated—this is definitely a destination restaurant. It has received *Wine Spectator*'s Award of Excellence every year since 1996. Lunch averages $12 for an entrée, less for salads and sandwiches; dinner is around $24 for an entrée. Venison chops, grilled ostrich, and sesame seed–crusted yellowfin tuna are typical menu items. Lunch is served Mon.–Fri., dinner is available daily.

PUFF (Pick-Up Fine Food), in the old train station on the premises of Montchanin Village, is a deli offering fresh-baked cookies, desserts, salads, quiche, and sandwiches for takeout. This is a good stop for a sophisticated picnic or light snack. It's open Mon.–Fri. 10 A.M.–6 P.M., Sat. 10 A.M.–2 P.M. Prices average $5.

Buckley's Tavern, 5812 Kennett Pike, Centreville, 302/656-9776, is another enormously popular local place that lives up to its reputation. The all-American menu is served up in pleasing portions by cheerful staff, and dining on the deck outside is a real treat in good weather. Buckley's is in a small shopping enclave with unpretentious antique and secondhand shops that are fun to stroll through. The restaurant is open daily for lunch (average $8) and dinner (average $16).

Also recommended: **Brandywine Brewing Company,** 3801 Kennett Pike (in the Greenville shopping center), 302/655-8000, an upscale brewpub with good food, $6–18.

West End of the County

Newark (pronounced as two separate words, NEW ARK) is the seat of the main campus of the University of Delaware. It's a good rest stop between Wilmington and Baltimore, and a handy place to pick up Fighting Blue Hen T-shirts. There are a couple of restaurants of note in town. Warning! The main street (named, oddly, Main Street) is parking ticket hell for the unwary. The meters run 8 A.M.–1 A.M. and gobble a quarter every 15 minutes. The **Iron Hill Brewery,** 147 E. Main St., 302/266-9000, has its own free parking lot in back, good-to-excellent brewpub food, and tasty beers. The atmosphere is upscale but comfortable, it's open for lunch and dinner Mon.–Sat., brunch on Sun., and prices average $10. It's definitely a first choice, if quality is high on your list.

The **Deerpark Tavern,** 108 W. Main St., 302/731-5315, www.deerparktavern.com, is the place to go if you want some college-style action (students and teachers), gallons of on-tap, high-volume chit-chat, and reasonably edible food. The building has history: Edgar Allan Poe is reputed to have hung out here, and the cast-metal ceilings are plenty authentic, but you might have a problem getting your shoes unstuck from the floor to take a tour. It's open for lunch and dinner, daily, and pub food prices average $6.

Nightlife: Newark has a booming late-night music scene. **The Stone Balloon,** 115 E. Main St., 302/368-2000, features live rock music, and the **East End Café,** 270 East Main St., 302/738-0880, offers a wide variety of alternative music, and a long list of imported and domestic beers by the bottle (it's a bit tamer than the Stone Balloon).

Wilmington

For many years despite Wilmington's slogan as "A place to be somebody," it really has been a place from which to go somewhere else. But things have turned around.

Our View, Opinion Page, The Wilmington News Journal, *1997*

Wilmington (and the State of Delaware and nearby Pennsylvania and New Jersey) got its start when the *Kalmar Nyckel* arrived from Sweden in 1638 with Swedish, Finnish, Dutch, and German settlers who built Fort Christina, in which were the first two log cabins in the New World (a Finnish form of architecture). By 1700, mills had been built along the swift-flowing Brandywine River. In 1731, Thomas Willing laid out "Willingtown" between the Christina and Brandywine Rivers. The Crown chartered the town as Wilmington in 1739, in honor of Spencer Compton, Earl of Wilmington. The site was laid out as a series of "farmlets." The du Pont family arrived in 1802 and began the gunpowder manufactory, but the town itself did not see

THE OCCUPATION OF WILMINGTON

After World War II, Wilmington experienced a great general flight from the city center, roughly the loss of 15,000 denizens over two decades. Since those who left tended to be more well off, the tax drain was enormous, and Wilmington began to ravel around the edges. After the assassination of the great humanitarian leader Martin Luther King Jr. on April 4, 1968, race riots broke out in several sections of town. Entire blocks were consumed by flame, and the city's mayor called in the National Guard and declared martial law. The city was occupied for nine months, under restrictive curfews—far longer than necessary, according to many Wilmingtonites. The city has taken years to heal and is just now beginning to grow.

much development until 1816, when the Industrial Revolution revved up the local economy. The Mexican War, the opening of the West, the building of the Transcontinental Railroad, the Civil War, Spanish-American War, two world wars, and the Great Depression brought booms and busts. The city's economy today is based on credit card banking and the chemical/pharmaceutical industries.

The riots of 1968 and subsequent National Guard occupation changed the face of the city for the worse, but Wilmington's recovery has been significant. The city is riding the crest of its own wave, much like Baltimore in the 1970s and Pittsburgh in the 1950s. Wilmington is a stew of ultra-wealthy international corporations such as DuPont, AstraZeneca, MBNA, Bank One, First Union Bank, and Wachovia; elegant homes built for the elite; and crowded, litter-strewn slums. It took a mighty strong love of place to stay when run-down neighborhoods turned dangerous and began to eat up block after block of a once-livable small city—especially when the economic means existed to flee to the suburbs. Many made that move. Those who stayed and those who have returned have been rallying—especially since 1990—to bring back Wilmington. In large measure, they have succeeded; though, as anyone who lives here will admit, there's still a distance before the race is won.

Indications for success are obvious. Wilmington's smaller size works for it. This city, like Baltimore, has good bones: a foundation of beautiful architecture, strong business and cultural support, and most important, people who are working to revive and revise the city. The 1970s restoration of the glorious Grand Opera House, built in 1871 by the Masons, got downtown revitalization rolling. The Amtrak Station was refurbished (and is the ninth busiest in the nation, with more than 70 trains daily). Downtown neighborhoods have become highly desirable for young families. Tall office buildings that were vacant as a result of corporate downsizing have been converted into luxury apartments,

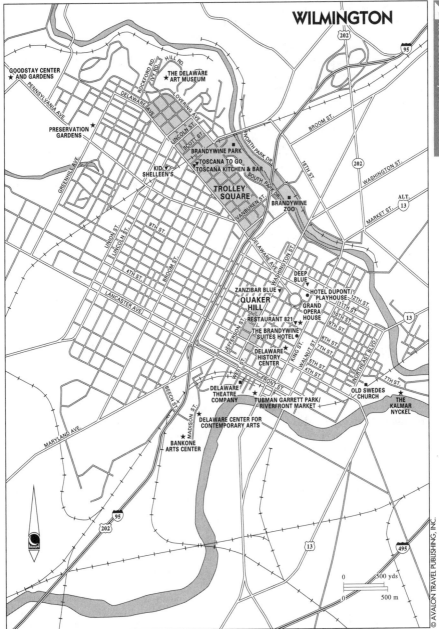

WILMINGTON

GOODSTAY CENTER AND GARDENS

THE DELAWARE ART MUSEUM

PRESERVATION GARDENS

KID SHELLEEN'S

BRANDYWINE PARK

TOSCANA TO GO
TOSCANA KITCHEN & BAR

TROLLEY SQUARE

BRANDYWINE ZOO

DEEP BLUE

ZANZIBAR BLUE
QUAKER HILL

HOTEL DUPONT PLAYHOUSE

GRAND OPERA HOUSE

RESTAURANT 821

THE BRANDYWINE SUITES HOTEL

DELAWARE HISTORY CENTER

DELAWARE THEATRE COMPANY

OLD SWEDES CHURCH

TUBMAN GARRETT PARK/ RIVERFRONT MARKET

THE KALMAR NYCKEL

DELAWARE CENTER FOR CONTEMPORARY ARTS

BANKONE ARTS CENTER

0   500 yds
0   500 m

© AVALON TRAVEL PUBLISHING, INC.

and people are moving into downtown. New top-quality restaurants have opened and are thriving. A new 221-seat art-film theatre that was opened in the Nemours Building in 2002 has had to add extra showings to its schedule.

The Wilmington Renaissance Corporation, an amalgamation of local businesses and citizen groups, is hard at work redeveloping the historic Ships Tavern District at the lower end of Market Street. The project is creating street-level boutique shops and upper-floor apartments in 19th-century buildings. New townhouses and condos are being built across the river from the train station. And the Riverfront Development Commission has led the way for public and private funds that have rebuilt the Riverfront, a project that includes the Bank One Center, the Shipyard Shops, the Riverfront Market, the Riverwalk, water taxis, and restaurants and museums.

Wilmington's downtown center is an area that's quite safe during the day and in the evenings when events are being held. Police and safety patrol are present and a network of surveillance cameras has been installed. Like all cities of any size in the northeast United States, there are neighborhoods that should be generally avoided unless you have family, friends, or (legal) business there.

SIGHTS

Delaware History Center

Don't let the storefront facade of this innovative museum fool you—it's one of the best things to see and do in downtown Wilmington. The center, 505 Market Street Mall, 302/656-0637, www.hsd.org, is set in a renovated 1940s Woolworth's, and is packed with cleverly presented information about the first state. Nostalgic memorabilia, artifacts, art, and scale-model historic scenes are interspersed with audiovisual displays and computer games.

For instance—do you have a future in the poultry industry? In the Distinctively Delaware exhibit, visitors are invited to play a computer game in which they invest in chickens; depending on the type of chicken, cost of feed, market demand, and other factors, either your invest-

ment will lay an egg or you'll advance in the corporate hierarchy of the Terrifically Big Cluck Company (pa-GAWK!). Other computer setups help visitors learn about transportation using real figures from history, including a colonial widow who made a go of her husband's plantation; visitors figure out how she did it by trying different ways of transporting her grain to market.

In the Made in Delaware exhibit, you'll learn the origins of Teflon, Tyvek, Gore-Tex (originally made as electrical ribbon cable, stretched to a thin layer), and polyester (there's a powder-blue leisure suit to die for). Adults were glued to the screens—never mind that kids were equally fascinated. Children will also enjoy Grandma's Attic, a discovery room with vintage dress-up clothes, an old-fashioned marketplace, and historic games and toys. The museum also features changing exhibits and has an excellent gift shop. This is one of those places that can occupy you for hours.

Another part of the museum is Old Town Hall, next door. This Georgian-style building served as the center of Wilmington government and social activity beginning in 1801, and now showcases changing exhibits. The Historical Society of Delaware operates the museum and town hall, as well as the Read House in New Castle. The museum and Old Town Hall are open Mon.–Fri. noon–4 P.M., Saturday 10 A.M.–4 P.M.; admission is $3.

Quaker Hill: Wilmington's First Neighborhood

In 1735, Willingtown consisted of 15 or 20 houses perched on the low banks of the Christina River. In May of that year, William and Elizabeth Shipley, Quakers from Ridley Township in Pennsylvania, moved to Willingtown. While still in Pennsylvania, Elizabeth Shipley dreamed of a forested hill above a river where they would settle—when she saw the rise above the Christina, she recognized it as the manifestation of her dream. The Shipleys built a one-story brick house near what is now 4th and Shipley Streets—the first Friends worship meeting was held in the Shipley home. By 1748, a new, larger structure was built, followed by a third Meeting House in

1816 that still stands today as an active community center on West Street between 4th and 5th Streets. The grounds contain more than 3,000 graves (often layered on top of one another to save space), including that of John Dickinson, a signer of the Declaration of Independence, and of Thomas Garrett, the famous Underground Railroad station master.

The 19th century saw much change in the small community. Now called Wilmington, the city became an industrial center, with factories lining the Christina River. Quaker Hill continued to appeal as a place to live for both workers and owners. As the economy boomed, many of the 18th-century structures were replaced. In the late 19th century, Quaker Hill became a predominantly working-class neighborhood, though a few prominent people, including the mayor, continued to live there.

A few homes from the 1700s can still be found. On West Street, between 7th and 8th Streets, 701 and 703 West St. were built in 1745 and 1760, respectively, by Joseph Woodward and his son Mordecai, two Quaker rope makers whose business was on the grounds.

The Cathedral of St. Peter on the corner of West and 6th Streets was built in 1816; it was the first Catholic church in the city, and was probably designed by Pierre Bauduy, architect of the town hall. The church features several examples of stained glass work from different periods. Six clerestory windows, and the windows above the altar and in the choir loft, are of particular interest. They appear to be from the Munich school, dating from approximately 1900; the intricate detail in the windows suggest they are the work of Franz Xavier Zettler, master glass painter to the Royal Court of Bavaria between 1870 and 1910, or possibly his pupil Franz Mayer. Their work is frequently seen in Baltimore and New York.

A block west on 6th Street (600 Washington St.), local ironworker Enoch Strotsenburg built an elegant home in 1798; the house was expanded by other owners and also used as a funeral home. A block south on Washington Street, 501 W. 5th was built by Joshua Heald, founder and president of the Wilmington and Western Railroad in 1860.

TAVERN REVIVAL

In the late 18th century, the 200 block of Market Street, near the Christina River in Wilmington, boasted a dozen or more taverns that served the thirsty sailors and stevedores who worked the docks a block away. The entire area, known as the Ships Tavern District, fell into disarray until early 2002. Investors saved several historic three-story buildings on the west side of the street from demolition—the early-19th-century structures literally had trees growing through their roofs—and rehabbed them into shops, apartments, and parking.

Returning to West Street, numbers 501 and 503 occupy the site of the first house built on Quaker Hill in 1738 by Thomas West. His great-great-grandson built the current homes on the site. The Quaker Meeting House and cemetery are on the next block toward the river. The 500 block of W. 4th Street, which can be seen clearly from the corner of 4th and West, was built around 1894–95, and is a nearly intact block of Victorian row houses and semidetached homes. Across 4th Street on West is one of the oldest remaining buildings on Quaker Hill. Built in 1750, the basement of the house at 310 West St. is believed to have been part of the Underground Railroad in the mid-1800s. Built between 1851 and 1865, 304 and 308 West St. were part of lumber merchant Joshua Simmons's family enclave that included 300 and 309 West St., since demolished. In 1871, 222 West St. was the home of David Woolman, owner of Wilmington Water Works. Later, the building became a Protestant mission. The oldest building in this block, 200 West St., was originally the home and butcher shop of Patrick Taylor in 1855.

During the 20th century, Quaker Hill went into decline, as the suburbs attracted many residents from the area. The housing stock deteriorated, and in 1971, an urban renewal project cleared the land south of 4th Street, removing the remaining 18th-century structures. The remaining buildings were designated a National Register Historic Landmark in 1978.

The Kalmar Nyckel

Formerly known as "the 7th Street folly," this reproduction of the tall ship that brought the first settlers to Wilmington is now everybody's darling—and it's precisely for that reason that visitors may not be able to see the ship at all when they're in town. Unlike static ship displays, the *Kalmar Nyckel* is fully Coast Guard–certified to carry passengers, and she is Delaware's sea-going Ambassador of Good Will.

Originally the brainchild of a group of history buffs, volunteers, and hobbyists in 1985, the project floundered due to lack of direction and funding until 1990. Then, thanks to the influence of new members of the board of directors and a loan from the Wilmington Riverfront Development Corp., the ship became a reality. The *Kalmar Nyckel* is a beauty—a 240-ton, triplemasted merchant vessel, authentic down to the carvings and 10 cannons aboard. Her mainmast rises higher than a 10-story building, and carries 7,600 square feet of sails.

Seventh Street, accessed through a rough-looking neighborhood, is home of the modest digs of the Kalmar Nyckel Foundation and shipyard. The shipyard will eventually be linked to other attractions on the Christina River, including the original landing place ("The Rocks," now Fort Christina State Park), Old Swedes Church, and the Hendrickson House. In the good-weather months you're likely to see the ship on the Christina and the Delaware Rivers—or in Norfolk, Washington, Philadelphia, Baltimore, New York, or Boston at sailing events. She's also in demand by Hollywood. Call 302/479-7447 to find out where she is, or check on www.KalNyc.org.

Old Swedes Church, 606 Church St., 302/652-5629, continues to hold Episcopal Sunday services Sept.–June at 9 A.M., July–Aug. at 10 A.M. The church houses a number of historically significant objects, including the oldest known pulpit in the United States. The graveyard predates the church by 60 years and is the final resting place of the early settlers as well as Revolutionary War soldiers and Thomas Bayard, Secretary of State under President Grover Cleveland. The Hendrickson House, built in 1690 in Chester, Pennsylvania, was brought to Wilmington in

1958 and restored on the church grounds; furniture and everyday objects from the 1700s are on display. The church offers tours Wed.–Sat. 1–4 P.M. Call to confirm tour times.

ART MUSEUMS AND GALLERIES

The **Delaware Art Museum**, 302/571-9590, www.delart.org, is located in the Bank One Center at the Riverfront through 2004 (800 South Madison St.) while its permanent home at 2301 Kentmere Pkwy. undergoes a $24 million expansion and renovation. The museum is distinguished by outstanding holdings in three areas: works by American illustrators; paintings and sculpture by American fine artists from 1840 to the present; and a world-class collection of paintings and decorative arts by the English group known as the Pre-Raphaelites.

The Brandywine Valley was home to America's most beloved illustrators at the dawn of the 20th century, when illustration meant fine art reproduced in popular magazines and books. Howard Pyle, a Wilmington resident, worked and taught extensively in the area. In 1912, the desire to keep 48 treasured works by Howard Pyle in Wilmington led to the founding of the Delaware Art Museum organization. Today, paintings and drawings by Pyle and his students, N. C. Wyeth, Frank Schoonover, and Maxfield Parrish, among others, are regularly exhibited. The work is delightful and of exceptional quality.

The museum's 19th- and 20th-century American art collections capture the best work of U.S. artists of all periods and styles, including contemporary works by Grace Hartigan and Claes Oldenburg. However, the Delaware Art Museum is perhaps best known for its unique 19th-century collection of Pre-Raphaelite art by English artists such as Dante Gabriel Rossetti and Marie Spartali Stillman. The collection, second only to that of the Victoria & Albert Museum in Britain, was bequeathed to the museum in 1935 by Samuel Bancroft, Jr., a wealthy Wilmington industrialist. The romantic paintings and objects represent a reaction to the increasing mechanization of the late 19th century.

THE PRE-RAPHAELITES

The Pre-Raphaelites were a group of English artists who, in reaction to the increasing industrialization and social upheaval of the world in the mid-19th century, developed a lush, sensual style based on the works of the Italian Renaissance before the period dominated by the painter Raphael. The group, consisting of Dante Gabriel Rossetti—who often used Jane Morris, the wife of his friend, designer William Morris, as a model—Edward Burne-Jones, John Everett Millais, Ford Madox Brown, and others, began painting around 1848.

Their works are characterized by rich colors, contrasts, sinuous rounded designs, and an almost medieval use of symbolism. Though the pictures appear romantic and decorative today, at the time, many were controversial for both subject matter and presentation. A full-lipped and seductive Mary Magdalene, for instance, drew criticism for its questionable representation of a sacred Christian figure.

The museum also features changing exhibits—a recent one illuminated the works of glassblower Dale Chihuly—and an excellent café and gift shop. It's open Tuesday, Thursday, and Friday 10 A.M.–6 P.M., Saturday 10 A.M.–5 P.M., Sunday 1–5 P.M., and Wednesday 10 A.M.–9 P.M. Admission is free every Saturday 10 A.M.–noon; otherwise it's $7.

In the mid-1970s, the **Delaware Center for the Contemporary Arts** (DCCA) started out in an unpainted, abandoned warehouse on French Street. In 1984, urban redevelopment forced the relocation of the DCCA to the historic Waterworks complex on the Brandywine River. But it soon outgrew that space, and in 2000 the organization moved from its improved but painfully small space of 2,200 square feet to the 33,000-square-foot historic Harlan & Hollingsworth Car Shop II in the heart of the rejuvenated Riverfront (S. Madison and West Streets, 302/656-6466, www.thedcca.org). The DCCA, a non-collecting museum, showcases work of regionally, nationally, and internationally recognized contemporary artists. It also is a venue for dialogue, promoting discussion with its programming, exhibitions, gallery talks, receptions, and symposia.

The DCCA has close ties to the community. Through Contemporary Connections, a model program, a professional artist works in a classroom with a teacher to develop an art project that connects students to core curriculum subjects. Recently, artist George Apostos worked with a ninth-grade math class using algebraic formulas to create a permanent ceramic-tile wall mural based on tessellation (that's patterning based on small squares, but you knew that). The DCCA's Visual Arts Residency Programs also touches the community. As part of the Art and Community Residency, artists make a full-time commitment to a community group to create works of art relevant to the participants' lives. In 2002, printmaker and sculptor Jennifer Schmidt worked with women and children from YWCA Home-Life Management Center to create books and collages that illustrated individual histories and identities.

Annually, the DCCA has more than 30 exhibitions of cutting-edge contemporary art in all media. Private tours can be arranged. The building houses seven galleries and 26 artists' studios, a high-tech auditorium, and a gift shop featuring one-of-a-kind handmade items. It's open Tuesday, Thursday, and Friday 10 A.M.–6 P.M., Saturday 10 A.M.–5 P.M., Wednesday 10 A.M.–8 P.M., and Sunday 1–5 P.M. Admission is $5. Saturday from 10 A.M.–noon, admission is free.

For individual gallery listings, see Trolley Square under Shopping.

PARKS AND GARDENS

The simple rock cottage that was to become **Goodstay Center and Gardens** was built around 1740. Over the years, the cottage was expanded and remodeled into a country mansion complete with formal Tudor gardens, now part of the University of Delaware adult extension campus, 2600 Pennsylvania Ave. In 1853, it became the boyhood home of Howard Pyle, who later wrote in *Woman's Home Companion,* "nowhere do I find a single place (except it be in those early childhood days) whereupon I may set my finger and say: 'Here my fortunes began.'" Famed for his book and magazine illustrations and writing, Pyle went on to teach Charles Dana Gibson, Ethel P. B. Leach, and N. C. Wyeth.

In 1868, the house was purchased by the Du Pont family and remained with them until gifted to the university in 1968. The mansion itself serves as a meeting place for various groups; the upper floors contain the Lincoln Collection, three rooms of pictures, memorabilia, and a library of books and documents pertaining to Abraham Lincoln. Though many of the artifacts are reproductions, the collection includes a Ford's Theatre playbill

LINCOLN'S SHAWL

One of the artifacts exhibited at the Lincoln Collection in Goodstay Center is a shawl worn by President Abraham Lincoln during the Civil War. Lincoln journeyed to western Maryland to visit General McClellan in October 1862. The president was unhappy with McClellan's handling of the Battle of Antietam a few weeks earlier and wanted a firsthand look at the troops and their leaders. One of McClellan's aides, Colonel John Schoonover, met the president and waited with him as he bathed his feet in an icy stream near the encampment. Schoonover shivered with the cold; Lincoln gave him the shawl he was wearing, commenting that there were many shawls in Washington, though they were needed much more on the battlefield. Schoonover kept the shawl; it was handed down to his descendants over the years, along with the story of his encounter with the president.

In spite of the legends that grew up around Abraham Lincoln, other items in the collection reveal a shrewd understanding of his public persona. The collection includes several versions of the Gettysburg Address, some by Lincoln himself, and others by those who reported it. In Lincoln's versions, he left spaces marked for "applause," and at the end, "long, continued applause."

from the night of the assassination, the shawl worn by President Lincoln during a visit to General McClellan during the Civil War, and several notes and documents with Lincoln's signature. The collection is open to the public Oct.–May, Tues. noon–4 P.M.; February 12 (Lincoln's birthday), 10 A.M.–4 P.M.; and the Sunday (noon–4 P.M.) and Monday (10 A.M.–4 P.M.) of President's Day weekend. Arrangements to visit at other times may be made by calling 302/573-4468.

The Goodstay Tudor garden, one of the oldest in Delaware, is open dawn–dusk, and includes a magnificent magnolia walk that ends in a circular pool that reflects a statue of Venus. The magnolias are best in April; early May is lilac time. Howard Pyle commented, "It was such a garden as you will hardly find outside of a story book. . . . I cannot remember anything but bloom and beauty, air filled with the odor of growing things, the birds singing in the shady trees." The garden is made of several "rooms" that offer floral displays year-round, and is an idyllic place far removed from the bustle of the nearby city. Free.

The **Marian Coffin Gardens at Gilbraltar,** 1405 Greenhill Ave., 302/651-9617, an estate owned by the Sharp branch of the Du Ponts, feature restored gardens designed by Marian Coffin, circa 1918. H. Rodney Sharp, who was largely responsible for the preservation of Odessa (see Central Kent County, in the Central Delaware chapter), married Isabella du Pont, sister of Pierre S. du Pont, and bought the "country" estate in 1909. Marble terraces are joined by a grand staircase, surrounded by shrubs, perennials, annuals, sculpture, garden ornaments, ironwork, a fountain, and reflecting pool. None of the Sharp heirs wanted to take on the renovation necessary to reclaim the estate for personal use. H. Rodney Sharp III, grandson of the original owners, said the restoration would not only cost millions, but would require a full staff to maintain. "You'd have to be a real aficionado of that kind of living," he said. "There are better things to spend your money on than living in a house with a huge staff." After five years of negotiation, the property came under the auspices of Preservation Delaware, Inc. As with most Du Pont properties, the garden is considered the best feature of the estate, though the house is being converted into a 31-room hotel and restaurant. The gardens are open Mon.–Fri. 9 A.M.–5 P.M. Free.

The **Delaware Center for Horticulture,** 1810 N. Dupont St., 302/658-6262, a nonprofit organization housed in a former city maintenance building, is focused on the greening of Wilmington. Members of the center work with citizens' groups to turn vacant lots into community gardens, plant trees on weed-strewn thoroughfares, and promote urban gardening skills; a program to prepare young people for work in the horticultural trades is one of its offerings. An annual Harvest Festival showcases the achievements of neighborhood groups throughout the city. At the center, visitors will find exhibits and workshops on urban gardening, and a seasonal garden-themed art exhibit. A rare plant auction is held annually in addition to spring and fall plant sales. The center also puts together group tours to explore private and public gardens in the city. The grounds that surround the modern building are planted as demonstration gardens that showcase urban planting/landscaping ideas and design. The center is open Mon.–Fri. 10 A.M.–5 P.M., and on Saturday during the summer. Free.

In **Brandywine Park,** North Park Drive, a pleasant, tree-shaded 180-acre urban park, the **Brandywine Zoo,** 302/571-7747, is the main attraction. The zoo, which remains small and intimate, was begun in 1905. Animals are largely from the western hemisphere, such as llamas, condors, and bobcats, with a tiger and a variety of monkeys thrown in for exotica. The hands-down most popular exhibit is the zoo's rambunctious pair of river otters, Jester and Delta. Possessing the camera savvy of supermodels, the otters offer shutterbugs a variety of comely poses in between frantic dips and frolics in the pool. Beloved by visitors and zoo personnel alike, the keepers say that Jester and Delta's favorite activities are "destroying and climbing on anything they can, as well as stealing stuff when we aren't looking." The zoo is open daily 10 A.M.–4 P.M. Admission is charged Apr.–Oct.: $3. The rest of the year, admission is free.

ENTERTAINMENT

The beautifully restored **Grand Opera House,** 818 N. Market St., 302/658-7897, hosts a year-round program of concerts, pop music, entertainers, and dance shows. It's home to **Opera-Delaware,** 302/658-8063, and features performances by the **Delaware Symphony Association,** 206 W. 10th St., 302/656-7374. The symphony also offers a music series in southern Delaware, small ensemble performances at Winterthur, and chamber concerts in the Hotel du Pont's Gold Ballroom. The **Delaware Theatre Company** supports a six-play season on the Christina Riverfront, 200 Water St., 302/594-1100, and **Candlelight Music Dinner Theatre** presents year-round musicals, revues, and comedies north of the city in the community of Arden (2208 Millers Rd., 302/475-2313). The **Christina Cultural Arts Center** at 705 N. Market St., Wilmington, 302/652-0101, offers exhibits, concerts, and special events. The **Playhouse** in the Hotel du Pont, 11th and Market Streets, Wilmington, 302/656-4401, presents touring companies of Broadway shows and New York–bound productions throughout the year. In addition to musicals, TLB presents a wide variety of celebrity shows and concerts. The **Best of Broadway Dinner Theatre,** 800 S. Madison, Wilmington, 302/478-6178, is located in the Bank One Center at the Riverfront and presents new and classic shows and revues.

SHOPPING

Trolley Square

The neighborhood bordered by Kentmere Parkway, Lovering Avenue, Delaware Avenue, and I-95 is a particularly pleasant place to have a cup of coffee and wander about. **Blue Streak Gallery,** 1721-23 Delaware Ave., 302/429-0506, features art and crafts, while **Carspencken-Scott Gallery,** 1707 N. Lincoln, 302/655-7173, concentrates on paintings and drawings. The **Sandy Hollow Herb Company,** 1715 Delaware Ave., 302/654-2911, also displays art among its herbal offerings.

ACCOMMODATIONS

The least expensive housing option close to Wilmington is a stay at the **Goldey-Beacom**

College dorm, 4701 Limestone Rd., 302/998-8814. Single and double rooms are available from June 15–Aug. 15, and run $20–40.

There are a number of moderately priced chain hotels in downtown Wilmington, including Courtyard by Marriott, the Sheraton Suites, and Economy Inn. **The Brandywine Suites Hotel,** 707 N. King St., 302/656-9300 or 800/756-0070, is a recently renovated lodging that caters to businesspeople and families. It's downtown, on a major thoroughfare just behind the Grand Opera House and town center, with easy access to the Bank One Center at the Riverfront and other attractions on the river. The hotel's 49 rooms are all suites: big, pleasant, and spotless, surrounding a light-filled atrium. The hotel offers complimentary van transportation to a nearby full-service health club and nearby attractions. Parking is in the lot across the street. A restaurant off the main lobby offers a complimentary continental breakfast. Rooms run $99–169.

The **Hotel DuPont,** 11th and Market Streets, 302/594-3100, is renowned for its luxurious accommodations, fine service, and dining. In fact, it's Delaware's only Mobil four-star/AAA four-diamond–rated hotel. All guest rooms have separate sitting areas and bathrooms big enough to accommodate a family of five (at one time); the hotel offers 24-hour room service and a business center. The hotel's parking garage is a half-block away, and valet parking is much appreciated, especially in this downtown location, which resembles nothing so much as a ghost town after

FESTIVALS AND EVENTS

From June through September, Wilmington is home to a number of ethnic celebrations, including the Greek Festival, 302/654-4446; St. Anthony's Italian Festival, 302/421-3790; St. Hedwig's Polish Festival, 302/652-8521; and the Caribbean Festival, 302/529-1392. Since contact numbers tend to change annually, contact the Greater Wilmington Convention & Visitors Bureau, 302/652-4088, www.visitwilmingtonde.com, for updates.

January/February

The **Wilmington International Exhibition of Photography,** often held on the University grounds in Newark, has been an annual event since the early 1930s. 302/478-6392.

The annual **Delaware Antiquarian Book Show/Sale** is a good place to scout for those rare first editions. 302/655-3055.

March/April

The **Delaware Art Museum** holds a special biennial exhibit on even years (2004, 2006, etc.). 302/571-9590.

May/June

See behind the scenes at **Wilmington Garden Day,** an annual tour of private gardens. 302/428-6172.

September/October

The artists' community of Arden has held its annual **Arden Fair** since 1907. 302/475-3126.

Delaware City celebrates **Delaware Authors Day** for those who write about the state. 302/577-2144.

November/December

Yuletide at Winterthur fulfills the fussiest decorating fantasy. 800/448-3883.

dark, though this is likely to change as the area becomes more gentrified.

The hotel features a lounge and two restaurants on the premises: the Green Room and the Brandywine Room, both four-star/four-diamond eateries. There's also a 1,230-seat theater that showcases Broadway musicals. The DuPont shrieks "luxe," and the prices ($289–450 and up) reflect it; however, it does offer weekend and romantic escape packages that are comparatively good deals.

FOOD

Toscana To Go, 1402 N. DuPont St., 302/655-8600, is the take-out arm of Toscana Kitchen. Items vary in quality and price, though both tend to be high. It's open daily.

Kid Shelleen's, 14th and Scott Streets, 302/658-4600, is the hip place to have a beer and hang out. Neither the service nor the food is special, but the place is really hopping in the evening with local 30-somethings. The restaurant features a full bar with an assortment of draft beers, and a pizza/burger/pasta/salad menu with a few fancy entrées such as enchiladas, blackened salmon, and bayou stew ($6–16). It's open every day, 11 A.M.–midnight.

Toscana Kitchen + Bar, 1412 Dupont St., 302/654-8001, was the first restaurant started by local celebrity chef/owner Dan Butler, and remains extremely popular. Butler started out as a dishwasher at the Hotel DuPont and worked his way up the kitchen prep lines to open Toscana at the age of 30. The menu is upscale Italian, and the crowd is dressy and hip. The roasted butternut squash ravioli in butter and sage sauce is a perennial favorite. Lunch Mon.–Fri., dinner Mon.–Sun.; prices average $18.

Which brings us to Dan Butler's other restaurant, **Deep Blue,** 111 E. 11th St., 302/777-2040, a major risk that's paid off handsomely. The restaurant was a gamble because of its downtown location (no-person's land after 5 P.M.) and the concentration on a very different type of menu: fresh seafood. Deep Blue has become the place the sophisticated suits meet after work, and the hip decor is a fitting background to the well-prepared fish and shellfish dishes (plus free-range chicken or beef tenderloin for those in a landlubber mood). Nearby parking is complimentary. It's open for lunch Mon.–Fri., dinner Mon.–Sat.; expect the bill to average $19 per entrée.

Also recommended is **Restaurant 821,** 821 N. Market St., 302/652-8821, www.restaurant 821.com, offering a $39 prix fixe dinner menu with such delicacies as Atlantic salmon with basil whipped potatoes, and baby clam with preserved lemon and tomato brodetto. The menu changes frequently and centers on fresh produce, some of which is grown on the restaurant's own farm in New Jersey. The lunch menu is more affordable, averaging $13 a plate. Dinner is served Mon.–Sat., lunch Wednesday only.

Zanzibar Blue, 10th and West Streets, 302/472-7000, www.zanzibarblue.com, is the Wilmington branch of a well-known Philadelphia jazz club. Dinner is served nightly to the strains of live jazz music, and entrées like the Mediterranean vegetable plate and braised beef short rib average $18. Lunch, served weekdays, averages $11 for pastas, salads, and sandwiches.

The **Riverfront Market,** next to Tubman-Garrett Park, 302/425-4454, www.riverfront wilm.com, is an upscale food court with Thai, sushi, pasta, and ice cream booths, among others, in a historic restored warehouse. It's open for three meals Tues.–Sat.

INFORMATION

The Greater Wilmington Convention & Visitors Bureau serves northern Delaware. Write to GWCVB, 100 West 10th St., Ste. 20, Wilmington, DE 19801, or call 302/652-4088 (in state) or 800/422-1181. The website is www.Visit WilmingtonDE.com. General information is also available at the I-95 Visitor Information Center, south of Wilmington in the middle of I-95 between Rte. 896 (exit 1) and Rte. 273 (exit 3—there is no exit 2). The center can also help with hotel and motel reservations, 302/737-4059. Another center, the Delaware Memorial Bridge Information Center, I-295 on the Delaware end of the bridge between Delaware and southern New Jersey, 302/571-6340, offers general information to walk-ins and callers.

Central Delaware

This is a place where you can hear fall coming for miles.

Charles Kuralt, Sunday Morning, *October 1986*

Central Delaware seems to be drenched in perpetual golden light, reflected off the endless stretch of wheat-covered farms and the waving sea grasses of the marshes. Home to the state capital, Dover, central Delaware is a place of quiet towns and fishing villages. The silence can be deceptive, however: Dover and Harrington jump with the pounding of horse hooves, squealing of race cars, and clanging of slot machines. Dover is also home to an exceptional Air Force museum at the nearby Air Force base. The county's long coastline is pocketed with dozens of small and scenic watermen's villages, and the back roads are a feast for the eyes.

Though "lower slower Delaware" traditionally starts south of the Chesapeake & Delaware Canal on the border of Kent County, the historic village of New Castle is included in this segment because of its proximity to Fort Delaware and the northern greenways, and its historic connection as the former state capital. There's plenty of history in central Delaware, captured in museums and shaped in architecture, but there's

New Castle

©JOANNE MILLER

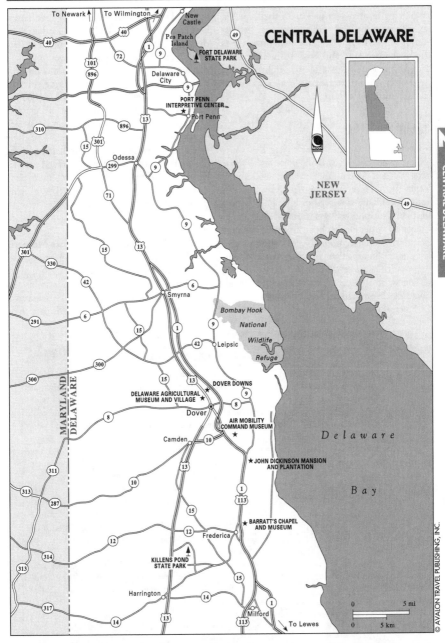

CENTRAL DELAWARE

To Newark To Wilmington
New Castle
Pea Patch Island
FORT DELAWARE STATE PARK
Delaware City
PORT PENN INTERPRETIVE CENTER
Port Penn
Odessa

NEW JERSEY

Smyrna

Bombay Hook
National
Wildlife
Leipsic
Refuge

DOVER DOWNS
DELAWARE AGRICULTURAL MUSEUM AND VILLAGE
Dover
AIR MOBILITY COMMAND MUSEUM
Camden

Delaware

JOHN DICKINSON MANSION AND PLANTATION

Bay

BARRATT'S CHAPEL AND MUSEUM

Frederica

KILLENS POND STATE PARK

Harrington

Milford
To Lewes

MARYLAND
DELAWARE

CENTRAL DELAWARE

0   5 mi
0   5 km

© AVALON TRAVEL PUBLISHING, INC.

also living history—farmers and fishers making a living from the land as they have since the first European settlers pulled their own plows across freshly cleared land and Native Americans laid nets in the water. It is a sweet, bright country, where, in the autumn, the calling geese really can be heard for miles.

NEW CASTLE

Once the capital and largest city in Delaware, New Castle is now a carefully preserved historic site. William Penn himself ordered the building of the town. The courthouse was Delaware's first, and New Castle served as an immigration port until Philadelphia eclipsed it. It was also a noted transport center: packet boats from Philadelphia transferred their cargo in New Castle to stagecoaches bound for Frenchtown, Maryland. Andrew Jackson, Stonewall Jackson, Davy Crockett, Osceola, and Black Hawk all passed through New Castle on their way to Washington, D.C.

Since 1804, the town of New Castle has been preserved to reflect its long heritage. Public historic homes are a short stroll from each other along rippling sidewalks raised by the roots of ancient trees. In the summer, they provide welcome shade and a dizzying display of color in the autumn. Your car tires will shudder in amazement on a few of the cobblestone streets. But historic New Castle is more than a museum—it's a living town, with cafés, restaurants, and shops on the streets, interspersed with residential areas. The town meets the Delaware River in a green and peaceful riverfront park frequented by joggers and strollers. It's a wonderful place to sit and watch the massive cargo ships move north on the Delaware River toward Wilmington and Philadelphia.

Sights
The Old New Castle Court House Museum, 211 Delaware St., 302/323-4453, www.newcastlecity.com, was the colonial capital of Delaware, though its history extends far beyond that time. A Swedish colony had settled near Wilmington in 1638; in order to isolate them

WHEN A BEACH IS NOT A BEACH

Many of the villages named "beach" in Delaware are fishing ports or residential areas with limited recreational opportunities for visitors. Beaches on the Delaware River north of Prime Hook tend to be gravel-covered and rough, as opposed to the fine sand beaches of Lewes, Rehoboth, Bethany, and Fenwick Island—they're also considerably more deserted, which has advantages and disadvantages (auto break-ins, etc.). The coastal areas are fun to explore, but if you're seeking sun and sand, use this information as a rough guide.

Slaughter Beach has a dune crossing (a designated area where people can cross over the dunes to the beach, in order to prevent erosion), a picnic pavilion, and bathing area, but no other facilities—most of the area is residential. Broadkill Beach also has a dune crossing and a little store, plus a residential area. The beaches of Bowers are separated by an ocean inlet and must be reached by two different roads: North Bowers Beach has a tiny maritime museum on Marin and Williams Streets, which is open weekends June–Aug.; South Bowers Beach has a small sandy beach on the bay. Kitts Hummock, Primehook Beach, and Pickering Beach are largely residential with limited parking. Bay View Beach, Big Stone Beach, Fowler Beach, and Bennetts Pier are fishing villages with few or no tourist facilities.

Woodland Beach features a boat launch, small beach, and fishing pier with pretty coast views. Woodland Beach, Augustine Beach, and Collins Beach all used to have boardwalks or amusement piers that were popular in the late 19th century; the hurricane and tidal wave of 1878 destroyed piers, buildings, roads, and tourist facilities, putting many of these resorts underwater. Facilities for visitors are limited. The Delaware Division of Parks and Recreation has the latest information on beaches, parks, and trails. It can be reached by calling 302/739-5285.

and control river traffic, Dutch governor Peter Stuyvesant established Fort Casimir in 1651, later renamed New Amstel (New Castle). Ownership of the site was continually disputed by the Swedes, Dutch, and English; the final dispute involved Lord Baltimore and William Penn over the boundaries of Maryland and Pennsylvania. In 1682, the Duke of York awarded Penn the "three lower counties of Pennsylvania" (Delaware), making him the largest landowner on both continents. New Castle was Penn's first landing site in the New World. The cupola on the courthouse is the point from which a 12-mile radius is measured that ensured Penn his freshwater port. When Delaware finally broke away from Pennsylvania in 1704, New Castle, then the largest city, was named capital of the new colony.

The courthouse contains paintings and artifacts that illuminate the town's multinational history; tour guides also provide insight. There is no charge to tour the New Castle Court House; it's open Tues.–Sat. 10 A.M.–3:30 P.M., Sunday

© JOANNE MILLER

New Castle Court House

1:30–4:40 P.M. Since volunteers maintain the courthouse and all historic buildings, hours are subject to change.

Two historic homes built for two different residents of New Castle are the **Dutch House, 32 E. 3rd St.,** 302/322-9168, and the **Amstel House Museum, 4th and Delaware Streets,** 302/322-2794. The Dutch house was built in the early 1700s and is one of the oldest in Delaware; it's typical of early colonial housing, with a double fireplace and a hip (some call it "gabled") roof. The illustrated Bible from 1714 and large carved Kas ("Kasht" in Dutch—a cupboard where most of the family goods were stored) are authentic to period. The Amstel House, 1738, was likely the home of Governor Van Dyke and the most elegant house in town when it was built. The structure seems cramped and cottage-like now, but few homes can boast a hearth honoring the attendance of George Washington at the governor's daughter's wedding, in 1784. The Staffordshire china and Venetian blinds on the windows were appropriate for a wealthy family of the time. Artfully decorated with period antiques, right down to the "klumpen" (wooden shoes), both homes are open Mar.–Dec., Tues.–Sat. 11 A.M.–4 P.M., Sunday 1–4 P.M. Each charges a separate admission of about $4, $6 for both.

The most "recent" of New Castle's public historic homes is the **George Read II House and Gardens, 42 The Strand,** 302/322-8411. Built in 1801 by the profligate son of a notable politician, the home is as elegant and modern as Mr. Read's (extensive) credit would allow. Read, an attorney, hoped to follow in his influential father's footsteps, and built a place to entertain his future friends. The kitchen had the latest steam system, including a "Rumford Roaster," powered by wood fires. Unfortunately, his dreams never materialized, and he died in bankruptcy. The house is, however, a real beauty, furnished to period. The Victorian-style gardens around the house were added by William Cooper, who grew up next door and bought the house in 1846. It's open Mar.–Dec., Tues.–Sat. 10 A.M.–4 P.M., Sunday noon–4 P.M., and weekdays by appointment Jan.–Feb. Admission is $5.

EXEMPLARY VERTUES

A twilight stroll through the cemetery at Immanuel Church in New Castle is a treat during the early fall, when the crickets still sing lazily to one another. While checking out the odd funerary furniture—two pieces look like a chaise lounge and table, ready for someone to plop down with a steamy novel and a cold drink—stop by the grave of Jane, the wife of William Read, one of New Castle's earliest settlers. It's instructive to learn the desirable character traits of a woman of MDCCXXXII:

Many were her Exemplary Vertues
Her temper meak and carriage obliging
Strict chastity prudent oeconomy
Piety without ostentation
And hospitality without crudgeing. . . .

Sounds like Martha Stewart (though the "prudent oeconomy" may be contested).

The **Old Library Museum,** 40 E. 3rd St., 302/322-2794, was designed with a series of skylights and light-sinks (glass floors) by Philadelphia architect Frank Furness in 1892. The unusual building no longer houses a library, but specializes in displays on the history of New Castle. It's open March–Dec. weekends only 1–4 P.M.; admission is free.

While strolling through the town, you'll pass **Immanuel Church,** 100 Harmony St. on the Green, 302/328-2413, the oldest Anglican parish in Delaware (1689), and the **Presbyterian Church,** founded in 1657 by a Dutch Reformed congregation; it's behind the George Read House on 25 E. Third St. These are open most of the time and are points of historical and architectural interest. On some evenings, you can catch choir practice; heavenly song wafts out of brightly lit stained glass windows just as it has for hundreds of years.

The Visitor's Bureau of Historic New Castle, P.O. Box 465, New Castle, DE 19720, 800/758-1550, www.visitnewcastle.com, publishes a brochure that details the historic structures

above and many more. Ask for "New Castle Heritage Trail."

Accommodations

The Armitage Inn, 2 the Strand, New Castle, 302/328-6618, armitageinn@earthlink.net, is surely the prettiest place to stay in New Castle. One of the oldest homes in town, the inn has portions that were built in the 1600s. Once referred to as the Van Leuvenigh House after its original owner, the inn faces the riverfront park, and some of the rooms look out over the Delaware River. Each of the five lavishly decorated rooms is equipped with private bath, cable television, telephone, and air-conditioning. Innkeeper Stephen Marks could have another career as a chef if he so desired, judging from the wonderful breakfast served in the morning. Rates range between $105–150.

At least two of the homes downtown across from the old marketplace have been restored into bed-and-breakfasts. One is **The William Penn Guest House,** circa 1682, 206 Delaware St., 302/328-7736. The four rooms can be set up as either two private rooms with baths, or four rooms with two shared baths. Rates range $75–95, including a continental breakfast.

Also recommended: The **Terry House Bed and Breakfast,** 130 Delaware St., 302/322-2505, www.terryhouse.com, features four spacious guestrooms with private baths, queen-size beds, and modern amenities in a lovely three-story 1860 Federal townhouse. The rooms offer a view of Battery Park or Market Square and the Court House and the Delaware River during the winter months. Rooms include a full country or continental breakfast; rates range $90–110.

Food

O'Donald's Ice Cream and Sandwich Shop, 302 Delaware St., 302/322-4272, is a casual place for a short sit-down in a Victorian setting with arched windows and tin ceiling. It offers coffee, tea, sodas, sweet rolls, bagels, ice cream, water ice, milkshakes, sandwiches, soups, salads, and a deli and grocery. O'Donald's is open Mon.–Fri. 8 A.M.–7 P.M., Saturday 8 A.M.–6 P.M., Sunday 8 A.M.–4 P.M.

Jessop's Tavern, 114 Delaware St., 302/322-6111, is the best place to eat in downtown New Castle, and the most popular. It serves a modified pub menu with a few old favorites, such as shepherd's pie and prime rib, plus hearty and fresh soups, sandwiches, and salads. Prices average $8–18, and it's open for lunch and dinner Mon.–Sat. Getting in early for dinner, especially on weekends, is a good idea.

The constant heavy traffic on U.S. 13 (Du Pont Parkway) south of the U.S. 40 intersection might make it easy to miss two restaurants that are worthy of note. The **Lynnhaven Inn,** 154 N. Du Pont Pkwy., 302/328-2041, might be mistaken for just another fast-food place until you walk into the elegant foyer. Inside, the candlelit dining room could be a million miles away from the rumbling trucks outside. A well-kept favorite of residents for years, the inn serves a variety of seafood and meats for dinner, and lighter fare for lunch; prices average $12–20. It's open for lunch and dinner Mon.–Fri., dinner only Sat.–Sun.

Though the food quality can be uneven, **Air Transport Command,** 143 N. Du Pont Hwy., 302/328-3527, should be on everyone's fun list. The name says it all; Air Transport Command is set up like a World War II field station, complete with vintage trucks and blown-out walls. The Andrews Sisters wail over the intercom, and vintage armed forces memorabilia lines the walls. The menu is American, prices average $8–22, and it's open daily for lunch and dinner.

Also recommended: **Casablanca Restaurant,** 4010 N. Dupont Hwy., 302/652-5344, for its exotic Moroccan atmosphere and food. Low tables, belly dancers, and contagious music heighten the gustatory pleasures of well-prepared chicken, couscous, lamb and other specialties. Dinner served Tues.–Sun.; prices average $20.

FORT DELAWARE STATE PARK AND ENVIRONS

Fort Delaware on Pea Patch Island in the Delaware River, 302/834-7941, was originally built in 1819 for the protection of Wilmington and Philadelphia. It was rebuilt in 1859, and served as a prison for 33,000 captured Confederate soldiers over the course of the Civil War. The prison was unusual not only because of its size, but also for the unique perspective of the man who ran it. General Albin

© JOANNE MILLER

Fort Delaware

THE WILD GREEN ROAD

The greenway that runs along the Delaware River from New Castle in New Castle County to Cape Henlopen in Sussex County is a prime feeding stopover for migratory shorebirds and other species; its importance is such that it was designated as the first reserve in the Western Hemisphere Shorebird Reserve Network. This system of easily accessible preserves is rife with local and migrating species.

Famed for its population of shorebirds, the area hosts sandpipers, plovers, avocets, stilts, oystercatchers, and four types of sandpiper, the red knot, sanderling, ruddy turnstone, and semi-palmated, among hundreds of other avian species. Shorebird migration is distinguished by two characteristics: the distance traveled (19,000 miles round-trip for the red knot, from Argentina to the Hudson Bay), and the fact that they seldom stop for food, so each stop is crucial. The Delaware Bay is one "staging area," due to its abundance of horseshoe crab eggs in late May and June. Shorebirds bent on doubling their body weight swarm the shoreline; a 50-gram sanderling will eat one crab egg every five seconds for 14 hours each day; the birds reach only the top layer of eggs, leaving the deeper ones to hatch later.

From spring through fall, flocks of bird species probe the mudflats for the food that means survival during their long journey. Birders and other naturalists can enjoy frequent sightings by driving south from New Castle on Route 9 and taking advantage of these viewing areas:

Battery Park Trail, which begins in New Castle, is a 1.25-mile ramble that runs along Army Creek and Gambacorta Marsh. Continuing along Route 9 to Delaware City, you'll pass through a major industrial complex—keep an eye out for trucks. The largest landholder is Star Enterprises, which has devoted 1,700 acres to a freshwater wildlife preserve, **Dragon Run.** In addition to migratory birds, this is a good place to spot muskrats and amphibians.

In Delaware City, take the *Delafort* to Fort Delaware and **Pea Patch Island,** a notorious hangout for ibis, herons, and egrets. On the way to Port Penn, you'll pass through the largest freshwater marsh in the state, **Thousand Acre Marsh.**

Reedy Island Quarantine Station in Port Penn was the Delaware River's main quarantine detention center until 1936. It can be seen from the Wetlands Trail in the **Augustine Wildlife Area.**

Continuing south on Route 9 past the Odessa turnoff, you'll come to Taylor's Bridge; its main characteristic is the Reedy Island Rear Range Light, a 135-foot cast-iron lighthouse created in the mid-1800s. As sailors cruised the waters of the Delaware Bay, they timed the unique pattern of flashes from each range light to aid navigation. Blackbird Creek, near Taylor's Bridge, is a research site for the Delaware National Estuarine Research Reserve, and is not open to the public.

Woodland Beach Wildlife Area, a 4,794-acre preserve, is a popular site for fishing, crabbing, and birding. A bird-watching tower is located nearby, with a good opportunity to see huge flocks of snow and Canada geese and other waterfowl. The town of Woodland Beach is a short detour east on Route 6.

F. Schoeph, a native Austrian freedom fighter, had lived in the United States for more than a decade and served as an engineer in the U.S. War Department when he was tapped to oversee prison operations in 1863. Educated in Vienna, Schoeph was familiar with the germ theory, and insisted on several innovations that saved the lives of his prisoners: smallpox inoculations, flush toilets, regular bathing, and the use of disinfectants in the two

hospitals on the island. Dysentery was the biggest killer of the Civil War: of 600,000 military deaths, two-thirds were from disease; but on Pea Patch Island, the death rate due to disease was 7.9 percent. The prisoners "were for saving," according to the warden.

Fort Delaware was known as a "country club" prison. It was very much like a city, with a grocery store, beer, evangelical staff, and vis-

Farther south on Route 9, **Bombay Hook National Wildlife Refuge** is one of the best places to view birds and other marshland wildlife. Three of the trails in the refuge have 30-foot observation towers, and visitors may rent high-power viewing scopes.

Port Mahon, a short detour east on Route 89 from Route 9, is a good spot to see shorebirds; however, the road is sometimes impassible due to flooding. Port Mahon once had a beautiful lighthouse and thriving fishing community; the lighthouse burned down in 1984, and the buildings rotted away. As a startling example of beach erosion, the Port Mahon lighthouse once stood 200 feet inland; its pilings are now in the bay.

The northern section of **Little Creek Wildlife Area** adjoins Bombay Hook. Most of the property is managed for waterfowl, with hunting blinds, photographic blinds, an observation tower, and a boardwalk. For more information on this developing area, call 302/678-9472.

Take Bergold Lane from Route 9 and follow it to Kitts Hummock Road and the entrance to **St. Jones Reserve.** The 700-acre reserve features a one-mile nature trail that includes a one-quarter-mile boardwalk across the marsh. Turn west on Kitts Hummock Road past the Dickinson Plantation, and take U.S. 113 south to Route 1. Turn east on Route 36, then north on Route 203, to reach the Mispillion Lighthouse, the sole surviving wood-frame lighthouse in Delaware. Route 203 will take you through the Cedar Creek section of the **Milford Neck Wildlife Area,** an excellent place to view shorebirds.

Slaughter Beach, southeast of the Mispillion Lighthouse, is one of the best places to see horseshoe crabs. Return to the Route 36 intersection and follow Route 204 along the shore. Take Route 224 to return to Route 1. Several roads heading east from Route 1 lead into the Prime Hook and the seashore; Route 220 to Route 221 to Route 199 leads to Fowler Beach; Route 198 to Route 222 to Route 38 leads to Primehook Beach (Shorts Beach). The main entrance is via Route 16 to Broadkill Beach.

Waters within **Prime Hook National Wildlife Refuge** are open for canoeing and boating, and four hiking trials include a boardwalk trail over the marshes. At Broadkill Beach, turn south from Route 16 to S. Bay Shore Drive to reach Beach Plum Preserve.

The northern half of **Beach Plum Island Nature Preserve,** a 129-acre barrier island, is open to the public. Roads within the area are open to off-road vehicles only, so plan to walk from the parking lot.

Return to Route 1 via Route 16, and head south toward Lewes (LOO-es). Route 1 becomes Route 9. Follow Route 9 (King's Highway) into Lewes, proceed east on Savannah Road, then south on Cape Henlopen Drive.

Former site of the famed Cape Henlopen Lighthouse, which blew down during a fierce storm in 1926, **Cape Henlopen State Park** offers several different environments in which to view wildlife and shorebirds.

itors. Prisoners came from every walk of life: officers and foreign nationals shared quarters with deserters, murderers, and thieves. Occasionally, a "political prisoner"—captured and held to interfere with pro-Confederate political processes—would be a guest at Pea Patch: F. R. Lubbock, governor of Texas, and Jefferson Davis's personal secretary, Burton Harrison, both did time in the prison.

The fort today consists of the main star-shaped brick building surrounded by a "wet ditch" (moat), a few additional buildings, and a 1855 New Columbia Rodman Cannon, with a range of four miles. The cannon is fired daily at 3 P.M.—don't miss this! Actually, you can't; the cannon is loud enough to stop and restart your heart. Inside the fort, costumed interpreters (often including General Schoeph himself) talk about day-to-day life in the prison. Many visitors bring a picnic lunch (grills are available) and spend the day on the pleasant, parklike island. No overnight facilities are available.

Because of its large waterfowl population, Fort Delaware is a birder destination. The fort also has many special events throughout the year; two popular activities are the Halloween Ghost Tour in October and the Garrison Weekend in August.

Fort Delaware State Park is reached via a half-mile boat ride aboard the 88-passenger *Delafort*. The boat is docked at the end of Clinton Street in Delaware City, a charming village with some unique shops (look for signs from Route 9). Battery Park in Delaware City, right next to the boat dock, delivers a beautiful view of the river. The *Delafort* runs May–Sept. weekends and holidays, mid-June–Labor Day Wed.–Sun.; call for the latest schedule. The boat ride is $6 for adults, $4 for children, and entry to the island is free.

When the **Olde Canal Inn,** 30 Clinton St., Delaware City, 302/832-5100, was built in 1826, it first housed canal workers, then served as a hotel for dignitaries, business leaders, and gentry. The dining rooms and tavern, designed with high ceilings in the style of the time, were ideal for this clientele. When the Chesapeake & Delaware Canal opened, the inn was in an important location on the water route from Philadelphia to Baltimore. The inn was completely renovated in 1999, and now offers six rooms, four suites, and a four-bedroom penthouse, most with private bath. The penthouse, all suites, and most rooms are waterfront or have water views. Prices range $49–199.

The inn also offers several restaurants. The Reybold Room is a fine-dining restaurant featuring seafood, veal, steaks, and other area delicacies. Reservations are suggested; lunch (averaging $8) is served Tues.–Fri., dinner (averaging $15) Tues.–Sun. The Riverfront Tavern has been the gathering place for politicians, businesspeople, rum-runners, and the like since the early 1800s. A light menu is available for lunch Tues.–Fri. and dinner Tues.–Sun. Weather permitting, the Waterfront Deck is also open for dining. This deck spans more than 100 feet overlooking the river,

with views of vessels of transport and leisure as well as Fort Delaware on Pea Patch Island.

The shops on Clinton Street include **Jim Pileggi's Furniture Shop.** Pileggi is a sixth-generation craftsman who works in the Shaker style.

Port Penn and the Augustine Wildlife Area

Port Penn is a tiny fishing village about four miles south of Fort Delaware on Route 9, and is the home of the Port Penn Interpretive Center, Market and Liberty Streets, 302/834-0431. The center is a one-room schoolhouse/folk museum that celebrates the lives of the watermen, hunters, fishers, and farmers who populate the area. Throughout the year, from early September to the end of October, the center offers special programs. One favorite is "Muskrats A-Z"; muskrats (also known as bog bunnies) have been trapped in the area for meat and fur from well before European settlement—the program explores the lives of the versatile little rodents. The drive from Fort Delaware, over a curving bridge through the open marshland of the Augustine Wildlife Area, is idyllic—since traffic is light, especially midweek, it would also be an excellent choice for bicyclists. In mid-September, Port Penn holds a Wetland Folk Festival with food (crab cakes!), storytelling, living history programs, and music. Call the Port Penn Interpretive Center or the Delaware Folklife Program, 302/834-7941, for dates and times. The Port Penn Interpretive Center is open Memorial Day–last weekend of Sept., Fri.–Sun. 10 A.M.–6 P.M. Free.

Kelly's Tavern, at the end of Market Street, Port Penn, 302/834-9221, is a good place to stop for a beer and a burger ($6). Kelly's has no sign, just a neon beer light in the window (there's a phone booth on the street in front). Several people raved about the crab cakes, but mine were loaded with cartilage.

CENTRAL KENT COUNTY
Odessa

It's easy to slip past Odessa on U.S. 13 without a glance down Main Street. However, those interested in architecture, American decorative arts,

LIFE ON THE WATER

In the late 1800s, floating cabins lined the wetlands of the Delaware River tidal basin—as common as cars are today, according to local watermen. The cabins were made up of one or two rooms, equipped with a small stove, table, and two to four built-in bunks. The cabin was mounted on a shallow-draught hull, which permitted it to be towed by a skiff, then staked near fishing grounds.

From late March through June, these cabins were lashed together to form communities, and used as residences by watermen who made their living catching shad and sturgeon as the fish migrated up the river to spawn. The men used their skiffs to fish from, and returned to the cabin community at night to eat, sleep, and swap stories.

Since the fishermen who used the floating cabins relied on the annual fish migration, the cabins fell into disuse in the early 20th century. One man said, "The 1920s was the end of the good times because the Delaware River got so polluted. . . . I've seen a man put in his net and come out with not one fish. Not a one." The cabins were sold, or deserted along the waterways, or brought inland and used as storage sheds, where they may still be seen today.

and living history would miss out on a lot. Odessa is a beautifully preserved small town in a rural area 23 miles south of Wilmington; several of the properties in the town—officially called the **Historic Houses of Odessa,** Main Street, 302/378-4069—are owned by Winterthur Museum (see Northern Delaware chapter). Three of the homes, the Corbit-Sharp House (circa 1772), the Wilson-Warner House (circa 1769), and the Brick Hotel Gallery (circa 1822), are open to the public by guided tour. The buildings are all furnished with exquisite period furniture and porcelain (including French pieces owned by the Du Ponts), and the collections are regularly rotated. The Brick Hotel Gallery features an exhibit of Belter furniture, the height of Victorian fashion.

Before European settlement, Lenni Lenape named the little port Appoquinimie, for which Appoquinimink Creek (ah-po-KWIN-a-mehnk) was named. In 1731, a man named Cantwell built a toll bridge over the creek, and travelers renamed the little settlement Cantwell's Bridge. The town was named Odessa in 1855 in the hopes that the tiny port would flourish like its Russian namesake, in spite of the fact that the railroad had bypassed the town by three miles. For a time, the name brought luck. But, when a viral disease, "the yellows," destroyed the local peach crop in the 1890s, the port declined and the town fell asleep.

The Du Pont family had used a property in Odessa as a retreat, and understood the value of the 200 years of colonial, Federal, and Victorian architecture in the town. Winterthur Museum acquired the buildings, opening them to the public and using them as living laboratories for students of American Studies at the University of Delaware and other institutions. Many homes in Odessa continue to be privately owned, but are opened to the public during "Christmas in Odessa," an extremely popular event held on the first Saturday in December each year.

Christmas is always a special time at the historic houses; each year, the buildings are decorated according to a theme, such as Peter Pan. Tours sometimes include a special tea or hearth-cooked meal based on current exhibits (call for a schedule). One specialty is Appoquinimink cakes, a forerunner of a modern tortilla; settlers modified the flour-and-water cakes eaten by the Lenni Lenape and used them as a base for both sweet and savory dishes. Visitors may be escorted through one ($5), two ($7), or three properties ($8). Historic Houses of Odessa is open Mar.–Dec., Tues.–Sat. 10 A.M.–4 P.M., Sunday 1–4 P.M. Reservations are not necessary, but the last tour is at 3 P.M. daily. Historic house tours start at the Brick Hotel on Main and 2nd Streets. A walking tour of the town, including most of the privately owned buildings, also starts from there.

Bombay Hook National Wildlife Refuge

Poets who know no better rhapsodize about the peace of nature, but a well-populated marsh is a cacophony.

Bern Keating, *"Birders' Heaven,"* Connoisseur, *April 1986*

Established in 1935, Bombay Hook (the word "hook" is derived from the Dutch term for a stand of trees) is one of the most important links on the Atlantic flyway. More than 16,000 acres of brackish marsh, freshwater pools, brush, timbered swamp, farms, and grassy upland are home to 256 identified species of birds, 33 species of mammals, and 37 species of reptiles and amphibians. The visitor center features wildlife exhibitions and a number of ranger-led programs; a 12-mile auto tour loop starts at the center. Along the auto route, five nature trails ranging from a quarter-mile to one mile in length are available to hikers and photographers. If you intend to leave your auto, insect repellent is a must! Throughout the warmer months, the marshes are filled with an equal number of biting insects and rainbow-hued wildflowers. During spring and fall migrations, the ponds are often crowded with thousands of egrets or Canada geese (Bombay Hook has the largest count in the United States); numerous other migratory species, such as bald eagles, take advantage of a safe stopover at the refuge. Late October is a peak season for shorebirds, warblers, reptiles, and amphibians. In April and May, both red and gray fox sightings are common. Along the auto route, you'll notice cultivated farm fields. The refuge permits farmers to work the land in exchange for a designated portion planted with crops favored by the park's wildlife. To reach the refuge from Route 9, turn east on Whitehall Neck Road; continue 2.3 miles to the visitor center, 302/653-6872. It's open Mon.–Fri. 8 A.M.– 4 P.M., Sat.–Sun. 9 A.M.–5 P.M. Visitors may rent a 2X sighting scope at the center. There are no overnight facilities, and a $5 fee is charged to enter the park.

The Allee House is one of the best-preserved early farmhouses in Delaware. Built by Abraham Allee in 1753, the property overlooks wood-

THE PARLOR AS THEATER

Victorian fascination with the study and control of nature found full expression in the parlors of American homes with the revival of rococo-style furniture. Henry Belter, a native of Germany who immigrated to New York and set up a furniture crafting business in 1850, became the best-known proponent of the style.

Belter and his many imitators created furniture of hand-carved rosewood and curved pieces made from a series of 7 to 21 thin wood veneers. New technology in the manipulation of sheets of laminated wood created rounded chair backs and sinuous table legs in stark contrast to the plain, functional styles of the past. Deceptively fragile-looking openwork provided the base for massive marble tabletops; delicate parlor chairs were engineered to support the weight of the heftiest tea sipper.

Belter furniture, made during 1840–1860 and sold for premium prices, was an updated version of the French Louis XIV style. Realistically carved fruit and leaf motifs, a variety of woodland animals, figures from mythology, and sinuous curves crowded together on table legs and chair arms. A parlor filled with the dark, heavy pieces—often upholstered in fine needlepoint—became a formal setting for guests dressed in voluminous satin and velvet, a place to see and be seen.

lands and broad fields in the Bombay Hook Refuge. The farmhouse, with quarters for servants and slaves, has remained unaltered in appearance. It is a private residence, but is open for tours on weekends in the spring and fall 2–5 P.M. Call 302/653-6872 for dates.

Harrington

Most recognized as home of the Delaware State Fair, the small town of Harrington has a few other sites of note. The **Messick Agricultural Museum,** Route 14W on Vernon Road, 302/ 398-3729, mostly displays the shiny green-and-gold equipment of the John Deere Company (the museum is in the warehouse of a farm-equipment company). It's open Mon.–Fri. and by appointment on weekends. The **Harrington**

Museum, 110 Fleming St., 302/398-9617, features local history; it's open the third Saturday of each month or by appointment; donations appreciated. **Harrington Railroad Museum,** Clark and Hanley Streets, 302/398-9617, is open the third Saturday each month and by request. It has a railroad car to explore and exhibits on train lore. Free.

For fans of gaming, Harrington is also home to **Midway Slots,** Delaware State Fairgrounds, U.S. 13, 888/88-SLOTS (888/887-5687). Midway also features harness horse racing in the autumn.

Barratt's Chapel and Museum

The "Cradle of Methodism," Barratt's Chapel was the site of the organization of the Methodist Episcopal Church in the United States. In 1780, Phillip Barratt donated land to the Methodist Society. John Wesley ordained America's first two Methodist clergymen, Dr. Thomas Coke and Rev. Richard Whatcoat, and in 1784, they administered the first American Methodist services in Barratt's Chapel. The simple brick building with its traditional Georgian architecture is one of the oldest houses of worship still extant in America. The museum features artifacts from the founding of Methodism in Delaware and an archival collection of memorabilia. The complex is one mile north of Frederica on U.S. 113, 302/335-5544. It's open on weekends, 1:30–4:30 P.M., and by appointment. Free.

KILLENS POND STATE PARK

Centrally located in the heart of Kent County, Killens Pond State Park, 5025 Killens Pond Rd., Felton, 302/284-4526, has something for everyone. The park's centerpiece is a 66-acre millpond, which was established in the late 1700s. Prior to the pond's creation, the Murderkill River and surrounding hardwood forest were sites of several Native American homes and hunting camps. Killens Pond became a state park in 1965. Killens Pond Water Park, a sort of super swimming pool, offers resort entertainment in a serene, natural setting.

Open year-round, the park's campground and cabins are popular retreats in every season. Play-

ground equipment and picnic areas are available, and four pavilions can be reserved for larger group events. A number of recreational programs are conducted during the summer, and autumn hayrides—the best way to view vivid fall foliage—are available by reservation after Labor Day through mid-November.

Hiking, Running, Biking: Hiking trails and a cross-country running course wind through several different native plant and animal habitats. The Ice Storm Trail gives hikers a chance to observe the forest's recovery from the devastating ice storms that struck the area in 1994. A bike path from U.S. 13 to the main entrance provides a leisurely passage into and out of the park.

Playing Fields: Game courts and ball fields are available to those with team play in mind, and an 18-hole disc golf course challenges players as well.

Boating: Canoes, rowboats, and pedal boats can be rented during the summer. A narrated pontoon boat tour of the pond is offered on summer weekends and holidays. The Murderkill River Canoe Trail provides a challenge for the more adventurous paddler.

Fishing: The pond is home to largemouth bass, catfish, carp, perch, crappie, bluegill, and pickerel.

Swimming: The Killens Pond Water Park is more than a pool; its innovatively designed zero-depth entrance makes getting in and out easy, and it also features three lap lanes along with interactive water features such as the Floating Lily Pad Fun Walk. Two 27-foot-high, 205-foot-long twisting and turning waterslides end in a specially designed splash pool. At the tot pool and tot lot, bubblers, ground water jets, small slides, and a poolside water play system give smaller visitors lots of fun on a warm summer's day. There's a swim shop and food concession nearby.

Overnight Facilities: The park offers 59 campsites with water and electric hookups accommodating both tents and recreational vehicles, 17 primitive tent campsites, and 10 cabins. One of the cabins, the Pond View Cottage, is a deluxe model with extra amenities and a view of the pond. Campsites are on a first-come, first-served basis, but reservations for cabins are accepted up to 120 days prior to the date of arrival. From Memorial Day weekend to Labor Day weekend, the park takes reservations for full-week rentals only. The cabins sleep four and feature an efficiency kitchen with an eating area, bedroom, bath with shower, air-conditioning, and heat. A picnic table, grill, and porch are located outside. Subject to availability, cabin rentals include the use of a canoe and rowboats. For reservations, call the park office at 302/284-4526.

DOVER AND ENVIRONS

Dover

Dover, the state capital, features several attractions within walking distance of the Delaware State Visitors Center, 406 Federal St. and Bank Lane, 302/739-4266, in the middle of town. The visitors center offers all the information you could ever want about the state; in back of the information desk is a store loaded with tempting Delaware souvenirs.

The **Sewell C. Biggs Museum of American Art,** 302/674-2111, is upstairs from the visitors center, accessed by a door near the information desk. The collection strongly emphasizes art from Delaware and the Delaware River Valley, including many of its illustrators; portraitist Charles Willson Peale, Hudson River School landscape painters Thomas Cole and Albert Bierstadt, and impressionist Robert Reid are also represented. The galleries contain a variety of sculptural pieces, porcelain, American-made silver, furniture, clocks, and an exhibit of paintings and book illustrations by Frank Schoonover from the golden age of publishing. The museum is open Wed.–Sat. 10 A.M.–4 P.M., Sunday 1:30–4:30 P.M. It's an excellent pastime, especially considering admission is free, though donations are accepted.

The **Meeting House Galleries I and II,** 316 S. Governor's Ave., 302 739-4266, are two old church buildings that have been converted to museums. Gallery I displays the archaeological history of Delaware through pictures and a mock burial site. Gallery II focuses on the state's small towns and more recent history, with a re-creation of an old print shop and an antique let-

terbox from a country post office. Ask to hear the "Grand Harmonica," a set of glass goblets that ring to individual notes when touched. The stained-glass windows in this former church are especially beautiful in the late afternoon. The galleries are open Tues.–Sat. 10 A.M.–3:30 P.M.; admission is free, and donations are accepted.

A truly unique collection, the **Johnson Victrola Museum,** Bank Lane and New Street behind the Meeting House Galleries, 302/739-4266, is a tribute to Delawarean Eldridge Reeves Johnson, who founded the Victor Talking Machine Company in 1901. The museum, which was greatly expanded in 1998, features a 1920s Victrola dealer's store complete with a variety of talking machines and early records. Photographs and memorabilia of recording artists from the era are on display, and Victor recordings play on modern and antique equipment. The original oil painting of Nipper, listening to his master's voice, is also on display.

The **State House** was built in 1792 as the Delaware Capitol building. It faces Dover's central green, a public area designated by William Penn in 1683. The interior of the building contains a courtroom and an exhibit on the building's history; on the ceiling, visitors can view the sunflower (base of the central chandelier) that is the symbol of Delaware's State Museums. The State House is open Tues.–Sat. 10 A.M.–4:30 P.M., Sunday 1:30–4:30 P.M. Free.

Amish Country Auto/Bike Tour

The Amish community around Dover is a fairly recent development. Unlike the colonial farms of eastern Pennsylvania, central Delaware's Amish families moved to the area from California and Indiana during the Great Depression when land prices were severely depressed. Old Order Amish, an ultraconservative branch of the Christian Mennonite sect, appear to have rejected—and perhaps transcended—the modern world. Amish distinguish themselves from the communities around them by conservative dress, the practice of traditional religious worship, adoption of strict codes of behavior, and disavowal of telephones, cars, electricity, government, advanced schooling, and many other "modern" aspects of life.

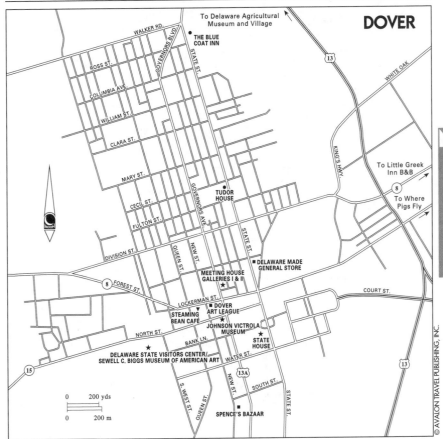

DOVER

To Delaware Agricultural Museum and Village

THE BLUE COAT INN

WALKER RD.

GOVERNORS BLVD.

STATE ST.

ROSS ST.

COLUMBIA AVE.

WILLIAM ST.

CLARA ST.

MARY ST.

CECIL ST.

FULTON ST.

DIVISION ST.

FOREST ST.

LOCKERMAN ST.

NORTH ST.

BANK LN.

WATER ST.

S. WEST ST.

QUEEN ST.

NEW ST.

SOUTH ST.

STATE ST.

GOVERNORS AVE.

QUEEN ST.

NEW ST.

STATE ST.

WHITE OAK

KING'S HWY

To Little Greek Inn B&B

To Where Pigs Fly

COURT ST.

TUDOR HOUSE

DELAWARE MADE GENERAL STORE

MEETING HOUSE GALLERIES I & II

DOVER ART LEAGUE

STEAMING BEAN CAFE

JOHNSON VICTROLA MUSEUM

STATE HOUSE

DELAWARE STATE VISITORS CENTER/ SEWELL C. BIGGS MUSEUM OF AMERICAN ART

SPENCE'S BAZAAR

0   200 yds
0   200 m

CENTRAL DELAWARE

© AVALON TRAVEL PUBLISHING, INC.

Old Order Amish retain a visible and powerful presence throughout central Delaware.

All Amish and Mennonites trace their roots to the Anabaptist ("new birth") movement in Switzerland in 1525, an offshoot of the Protestant Reformation. Toward the end of the 17th century, the Anabaptist movement split over several issues, chiefly the practice of "shunning": social ostracism of community members for disobedience. Old Order Amish, a sect dwelling primarily in the Alsace region of France, chose to continue the practice. Anabaptists separated into two main camps, the Amish and the more liberal Mennonites. Since the original schism, each of the main branches has split many times. Almost obliterated in their European homeland, the Amish have flourished in the New World. One thing is true of all Amish—the religious basis of their lives demands that they be aware of the larger world, but not participate in it.

Amish who reside around Dover are unselfconscious and comfortable in their worldly surroundings. The area west of Dover consists of numerous Amish farms; buggies on back roads and steam-powered farm equipment are common. Conservatively dressed men in their black felt or straw hats, and women with long skirts and capped hair, pick up basketfuls of produce at local stores. The loop represented by this tour is only a small portion of the Amish community.

INSPIRATION

Felix Darley may have been the first artist/illustrator in Delaware to gain national fame, but he wasn't the most well known (see the special topic "A Maker of Pictures," Northern Delaware chapter). In the last years of the 20th century, Wilmington resident Howard Pyle often illustrated stories and nonfiction work for *Harper's Monthly*, and was celebrated for his ability to bring historic subjects to life. Pyle's talent was no accident; he researched each illustration meticulously, making sure that the garments worn by a colonial tradesman—and the tack on his horse—was historically accurate. Pyle founded the Brandywine school of painting, noted for its dreamy, luminous backgrounds portraying "natural" sites and glowing, surreal figures. His teaching is readily evident in the work of his student, Maxfield Parrish.

Another of Pyle's famous students, N. C. Wyeth, found fame for his book illustrations. *Treasure Island* is one of several books illustrated by Wyeth that bring big prices from collectors.

In the early 1900s, Ethel Pennewill Brown became the most successful American illustrator of her day at a time when a woman earning a living as an artist was a rarity. In her early 20s, she overcame social, financial, and geographic barriers to attend the prestigious Art Students League of New York. She then studied with Howard Pyle at his studio in Wilmington. Ethel Brown was one of Pyle's first female students.

Later, she went to France and studied and exhibited in Paris. Brown appreciated the modern style of Matisse and Picasso, but preferred a more realistic style, similar to that of another American expatriate, Mary Cassatt of Pittsburgh.

While a student, Brown worked as an illustrator, and as her popularity grew, her work appeared in major magazines in the early 1920s, such as *Good Housekeeping, Harper's Bazaar,* and *Harper's Monthly.* She also illustrated books, notably the Betty Baird series and works by Louisa May Alcott.

At the age of 45, Brown married fellow Delaware artist William Leach, and the couple settled in Frederica. She then turned from illustration to serious painting. Ethel P. B. Leach played a pivotal role in the creation of the Rehoboth Art League in Rehoboth Beach, and generously encouraged the work of other artists throughout her life. Her paintings include landscapes of Delaware and numerous portraits.

Much of the farmland in eastern and southern Kent County is farmed by Amish or Mennonites, and is recognizable by the lack of motorized vehicles and phone and power lines.

This easy 16-mile round-trip tour starts in downtown Dover on the corner of Loockerman (LAHK-er-mehn) and Queen Streets. All distances are approximate. Loockerman becomes Forest Avenue/Route 8; follow the signs for Route 8 west out of town and stay on the road until the intersection of Rose Valley School Road, in less than five miles. **Byler's Country Store,** a bulk market, is on the corner, and you may see a buggy or two parked outside. Turn left (south) on Rose Valley School Road. Look for the Amish School with its his-and-hers outhouses. For a shorter trip, continue on Rose Valley School Road to Hazlettville

Road and return to Dover, as below. Otherwise, look for the intersection of Yoder Drive (.75 mile south of Route 8) and turn right onto it (west). Follow Yoder about two miles to Pearsons Corner Road and turn left (south). In little over a mile, you'll come to the intersection of Hazlettville Road; turn left (east). Dover is about seven miles away; you'll pass **Eden Hill Farm,** a nursery with a U-pick pumpkin patch in the autumn. Once in Dover, make a left on Queen to return to the start.

As with anywhere else, don't trespass on private property, nor photograph people without permission; many, though not all, consider a photograph in which they may be identified as a "graven image" or a sign of vanity, and therefore a violation of biblical precepts—not to mention a major invasion of privacy.

Delaware Agricultural Museum and Village

A wide variety of displays beyond old farm equipment makes this museum well worthwhile—not to discount the equipment, much of which is remarkable for its size, decoration, or weirdness of function. The museum offers a number of farm buildings to explore, as well as farm-related professional art exhibits and programs and special events that change regularly. One of the most amusing permanent offerings is a collection of woodcarvings by Jehu Camper. The rustic carvings depict stories and scenes of farm life around the turn of the 19th century. Camper, who was born in nearby Harrington and died in 1989, gave advice to others who might be interested in "whittlin'": "The first thing you do is get yourself a piece of wood . . . then get yourself some band-aids and a few cuss words and start in." The museum is continually expanding, and is enjoyable for all ages. Tots go for the live chickens pecking around the chicken industry exhibit, and the playroom, where they can "drive" an Amish buggy to market; seniors will be reminded that agriculture was once a way of life rather than big business. The museum is on U.S. 13 at State Street, 866 N. Du Pont Hwy., Dover, 302/734-1618. It's open Jan.–Mar., Mon.–Fri. 10 A.M.–4 P.M.; Apr.–Dec., Tues.–Sat. 10 A.M.–4 P.M., Sunday 1–4 P.M. Admission is $5.

The Air Mobility Command Museum

To get to this museum on Dover Air Force Base, visitors must enter from Route 9 south of the base through the fenced entrance. When the base is on alert, the museum may not be open to the public. It's one of the most unique collections anywhere: inside the main hangar, restored airplanes from all phases of military use and history glimmer brightly; outside, more airplanes, including racy jet fighters and huge transports, are open to explore. Roaring jets stationed at the base maneuver overhead, then land in the airfield nearby. Military personnel sometimes staff the cockpits and answer questions about modern flying and the Air Force's air mobility command, in the business of moving men and equipment all over the world.

The museum features an exhibit on WASPS, World War II women pilots who flew transport. The women pilots were organized at the New Castle Air Base; 25,000 applied for the job, and 916 made it through training. Of these, 38 died in service. Because WASPS performed ferrying services, they were never military personnel, and the families of women who died were never compensated. WASPS were finally granted veteran status in 1979. The museum also features a number of rare and unusual aircraft: a C-47 Gooney Bird used in the D-Day troop drop, an O-2A used for rescue in Vietnam, and the last C-54M

© JOANNE MILLER

Air Mobility Command Museum, Dover

CENTRAL DELAWARE

CENTRAL DELAWARE

THUNDER ROAD

Stock car racing is one of America's fastest-growing spectator sports. Since 1991, attendance at races affiliated with NASCAR (National Association for Stock Car Auto Racing) has grown by 70 percent. In 2003, 200,000 people attended the 45th annual Daytona 500 in Florida, and television polls showed that an additional 29.4 million viewers tuned into some part of the race. The Daytona 500 is part of the Winston Cup, a 33-race series—and one of many public races on tracks all over the East Coast.

Nearly half of all stock car racing fans are women. Fans attribute the popularity of the sport to everything from the drama of "cautions" (track accidents) to the fact that fans have two things to get excited about: the personalities of the racers and their vehicles. One speedway promoter referred to this combination as "mechathletes"—perhaps in the future, the two will join permanently to form a *Robocop*-style competitor. Fans also spend a great deal of time inspecting and appreciating the mechanical accessories that are a necessity of the sport: the race cars, their tires and engines; the truck-like rigs that tow them; and the colorful custom buses that house the top drivers. In fact, most fans travel the stock car circuit in their own mechanical mini-versions of home: before each race, the lots are full of motorhomes, trucks, and travel trailers.

Stock car racing was born on the dirt roads of southeastern America after the second World War; the predecessors of today's racers might have been back-country bootleggers hauling their wares to market in the first supercharged versions of street cars. Though today many commercial racetracks are paved, the slick clay soil of the Piedmont Plateau that stretches between the Appalachian Mountains to the Atlantic Ocean, from New York to Alabama, continues to provide some of the best racing dirt in the world. Both Delaware and Maryland have dirt tracks of varying sizes. Dover Downs International Speedway in Delaware hosts one of the Winston Cup races along with slot machines and harness horse racing.

The cars themselves, standard-issue street cars on the outside, are driven by 500-horsepower engines with a top speed of nearly 200 miles per hour. NASCAR rule makers continually come up with technical impediments to slow the cars down, and racing teams spend enormous amounts of time and money to circumvent them—secrecy is as tight as a war room, but leaks are common, as are private and public disagreements both on and off the raceway.

Race car driving is labor-intensive. NASCAR crews work 12-hour days, six days a week, then race on Sunday. On smaller tracks, local racers often have full-time jobs but spend their evenings in the garage. Most winnings are poured back into improving the vehicle. Anyone who opts for a career in racing needs sponsorship, and stock-car racing has been given an enormous boost by corporate sponsors. Large corporations have found that the loyalty of racing fans for their heroes extends to the products whose logos cover the cars. The first of these was R. J. Reynolds, the tobacco giant, which sponsors the Winston Cup, among other events.

Stock-car racers have reached nearly godlike popularity. Four-color images of NASCAR Winston Cup 2000 champion Bobby Labonte, 2003 Daytona 500 winner Michael Waltrip, and other road warriors grace T-shirts, baseball caps, trading cards, soft drink machines, and a host of other items. If stock car racing hasn't thundered into a town near you, it's only a matter of time.

in existence, used to haul coal during the Berlin airlift. The Dover Air Force Base is on U.S. 113, two miles south of Dover, 302/677-3376. It's open Mon.–Sat., 9 A.M.–4 P.M. There is no admission charge.

John Dickinson Mansion and Plantation

This plantation, Kitts Hummock Road off U.S. 113, six miles south of Dover, 302/739-3277, is a reconstructed farm complex built in the mid-1700s by Samuel Dickinson. His son, John Dickinson, a framer and signer of the U.S. Constitution, grew up on the plantation and supported the farm through his work as a lawyer. His "Letters from a Pennsylvania Farmer," published in major newspapers of the day, stated his opposition to British taxation of the colonies.

The property contains a Georgian mansion, a log building similar to the original slave's quarters (Dickinson's slaves were manumitted in 1787), and all the outbuildings necessary to maintain a self-contained plantation lifestyle. Costumed interpreters guide visitors through plantation life during Revolutionary times. The oddly named St. Jones River borders the plantation; apparently, Mr. Jones, an early landowner, designated the waterway as the "stream of Jones." Since all deeds and maps were hand-lettered in the early 1700s, the term was abbreviated to "str. of Jones," which eventually became St. Jones. The plantation is open Tues.–Sat. 10 A.M.–3:30 P.M. and Sunday 1:30–4:30 P.M. Admission is free.

Dover Downs

Dover's hot spot, the Downs, U.S. 13, 302/674-4600, features the "Monster Mile" of car racing challenges, a steeply banked (24 degree) track that hosts the NASCAR Winston Cup twice each year. When professionals aren't using the track, racing wannabes can test their mettle by signing up for **Monster Racing Excitement,** 800/GO-TO-WIN (800/468-6946). For $75, a racing instructor will take you around the track four laps in a Winston Cup racing car or truck— for $300 and up, you can drive the Monster yourself. Stock car racing takes place late spring and late fall.

November through April brings on the ponies for harness racing and simulcasts. Call Dover Downs, 800/711-5882, for entries and results, or visit the website at www.doverdowns.com.

Dover Downs' video lottery gaming terminals—better known as slots—are available every day. The casino is a mini–Las Vegas with a Sistine Chapel–like ceiling that gives the illusion of being outdoors on a fresh spring day. Otherwise, it's full of eau de gambling: the throaty pitch of possibility tempered by the sugary scent of exotic drinks. The former third element, cigarette smoke, is no longer allowed in public places. The slots draw a truly mixed crowd, a few of whom look like they should be saving their quarters in a coffee can rather than donating to a one-armed bandit—er, a video lottery gaming terminal. But Lady Luck may be electronically hovering over your Stampede, Piggy Bankin', or Lucky Ladies machine, who knows? Two restaurants, the Garden Café, which serves decent meals for around $10 and often has good entertainment at night, and the Buffet, a real bargain at $7.50 for lunch and $9 for dinner combined with a fine view of the track, are worthwhile places to stop for a meal.

Shopping

In addition to the bulk market mentioned in the Dover Amish Country Tour, **Spence's Bazaar,** South and New Streets, Dover, 302/734-3441, is a fun place to browse for both food and junque. It's a combination produce market, auction, and flea market; the Amish community is well represented. The bazaar operates on Tuesday and Friday.

The **Delaware Made General Store,** in the historic John Bullen House, 214 S. State St., Dover, 302/736-1419, is a showcase of gifts from many talented Delaware craftspeople. The shop sells souvenirs, pottery, tinware, art, candy, jams, cards, antiques and collectibles, and much more.

Loockerman Street, between S. Queen and S. State Streets, features a stroll's worth of shops and cafés. One place of note is the **Dover Art League,** 21 Loockerman St., a sales gallery that displays juried work of local artists.

FESTIVALS AND EVENTS

June

Separation Day in old New Castle celebrates Delaware's separation from Pennsylvania with a fair and fireworks. 302/322-9802.

July/August

One hundred antique dealers trot out their wares at the **Battery Park Antique Show** in New Castle. 800/758-1550.

The tiny town of Delaware City holds a **Town-Wide Yard Sale** for those who just can't resist a bargain. 302/823-1890.

September/October

The Delaware Agricultural Museum and Village present the **Demarvalous Feast.** 302/734-1618.

Delaware's governor hauls the skeletons out of the closet for the **Governor's Annual Haunted House,** held in Woodburn. 302/739-5656.

November/December

Miniature farmers will enjoy the **Toy Tractor Show and Sale** at the Delaware Agricultural Museum in Dover. 302/734-1618.

Caroling on the Green (302/736-7050) and a **Candlelight Tour of Homes** (302/653-2355) are wonderful ways to celebrate the season in Dover.

Accommodations

Rose Tower Bed & Breakfast, 228 E. Camden-Wyoming Ave., Camden, 302/698-9033, is a spacious home built in 1807 that is now listed on the National Register of Historic Places. Jane and Ed Folz have decorated the rooms in the style of the historic houses of Odessa. Though the house is on the main street of the old section of Camden, it's very quiet and peaceful, and the rose garden in bloom is a delight to behold. Each of the rooms has a private bath, and reservations are necessary. Rates range from $76–120.

Also recommended: the **Little Creek Inn B&B,** 2623 N. Little Creek Rd., Dover, 302/730-1300, www.littlecreekinn.com. Five rooms, all with baths, plus down pillows and comforters, in an 1860 Italianate-style home with swimming pool. Rooms come with a full breakfast. Rates range $90–195.

Food

The Blue Coat Inn, 800 N. State St., 302/674-1776, is one of Dover's finest dining establishments and an old favorite of the town's cognoscenti. The view over Silver Lake at sunset

is spellbinding. The setting is elegant, and prices on the seafood/beef/chicken menu average $18.

The **Steaming Bean Café,** 25 West Loockerman St., 302/734-2526, is an excellent place to stop for a cappuccino or light lunch ($5).

Where Pigs Fly, 617 E. Loockerman St., Dover, 302/678-0586, is a great place to get huge helpings of messy barbecue for lunch or dinner. Sandwiches and platters are priced $5–12.

Sambo's Tavern, Front Street, Leipsic, 302/674-9724, has the best crab cakes in central Delaware. Am I prejudiced? You bet! In the constant search for creamy, crusty, crabby crab cakes, Sambo's wins, claws down. This comfortable roadhouse on the water is open Mon.–Sat. 11 A.M.–10:30 P.M.; the bar opens earlier and closes later. Since Sambo's is a tavern, no one under 21 is admitted. Seafood platters average $10, and seafood is served only in season.

INFORMATION

For more information, contact Kent County Tourism, P.O. Box 576, Dover, DE 19903, 800/233-KENT (800/233-5368).

Southern Delaware

Any parent who has ever found a rusted toy automobile buried in the grass or a bent sand bucket on the beach knows that objects like these can be among the powerful things in the world. They can summon up in an instant, in colors stronger than life, the whole of childhood at its happiest.

Editor's note, *"The Timeless House of Children's Games,"* Sports Illustrated Magazine, *1960*

For lovers of sea and sand, the southern shore *is* Delaware. Cape Henlopen and Delaware Seashore draw the largest number of visitors in the state, surpassing all other attractions. Each resort town is unique: Rehoboth Beach and Lewes,

Fenwick Island and Bethany Beach each attract aficionados for different reasons. However, southern Delaware is far more than the beaches. Quiet historic towns like Laurel, Seaford, and Blades, once known for shipbuilding, provide a quaint respite from grit and glare. Prime Hook National Wildlife Refuge affords a glimpse into a rare ecological system, one of the busiest stops on the Atlantic flyway.

Speaking of birds, southern Delaware is also a major agricultural area; it contains the largest population of broiler chickens on the Delmarva Peninsula. More in evidence, though, are the bounty of fruits and vegetables the region produces. In the summer, interior villages burst with roadside stands.

© JOANNE MILLER

Woodland Ferry

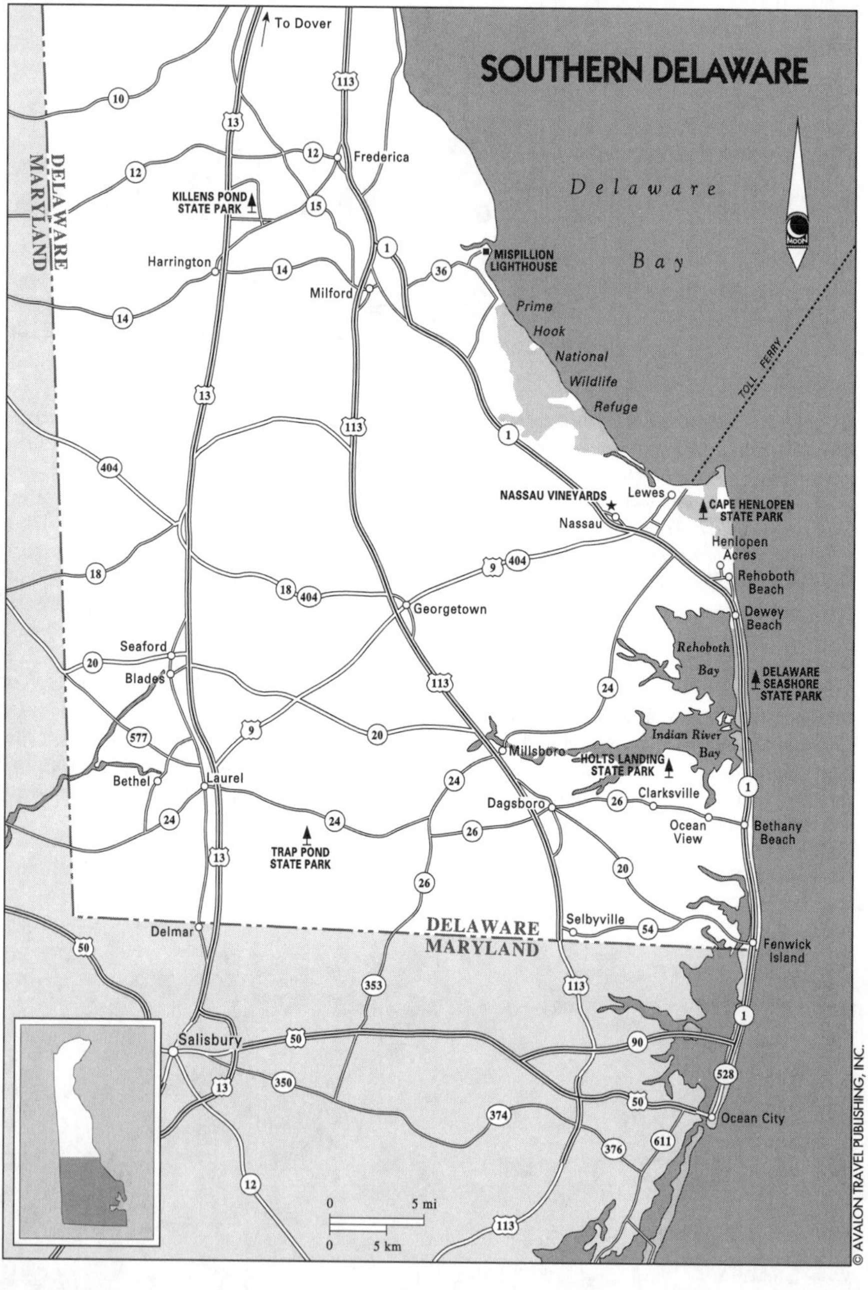

SOUTHERN DELAWARE

To Dover

113

10

13

12

Frederica

12

DELAWARE
MARYLAND

KILLENS POND
STATE PARK

15

Harrington

14

Milford

36

MISPILLION
LIGHTHOUSE

Delaware

Bay

Prime

Hook

National

Wildlife

Refuge

14

13

404

1

18

113

NASSAU VINEYARDS

Lewes

CAPE HENLOPEN
STATE PARK

Nassau

Henlopen
Acres

9 404

404 18

Rehoboth
Beach

Georgetown

Dewey
Beach

Seaford

113

*Rehoboth
Bay*

20

Blades

24

DELAWARE
SEASHORE
STATE PARK

577

9

20

*Indian River
Bay*

Bethel

Laurel

Millsboro

HOLTS LANDING
STATE PARK

24

24

Dagsboro

26

Clarksville

1

Ocean
View

Bethany
Beach

24

26

20

TRAP POND
STATE PARK

13

26

Selbyville

54

Delmar

DELAWARE
MARYLAND

Fenwick
Island

50

353

113

1

Salisbury

50

90

528

13

350

50

Ocean City

374

12

611

376

113

0   5 mi

0   5 km

© AVALON TRAVEL PUBLISHING, INC.

TOLL FERRY

All year, antique hunters can find a surfeit of choices and equally choice scenery along the back roads. Though beach towns tend to be seasonal, the tourist "year" is expanding from May well into November. The least-crowded time to visit is during the spring and after Labor Day. The beaches are spectacularly uncrowded, and, especially in the fall, the water and weather are warm and welcoming.

PRIME HOOK NATIONAL WILDLIFE REFUGE

This refuge, transected by four state highways, was established in 1963 to preserve coastal wetland for migratory waterfowl. Most of the 8,817-acre refuge is marshland, and water levels are manipulated through a system of dikes and water control structures to stimulate growth of plants used by wildlife. As in Bombay Hook (Central Delaware), the upland fields are managed under an agreement with local farmers who leave a portion of their crops in the field to provide supplemental food and cover.

© JOANNE MILLER

Mispillion Lighthouse

All tidal waterways and enclosed ponds are open to **sportfishing; hunting** is permitted within season. Special regulations apply for all hunters: more information is available from the refuge headquarters, c/o Refuge Manager, Prime Hook National Wildlife Refuge, RD3, Box 195, Milton, DE 19968, 302/684-8419.

Canoeing and boating enthusiasts have more than 15 miles of streams and ditches to explore. Several boat-launching ramps are available (maps may be requested from the refuge headquarters).

Two trails are open for **hiking, photography, and wildlife observation.**

The **Mispillion Lighthouse** is the oldest surviving wood lighthouse in Delaware—and the lack of public or private interest in preserving the structure is evident. Located north of Prime Hook National Wildlife Refuge near Slaughter Beach off Route 36 on Lighthouse Road, the frail lighthouse is only a few feet away from the encroaching bay. Riprap, broken concrete slabs reinforced with rebar, line the edges of the water in an attempt to hold back the insistent power of erosion.

LEWES

The charming town of Lewes (LOO-iss) provides a redoubt from the nearby sun-and-fun frenzy of Rehoboth. Many visitors to the area prefer to stay in this quiet town and visit the local small beach or larger beaches during the day. The town also features sophisticated restaurants, shopping, and a healthy dose of history. Lewes, "the first town in the first state," was the site of the original settlement in Delaware in 1631, named Zwaanendael (Valley of the Swans).

The **De Vries Monument,** Pilottown Road, commemorates the Dutch West India colony that existed here until cultural misunderstandings between the Dutch and Native Americans of the area culminated in the extermination of the Europeans by the locals. Apparently, a tribesman had pried the metal shield off the front of the fort because he liked the unicorn symbol on it. When the Dutch traders complained, the chief had the "thief" killed and sent his head to the leader of the Dutchmen. The Dutch were aghast at the severity of the penalty, and dressed down the chief for his action. Deeply insulted that their kinsman had made restitution with his life and it was still unacceptable, the thief's relatives massacred the encampment. Who can understand these hard-to-please Europeans?

The **Zwaanendael Museum,** Kings Highway and Savannah Road, 302/645-1148, tells the story of the early encampment, and has a copy of the goofy-looking red unicorn that proved such a fatal attraction (the unicorn is the symbol of the town of Hoorn in the Netherlands, the origin of most of the early Dutch traders). The museum itself, built in 1931, is a striking replica of the Town Hall of Hoorn. In addition, the museum features changing exhibits on other historical aspects of the area. One such exhibit delved into the area's maritime connections, including information on *slops* (regulation British sailors clothing), *long toggies* (sailors in civilian clothing—getting a set of slops was imperative for new sailors), and *Welsh wigs* (worsted knit caps worn by sailors). The Zwaa-

Zwaanendael Museum

nendael is open Tues.–Sat. 10 A.M.–4:30 P.M., Sunday 1:30–4:30 P.M. Donations are welcomed.

Lewes Historical Complex

The town's historical society maintains a group of restored buildings, many of which were moved from other areas. The first of these is the **Burton-Ingram House,** Shipcarpenter and 3rd Streets; it features hand-hewn timbers and cypress shingles (drawn from fallen trees in the Pocomoke cypress swamp that once covered the area), and a cellar made from ship's ballast stones. The **Rabbit's Ferry House,** 3rd Street, serves as the visitor's center; the building consists of an early-18th-century farmhouse, expanded into a second room in later years.

The **Thompson Country Store,** 3rd Street, has many of its original appointments, and has remained essentially the same as when it operated full-time from 1888–1962. The **Ellegood House** behind the country store contains the historical society's excellent gift shop, full of handcrafted items. Also behind the country store, the **Early Plank House** is an example of a Swedish-type settler's cabin.

The **Doctor's Office,** near the Plank House, is a handsome Greek Revival structure built around 1850. It has been outfitted as a late-19th-century doctor's office. The **Hiram R. Burton House,** 2nd Street and Shipcarpenter Square, was the home of Hiram Burton, Lewes physician, president of the Medical Society of Delaware, a Queen Anne's Railroad director, and a member of Congress in 1904; a Delaware history reading room is on the premises.

The **Ryves Holt House,** 2nd and Mulberry Streets, is believed to be the oldest house in the state. Once a colonial inn, the building was dated to 1665 through core samples of the structure.

Self-guided tours of these historic buildings originate at the Rabbit's Ferry House. The buildings are open mid-June–Labor Day, Tues.–Fri. 11 A.M.–4 P.M., Saturday 10 A.M.–1 P.M. Admission is $6.

The **Cannonball House Marine Museum,** Front and Bank Streets, is also administered by the historic society. So named because it was struck by a cannonball during the bombardment of Lewes by the British during the War of 1812, the museum houses an ever-increasing number of nautical exhibits, including model sailing ships and artifacts. The Cannonball House is open in summer Mon.–Sat. 10 A.M.–4 P.M. This museum is included in the tour ticket of the historic complex. For more information, call Lewes Historical Society, 110 Shipcarpenter St., 302/645-7670.

Recreation

In addition to lolling about the pretty public beach on Cape Henlopen Drive, visitors can join a sportfishing expedition aboard one of the many party boats docked at **Anglers Marina** on An-

gler's Road. Dolphin and whale-watching cruises are also available.

The Cape May–Lewes Ferry leaves daily from the dock on Cape Henlopen Drive. The 70-minute trip across Delaware Bay ends in the Victorian town of Cape May, New Jersey. A farmer's market is held at the ferry landing during the summer. During the week, the ferry leaves Lewes at 8 A.M., 9:15 A.M., 11:15 A.M., 12:45 P.M., 2:45 P.M., 4:15 P.M., and 7:45 P.M., with extended hours on weekends and June–Sept. Foot passengers pay $6–8 (less for children under 5), and vehicle and driver pay $18–25 (passengers pay the same as foot passengers). Bicycles are an additional $6–8. For reservations, call

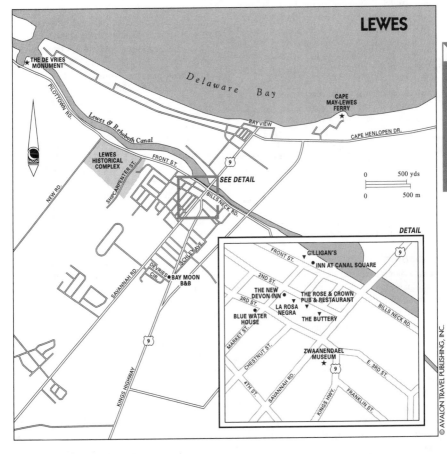

SOUTHERN DELAWARE

© AVALON TRAVEL PUBLISHING, INC.

HOUSES IN MOTION

The uprooting of entire buildings from their foundations and subsequent transportation to a new location has long been practiced in Sussex County. More than 85 homes and commercial structures were built and put to use many miles from Lewes before they came to rest in that town. One early instance was the 1825 relocation of the Burton homestead from the town of Angola to Savannah Road near the canal bridge. The old Methodist Meeting House, corner of Mulberry and 3rd Streets, was moved three times.

So common was the movement of houses that in 1983, a pair of entrepreneurs created Shipcarpenter Square in Lewes, an 11-acre community of 38 buildings that were brought to the site from within a 40-mile radius and then restored. Lewes's second-largest enclave of "scooter houses" (moved dwellings) belongs to the Lewes Historical Society: seven of the eight buildings (the Ryves Holt House, on 2nd Street, is in its original location) have been transported. The Doctor's Office is on its fifth site.

Early scooter houses were pulled by oxen on skids; today, homes can still be seen rolling down the road on tractor-trailers. Modern times have brought changes, though; it's often necessary to dismantle a building to allow passage under overhead utility wires.

800/64-FERRY (800/643-3779); it's a good idea to arrive 30 minutes before departure.

Shopping

A two-block-long section of **Second Street** off Savannah Street is the shopping district in Lewes, with a number of upscale clothing, antique, and collectible shops. Blown glass, oriental rugs, and house and garden items are plentiful. A few shops are seasonal, but most are open year-round. Notable stops are **2nd St. Popcorn,** which features exquisite candied apples including old-fashioned red cinnamon, Heavenly Hash (chocolate, marshmallows, and walnuts), and gooey caramel; **Gerties Greengrocer** sells organic produce; **Books by the Bay** features publications with a local twist, and **King's Ice Cream** is the place for frozen treats.

A block away on 3rd Street, **Preservation Forge,** an old-fashioned forge complete with blacksmith, sells metal items.

Accommodations

The New Devon Inn, downtown at 2nd and Market Streets, 302/645-6466, was built in 1926, and has been thoroughly updated. It's open all year. Rooms run $50–130 depending on day and season; some suites are available, $90–170.

Also open all year, the **Inn at Canal Square,** 122 Market St., 302/644-3377 or 888/644-1911, innatcanalsquare@ce.net, offers the most modern lodgings in town, with 19 spacious suite rooms and full baths. All have a water view, and 17 rooms have private balconies. A modest continental breakfast is served. The inn offers specials and packages, especially during the Lewes Jazz Festival, held the third weekend in October. The inn is closed Dec. 18–26. Rates vary with the season and location, from a low of $105 per night in winter to $250 in summer.

The **Bay Moon Bed and Breakfast,** 128 Kings Hwy., 302/644-1802 or 800/917-2307, is an older home that attracts guests from all over the world. Each of the three pleasant rooms has a full bath, and one is a deluxe suite with a parlor and deck. Innkeeper Pam Rizzo cooks up a sumptuous breakfast in the morning, and the inn is only a few blocks from Lewes's shopping and restaurants. The inn supplies guests with beach paraphernalia and ice for coolers. Rates are $115–150 per night.

The **Blue Water House,** 407 E. Market St., 302/645-7832 or 800/493-2080, www.lewesbeach.com/welcome2.htm, brings a touch of the Caribbean to its brightly colored exterior and four guest rooms, all with private bath. It caters to families, with rooms large enough for cots, and a variety of toys—boogie boards, bikes, towels, umbrellas, movies, and an open-air patio—to satisfy everyone. A hot breakfast is served in the morning. During the high season, May 26–Sept. 7, rates range $140–210, less in winter.

Food and Wine

The Buttery, in the Destiny House, 2nd and Savannah Streets, 302/645-7755, has a well-deserved reputation for fine dining. The bistro-like restaurant serves lunch, dinner, and Sunday brunch; prices average $10–28. They offer a $21 three-course prix fixe dinner between 5–6:30 P.M. daily.

Gilligan's, Front and Market Streets, 302/645-7866, is one of the most popular places to eat in town. The outside bar that fronts the channel is a meeting place for locals and visitors alike. The menu is American, featuring seafood, beef, and chicken; lunch dishes average $7, dinner entrées $20.

La Rosa Negra, 128 2nd St., 302/645-1980, is packed during the evenings with those who appreciate fine seafood-filled ravioli and Italian cuisine. It serves lunch and dinner during the summer, dinner only the rest of the year; prices average $16. La Rosa's desserts are baked on premises.

The Rose & Crown Pub and Restaurant, 108 2nd St., 302/645-2373, serves wonderful light pub food under a skylighted ceiling and features a lobster special on Thurs. from 5–6 P.M. They serve lunch and dinner; the bar crowd meets here at night, and the place gets boisterous and a little smoky. Prices average $8–15.

Here's something visitors don't expect to find: **Nassau Vineyards,** 36 Nassau Commons, 302/645-9463, bills itself as "The First Winery in the First State," and the wines, made from local grapes, are quite good. Winemaker Peg Raley was trained in France and Spain, and really knows her stuff. See for yourself—the vineyard has a wine tasting room, open Tues.–Sat. 11 A.M.–5 P.M., Sunday noon–5 P.M. Nassau Commons/Nassau Vineyards is located just off of Route 1, west of Lewes.

CAPE HENLOPEN STATE PARK

In 1682, when the current lands of the state of Delaware were granted to William Penn, he proclaimed Cape Henlopen and its natural resources were to be for the common usage of the citizens of Lewes and Sussex County, thus establishing some of the nation's first "public lands." Cape Henlopen's strategic location at the mouth of the Delaware Bay contributed to its importance in local shipping and military history.

The long-lamented Henlopen Lighthouse no longer helps to guide vessels through the treacherous bay waters (it blew down in a windstorm in the 1920s), but the two stone breakwater barriers off the point of the Cape, completed in 1869 and 1901, still form a safe harbor for boats during rough seas.

In 1941, the U.S. Army established a military base at Cape Henlopen. Bunkers and gun emplacements were camouflaged among the dunes, and concrete observation towers (one of Henlopen's notable sights) were built along the coast to spot enemy ships. In 1964, the Department of Defense declared 543 acres of the Cape lands as surplus property, and the State of Delaware established Cape Henlopen State Park.

In addition to expansive bay and ocean beaches, the 3,143-acre maritime park contains Gordon's Pond Wildlife Area, a unique saltwater impoundment. Along the coast, the Great Dune rises 80 feet above sea level, and further inland, "walking dunes" slowly move across the pine forests. A broad salt marsh stretches along the park's western boundary. The variety of habitats within the park makes it a valuable home to many species of birds, reptiles, and mammals, including threatened shorebirds.

The park also features a picnic pavilion, 19-pole disc golf course, and basketball courts. Winter hunting is permitted in some areas of the park; a hunting permit is required, and information can be obtained from the Park Office. Annual events such as the Kite Festival and the Halloween Spook Trail are family favorites. The park conducts a variety of entertaining recreational programs such as the annual Shoretalk series, outdoor concerts, seaside seining, and bird-watching. For more information on Cape Henlopen State Park, contact Park Headquarters, 42 Cape Henlopen Dr., Lewes, DE 19958, 302/645-8983.

The **Seaside Nature Center** offers environmental education programs and recreational activities year-round, and is a good place to stop for park information. Marine aquariums and displays there let visitors meet ocean creatures face to face. An auditorium for audiovisual programs and gift shop complete the attractions at this popular facility. Call for more information: 302/645-6852.

Hiking: Hiking trails and interpretive displays throughout the park help visitors to learn about the area's unique natural features. In addition, several World War II–era bunkers provide scenic overlooks, and one of the concrete observation towers has been renovated to provide a panoramic view of the cape.

Fishing: A quarter-mile-long pier provides convenient access to Delaware Bay. The bait and tackle concession at the pier offers fishing supplies and snack foods, and transportation along the pier is available for people with disabilities from Apr. 1–Oct. 31. Surf fishing is a year-round activity along the park's ocean beaches. Dune crossings allow pedestrian and vehicle access to the designated fishing areas. A surf fishing vehicle permit is required in order to drive onto the beach. Permits are available at the park office.

Swimming: Cape Henlopen's beaches attract thousands of visitors who enjoy ocean swimming and sunbathing. Two designated swimming beaches are guarded Memorial Day–Labor Day. The northern swimming area also features a modern bathhouse with showers, changing rooms, and a food concession. Umbrellas are available for rent during the summer.

Overnight Facilities: Pine-covered dunes surround 159 spacious sites, each with a water hookup. Camping is available Mar. 1–Nov. 30; call 877/98-PARKS (877/987-2757) for reservations.

Beach Plum Island Nature Preserve is a satellite of Cape Henlopen State Park. Located north of the city of Lewes, with vehicle access from Broadkill Beach, most of this 129-acre barrier island is protected to preserve habitat for native plant and animal species, but surf fishing and beachcombing are permitted along the Delaware Bay shore.

REHOBOTH BEACH AND DEWEY BEACH

If there ever was an archetypal beach town, Rehoboth is it. An endless boardwalk filled night and day with throngs of scantily clad humans, thrill rides, T-shirt booths, junk food, and miles of sugary sand, striped umbrellas, and roasting people. What distinguishes Rehoboth are its humble beginnings as a Methodist summer camp (Carey's Camp Meeting Ground is still in operation for revival meetings during the summer), and its death and resurrection. After World War II, Atlantic beach resorts took a beating as families found other forms of recreation. The once-thriving community decayed; during the real estate mania of the 1980s, farsighted investors, many of them gay, bought up property there. The town came back better than ever. Though its reputation as a "gay" resort kept some families away during the late '80s, that's no longer true. People of every hue, persuasion, spiritual leaning, and nuclear grouping shuffle along the sidewalks of the bustling little town. And the restaurants are top-notch!

A few miles south, the habitués of Dewey Beach play in a different scenario—the town has the reputation of a high-time, hard-partying nightlife scene, a reputation that delights the nightlife crowd and disturbs more than a few of the residents. The bars are packed during summer nights, but the town immediately quiets down again when autumn winds blow. The beaches are a continuation of Rehoboth perfection.

The best time to visit the beaches is during the first two weeks of September (if you're looking for hot, sunny days and an active nightlife) and mid-September to late October if your beat is still the beach without the night action. Most of the restaurants are open, the crowds have thinned to a trickle, and the "permit parking only" restrictions on roads leading to Rehoboth and Dewey Beaches end around mid-September, making it easy to drive right up to the beach of your choice and hop out of the car for a few hours to work on your tan.

Rehoboth Beach

The Boardwalk on the beach extends from Virginia Avenue on the north end of town 16 blocks south to Penn Street. The active part—with shops and food concessions—runs from Olive Avenue in the north down to Laurel/Philadelphia Street in the south. **Funland** (rides and games) is clustered at the terminus of the three main streets

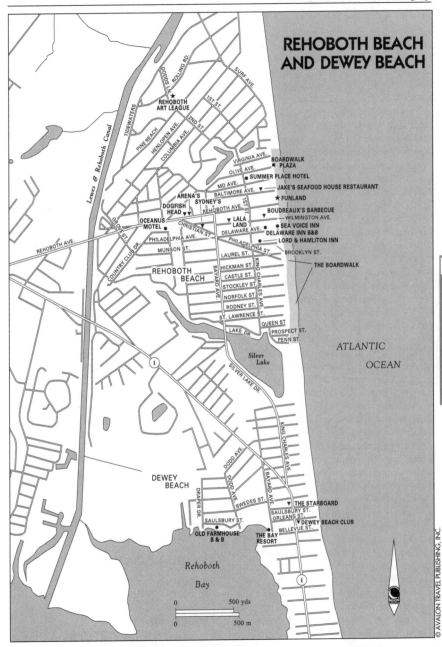

REHOBOTH BEACH AND DEWEY BEACH

REHOBOTH ART LEAGUE

DODDS RD.

ROLLING RD.

SURF AVE.

1ST ST.

2ND ST.

COLUMBIA AVE.

HENLOPEN AVE.

PINE REACH

TIDEWATERS

Lewes & Rehoboth Canal

VIRGINIA AVE.

OLIVE AVE.

BOARDWALK PLAZA

SUMMER PLACE HOTEL

MD AVE.

BALTIMORE AVE.

JAKE'S SEAFOOD HOUSE RESTAURANT

ARENA'S

SYDNEY'S

FUNLAND

DOGFISH HEAD

REHOBOTH AVE.

BOUDREAUX'S BARBECUE

WILMINGTON AVE.

LALA LAND

OCEANUS MOTEL

CHRISTIAN ST.

DELAWARE AVE.

SEA VOICE INN

DELAWARE INN B&B

GROVE ST.

PHILADELPHIA AVE.

LORD & HAMILTON INN

PHILADELPHIA ST.

MUNSON ST.

BROOKLYN ST.

REHOBOTH AVE.

COUNTRY CLUB DR.

LAUREL ST.

THE BOARDWALK

HICKMAN ST.

REHOBOTH BEACH

CASTLE ST.

BAYARD AVE.

STOCKLEY ST.

KING CHARLES AVE.

NORFOLK ST.

RODNEY ST.

ST. LAWRENCE ST.

QUEEN ST.

LAKE DR.

PROSPECT ST.

PENN ST.

Silver Lake

ATLANTIC OCEAN

SILVER LAKE DR.

1

DEWEY BEACH

DRAPER DR.

DODD AVE.

DODD AVE.

KING CHARLES AVE.

SWEDES ST.

BAYARD AVE.

THE STARBOARD

SAULSBURY ST.

ORLEANS ST.

SAULSBURY ST.

DEWEY BEACH CLUB

OLD FARMHOUSE B & B

BELLEVUE ST.

THE BAY RESORT

Rehoboth

Bay

1

0   500 yds

0   500 m

SOUTHERN DELAWARE

© AVALON TRAVEL PUBLISHING, INC.

in town: Baltimore, Rehoboth, and Wilmington Avenues. In the warm evenings, it's a pleasure to walk past the hundreds of little gaming booths and rides and see the glowing faces of small children reflected in the bright lights. It's an old-fashioned style of family fun, but one that hasn't lost its sheen during the past century.

The **Rehoboth Art League,** 12 Dodd Ln., Henlopen Acres, 302/227-8408, is an unexpected oasis of calm in a wealthy suburb of Rehoboth Beach. The league was founded in 1938 to encourage interest and participation in cultural and artistic activities. The league's buildings, including the 1743 Peter Marsh Homestead, sit on 3.5 heavily forested acres. The league offers concerts, lectures, classes, workshops, and art exhibitions year-round. The Corkran/Tubbs Gallery and Marsh Homestead house show exceptional art exhibits by league members. The grounds offer pleasant strolling, the art is all for sale, and there is no fee to enter. The Corkran/Tubbs Gallery and the Marsh Homestead House are open year-round, Mon.–Sat. 10 A.M.–4 P.M., Sunday noon–4 P.M.

Shopping

Shop-a-rama! **The Outlets,** which stretch between Lewes and Rehoboth Beach, deserve special notice—not because they don't duplicate a lot of the outlet malls you can find in Anywhere, USA (they do), but because they duplicate *all* of them: every outlet store in existence is there plus a few more, and there's no sales tax in Delaware. Genius! The outlets consist of three major shopping centers interspersed with several minor ones on "mall mile" (Route 1). Contact the outlets at 302/226-9223, www.shoprehoboth.com, for a map of who's where.

One unique store in the outlets is **Peppers,** Outlet #3, 800/998-FIRE (800/988-3473), peppers@peppers.com. If you're a macho peppermeister or just looking for an unusual gift, this is the place. Proprietor Luther "Chip" Hearn and his sister Randi have gathered the largest collection of fiery condiments in the world—more than 3,000 sauces and 50 salsas—and have added a few prize-winning combinations of their own. The sauces sold at Peppers are all rated for heat factor; a few—such as Pure Cap and Dave's

CHRISTMAS IN JULY

While you're on beach leave during the warm months of the year, it's a good time to think about Christmas—shopping, that is. The outlets, especially with their lack of sales tax, make shopping for everyone on your list a sea breeze. Many of the shops will ship bigger items, and your beach lodging may help you forward any cartons to your home via their UPS connection.

The secret to shopping in July is planning. Like Santa, you have to make a list and check it twice, including everybody's sizes and preferences (getting a map listing the available stores in the outlets is a good idea). Not only do you avoid the Christmas crowds, you have the fun of adding shopping to your sunshine holiday activities. Just make sure you shake out the sand before you tie the shiny red bow.

Gourmet Insanity Sauce, Private Reserve—are so hot that customers must sign a waiver before purchase. Peppers has a salsa bar where you can taste before you buy, hot pepper jelly beans, and a collection of "pepperwear" aprons and cooking accessories. The brightly colored store started out as a hobby, an adjunct to the Hearn's popular Starboard Restaurant and Bar in Dewey Beach. They have a catalog for those who just can't get enough of that endorphin rush.

For pure beach-mania overload, **Rehoboth Avenue** is a must-see. You'll pass more ocean-themed shops, seashell stores, and saltwater taffy places than you ever realized existed. But the real draw is the parade of people, from nattily dressed ladies with poodles to teen-age punks, from deeply tanned bikini-wearers (male and female) to pale whales in pastel plaid.

ACCOMMODATIONS

Rehoboth and Dewey have dozens of places to stay, fitting every taste and budget. Here are a few:

Bed-and-Breakfasts

The restful lodgings noted below are all close to the center of town, but a few blocks away from the beach. Some B&Bs limit their lodgings to guests over the age of six; check before making reservations. The rates shown are for high season, Memorial Weekend–Labor Day; rates are reduced by 10–30 percent in other seasons.

The **Delaware Inn Bed and Breakfast,** 55 Delaware Ave., Rehoboth, 302/227-6031 or 800/246-5244, has been in operation since the late 1920s, and features single rooms with private or shared baths. Open year-round, they offer off-street parking, which is at a premium close to the beach. Rates average $105–190.

Sea Voice Inn, 14 Delaware Ave., Rehoboth, 302/226-9435 or 800/637-2862, is a big yellow house half a block from the beach. This accommodation offers single rooms with private or shared baths, and suites with private baths; innkeepers Susie and Jeff Bond serve a full breakfast. Open year-round, rates range from $70–120, depending on room and season. Suites are $160–385.

The **Lord & Hamilton Seaside Inn,** 20 Brooklyn Ave., Rehoboth, 302/227-6960 or 877/227-6960, is an elegant Victorian built on the original plot of land purchased by the Rev. R. W. Todd, founder of Rehoboth Methodist Campground. Open year-round, the inn offers six individually decorated guest rooms with private bath. High-season rates, depending on location, range from $130–225.

The **Old Farmhouse Bed and Breakfast,** 204 Saulsbury St., Dewey Beach, 302/227-2359, www.oldfarmhousebnb.com, sits on Rehoboth Bay; it was built in 1832 and moved from the town of Millsboro in 1956. Looking out the window from the upper floor, you'd swear you were on a boat; this is the closest you can come to being on the water in complete comfort. The house has a view of Thompson's Island, a nature preserve and archaeological site that holds evidence of habitation from around 500 B.C. A paddleboat is available for guests a few feet from the back porch. Inevitably, the town of Dewey Beach has grown up around the once-remote site, and neighbors' parties are a rare but real nuisance. The Old Farmhouse is open May–Oct., and a two-night minimum is required on weekends. Rooms all have private baths; rates range from $159–179 in season, with special prices in effect in October.

Hotels and Motels

Paper chaos in the lobby of the **Summer Place Hotel,** 1st and Olive Streets, Rehoboth, 302/226-0766 or 800/815-3925, may put some visitors off, but the rooms and condos are in a convenient and quiet location. This small hotel is open year-round; room rates range from $39–160, and condos are priced $50–190, with price breaks for weeklong stays.

The **Oceanus Motel,** Six 2nd St., Rehoboth, 302/227-8200 or 800/852-5011, is just off Rehoboth Avenue, two blocks from the beach. A two-night minimum is required in season. Rooms feature private baths and refrigerators; some have microwaves. The Oceanus is open from the last week in March to the first week in November. Expect tariffs of $59–199.

In Rehoboth, the attractive **Boardwalk Plaza** at the end of the boardwalk on Olive Street, 302/227-7169 or 800/332-3224 (33-BEACH), features a variety of rooms, efficiencies, and apartments. Open all year, the hotel, complete with sundeck, heated indoor-outdoor pool, and grand Victorian decor, is one of the better buys in town. Rates run $59–519, with discounts off-season.

Another good value, **The Bay Resort,** 126 Bellvue St. at Bayard Street, Dewey Beach, 302/227-6400 or 800/922-9240, is off the beaten path in Dewey, but still within a few blocks of the beaches and nightlife. The resort is open Apr.–Oct., and requires a two-night minimum stay in season. All rooms are efficiencies and some overlook Rehoboth Bay: $54–249.

FOOD

Fast Food

Boudreaux's Barbecue is nothing more than a walk-up window midway between the boardwalk and 1st Street on Wilmington Avenue, but it's a handy place for southern-style snacks ($5).

Grotto Pizza, 36 Rehoboth Ave., 302/227-8978, and just about everywhere else in southern Delaware, has good pizza by the slice or pie ($9).

Breakfast/Lunch

Java Beach Café, 167 Rehoboth Ave., Rehoboth Beach, 302/226-3377, is a reliable source for coffee, pastries, sandwiches (including fried egg), and salads. It's open daily 7 A.M.–10 P.M. ($5).

The **Eden Café,** 122 Rehoboth Ave. #A, Rehoboth, 302/227-3330, serves imaginative sandwiches and fish platters for lunch and dinner. Prices range $6–15.

Arena's, in the Village By the Sea mall off Rehoboth Avenue between 1st and 2nd Streets, Rehoboth, 302/227-1272, has great build-your-own sandwiches and microbrews. It features quiet indoor-outdoor dining during the day and becomes a hopping sports bar at night.

Fancy Food

LaLa Land, 22 Wilmington Ave., Rehoboth, 302/227-3887, has captured a couple of "Best of Delaware" Awards from *Delaware Today* magazine, and was noted by *Wine Spectator* magazine for its wine list. It's open for dinner every day, and prices average $25. The menu features vegetarian, fish, and rack of lamb entrées, among others.

Planet X Cafe, farther down the street at 35 Wilmington Ave., 302/226-1928, has a more adventurous decor and menu. Dinner prices average $26. The restaurant is open for dinner every day during the summer, and Fri.–Sun. in fall.

Victoria's Restaurant, in the Boardwalk Plaza Hotel, Olive Avenue on the boardwalk, Rehoboth, 302/227-0615, features excellent regional American cuisine in lush Victorian surroundings combined with ocean views. The fresh local fish is impeccably prepared ($18–29).

Jake's Seafood House Restaurant, 29 Baltimore Ave., Rehoboth Beach, 302/227-6237, www.jakesseafood.com, has been around since 1929, and is reputed by a writer from *Delaware Today* magazine to have the best crab cakes on the beach. This is actually the second incarnation of Jake's—the original was in Baltimore, and Jake's daughter and grandson opened the Rehoboth branch in 1988. It's open for lunch and dinner every day and features the usual seafood house menu; entrées average $18.

Nightlife Plus

Rehoboth has several free newspapers with event listings, and one of the most entertaining is *RBG*, Rehoboth Beach Gayzette. It's a great resource for information on men's and women's clubs and nightlife in general; most of the clubs listed are straight, but gay-friendly.

Sydney's Blues & Jazz Restaurant, 25 Christian St., Rehoboth Beach, 302/227-1339, is the local club for live blues, jazz, and R&B. They also serve a Creole menu, like Cajun but not as spicy: lots of seafood smothered with tomatoes and onions, and brown-sugar-glazed pork chops with sweet potatoes. Dinner is served nightly, and prices average $19.

Dogfish Head Brewings & Eats, 320 Rehoboth Ave., Rehoboth Beach, 302/226-BREW (302/226-2739), www.dogfish.com, ferments its own ales and serves them up with organic wood-grilled pizzas, seafood, and steaks ($18). Dogfish Head has a craft brewery in Milton, 6 Cannery Village Center, 302/684-1000 or 888/8DOG-FISH (888/836-4347); it's open Mon.–Fri. 10 A.M.–4 P.M. Tours are given Thursday 1–3 P.M.

The Starboard, corner of Salisbury Street and Route 1, Dewey Beach, 302/227-4600, has a Bloody Mary smorgasbord where you can make your own, and an extensive Cajun/pub menu. The Starboard is open daily 7 A.M. for breakfast until 1 A.M. during the warm months and 24 hours on weekends. They have a big blowout party in September to close down for the winter.

Dewey Beach Club, 1205 Rte. 1, Dewey Beach, 302/227-0669, is open year-round, and features pub food with lunch and dinner specials. Spoon's Saloon hops at night.

BETHANY BEACH AND FENWICK ISLAND

The state's quieter resorts are south of Delaware Seashore State Park. Bethany Beach is a microversion of Rehoboth, a small enclave of mostly residential dwellings with a fairly sedate two-block-long city/shopping area. Fenwick Island is joined at the hip with Ocean City, Maryland; so much so that the boundaries between the states collide and disappear. As it passes through Fenwick, Route 1 becomes festooned with beach shops and hotels, all threatening to blend into one another.

© JOANNE MILLER

Indian River Inlet Lifesaving Station Museum

Delaware Seashore State Park

This 2,825-acre state park covers the narrow strip of land that separates the Atlantic Ocean from Rehoboth Bay between Dewey Beach and Bethany Beach on Route 1. A barrier island, the sandy spit was largely inaccessible until 1939, when the federal government built two iron and stone jetties, stabilizing Indian River Inlet and permitting a road to be built. Information and maps may be requested from Delaware Seashore State Park, Inlet 850, Rehoboth Beach, DE 19971, 302/227-2800.

Swimming areas on both the ocean and bay are lifeguarded from Memorial Day to Labor Day. Two of the larger public areas, Tower Road Ocean Beach and Southeast Day Area, feature bathhouses, umbrella and raft rental, a picnic area, and food concessions—the day area even has a designated surfing beach. Surf fishing vehicles may be driven on designated beaches with a permit (available from the park office). Swimming outside the guarded areas is discouraged, as is crossing the fragile dune system at any point other than clearly designated dune crossings.

Near the park office on Indian River Inlet, a 1.5-mile nature trail leads to Burton's Island, and the Indian River Marina sells bait and tackle; a boat ramp and charter boats are also available. On the south side of the inlet near the Southeast Day Area, the park offers a small campground with hookups and tent sites (call 877/98-PARKS, or 877/987-2757, for campground information). There is a fee to use the park during the summer (through Labor Day) and on spring and fall weekends.

Indian River Inlet Lifesaving Station Museum, Route 1, one mile north of Indian River Inlet, 302/227-0478, features an interesting small museum chronicling the history and duties of the men who risked their lives to save shipwrecked sailors during the late 19th century. These surfmen lived sometimes-tedious lives in primitive conditions waiting for the cry "Ship Ashore." They then launched their wooden boats into the stormy sea and set out to rescue crew and passengers from vessels torn by the Atlantic's rocky coast. The restored stationhouse—the only one left standing in its original location on the East Coast—is next to the museum. Both are open Tues.–Sun. 10 A.M.–5 P.M., with reduced hours in winter. Admission is $4.

© JOANNE MILLER

Fenwick Island Lighthouse

Sights

The beautifully preserved, 89-foot **Fenwick Island Lighthouse,** off Route 54, Fenwick Island, looms over the low commercial buildings that surround it; the tower was built in 1852, when farmland covered the area. In 1869, one of the duties of the assistant lighthouse keeper—paid the grand sum of $660 a year—was to stay up all night to watch for smoking whale oil that might obscure the light. The lighthouse is on the Transpeninsular line, the east-west boundary between Pennsylvania's "three lower counties" and Maryland, from which Mason and Dixon sighted their eponymous border in 1750. The Fenwick Island light was decommissioned during World War II.

Though visitors can't go up into the tower for insurance reasons, the entranceway to the lighthouse is open two Wednesdays a month or by appointment (when volunteers are available). Paul Pepper, whose grandfather was the third lighthouse keeper at this station, grew up in the house next door. He was, along with his late wife, the person most responsible for restoration of the historic landmark. Contact the Bethany/Fenwick Chamber of Commerce, 800/962-SURF (800/962-7873), for hours and to make an appointment.

DiscoverSea Museum, 708 Ocean Hwy. (above Sea Shell City), Fenwick Island, 302/539-9366 or 888/743-5524, was created through the efforts of one man, professional diver Dale Clifton. Dale has hundreds of underwater hours to his credit—he worked on the raising of the *Atocha,* featured in Georgetown—and has dedicated his life to revealing the romance and history of treasure ships. All material in the museum has been recovered by Dale himself from pre-1860 Delmarva Peninsula shipwrecks. The china, jewelry, pottery, buttons, shoes, weapons, and reams of other found objects represent only about one-tenth of his collection. Visitors quickly understand that Dale's concept of "treasure" means not only gold and silver—there's plenty of that—but also items that were dear to the hearts of those who died beneath the waves: a pocket watch from 1541, a doll's face, a tiny "moon" cannon that would fire on the hour. DiscoverSea features a combination of classic display cases and high technology; the displays are changed twice each month. Each visitor gets a personalized tour tailored to their interests, though most of the younger set are fascinated by "Crabby," the blue crab who marches around one of the aquarium cases waving his arms frantically (he may be waving hello, or he may be filtering oxygen-heavy water through his gills; probably both).

DELMARVA'S SIREN CUSS

The Delmarva Peninsula is the site of several hundred shipwrecks. Besides those caused by storms, rough waters, and rocks, there were manmade causes. A good living was made in the salvage industry by "moon cussers," pirates who cursed the full moon because it put them out of business. On the blackest nights, they would lead a lantern-laden donkey along the ridges near rocky shoals, or light tin drums afire, simulating the lights that burned to guide ships up the coast into the Delaware River. The false lights would bring the ships too close to the shore, running them aground. After the crew and passengers were safely rescued and brought ashore by the local surfmen, the moon cussers would raid the ship, taking whatever valuables they could find.

The museum is open daily Memorial Day–Labor Day 10 A.M.–9 P.M., weekends only Sept.–May 11 A.M.–4 P.M. The museum is free to enter, but donations are encouraged.

Who says corn can't be fun? **Magee's Maize Maze,** Magee's Farms, Route 54, Selbyville, 302/436-5589, is a gigantic cornfield maze that appears every summer in different shapes such as a football-field-size chicken or a fire engine; participants have said that it's a lot harder than you'd think to find your way around, but it's great fun. The maze is open every day July–Sept., 10 A.M.–6 P.M., and weekends only Labor Day–mid-Oct., weather permitting. There's also a petting zoo, picnic area, and straw bale maze. Admission is $6 for adults, $4 for children.

Recreation

Bethany has a beautiful beach and a short board-walk with a few shops on it, but no rides or games. Fenwick's beaches are often private, or fronted by major hotels.

Sweet Meadow Stables, Route 54 in Selbyville, offers trail rides (302/539-5652).

Thunder Lagoon Water Park, Route 1 at Route 54, 302/539-1644, offers a pair of 25-foot twister slides, a kiddie pool, a 3,000-square-foot activity area, and other features for those who prefer their water less salty.

Shopping

Bethany Beach town center at Atlantic and Garfield Streets features a small mall and several shops selling clothing, books, candy, and jewelry.

The **Inland Drive** on Route 26 west from Bethany Beach to Dagsboro, then south on Route 20, then east on Route 54 to Fenwick Island, passes a bulk store and a number of collectible, antique, and art shops, especially on the first leg through Ocean View and Millville. The drive is especially scenic, and passes through farmland and ocean marshes. In Selbyville, turn west on Route 54 to visit the **Route 54 Flea Market** and **Magee's Maize Maze** and farm store.

Accommodations and Food

A pleasant, functionally modern lodging alternative in Bethany Beach is the **Blue Surf Motel,** oceanfront at Garfield Parkway, 302/539-7531. Each of the rooms has a balcony and small kitchen; some face the ocean. The Blue Surf is open all year; rates range $50–185, with the high season from June 19–Sept. 6, and lower prices in effect during the off-season. Book as far in advance as possible; many of the motel's patrons return here year after year.

The **Addy Sea,** on the oceanfront at 99 Ocean View Pkwy. and N. Atlantic Avenue, Bethany Beach, 302/539-3707 or 800/418-6764, offers secluded charm. Fronting the quiet beach, this three-story Victorian was built in 1901 as a home for the wealthy family of a pastor of the Church of Christ. One of their contemporary descendants, Martha Jean Addy, manages the historical museum downtown. The family sold the house; since 1974, it has been run year-round as an inn. True to its past, several rooms on each floor share one shower/bath, though each room has a small toilet (sometimes in the closet!) and sink. Decor is a mix of authentic and faux-period pieces. The measured pace of time in the town and inn seems to make the hours slow down. A continental breakfast is served in the parlor in the morning, sometimes to the accompaniment of stories of ghost sightings during the early days of the inn. Rates are $150–300, depending on day and season; discounts for longer stays and off-season.

Becky's Country Inn, 401 Main St., 302/732-3953, is in the hamlet of Dagsboro, off the beaten path—perfect if you're biking the back roads or making the inland drive. This cute little 1850 farmhouse has three rooms with private baths, all of which open onto a deck. Be prepared, however: the inn faces the main road through Dagsboro, and the agricultural trucks may be noisy in the morning. High-season rates run $65–85.

Food: Bethany Beach has a number of upscale restaurants in town; one of the local favorites is **The Parkway,** in the Antal Building on Garfield Parkway, 302/537-7500, which serves an American menu in a casual setting. It's open for dinner, and prices average $26.

If a bowl of inexpensive, good, homemade chicken soup is what you're after, drive out Route 26 to Ocean View, and keep an eye out for the **Ocean View Deli and Restaurant,** on the south side of the road, 302/539-4864 (there's no address, but it's between the bridge and the traffic light). This family-run, family-style diner isn't fancy, but the food is good and the prices are great. It serves breakfast, lunch, and dinner, $3–10.

SUSSEX COUNTY INLAND

The beaches of Sussex County are the destinations for most travelers. However, for a break from surf and sand, go west. A couple of Delaware's most popular parks, plus a scattering of small-town attractions, await the adventurous.

Millsboro

A former mill town, Millsboro is now the center of Delaware's broiler chicken industry, a fact that's celebrated in June by the annual Delmarva chicken festival, featuring the world's largest frying pan among other oddities. The area's tree-shaded farmlands are also home to the Nanticoke Indian tribe, whose villages once covered the area from one coast of the Delmarva Peninsula to the other.

The **Nanticoke Indian Museum,** on Route 24, 12 miles west of the Route 1 intersection, 302/945-7022, tells the history of the Nanticoke through displays and written information. The museum was converted from the former Indian school by members of the tribe in the early 1980s, and features a research library with information on the Nanticoke and other Native American peoples. In September of each year, the tribe holds an exceptional powwow that's open to all. Donations are appreciated.

Georgetown

The **Delaware Technical & Community College,** Route 18 just west of U.S. 113, has two exhibits in the library building that will interest visitors. The first is **Treasures of the Sea,** 302/856-5700, a museum-like exhibit created by a group of Delmarvans who had invested in the

---

THE NANTICOKE POWWOW

In precontact days, the Algonquian word *pauwau* referred to the healing and curing ceremonies conducted by Indian spiritual leaders to drive sickness and negative energy away. Nanticoke see the powwow not only as a tool to preserve their heritage, but also as a device to cure misconceptions about the beliefs and values of the first people. The Nanticoke powwow began in 1921, in an attempt by tribal elders to hold on to the vestiges of native culture that were slipping away. World War II halted the festivities for a few years, but the powwow was revived and has grown bigger than ever.

Every year in mid-September, the Nanticoke tribe of southern Delaware holds its powwow weekend west of Rehoboth Beach near the Nanticoke Indian Museum outside Millsboro. The powwow, set in a cool and peaceful grove, is open to everyone, and word of the friendly reception to other Native Americans and non-Indians has spread, increasing the size of the get-together every year.

Dancing, which is the major activity, is primarily for Nanticoke tribal members and visitors from other tribes across the nation. On Saturday, the festivities start at noon with the "Grand Entry"; all dancers follow behind U.S. and tribal flags. The entry is followed by an invocation to the Great Spirit, lighting of the peace pipe, and herbal purification. For the next few hours, dancers perform traditional and specialty dances, followed by an hour of storytelling until 4:30; the dancing then continues until 7 P.M. On Sunday, a Christian church service with singing takes place 11 A.M.–noon, and the dancing continues 2–5 P.M. Both days, booths around the dance area featuring handmade goods, fry bread, Indian tacos, and more are open 10 A.M.–8 P.M. Though some seating is provided for the elderly and infirm, visitors are expected to bring their own folding chairs.

RESULTS! RETURN DAY IN SUSSEX COUNTY

Since 1792, citizens have been returning to the county seat of Georgetown two days after each major election to hear election results and bury the hatchet, accepting both wins and losses. By 1888, "Return Day" drew several thousand people in a carnival-like atmosphere that included attendees "dressed in costumes which were used in primitive times, and others purposely arraying themselves in an outlandish manner to give more zest to the spirit of the occasion," according to Thomas Scharf in *The History of Delaware*. People decorated their horses, oxen, and wagons, as well as themselves.

The advent of radio in the early part of this century dampened down the festivities, but Return Day was revived by that rarest of animals, a donkephant—members of local Democratic and Republican parties worked together to revive the custom in the early 1950s. Today, Return Day is a legal half-holiday for Sussex County, and voters from all over make a special trip to Georgetown for the roasted ox sandwiches, arts and crafts vendors, and parade that seats winners and losers together in decorated carriages and convertibles. The leaders of the local political parties actually do bury a hatchet—until the next major election.

raising of the Spanish treasure ship the *Nuestra Señora de Atocha*. The ship, a seagoing fortress with 20 cannons, went down in a hurricane in 1622. The exhibit tells the story of Spanish shipping in the Indies and the process of finding shipwrecks. The *Atocha* yielded gold, silver, and more than 300 uncut emeralds; some of the gold and jewelry is on display, in addition to a video and artifacts from the raised vessel. The exhibit is open Mon.–Tues. 10 A.M.–4 P.M., Friday noon–4 P.M., and Saturday 9 A.M.–1 P.M. Admission is $2.50.

While visiting the library, make sure and stop by the **Elsie Williams Doll Collection,** 302/856-9033, available for viewing during library hours (8:30 A.M.–1 P.M.). Hundreds of different types of dolls are represented, including Hopi kachinas, bisque pattern dolls from the 19th century, and an "Easter Egg Doll" from 1860, filled with candy. Free.

The grounds of the college also feature the **Trees of the States Arboretum,** a self-guided walking tour of 51 trees representing 50 states plus the District of Columbia. Florida's sabal palm is there, along with California's sequoia and Maryland's wye oak. The grounds are open during college hours. Call 302/856-5400 for information.

Trap Pond State Park

A popular destination for Delawareans, Trap Pond, Route 449 east of Laurel, 302/875-5153,

is a freshwater swamp featuring the northernmost natural stand of bald cypress trees in the United States. The park is laced with hiking trails, and fishing and boating in the swamp are major activities. Rowboats, pedal boats, and canoes may be rented from a concession near the park office; a park interpreter narrates pontoon boat tours on weekends and holidays during the summer months. There is a guarded swimming area and bathhouse nearby. Picnic sites, volleyball courts, and horseshoe pits are available for those who prefer drier fun.

The park offers 152 campsites for both tents and RVs; half are equipped with water and electric hookups. Call 302/875-2392 for campground information.

River Towns Highlights Tour

This tour begins in Laurel and ends a few miles north in Seaford. The distance traveled is approximately 17 miles, with a 13-mile return to Laurel via Route 13 A. The route is very flat, and could easily be biked as well as driven.

One mile east of Laurel off Route 24, **Old Christ Church,** Chipman's Pond Road, built in 1771, is one of the few churches to survive unaltered from America's prerevolutionary past. Stepping inside has been likened to "entering 18th-century England." It's open on Sunday and July 4, 1–4 P.M.

RIVER TOWNS

Location, location, location: Some may be puzzled that Seaford, Bethel, and Laurel—so far inland—prospered from the water transport of agricultural and forestry products, and then made new fortunes in the shipbuilding industry. But location is everything: Seaford is on the Nanticoke River; Bethel and Laurel are both on Broad Creek. When the Nanticoke Tribe inhabited this region, Laurel was known as "the wading place," the last crossing before Broad Creek widened and met the Nanticoke River on its way west to the Chesapeake Bay. These small towns, in the center of Delmarva Peninsula's great agricultural area, profited from the sending of goods west to the bay, Baltimore, and the Atlantic seaboard beyond. Bethel, famous for its shipbuilding, became an enclave of Victorians built for sea captains by ships' carpenters.

Up until World War I, Bethel, Laurel, and Seaford experienced intermittent economic booms, which resulted in a number of grand homes. Laurel has more than 800 buildings listed on the National Register, and the entire town of Bethel is listed. Though now the towns afford a quiet grace, they continue to retain the charm of small-town America. In fact, Seaford ranked 28th in the second edition of *The Best 100 Small Towns in America.*

Before exploring the elegant neighborhoods of Laurel—it was the wealthiest town in the state around 1900—stop by **Bargain Bill's, The Shore's Largest Flea Market,** U.S. 13 and Route 9E, Laurel, 302/875-9958. This covered/open market sprawls over several acres and is open year-round, Fri. 8 A.M.–4 P.M. and weekends 8 A.M.– 5 P.M. Friday is a fairly slow day, but the weekends are bursting with people, particularly in the summer. You can find it here, and usually for the price you want to pay. If you're still in a shopping mood, consider a side trip: drive south on U.S. 13 to the corner of U.S. 13 and Delaware Avenue to **O'Neal's,** a store/pawn shop with occasional good buys on estate jewelry.

Drive west into Laurel, exploring the streets in the older part of town, around Route 24. This street intersects Route 492 in the western part of town. Follow Route 492 through the country to 493, where you'll cross Broad Creek into **Bethel.** Once a busy shipbuilding center, this quiet community of seafarers' homes is listed on the National Register of Historic Places. Continue on Route 493 to Route 78. Turn left onto Route 78. You'll see signs for the Woodland Ferry. Travel to the end of Route 78 and you'll be at the ferry crossing.

The **Woodland Ferry** is a bit of old Delaware that continues on. The drive to the ferry (which crosses the Nanticoke River) is a scenic one. The ferry, which can carry two or three cars, is free. When you get to the other side of the narrow but deep river, take time to enjoy a picnic in the tiny Woodland Park next to the ferry.

Drive from Woodland a short distance, then turn right onto Route 78 toward Seaford. Proceed 3.6 miles to Gethsemene United Methodist Church (referred to locally as "the burned church") and turn right onto Route 20 East. You will drive through the country on Route 20 and then enter the town of Seaford. You'll pass the Nylon Capitol Shopping Center on your left. Seaford is the site of the world's first nylon plant—in fact, the DuPont Highway, U.S. 13, was built by the Du Ponts in order to transport supplies and materials to Wilmington. There will be a sign on the right side of the road that says "Library." You'll need to make a bit of a loop to get to the other side of the road. Go across the bridge and make the first right as soon as you reach the foot of the bridge onto Pine Street. Turn right when you reach the first road to your right (6th Street). Take this road until you reach Cedar Street (6th Street dead-ends on Cedar). Make a right onto Cedar. This will take you under the bridge. Follow Cedar around. At the first intersection, make a right onto Oak Street, then a left back onto Pine Street. Continue one-half mile to the Ross Plantation. You will see an orange Victorian cottage on the right. Turn toward the cottage and park.

The lovely Italian villa–style **Governor Ross Mansion and Plantation,** N. Pine Street, Seaford, 302/628-9500, was built in 1854, as the Delaware governor was finishing his term in office. Governor Ross, a slaveholder, was a Southern sympathizer; branded a traitor, he was forced to spend the Civil War years traveling in Europe after President Lincoln issued a warrant for his arrest. Governor Ross brought the railroad to southern Delaware, installing a station on his 1,400-acre plantation, but the family went bankrupt within a few generations. The furnished mansion, grounds, and outbuildings, including the slave quarters, are open to the public the fourth Sunday of each month from 1–4 P.M. and other times by appointment (call 302/628-9500). Admission is $2.

Accommodations and Food

Spring Garden Bed and Breakfast, Delaware Avenue Extended, Laurel, 302/875-7015 or 800/797-4909, takes care of quite a few guests who visit nearby Trap Pond. The innkeepers are heavily involved in local ecotourism, and are a good resource for information on the topic. This 18th-century country manor was once a working farm and sea captain's home. Four spacious rooms either share a bath or have private baths; a suite is available. All are complemented by a full breakfast in the morning. Next door, the property's old barn houses antiques and artist's workshops.

FESTIVALS AND EVENTS

March/April

How much chocolate can you eat? Rehoboth Beach hosts an annual **Chocolate Festival** and researchers are standing by. 302/227-2772.

Fly high at the **Great Delaware Kite Festival,** Cape Henlopen State Park. 302/227-6996.

June/July

Celebrate Independence on the beach at **Rehoboth's Beach Fireworks.** 302/227-2772.

August/September

The *Delaware State News* sponsors the annual **Sandcastle Contest** at Rehoboth Beach. 800/282-8586.

The Rehoboth Art League invites visitors to its annual **Art League Outdoor Fine Art and Craft Show.** 302/227-8408.

For a wonderful cross-cultural experience, try the **Nanticoke Indian Pow Wow,** in Millsboro. 302/945-7022.

October/November

The scenic town of Laurel hosts an annual **Antique Show and Sale.** 302/875-3983.

The annual **Sea Witch Halloween & Fiddler's Festival** includes creative parades, contests, and lots of great fiddle music. Costumed kids can trick-or-treat at many of the shops in town. 302/644-2401.

The general revelry around **World Championship Punkin' Chunkin',** Harbeson, is something a few locals would rather forget—but it's impossible to ignore giant squash flying over fields of stubble, powered by homemade catapults. Distance matters. Call 302/856-1444 or visit the website at www.punkinchunkin.com.

The annual **Rehoboth Beach Independent Film Festival,** begun in 1998, screens several days of carefully chosen independent films. Call 302/645-9095 or email info@rehobothfilm.com.

December

Lewes celebrates the holidays with a **Christmas Parade, Tree Lighting, and Caroling.** 302/645-8073.

Rehoboth Beach sponsors a **Hometown Christmas Parade.** 302/227-6181.

Though the B&B is easy to get to, lack of street signage makes it difficult to find; call for exact directions when making your reservation. Rates run $75–95.

Smith's Family Restaurant, 115 E. Market St., Georgetown, 302/855-0305, is an excellent stop for lunch. It's a casual, inexpensive, home-cooking-style place, open all day, every day except Sunday. Prices hover around $3–10. While you're there, driving around the town's central circle, check out the historic homes on the surrounding streets; many were built in the early 1800s, after the county seat was moved to Georgetown from Lewes.

The **Bon Appetit Restaurant,** 312 High St., Seaford, 302/629-3700, is one of those unexpected places lucky travelers run across. The place is well known in the area for its gourmet French menu and prix fixe meals. Highly recommended: $34 for the five-course prix fixe.

Britts Dutch Inn, 1012 S. Central Ave., Laurel, 302/875-7158, on the other hand, is the down-home kind of place where people stop by for a cup of coffee and a tuna sandwich ($5).

The **Old Mill Crab House and Restaurant,** Route 54 and Waller Road, Delmar, 302/846-2808, is a big favorite of the locals. It serves dinner only ($12) and is open Mar.–Nov.

SOUTHERN DELAWARE TOURS

If you can't get enough of that shipwreck stuff, spend an afternoon with marine biologist Bill Winker on a **TreasureQuest Tour.** The tour includes an introduction to identifying artifacts and beachcombing tips; it ends on the beach, at the site of several 18th- and 19th-century shipwrecks. Call 302/537-5334 for reservations.

Sea Dogs of Bethany Beach, 888/371-7888, offers **Golf Getaways** all over the Delmarva Peninsula, complete with accommodations and green fees.

Biking Inn-to-Inn takes participants on a four-day, three-night biking and bed-and-breakfast tour from Laurel to Lewes and back. Call Ambassador Travel, 800/845-9939, for more information.

INFORMATION

The Sussex County Convention and Tourism Commission provides a free vacation-planning guide. It can also provide information and contact numbers about individual towns, attractions, and areas. Call the information line, 866/284-7483, or visit the website at www.visitdelaware.com.

Side Trip to D.C.

History

On June 20, 1783, hordes of unpaid soldiers descended on Philadelphia, demanding back pay from the War of Independence. A nervous Congress was quickly convinced that the fledgling United States needed a federal city where its lawmakers could govern in relative peace. Creating one would be no easy task: the 13 colonies were united in freedom but divergent in interests; there was no president yet; and the war had left the national coffers nearly empty.

The location for the country's new capital was decided by a combination of political compromise and pragmatism. Southern states, who helped bail out their northern brethren after the war, insisted in return that the city be located to the south. Newly elected president George Washington decided on a spot near where the Anacostia River meets the Potomac, for its economic potential near the tobacco market of Georgetown and a planned canal across the Cumberland Gap to the western frontier.

French engineer and revolutionary volunteer Pierre L'Enfant was given the task of designing the nation's capital, which he planned on a grand scale in the spirit of his beloved Paris. A bold grid pattern, anchored by great parks and monumental squares, was overlaid with diagonal avenues named for the states and radiating outward from the White House and the Capitol

Capitol building

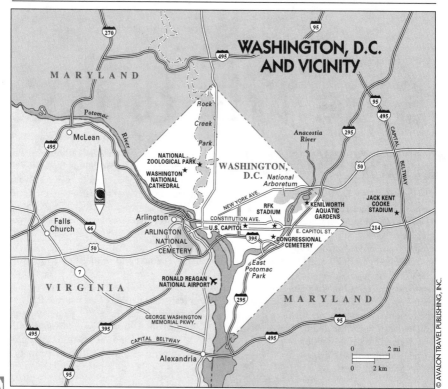

WASHINGTON, D.C. AND VICINITY

© AVALON TRAVEL PUBLISHING, INC.

building, both of which were begun in 1793. In October 1800, the governmental archives and general offices were shifted to Washington from Philadelphia, President John Adams moved into the White House, and Congress met for the first time in the Capitol.

Critics soon began to attack D.C.'s seemingly arbitrary location. What was conceived as a "city of magnificent distances" was derided as the "Capitol of Miserable Huts," and members of both Congress and the national press tried to have the capital moved to a more accessible location. National outrage over the British invasion in 1814, however, firmly seated Washington, D.C., as America's capital in the minds of her citizens. The city's key role in the Civil War, as the heart and brain of the victorious Union, further solidified its symbolic image.

A sudden influx of 40,000 freed slaves more than doubled D.C.'s population and set it on a course of racial diversity that eventually would embrace immigrants from every country in the world. In the 21st century, the capital's identity continues to evolve and mutate, as wealthy neighborhoods stand next to slums, and homeless people sleep in the shadows of the country's greatest monuments. Our most monumental, symbolic, and international city serves as a reminder of all that is desirable—and much that is not—in the country it embodies.

The Mall Sights

The area between Constitution Avenue NW and Independence Avenue SW is truly America's backyard. The grassy expanse, wide as a football field, stretches 2.5 miles from the Capitol at the east end to the Lincoln Memorial at the west. Along both sides stand many of the Smithsonian museums, and just north is the White House. The Mall itself encloses monuments to George Washington and Vietnam veterans, outstanding national gardens, the Reflecting Pool, and even a charming merry-go-round.

For information on any of the free attractions on the Mall, write or call Superintendent, National Capital Parks Central, 900 Ohio Dr. SW, Washington, DC 20242, 202/485-9880, or visit the website at www.nps.gov/nama. Be aware that access to many sites in the D.C. area may be limited due to security concerns.

Constitution Gardens

The last of the unsightly "temporary" buildings marring the Mall was finally removed in the mid-1970s and replaced by this tranquil oasis of landscaped gardens, meandering footpaths, and a duck pond. A willow-shrouded island at the center of the pond contains a roster of the signers of the Declaration of Independence, inscribed on a granite-and-gold plate.

Lincoln Memorial

While more than a century elapsed before the Washington Monument moved from contemplation to completion, the Lincoln Memorial was built in 60 years. Henry Bacon's white marble temple is another D.C. testimonial to the Greeks, while the 19-foot statue of Lincoln by Daniel French that sits inside the temple bears signs of Roman influence, especially in the chair arms bearing *fasces,* symbols of Roman imperial power. Although the 1922 unveiling ceremonies were segregated, the site began a long association with the civil rights movement 17 years later when contralto Marian Anderson sang from the steps after she was barred from performing at nearby Constitution Hall. Anderson ascended the steps again in 1963, preceding the Reverend Martin Luther King, Jr.'s momentous "I Have a Dream" speech.

During World War II, the Lincoln Memorial was the only edifice in D.C. to come under friendly fire: a nervous trooper manning the big guns atop the Department of the Interior building managed to blow off bits of the marble rooftop. Located at the west end of the Mall, the memorial is best visited at night, when the spirit of the place is most alive. Like other Mall attractions, the Lincoln Memorial is open all day every day. Rangers are on duty 8 A.M.–midnight daily except Christmas Day.

Korean War Veterans Memorial

The centerpiece of the Korean War Veterans Memorial, dedicated in 1995, is the triangular "field of service," depicting a wedge of soldiers slogging through the countryside. This symbolic patrol of 19 stainless-steel figures is made up of members from each of the four main branches of the armed services. The memorial is most haunting when the seven-foot-tall soldiers are softly illuminated at night. Staffed by park rangers 8 A.M.–midnight every day except Christmas, the memorial is just south of the Reflecting Pool near FDR Memorial Park.

Vietnam Veterans Memorial

The revolutionary work that designer Maya Lin described simply as "a rift in the earth" doesn't trumpet the glory of struggle or the legacy of some lauded general. Instead it lists, in neat, simple, endless columns, the name of every person killed in America's longest war. More than 58,000 names are carved into the 492-foot wall of black granite, the polished surface of which reflects the faces of those who visit to pay homage. The names are listed chronologically in the order of death, and at each end of the memorial are paperback registers listing the names alphabetically with a key to their location on the wall.

Vietnam veteran Jan Scruggs raised the funds to construct the memorial through a nonprofit organization, and today it is America's potent shrine, a place of grief and cleansing where every year tens of thousands of people bring offerings of poems and rings, harmonicas and sardines for lost friends, lost sons, or for the parent they never knew. Some leave only their thoughts for future generations, such as, "Understand that if the time comes when you must kill, it will destroy you for all of this life."

Vietnam Women's Memorial

This bronze sculpture portraying three women and an injured soldier was dedicated on November 11, 1993. Artist Glenna Goodacre honors the women who served in Vietnam with a solid, uncomplicated piece that communicates the emotional bond that formed between the male soldiers and women who served primarily as nurses and support staff.

Washington Monument

According to federal law, no structure in the capital can be built higher than the 555-foot tapered shaft of the Washington Monument. In 1783, the Continental Congress first suggested a monument honoring the nation's inaugural president, but more than a century passed before the idea became reality; from cornerstone to completion took 40 years. During one embarrassing interlude from 1854 to 1876, the obelisk languished as an unsightly stump of 150 feet, described by Mark Twain as "a factory chimney with the top broken off."

When work began again, the marble originally drawn from a Maryland quarry had been exhausted; thus the noticeable change in shade of the remaining 400 feet. The monument finally opened in 1888 with women and children dutifully trudging up the 898 steps (the elevator designed by Mr. Elisha G. Otis was considered patently dangerous, braved only by men). Today everyone rides the elevator, ascending to 360-degree views of the capital's historic heart through narrow windows.

The monument is open daily 9 A.M.–5 P.M., every day except Christmas, with extended summer hours for nighttime viewing. Tickets are required. Depending on the availability of staff,

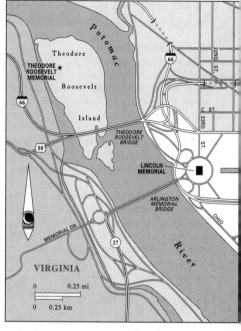

summer weekend walking tours down the steps are also offered. For more information, call 202/426-6841, or write Superintendent, the Washington Monument, 1100 Ohio Dr. SW, Washington, DC 20242, or visit the website at www.nps.gov/wamo.

National Gallery of Art

In the 1930s, this museum's west wing sprang full-grown from the wallet of rapacious banker Andrew Mellon, who wisely declined to append his name to the edifice. I.M. Pei designed the angular east wing, which was built in 1978. Both wings are constructed of pink Tennessee marble, but there the similarity ends: the east displays 20th-century works by the likes of Miró, Magritte, and Matisse, while the homier, more crowded west wing is the domain of classic art by the likes of Raphael, Rembrandt, and Renoir. Historians of the presidency are invariably drawn to the west wing, which sits over the bones of the old B&P Railroad Station where, in 1881, President James A. Garfield was shot twice in

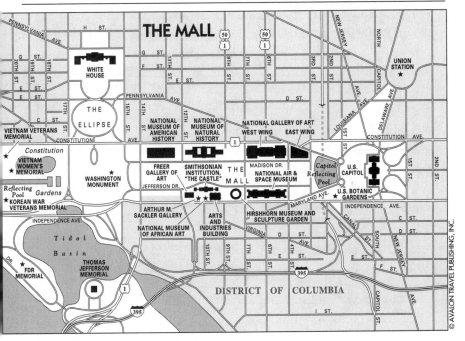

the back by Charles Guiteau. The gallery, 600 Constitution Ave. NW, 202/737-4215, www .nga.gov, is open Mon.–Sat. 10 A.M.–5 P.M., Sunday 11 A.M.–6 P.M. Closed New Year's Day and Christmas Day; free.

Mall Merry-Go-Round

On the grounds of the south side of the Mall, a small carousel offers a pleasant respite from the solemnity of its monumental surroundings. A circular journey or two aboard gaily painted horses, serenaded by cheery carnival tunes, can serve as a bracing antidote to historic dates and endless museum rounds. The carousel spins just east of the Smithsonian Castle and is open daily 9 A.M.–5 P.M., depending on the weather, closed major holidays. Admission is $1.

SMITHSONIAN INSTITUTION
Smithsonian Castle

In 1829, eccentric English chemist James Smithson passed on, leaving to the United States—

a country he had never seen—105 bags of gold sovereigns "to found an establishment for the increase and diffusion of knowledge." After no small amount of puzzlement and a fair amount of wrangling, Congress decided in 1846 to spend Smithson's largesse on an institute of scientific research. In 1855, James Renwick completed the fairytale red sandstone structure popularly known as the Castle.

The institution quickly outgrew these grand confines, and today the building serves simply as an information center guiding visitors to the Smithsonian's scattered holdings. Smithson's dusty remains rest in a crypt beneath the castle, his corpse having gained these shores at last in 1904. Most Smithsonian attractions are on the Mall, though the National Museum of American Art, the National Portrait Gallery, the Anacostia Museum, and the National Zoological Park are elsewhere in the city. The Castle sits at 1000 Jefferson Dr. SW, Washington, DC 20560, 202/357-2700, and is open daily 10 A.M.–5:30 P.M. Closed Christmas Day.

USING THE METRO IN D.C.

Location	Metro Station/Line
Botanical Gardens	Federal Center SW/Blue or Orange
FBI Building	Archives-Navy Memorial/Yellow or Green
Federal Triangle	Federal Triangle/Blue or Orange
Folger Shakespeare Library	Capitol South/Blue or Orange
Ford's Theatre	Metro Center/Blue, Orange, or Red
Kennedy Center/Watergate	Foggy Bottom/Blue or Orange (walk south along New Hampshire Avenue)
Library of Congress	Capitol South/Blue or Orange
MCI Center	Gallery Place/Green, Red, or Yellow
National Aquarium	Federal Triangle/Blue or Orange
National Archives	Archives-Navy Memorial/Yellow or Green
National Building Museum	Judiciary Square/Red
National Mall	Smithsonian/Blue or Orange
National Museum of American Art	Gallery Place/Green, Red, or Yellow
National Portrait Gallery	Gallery Place/Green, Red, or Yellow
Rosslyn	Rosslyn/Blue or Orange (walk north across Francis Scott Key Bridge)
Shakespeare Theatre	Archives-Navy Memorial/Yellow or Green
Union Station	Union Station/Red
Washington National Cathedral	Woodley Park-Zoo/Red (walk west along Woodley Road)
White House	Metro Center/Blue, Orange, or Red
Zoological Park	Woodley Park-Zoo/Red

Metro Transfer Stations include L'Enfant Plaza, Gallery Place, King Street, Metro Center, Pentagon, Rosslyn, and Stadium-Armory.

National Air and Space Museum

Year after year, this is the most visited attraction in the city. People just can't get enough of the model of *Sputnik,* the 1903 Wright Brothers *Flyer,* Charles Lindbergh's *Spirit of St. Louis,* a knockoff of the Hubble space telescope, and a walk through a full-scale reproduction of the Skylab space station. Perhaps the most popular item on display is the four-billion-year-old shard of lunar rock brought back by the astronauts of *Apollo 17;* hardly anyone can resist running fingers over this chunk of another world. The museum is open daily 10 A.M.–

5:30 P.M. with extended summer hours determined annually; closed Christmas Day. Admission is free, though a fee of $2–7 is charged to view IMAX films in the museum's Albert Einstein Planetarium and Samuel P. Langley Theater. Visit the Castle, call 202/357-1400, or check the website (www.nasm.si.edu/visit/visit.htm) for more information.

Arthur M. Sackler Gallery

This eye-boggling three-tiered subterranean museum at 1050 Independence Ave. SW houses

SIDE TRIP TO D.C.

Smithsonian Castle

5,000 years of Asian art. Highlights of the Sackler's unequaled permanent collection include Chinese bronze, jade, and lacquerware; delicate Persian paintings; Near Eastern works in silver, gold, bronze, and clay; and a pantheon of Buddhist and Hindu deities executed in stone and bronze. Open daily 10 A.M.–5:30 P.M., closed Christmas Day. Tours begin at 11 A.M. except Wednesday. Admission is free. Visit the website at www.asia.si.edu or write Office of Public Affairs, Arthur M. Sackler Gallery, MRC 707, Smithsonian Institution, Washington, DC 20560, or call 202/357-3200 for information.

Arts and Industries Building

At the conclusion of the 1876 U.S. International Exposition in Philadelphia, most exhibiting nations and many U.S. states craftily donated their exhibits to the U.S. government, thus saving the costs of shipping them home. It took 60 trains to transport all these objects to the Smithsonian,

increasing its holdings fourfold and requiring the construction of this Victorian edifice to house it all. Today, the Arts and Industries Building, 202/357-1300, fax 202/357-2700, features a variety of special changing exhibitions and is also noteworthy for the Discovery Theater, which offers diverse programs for young children. Located at 900 Jefferson Dr. SW, the museum is open daily 10 A.M.–5:30 P.M. Closed Christmas Day. Admission is free. For more information, visit the Castle or the website www.si.edu/ai.

Freer Gallery of Art

Charles Lang Freer raked in millions designing railroad cars, then began to spend his accumulated wealth on fine art. Freer first became enamored of the prints, pastels, oils, and watercolors of James Whistler, then, at the artist's urging, began accumulating Asian art. When Freer died in 1919, his entire collection went to the Smithsonian; this gallery opened four years later. Today the Freer houses more than 26,000 objects, which includes more than 1,200 works by Whistler, the largest collection of the artist's work found anywhere. On Jefferson Drive SW, 202/357-4880, the gallery is open daily 10 A.M.–5:30 P.M. Closed Christmas Day. Admission is free. Visit the Smithsonian Castle or website www.asia.si.edu for more information or write Office of Public Affairs, Freer Gallery-MRC 707, Washington, DC 20560.

Hirshhorn Museum and Sculpture Garden

Created to quiet critics who complained that the Smithsonian cared only for classic art, the Hirshhorn is built around the extensive 11,000-piece modern art collection of uranium tycoon Joseph Hirshhorn. The museum's revolving exhibitions are dedicated to promulgating appreciation for "the art of our time." The museum, located on Independence Avenue and 7th Street SW, is open daily 10 A.M.–5:30 P.M. (the garden is open 7:30 A.M.–dusk). Closed Christmas Day. Admission is free. Call 202/357-2700 or visit the website at www.hirshhorn.si.edu for more information.

National Museum of African Art

Founded as a private institution in 1964 and absorbed by the Smithsonian in 1979, this underground museum focuses primarily on the traditional arts of sub-Saharan Africa. Permanent exhibits include pieces from the royal court of the kingdom of Benin as it was before British colonial rule; traditional and modern ceramic works from many regions of the continent; and a display of utilitarian objects, each an example of the aesthetics found in daily African life. At 950 Independence Ave. SW, the museum is open daily 10 A.M.–5:30 P.M. Closed Christmas Day. Admission is free. For more information, call 202/357-4600, visit the Castle, or go to website www.si.edu/nmafa.

National Museum of American History

Living up to the nickname "America's attic," this museum is as big, rich, and sprawling as the country from which it collects. The sheer quantity of material is staggering; it would require several hours to appreciate the intricate, painstaking, exhaustively informative light bulb display alone. Nothing is too big for the museum's curatorial staff, who have hauled in a full-size gunboat and an entire post office, among other things. See Foucault's pendulum, proof the earth still turns; and the tattered fabric Francis Scott Key immortalized as "The Star-Spangled Banner," proof the flag *is* still there. Discover the charge in a kiss in the Hall of Electricity, and on the third floor review the heartbreaking collection of effects left at the Vietnam Veterans Memorial. It's located at 14th Street and Constitution Avenue NW, and is open daily 10 A.M.–5:30 P.M. with extended summer hours determined annually. Closed Christmas Day. For more information, call or visit the Castle, or go to www.si.edu/nmah on the Internet.

National Museum of Natural History

Here you'll find an endless amalgamation of artifacts—animal, vegetable, and mineral—from the jaws of a prehistoric shark large enough to swallow entire automobiles to the Hope diamond. A 13-foot-tall stuffed African elephant and a great stone head from Easter Island round out the collection. An extensive exhibit on Native Americans inspired Rudyard Kipling to ponder "the wonder of a people who, having extirpated the aboriginals of their continent more completely than any other modern race had ever done, honestly believed that they were a Godly little New England community, setting examples to brutal mankind." Hands-on displays in the Discovery Room (open afternoons by ticket only) are geared toward children. The museum, located on Constitution Avenue NW, is open daily 10 A.M.–5:30 P.M., with extended summer hours. Closed Christmas Day. For more information, go to www.mnh.si.edu, call 202/357-2700, or write National Museum of Natural History, Smithsonian Institution-MRC 106, Washington, DC 20560, or call or visit the Castle.

More Capital Sights

TIDAL BASIN

Separating West Potomac Park from East Potomac Park, the Tidal Basin was originally dredged as a reservoir but soon proved popular as a recreational area. From 1917–1925, white Washingtonians flocked to a segregated beach located where the Jefferson Memorial now stands. Today the basin is famous worldwide for the 1,300 cherry trees along its banks. The first batch, a peace offering from Japan, arrived in 1909, but the trees were contaminated with insects and were immediately destroyed. In 1912, a second shipment fared better and thrived through World War II, notwithstanding occasional efforts by enraged citizens to fell them. These days you can cruise the basin on rented paddleboats (two-seaters for $8 and four-seaters for $16, picture ID required), available daily 10 A.M.–6 P.M.; for information, call 202/479-2426. A public area, the Tidal Basin is officially open 8 A.M.–midnight daily. For more information, write Information—Superintendent, National Capital Parks Central, 900 Ohio Dr. SW, Washington, DC

20242, or call 202/485-9880. Be aware that access to many sites in the D.C. area may be limited due to security concerns.

FDR Memorial

Composed of four outdoor rooms, one for each of Franklin Delano Roosevelt's terms in office, this granite structure spreads along the banks of the Tidal Basin in West Potomac Park. Visitors to the memorial enter past an inscribed FDR quote—"This generation of Americans has a rendezvous with destiny"—and a bronze bas-relief of the presidential seal as it appeared at FDR's first inauguration in 1933. The interiors of each room include waterfalls, plants, shrubs, and trees, as well as sculpture and inscriptions highlighting FDR's accomplishments as president, from bringing the nation out of the Great Depression to leading the United States during World War II. The fourth room includes FDR's "four freedoms": Freedom of Speech, Freedom of Worship, Freedom from Want, Freedom from Fear—symbolizing what the United States was fighting for during the war. It also presents the contributions of First Lady Eleanor Roosevelt as U.N. ambassador after her husband's death.

There was some controversy over the memorial at its unveiling. Initially the memorial completely neglected the fact that Roosevelt used a wheelchair for most of his life because of the polio he contracted as a child. After protests by historians and the disabled community, the memorial's designers agreed to include images of FDR in his wheelchair. Park staff are on duty 8 A.M.–midnight every day but Christmas. Admission is free. For more information, write Information—Superintendent, National Capital Parks Central, 900 Ohio Dr. SW, Washington, DC 20242, or call 202/426-6841, or visit the website at www.nps.gov/fdrm/home.htm.

Jefferson Memorial

Though the Jefferson Memorial has stood only since 1942, it is today under almost constant repair, its columns cracked by the effects of auto exhaust and acid rain. Nevertheless, the 19-foot-tall hollow bronze of Thomas Jefferson in furs is undeniably impressive, centered in an open-air ro-

tunda surrounded by massive Ionic columns, an architectural copy of Jefferson's own rejected plans for the White House. The interior walls are crammed with quotes from Jefferson's voluminous writings, although not all are accurate: there are more than a dozen errors in the excerpt from the Declaration of Independence alone. Located on the south shore of the Tidal Basin, the memorial is open all day, every day. Park staff are on duty 8 A.M.–midnight. Closed Christmas Day. Admission is free. For more information, write Information—Superintendent, National Capital Parks Central, 900 Ohio Dr. SW, Washington, DC 20242, or call 202/426-6821, or visit the website at www.nps.gov/thje/home.htm.

"The Awakening"

Brave the gauntlet of joggers and golfers in East Potomac Park to arrive at J. Seward Johnson's bold, boisterous sculpture of a great bearded giant angrily erupting from the chains of the earth. Only the head and portions of each naked limb have broken through the grass at the tip of Hains Point, but the wild look in his eyes promises a great awakening indeed. Children can't resist reaching inside the great shouting mouth. Located at Hains Point in East Potomac Park at the southernmost point of Ohio Drive SW, "The Awakening" is viewable all day, every day. For more information, write Superintendent, East Potomac Park, Ohio Dr. SW, Washington, DC 20024, or call 202/485-9880.

Theodore Roosevelt Island

Those proposing a memorial for the nation's 26th president decided nothing less than an entire island would do, choosing 88 wilderness acres in the middle of the Potomac. Three miles of flat, easy trails wander through the swampy, wooded expanse of willow and ash, mud and muskrat. Rocky beaches with D.C. city views compete for visitors' attention with Paul Manship's 17-foot-tall bronze statue of the conservation-minded Roosevelt. There is only one way to get to the island: drive from D.C. into Virginia across the Theodore Roosevelt Bridge, veer right onto the northbound lanes of George Washington Parkway, pull into the poorly signed Roosevelt Island lot, and walk across the pedestrian footbridge that provides access to the island. The island memorial to the Bull Moose candidate is open 8 A.M.–dusk daily. Closed New Year's Day and Christmas Day. Admission is free. For nature/historical tours, call 703/289-2500 at least seven days in advance; no winter tours are offered. For more information, write Information—District Ranger, Theodore Roosevelt Island, George Washington Memorial Pkwy., c/o Turkey Run Park, McLean, VA 22101, or visit the website at www.nps.gov/this.

Bureau of Engraving and Printing
Here some 2,300 people labor around the clock to produce more than $100 billion in paper currency each year. Through plates of thick glass, visitors can watch workers inking, stacking, cutting, and examining millions of dollars a day. There's also an interesting exhibit on the curious history of money and, yes, bags of shredded bills are for sale in the gift shop (*everyone* considers trying to glue them back together, but it's futile). The Bureau, at 14th Street and C Street SW, 202/874-3019, is open Mon.–Fri. 9 A.M.–2 P.M. Closed federal holidays. Admission is always free, though tickets, available inside the building, are required from Easter to Labor Day. For more information, visit the website at www.moneyfactory.com.

United States Holocaust Memorial Museum
A truly wrenching experience, the Holocaust Museum is one of the most moving exhibits in this or any other city. From the outside, the building intentionally resembles the high brick ovens used to dispose of the bodies of millions of European Jews; inside, exhibits methodically trace the rise of Nazi Germany and its systematic implementation of its policy of genocide. The displays make clear that government officials in the United States and elsewhere were well aware of Hitler's implementation of the "Final Solution" but chose to do nothing. Visitors will witness many depictions of horrific atrocities, but perhaps the most affecting items are the heaps of personal effects collected by the Nazis from those they murdered:

mute piles of shoes, brushes, hair. Not recommended for children under age 11.

It's located at 100 Raoul Wallenberg Place SW (formerly 15th Street) at Independence Avenue right off the Mall, 202/488-0400, www.ushmm .org. The museum is open daily 10 A.M.–5:30 P.M., with occasional extended hours. Admission is free, though you must have tickets to enter. There are two ways to get tickets: reserve tickets in advance from Ticketmaster, which charges a service charge (from D.C. call 800/400-9373); or get same-day tickets at the museum box office. Allow at least 4–5 hours to visit.

CAPITOL HILL
Library of Congress
In 1800, the nation's legislators allocated a modest $5,000 "for the purchase of such books as may be necessary for the use of Congress." The collection was contained in a single room and was consulted as much to settle bets as to determine fine points of law. In 1814 the British put the entire nascent library to the torch. Fortunately for the nation, Thomas Jefferson was suffering through one of his periodic spasms of acute financial distress around the same time and sold to Congress his entire personal library of 6,500 volumes to rebuild the collection after the fire.

Today "Mr. Jefferson's Library" consists of more than 28 million books, with an additional 90 million holdings of film, photographs, music, other media, and splendid exhibitions. The library complex consists of three structures and 532 miles of shelves; start at the stunning Jefferson Building, completed in 1897 and offering a feast of mosaics and murals, sculptures and bas-reliefs. The Main Reading Room, with 236 desks arranged in an elegant circular pattern beneath a 160-foot dome, is one of the most beautiful sights in the city. The Library of Congress is not a lending library—materials must be perused on site. Located on 1st Street SE between Independence Avenue and East Capitol Street, the library is open Mon.–Sat. 10 A.M.–5:30 P.M. Closed New Year's Day and Christmas Day. Call 202/707-5000 or 202/707-8000 or check www .lcweb.loc.gov for library events.

Union Station

When it was completed in 1907, Union Station, modeled after the Baths of Caracalla in Rome, was the largest train station in the world. For the next 50 years, most visitors to the city first set foot in D.C. upon the station's elegant marble floors. By the 1970s, however, the place had become a national embarrassment: the floors buckled, torrential rains caved in portions of the roof, and a runaway train had slammed into the station, scattering spiraling shards of cars.

In 1981, Union Station was shut and sealed, until a business/government consortium invested $160 million to restore it to its former grandeur. Today visitors revel in acres of white marble flooring, bronze grilles, coffered ceilings, gold leaf, Honduran mahogany, and a plethora of stone carvings and statues. Being a working train station, Union Station is open all day, every day, and there is no admission charge. Visit Union Station at 40 Massachusetts Ave. NE, 202/371-9441, www.unionstationdc.com.

U.S. Capitol

Any first-time visitor to D.C. should take advantage of the opportunity to peek at our elected congressional officials at work. The small but well-appointed Senate chamber offers each senator a private desk separate from the rest, whereas House representatives are jammed together in long curved pews. The rest of the building presents its own peculiar charms: halls and rotundas stuffed with statues, and the frenzied frescoes of Constantino Brumidi, whose work was incisively described by Mark Twain as "the delirium tremens of art." A word of warning: much of the Capitol is off-limits to nonofficeholders, and visitors must heed the guidance of Capitol police.

To observe the House and Senate in session, U.S. citizens must obtain passes from the office of their senator or representative. International tickets are available in the Capitol for visitors from foreign countries (picture ID is required for visits to the House gallery). Another option is simply to cruise through the congressional office buildings across from the Capitol, where you're often more likely to experience the hustle and bustle of the political scene. The Senate buildings are to the north, on Constitution Avenue, and the House buildings are south of the Capitol on Independence Avenue. The Capitol is open to visitors Mon.–Sat. 9 A.M.–4:30 P.M. Closed New Year's Day, Thanksgiving Day, and Christmas Day. Free guided tours depart every 30 minutes 9 A.M.–3:30 P.M. from the information desk beneath the rotunda. Reservations are recommended; tickets are free and available on site. For more information, write Information—United States Senate/House of Representatives, U.S. Capitol Building, Washington, DC 20510 (20515 for the House), 202/224-3121. Be aware that, as with all D.C. sights, access to the Capitol building may sometimes be limited due to security concerns.

Capital Children's Museum

The guiding principle of this elaborate, realistic educational experience is encapsulated in the Chinese proverb, "What I hear, I forget; what I see, I remember; what I do, I understand." From learning how to make animated cartoons to sliding down a fire pole, children learn how the world works by taking the controls. Luckily, there's enough here to keep most grown-ups interested, too. Climb inside a soap bubble (adults welcome), visit Mexico, and tour the Ice Age in a collection of exhibits that change almost daily. The museum is open daily 10 A.M.–5 P.M. Admission is $7 per person, $5 seniors. Kids under two are admitted free. Located at 800 3rd St. NE, right at the Union Station Metro stop on the red line, the Capital Children's Museum fits easily into a tour of the Capitol Hill area. Call 202/675-4120 or visit www.ccm.org for more information.

Folger Shakespeare Library

The Bard lives on at this combination research library, museum, and theater, brimming with art, music, and literature. Inside is an eerie and delightful working reconstruction of an Elizabethan theater, where family events are held and the Shenandoah Shakespeare Express performs Shakespeare's finest. Poetry readings attract the likes of Robert Haas, Czeslaw Milosz, Octavio Paz, and John Updike. The Folger Consort, a chamber music ensemble, performs works from the 12th through the 18th centuries. The marmoreal facade of this great museum fits neatly between the imposing Library of Congress and the august Supreme Court building. The Folger is open Mon.–Sat. 10 A.M.–4 P.M. at 201 E. Capitol St. SE; free. Call 202/544-4600 for more information, or visit www.folger.edu on the Internet.

U.S. Supreme Court

Completed in 1935, this structure is undeniably opulent, with lush curtains, grandiose statues, and portentous inscriptions at every turn. The main chamber is particularly impressive, with the seats of the nine justices placed high above the rest of the court.

Check the schedule in advance to find out when the Court hears oral arguments. The public is welcome to attend, but there is limited seating, allocated on a first-come, first-served basis to those willing to line up outside the building. When the Court is not in session, visitors can attend courtroom lectures on the half hour 9:30 A.M.–3:30 P.M. The Supreme Court Building, at One 1st St. NE, Washington, DC 20543, 202/479-3030, is open Mon.–Fri. 9 A.M.–4:30 P.M. Closed on federal holidays. Admission is free.

Congressional Cemetery

In the early 19th century, D.C. was a remote, pestilential city, which sometimes proved fatal to those sent to govern from it. Congressional corpses

faced weeks of daunting travel on slow roads and primitive waterways to reach hometown interment, so it was much easier to bury them in the city itself. In 1812, Congress purchased 100 plots in a five-year-old cemetery, which eventually held 14 senators and 60 representatives.

A peaceful, rarely visited, and ultimately desolate place, the cemetery is mostly full of children because of the high infant mortality rate in the 19th century. Others among the 60,000 souls laid to rest here include FBI director J. Edgar Hoover and his longtime companion, Clyde Tolson; Taza and Push-ma-ta-ha, two native chiefs felled by disease while visiting D.C.; and David Herold, hung for his role in the assassination of Lincoln and quietly buried in a grave unmarked to this day. Dozens of cenotaphs honor members of Congress actually buried elsewhere. In this working cemetery, someone can usually be found around the small gatehouse just inside the E Street entrance; ask for the walking-tour brochure. The cemetery grounds are open daily 6:45 A.M.–dusk. For more information, write Information—Association for the Preservation of Historic Congressional Cemetery, 1801 E St. SE, Washington, DC 20003, or call 202/543-0539.

U.S. Botanic Garden

Another lovely idea of Thomas Jefferson's, this humid haven has enchanted visitors since 1820. Wander amid a wealth of tropical, subtropical, and desert plants; guide dinosaur-entranced young ones to the garden of the Jurassic; or picnic on a flowery terrace overlooking the Capitol reflecting pool. Located at 100 Maryland Ave. SW, 202/225-8333, near the east end of the Mall, the gardens are open daily 10 A.M.–5 P.M. Closed Christmas Day. For more information, write Information—United States Botanic Garden, 100 Maryland Ave. SW, Washington, DC 20024, or visit the website www.aoc.gov/usbg/ usbg_overview.htm.

THE WHITE HOUSE

First occupied by John Adams, the mansion at 1600 Pennsylvania Ave. NW was known as the President's House until it was whitewashed to cover smoke damage from the 1814 British burning of the city. It's not nearly as accessible today as it was during Jefferson's time, when enthusiastic dairymen would bustle in to deposit huge cheeses in the East Room. Nevertheless, it's the only chief executive's abode in the world that opens itself to tourists five days a week. When visiting the White House, don't step across the boundary ropes or make other foolish moves—those friendly men patrolling the halls can turn serious suddenly.

Tours of the White House are free, though tickets are required in spring and summer. Calling first is recommended. Only group tours are allowed. Tickets are available at the White House visitors center at the corner of 15th and E Streets, 202/456-7041, open 7:30 A.M.–4 P.M. Arrive early if you plan on touring the mansion the same day; there are usually no more tickets available after 8:30 A.M. The White House is open Tues.–Sat. 7:45 A.M.–noon. Closed major holidays and for official functions. No public restrooms or telephones are available. No photograph taking or videotaping allowed. For more information, write Information—White House Historical Association, 740 Jackson Pl. NW, Washington, DC 20560, or call 202/737-8292, or visit the website www.whitehouse.gov. Be aware that access to the White House is sometimes limited due to security concerns.

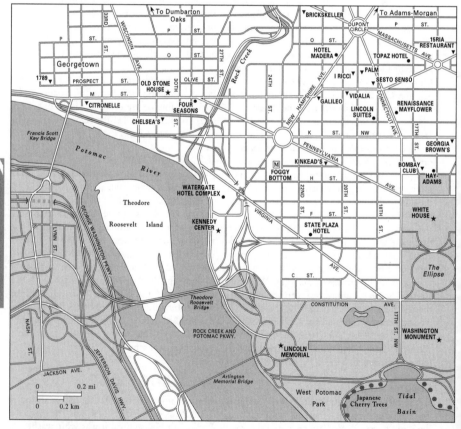

OLD DOWNTOWN AND THE FEDERAL TRIANGLE

The area enclosed by Pennsylvania Avenue, Constitution Avenue, and 15th Street is home to such stern, solemn edifices as the IRS and Justice Department buildings. For many years, the area was the most notorious neighborhood in D.C., popularly known as "Murder Bay." During the Civil War, the region was redubbed "Hooker's Division" in honor of the prostitutes encamped there. The place didn't get straight until the U.S. government bought up the land in the 1930s, razing the shacks and replacing them with grim granite.

The area north of Federal Triangle, between the White House and the Capitol Building, and bordered to the north by New York and Massachusetts Avenues, was the city's original downtown area. Popular restaurants and theaters, fashionable tailors' shops, and other, more practical business kept those in office from having to stray too far from their seats of power for dining, entertainment, and life's necessities. Between the time that the buildings of the Federal Triangle were built and the late '60s, the area became quite rundown, gaining the name "Old Downtown" to separate it from "New Downtown"—the area north of the White House, where new businesses opened shop next door to vendors fleeing rundown Old Downtown. The entire Old

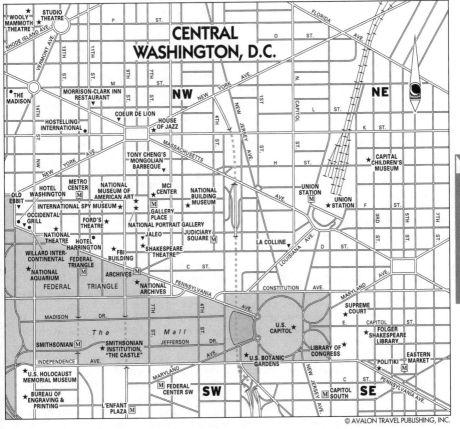

© AVALON TRAVEL PUBLISHING, INC.

Downtown area, especially Pennsylvania Avenue, gained a major facelift in the '80s. Today, the area again boasts popular restaurants and galleries, as well as landscaped plazas and memorials.

National Building Museum

In 1885, the general-cum-architect Montgomery Meigs erected the Pension Building. Damned at its dedication as an "unsightly monstrosity," the structure is recognized today as a masterpiece. Built of more than 15 million bricks, it features a 1,200-foot-long terra cotta frieze of Union soldiers forever filing for pensions. Eight central Corinthian columns, the largest in the world, dominate a great hall large enough to contain a 15-story building.

Today the eccentric old edifice is home to the National Building Museum, the only institution in the United States dedicated to architectural achievements. On permanent display are exhibits dedicated to D.C. and the Pension Building itself. Past temporary shows covered the humble, classic American barn, the aftermath of the April 1995 bombing of the federal building in Oklahoma City, and design proposals for the new World Trade Center. Located at 401 F St. NW, the museum is open Mon.–Sat. 10 A.M.–5 P.M., Sunday 11 A.M.–5 P.M. Closed New Year's Day, Thanksgiving Day, and Christmas Day. Call 202/272-2448 or fax 202/272-2564, or go to www.nbm.org on the Web.

International Spy Museum

Double-O-Seven had nothing on this museum, 800 F St., NW, 202/654-0946, www.spymuseum.org. It, however, has something of his—the oil-spewing, top-popping Aston-Martin DB5 he drove in **Goldfinger.** Everything you ever wanted to know about spies and spying is here, from the German Enigma cipher machine, button cameras, and guns that look like a tube of lipstick to fake dog poop (it signals a target to bombers flying overhead). You'll learn about the devious doings of male and female spies, among them George Washington, Mata Hari, and Julia Child (!), famed TV chef. There's something for everyone in this extensive and thorough collection. Archival films of OSS and C-130 training

films from WWII, toys developed from popular TV programs like *Mission Impossible* and *The Avengers,* and cleverly lit and well-thought-out displays are both informative and entertaining. It's open April–Oct. 10 A.M.–8 P.M., Nov.–Mar. 10 A.M.–6 P.M. every day except major holidays. Admission is $11.

National Museum of American Art

Housed in an imposing edifice Philip Johnson once adjudged "the greatest building in the world," this eclectic collection of two centuries of American art includes truly marvelous works in the folk and ethnic traditions. (The building is closed for renovation until 2006. Programs take place at other sites. See website www.nmaa.si.edu for more information.) See especially D.C. janitor James Hampton's *The Throne of the Third Heaven of the Nations' Millennium General,* the fruit of some 15 years of cementing together found objects such as light bulbs, electrical cables, and aluminum foil; and the spirit-rich *Man on Fire* by Luis Jiminez, sprung from a legend of an unlucky Aztec man put to the torch by 16th-century conquistadores. Additional offerings include giraffes constructed solely of bottle caps and the psychedelic stain paintings of Morris Louis.

Located at 8th and G Streets NW, the museum is closed for renovation until July 2006. For more information, write Information—Smithsonian Information Center, 1000 Jefferson Dr. SW, Washington, DC 20560, or call 202/357-2700.

National Portrait Gallery

On the site where D.C. designer Pierre L'Enfant once wished to build a national cathedral stands this fascinating gallery of America's heroes and villains portrayed in sculptures, paintings, and photographs. (The building is under renovation and will not reopen until 2005. Programs take place at other sites. See website www.npg.si.edu for more information.) See especially the serious and sardonic self-portraits, the dizzying diversity of the Gallery of Notable Americans, and the treasury of 19th-century black-and-white photography. At 8th and F Streets NW, the museum is closed for renovation until 2005. For information, write

Information—Smithsonian Information Center, 1000 Jefferson Dr. SW, Washington, DC 20560, or call 202/357-2700.

The National Aquarium

Besides the usual collection of fish-tank fare, the nation's oldest public aquarium offers belligerent fiddler crabs banging on the glass, sleepy sloe-eyed alligators, gape-mouthed eels exuding yellow slime, and pale moist axolotl salamanders. A touch pool allows young ones to gently maul the likes of horseshoe crabs, while a small sign puts the whole shark business in perspective: people kill and consume 10 million sharks each year, while sharks rarely kill humans. The aquarium holds shark feedings Monday, Wednesday, and Saturday at 2 P.M., and piranha feedings Tuesday, Thursday, and Sunday. Regular hours are 9 A.M.–4:30 P.M. daily. Closed Christmas Day. Admission is $3.50. The entrance to the aquarium, which is located in the basement of the Commerce Building, is on 14th Street NW. There is no street address, but you can write to U.S. Department of Commerce Building, Room B-037, Washington, DC 20230, call 202/482-2825, or visit the website at www.national aquarium.com for more information.

J. Edgar Hoover FBI Building

The free one-hour tour of FBI headquarters, 935 Pennsylvania Ave. NW, offers an extremely selective history of the bureau, including Dillinger, drugs, and a firearms demonstration by an FBI sharpshooter. (The building is under extensive renovation and will reopen for tours in late 2004.) Guided tours (mandatory) depart eight times a day Mon.–Fri. 8:45 A.M.–4:25 P.M. The tour entrance is on E Street NW, and reservations are recommended. Plan well ahead; this is a popular attraction. Arrange your visit by phoning the bureau or through your congressional representative. Admission is free. For more information, call 202/324-3447 or visit www.fbi.gov. Closed federal holidays.

District of Columbia Courthouse

This Greek Revival edifice at 500 Indiana Ave. NW originally served as Washington's first city hall; it also saw duty as a hospital, patent office, and slave market. For more than 100 years, it's been the D.C. courthouse, the place where accused local lawbreakers are processed through the criminal justice system. In 1881, Charles Guiteau, the lunatic assassin of President James Garfield, babbled and bellowed through his trial in these rooms, then ascended the gallows reciting poetry until he was stopped by the rope. There are information pamphlets at the Public Information Desk to the left of the entrance. Stop here, after passing through the metal detector, for the lowdown on the juicy trials of the day. The courthouse is open Mon.–Fri. 9 A.M.–5 P.M. Closed all federal holidays. Admission is free; call 202/879-1010 for more information.

Old Post Office

When it was completed in 1899, this former home of the U.S. Postal Service was denounced as a monstrosity, "a cross between a cathedral and a cotton mill." These days, surrounded by the abominations of modern architecture, the old joint looks pretty good, housing federal workers for such agencies as the National Endowment for the Arts (NEA) and the National Endowment for the Humanities (NEH). Take the glass elevator to the clock tower; at 315 vertical feet, it offers one of the finest aerial views in the city. It's located at 1100 Pennsylvania Ave. NW, 202/289-4224, www.nps.gov/opot/index2 .htm; admission to the building is free. The tower is open daily June– Sept. 9 A.M.–7:45 P.M., except Thursday when it closes at 5:30 P.M., Oct.–May 9 A.M.–5 P.M.; the shops are open Mon.–Sat. 10 A.M.–7 P.M., Sun. noon–6 P.M. Closed Christmas Day.

National Archives

Preservationists of "the nation's memory," archivists here determine the worth of billions of documents generated annually by the world's busiest government. Pride of place goes to the Declaration of Independence, the Constitution, and the Bill of Rights, which are displayed daily, then mechanically lowered into a 50-ton vault to shield them from vandals and nuclear attack. Famous primarily as a center of genealogical research, the Archives have in recent years become a pilgrimage site for those wishing to listen to Nixon's Watergate tapes. At 8th Street and Constitution Avenue NW, the Archives are open daily 10 A.M.–5:30 P.M. Closed Christmas Day. Reservations are required and are available by appointment only. Call 202/501-5205 for details. For more general information, write to the archives (zip code 20408), or call 202/501-5400 or visit the website www.nara.gov.

Ford's Theatre National Historic Site

In one of history's tragic ironies, President Abraham Lincoln was shot in Ford's Theatre just five days after Confederate general Robert E. Lee surrendered at Appomattox. Today the basement of the theater is a shrine to the martyred president, while upstairs the show goes on. See the bronze of a slumping, exhausted Lincoln; the simple contents of his pockets at the time of his death, from an Irish linen handkerchief to Confederate money; and the .44 single-shot derringer used by assassin John Wilkes Booth. Located at 511 10th St. NW, the theater is closed to visitors during rehearsals and matinees (usually Thursdays and weekends), but the museum is always open. Admission to the museum is free. For theater box office information, call 202/347-4833. The box office is open Mon.–Fri. 10 A.M.–6 P.M. Closed Christmas Day. For more information, write Information—Superintendent, National Capital Parks Central, Washington, DC 20242, or call 202/485-9880, or visit the website www.nps.gov/foth.

Petersen House

After his shooting by John Wilkes Booth, Abraham Lincoln was carried from his box in Ford's Theatre across 10th Street to the boardinghouse of William Petersen, a German-born tailor. Today, three rooms of the Petersen domicile are preserved as they were that night in April 1865; the front bedroom that Secretary of War Edwin Stanton turned into a temporary White House; the parlor where Mary Lincoln waited and prayed; and the room where Lincoln died, which had been commandeered from William T. Carl, a

young man out on the town that night celebrating the end of the war. The house is open daily 9 A.M.–5 P.M. Closed Christmas Day. Admission is free. For more information, write Information—Superintendent, National Capital Parks Central, 900 Ohio Dr. SW, Washington, DC 20242, or call 202/426-6830.

ADAMS-MORGAN

Adams-Morgan is D.C.'s version of New York City's East Village, only smaller. Most of this teeming quarter's nightlife takes place along two main drags: Columbia Road and 18th Street, joined together in a V at their northern apex. A little bit tony, a little bit tawdry, Adams-Morgan is a place where Washingtonians feel free to step outside the bars of their pinstriped suits.

Where yankee-doodle Washington is built on a monumental scale, Adams-Morgan is a concrete redoubt, an urban refuge. The streets actually become more crowded after 6 P.M., while the rest of D.C. rolls up its sidewalks. Here it's safe to be neurotic, to be gay, to be straight, to stay up late, to drink too much, to pretend.

Once a row of tired Ethiopian restaurants scrunched cheek-by-jowl into red brick townhouses, Adams-Morgan has hip-hopped into its own over the last decade, as Washington discovered that there was life after legislation. This is an immigrant neighborhood, a largely Hispanic enclave that is also home to wealthy Anglos and a veritable United Nations of other ethnicities.

When the world starts getting you down, there's room enough for two (and plenty more) on Adams-Morgan's roofs; rooftop partying is de rigueur. There's **Perry's,** 1811 Columbia Rd., 202/234-6218, that offers sashimi by starlight. There's also **Roxanne's,** 2319 18th St., where you can enjoy eclectic Cajun cuisine under the stars.

One way to get your bearings in Adams-Morgan is by zigging and zagging. Best to zig down to 18th Street and to zag up to Columbia Road. Such an erratic route will take you up and down (mostly up, for Adams-Morgan is hilly) delightfully leafy lanes lined with elegant townhouses, many of which come with huge picture windows.

A big problem is that there are no convenient Metro stops near Adams-Morgan. It's a long walk from the two nearest stations, Dupont Circle and Woodley Park-Zoo, to the heart of the quarter. It's best to pay for taxis or, better yet, let a friend drive: finding a parking spot in Adams-Morgan has been known to reduce would-be visitors to tears. There is one convenient parking lot at 2419 18th St.

Club Heaven, 2327 18th St. NW, 202/667-4355, provides an antidote for the fiendish parking. Appropriately, Club Heaven shares its townhouse venue with—you guessed it—Club Hell, downstairs. (Just in case you're wondering about the afterlife, Club Hell has the trendier crowd—and a larger dance floor.)

In addition, Adams-Morgan offers a wide variety of good restaurants and entertainment. This is the only area of town apart from Georgetown where it's possible to shop, relax over drinks, then walk down the street to find dinner. Afterward, you can stroll up the block to a club to close the night, unwind with some dancing, or just relax and listen to good music.

UPPER NORTHWEST

A series of residential neighborhoods, arranged in a succession of rings, gives the Upper Northwest its own distinct character and allure. Arguably, **Dupont Circle** marks the center of the area that fills the district's borders between Adams-Morgan and the Maryland state line. On one side of the circle sits some of the city's great think tanks, such as the **Brookings Institution,** 1775 Massachusetts Ave., 202/797-6000, established in 1927. Near the circle along Connecticut Avenue, you'll find good restaurants in a variety of price ranges. To the north, **Kramerbooks & Afterwords,** 1517 Connecticut Ave. NW, 202/387-1462, is a D.C. institution. The bookstore offers a café in back, where, after browsing the aisles, you can hear live music Wed.–Sat. On Friday and Saturday, Kramerbooks stays open 24 hours for late-night literary binges.

One ripple out from Dupont Circle is **Woodley Park,** known principally for the National Zoo. The area also claims to be home to more

international restaurants than anywhere in D.C., which in this international metropolis is saying a lot.

Beyond Woodley Park is exclusive **Cleveland Park,** where former President Grover Cleveland built his "summer White House," and consequently lent his name to the neighborhood. Today, the area is home to former senator Bill Bradley, Jim Lehrer of the *NewsHour,* and satirist Mark Russell. If you're here at lunchtime, try the local Irish pub **Ireland's Four Provinces,** 3412 Connecticut Ave. NW, 202/244-0860, serving shepherd's pie and Irish brew.

Heading farther north, the campus of **American University,** alma mater of Willard Scott and novelist Anne Beattie, covers 84 acres in the area known as Tenleytown. The final reaches of the Upper Northwest extend out to Friendship Heights and Chevy Chase at the border of Maryland. **Friendship Heights** is a busy entertainment/shopping district offering the tony urban mall known as Mazza Gallery, and **Chevy Chase** is an exclusive address where you'll find one of the best movie palaces in Washington: the **Cineplex Odeon Avalon 2,** built in 1925, with 679 seats in the main theater.

Washington National Cathedral

Medieval cathedrals often required centuries to complete, so perhaps it's not so embarrassing that 199 years passed before this one was considered finished. In 1791, D.C. designer Pierre L'Enfant envisioned a "church intended for national purposes, and assigned to the special use of no particular Sect or denomination, but equally open to all." In 1893 Congress finally allocated funds for the edifice, and in 1990 the last stone was placed atop a west front pinnacle.

The cathedral is a truly magnificent structure, and its stone and wood carvings, stained glass, and metalwork are unsurpassed on these shores. The Gothic wonderment is constructed of Indiana limestone, with all details carved from the walls by hand. High above dwell angels, gargoyles, and grotesques; outside, visitors to the 57-acre grounds can stroll a medieval walled garden of roses and herbs. The cathedral is located at Massachusetts and Wisconsin

Streets NW, 202/537-6207, www.cathedral.org/cathedral. Open Mon.–Fri. 10 A.M.–5:30 P.M., Saturday 10 A.M.–4:30 P.M. Sunday 8 A.M.–6:30 P.M. Admission is free. Evening services are held at 7:30 P.M. Mon.–Sat., call for other service times, and the Chapel of the Good Shepherd is always open.

National Zoological Park

Under the auspices of the Smithsonian Institution, the National Zoo is one of the nation's more humane animal parks. More than three miles of trails wander past 2,800 animals caged on 163 hilly acres at the edge of Rock Creek. Visitors will find no class hierarchy here: paramecia and leafcutter ants are displayed as proudly as lions, tigers, and bears. An enclave of naked mole rats even get exposure via the Internet with the zoo's live naked mole rat webcam (http://natzoo.si.edu/Animals/AfricanSavanna).

Visitors can "ooh" and "aah" over such rarities as Komodo dragons, watch the cuttlefish transform from a mass of transparent jelly into a voracious predator, or ponder the ways animals use their brains, described in the Think Tank exhibit. The rainforest environment of the Amazonia exhibit approaches D.C.'s own August heat and humidity. Admission to the zoo, at 3001 Connecticut Ave. NW, is free, though there is a somewhat steep charge for on-site parking (maximum $11); 202/673-4800, http://natzoo.si.edu. The zoo grounds are open daily May 1–Sept. 15, 6 A.M.–8 P.M., Sept. 16–Apr. 30, 6 A.M.–6 P.M. Closed Christmas Day. Zoo buildings are open May 1–Sept. 15, 10 A.M.–6 P.M., Sept. 16–Apr. 30, 10 A.M.–4:30 P.M. Closed Christmas Day.

Rock Creek Park

These 1,750 acres were purchased in 1890 by Congress for the "pleasant valleys and ravines, primeval forests and open fields, its running waters, its rocks clothed with rich ferns and mosses, its repose and tranquility, its light and shade, its ever-varying shrubbery, its beautiful and extensive views." Rock Creek Park still offers all that, as well as more than one million wildflowers.

Bordering the Upper Northwest to the east, the city's largest park is a magical ribbon of green.

Here hikers, horseback riders, and joggers have the right of way, and on Sunday, with long sections of the park's roads closed to cars, they take control. Rock Creek Park offers some 15 miles of hiking trails, from toddler-friendly to quite rugged. Trail maps are available at both the park headquarters and the nature center. An 11-mile bike path from the Lincoln Memorial to the Maryland border runs the full length of the park; it's paved the entire distance and closed to vehicular traffic on weekends and holidays. Numerous access points make visiting the park on bike or on foot an easy day's outing. Trail rides ($25) are available Sat.–Thurs. at the **Rock Creek Park Horse Center,** 5115 Glover Rd. NW, 202/362-0118. Closed Mondays, Thanksgiving Day, Christmas Day, and New Year's Day.

The cemetery in Rock Creek Park is the oldest in the city and home to one of the most arresting statues in D.C. In 1883, Marian Adams, wife of historian Henry Adams, downed enough photographic chemicals to end her life. Her husband interred her in Rock Creek Cemetery, then commissioned sculptor Augustus Saint-Gaudens to create a monument in bronze, adding "no attempt is to be made to make it intelligible to the average mind." When the work was ready the grave-keepers were horrified, saying they wanted no part of it. But Adams persisted, and the cloaked, hooded lady was set among holly and ivy in section E. Adams called it *The Peace of God,* the sculptor *The Mystery of the Hereafter,* but most visitors agree with Mark Twain that the most appropriate designation is simply *Grief.*

The cemetery is located on Rock Creek Church Road NW and open daily 7:30 A.M.–dusk. Admission is free. The nature center is open Wed.–Sun. 9 A.M.–5 P.M. Pierce Mill (202/426-6908), a working cornmeal and wheat flour gristmill, where visitors can purchase the mill's products, make the flour and meal themselves in small handheld grinders, or just come in and watch, is closed for repairs until mid-2004. Both the nature center and mill are closed on major holidays. For more information, write Rock Creek Park Superintendent, 3545 Williamsburg Ln., NW, Washington, DC 20008, or call 202/895-6070, or visit the website www.nps.gov/rocr.

Society of the Cincinnati

Established in 1783 by George Washington and the officers in his Continental Army, the Society still limits membership to only one direct descendant per original officer. For 15 hours each week (call for hours; closed federal holidays), the society's beautiful beaux arts mansion is thrown open to the public, and visitors may walk among elegant furnishings and priceless artwork, or peruse the excellent Revolutionary-era reference library. Admission to Anderson House, 2118 Massachusetts Ave. NW, 202/785-2040, is free.

GEORGETOWN

President Kennedy lived in Georgetown 1957–1961 during his pre-presidential term as a U.S. senator and before becoming president. Syndicated columnist George Will keeps his office here. The latter was a New Deal Democrat, then later a staunch Republican. Still, they hailed from the same place, a neighborhood sandwiched between Rock Creek and the Potomac River known as Georgetown. No one is certain who named the quarter: some say it was named after one of the King Georges or one or another of the area's founders. Georgetown didn't become part of the District of Columbia until after the Civil War.

Since then, it has had ups and downs, good times and bad, but the present moment is decidedly up. Between the peaceful towpaths of the old C&O Canal to the south and what has come to be known as "the most civilized square mile in America" to the north abides some of the most expensive real estate on earth. An average-sized, even smallish house in Georgetown runs into the millions of dollars. Like Beverly Hills in Los Angeles, the homes in Georgetown are pedigreed, known by their former famous owners, like the house at 3017 N St. where Jacqueline Kennedy lived for a time.

History and personality blend in Georgetown's streets. Many great authors, such as Katherine Anne Porter and Sinclair Lewis, have called the neighborhood home. Herman Wouk still lives here, as does celebrity biographer Kitty Kelly. Historical figures such as Alexander Graham Bell called Georgetown home, as did Dr. Walter Reed, the American Army surgeon who proved yellow fever was carried by mosquitoes.

along the C&O Canal in Georgetown

Georgetown's main crossroads are M Street and Wisconsin Avenue, a bustling area of boutiques, jazz clubs, and good restaurants. Just south of Wisconsin on M Street, **Canal Square,** built in 1842, was first used as a grain warehouse, then as a cooperage, and finally as home to a census bureau contractor known as the Tabulating Machine Company. Though its headquarters are currently in Armonk, New York, you'll recognize the company's more recent acronym: IBM.

From Canal Square, a block south of M Street toward the Potomac you'll find lock number 4 of the **Chesapeake and Ohio Canal.** Operated by National Park Service rangers dressed in 19th-century costumes, a working barge takes visitors under the bridge and through the locks on a half-mile mule-towed journey through the past. A bit farther south is **Washington Harbor,** known by some as "Baghdad on the Potomac." This terraced extravaganza is a riverfront development of condominiums, shops, and restaurants. Once something of a joke, the Harbor has grown into a delightful and popular setting of nightspots. With lots of fun restaurants, gushing fountains, bright lights, fluttering flags, fabulous river views, and a romantic promenade, the harbor makes for great people-watching.

Despite being 20 minutes by foot from the nearest Metro station, Georgetown definitely deserves, and can easily consume, a day or more of touring. Walk the historic homes, idle at Dumbarton Oaks, and dine in town.

Dumbarton Oaks

The crown jewel of Georgetown is Dumbarton Oaks, 1703 32nd St. NW, a former estate that is now a museum and 43-acre garden spot. In 1944, as World War II moved into its final climactic phase, the leaders of the United States, Britain, China, and the Soviet Union met here to lay the groundwork for what was to become the United Nations.

For visitors to Dumbarton Oaks, it's easiest to think of the estate in three parts. The first is the 16-acre compound owned by Harvard University and known as the Dumbarton Oaks Research Library and Collection. Here you'll find the estate's renowned collection of some 1,500 eastern Mediterranean artifacts dating from 330 to 1453 A.D. The library holds more than 12,000 Byzantine coins, one of the most complete collections in the world. Next comes the 27-acre Dumbarton Oaks Park, 202/339-6410 (open daily until dusk). Ten acres of the park are given over to one of the finest examples of European-styled formal gardens in America, with nearly 1,000 rose bushes, 10 pools, and nine fountains. The entrance is on R Street, and it's open Mar.–Oct. 2–6 P.M.; $5 admission, Nov.–Mar. 2–5 P.M.; free admission. The remaining 17 acres of the Dumbarton Oaks estate are covered by well-groomed parkland. Call 202/339-6401 or visit www.doaks.org for more information.

Georgetown University

Another cornerstone of the community is the 104-acre main campus of Georgetown University, one of the nation's premier schools for law and international affairs, and the oldest Catholic university in the nation. Free maps and brochures on the campus and environs are available at the main gate, 37th and O Streets NW. Be sure to visit the Gaston Hall collections of Victorian dolls and Indian artifacts. For more information on the university, check out www.georgetown.edu or call 202/687-0100.

Old Stone House

The oldest standing structure in the city, the house was built in 1765 by a cabinetmaker named Christopher Layman in what was then the Town of George. Over the years, the dwelling also served as boardinghouse, tavern, bordello, and artists' studio. Today its low doorways and lumpy beds are preserved as a relic of working-class life in pre-Revolutionary times. Rumor that Pierre L'Enfant worked here while designing D.C. helped secure congressional protection for the structure in the 1950s. It is said that children are those most likely to encounter the many ghosts inhabiting the structure. The house, 3051 M St. NW, 202/426-6851, is open Wed.–Sun. noon–5 P.M. Closed Christmas and New Year's Day; free.

EAST OF THE CAPITOL

Kenilworth Aquatic Gardens

This 12-acre haven along the Anacostia River is the only U.S. national park devoted exclusively to water plants. Beginning in 1880, one-armed Civil War veteran Walter Shaw and his industrious daughter methodically dredged a series of ponds here, growing lilies and lotuses that they marketed to plant-happy Washingtonians. The government acquired the property in 1938, and today a network of trails crisscrosses levees separating dozens of bright marshy ponds.

Don't miss the lotus, once thought to be extinct, which was grown from 900-year-old seeds unearthed in a dry Tibetan riverbed; be on the lookout too for frogs, salamanders, snakes, mallards, and turtles. Admission to the gardens, located at 1900 Anacostia Dr. NE, 202/426-6905, is free. The entrance is just off Anacostia Avenue near Quarles and Douglas Streets. Kenilworth Aquatic Gardens is open daily 7 A.M.–4 P.M. Closed Thanksgiving, Christmas and New Year's Day.

Tours and walks can be made by arrangement. Visit the website at www.nps.gov/nace/keaq.

U.S. National Arboretum

Along the Anacostia River lies this 444-acre natural jewel, featuring stunning collections of bonsai, dwarf conifer, dogwood, and azalea. There are nine miles of paved roads, but it's more enjoyable to park somewhere and get out and walk. At the center of the arboretum are 22 ghostly Corinthian columns rising from a grassy knoll; for 125 years they supported the east portico of the Capitol. Other highlights of the arboretum include the National Herb Garden, containing more than 800 useful herbs from around the world, and the National Grove of State Trees, a perfect place for picnicking. The arboretum staff is currently attempting to reintroduce bald eagles to the nation's capital. Admission to the arboretum is free; 3501 New York Ave. NE, 202/245-2726, fax 202/245-4575, www.usna.usda.gov. Hours are daily 8 A.M.–5 P.M. Closed Christmas Day.

Accommodations

For the most part, accommodations in the District are pricey. There are exceptions to that rule, though, and your options increase dramatically if you consider staying outside of D.C. in Maryland or Virginia.

UNDER $50

The **Washington, D.C., Hostel** is centrally located downtown at 11th and K Streets NW, near the Smithsonian Museums, the White House, and other attractions. Only a four-block walk from Metro Center station, the renovated eight-story hotel offers 270 beds, kitchen and laundry facilities, lockers/baggage storage area, and wheelchair accessibility. For night owls, the hostel offers 24-hour access; there are also tours, movies, and other special programs. Rates run approximately $29–35. The DC Hostel is open year-round and private rooms are available on a limited basis. Groups are also welcome, but reservations are required, 202/737-2333, fax 202/737-1508, or email reserve@hiwashingtondc.org. Reservations are accepted by phone or fax with 24-hour advance notice and credit card confirmation and can also be made using the Hostelling International toll-free number (within the U.S. only); have your credit card ready and dial 800/909-4776, then enter the DC Hostel two-digit access code (04) to be connected. Visit www.hiwashingtondc.org for more information.

$50–100

Adam's Inn, 1744 Lanier Place NW, 202/745-3600 or 800/578-6807, fax 202/319-7958, adamsinn@adamsinn.com, www.adamsinn.com, consists of three brick townhouses and a carriage house hidden away on a leafy residential street two blocks from the heart of the Adams-Morgan district. Built around 1913, the inn has a definite Victorian feel, with some modern touches. The common rooms are equipped with TV and computers for Internet access. A lavish continental breakfast is included in the price of your stay. A total of 25 rooms are available with private baths ($85 s, $95 d) or shared baths ($70 s, $80 d). As elsewhere in Adams-Morgan, parking is limited.

The charming, inexpensive **Kalorama Guest House,** 1854 Mintwood Place NW, 202/667-6369, fax 202/319-1262, consists of six Victorian townhouses filled with creative antique furnishings, like brass beds and Oriental rugs, set off by fresh flowers. Enjoy a sherry in front of the fire or lemonade on the patio, then take the short walk to many of the finest restaurants in the city. Really two venues, one at this location in Adams-Morgan and another in Washington's pleasant Woodley Park neighborhood, the guest house offers 30 air-conditioned rooms ($70 s, $75 d), all nonsmoking. Reservations with full payment are required.

Located a few blocks from the White House, the **Center City Hotel,** 1201 13th St. and M Street NW, 202/682-5300, fax 202/371-9624, offers 100 traditional-style guest rooms at decent rates ($89–125). There are free movies in all the rooms, refrigerators in some, and a restaurant on the premises. Nonsmoking rooms are available. In regard to pets, the front desk says, "We take small animals, but no snakes!"

The venerable, friendly **Hotel Harrington,** 436 11th St. NW, 202/628-8140 or 800/424-8532, fax 202/343-2311, www.hotel-harrington.com, is downtown, only two blocks from the Smithsonian. The excellent location makes the Harrington a particular favorite of international travelers. The Harrington also offers a restaurant, and is wheelchair accessible. The 245 rooms and 26 suites must be booked in advance. Parking is available at a lot a few blocks away. The large rooms ($89) are clean and comfortable.

The **Savoy Suites Georgetown,** 2505 Wisconsin Ave. NW, 202/337-9700 or 800/944-5377, fax 202/337-3644, features fine, large rooms. The 152 suites, some with excellent views of the D.C. skyline, run $89–99. The hotel restaurant, a favorite of locals, offers outdoor dining in season and serves as gallery space for area artists. Area transportation services are available at the Savoy, including a D.C. Metro shuttle.

International visitors feel welcome at the **Swiss Inn,** 1204 Massachusetts Ave. NW, 202/371-1816 or 800/955-7947, with managers who speak a plethora of European languages. The inn's seven air-conditioned apartments ($89–119) have bathrooms and kitchenettes with refrigerators. During the off-season (November 15 through the end of February), the apartments rent for $420 per week. If you need a ride from the airport or bus stop, just give the place a call, and a staff member will come pick you up.

$100–150

Located by the Lincoln Memorial, the Mall, and George Washington University, the **State Plaza Hotel,** 2117 E St. NW, 202/861-8200 or 800/424-2859, fax 202/659-8601, is a favorite among those Kennedy Center performers who aren't staying at the posh and expensive Watergate. The 223 suites ($145 and up) are pleasant and spacious, with full kitchens. The State Plaza has a restaurant on premises, a fitness center, and coin-operated washing machines. For those needing to get out of the city or wishing to visit Arlington Cemetery, the State Plaza is conveniently located just blocks from Memorial Bridge.

D.C.'s only waterfront hotel, the **Channel Inn,** 650 Water St. SW, 202/554-2400 or 800/368-5668, fax 202/863-1164, peers out over Washington Channel toward the island of East Potomac Park. Each of the 100 rooms ($150) offers a balcony, and some provide fine views of the boats in the harbor. Try the raw bar at the hotel restaurant, the Engine Room.

$150–250

The **Radisson Barcelo Hotel DC,** 2121 P St. NW, 202/293-3100 or 800/333-3333, fax 202/331-9719, is the first D.C. joint venture of the Mallorca-based Barcelo chain, offering European service at decent American prices. The 301 marble- and mahogany-decorated rooms run $149 and up. The hotel restaurant, **Gabriel,** is excellent, and the hotel bar is popular with locals. Enjoy swimming in the rooftop pool while watching the stars.

Located close to Dupont Circle, the cozy **Tabard Inn,** 1739 N St. NW, 202/331-8528, fax 202/785-6173, is an unspoiled mark of good taste. This country inn in the heart of Washington offers doubles with baths starting at $180, but don't be fooled by the bargain. The Tabard's indoor-outdoor restaurant is without peer in its business-class price range.

The friendly, 10-story **Hotel Madera,** 1310 New Hampshire Ave. NW, 202/296-7600, fax 202/293-2476, has 82 spacious rooms, most with two double beds ($189). This Dupont Circle hotel also has "specialty rooms" that offer amenities varying from in-room exercise equipment to DVD libraries, free Internet access, and "smart phones" offering access to a bewildering variety of services.

The **Henley Park Hotel,** 926 Massachusetts Ave. NW, 202/638-5200 or 800/222-8474, fax 202/638-6740, www.washingtonplazahotel .com, is a converted 1918 seven-story Tudor structure featuring faux 18th-century furnishings, a facade bristling with 118 gargoyles, and a telephone in every bathroom. The 90 air-conditioned rooms run $175–1,000. Ask if there's a four-poster bed available, and be sure to take afternoon tea in the Wilkes Room. Think dark wood and tiny golden lamps.

The **Carlyle Suites,** 1731 New Hampshire Ave. NW, 202/234-3200 or 800/964-5377, fax 202/387-0085, is a wonder. The bold exterior and accompanying interior frills are pure art deco, a motif abandoned only in the suites, which are washed in pastels splashed with charcoal and gray. The on-site Neon Café is stuck firmly in the 1940s: here you can dig into a large steak while swinging to the sounds of live weekend jazz. Located on a pleasant residential street near Dupont Circle, the eight-story Carlyle features 170 guest suites ($179–189) with sitting areas, kitchenettes, and limited complimentary parking.

The Gaelic place in DC—the **Phoenix Park Hotel,** 520 N. Capitol St. NW, 202/638-6900 or 800/824-5419, fax 202/393-3236—is nine stories of Irish linen, hospitality, finery, and food. The Phoenix Park features 150 rooms ($150) and regular live entertainment, both scheduled and unscheduled. AAA members can secure drastic rate reductions.

The **Washington Courtyard,** 900 Connecticut Ave. NW, 202/332-9300 or 800/ 321-2211, fax 202/328-7039, is surprisingly affordable for all that it offers: chandeliers in the lobby, mahogany armoires, and phones with modems, for starters. The hotel is also host to the pricey **Claret's** for eats and the clublike **Bailey's** for drinks. Children under 18 sleep with their parents for free. Prices at this 147-room hotel range from $179–290 depending on the season and availability. Located in Kalorama, an upscale residential neighborhood near Embassy Row, the hotel hosts many foreign diplomats, who undoubtedly enjoy the marble baths and fax machines of the executive rooms. All guests can enjoy the outdoor pool and the fitness room.

Situated only five blocks west of the White House, the **Hotel Lombardy,** 2019 I St. NW, 202/828-2600 or 800/424-5486, fax 202/872-0503, www.hotellombardy.com, provides sumptuous accommodations including cherry-wood furnishings, dusty rose carpeting, and fine art on the walls. Most of the 132 rooms ($130) offer fully equipped kitchens, but the Lombardy features a fine restaurant as well. Rates are reduced sharply in the off-season.

The **Topaz Hotel,** 1733 N St., NW, 202/232-8000, www.topazhotel.com, is one of several Kimpton Group hotels in Washington that represent a bright and lively new face of the lodging industry (the group also owns and manages Hotel Rouge and Hotel Monaco). The rooms are spacious and comfortably modern, and several offer amenities such as a workout (energy) alcove or yoga alcove complete with equipment and videos. The Topaz also offers breakfast, lunch and dinner to order in-room, and a very popular bar. Rates range $145–275.

The 10-story **Washington Suites,** 2500 Pennsylvania Ave. NW, 202/333-8060, fax 202/338-3818, offers 124 spacious one- and two-bedroom suites ($139), with kitchens. If you're absolutely determined not to get away from it all, this is the place: some rooms offer two telephones and two TVs.

OVER $250

When it's time to inaugurate a president, no hotel offers better views of the parade than the 80-year-old **Hotel Washington.** With 344 rooms, you couldn't get much closer to the Treasury Building and the White House. Located at 15th Street and Pennsylvania Avenue, it offers two top-floor restaurants, the informal Sky Terrace and the more formal Sky Room, that offer spectacular vistas of the White House, the Ellipse, and the Washington Monument. It was from here Woodrow Wilson reviewed U.S. troops marching off to war. Rooms range upwards from $265 to the $700 suites. For reservations, call 202/638-5900 or 800/424-9540, or visit the website at www.hotelwashington.com.

Built by D.C. hotel magnate Harry Wardman, **The Jefferson,** 1200 16th St. NW, 202/347-2200 or 800/368-5966, fax 202/331-7982, www.thejeffersonhotel.com, offers 100 air-conditioned rooms and suites ($309–329). Hailed by some as one of the top 10 hotels in the world, it's the sort of place where, even after a single visit, the staff will recall every detail of your preferences and peculiarities. A favorite since 1923 of arty types such as Vivien Leigh, Van Cliburn, and Leonard Bernstein, the hotel's legendary discretion also made it a favorite of reporters such as Edward R. Murrow and H. L. Mencken.

The 150-year-old **Willard Intercontinental Hotel,** 1401 Pennsylvania Ave. NW, 202/628-9100 or 800/327-0200, fax 202/637-7326, http://washington.intercontinental.com, is the grand dame of Pennsylvania Avenue, located just around the corner from the White House. Its architect, H. J. Hardenberg, designed New York's prestigious Plaza, but did his best work in Washington. The hotel also features the locally popular Occidental Grill. Special weekend rates are $265 per night, but prices go much higher during the week. Prices for suites like the 1,550-square-foot Oval Room with marbled foyer aren't even listed.

The aristocratic edifice of the **Hay-Adams,** One Lafayette Square NW, 202/638-6600 or 800/853-6807, fax 202/638-2716, www.hayadams.com, was erected in 1927, the work of tireless D.C. hotel

builder Harry Wardman, who intended it "to provide for the socially elite as well as men who loom large in the country's life." It was named for the structures it replaced, the homes of McKinley cabinet member John Hay and historian Henry Adams. Years before, Confederate arch-spy Rose Greenhow plied her duplicitous trade on this site. Each of the 145 rooms ($300–4,200) offers luxurious antiques, ornaments, and amenities.

The venerable **Stouffer Renaissance Mayflower Hotel,** 1127 Connecticut Ave. NW, 202/347-3000 or 800/468-3571, fax 202/466-9082, www.renaissancehotels.com, was snapped up by the Stouffer chain in 1991 for a cool $100 million. Formerly the haunt of political stalwarts such as Huey P. Long and J. Edgar Hoover, the stately Mayflower is Washington's answer to New York City's Waldorf-Astoria. Lines of black limos parked around the hotel signal that government dignitaries have dropped by for a meal or are staying for the night in one of 660 air-conditioned rooms ($349 and up). Hoover arrived at the Mayflower Grille Room every day of the last 20 years of his life for his regular meal of chicken soup, grapefruit, and cottage cheese. Franklin Delano Roosevelt wrote "the only thing we have to fear is fear itself" in suite 776.

For a price, you can stay in the ritzy hotel wing of the complex that brought down a president. On June 17, 1972, Watergate security guard Frank Wills surprised five men burgling the offices of the Democratic National Committee; a little more than two years later the burglars' employer, Richard Nixon, was a disgraced ex-president on his way home to San Clemente. The **Watergate Hotel,** 2650 Virginia Ave. NW, 202/965-2300 or 800/424-2736, fax 202/337-7915, www.swissotel.com, has long been a favorite of the high and mighty—Attorney General John Mitchell, who authorized the Watergate break-in, maintained an apartment here, as did would-be chief executive Robert Dole. Monica Lewinsky, too. Many of the actors, dancers, and musicians who appear at the Kennedy Center across the street enjoy shorter stays in one of the hotel's 250 rooms ($335). On the weekend, singles and doubles start at $159.

Food

POLITICALLY CORRECT

Washington's answer to New York's Sardi's, **The Palm,** 1225 19th St. NW, 202/293-9091, fax 202/775-1468, www.thepalm.com, features an earnest menu that only occasionally misses the mark. Steaks are another matter—get one. Enjoy the brilliant waiters and see what it feels like to be treated as a power broker. Reservations are recommended, and make sure you ask for the main dining room.

In French, **La Colline,** 400 N. Capitol St. NW, 202/737-0400, means "The Hill," as in Capitol Hill. The food is good, the service is solid, but the restaurant itself sometimes suffers from a slight case of the conventional. There always seems to be enough room, so reservations are not usually necessary.

Relaxed but stately, the **Old Ebbitt Grill,** 675 15th St. NW, 202/347-4801, www.clydes.com, offers wonderful service and very good food. The bar is long on character and the Kumamoto oysters are magnificent. Call for reservations and ask for the main room to catch the power-lunch scene. Try breakfast; it's a pleasant surprise.

When White House staff members take a break to celebrate a political victory, the courtly **Occidental Grill,** 14th and Pennsylvania Streets (part of the Willard Hotel complex), 202/783-1475, known locally as the "Oxie," is their destination. Straighten your tie, make your reservations, and admire the century-old trophy wall of 1,800 photographs portraying Washington's famous faces. Don't miss out on the martini with quail eggs.

Bullfeathers, 410 1st St. SE, 202/543-5005, is beery, a bit overpriced (but still cheap by D.C. standards), and loud, so have a drink at the bar if there's room. It's hamburgers for lunch and happy hour for those in the nearby House office buildings who need to change their mood.

Georgia Brown's, 905 15th St. NW, 202/393-4499, is unique in Washington for its soul-food version of haute cuisine—collard greens and black-eyed peas never looked this fancy. Enjoy the handsome crowds, smashing ambience, and tantalizing menu descriptions.

EXPENSIVE

D.C. Coast, 1401 K St. NW, 202/216-5988, is one of the city's hot new eateries—boldly designed, on two levels, its decor is matched only by its cuisine. Chef Jeff Tunks's specialty is seafood, and he describes his cuisine as "tri-coastal," meaning the Atlantic, the Pacific, and the Gulf. Pay special attention to his Louisiana-style fare. The place is pricey, with entreés in the upper $20s, but the evening is its own reward.

Roberto Donna is one of D.C.'s culinary kings. Elegantly Italian with an outdoor terrace to enjoy summer, Donna's flagship restaurant, **Galileo,** 1110 21st St. NW, 202/293-7191, www.roberto donna.com, is a showcase of Piedmontian cuisine. Make reservations for the chef's table and watch a great kitchen at work.

Kinkead's, 2000 Pennsylvania Ave. NW, 202/296-7700, www.kinkead.com, is a gleaming red-white-and-blue answer to a French bistro. Seafood is Chef Bob Kinkead's specialty—try the tapas or the Carolina shrimp with corn pudding and Virginia ham.

Makoto, 4822 MacArthur Blvd., 202/298-6866, could well be among the top five Japanese restaurants in the United States. There are only four tables, with just 10 seats at the sushi bar. Try the "kaiseki" fixed-price (very expensive) dinner.

The setting at **I Ricchi,** 1220 19th St. NW, 202/835-0459, www.iricchi.net, is romantic, the service is personable and relaxed (and very professional), and the food would make a Florentine jealous. This is hands-down one of the finest and most consistent restaurants in the city.

Vidalia, 1990 M St. NW, 202/659-1990, is a southern belle of a restaurant known for its roasted Vidalia onion appetizer and manicured Southern cooking. But don't be misled: the food here is elegant and imaginative, and the menu is a palette for the palate. All this and valet parking, too.

With a glass-enclosed wine "cellar" surrounding the newly renovated dining room, **Citronelle,** 3000 M St. NW, in the Latham Hotel, 202/625-2150, www.citronelledc.com, is one of Washington's finest restaurants. If you consider how French wines were reborn in the Napa Valley, then you might imagine how French cuisine would fare when transplanted and ripened to perfection here in Washington.

The setting for **1789,** 1226 36th St. NW, 202/965-1789, www.clydes.com, is a Federal-style townhouse overlooking Georgetown. The oak-walled bar serves perfect silver bullets, while Chef Ris Lacoste conspires to fuse East and West with soys, peanut flavors, and lime marinades.

The **Bombay Club Restaurant,** 815 Connecticut Ave. NW, 202/659-3727, prepares the best Indian food in Washington, served in a setting as elegant as the best of India's famed Hill Stations. The service is magnificent and courtly, a relief from the earnest and overly eager professionalism in most city restaurants.

Morton's of Chicago is now in Washington, 1050 Connecticut Ave. NW, 202/955-5997, fax 202/338-8033. Situated in one of the city's prime business corridors across from the Mayflower Hotel, this is a classic martini-and-steak house. Waiters are part of the entertainment, as they present the day's fresh vegetables, meats, and treats (the lobsters don't bite). This is a place for power lunch and power dinner, and don't be afraid to remind your attentive waiter about the pet you left back at the hotel—no one can eat Morton's proportions.

The Henley Park Hotel restaurant, **Coeur de Lion,** 926 Massachusetts Avenue, NW., 202/638-5200, www.washingtonplazahotel.com, continually receives top ten ratings in the *Zagat Survey* for food, service and decor—the glass-enclosed dining room is filled with light in the morning hours, when white-gloved waiters pour golden orange juice into your glass. The innovative menu features new American cuisine with regional seasonal inspirations. It's open for breakfast daily ($9), lunch Mon.–Sat. ($16), and dinner daily ($23).

The restaurant at the **Morrison-Clark Inn** has been named one of the city's finest in *Condé Nast Traveler, Wine Spectator,* and the *Zagat Guide,* as well as being consistently ranked in the *Washington Post's* Top 50 list. Gilded mirrors, Italian marble fireplaces, and lace curtains highlight the main dining room, converted from an elegant townhouse. Chefs Richard and Peggy Thompson offer a seasonal menu of contemporary American cuisine; during pleasant weather, guests may be served alfresco in the protected brick courtyard. It's open for dinner daily; entrées average $25.

FUN

Ah, beer! Miles of beer. The **Brickskeller,** 1523 22nd St. NW, 202/293-1885, is Washington's monument to the mighty brew, packing more than 800 varieties from 50 countries, including 400 from the United States alone. The owners claim to have served 5,000 different styles of suds since opening in 1957. Enjoy the upstairs game room and buckets of mussels at good prices.

The cuisine at **Jaleo,** 480 7th St. NW, 202/628-7949, is Spanish and the tapas are terrific. Heft a jug of sangria and settle in at this exuberant restaurant in the renewed area near downtown known as Penn Quarter.

If a restaurant can be sexy and reasonably priced, **Sesto Senso,** 1214 18th St. NW, 202/785-9525, certainly qualifies. The people-watching is excellent, even at lunch: Mick Jagger eats here when in town. The menu ranges from fair to very fine, and the service is as good as you make it, so take advantage of it.

Kids love **Tony Cheng's Seafood Restaurant,** 619 H St. NW, 202/842-8669, the home of kung fu cooking. Patrons circle the huge round griddle that dominates the restaurant, selecting foods from surrounding trays. Chefs then fry up the selections and swipe the finished dinners onto small round plates without dropping so much as a soybean.

If your imagination runs to the great backroom dives of Tijuana, **Cactus Cantina,** 3300 Wisconsin Ave. NW, 202/686-7222, manages the atmosphere without any of the grit. A fun place for Sunday brunch or a relaxed dinner.

Coppi's, 1414 U St. NW, 202/319-7773, is

a local neighborhood eatery that just happens to serve exquisite food—baby artichokes and sheep's milk cheese. This is serious dining, but casual too.

15ria Restaurant, 1515 Rhode Island Ave., NW, 202/232-7000, in the Washington Terrace Hotel, is building a fine reputation for fresh food delivered from local purveyors. The menu is American with a twist: blue cheese buttermilk onion rings, and grilled Amish chicken with preserved lemon, olives, and mashed potatoes. It's open for breakfast daily ($9) lunch Mon.–Fri. ($15) and dinner daily ($18). The full bar specializes in fine bourbon. In case you're wondering, it's pronounced Fifteen Ar Eye Ay, as in "15 Rhode Island Avenue."

Entertainment and Nightlife

CLUBS

The classy **Habana Village,** 1834 Columbia Rd. NW, 202/462-6310, seemingly offers one activity for each of its four rooms: food, entertainment, dance, and a singles scene. The restaurant ambience is wicker and white wine. Cigars are allowed. Upstairs it's dance and the singles set, and above that, two heavenly lounges (with Latin music, of course).

Redheads get half price on all drinks at **Madams Organ,** 2467 18th St. NW, 202/667-5370. This blues/reggae house features live bands and Southern cooking. The motto: "Where the beautiful people go to get ugly."

At **Politiki,** 319 Pennsylvania Ave. SE, 202/546-1001, the trilevel bar (basement: tiki bar; ground floor: sports bar; upstairs: swing dancing) serves fruity drinks in tiki bowls. You may even find people here who don't work on the Hill.

A Georgetown landmark (assuming you can find it), **Blues Alley,** 1703 Wisconsin Ave. NW, 202/337-4141, www.bluesalley.com, is a side-street success. The 130-seat club attracts top acts to the town that gave birth to Duke Ellington. Covers are high, from $13 to more than $40. Usually, you get what you pay for.

The **9:30 Club,** 815 V St. NW, 202/393-0930, hosts the likes of Sean Lennon and Ziggy Marley. This pantheon of punk can hold up to 1,000 dancing, drinking guests within its walls. Parking is secure. Check out the downstairs bar to escape the crush. Visit the club's website, www.930.com, for concert information and to view the beer list and bar menu.

Looking like nothing so much as a below-ground Paris jazz cave, tiny **U-topia,** 1418 U St. NW, 202/483-7669, has become a part of the city's U Street scene. U-topia offers a bit of everything, from take-out food to jazz and blues.

Comfy velvet couches and Peruvian appetizers are the signatures of the dimly lit **Chi Cha Lounge,** 1624 U St. NW, 202/234-8400. It's often crowded, with semiregular live jazz music, but it's still intimate enough for conversation.

THEATER AND CONCERTS
John F. Kennedy Center for the Performing Arts

This D.C. landmark, New Hampshire Avenue and Rock Creek Parkway NW, 202/467-4600, www.kennedy-center.org, is home to the **National Symphony Orchestra** (NSO) and the **Washington Opera.** Founded in 1931, the National Symphony Orchestra has enjoyed a succession of brilliant musical directors—Antal Dorati, Mstislav Rostropvoich, and, today, Leonard Slatkin. The NSO has promised to visit all 50 states, but don't miss them while in Washington.

Artistic Director Placido Domingo gives the 42-year-old Washington Opera Company the sex appeal and gravitas it so much deserves, making D.C. one of the nation's centers for song. The Kennedy Center Opera House and the center's Eisenhower Theatre offer a prolific 74 performances of about eight operas annually.

The Kennedy Center also presents Broadway shows, repertory theater, jazz, Shakespeare, and more. Free performances are held every day at 6 P.M. on the Millennium Stage featuring performers from the local area and around the world. Tours of the center's main theaters and selected art holdings are offered 10 A.M.–5 P.M. during the week, and 10 A.M.–1 P.M. on weekends.

Other Venues

The **National Theatre,** 1321 Pennsylvania Ave. NW, 202/628-6161, www.nationaltheatre.org, is Washington's only Broadway-style theater and the city's oldest cultural institution. *West Side Story* had its world premiere here, as did *Hello, Dolly!* The theater's acoustics are excellent, but watch out for the distant seats in Balcony Two. The Helen Hayes Gallery (a workshop-sized auditorium) hosts free events weekly.

The classical and Shakespearean adaptations for which the **Shakespeare Theatre,** 450 7th St. NW, 202/547-1122, www.shakespearedc.org, is known are vivid and nontraditional productions, attracting big-name actors and actresses. The company regularly returns to more traditional presentations, such as Tennessee Williams's *Sweet Bird of Youth.*

The **Folger Elizabethan Theatre,** 201 E. Capitol St. SE, 202/544-7077, inside the Folger Library, is a full-scale re-creation of a 250-seat Elizabethan theater. Here one can experience life as a "groundling," as well as allowing the children to discover something of the life of Elizabethans, including William Shakespeare.

From repertory classics to musicals, the three stages at the **Arena Stage,** 1101 6th St. NW, 202/488-3300, www.arenastage.org, have pulled down 54 prestigious Helen Hayes theater awards. The Arena was the first theater outside New York to capture a coveted Tony Award. James Earl Jones, Dianne Wiest, Kevin Kline, James Woods, and many other notable actors and actresses have graced its stages.

The **Woolly Mammoth Theatre,** 1401 Church St. NW, 703/218-6500, is Washington's off-Broadway-style venue for experimental cutting-edge works. Productions are first-rate, and free parking is just across the street. Be careful when buying seats because the quality of the views ranges widely.

The **Studio Theatre,** 14 and P Sts. NW, 202/332-3300, www.studiotheatre.org, has grown more ambitious each year and recently renovated its two theaters, the Mead and the Milton, to

Shakespeare Theatre

allow longer show runs. The productions are contemporary and first quality.

COMEDY

People say Washington's a funny town, and when they're talking about humor, they're probably referring to the **D.C. Improv** at 1140 Connecticut Ave. NW, 202/296-7008. Open Tues.–Sun., show time is usually 8:30 P.M. but sometimes varies, so call or check www.dcimprov.com. Tickets are usually $15 but can range up to $30. Lunches and dinners are reasonable, around $10 for entreés, and diners get the best seats for the shows. Try the 57 Chevy for a cocktail—vodka, amaretto, and lots of vitamin C.

MORE EVENTS AND ENTERTAINMENT

Located in the heart of Chinatown, the **MCI Center,** 601 F St. NW, 202/628-3200, www .mcicenter.com, is not your typical sports venue. Home to the NHL's Washington Capitals, NBA's

Wizards, and WNBA's Mystics, the center features a video center showcasing historic moments in athletics, a sportscasters hall of fame, a sporting goods store, and the Discovery Channel's three-story, 25,000-square-foot interactive store. **Robert F. Kennedy Memorial Stadium,** 2400 E. Capitol St. SE, 202/547-9077, was once home to the Washington Redskins, but now hosts the city's pro soccer team, D.C. United, as well as rock concerts and the occasional outdoor convention. (The Redskins moved out of the city in 1996 and now play at **Jack Kent Cooke Stadium** in Landover, Maryland.) There are numerous ticket outlets in the D.C. area—check the local yellow pages or www.redskins.com or call 202/432-7328 or 800/551-7328. Parking at the stadium may cost $20 (the Redskins are fighting a parking war with fans), but extra Metro buses and trains make the journey to Maryland much more convenient. Contact WMATA headquarters, 202/637-7000, TDD 202/638-3780, www .wmata.com, for information.

The 4,200-seat **Carter Barron Amphitheatre,** 4850 Colorado Ave. NW, 202/426-0486, could host a major tennis tournament but more often offers free concerts during the summer. Located along the 16th Street corridor, it is also easily accessible. **Ford's Theatre,** 511 10th St. NW, 202/347-4833, the site of President Lincoln's last act and still a working theater, produces plays and musicals aimed at portraying the eclectic character of American life.

Washington is a monumental city, a city of lights. A fine way to capture the capital's dramatic sights is by cruising its feisty boundary, the Potomac River. **Odyssey Cruises,** 600 Water St. SW, 202/488-6000, www.odysseycruises.com, offers river tours, serving lunch, brunch, or dinner on board. **The Wharf,** 900 Water St. SW, offers another way to look at the Potomac, through its floating seafood stalls, shelling out everything from octopus to Carolina crabs. The river complex offers historic sites, quality restaurants, and fresh seafood.

Transportation

GETTING THERE

By Air

The Washington area is served by three major airports: Dulles International Airport receives both international and domestic arrivals; National Airport primarily takes domestic arrivals; and Baltimore-Washington International Airport (BWI) also receives international and domestic flights. Expect between 20 and 45 minutes driving time to reach downtown from any of the airports, longer at rush hour. Taxis downtown from Dulles (26 miles west in Virginia) and BWI (25 miles northeast in Maryland) will run $40–50, from National (four miles south of downtown) about $15.

Shuttle service is also available from all three airports. The Washington Flyer Express bus (888/927-4359) runs every 30–60 minutes from National (daily 6 A.M.–9 P.M.; $8 one-way, $14 round-trip) and from Dulles (daily 5 A.M.–10 P.M.; $16 one-way, $26 round-trip) to its city terminal

at 1517 K St. NW. There is another Washington Flyer Express bus from Dulles to the West Falls Church Metro station every 20–30 minutes (Mon.–Fri. 6:30 A.M.–10:30 P.M., Sat.–Sun. 7:30 A.M.–10:30 P.M.; $8 one-way, $14 round-trip). Trains run from this station to Metro Center station and on to downtown. Courtesy shuttles are available at the Washington Flyer terminal at Dulles to various downtown hotels. The BWI Super Shuttle offers hourly departures (daily 6 A.M.–1 A.M.; $19 one-way, $29 round-trip) to the 1517 K St. NW terminal.

National is the only airport with direct Metrorail service. The station is across from North Concourse and links directly with Metro Center and other stops along the Yellow Line. From BWI, the Maryland Rail Commuter Service (MARC) offers peak-hour service (Mon.–Fri. only, 5:30 A.M.–8 A.M. and 3:45 P.M.–6:45 P.M.; $5 one-way, $8.75 round-trip) to Union Station. Amtrak offers daily service ($12 one-way, $24 round-trip) from BWI to Union Station.

Both MARC and Amtrak take about 45 minutes to reach the city.

By Rail

The Amtrak train pulls into Washington, D.C., at Union Station. Call 800/USA-RAIL (800/872-7725), or access the website at www.amtrak.com.

The Amtrak line connects directly to the Maryland Area Rail Commuter (MARC) system, a Monday–Friday commuter service with 75 trains on three lines in the Baltimore-Washington corridor, eight Maryland counties, and northeastern West Virginia. Call 800/325-RAIL (800/325-7725) for routes and schedules.

GETTING AROUND

Most of the major sightseeing highlights in central Washington—the Mall, the White House, the Tidal Basin area—are within walking distance of each other, so using public transportation is only an option. If you want to see anything away from these areas or need to travel to any of the outlying neighborhoods, you'll be happy to know Washington has one of the best subway systems of any major city in the world. The related bus service is quite reliable, and there are always plenty of taxis and rental car options. Driving around downtown should always be your last choice: besides the confusing layout of the streets and the accompanying confusion of trying to read a map, parking fees are astronomical.

By Subway

The Washington Metropolitan Area Transit Authority (WMATA) operates the Metrorail, the D.C. subway system that's known by residents simply as "the Metro." It covers the downtown area and the suburbs (except Georgetown), but expansion is almost constant. Metro stations are identified by a large letter "M" atop a brown pylon.

You can purchase magnetic **fare cards** from vending machines at your departure station. Simply insert the card into the turnstile, and when you get where you're going use the card to exit. The turnstile will magnetically record the remaining value on your fare card. Cards can be purchased for the base fare of $1.20, or for as

much as $45. Should your card not have enough credit for you to exit the station, use one of the special exit-fare machines and try the turnstile again. Children under the age of four ride free when accompanied by a paying adult, up to a limit of two children.

On average, expect to pay between $1.20 and $3.60 during peak times (5:30–9:30 A.M. and 3–8 P.M.) and between $1.20 and $2.20 at other times. Metro trains run Mon.–Thurs. 5:30 A.M.–midnight, Friday 5:30 A.M.–3 A.M., Saturday 7 A.M.–3 A.M. and Sunday and most public holidays 7 A.M.–midnight. The trains arrive/depart every 5–6 minutes during peak times and every 10–15 minutes at other times.

The Metro also offers a variety of useful **train passes.** For $6 you can purchase a one-day pass valid from the time of purchase until closing (but not before 9:30 A.M. on weekdays). If you plan on being in the capital for a while, you might consider purchasing the $50 Fast Pass, good for 14 consecutive days of unlimited rail travel. For even longer stays, WMATA offers the $100 28-Day Pass, good for unlimited rail travel for almost a month. Another good option, especially if you plan on riding the Metro buses in addition to the trains, is the $65 Bus/Rail SUPER Pass, good for 14 consecutive days of unlimited bus and rail travel. If you don't want to spend the money or don't plan on staying for two weeks, rail-to-bus transfers are available on the train platform for only $.35.

Passes are available at the WMATA headquarters, 600 5th St. NW, Washington DC 20001, 202/637-7000, TDD 202/638-3780, www.wmata.com; and at the Metro Center station sales office at 12th and F Streets. NW. Some banks and liquor stores and some Safeway and Giant grocery stores also sell rail and bus passes. Metro **route maps** are available for $2 from the marketing office at WMATA headquarters.

By Bus

Like the subway, the Metrobus base fare is $1.20, and buses run at the same times as the trains, although some operate until 2 A.M. Rail-to-bus transfers are available ($.35), and so are bus-to-bus transfers (only $.10)—simply hand your bus-transfer pass, which you must purchase for each transfer, to the driver of the second bus. Bus fare is acceptable either as cash or in the form of tokens worth $1.10 and available in rolls of 10 or 20. You can also purchase a $25 Flash Pass, good for 14 consecutive days of unlimited bus travel.

By Taxi

Because not every D.C. neighborhood is served by the Metro (most notably Georgetown and Adams-Morgan), the capital's taxicabs are a nice complement to the subway and bus systems. A few reliable taxi companies include **Super Shuttle,** 800/258-3826, **Capitol Taxi,** 202/546-2400, and **Yellow Cab,** 202/544-1212. For information on cabs and fares in Washington, call the Taxicab Commission at 202/767-8319.

Rental Car

Most rental car agencies have offices at Dulles International Airport, National Airport, and Union Station, although you probably won't need a car if you're planning on staying within the city limits.

Resources

Suggested Reading

Arts and Crafts

Bethke, R. and J. Camper. *Americana Crafted: Jehu Camper, Delaware Whittler.* Jackson, MS: University Press of Mississippi, 1995. All about whittlin' and the constructed wooden folk art of Jehu Camper.

Delaware Art Museum. *American Illustration Collection of the Delaware Art Museum.* Wilmington, DE: Delaware Art Museum, 1991. A broad and varied look at the work of local illustrators.

Delaware Art Museum. *Wondrous Strange.* Wilmington, DE: Bulfinch Press, 1998. This illustrated book showcases the work of Delaware's best-known illustrators and painters: Howard Pyle, N. C. Wyeth, Andrew Wyeth and James Wyeth.

Fenimore, D., R. Trent, and E. Fowble. *Eye for Excellence: Masterworks from Winterthur.* Winterthur, DE: Winterthur Museum Press, 1997. When only the best will do.

Description and Travel

Chase, H., ed. *In Their Footsteps.* New York: Henry Holt and Co., 1992. Chase, the editor of *American Visions* magazine, has compiled this book of black heritage sites all over the United States.

Corddry, M. and E. Corddry. *City on the Sand: Ocean City and the People Who Built It.* Centreville, MD: Tidewater Publishing, 1991. An illustrated history of the resort.

Gallagher, C., ed. *Antietam: Essays on the 1862 Maryland Campaign.* Kent, OH: Kent State University Press, 1989. This well-received series of short pieces from different sources cov-

ers Civil War history in depth. Gallagher also edited another series of essays in 1999 (*The Antietam Campaign*), published by University of North Carolina Press.

Hanna, J. *Tales from Delaware Bay.* Salisbury, MD: Cherokee Books, 2000. Crabbing, boating, and life on the water—watermen tell the stories of their lives in their own words.

High, Mike, *The C&O Canal Companion.* Baltimore, MD: Johns Hopkins University Press, 1997. A definitive and well-written guide to C&O Canal National Historical Park history, points of interest, and recreation.

Horton, T. *An Island Out of Time.* New York: Vintage Books, 1997. Tom Horton, an environmental writer for the *Baltimore Sun,* moved his family to Smith Island for two years. This is an affectionate memoir of their stay.

Sherwood, J. *Maryland's Vanishing Lives.* Baltimore, MD: Johns Hopkins Press, 1995. These short essays are all about people who are unique to the Tidewater by virtue of their occupations, such as a teacher in a one-room school and a bridge operator. With the growth of the region, many of these jobs are disappearing, and with them a way of life.

Simon, D. and E. Burns. *The Corner: A Year in the Life of an Inner-city Neighborhood.* New York: Broadway Books, 2000. Guess which inner city? If the bucolic countryside has lost its charm, try this rough-edged true tale of Baltimore's seamier side. HBO based a TV special on this book.

Turner, W. *Chesapeake Boyhood: Memoirs of a Farm Boy.* Baltimore, MD: Johns Hopkins University Press, 1997. It was a different world in the 1940s and '50s, and this good story-teller spins a warm and entertaining tale of life on a Tidewater farm.

Warner, W. *Beautiful Swimmers.* New York: Little Brown/Back Bay Books, 1999. A lovely "little" book that's an excellent companion to travels in Talbot County. The title refers, of course, to blue crabs.

Fiction

Barth, J, and M. Johnston. *Tidewater Tales.* Baltimore, MD: Johns Hopkins University Press, 1997. Maryland's most famous contemporary author, John Barth has based a number of his novels on his life on the Chesapeake. This one is a fictional family drama told in a series of stories about the Tidewater.

Cherry, L. *Flute's Journey—the Life of a Wood Thrush.* New York: Harcourt Brace & Co, 1999. An entertaining and educational book for children about the challenges facing wildlife in modern times. Flute, a wood thrush, faces habitat loss and food shortages in his search to start his own family. The book is based on an endangered old-growth forest in Maryland that Ms. Cherry, working with others, managed to save.

Michener, J. *Chesapeake.* New York: Fawcett Books, 1990. The classic story of history on the bay, starting from precolonial times. It's big, and it slows down a bit here and there, but Michener did his homework, so it's a good read for history and adventure buffs.

Food

Junior League of Baltimore. *Hunt to Harbor: A Maryland Cookbook.* Baltimore, MD: Perry Publishing, 1996. This is the real thing, Hon—straight from the horsey set's mouth. It features all sorts of general recipes plus "Ethnic Festival Menus."

Shields, J. *Chesapeake Bay Cooking with John Shields.* New York: Broadway Books, 1998. This is the companion book to John Shields's popular TV program of the same name. You'll find ham pâté and beaten biscuits in addition to pan-fried chicken and seafood galore.

History

Bready, J. *Baseball in Baltimore—The First 100 Years.* Baltimore, MD: Johns Hopkins University Press, 1998. Covering 1859 to 1954 (when Baltimore returned to the major leagues), Bready unearths enough diamond trivia to satisfy the most ardent fan—did you know that one Baltimore franchise won three Negro League titles?

Dickens, C. *American Notes.* New York: St. Martins Press, 1985. Charles Dickens's record of his travels across the United States 1840–1842.

Fetzer, D., B. Mowday, and L. Jennings. *Unlikely Allies, Ft. Delaware's Prison Community in the Civil War.* Mechanicsburg, PA: Stackpole Books, 2000. How to run a prison right—a look at Pea Patch Island during the conflict. Dale Fetzer is one of the park's living history guides—he not only researched his subject, he plays the part of the enlightened prison commandant several days a week.

McElvey, K. *Early Black Dorchester, 1775–1870.* This book is a private publication and may be ordered by calling 800/521-0600 and asking for #9133192, 1998. This is a scholarly research paper that is an excellent reference source for anyone interested in Harriet Tubman and the actual lives of slaves in the colonies.

Rouse, P. *The Great Wagon Road: From Philadelphia to the South.* New York: McGraw-Hill, 1973. A kaleidoscopic picture of colonial times, when it was, as Rouse quotes, "a great life for dogs and men, but . . . hell on women and steers."

Shivers, F. *Maryland Wits and Baltimore Bards: A Literary History.* Baltimore, MD: Johns Hopkins University Press, 1998. The gang's all here. Contemporary authors John Barth and Adrienne Rich put in a word or two as Mr. Shivers chronicles the state's literary luminaries—among them E. A. Poe, and F. Scott Fitzgerald.

Weslager, C. *The Delaware Indians: A History.* Piscataway, NJ: Rutgers University Press, 1990. Despite his odd lapse in reference to the Lenni Lenape by their European name, Weslager's book is generally perceived as quite accurate. Until we see a history written by tribe members, this will have to do.

Maryland-Delaware Personages

Banks, R. *Cloudsplitter.* New York: HarperCollins, 1999. A best-selling fictional account of John Brown's life, written from the point of view of his atheist son and companion, Owen (several of Brown's sons and daughters followed him to Maryland for the Harpers Ferry rebellion).

Bradford, S. *Harriet Tubman, Moses of Her People.* Applewood Books, 1994. This is an inspiring classic, written while Tubman was alive. Her vision of freedom is shown from her own deeply spiritual perspective.

Colby, G. *Dupont Dynasty: Behind the Nylon Curtain.* New York: Lyle Stuart, 1984. This is a muckraking look at the history and dealings of the Dupont clan—you can be sure that Mr. Colby never did lunch in Delaware again after this book.

Oates, S. *A Woman of Valor: Clara Barton and the Civil War.* New York: Free Press, 1995. Though this book only covers Ms. Barton's Civil War years, it uses many quotes from her personal correspondence to bring the era to life.

Olds, B. *Raising Holy Hell.* New York: Penguin, 1997. Another account of John Brown's life, told through a pastiche of journal excerpts, news articles, and popular songs of the time.

Internet Resources

Most of these websites will link to many other points of interest:

History

http://woodshole.er.usgs.gov/epubs/bolide
The US Geological Survey explores the bolide (big crash from a celestial object faster than a speeding bullet—no kidding, that's the definition) that created the Chesapeake Bay.

www.mariner.org/baylink
A general history of the bay courtesy of the Mariner's Museum, Newport News, Virginia.

www2.cr.nps.gov/abpp/civil.htm
Scholarly site with Civil War history and battle details.

http://memory.loc.gov/ammem/cwphtml/cwphome.html
Wonderful site from the Library of Congress with selected Civil War photographs.

Media

www.sunspot.net
The award-winning *Baltimore Sun* newspaper online.

www.cbmmag.net
Glossy and full of interesting articles of Maryland life, this is *Chesapeake Bay Magazine* online.

In and Around Chesapeake Bay

www.baydreaming.com
Features an excellent listing of marinas and boating facilities plus tips on fishing, and general information on the bay.

www.thebayguide.com
A site by boaters for boaters.

www.fws.gov/r5cbfo
U.S. Department of Fish and Wildlife, Chesapeake Bay region.

www.thechesapeakebay.com
Calendar for bay events and general articles on the Chesapeake.

www.baygateways.net
A website that links to all the public access parks around the bay, plus additional information, articles, and a calendar.

Conservation Organizations

www.cbf.org
Chesapeake Bay Foundation—the largest and best known.

www.acb-online.org
Alliance for the Chesapeake Bay also offers guided trips.

Maryland General Information

www.mdisfun.org
Maryland's official tourism website.

www.dnr.state.md.us
Maryland's State Forest and Park Service; information on all state parks, camping, etc., plus links to boating and fishing license information and forms.

Maryland Towns and Places of Interest

www.baltimore.org
All about the city of Baltimore.

www.visit-annapolis.org
Site for the town of Annapolis.

Internet Resources

www.cvbmontco.com
Montgomery County information.

www.somd.com
A good general website for southern Maryland.

www.co.cal.md.us/cced
Calvert County's website.

http://sba.solomons.md.us
Village of Solomons Island and the surrounding area.

www.visitwesternmaryland.com
A good general site for all of western Maryland.

www.hdgtourism.com
Site for the town of Havre de Grace.

www.chestertown.com
All about Chestertown and the surrounding area.

www.stmichaelsmd.org
Information on the town of St. Michaels.

www.salisburymd.com
Site for the city of Salisbury.

www.ococean.com
All about Ocean City.

Delaware General Information

www.visitdelaware.com
Delaware's official tourism website.

www.destateparks.com/index.asp
Guide to Delaware state parks, greenways and trails, with information on camping and trail updates.

Delaware Towns and Places of Interest

www.visitwilmingtonde.com
Site for the city of Wilmington and the surrounding Brandywine Valley.

www.beach-fun.com
Rehoboth Beach and Dewey Beach share this website for fun in the sun in southern Delaware.

Index

A

Aberdeen Proving Ground: 237–238
Accokeek National Colonial Farm: 32, 127, 130
accommodations: general information 40–42; Annapolis 107–108; Baltimore 81–85; Delaware 336, 337; Ocean City 299–301; Washington, D.C. 423–426; *see also specific place*
Adams-Morgan: 418–419
African-American Heritage Society: 144
airlines: 44
air travel: 44–45, 95–96, 337, 431–432
Allee House: 372
American Chestnut Land Trust: 154
American Discovery Trail: 31, 34, 331
American Film Institute (AFI) Silver Theatre and Cultural Center: 121–122
American University: 419
Amish: 26, 145, 152, 216, 374–376
amphibians: 9–10, 318
amusement parks: 131, 295, 296–297, 388, 390, 395
Anglers Marina: 385
animals: *see* fauna
Annapolis: 18, 32, 98–111
Annapolis Visitor Center: 105
Anne Arundel County: 98–111
Annmarie Garden: 33, 158–159
Antietam Cemetery: 185
Antietam National Battlefield: 184–185
antiques: *see specific place*
Appalachian Mountains: 5, 7
Appalachian Trail: 31, 190
aquariums: 32, 71–72, 417
Arena Stage: 430
Armel-Leftwich Visitor Center: 100
arts and culture: 37–38, 73–75, 105–107
Arts and Industries Building: 408
Aspin Hill Pet Cemetery: 118
Assateague Island: 307–309
Assawoman Canal: 331
Atlantic Coastal Plain: 4–5, 7
Atlantic House: 296
ATMs: 50
Augustine Beach: 364
Augustine Wildlife Area: 368, 370

Art Centers and Galleries

Academy of the Arts: 269
African American Gallery & Gift Shop: 206
African Art Museum of Maryland: 114
American Visionary Art Museum: 32, 75
Arthur M. Sackler Gallery: 406, 408
Art League of Ocean City: 298
Arts and Industries Building: 408
Baltimore Museum of Art: 74–75
Carroll Arts Center: 225
City Gallery: 75
Delaplaine Visual Arts Center: 172
Delaware Art Museum: 356–357
Delaware Center for the Contemporary Arts: 357
Dorchester Arts Center: 275
Dover Art League: 379
Esther Prangley Rice Gallery: 225
Freer Gallery of Art: 408
Gallery of Ships: 103
Gallery on the Circle: 106
League of Maryland Craftsmen: 105–106
Maryland Institute College of Art: 75
Mattawoman Creek Art Center: 141
Meeting House Galleries I and II: 374
Meyerhoff Gallery: 75
Mitchell Gallery: 106
Montpelier Mansion and Cultural Arts Center: 130
Nancy Hammond Editions: 106–107
National Gallery of Art: 404–405
National Museum of African Art: 408–409
National Museum of American Art: 416
National Portrait Gallery: 416–417
Ocean Gallery: 298
Rehoboth Art League: 390
Scott Center for Fine and Performing Arts: 225
Sewell C. Biggs Museum of American Art: 339, 374
Spruce Forest Artisan Village: 215
Walters Art Museum: 32, 73–74
Ward Museum of Wildfowl Art: 33, 279
Washington County Museum of Fine Arts: 33, 192–193

Index

B

auto racing: 152, 195, 378, 379
Avalon Theatre: 269
Avelon Inn: 296
"Awakening, The": 410

B
backpacking: 31, 34
Baja Amusements: 297
Ballad of George and Mattie: 186–187
Baltimore: accommodations 81–85; food 85–95; neighborhoods 54–57; recreation and entertainment 76–80; shopping 79–80; sightseeing highlights 57–76
Baltimore-Annapolis Trail: 110
Baltimore Conservatory: 76
Baltimore County: 230–232
Baltimore-Washington International (BWI) Airport: 44, 95–96
Baltimore Zoo: 32, 72
Bancroft Hall: 103
Bargain Bill's, The Shore's Largest Flea Market: 398
bars: 78, 78–79
Barton, Clara: 117
baseball: 175–176, 237
Basilica of the Assumption: 70
baskets: 241
Battery Park Trail: 368
Battle Creek Cypress Swamp: 154
Battle of Gettysburg: 185–186
Battle of South Mountain: 182, 184
Bay View Beach: 364
beach dunes: 333, 364
beaches: 339, 364
Beach Plum Island Nature Preserve: 369, 388
bed-and-breakfasts (B&Bs): 42; see also accommodations; specific place
beer/breweries: 43–44, 110, 112–113, 178, 337, 428; see also specific place
Belmont-Hearn Hotel: 296
Belter, Henry: 372
Beltsville Agricultural Research Center: 124–125
Belvedere: 54, 55–57
Benjamin Banneker Historical Park: 113–114
Bennetts Pier: 364
Berlin: 293–294
Bethany Beach: 392–396
Bethel: 398
Bethesda: see Montgomery County
bicycling: 31, 34, 144, 198, 199, 333

Big Savage Mountain Trail System: 214
Big Stone Beach: 364
Billy Goat trail: 119
birds/birding: 9, 124, 145, 316–318, 368–369; see also hunting; state parks; waterfowl
biscuits: 259
"Black Panther" German submarine: 150
black population: 24–25, 324
black powder: 344
Blackwater National Wildlife Refuge: 33, 274
Blades: 339
Blair Witch Project, The: 151
Blake, Eubie: 68
Blob's Park Biergarten: 110
blue crabs: 10, 334
Boardwalk (Ocean City): 294–296
Boardwalk (Rehoboth Beach): 388
boating: 35–36, 46, 333; see also specific place
Boatwright, George: 186–187
Bollman Truss Railroad Bridge: 114
Bolton Hill: 54
Bombay Hook National Wildlife Refuge: 339, 369, 372
bookstores: 80, 103, 235, 419
Boordy Vineyards: 230–231
Booth, John Wilkes: 127, 128–129, 136–139, 141, 222
Booth, Junius Brutus: 222
Brandywine Park: 359
Brandywine Valley: 343–351
Brandywine Zoo: 359
bread crumb pancakes: 283
Breezy Point Beach: 161–162
Brent, Margaret: 147
bridges: 239
Brighton Dam Azalea Garden: 120–121
Broad Creek Greenway: 331
Broadkill Beach: 364
Broadkill River: 331
Bromo Seltzer Tower: 69
Brookings Institution: 419
Brookside Gardens: 120
Brown, Ethel Pennewill: see Leach, Ethel Pennewill Brown
Brown, John: 165, 179–181
Bucktown: 273
Bufano Sculpture Garden: 76
Bureau of Engraving and Printing: 411
Burrows, Martha Jane: 186–187
Burton-Ingram House: 384

bus travel: 46, 96, 109, 219, 338, 432–433
Byler's Country Store: 376

C

C&O Canal National Historical Park: 33,
    119–120, 196–198
C&O Canal towpath: 34
Calvert, Cecil: 14–16, 147, 320
Calvert, Charles: 16, 320
Calvert Cliffs Nuclear Plant: 156
Calvert County: 153–163
Calvert, George: 13–14, 25
Calvert, Leonard: 14, 136, 147
Cambridge: 272, 275
camping/campgrounds: 40–41, 332, 333; *see also
    specific place*

Canal Place: 202–203
canals: 197, 244–245, 422; *see also* C&O Canal
    National Historical Park; museums
Canal Square: 422
canoeing: 36, 198
Canton: 54, 81, 84, 91–92
Cape May-Lewes Ferry: 385–386
Capitol Hill: 411–413
Carol County Court House: 226
carousels: 295, 405
carriages: 27, 204
Carroll, Charles: 19–21, 62–63, 99
Carroll County: 223–230, 225–228
Carroll County Historical Society and Visitors
    Center: 225
Carter Barron Amphitheatre: 431

Civil War

general information: 21–22, 165–166,
    178–188, 225–227, 322
Antietam Cemetery: 185
Antietam National Battlefield: 184–185
Ballad of George and Mattie: 186–187
Baltimore Civil War Museum: 60–61
Barbara Fritchie Museum: 169
Battle of Gettysburg: 185–186
Battle of South Mountain: 182, 184
Boatwright, George: 186–187
Boonsboro Museum of History: 188
Booth, John Wilkes: 127, 128–129, 136–139,
    141, 222
Brown, John: 165, 179–181
Burrows, Martha Jane: 186–187
Carol County Court House: 226
Carroll County: 225–228
Clara Barton National Historic Site: 117
Confederate Soldier's Monument: 171
Corbit's Charge: 226
Crouse House: 226
Dr. Samuel A. Mudd House Museum:
    138–140
Early, Jubal: 186–187
Fort Delaware State Park: 367–369
Fort Frederick State Park: 198–199
Fort McHenry: 57, 60
Frederick vicinity: 169–172
Fritchie, Barbara: 169, 170

Gathland State Park/National War Correspon-
    dent's Memorial: 188–189
Grant, Ulysses S.: 186–187
Harpers Ferry National Historical Park: 179–181
Hill, D. H.: 181–182
historical background: 21–22, 165–166,
    169–172, 178–191, 225–228, 322,
    367–369
Kennedy Farm: 179
Lee, Robert E.: 165–166, 180–186
Lincoln, Abraham: 128–129, 136–137, 138,
    141, 358
Maryland Historical Society Museum and Li-
    brary: 62
McClellan, George B.: 181–184, 358
Monocacy National Battlefield: 186–188
Mount Olivet Cemetery: 169, 171
National Museum of Civil War Medicine:
    171–172
Newcomer House Museum: 185
Odd Fellows Hall: 226
Point Lookout State Park: 148–149
Shellman House: 226
Stuart, J. E. B.: 225–228
Surratt, Mary Elizabeth: 127, 128–129, 141
Trumbo/Chest House: 226
Turner's Gap: 182
Union Mills Homestead: 227–228
Wallace, Lew: 186–187

car travel: 46, 47, 96, 197, 219, 338; *see also*
    rental cars
Castle, The: 207–208
Cathedral of St. Peter: 355
Cathedral of the Annunciation: 70
Catoctin Iron Furnace: 171
Catoctin Mountain National Park: 175
caverns: 188
Cecil County: 240–246
Cedar Island Marsh Sanctuary: 288
cemeteries: 118, 185, 192, 366, 413, 420
Charles Carroll House: 99
Charles County: 138–146
Charles Street: 87–88
charters: 151–152, 161, 249, 266, 275
Chesapeake & Delaware (C&D) Canal: 244–245
Chesapeake and Ohio Canal: 422
Chesapeake Bay: 6, 10–12
Chesapeake Beach: 157
Chesapeake Beach Water Park: 157
Chesapeake City: 33, 242–243
Chesapeake Farms Agricultural and Wildlife
    Management Area: 250
Chestertown: 33, 246–248
Chevy Chase: 419
children, traveling with: 72, 173
Chincoteague National Wildlife Refuge: 308,
    309
Claiborne, William: 13, 14, 16
clamming: 334–335
Clara Barton National Historic Site: 117
Cleveland Park: 419
climate: 7–8, 315
clothing tips: 51, 315
clubs: 429
Coastal Heritage Greenway: 331
Cobb Island: 138
Collins Beach: 364
colonial architecture: 17
comedy clubs: 79, 430
Community Bridge: 172–173
commuter trains: 46
Cone, Claribel: 57, 74, 75
Cone, Etta: 57, 74, 75
Confederate Soldier's Monument: 171
Congressional Cemetery: 413
Conowingo Dam: 240
Constitution Gardens: 403
Corbit's Charge: 226
corn mazes: 395

Costen House: 291
covered bridges: 167, 169, 243
Cozy, The: 178
crabs, blue: 10, 334
crabs, horseshoe: 318, 319
Crescent Lawn: 203
Crisfield: 287–290
Cromwell, Oliver: 16
Crouse House: 226
cruise ships: 46, 286
Crystal Grottoes Cavern: 188
Cumberland: 201–208
Cumberland, The: 203
currency: 49–50, 411
Cutts & Case: 268
Cylburn Arboretum: 76

D
dancing: 79, 325
Dan's Rock Overlook: 206
Darley, Felix Octavius Carr: 349
Deal Island: 284–285
Deep Creek Lake: 33, 37, 210–211
Deer Park: 216
Delaware Center for Horticulture: 359
Delaware History Center: 339, 354
Delaware Technical & Community College:
    396–397
Delmarva Peninsula: 394
De Vries Monument: 383–384
Dewey Beach: 388–392
disabilities, travelers with: 47, 49
District of Columbia Courthouse: 417
Dixon, Jeremiah: 321
Doctor's Office, The: 384
doll collections: 397
Dolle's Candyland: 295
domestic customs: 194
Dorchester County: 272–278
dormitory rooms: 42
Douglass, Frederick: 104, 262
Dover: 339, 374–380
Dover Downs: 379
Dragon Run: 368
driving tours: Amish country 374–376; Carroll
    County 228; Cecil County 244–245;
    Conowingo Dam 240; Dorchester County
    272–274; Frederick Douglass Driving Tour
    269; Kent County 251; Oxford 267; Sussex
    County 397–399; Whitehaven Loop 278–279

Druid Hill Park: 76
Dumbarton Oaks: 422
Dumser's: 296, 302
Dupont Circle: 419
Du Pont family: 314, 343–348
Dutch House: 365

E

Eagle Roll Mill: 344
Early, Jubal: 186–187
Early Plank House: 384
East Coast Greenway: 330
Eastern Neck National Wildlife Refuge: 250–251
East New Market: 272–273
Easton: 33, 268–272
economy: 23, 323–324
Eden Hill Farm: 376
Edgar Allan Poe House: 64
education: 24, 324
electrical voltage: 51
Elk Neck Forest: 244
Ellegood House: 384
Ellicott City: 111–113
Elsie Williams Doll Collection: 397
Elsmere pathway: 330
emergency services: 49
Enoch Pratt Free Library: 65
entertainment: 37–38, 429–431; *see also specific place*
environmental protection: 11–12, 319
ethnography: 324
European settlement: 13–20, 165, 320–321
Ewell: 285

F

Fair Hill Nature and Environmental Center: 243
farm markets: 43, 80, 123, 152, 195, 228–229
Farm Tour Harvest Sale: 122
fauna: 8–11, 316–319
FDR (Franklin Delano Roosevelt) Memorial: 410
Federal Hill: 54, 84–85, 93–94
Federal Hill Park: 76
Federal Triangle: 415–418
Fell's Point: 54, 84, 90–91
Fenwick Island: 392–396
ferries: 47, 120, 286, 385–386, 398
festivals and events: Baltimore 92–93; central Delaware 380; central Maryland 132–133;
Delaware 335–336; Eastern Shore 304–305; Frederick 212–213; Jefferson Patterson Park and Museum 154; Maryland 38–40; north-central Maryland 252; northern Delaware 360; Ocean City 304–305; southern Delaware 399; southern Maryland 162–163; western Maryland 212–213; Wilmington 360
First Thursdays: 77, 92
fish/fishing: 10–11, 34–35, 318, 334–335; *see also specific place*
Fitzgerald, F. Scott: 118
Fitzgerald, Zelda: 118
Flag Ponds Nature Park: 155
floating cabins: 371
flora: 8, 315–316
Folger Elizabethan Theatre: 430
Folger Shakespeare Library: 413
food: general information 43; Annapolis 108–109; Baltimore 85–95; Delaware 336–337; Ocean City 301–303, 306; Washington, D.C. 427–429; *see also specific place*
Ford's Theatre National Historic Site: 418, 431
Fort Delaware: 339
Fort Delaware State Park: 367–369
Fort Frederick State Park: 198–199
Fort McHenry: 32, 57, 60
Fort Washington National Park: 130
Fowler Beach: 364
Frederick: 33, 167–178
Frederick Douglass Driving Tour: 269
Frederick vicinity: 169–172
French and Indian War: 18
freshwater fishing: 334
Fresnel, Augustin: 160
Friendship Heights: 419
Fritchie, Barbara: 169, 170
Frontier Town Western Theme Park: 297
Funland: 388, 390
Furnace Town: 291
furniture: 370, 372

G

gambling, legal: 325, 335, 373, 379
game animals and birds: 35
Garrett County: 209–219
Garrett County State Forest: 211–212
Gathland State Park/National War Correspondent's Memorial: 188–189
General Smallwood Retreat House: 140–141
geography: 4–7, 314–315

George Meany Center for Labor Studies and Memorial Archives Library: 118–119
George Peabody Library: 64
George Read II House and Gardens: 365
Georgetown: 396–397, 421–422
Georgetown University: 422
George Washington's Headquarters: 205–206
ghosts: 225
Glen Echo Park: 117–118
Goddard, Robert H.: 126
golf: 35, 121, 303; *see also* miniature golf; *specific place*
Gonzalez, Elian: 258
Goodstay Center and Gardens: 357–358
Gordon-Roberts House: 204–205
government: 22–23, 322–323
Governor Ross Mansion and Plantation: 398–399
Grant, Ulysses S.: 186–187
Great Falls of the Potomac: 5, 119–120
Greektown: 54, 92
Green Ridge State Forest: 199
greenways: 328–331
grocery stores: 80
Grotto of Lourdes: 174
gunpowder: 344

H
Hager House: 192
Hagerstown: 165, 192–196
Hagerstown Speedway: 195
Hallowing Point Park Tobacco Barn: 157
Halsey Field House: 100
Hammond-Harwood House: 99
Hampden: 54
Harborwalk Promenade: 76
Harford County: 232–240
Harpers Ferry National Historical Park: 179–181
Harrington: 372–373
Havre de Grace: 232–236
Helen Avalynne Tawes Garden: 103, 105
Henry Clay Mill: 343
Herrold, David: 136–137, 138–139, 141
Highlandtown: 91–92
High Street (Cambridge): 275
hiking: 31, 34, 331, 333; *see also* greenways; state parks; *specific place*
Hill, D. H.: 181–182
Hiram R. Burton House: 384
Historical Society of Frederick County: 172

Historical Society of Talbot County: 269
Historic Annapolis Foundation: 105
Historic Houses of Odessa: 371
Historic St. Mary's City: 32, 146, 148
history: Delaware 320–322, 352; Maryland 13–22, 134, 136–138, 164–167; *see also* Civil War
H. L. Mencken House: 64
Holocaust Memorial: 70
Hooper Island: 273
horseback riding: 199, 215, 395, 420
Horsehead Wetlands Center: 257
horse racing: 38, 77, 92, 131, 231
horseshoe crab: 318, 319
hostels: 41–42
hotels: 41–42, 81–85, 337
Howard County: 111–116
hunting: 35, 241, 248, 281, 335; *see also* birds/birding; *specific place*

IJ
ice cream: 65, 196, 230, 236, 249
ice fishing: 37
Immanuel Church: 366
immigration: 47
indigenous peoples: 13–15, 18–19, 165, 284, 320–321, 325
industry: 322, 323–324
insects: 318–319
Internet resources: 439–440
Jack Kent Cooke Stadium: 431
J. Edgar Hoover FBI Building: 417
Jefferson Memorial: 410
Jefferson Patterson Park and Museum: 153–154
jet-skiing: 37, 249
John Dickinson Mansion and Plantation: 379
John F. Kennedy Center for the Performing Arts: 429–430
Jolly Roger: 296
Jones, John Paul (crypt): 103

K
Kalmar Nyckel: 356
kayaking: 36, 198, 249
Kenilworth Aquatic Gardens: 423
Kennedy Center: 429–430
Kennedy Farm: 179
Kent County (Delaware): 370–373
Kent County (Maryland): 246–253
Kent Fort Farm: 257
Key, Francis Scott: 169

KidZone: 72
Kimmey House: 225
King's Landing Park: 155
Kitts Hummock: 364
Korean War Veterans Memorial: 403
Kramerbooks & Afterwords: 419

L

lacrosse: 68–69, 77
Ladew Topiary Gardens: 33, 236–237
language: 25
Lankford Hotel: 296, 300
laser tag: 297
Latrobe, John H. B.: 55
Laurel: 339, 397, 398
Laurel Park Race Track: 131
La Vale Tollgate House: 206
Leach, Ethel Pennewill Brown: 376
Lee, Robert E.: 165–166, 180–186
Lejeune Physical Education Center: 100
Lenni Lenape: 320
Lewes: 383–387
Lewes Beach: 339
Lewes Greenway: 331
Lewes Historical Complex: 384–385
Liberty Tree: 106
Library of Congress: 411–412
licenses, fees, and permits: boating 36, 333–334;
    camping/campgrounds 332; fishing 34, 334;
    hunting 35, 335; snowmobiling 335
Lilypons Water Gardens: 173
Lincoln, Abraham: 128–129, 136–137, 138,
    141, 358

Lincoln Memorial: 403
liquor laws: 27, 325
Little Creek Wildlife Area: 369
Little Italy: 54, 89–90
log canoes: 263
Lonaconing: 206
London Town: 110
Lovely Lane United Methodist Church: 70
Lover's Leap: 206
Lower Christina River Greenway: 330
loyalists: 247
Loyola Retreat House: 144
Lyme disease: 48, 251

M

magazines: 50
Magee's Maize Maze: 395
Mallows Bay: 145
Mall, The: 403–409
mammals: 8–9, 316
map sources: 51
Marian Coffin Gardens at Gilbraltar: 358–359
markets: 80, 176, 216, 398
Martha Lewis: 234–235
Martin National Wildlife Refuge: 286
Maryland Archaeological Conservation Labora-
    tory (MAC): 154
Maryland International Raceway: 152
Maryland Science Center: 72
Maryland state anthem: 227
Maryland State House: 99
Maryland Theatre: 195
Mason, Charles: 321
Mason-Dixon Marker: 280–281, 321
mass transit: 46–47, 96, 432; *see also specific place*
McCardell, Claire: 173
McClellan, George B.: 181–184, 358
McCrillis Gardens: 120
MCI Center: 430–431
Meadow Mountain Trail System: 214
Meany, George: 119
measurement systems: 51
medical services: 49, 338
Medieval Times Dinner & Tournament: 110
Meeting House Galleries I and II: 374
Memorial Hall: 103
Mencken, H. L.: 56–57, 64
Mennonites: 374–375
Merkle Wildlife Sanctuary: 130
Merry Sherwood Plantation: 294

Lighthouses

Brandywine Shoal: 316
Concord Point Lighthouse: 234
Delaware Breakwater: 316
Fenwick Island Lighthouse: 394
Fourteen Foot Bank: 316
Fresnel, Augustin: 160
Harbor of Refuge: 316
Miah Maull: 316
Mispillion Lighthouse: 383
Piney Point Lighthouse and Park: 150
Seven-Foot Knoll Lighthouse: 63–64
Ship John Shoal: 316
Turkey Point Lighthouse: 243–244

Museums

Accokeek National Colonial Farm: 32, 127, 130
African Art Museum of Maryland: 114
Air Mobility Command Museum, The: 339, 377, 379
Allegany County Museum: 203
American Visionary Art Museum: 32, 75
Amstel House Museum: 365
Annapolis Maritime Museum: 105
Babe Ruth Birthplace and Orioles Museum: 32, 68
Baltimore Civil War Museum: 60–61
Baltimore Maritime Museum: 63–64
Baltimore Museum of Art: 74–75
Baltimore Museum of Industry: 32, 65
Baltimore Public Works Museum: 66
Baltimore Streetcar Museum: 66
B&O Railroad Museum: 32, 61–62
B&O Railroad Station Museum: 111
Banneker-Douglass Museum: 105
Barbara Fritchie Museum: 169
Barratt's Chapel and Museum: 373
Belair Mansion and Stable Museum: 127
Benjamin Banneker Historical Park: 113–114
Boonsboro Museum of History: 188
Brannock Maritime Museum: 275
Calvert Marine Museum: 33, 158
Calvin B. Taylor House Museum: 293
Cannonball House Marine Museum: 384–385
Capital Children's Museum: 412–413
Carroll County Farm Museum: 223–225
Chesapeake & Delaware (C&D) Canal Museum: 242–243
Chesapeake Bay Maritime Museum: 33, 262–263
Chesapeake Beach Railway Museum: 157

College Park Aviation Museum: 32, 126
Cryptologic Museum: 113
Delaware Agricultural Museum and Village: 339, 377
Delaware Art Museum: 356–357
Delaware Museum of Natural History: 339, 348
Delaware Toy & Miniature Museum: 345
DiscoverSea Museum: 394–395
Dr. Samuel A. Mudd House Museum: 32, 138–140
Dr. Samuel D. Harris National Museum of Dentistry: 32, 67–68
Eubie Blake National Jazz Museum and Cultural Center: 68
Evergreen: 63
Fell's Point Maritime Museum: 64
Fire Museum of Maryland: 232
Fort Frederick State Park: 198–199
Garrett County Historical Museum: 215
George Read II House and Gardens: 365
Gordon-Roberts House: 204–205
Governor J. Millard Tawes Historical Museum: 287–288
Great Blacks in Wax: 69
Hager House: 192
Hagerstown Roundhouse Museum: 193, 195
Hagley Museum/Eleutherian Mills: 322, 339, 343–345
Harrington Museum: 372–373
Harrington Railroad Museum: 373
Havre de Grace Decoy Museum: 33, 233–234
Hirshhorn Museum and Sculpture Garden: 408
Homewood House Museum: 63
Indian River Inlet Lifesaving Station Museum: 393

metro system (Washington, D.C.): 406, 407
Middleton House: 285–286
Milford Neck Wildlife Area: 369
Mill Creek Hundred: 330
Millsboro: 396
miniature golf: 298
Mispillion River Greenway: 331
Mispillion Riverwalk: 331
money: 49–50, 411
Monocacy National Battlefield: 186–188

Monroe Run: 214
Montgomery County: 116–123
mosquitoes: 318–319
motels: 41–42, 337
Mother Seton House: 70–71
Mount Harmon Plantation: 244
Mount Olivet Cemetery: 169, 171
Mount Vernon: 54, 55–57
Mount Vernon Cultural District: 77
Mount Vernon Place United Methodist Church: 71

International Spy Museum: 416
James B. Richardson Maritime Museum: 275
Jefferson Patterson Park and Museum: 153–154
Jewish Museum of Maryland: 70
Johnson Victrola Museum: 339, 374
Julia A. Purnell Museum: 290–291
Lacrosse Museum and National Hall of Fame: 68–69
Life-Saving Station Museum: 33
Maryland Historical Society Museum and Library: 32
Meeting House Galleries I and II: 374
Meredith House and Nield Museum: 275
Messick Agricultural Museum: 372–373
Miller House Museum: 192
Mount Clare Museum: 62–63
Mt. Zion One Room School Museum: 291
Nanticoke Indian Museum: 396
National Air and Space Museum: 406
National Building Museum: 416
National Museum of African Art: 408–409
National Museum of American Art: 416
National Museum of American History: 409
National Museum of Civil War Medicine: 33, 171–172
National Museum of Natural History: 409
Newcomer House Museum: 185
Ocean City Life-Saving Station Museum: 295, 297
Old Library Museum: 366
Old New Castle Court House Museum: 364–365
Oxford Museum: 267–268
Pax River Naval Air Museum: 149–150
Piscataway Indian Museum: 144
Queen Anne's Museum of Eastern Shore Life: 257

Reginald F. Lewis Museum of African American History and Culture: 69
Ripken Museum: 237
Rockwood Mansion: 348
Schifferstadt Architectural Museum: 169
Sewell C. Biggs Museum of American Art: 339, 374
Shiplap House Museum: 98
Smith Island Center: 286
Sotterley Plantation: 150
Star-Spangled Banner Flag House and Museum: 63
St. Clement's Island—Potomac River Museum: 32, 149
Steppingstone Museum: 239
Surratt House Museum: 32, 127, 137
Susquehanna Museum of Havre de Grace at the Lockhouse: 234
Tawes Historical Museum: 33
Thrasher Carriage Museum: 33, 204
Tolchester Beach Revisited Museum: 249
Top of the World Observation Level and Museum: 69
Treasures of the Sea: 396–397
United States Holocaust Museum: 411
Upper Bay Museum: 241
U.S. Army Ordnance Museum: 33, 237–238
U.S. Naval Academy Museum: 103
Walters Art Museum: 32, 73–74
Ward Museum of Wildfowl Art: 33, 279
Washington County Museum of Fine Arts: 33, 192–193
Waterman's Museum: 249
Western Maryland Railway Station: 202–203
Winterthur: 339, 346–348
Zwaanendael Museum: 384

movie theaters: 419
Mudd, Dr. Samuel A.: 137, 138–140, 141
Murderkill River Greenway: 330–331
music: 78, 359
Myrtle Grove Game Refuge: 145

N
Nancy Hammond Editions: 106–107
Nanjemoy Creek Great Blue Heron Sanctuary: 145

Nanticoke Powwow: 325, 339, 396
Nanticoke River: 331
Narrows: 206
NASA/Goddard Space Flight Visitor Center: 32, 125–126
Nassawango Cypress Swamp: 291–292
National Aquarium: 417
National Aquarium in Baltimore: 32, 71–72
National Archives: 417–418
National Historic Seaport of Baltimore: 57

National Institutes of Health (NIH): 119
National Library of Medicine: 119
National Parks: 30
National Pike: 45
National Road: 45, 166, 206
National Shrine of St. Elizabeth Ann Seton: 33, 173–174
National Symphony Orchestra (NSO): 429
National Theatre: 430
National Wildlife Refuge System: 124
National Zoological Park: 420
Native Americans: 13–15, 18–19, 165, 284, 320–321, 325
Navy chapel: 100, 103
Nemacolin's Path: 45
Nemours Mansion and Gardens: 339, 345
New Castle: 339, 364–367
newspapers: 50, 95, 98, 339
nightlife: 78–79, 303, 392, 429–431
North Beach: 157
North Bowers Beach: 364
North East: 240–242
Northern Delaware Greenway—East Link: 330
Northern Delaware Greenway—West Link: 329–330
nuclear power plants: 156

O

Ocean City: 33, 37, 294–309
ocean fishing: 334
Odd Fellows Hall: 226
Odessa: 339, 370–371
Old Christ Church: 397
Old Downtown: 415–418
Olde Canal Inn: 370
Old Post Office: 417
Old Stone House: 422
Old Swedes Church: 356
Old Third Haven Meeting House: 33, 269
Old Town Laurel Walking Tour: 130–131
Old Trinity Church: 273–274
Old Wye Church: 259
O'Neals: 398
opera: 78, 429
Orchard County: 196–200
Orrell's Maryland Beaten Biscuits: 259
Otterbein: 54
outlet malls: 390
Oxford: 267–268
Oxford Bellevue Ferry: 267

P

parking: 110
parks: 30–31
passenger pigeons: 281
passports: 47
Patapsco Female Institute Historic Park: 111–112
Patterson Park: 76
Patterson Theater: 76–77
Patuxent Research Refuge/National Wildlife Visitor Center: 32, 123–124
Paw Paw Tunnel: 198
Peabody, George: 64–65
Pea Patch Island: 317, 367–370
Pemberton Hall: 278
Pemberton Historical Park: 280
Pencader Hundred: 330
Penn Station: 32, 66
Penn, William: 16, 18, 320, 365
performing arts: 78, 176, 195, 225, 335, 359, 429–430
Petersen House: 418
Phillips Seafood Tour: 69
Pickering Beach: 364
Pickering Creek Audubon Center: 269
picnicking: 174, 175
Piedmont Plateau: 5, 7
Pimlico Race Course: 77
Pintail Point: 258–259
piracy: 264
Planet Maze: 297
plantations: 17, 244, 379, 398–399
plants: *see* flora
Poe, Edgar Allan: 55, 64
Point Lookout State Park: 148–149
police: 27–28, 49, 325–326, 338
politics: 22–23
pollution: 11–12
Pomfret: 144
Pope's Creek: 144
Poplar Hill Mansion: 280
population: 24–25, 324–326
Port Discovery: 32, 72–73
Port Mahon: 369
Port of Crisfield Escorted Walking Tour: 288
Port Penn: 370
Port Republic School Number 7: 155, 157
Port Tobacco Historic District: 141, 143–144
Post, Emily: 57
Potomac River Trail System: 212

Potomac Speedway: 152
Potomac State Forest: 213–214
Pratt, Enoch: 65
Preakness: 38, 77, 92
Preble Hall: 103
Pre-Raphaelites: 357
Presbyterian Church: 366
Primehook Beach: 364
Prime Hook National Wildlife Refuge: 339, 369, 383
Prince George's County: 123–133
Prince George's Equestrian Center: 131
Princess Anne: 284
Pyle, Howard: 376

QR
Quaker Hill: 354–355
Quakers: 26–27, 354–355
Queen Anne's County: 257–262
Rabbit's Ferry House: 384
race relations: 24–25, 352
radio stations: 50, 95
railroad bridge: 239
recipe, bread crumb pancakes: 283
recommended reading: 436–438
recreation: Anne Arundel County 110–111; Baltimore 77; Brandywine Valley 349–350; Calvert County 153–155, 161; Cape Henlopen State Park 387–388; Charles County 144–145; Cumberland 206; Delaware 328–335; Dorchester County 272–276; Frederick 174–176; Garrett County 209–215; Hagerstown 195; Harford County 238–240; Howard County 114–115; Kent County 249–251; Killens Pond State Park 373–374; Lewes 385–386; Maryland 30–37; Ocean City 306–309; Orchard County 196–199; Prime Hook National Wildlife Refuge 383; Prince George's County 127, 130–131; Queen Anne's County 257–258; St. Mary's County 151–152; Salisbury 281–282; Somerset County 288–289; Talbot County 263, 266; Worcester County 292; *see also* state parks; *specific activity*
Rehoboth Beach: 339, 388–392
religion: 16, 25–27, 324–325
rental cars: 96, 433; *see also* car travel
reptiles: 9, 318
restaurants: *see specific place*
Return Day: 397

Revolutionary War: 20, 247, 321
Rhodes Point: 285
rivers: 5–6, 36, 145, 314–315
Robert F. Kennedy Memorial Stadium: 431
Rockawalkin schoolhouse: 278
Rock Creek Park: 420
Rock Hall: 33, 248–250
Rockville: *see* Montgomery County
Rockwood Mansion: 348
Rocky Gap: 37
Rodney, Caesar: 323
Rosecroft Raceway: 131
Rose Hill Cemetery: 192
Rose Hill Manor Park: 173
Ruth, George Herman "Babe": 67, 68
Ryves Holt House: 384

S
safety tips: 47, 49, 95, 338
sailing: 36, 333
Sailwinds Park: 272
sainthood: 26
Salisbury: 279–283
Salisbury Zoo: 279
Salyer, J. Clark: 124
Samples Manor: 179
Savage Mill: 114
scooter houses: 386
Scott, Dred: 21
Seaford: 339, 398
Seaside Nature Center: 387–388
seasons: 7–8, 315
Secretary: 273
Seton, Elizabeth Ann: 26, 173–174
Shakespeare Theatre: 430
Shamrock, The: 178
Shellman House: 226
Ships Tavern District: 355
shipwrecks: 394
shopping: 37, 79–80, 335, 390; *see also specific place*
Shriver family: 227–228
Sideling Hill Exhibit Center: 200
Simpson, Wallis Warfield: 56, 57
Sinclair, Upton: 56
Six Flags America: 131
65th St. Slide & Ride: 297
skiing: 37, 189, 199; *see also* state parks
skipjacks: 234–235, 263
Slaughter Beach: 364, 369

State Parks

general information: 30–31, 328
Assateague State Park: 34, 37, 307
Bellevue State Park: 349–350
Big Run State Park: 209–210
Brandywine Creek State Park: 349
Calvert Cliffs State Park: 32, 154–155
Cape Henlopen State Park: 332, 339, 369, 387–388
Casselman River Bridge State Park: 209
Cunningham Falls State Park: 37, 174–175
Dan's Mountain State Park: 206
Deep Creek Lake State Park: 33, 37, 210–211
Delaware Seashore State Park: 332, 339, 393
Elk Neck State Park: 243–244
Fort Delaware State Park: 367–370
Fort Frederick State Park: 198–199
Gambrill State Park: 175
Garrett County State Forest: 211–212
Gathland State Park/National War Correspondent's Memorial: 188–189
Greenbrier State Park: 189
Green Ridge State Forest: 199
Greenwell State Park: 150–151

Gunpowder Falls State Park: 34
Herrington Manor State Park: 210
Jane's Island State Park: 33, 37, 288–289
Killens Pond State Park: 332, 373–374
Lums Pond State Park: 332
New Germany State Park: 209
Palmer State Park: 238
Patapsco Valley State Park: 114–115
Point Lookout State Park: 32, 37, 148–149
Potomac State Forest: 213–214
Rocks State Park: 238–240
Rocky Gap State Park: 206
Sandy Point State Park: 34, 37, 110
Seneca Creek State Park: 121
Smallwood State Park: 140–141
South Mountain State Park: 189
St. Mary's River State Park: 34
Susquehanna State Park: 238–240
Swallow Falls State Park: 33, 37, 210
Thomas Point State Park: 110–111
Trap Pond State Park: 332, 397
Tuckahoe State Park: 257–258
Washington Monument State Park: 189–190

slavery: 21, 143, 322
Smith Island: 33, 285–287
Smith Island Center: 286
Smithsonian Castle: 405
Smithsonian Institution: 405–406, 408–409
Smyrna Trails: 330
Snow Hill: 290–293
snowmobiling: 37, 335
snowshoeing: 37
Society of Friends: *see* Quakers
Society of the Cincinnati: 421
Solomons: 157–158
Somerset County: 284–290
Sotterley Plantation: 150
South Bowers Beach: 364
South Mountain: 7, 182–184
spectator sports: 77–78, 175–176, 335, 430–431
Spencer-Silver Mansion: 235–236
Spocott Windmill: 275
Sportland Arcade: 297
State House (Dover): 374
Statue of Tecumseh: 103

Stein, Gertrude: 57, 74
St. Ignatius Catholic Church: 143
St. John's College: 106
St. Jones Reserve: 369
St. Jones River Greenway Commission: 330
St. Jude Shrine: 70
St. Mary's: 14, 136
St. Mary's County: 146–153
St. Michaels: 33, 262–266
Stony Demonstration Forest: 238
stool pigeon: 281
Stream Corridor Greenways: 328–329
Stuart, J. E. B.: 225–228
Studio Theatre: 430
submarines: 150
subways: 46, 432
Suicide Bridge: 277
Sultana: 246
surf fishing: 334
surfing: 37, 333
Surratt, Mary Elizabeth: 127, 128–129, 141
Sussex County: 396–400
swimming: 37, 175, 189, 333

T

Talbot County: 262–272
Tangier Island: 286
taverns: 355
taxes: 51
taxis: 96, 109, 433
Taylors Island: 273
Taylor's Ocean Pier: 295
Teackle Mansion: 284
television stations: 50
temperatures: 51, 315
theater: 76, 78, 246, 269, 359, 429–430
theft: 49
Theodore Roosevelt Island: 410–411
Thomas Stone House: 143–144
Thompson Country Store: 384
Thousand Acre Marsh: 368
ticks: 48, 251
Tidal Basin: 409–411
Tidewater: 4–5
Tilghman Island: 266–267
time zones: 51
tobacco: 15, 142
Tocqueville, Alexis de: 20
toll roads: 46
tourist information: 50–51, 95, 339–340; see also
    specific place
tours: boats 275–276, 289; Chestertown 246;
    cruises 105, 263, 431; Ellicott City 112;
    NASA/Goddard Space Flight Visitor Center
    125–126; Phillips Seafood Tour 69; St.
    Michaels 263; southern Delaware 400; Tawes
    Historical Museum 33; U.S. Naval Academy
    (USNA) 100; walking tours 33, 55–57, 77,
    130–131, 239, 288; see also museums
Town Drummer: 108
trails: see greenways; hiking
train travel: 45, 46, 96, 219, 338, 432
transportation: 44–47, 95–96, 306–307,
    337–338, 431–433
Trees of States Arboretum: 397
Trestle Walk/Promenade: 203
Trimper's Rides and Amusements:
    295, 296
trolleys: 250
Trolley Square: 359
Trollope, Frances: 194
Trumbo/Chest House: 226
Tudor Hall: 222
Turner's Gap: 182

Twin Beaches: 157
Tylerton: 285

UV

Underground Railroad Gift Shop: 275
Union Mills Homestead: 227–228
Union Station: 412
Upper Christina River Greenway: 329
Upper Northwest District: 419–421
U.S. Botanic Garden: 413
U.S. Capitol: 412
U.S. National Arboretum: 423
U.S. Naval Academy (USNA): 99–100, 103
U.S. Naval Institute Bookstore: 103
U.S. Supreme Court: 413
vegetation: see flora
Vienna: 273
Vietnam Veterans Memorial: 403–404
Vietnam Women's Memorial: 404
visas: 47

WXYZ

Waldorf: 144
Wallace, Lew: 186–187
Walters, William: 74
Ward Brothers Workshop: 288
Warfield, Wallis: see Simpson, Wallis Warfield
War of 1812: 21
Washington, D.C.: 401–433
Washington D.C. Mormon Temple: 121
Washington, George: 18, 20, 205
Washington Harbor: 422
Washington Monument: 32, 66–67, 404
Washington National Cathedral: 419–420
Washington Opera: 429
Washington Street: 202–203
waterfowl: 241, 248; see also birds/birding
Waterfront Warehouse: 98
water parks: see amusement parks
water sports: 175, 189, 199, 209, 210; see also
    state parks
water taxis: 96, 109, 338
weather: 7–8, 315
Western Maryland Railway Station: 202
Westminster: 223–230
Westminster Cemetery Hall and Burying
    Ground: 64
Wheels of Yesterday: 297
White Clay/Middle Run (Northern Delaware
    Greenway—West Link): 329–330

Whitehaven Ferry: 278–279
Whitehaven Loop: 278–279
White House, The: 413–414
White's Ferry: 120
white-water rafting: 215
Whittier, John Greenleaf: 170
Wicomico County: 278–284
wild horses: *see* Assateague Island
wildlife management areas: 31
wildlife refuges: 328
William Paca House and Garden: 98–99
Wilmington: 322, 352–361
Wilmington Walkways: 330
wine/wineries: 43, 80, 230–232
winter sports: *see specific sport*
Winterthur: 339, 346–348

Wisp Resort: 214
witches: 151
Woodhall Wine Cellars: 231–232
Woodland Beach: 364
Woodland Beach Wildlife Area: 368
Woodland Ferry: 398
Woodley Park: 419
Woolly Mammoth Theatre: 430
Worcester County: 290–294
worship meetings: 27
Wye: 33
Wye Grist Mill: 259
Wye Island: 33, 258–259
Wye Oak: 259
Wye School: 259
zoos: 32, 72, 279, 359, 420

Acknowledgments

This book is made possible through the help and cooperation of many. Erika Howsare was responsible for gathering much of the updated contact information, and Vera Gross also contributed her time and talent. In Maryland, Mindy Bianca of the Maryland Department of Business and Economic Development was invaluable, along with her cohorts, Angela Reynolds, Allegany Co.; Erin Long, Annapolis and Anne Arundel Co.; Larry Noto, Baltimore; Herman Schieke, Calvert Co.; Barbara Beverungen, Carroll Co.; Sandy Turner, Cecil Co.; Joanne Roland, Charles Co.; Natalie Chabot, Dorchester Co.; Beth Rhoades, Frederick Co.; Diane Molner, Harford Co.; Melissa Arnold, Howard Co.; Bernadette Van Pelt, Kent Co.; Kelly Groff, Montgomery Co.; Carl Smith Jr., Prince George's Co.; Barbara Siegert, Queen Anne's Co.; Carolyn Laray, St. Mary's Co.; Julie M. Horner, Somerset Co.; Debbi Dodson, Talbot Co.; Gigi Yelton, Hagerstown/Washington Co.; Sandy Fulton, Wicomico Co.; Lisa Challenger, Worcester Co.; and Martha Clements, Ocean City. In Delaware, Jennifer Boes of the Delaware Tourism Office and her associates J. Harry Feldman and Josie Jeker, Greater Wilmington, and Mary Skelton, Kent Co., were enormously helpful.

Avalon Travel Publishing has given me the opportunity, once again, to come to know and appreciate another piece of America. Editors are the unsung champions of the book world; this book was gracefully brought to life under the sharp eyes of Kathryn Ettinger. Thanks also to Kevin Jeys, original author of much of the Washington, D.C., chapter, as well as a slew of able editors and updaters who contributed to that chapter. Thank you and blessings to all.

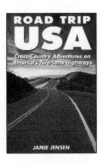

U.S.~Metric Conversion

1 inch = 2.54 centimeters (cm)
1 foot = .304 meters (m)
1 yard = 0.914 meters
1 mile = 1.6093 kilometers (km)
1 km = .6214 miles
1 fathom = 1.8288 m
1 chain = 20.1168 m
1 furlong = 201.168 m
1 acre = .4047 hectares
1 sq km = 100 hectares
1 sq mile = 2.59 square km
1 ounce = 28.35 grams
1 pound = .4536 kilograms
1 short ton = .90718 metric ton
1 short ton = 2000 pounds
1 long ton = 1.016 metric tons
1 long ton = 2240 pounds
1 metric ton = 1000 kilograms
1 quart = .94635 liters
1 US gallon = 3.7854 liters
1 Imperial gallon = 4.5459 liters
1 nautical mile = 1.852 km

To compute Celsius temperatures, subtract 32 from Fahrenheit and divide by 1.8. To go the other way, multiply Celsius by 1.8 and add 32.

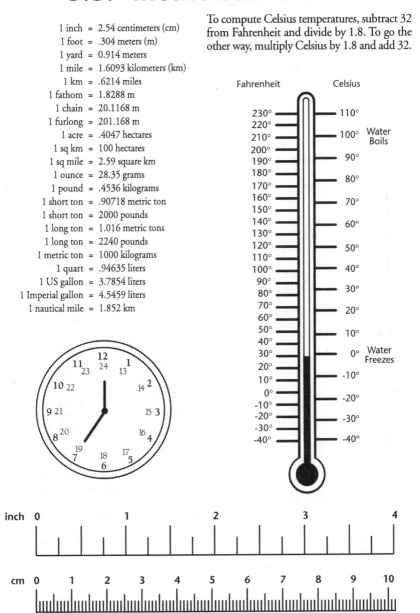

Keeping Current

Although we strive to produce the most up-to-date guidebook humanly possible, change is unavoidable. Between the time this book goes to print and the moment you read it, a handful of the businesses noted in these pages will undoubtedly change prices, move, or even close their doors forever. Other worthy attractions will open for the first time. If you have a favorite gem you'd like to see included in the next edition, or see anything that needs updating, clarification, or correction, please drop us a line. Send your comments via email to atpfeedback@avalonpub.com, or use the address below.

Moon Handbooks Maryland & Delaware
Avalon Travel Publishing
1400 65th Street, Suite 250
Emeryville, CA 94608, USA
www.moon.com

Editor: Kathryn Ettinger
Series Manager: Kevin McLain
Copy Editor: Emily McManus
Graphics Coordinator: Susan Mira Snyder
Production Coordinator: Darren Alessi
Cover Designer: Kari Gim
Interior Designers: Amber Pirker,
   Alvaro Villanueva, Kelly Pendragon
Map Editor: Naomi Adler Dancis
Cartographers: Olivia Solís, Landis Bennett,
   Chris Folks
Indexer: Judy Hunt

ISBN: 1-56691-621-6
ISSN: 1531-5592

Printing History
1st Edition—2001
2nd Edition—February 2004
5 4 3 2 1

Text © 2004 by Joanne Miller.
Maps © 2004 by
Avalon Travel Publishing, Inc.
All rights reserved.
Metrorail Map © 2000 Washington
Metropolitan Area Transit Authority

Avalon Travel Publishing is a division of
Avalon Publishing Group, Inc.

Some photos and illustrations are used by permission and are the property of the original copyright owners.

Front cover photo: © Folio, Inc.
Table of Contents photos: © Joanne Miller

Printed in the United States by
Malloy Lithography